Southern cultures

Southern cultures

Edited by
Harry L. Watson
and Larry J. Griffin
with
Lisa Eveleigh,
Dave Shaw,
Ayse Erginer,
and Paul Quigley

The
Fifteenth
Anniversary
Reader

The University *of*
North Carolina Press
Chapel Hill

© 2008 The University of North Carolina Press
All rights reserved
Designed by Kimberly Bryant
Set in Monotype Garamond by Keystone Typesetting, Inc.
Manufactured in the United States of America

The paper in this book meets the guidelines for permanence
and durability of the Committee on Production Guidelines for
Book Longevity of the Council on Library Resources.

Library of Congress Cataloging-in-Publication Data

Southern cultures: the fifteenth anniversary reader / edited by
Harry L. Watson and Larry J. Griffin; with Lisa Eveleigh,
Dave Shaw, Ayse Erginer, and Paul Quigley.
p. cm.
Includes bibliographical references and index.
ISBN 978-0-8078-3212-7 (cloth: alk. paper)
ISBN 978-0-8078-5880-6 (pbk.: alk. paper)
1. Southern States—Civilization. 2. Southern States—Social life
and customs. I. Watson, Harry L. II. Griffin, Larry J.
III. Eveleigh, Lisa. IV. Shaw, Dave, 1966– V. Erginer, Ayse.
VI. Quigley, Paul. VII. Southern cultures.
F209.S733 2008
975—dc22

                                           2007042150

A Caravan book. For more information,
visit www.caravanbooks.org.

cloth   12 11 10 09 08   5 4 3 2 1
paper   12 11 10 09 08   5 4 3 2 1

For

JOHN SHELTON REED,

Founding Editor of Southern Cultures
*and Co-founder of The UNC Center for
the Study of the American South*

Contents

The New Days of Yore

Country music, the blues, Atticus Finch, and southern childhoods aren't what they used to be—and perhaps never really were.

Colliding Cultures

Peoples and powers intersect, forging and reshaping the South and its southerners.

Regional Stereotypes

Kudzu, hogs, rednecks, feuding, and rasslin' have real stories behind them.

Southern Traditions

*What interests, guides, and defines southerners is a diverse collection we can
only begin to sample here.*

front porch

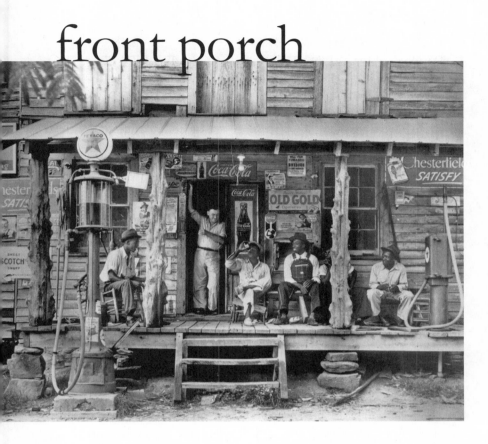

The old bluesmen of Tin Pan Alley had a famous question: "Is It True What They Say about Dixie?" In some contemporary quarters, the follow-up question might be, "Why does it matter?"

By now, we all know the sound bite: mass media, mass culture, the Internet, instant messaging, and all the rest rocket information from one end of the world to the other, flattening local distinctions and particular places at every turn. The rap that rocks L.A. this morning will be just as popular in Atlanta, Cape Town, and Tokyo by nightfall. People move around almost as fast, from immigrants changing continents, to refugees fleeing warfare, to "evacuees" trying to escape the effects of the weather. Think about what the Atlanta suburbanite said to his new neighbors:

above:

The very first issue of Southern Cultures *featured this classic front porch on the cover. Photograph by Dorothea Lange, courtesy of the Collections of the Library of Congress.*

"You'll love this development. There isn't a southerner for miles." The same global forces that send executives from no place in particular to everywhere at once depress local economies in some places and inflate new boomtowns somewhere else. Money flies even faster than goods, with capital skipping from stock exchange to stock exchange at click-of-a-mouse speed. The process has thrust up financial giants in Charlotte (of all places) while wreaking havoc in once-sturdy communities like Kannapolis, just up the road. In a famous essay of 1958, historian C. Vann Woodward described a "Bulldozer Revolution" that was wrecking old landmarks, building new ones, and transforming the South of his day.[1] For nearly five decades, globalization has outstripped mere machinery as an agent of destruction and construction. In the midst of all this ultra-bulldozing, what's left of the South?

Back in 1992, a few of us at the University of North Carolina at Chapel Hill defied the general trend away from locality and started up a journal about the South. You can be pretty sure that the late Governor George Wallace would have called most of us pointy-headed intellectuals who couldn't even park our bicycles straight, but we still cared about the South and wanted to talk about it. We wanted some space where academics and general readers could swap stories about culture and place, and where scholars of different specialties could learn from each other and from people who wouldn't ordinarily pick up an academic journal. We were very aware that past South-watchers have sometimes erred in assuming that there has been only one "real" South: the South of white people, especially upper-crust white people like plantation belles and beaux. Ulrich B. Phillips made that mistake when he declared that "the cardinal test of a Southerner and the central theme of Southern history" was "a common resolve indomitably maintained—that it shall be and remain a white man's country."[2]

Instead, we thought of the South as a plural place with endless diversity and no single defining set of traits and customs. Hoping to reach even wider than a biracial South, we chose a deliberately plural name: *Southern Cultures*. Our inaugural issue invited readers to enter into an ongoing conversation, and somehow we're still at it. Our founding editor and tutelary genius, John Shelton Reed, has moved on to other projects, but others have taken up the thread. Time has passed, but the conversation has kept us interested.

The world was a lot different back then. One of us remembers getting his first e-mail connection when *Southern Cultures* began to take shape, ostensibly to communicate with the staff. In fact, he was humoring the rest of them and couldn't imagine what he was really going to do with something so frivolous. Now you can't pry him away from it.

But while the high-tech world was just getting started, the trend line was clear, and the smart money was betting that the American South was a thing of the past. Walls were coming down everywhere, not just in Berlin, and one reckless prognosticator was predicting the "end of history." Global was in, local was out. For a region that had always seemed choked with history, the future did not look good. In 1990, Hodding Carter III, a Mississippian of flawless southern pedigree, pronounced the epitaph. "The South as South, a living, ever regenerating mythic land of distinctive personality, is no more," he announced in *Time* magazine. "At most it is an artifact lovingly preserved in the museums of culture and the shops of tourist commerce precisely because it is so hard to find in the vital centers of the region's daily life. . . . The South is dead. . . . What is lurching into existence in the South is purely and contemporaneously mainstream American, for better and for worse."[3]

But the disappearance of the South is one of the most enduring clichés of American social commentary. To no avail, legions of northern reformers vowed to enlighten the benighted South in the aftermath of its ill-starred bid for independence. No such luck. By the 1920s, industrialization threatened another cultural takeover, and the famous Nashville Agrarians took their stand to stop it. They couldn't, of course, and manufacturing became the backbone of the southern economy—but it was still the South. In the 1960s, liberals and conservatives alike wondered if the South could survive—the former because they hoped that segregation might collapse, and the latter because they feared it would. And legally mandated segregation did collapse—but the South did not. In a famous essay, C. Vann Woodward reminded us that the South would not disappear because its history, what he called "the collective experience of the southern people"[4] could not be effaced. Today, "the southern people" include many whom Woodward would never recognize as southerners— but the South is still here. Veteran South-watcher James C. Cobb captured an imprecise certainty when he observed in 2005 that "for all the contemporary statistical data documenting regional convergence and the physical evidence of it afforded by skyscrapers, suburban sprawl, and gridlocked expressways, I have yet to encounter anyone who has moved into or out of the South and did not sense that, for better or worse, living here was different from living in other parts of the country."[5]

Explanations abound for the persistence of southern identity. Echoing James Cobb's observation, many insist that cultural convergence is overrated, whether in the United States or around the world. In fact, some say, the South really *is* different from other places, and they can point to a million different traits and factors, and tell a million stories, to prove it. Truth be told, a lot of those stories have appeared in *Southern Cultures*. And echoing Woodward, some of us still point to southern history, and especially southern memory, as the fountainhead of regional identity. After all, there are still many of us who did *not* come here from somewhere else and who remember whispered family stories that don't get told around Plymouth Rock. Like the time great-granddaddy witnessed a lynching. Or worse, the time great-granddaddy was almost lynched.

Another set of explanations hinges on the same forces of mass culture and homogenization that supposedly undermine regional identity. In a world of mass-marketed consumption and mass-produced uniformity, people long for distinctiveness and authenticity. In this view, local and particular identities become even more important in mass society, not less. All across the planet, provincial cultures are being reasserted in the face of globalization, as national identities weaken and local, even tribal, identities come forward. In this view, being southern is like being Scottish or Catalan or Tamil or Kurdish—a cherished aspect of personal and family identity that resists incorporation by a distant or domineering other. Here at home, the eccentrics of the League of the South compare themselves explicitly to the regional nationalists of places like Lombardy and Quebec to justify their renewed campaign for southern independence. Sometimes these local assertions are benign and tolerant of the neighbors, but we all shudder at the cases where the very opposite is true. Ironically, nothing abets this tribalizing urge more effectively than the Internet, where every conceivable faction and subculture can find its own site, its own chatroom, and its own faceless community of insiders who plot their revenge against the rest of us. God forbid that southern consciousness should ever go down that path again.

The greater danger here is that the yearning for unique identity is pathetically easy to co-opt and commercialize. If the customers want authenticity, then sell 'em authenticity, the purveyors of kitsch decide, and the "mass" market is promptly subdivided into any number of niches, each hawking its own subculture. And there's no reason to limit one's cultural choices to one niche—it's a free country and a free market, so you can mix and match as much as you want. So thus we have worldwide examples of "authentic" Irish pubs and Mississippi juke joints, all nestled comfortably beside McDonald's and the Hard Rock Café, all cashing in with an ersatz version of down-home culture. In London, John Shelton Reed has discovered an especially striking example of this widespread phenomenon: an Arkansas barbecue joint that claims to serve the real thing "by appointment to his Excellency the American Ambassador."[6] But if southern persistence is no more significant than any other consumer selection, and no more authentic than Dollywood, who needs it?

And finally there are those who maintain that the South persists because the rest of the world demands it. According to long-established stereotypes, the South is lazy, backward, ignorant, racist, and superstitious, while the rest of America is hardworking, progressive, intelligent, tolerant, and enlightened. There is certainly some historical reality behind these negative descriptions of the South, but it's also true that the rest of America has occasionally deserved them as well. In this view, the American majority learns to live with its own shortcomings by blaming them all on its evil twin, the South. So the idea of a South that's fundamentally different from the rest of the country persists as a necessary scapegoat, whose obvious sins make the rest of America look and feel so much better. If these theorists are right, the South won't disappear for the same reason some comedian once said that the British will never abolish their monarchy: the American people wouldn't stand for it. For an extended treatment of this idea, take a look at "Southern Distinctiveness, Yet Again," this volume's lead essay.

Whatever its attractions, the scapegoat idea can't settle the question of southern identity or distinctiveness. If "America" clings to southern distinctiveness because that makes nonsoutherners feel better about themselves, then why do southerners themselves feel distinctive? While polls show that the proportion of white and black people who call themselves "southern" is steadily declining, the number still exceeded 70 percent of the South's residents as recently as 2001.[7] If all these people still think they are "southern," what does that say about them and the region they claim to belong to?

Where so many have tried and fallen short, we are not about to propose our own answer to that question now. Instead, we're offering this volume as a selection of different answers to lots of questions about the South, including that one. All these essays originally appeared in *Southern Cultures* during its first fifteen years. Readers can treat it as a retrospective that brings some of our most-requested pieces together for easy reacquaintance. Or they can take it to another level, as a series of questions and answers about regional history and culture, each of which call for more of the same.

The authors in our first section get right to the point: what exactly *is* the South? Taken together, their essays suggest that there are no rigid answers, for definitions of the South expand and contract with the needs of the definers. The South is a place that southerners and nonsoutherners have invented, so no two definitions are exactly the same. Subsequent sections ask how the South operates today. Are there distinctive southern arts or rituals? What happens when southerners are different from each other? What about southern stereotypes? Or living southern traditions? Different sections of the pages that follow are dedicated to each of these inquiries.

As they address these questions, our authors call on every southern image, reality, and caricature. The Confederate flag is here, and country music. The southern accent turns up, and so does southern migration. Jewish southerners meet Hispanic southerners meet rednecks meet sorority sisters. Confederate memorials are entwined with kudzu, and Bear Bryant lies down to rest with Booker T. Washington. They're all here, so come on in and join the crowd.

No one is likely to settle the question of southern identity or distinctiveness for long. As editors, we have learned most clearly from *Southern Cultures* that southernness is a set of stories that southerners tell about themselves, making themselves up as they go along, always combining new materials and worn-out scraps. Pursuing this conversation is sometimes fun and sometimes grim, but always interesting.

Is it true what they say about Dixie? We don't always know, but here, at least, you can find out what people are saying.

Harry L. Watson and Larry J. Griffin

NOTES

1. C. Vann Woodward, "The Search for Southern Identity," in *The Burden of Southern History*, 3rd ed. (Baton Rouge: Louisiana State University Press, 1993), 6.

2. Ulrich B. Phillips, "The Central Theme of Southern History," *American Historical Review* 34 (1928): 31.

3. Hodding Carter III, "The End of the South," *Time*, 6 August 1990, 82.

4. Woodward, "The Search for Southern Identity," 16.

5. James C. Cobb, *Away Down South: A History of Southern Identity* (New York: Oxford University Press, 2005), 336–37.

6. John Shelton Reed, "Queuing up for Q in London's East End," *Southern Cultures* 11:3 (Fall 2005): 82–87.

7. Larry J. Griffin and Ashley B. Thompson, "Enough About the Disappearing South: What About the Disappearing Southerner?" *Southern Cultures* 9:3 (Fall 2003): 51–65.

A Moveable Mason-Dixon Line

Where is the South? Which South?
Where isn't the South?

Southern Distinctiveness, Yet Again, or, Why America Still Needs the South

Larry J. Griffin

Juxtaposing America and the South in a way that focused attention almost exclusively on the region's racial crimes quite possibly stunted the rest of the nation's willingness to confront its own racism. Rally at the state capitol, Little Rock, Arkansas, courtesy of the Collections of the Library of Congress.

n 1976 the Democratic Party nominated a true blue son of the South—Jimmy Carter—to be its presidential candidate. During that campaign, and especially after Carter's election, things southern—from rednecks and born-again Protestantism to potlikker and red-eye gravy—were the journalistic rage. Southerners did things differentially, they—we—spoke differently, we ate different kinds of food, we believed and acted differently, and, during those early Carter years, the national media seemed entranced by the "southernness" of it all, believing themselves, I suppose, called first to understand the South and then to help the American people—or at least the nonsoutherners among us—understand it too. I was finishing graduate school in Baltimore at the time, and I remember my Yankee friends asking me an inordinate number of questions about the South, about being southern. Of course, I was neither the first nor the last southerner to have enjoyed that particular pleasure: southerners have been explaining, telling about, the South for generations.[1]

We saw some of the same curiosity—this attention to southernness—in the 1992 presidential election, but by then the novelty of a southerner sitting in the White House had worn off, and, anyway, Arkansan Bill Clinton gave the country other things to talk about. And if sometimes-southerner Al Gore wins the 2000 election, I doubt very much that the region will again be scrutinized and stared at as it was in the late 1970s. Still, Gore's "real but delicate" Tennessee roots, as the *Los Angeles Times* puts it, have motivated some media attention already, and I suspect more is to come. "The past is never dead. It's not even past," William Faulkner once said, and I think he's right.[2] In the South, to be sure, the past is not past, but even in America, the past is not even past, if the topic is the South.

The reasons for this are easy enough to understand. All know that until quite recently—say, the 1970s—the relationship between the South and America was strained, to say the very least, and it had been so for two centuries or more: from the antebellum slavery debates through the Civil War and Reconstruction to the modern civil rights movement of the 1950s and 1960s, region and nation were at odds. Indeed, the South and America fought—politically, legally, culturally, and even militarily—and that conflicted, sorrowful past is not easily forgotten. As the title of a 1998 *New York Times* article has it, "The South's History Rises, Again and Again." No culture, of course, exists only in the present: all draw on, hark back to, a past significant precisely because of its continued moral, identity, and emotional utility. In this the South is no different, but what is unusual is how explicitly, how routinely, and how pervasively the region's history, that very particular southern past, is evoked in the present: the South of *then* is recreated and oddly memorialized, concretized in a sense, in the South of *now*.[3]

Images abound of the South's past continuing to rise again and again, and some of those most sharply etched—in particular, those that portray in one way or another the conflict between nation and region, or the South's outcast nature—are found in today's newspaper. A special section of the very first issue of the *New York Times* to appear in the new century, titled "Reflections on the Century Past and the Decades Ahead," included interviews with individuals for whom the twentieth century's "signal moments" remain "vivid memories" and with those who, according to the *Times*, "inherit this history." Not surprisingly, the people interviewed were from places with histories heavy with drama and death, shame and struggle, pain and possibility: India, Cambodia, and Germany, Russia and China, South Africa and the Middle East, and Detroit and the American South. Two southerners were interviewed about the past and future of race and rights in the region, and, perhaps paradoxically suggesting continuity amidst change, were from localities about as opposite in cultural trajectory as one could imagine, that New South symbol (or perhaps the "No-South" symbol), Atlanta, and what historian James Cobb has called "the most Southern place on earth," the Mississippi Delta.[4]

A cursory Lexis-Nexis search of selected newspapers published in the last few years revealed a very large number of similar articles. A handful of such titles appear here, roughly grouped by whether the article is largely about the past itself ("Old Times Are Not Forgotten"), reports significant current events by evoking, or linking them to, the region's past ("The Past in South's Present"), or makes analogies between the history of the South (in this case, just Mississippi) and happenings, past or present, in other localities. Where the meaning of the story's title is not self-evident, I have included brief excerpts and emphasized particular passages from the article to suggest its flavor.

OLD TIMES ARE NOT FORGOTTEN

1. "Revisiting a Watershed Era; Photo Show Reflects Turmoil of the Civil Rights Battle," *New York Times*, 18 January 1999.

2. "Fighting an Enemy Called Segregation. World War II Army Captain Recalls a Different Battle: Breaking Racial Barriers," *Kansas City Star*, 24 February 1999.

    "But neither had [Benjamin Dennis] experienced segregation and intense racial discrimination until arriving at Camp Van Dorn in Mississippi in 1943. . . . *'I'd grown up in a good state,' Dennis said, 'but when I got to Mississippi and saw signs for 'colored' restrooms and 'colored' water fountains, you can bet your life I didn't try anything else. . . . Southern England was just like Mississippi (in terms of discrimination).'*"

3. "A New Lesson Plan; Area Schools Take Black History Seriously," New Orleans *Times-Picayune*, 28 February 1999.

    "When Chris Reuter started to teach his students . . . about the civil rights movement, he didn't plan to follow the textbook's cue that it was born from Rosa Parks' refusal to give up her seat. . . . *The catalyst was the death of Emmett Till, a black teenager who was beaten to death in Mississippi by white supremacists. It happened Aug. 28, 1955.*"

4. "Trying to Understand Racial Tension," Dublin *Irish Times*, 1 March 1999.

    "I recently watched again the excellent 1988 film *Mississippi Burning*. . . . *The film movingly depicts the racial tensions and the hatred directed against black people in Mississippi in the early 1960s.*"

5. "Ride Recalls Mississippi Slayings; Atlanta Among Stops as Caravan Travels South," *Atlanta Journal and Constitution*, 19 June 1999.

6. "In Memory of Emmett," *Chicago Sun-Times*, 23 August 1999.
    "*A 14-year-old Chicago boy, Emmett was brutally murdered on Aug. 28, 1955, ostensibly because he had whistled at, or made a flirtatious remark to, the wife of a white store owner in the town of Money, Miss.* . . . The crime, and the kangaroo trial that followed . . . were galvanizing events in the fight for civil rights."

7. "A Witness to History," *Chicago Sun-Times*, 2 January 2000.
    "*[In 1962] I watched a crowd of heckling but good-humored young Americans turn into a murderous mob that heaved bricks at U.S. marshals with no more thought than that of a small boy breaking*

*windows in a greenhouse. . . . Beyond the park is the Lyceum Building,
the main administrative offices of 'Ole Miss'. . . .* At first, no one
seemed in a bad mood. The crowd was enjoying itself, milling
about and chanting: 'Two, four, six, eight, we don't wanna
integrate.' But things got meaner."

8. "Project Understanding: As Part of a Freshman Class Project,
Seward High Students Learn that Racism and Hatred Exist
Outside of the Midwest," *Omaha World-Herald*, 4 January 2000.
"Twenty-four freshmen, led by their teacher, solicited accounts
of racism from across the country and tacked them on their
classroom bulletin board. . . . *after reading John Howard Griffin's
"Black Like Me," a book in which the white author darkens his skin to
appear black and travels through Mississippi. He finds that racism goes
deeper than cross burnings. It's in the way people look at and speak to
blacks."*

9. " 'And Justice For All'; New Play Explores Message in Death of
Young Civil Rights Martyr," *Houston Chronicle*, 15 January 2000.

THE PAST IN THE SOUTH'S PRESENT

10. "In Mississippi, a New Look at Old Hostilities," *The Washington
Post*, 20 March 1998.
"Since the secret files were first made public Tuesday, Sarah
Rowe-Sims, a state archivist here, *has watched the faces of the steady
stream of visitors who have searched a thick book containing names of
activists and just plain folks who were spied on by the Mississippi
Sovereignty Commission during the civil rights movement. 'There's a look
of disbelief when they see their name,' said Rowe-Sims. The initial reaction
sometimes is followed by tears."*

11. "Justice Catches Up With KKK Killer 32 Years On; The Family of a
Black Civil Rights Activist Has Seen Him Avenged at Last—After
Four Unsuccessful Trials," London *Observer*, 23 August 1998.

12. "Ex-Klansman Charged in '66 Race Slaying Dies," *New York
Times*, 20 September 1998.

13. "Too Slowly for Many, Mississippi Faces a Hurtful Heritage,"
Washington Post, 24 October 1998.

14. "Civil Wrongs; Pressure Builds to Reopen the Unsolved Murders of Rights Activists in 1960s," *Atlanta Journal and Constitution*, 21 February 1999.

15. "In Miss, a Bombing Reopens Racial Wounds," *Philadelphia Inquirer*, 15 March 1999.

16. "NAACP Tours Sites of Alleged Army Slaughter; Writer Brings ww 11 Legend into Limelight," New Orleans *Times-Picayune*, 23 March 1999.

17. "Activists Converge on S.C. Capital," *Atlanta Journal and Constitution*, 7 January 2000.
    "[A member of the] Sons of Confederate Veterans . . . said if the [NAACP] succeeds in forcing down the flag in South Carolina, it next would target the Confederate emblem incorporated into the Georgia and Mississippi state flags. 'We've got to hold the line somewhere. They want to eradicate all of our heritage,' [he said]. 'That is why all of the (old) Confederacy is so concerned about South Carolina.' "

MISSISSIPPI: EVOCATIONS, ANALOGIES, METAPHORS

18. "No Kennedy Likeness," *Journal of Commerce*, 9 January 1998.
    "The massacre of 45 Tzotzil Indians . . . in the southern [Mexican] state of Chiapas . . . [is compared] with the U.S. civil rights struggle in the early and mid-1960s. '*It would be a fair comparison to say this is like the Old South, and Chiapas is Alabama or Mississippi,' political scientist Federico Estevez recently told* The New York Times."

19. "Secret Files Unlocked: Spies Hounded Black Activists; Mississippi Ran a Stasi-style Network that Targeted 1960s Civil Rights Campaigners," London *Guardian*, 19 March 1998.

20. "Horror and Fear Haunt Streets of Race-murder Texas Town; The Brutal Killing Had the Hallmarks of the Movie *Mississippi Burning*," London *Guardian*, 12 June 1998.

21. "Flare-up of Racial Tension in Oakland; Outrage over Remarks by Schools' Adviser," *San Francisco Chronicle*, 1 March 1999.
    "Oscar Wright [who] ignited a debate about anti-Semitism

because of his remarks . . . [on] the struggle over who runs the Oakland schools . . . *was born into a sharecropper family on a Mississippi plantation where black boys were not allowed to go to school.*"

22. "Protests in Police Killing of Diallo Grow Larger, and More Diverse," *New York Times*, 25 March 1999.
    "Blocking the door was a group of 17 elderly white women, *including Carolyn Goodman, 83, whose son, Andrew, a civil rights worker, was murdered in Mississippi in 1964.*"

23. "When Justice Is a Game," *New York Times*, 23 January 2000.
    "*This book about the life and trials of Rubin Carter recalls much of what was good and terrible about the United States during the last four decades: racism that was as virulent in New Jersey as it was in Mississippi.*"

When the cumulative weight of these titles and articles is tallied, one very much has the sense that the South's past, especially its racial past, is, to quote Faulkner again, "not even past." Indeed, that past—a past of racial injustice and brutality, of freedom rides and anti-desegregation riots by white university students—is recycled, and then recycled again. Perhaps the best illustration of this is the *Irish Times* article "Trying to Understand Racial Tension" (#4), which is a 1999 commentary on a 1988 movie, *Mississippi Burning*, about Mississippi's 1964 Freedom Summer. Because the South's past is seemingly ever renewed in the present, that past becomes an important lens, possibly one of the most important lenses, through which particular *contemporary* moments or events are cognitively and emotionally apprehended, thereby framing how readers make moral and intellectual sense of current happenings both in the South and elsewhere. The headlines of a London newspaper, for example, compared the infamous 1998 murder by dragging of James Byrd Jr. in Texas to *Mississippi Burning* (#20), and articles (#'s 21 and 22) situate recent racial incidents in Oakland, California, and in New York City in the context of Mississippi's troubled racial past, possibly as a moral compass to orient readers or perhaps simply to make the stories more dramatic.

The region's past, too, is sometimes linked, historically or metaphorically, to deliberately inhumane circumstances elsewhere, thereby both projecting onto the South a particular (and, obviously, near-barbaric) meaning and, by that very process, enabling readers to evaluate morally those nonsouthern situations. The "January 1, 2000" issue of the *New York Times* mentioned earlier does this subtly by grouping the South with other horrific twentieth-century hotspots across the globe (Germany, Cambodia, South Africa, etc.). Less nuanced are the pieces explicitly likening racism in New Jersey (#23) and in southern England (#2) to that in Mississippi. But much more pointed examples include the article in which a Mexican political scientist, commenting on the murders of forty-five Tzotzil Indians in the southern Mexican state of Chiapas, stated that "it would be a fair comparison to say this is like the Old South, and Chiapas is Alabama or Mississippi" (#18), and the one titled "Secret Files Unlocked" (#19), in which the London *Guardian* equated (probably accurately) Mississippi in the 1950s and 1960s to East Germany during the Communist era because both regimes established elaborate state structures to spy on their own citizens and to punish those deemed insufficiently loyal.[5]

These stories represent only a fraction of the *hundreds* of functionally equivalent articles I turned up for just the last few years using only two keywords to guide the Lexis-Nexis search: "race" and "Mississippi." With more diligent searching, using, say, the names of all ex-Confederate states and going back a decade or two, I suspect I could have found literally thousands of such articles. Add to all this the wide geographic scope of these newspapers—from London and Dublin to New York, Chicago, Kansas City, and San Francisco—and the extraordinarily high prestige of many of them, and one has a clearer sense still that the South's past *must* retain profound moral significance, for the region, the nation, and beyond. In a very special and important way, then, that past can't die, can't become fossilized, can't be relegated to history books or museums; it *can't* become simply "past."

One thing most of these titles suggest is how seriously aberrant the South (or at least Mississippi) was from "American" public life, and they thus signal, yet again, the conflict between region and nation. At root, this conflict revolved around differences in definitions and practices, around what it meant to be southern, and how southerners acted, and what it meant to be American, and how Americans acted, or were supposed to act. So significant, in fact, were these differences that the search for the origins, expressions, and consequences of "southern distinctiveness" has been a journalistic and academic staple for decades. Whether the South was thought "savage," or "benighted," or an "American problem," on the one hand, or "traditional" or "authentic," on the other, almost everyone was sure that it was different, different from the Northeast, different from the Midwest and West. This belief was at the root of the attention to the region during the Carter years and, of course, for decades before that. But the South wasn't just different, it was *really* different, *importantly* different; more, in the differentness of its history and its culture and in the way it meshed, or did not mesh, with mainstream America, the South was constructed to be something larger than the totality of its history and its people and their practices.[6] And the region continues to this day to be depicted and understood metaphorically—not only as the negative standard used to assess the civic immorality of other places, but also as an object lesson, a morality tale, about what America was or was not, or could be, or most certainly should not be.

So it was that thirteen years ago, when a young African American, Michael Griffith, was beaten to death by white racists in Howard Beach, Queens, New York City, for no apparent reason other than the fact that he was black, the outraged then-mayor of New York, Ed Koch, told a national television audience that he would "expect this kind of thing to happen in the Deep South," adding that the attackers were no better than "lynching parties that existed in the Deep South." Whites in Queens apparently took umbrage at being equated with those from Dixie and, according to the *Los Angeles Times*, booed Koch out of a church in which he was speaking. Much more recently, in the last days of 1998, another African American, nineteen-year-old Tyisha Miller, was killed by Riverside, California, police officers, who shot her at least twenty-seven times even though she was apparently unconscious in her car. Understandably outraged, a family friend accused the officers of acting like a lynch mob, saying, too, "This might as well be Mississippi."[7] Implicit in this man's moral geography, and in Koch's as well, was the silent yet unmistakable presumption that such racist violence could not, should not, happen in California or in New York City or in any other place in America except the Deep South, in Mississippi. Southern distinctiveness, indeed.

The idea that the South exists on a visibly lower ethical plane is, quite clearly, alive and well, now, today, in the minds and words of Americans who must make sense of the senseless, and who do so by latching on to emotional and moral imagery they can understand, here the history of racial barbarism of the Deep South. Note on this score the raw anger and anguish of *New York Times* editorial-columnist Bob Herbert, who wrote in a May 1999 "In America" op-ed piece: "I stood beside the cotton field in the morning quiet of the Delta and listened to the echoes of the tortured souls from years and decades and centuries past. To enter Mississippi has always been, in my view, to descend to a lower place, a world of fanatical race hatred in which blacks were condemned by whites to a perpetual state of humiliation and often gruesome suffering."[8] Again, southern distinctiveness, indeed.

If for no other reason than that signified by these images and representations, the idea of southern distinctiveness clearly warrants continued discussion. But it is worthwhile for another reason as well. Merely to ask whether the South is still significantly different leads us to examine the remarkable changes that have occurred in the region in just the past generation: the end of legalized racial segregation; large-scale return migration by African Americans from the North and the West; marked ethnic heterogeneity; urbanization unmatched by any other region in the country; growing economic affluence for many southerners; the rise of a two-party political system; the political presence and electoral clout of African Americans; and what political scientists Earl and Merle Black have called "the great white switch," the exodus of white southerners from the Democratic party to the party of Abraham Lincoln.[9] By thinking about what may seem to be a staid, even hackneyed, question—Is the South still different?—we are driven to ponder social change of the highest order.

Despite the continued relevance of the question of southern distinctiveness, for it to yield all the intellectual and moral riches it possesses, we need to ask it in new ways, ways that lay bare some of its hidden and problematic assumptions. We need also to ask further questions motivated by the question of southern distinctiveness itself. Consider, for example, the enormously influential essay "The Search for Southern Identity," written in the 1950s by C. Vann Woodward. Woodward defined southern distinctiveness in terms of what he called the "historical experiences" of the southern people, experiences that were really the negation of what he took to be the mythical, idealized experiences of the "American people."[10] To Woodward, where America was created morally pure and innocent, providentially decreed by a Supreme Being to be "a city on a hill" and free of the Old World evils of tyranny and class privilege, the South was steeped in sin—guilty first of the evils of slavery and later of enforced racial segregation. Second, where America was the land of prosperity and plenty, the South was poor, desperately bereft of economic opportunity and economic justice, and proclaimed the nation's "number one economic problem" by President Franklin Roosevelt in 1938. Finally, where America was victorious in its military quests (at least in those sunny days before Vietnam) and the global prototype for successful nation-building, the South's fleeting attempt at nationhood in 1861 was a dismal failure, shot down in defeat in the costliest war in terms of American (including Confederate) casualties this nation has ever fought. Guilt, poverty, and defeat, then, are at the root of southern distinctiveness in Woodward's view.

Now, there is something wrong—factually wrong, I think—with these sorts of understandings. Poverty there was, more than enough to go around, but guilt? defeat? No. "The southern people," generally speaking, could not have been guilty of racial tyranny because a large minority of southerners—*black southerners*, to be precise—were its victims, not its perpetrators. No guilt there. Defeat? Again, no. Contrary to Woodward and many others, "the southern people" did not lose the Civil War; the *Confederacy* lost the War, to be sure, but a large minority of southerners— again, *black* southerners—in fact won the War and thus their legal freedom. And the implication of these observations about guilt and defeat, unfortunately, is as arresting as it is unavoidable: the only way that Woodward, a man of obvious goodwill and enormous learning, the *only* way he could possibly be correct in his reasoning about southern distinctiveness was to assume—implicitly to be sure—that African Americans, a people with roots in the soil and the toil of the South going way back, further back than that of most southern whites, were not in fact southerners. They were blacks; southerners, *real* southerners, by unconscious but consensual definition, were white.

Woodward's definition of southern identity nonetheless is shrewder than some might realize. He also argued that in its poverty, defeat, and guilt, "the South" had much more in common with the rest of humanity than did its opposite, "America," whose "opulence, success and innocence" thus rendered it by global standards the truly distinctive nation-state. Though some South-watchers, such as James Cobb in *The Most Southern Place on Earth* and elsewhere, have extended Woodward's insight by positing the "universality" of the South's historical experiences, most have honored it only in breach, focusing instead on his formulation of southern distinctiveness vis-à-vis America.

In retrospect, it is clear that had Woodward brought African Americans centrally into his definition of "the southern people" in his essay, as he later did, his important notion of "Southern (global) commonality" would have enjoyed greater empirical grounding and political resonance. However, for decades his "Southerner-as-white" held sway, probably because it seemed so natural, so *right*, to so many who, in the midst of extraordinary challenge and change, were striving so hard to normalize and thereby positively (if ironically) affirm their regional identity. But despite the "commonsensical" and "taken-for-granted" nature of Woodward's and similar definitions, they obscure at least as much as they illuminate, and, as I've said, sometimes they are flat wrong. Note, for example, the seemingly "natural" logical move Woodward and others make, from the *Confederacy* to the "South" to southerners, the easy, almost unconscious, identification (cognitively, yes, but also politically and morally) of the very last construct in that false syllogism with the first one. The problem with definitions of this sort, and with the logic upon which they are built—a problem shared by much analysis of southern identity and distinctiveness, and certainly by those who defend the display of the Confederate battle flag by appeals to what they mistakenly call "Southern Heritage"—is that "the South" was always both more and less than the Confederacy. Thus, when we define "the South" and when we ask how it differed from America, we must understand what we are doing, and what we are doing is affirming and thereby imposing on ourselves and on others "*a South*" and "*an America*" that are seamless, unitary, undifferentiated notions—"*a South, an America; one South, one America.*" These are definitions of peoples and places artificially devoid of significant internal diversity and schism. That black southerners were also *southerners*, as well as, crucially, Americans of African descent, is the most glaring contradiction here, but hardly the only one.[11]

When we talk about "the South," for example, which South, exactly, are we talking about? The glittering Sun-Belt, franchise-laden South of Houston, Atlanta, Nashville, Charlotte, or the rural, small-town and disappearing South of coalminers in eastern Kentucky, sharecroppers in the Mississippi Delta, textile workers in small Carolina towns throughout the Piedmont? In our definitions of southerners, do we include the Chinese in Mississippi and the Cherokee in Georgia? The Cuban Americans in Miami and the forty thousand or so Hispanics in Nashville? The Cambodians in Atlanta and the Vietnamese along the Texas Gulf Coast?

When we speak of "the South," do we have in mind the South of Birmingham's racist Commissioner of Public Safety, Bull Connor, who in 1963 unleashed police dogs and turned fire hoses on black children? Is it that South? Do we perhaps think of the very similar South of Mississippi's Sam Bowers, the former Klan leader so often mentioned in those newspaper articles from 1998 for the murder more than thirty years earlier of civil rights leader Vernon Dahmer? Or is it the South of Martin

Luther King and Fannie Lou Hamer and John Lewis, of whites like Will Campbell and Virginia Durr and Duncan Gray, who worked with King and Hamer and countless other African Americans for racial justice? Is it the South of today's big-city black mayors like Willie Herenton of Memphis and Richard Arrington of Birmingham, of award-winning African American novelists such as Ernest Gaines and Alice Walker?

When we see "the South" portrayed in popular culture, do we see the South of the movie *Mississippi Masala*, a film that suggests that life in today's Deep South is far richer and much more multihued than many might believe possible? Do we see the South of the movie *Down in the Delta*, a South sweet with healing for African Americans no longer living in, but nevertheless indelibly of, the South? Or is it the South of *Mississippi Burning*, of Phil Ochs's early 1960s protest song, "Mississippi, Find Yourself Another Country," of Nina Simone's 1950s song "Mississippi Goddamn"? When we speak of the music of the South, what do we have in mind? Contemporary country at the Grand Ole Opry, or bluegrass from the East Tennessee mountains, or rock-and-roll from Athens, Georgia, or, still again, the music that was played thirty years ago when I listened to it on Memphis radio station WDIA, home of the blues in the mid-South? When we talk of the South, are we talking about the South of the magazine *Southern Living*, an enviably affluent South peopled almost exclusively by gracious whites who seem to do little more than cook gourmet meals and tend to their luscious gardens, or are we talking about the South of the magazine *Southern Exposure*, an economically exploitative, racist, homophobic, misogynist, genuinely ugly South?[12]

Again, then, which South? Whose South?

And, now, *America*. When we speak of "America," which America, exactly, is used to judge and damn the South? Is it the America of the movie *You've Got Mail*, America as Manhattan's Upper West Side writ large, enviably affluent and also very white, just about as white as the South of *Southern Living*? Or is it the America of social critic Jonathan Kozol, who in his book *Amazing Grace* describes the brown and black south Bronx, a huge pocket of almost unimaginable poverty and brutality, an area of New York City used by the city's hospitals as a dumping ground for amputated body parts and bloody bandages and where city authorities paint warm scenes of stable domesticity on the expressway sides of gutted buildings so that, perhaps, just for a moment, suburban commuters who see these murals can believe they are looking into the windows of an America not so unlike their own? Is it the America of

Buford Furrow and Benjamin Smith, murderous racists full of lethal hatred from Los Angeles and Chicago respectively, who, in the summer of 1999, succeeded in stunning a nation *deeply* jaded by decades of civil violence? Or is it the America of Robert Kennedy, who dreamed of things that never were and asked why not? Is it the America of the Indian Removal Act, as it was officially known, or the America of the Voting Rights Act?

Which America, then, and which South? And now another question— Who decides the answers to these questions?

As a university teacher and a social scientist, I know that reality can't be portrayed in all its nuance and complexity, and I know, too, that those of us who talk of and teach the South must simplify, homogenize, exaggerate, smooth away inconsistencies and contradictions. Organizing frames must be forged, narrative plots and story lines developed, central themes discovered, and of necessity this means that "reality" will be massaged, if not consciously lied about. But this need to find, or manufacture, intellectual coherence neither precludes the portrayal of multiple Americas and multiple Souths—simply put, of southern *cultures* rather than southern *culture*—nor specifies exactly *which* America(s) and *which* South(s) will be constructed and reconstructed.[13]

My third question, then, is this: Why *this* America rather than *that* America? Why *this* South and not some *other* South? Perhaps it's the simple, unavoidable facts of history that lead us naturally to some understandings of nation and region and not to others. Some facts are so glaring, so historically patterned, so obviously important or morally appalling that they can't be ignored, that they *must* be what the newspaper story, or the college course, is *really* about. Perhaps. That is indeed how I organize my own course on the U.S. South. But consider also this fact: C. Vann Woodward's book *The Strange Career of Jim Crow*, a book about the rise and demise of the South's segregation laws, a book that Martin Luther King once called the "bible" of the civil rights movement and from which he read passages to Selma marchers in 1965, shows that America—its courts and laws, its politicians and its newspapers, too often its public—was deeply complicit in the white South's oppression of black southerners. The nation exported Jim Crow laws to the South; it was the *U.S.* Supreme Court that sanctified "separate but equal" Constitutional constructions, and all the while "America" proudly championed an imperial white supremacy, thereby subjugating people of color abroad and ignoring the pain and yearnings of African Americans at home. "As far as

I am concerned," Malcolm X once shrewdly observed, "Mississippi is anywhere south of the Canadian border."[14] Yes, the white South inexcusably committed racial atrocities that today would rightly be (and should have been at the time) punished as criminal, but it did so in part— *only* in part, but nonetheless *in part*—because it was permitted to do so— maybe encouraged to do so, with a wink and a nod, and by example—by America, or more precisely, by white America. These are facts, too, and they subvert easy invidious comparison of America and the South.

Given all of this—given, that is, that conventional juxtapositions of region and nation both presuppose and perpetuate understandings of (one, largely seamless) "America" and of "the (single, solid) South"— given that, in truth, region and nation have shared and together made a common history and thus are tied, inextricably, one to the other—given all of this, then my last question is as follows: What intellectual interests are being served, what political functions are being met, by posing the question of southern distinctiveness? Which group or social practice is elevated by the query and which denigrated? In the academic parlance of today, what "culture work" is accomplished by posing this question in the way it is typically raised?

Allow me to offer a few suggestive answers to those questions.

First, juggling such oppositional dichotomies as "America" and "the South" sharply etches into popular consciousness morally vivid definitions of both region and nation. When one understands the South as the negation of America—as Woodward and others have argued—one is also likely to understand more deeply what America is, and what it is (or ought to be), in particular, is the opposite of the South. This is what Koch was saying, what the critics of the Riverside, California, police-killing of Tyisha Miller were saying: regardless of where these racial horrors actually happened, they could really, should really, have happened only in the Deep South. So if the South is the repository of brutal racism, then America, by way of stark contrast, is the repository of the ideals of justice, freedom, equality, where character, not color, supposedly imparts individual worth and where all individuals are to be treated with dignity.

Second, unfavorably comparing the South to America can motivate and legitimate political action to bring the social reality—that is, "the South"—closer to the abstract ideal; that is, "America." In his magisterial "Letter from the Birmingham Jail," Martin Luther King, for example, drew on centuries of racial injustice against southern blacks to project onto the conscience of the nation "a South" that had no place in a morally just America, and then he contrasted that South to what he called the "goal of America"—"freedom"—to validate and to sustain a militant nonviolence so massive, so profound, and so extraordinarily essential as to prove transformative for my generation of southerners, black and white.[15]

Third, juxtaposing America and the South in a way that focuses almost exclusive attention on the region's racial crimes quite possibly stunted the nation's willingness to confront *its* own racism. Again, if the white South is understood to be the "real," the "main," perhaps even the exclusive source of racial barbarism, then America is permitted to distance itself from its racial problem, to localize and thereby regionally contain it—in the South. Thus, even as the white South's distinctive, and immoral, racial practices mobilized the outrage, sacrifice, and heroism of some Americans, mostly African Americans, for much too long it also insulated millions of nonsouthern white Americans from looking too closely at their own unearned wages of whiteness. Despite Fannie Lou Hamer's admonition—"So this ain't just Mississippi's problem. It's America's problem"— the South (again more precisely, the white South), not white America, was in need of reconstruction; the South, not America—or so the argument went—must change its ways.[16]

Given what I've thus far said, I suppose some might wonder if I am *really* saying that the South was used as a scapegoat for America's sins— that, in Willie Morris's words, the region "has always been the toy and the pawn, in greed and righteousness, of all the rest of America: the palliative of national guilt"—and that too much attention, in movies, on TV, in books and newspapers such as those discussed here, continues to be paid to the seamier side of the South's history; they might wonder if I'm *really* saying that it's time to put that unfortunate past behind us and just get along.[17] Am I *really* saying these things?

No, that is not what I am saying. The moral and political gravity of those times—of the events etched in memory and chronicled still in current newspaper articles and elsewhere—is too painful and thus too precious to be allowed to wither, to become, simply, "past." The white South exhaled such toxicity for so long on the nation, and most particularly on its own people of color, that if the very word "South"—or Mississippi— has indeed become a metaphor, a symbol, for evil, so be it. Now that well-argued calls for national reparations to African Americans are in the air, that is small enough price to pay, too small perhaps. "The South owes," says Leslie W. Dunbar. "It ought to compensate."[18] We as a people therefore continue to need to read about and to teach those times, those happenings; we need to learn about and to memorialize—in Memphis and Montgomery, Birmingham and Oxford—the historical "why" animating the present-day symbol. For without historical reckoning, there can be no repentance, and without repentance, there can be no reconciliation and no redemption. So, again, no, I am saying none of those things.

What I *am* saying is this: there are many Souths and many Americas, that region and America are both rural and urban, cosmopolitan and provincial, moral and immoral, radical and reactionary, rich and poor, brown and red, and yellow and black and white, and when the issue of southern distinctiveness is raised, as it clearly continues to be in today's newspapers and as it likely will be in one guise or another in the months to come, I believe it both useful and fair to ask, *Which* America? *Which* South? To ask, Why *this* South? Why *that* America? To ask which issues are being illuminated and which obscured by this question; to ask, in brief, what culture work is accomplished, intentionally or otherwise, by the timing and phrasing of the question of southern distinctiveness.

NOTES

This is a revision of talks given at Vanderbilt University and the University of Mississippi. I would like to thank the following for their comments on earlier drafts: Elizabeth Boyd, Jimmie L. Franklin, Larry Isaac, Yollette Jones, John Shelton Reed, Peggy Thoits, and Harry Watson.

1. See, for example, Fred Hobson, *Tell About the South: The Southern Rage to Explain* (Louisiana State University Press, 1983).

2. Faye Fiore, "Run for Presidency Begins for the Man from Carthage; Politics: On Town's Courthouse Steps Today, Gore Will Showcase His Real But Delicate Roots in Tennessee Soil," *Los Angeles Times*, 16 June 1999; see also Al Cross, "Gore Goes Back to Rural Roots; He'll Begin Run For Presidency in Tennessee," Louisville *Courier-Journal*, 16 June 1999. William Faulkner, *Requiem for a Nun* (Random House, 1951), 85.

3. Kevin Sack, "The South's History Rises, Again and Again," *New York Times*, 22 March 1998. I would like to thank Harry Watson for gently pushing me to think more deeply about this part of my argument.

4. " 'They Just Moved a Brick, Because the Brick Was Right in Their Face,' " *New York Times*, 1 January 2000; James Cobb, *The Most Southern Place on Earth: The Mississippi Delta and the Roots of Southern Identity* (Oxford University Press, 1992);

for a lively discussion of the "No-South South," see James Cobb, *Redefining Southern Culture: Mind and Identity in the Modern South* (University of Georgia Press, 1999), 150–86.

5. See, for example, James Silver, *Mississippi: The Closed Society,* new enl. ed. (Harcourt, Brace & World, 1966).

6. See Robert M. Pierce, "Jimmy Carter and the New South: The View from New York," ed. Merle Black and John Shelton Reed, *Perspectives on the American South*, vol. 2 (Gordon and Breach, 1984), 181–94. Edward Ayers, "What We Talk about When We Talk about the South," Edward Ayers, Patricia Nelson Limerick, Stephen Nissenbaum, and Peter S. Onuf, *All Over the Map: Rethinking American Regions* (Johns Hopkins University Press, 1996), 62–82.

7. Joyce Purnick, "Koch Comment on 'Deep South' Angers Mayors," *New York Times*, 25 December 1986; John J. Goodman and Lee May, "The Howard Beach Story: Ordinary Night Explodes," *Los Angeles Times*, 8 February 1987; James Langton, "Los Angeles Simmers after Shooting," London *Sunday Telegraph*, 3 January 1999; see also Montreal *Gazette*, 4 January 1999.

8. Bob Herbert, "In America; Mississippi Learning," *New York Times*, 13 May 1999.

9. Carol Stack, *Call To Home: African Americans Reclaim the Rural South* (Basic, 1996); Earl Black and Merle Black, *The Vital South: How Presidents Are Elected* (Harvard University Press, 1992); Hugh Davis Graham, "Since 1965: The South and Civil Rights," in *The South as an American Problem*, eds. Larry J. Griffin and Don H. Doyle (University of Georgia Press, 1995), 145–63.

10. C. Vann Woodward, *The Burden of Southern History*, rev. ed. (Louisiana State University Press, 1968), 3–25.

11. I would like to thank Elizabeth Boyd for urging me to acknowledge Woodward's insight about the South's universality. In his 1965 essay "From the First Reconstruction to the Second" in *The South Today: 100 Years After Appomattox*, ed. Willie Morris (Harper and Row, 1965), Woodward used the phrase "Negro Southerner." On the "southernness" of the region's African Americans and their claims on the region and its identity, see Jimmie Lewis Franklin's 1993 presidential address to the Southern Historical Association, "Black Southerners, Shared Experience, and Place: A Reflection," *Journal of Southern History* 59 (February 1994): 3–18; Charlayne Hunter-Gault, *In My Place* (Farrar Straus, 1992); Carol Stack, *Call to Home*, and James Cobb in *Redefining Southern Culture*, 125–49. My debt to Ed Ayers in the next few pages will be obvious to all who know his sparkling, provocative essay, "What We Are Talking about When We Talk about the South."

12. On the magazine *Southern Living*, see Diane Roberts, "Living Southern in *Southern Living*," in *Dixie Debates: Perspectives on Southern Cultures*, ed. Richard H. King and Helen Taylor (New York University Press, 1996), 85–98, and James Cobb, *Redefining Southern Culture*, 141.

13. This notion is hardly original. See, for example, Frank Vandiver, ed., *The Idea of the South: Pursuit of a Central Theme* (University of Chicago Press, 1964); Jack Kirby, "The South as a Pernicious Abstraction," in *Perspectives on the American South*, vol. 2, 167–79; and Edward Ayers, "What We Talk about When We Talk about the South." On southern *cultures* rather than southern *culture*, see Richard Gray, "Negotiating Differences: Southern Culture(s) Now," in *Dixie Debates: Perspectives on Southern Cultures*, 218–27.

14. C. Vann Woodward, *The Strange Career of Jim Crow* (3rd rev. ed. Oxford University Press, 1974). King's reaction to and use of the book is discussed by C. Vann Woodward, *Thinking Back: The Perils of Writing History* (Louisiana State University Press, 1986), 92. Malcolm X, with the assistance of Alex Haley, *The Autobiography of Malcolm X* (Ballantine, 1965), 417.

15. Martin Luther King Jr., *Why We Can't Wait* (New American Library, 1964), 93.

16. Quoted in John Egerton, *A Mind to Stay Here: Profiles from the South* (Macmillan, 1970), 103.

17. Willie Morris, *Terrains of the Heart and Other Essays on Home* (Yoknapatawpha Press, 1981), 75.

18. Leslie W. Dunbar, "The Final New South?" *Virginia Quarterly Review* 74 (Winter 1998): 49–58. Randall Robinson, *The Debt: What America Owes to Blacks* (Dutton, 2000), makes a provocative case for national reparations that is not so easily dismissed.

Chicago as the Northernmost County of Mississippi

Anthony Walton

"It took my experience in the North to teach me that I am first and last a southerner." Migrants preparing to leave the South in Goin' to Chicago, *courtesy of California Newsreel.*

was born August 27, 1960, in Saint Joseph's Hospital, a diocesan Catholic institution in Aurora, Illinois, where my mother was employed as a nurse's aide and therefore acquainted with most of the personnel, including a couple of dozen priests and nuns. This fact is noteworthy because it indicates that I was fussed and prayed over more ferociously even than most newborns, which is to say, quite a bit. My mother was a staunch hard-shell black Baptist, but I'm sure she didn't mind all the extra spiritual armor. She had suffered a miscarriage before my birth, was worried about having children at all, and dearly wanted this child—me—to survive.

The town I was born in, Aurora, wasn't that unique a place in the northern, or say middle northern, Midwest of that time. It was, however, the sort of place that doesn't really exist anymore: a rugged industrial town of fifty- to sixty-thousand people, where a garden variety of ethnic whites—Irish, Italian, and Polish Catholics, Romanians and Greeks, Serbs and Croatians—vied with blacks and Hispanics for the good jobs in the mills and factories of the city. These were *very* good jobs, the kinds of jobs where an illiterate man with a strong back and a strong will could make twenty, thirty, even forty dollars an hour as he gained expertise and value to the company. These jobs are now in Mississippi, Tennessee, and Alabama—if they are in the United States at all—and even more likely to be in Mexico if not the Dominican Republic or Ireland or India due to the ongoing process of downsizing and globalization, now twenty years old and continuing in the Midwest.

These ethnic groups, which made up a distinct working class, were overseen by a middle class of stolid midwesterners—Presbyterians, Methodists, and Lutherans of mostly Anglo-American, Scandinavian, and Scottish (not Scots-Irish) stock, who were in turn superseded in authority and influence by an elite of a few wealthy Irish Catholics, a strong core of Swedish Lutherans, and, surprisingly, Christian Scientists, and the usual sprinkling of Anglo founders' descendants refusing to relinquish their advantage. O'Brien, Copley, Erickson. Those were the town names of consequence and weight, but it wasn't all tamped down. My father, a Mississippi migrant, was befriended by Mr. Erickson, one of the wealthy Scandinavian Christian Scientists from over on Downer Place. My father would go by Mr. Erickson's office after-hours at the bank on Saturdays and they'd talk about things—sports, their families, world affairs, the Masonic secrets of money. My father often credited this friendship and these talks with helping him find his way. He learned how things work, at least in that town, and he learned not to be intimidated by whites. This information he passed on to his children, to *our* great advantage as we grew up in the North and had to learn to decipher things, to read the writings on the wall, as it were.

The preceding description is, of course, a great simplification of a place and its people, and even of my family. But I lay it out to offer a sort of *genius loci*, as the term is used by anthropologist Victor Witter Turner and literary critic Robert Stepto—"my site of generation," the place I sprang from—in the hopes of providing a larger context of the surrounding American culture of the 1960s and 1970s and attempting to live up to my slightly woofing title: "Chicago as the Northernmost County of Mississippi." The older I get, the more I am convinced that this is what happened, or what mostly happened, as my personality and psyche were formed and as I became the person who stands before you today, a resident of the resolutely Yankee state of Maine, born and raised in late-century Chicago (or Chicagoland, as we call it), yet allowed, with not incredible overreaching, to claim kinship to the South.

If that's even what I'm doing. I don't know if I can claim to be a southerner the way my friends Richard Ford, Franklin Burroughs, and Richard Howorth are—somewhat conflicted by their fierce pride in the legacy of their forebears, if not exactly foursquare with all that happened back then (and I'm taking a huge liberty of putting words in their mouths). And I'm not exactly a southerner the way my Uncle Elton Cummings or my Aunt Hazel Simmons or my cousins Kenny and Ray McKenzie are—Christian, friendly, thoughtful, but also quietly content in a largely black world that hasn't changed much since the end of segregation.

Still, the more I travel the nation, the more time I spend in Maine, or Miami, or Los Angeles, or Chicago, the more I feel like a southerner. I look around me and most of my friends are southerners or people with strong southern roots. I even find, most strangely, that most of my enduring business relationships are with southerners.

How, then, did this come to be? What does it mean? My father went north with the intention of leaving Mississippi in his rearview mirror, and he still largely feels that way. My mother, on the other hand, longs for New Albany and Oxford, for the stretch of Lafayette County that lies between them, where she grew up in a more gentle and privileged (if that is the word) environment. My father, who endured some of the worst of life for African Americans in Mississippi, can often be heard to say, "I call it 'Sippi 'cause I don't miss it," or, more trenchantly, "It wasn't Lincoln who freed the slaves, it was the Illinois Central." My father says he *hates* Mississippi, and to get him to move back there you'd have to take him in a pine box. So why do I embrace this place that my good father doesn't care to see again and would not return to were he not forced to from time to time by his wife, my mother?

Those journeys back, to visit my mother's family in Mississippi, are a large part of the answer. I can't even call those thousand-mile trips in a Ford woody station wagon loaded with kids and cold drinks and sandwiches epic, because that isn't how they seemed to me then. (Although I'm sure that's how they seemed to my Air Force mechanic father, who planned them with the precision of a bombing run through enemy territory.) They were simply a part of my daily life. I spent many summers there when I was young, at my grandparents' house in New Albany, at my great-grandmother's cabin way back up in the woods, at my Aunt Hazel's beauty parlor/hamburger shack/pool hall, and we often traveled down during the year at Thanksgiving, Christmas, or just for the heck of it.

We weren't the only ones. More than half the people in my neighborhood traveled just as often to Mississippi in *their* Ford or Chevy wagons. In the distorted geography of childhood, based on the world I had seen and experienced, Chicago and Mississippi stood out over everything else, with the long stretch of U.S. Highways 55 and 57 running like a lifeline between them. In my neighborhood the question, "Where are your people from?" was not answered by "Mississippi"—that was generally assumed —but by the name of a county (Amite, Lafayette, Coahama) or a town (Chulahoma, Tupelo, Byhalia), with a family member, near or distant, often discovered in common.

Looking back on my childhood from the aerial view of my adult years, I realize that I grew up in what was essentially an enclave of southerners. There were many other enclaves like mine, southern neighborhoods spread out between the Puerto Ricans on the next street and the blocks of Italians, Poles, and Croats in the industrial working-class towns all around Chicago.

These neighborhoods weren't drawn solely along racial lines. A few houses down from mine was a white family from Kentucky and a little further on a white family from Tennessee. Both of these families came north at about the same time and with many of the same dreams as my parents had. This was also the beginning of the great Latino surge into Chicago, yet another set of migrations that will leave the City of Big

Shoulders with as decidedly a Spanish accent as the City of Angels. I remember those kids and their families, as well: Angel, whose family lived in an old railroad car, and Wanda, one of my mother's best friends, always ready with candy or a kiss.

The fathers of many of my black friends rode around in cowboy hats and pickup trucks, some of them listening to Merle Haggard and George Jones. My neighborhood had the feeling of an extended family so characteristic of towns in the South. In fact, my Aunt Virginia lived next door, and my Aunt Shorty and my godmother, Mary Smith, lived at either end of the block, along with various cousins actual and assumed. If I were ever past the point where I was supposed to be on our street, doing something I wasn't supposed to be doing, my aunts or any of the other mothers—with a terse, "You're Dorothy's boy, aren't you?"—would discipline me themselves and send me on home. By the time I got there, they'd have called my mother and told her about it, so I'd end up getting it not once but twice, or if the offense were really bad, even a third time when my father got home from his twelve-hour day at work and took off his work boots with deliberate slowness, seemingly, to my self-centered mind, to prolong my agony. It never occurred to me that he might be tired.

We had the same church sermons and suppers, the same food, as our families had in the South, sermons and food—black-eyed peas, collard greens, sweet potato pie—quite different from that of the mainstream North. We were made to quote verses from the King James Bible every day—John 3:16, Romans 8:28, the 23rd Psalm. I can still quote, to the last semicolon of pregnant and proper pause, John 3:16: *For God so loved the world, that He gave His only begotten Son, that whosoever believeth in Him should not perish, but have everlasting life*. I still say it to myself at times, sometimes to hear the language, sometimes to "get a hold of myself," as I was so frequently admonished.

And many of the black folks around me, just a generation or two, if that, out of the South, loved country music, and not just those with pickup trucks and cowboy hats. When my mother was a child in New Albany, she and her family would spend Saturdays—the only day off for blacks—around the radio, listening first to Notre Dame football (it was a tradition among blacks, a kind of quiet rebellion, to root for the Catholic team) and then to the Grand Ole Opry. I believe those Saturday evenings by the radio with her six older sisters are her most cherished memories. When she moved north she brought this tradition with her. TV had replaced radio, but every week we'd watch *Hee Haw*—yes, *Hee Haw*—and the show Johnny Cash had for a while. And when Tammy Wynette or Charley Pride was going to be on the Ed Sullivan show, we'd tune in just to watch them, along with the Jackson Five or Smokey Robinson or whomever. My mother was very proud, in a deeply unironic way, of Tammy—born Virginia Wynette Pugh—for making it out of the fields just like she had.

When I was seven or eight years old I'd walk around the house singing "Your Cheatin' Heart" and "T for Texas." When I was younger still, my mother would dance with me to her country records, and I remember in particular turning around the kitchen to the sound of the "Tennessee Waltz" playing on the old record player in the next room. *I was dancin' with my darlin'*, too young to know what a darling was, or whose darling I was.

When I went to college, the black people I met who were a few more generations out from the South—and used "country" in general as a derogatory adjective implying a lack of sophistication—looked down on my love of this music. To them I think it carried connotations of a nostalgia among whites for the Old South, for a "simpler" time when blacks, by implication, were kept in their place. And I don't know, it's possible that this is part of its appeal for whites. But as Kenneth Burke and Ralph Ellison chronicle, cultural strategies created for one purpose can be used for quite another, and I still love country music in some ways as much as I love the blues, maybe because of those waltzes with my mother.

To her the deep loss and sadness of those songs carries the memory of and longing for her childhood in Mississippi—not that that was a better place or time. Even with her relatively gentle upbringing she remembers in detail and with bitterness the many insults of Jim Crow, but it was a time when she was with her family and when they all had the pure hope, unsullied by reality, of better things to come, in particular in the North. Music (country, blues, rhythm and blues) and the black Baptist church (gospel, spiritual, Holy Ghost) have shaped who I am and the extended family of my neighborhood, as did my father's reticence and carefulness and my mother's stern emphasis on manners. All of this I consider largely and distinctly a southern heritage.

But it has taken me almost until the age of forty to learn this. For a long time, as I left college in the Midwest and moved to Providence, Rhode Island, and later New York, I thought of myself as a northerner. I tried to *be* a northerner because this was what I thought it would take to make it. There is a saying, "The richest man in Chicago feels like a pauper in New York"; well, I intended to be a rich man in New York. This was what I thought the whole point of my parents' journeys north had been; my success would redeem all their work and everything they and everyone all the way back to Africa had suffered.

What I found in New York was not quite—not remotely, in fact—what I had expected. In New York I was both metaphorically and not-so-metaphorically beaten. The frenetic pace and random everyday cruelty of the big city were startling and wearing enough. But my disorientation went beyond that and stemmed from causes beyond my being young and naïve—though I certainly was both of those things. My time in New York felt like nothing so much as a hall of mirrors. As an aspiring young writer I was constantly being made promises by magazine editors, older writers, writers who were my peers, and few if any were kept. My confusion at all of this was sufficiently deep that it would take me years away from New York even to begin to unravel it. And, I am sure, New York is not the only place where this kind of initiation happened. Maybe the same thing would have happened in Chicago; I am sure it would have in Los Angeles. New York is where it happened to *me*.

Looking back on New York, I realize that much of my confusion there—much of its fun-house effect in my mind—had to do with issues of race, experience, and, most tellingly, class. And geography. I was surrounded by northeasterners, but all my frames of reference were southern, because *those were the people who had raised me. I* did not know, I could not have known, that in New York it seems to be accepted that words are a different thing than actions, that everyone was pressing for advantage in the same game, and that the majority of the actions I took out of what I perceived to be the codes of valor, duty, and honor would be interpreted as weakness and often held against me.

It took my experience in the North to teach me that I am first and last a southerner, as I was raised to be. It is no coincidence that my best friends are southerners; our frames of reference are the same, and my father's words have proven true. It was Faulkner who said—with his usual uncanny insight—that the son of the slave and the son of the slaveholder may prove to understand each other best of all. But I don't romanticize the South. I know how my father suffered there; I know why he doesn't want to come back; I know about Emmett Till and Schwerner, Chaney, and Goodman; I know the conditions in which most of the blacks in Mississippi—in the Delta in particular, but elsewhere as well—still live.

But I don't romanticize the North either, and more than anything I don't romanticize the connection between the regions. My father worked hard and spent a great deal of time and money and probably took years off his life to bring the rest of his extended family from the enforced rural poverty of Mississippi to what he perceived to be the freedom of the North. But the devastation of his family there has been almost total. The next generation has suffered grievously from gangs, prison, and AIDS, among other things, in the enforced urban poverty of Chicago and its more ruthless segregation and brutality.

As I have come to understand about myself that I am a southerner, I have come to understand this also about the generations of blacks who traveled north to find freedom and have found only the projects of Brooklyn or the miles of Chicago's Robert Taylor Homes, hard by the expressway. I have come to see that Chicago is the northernmost county of Mississippi in another, deeper way and that the story of Mississippi is first and last a tragedy of incalculable human scope, made all the more tragic by the deliberateness with which the tragic circumstances were administered.

For all the southern virtues I have named, there are corresponding flaws, or patterns of thought and belief which, while developed in response to the specific sociohistorical situations of the South and counting as strengths in those contexts, have only worked against millions of blacks in the North. I'm thinking in particular of fatalism, which my great-grandmother used to express in the beautiful if sad phrase "Come-day, go-day," meaning anything that was gained today usually was to be used today. You would never get ahead. Black and white southerners both are well acquainted with defeat. The tragicomic awareness of the blues, of which Ralph Ellison so eloquently writes, which enabled blacks to keep their souls and lives intact when there was nothing they could do, became in the North a circumscription. "Been down so long that down don't bother me," when taken to the North, with its scattered opportunities to rise against what is otherwise an unrelenting brutality, becomes a self-limiting pattern of thought, damning blacks as much by that brutality as by their bewildered, often inevitable acceptance of it. And in the North blacks found less help in survival from whites than they had received in the previously demonized South, Mayor Daley and the good Catholics of Chicago working with an efficiency of which Bilbo and Vardeman and the poor whites of Mississippi could not have dreamed.

In the North Robert Johnson's "Crossroads" evolved—or devolved—

into the "Crossroads" of the rap group Bone, Thugs-N-Harmony's song by that name, for my money the greatest pop song of the nineties in its attempt to encompass the devastation experienced by blacks in the North, from gun violence to drug abuse to AIDS. But the song is also deeply disturbing in that it represents almost a cult of death, a too eager, too fatalistic embrace of the inevitability of defeat, a celebration of the young friends and heroes who have gone on to some sort of hip-hop Valhalla.

This fatalism goes hand-in-hand, as most extremes do, with its opposite, magical thinking—the desire for success now, the belief that this is possible by any means and without any cost—so different from the work ethic of the South. The two taken together have led to the violent, empty, soulless, and grossly materialistic gangsta culture of the inner cities. This is the dark side of the rap myth, which is as problematic for young blacks as any myth—white supremacy, black inferiority, the futility of honest effort—that has passed previously.

Consider, along with fatalism and magical thinking, other southern virtues-as-flaws: the transformation of the extended families that enabled survival in my childhood and in the South into, in some quarters, the corrupted extended families of gang culture and the insular, church-based communities of the kind I grew up in that are so self-contained as to be removed from the main sources of information about opportunities to rise in the northern economy and now in the new global economy. Consider globalization itself and its crippling effects in terms of lost jobs and the corresponding loss of male providers and male leaders in black communities (see, for example, William Julius Wilson's work). Consider all this and it seems to me that blacks in general who moved to the North did not have much of a chance.

Chicago is the northernmost county of Mississippi. I think of this whenever I hear the latest gothic trauma on the news, with blacks either as villains or as victims; I think of this when I hear of the endless battles over busing and school resources; I think of the price that has been paid, the price that continues to be paid, by the millions whose only crime was hope, the same hope held by the millions of Irish, Italian, German, and Slavic immigrants and their descendants, who have so grimly opposed the black advance in the urban North. And I remember dancing with my mother to the "Tennessee Waltz." I think of the longing and loss that that song—that all of her beloved country songs—carries for my mother, of the endless catalog of suffering that she and her family would face in Chicago, of the pure hope for something better that was betrayed.

Perhaps the truest thing to say in the end is not that I am a southerner, but that I am an American. I've been shaped by the South and by the North, and by the East and West as well. (My mentor, Michael Harper, grew up in Brooklyn and Los Angeles.) I think of my aerial map of Chicago, those thousands of neighborhoods and towns like my childhood Aurora, of the rustbelt in general, and I realize there are two hundred million stories like mine. Different epochs, different histories, different places and times can exist side by side in the same city and in the same soul.

It is, I think, our great challenge as Americans to shake our persistent desire to believe there is only the eternal present—epitomized by MTV and the Internet and air travel and cosmetic surgery and personal fitness —to shake our love and chase of the new and the big. We spent a trillion dollars on a Star Wars system that did not work, but we could not defend Columbine High School. We need to start listening to these stories, *all* of these stories, because it is the stories that are not heard—for example, those of gangbanging young black kids and those of locked out poor whites—that often come back to bite us in violence and social misery. We need to start listening to these stories for what they can teach us about ourselves and our country, for what they can teach us about the two-hundred-and-fifty-year experiment that is the United States as it enters the next millennium.

Teaching *Gone with the Wind* in the Socialist Republic of Vietnam

Mart Stewart

With Gone with the Wind, *Margaret Mitchell (here) authored a global phenomenon that has sold over thirty million copies and has been issued in nearly two hundred editions in forty countries. Courtesy of the Atlanta History Center.*

n his tour through modern Georgia in search of memories of the Old South, Tony Horwitz marveled at Japanese tourists' fascination with *Gone with the Wind* and observed the exchanges between them and a busy Vivien Leigh–Scarlett O'Hara impersonator, Melly Meadows. Meadows had taken her act to Tokyo and boasted that she had once shown her red pantalets to a delighted Japanese Empress. She had learned some Japanese to banter with the tourists who contracted for her appearances in Atlanta, and from these exchanges, she speculated that the Japanese had a "special affinity" for *Gone with the Wind* (GWTW) because of a kindred attraction to traditional notions of femininity and because they, like southerners, had rebuilt their country after a devastating war. Horwitz mentions other sources of attraction: Scarlett's loyalty to family, her strength, and the "subtle, mannered code" that both Japanese and southern culture seem to share.[1]

It is no news to GWTW watchers that Margaret Mitchell's 1936 book and subsequent film have been embraced by fans around the world. By the late 1930s *Gone with the Wind* was enormously popular in the United States; it had won a Pulitzer and almost a million and a half volumes were published in the first edition. Today, GWTW is a global phenomenon that has sold over thirty million copies and has been issued in nearly two hundred editions in forty countries. The film, released in 1939, became one of the most popular escapist events of the hard 1930s in the United States, winning eight Academy Awards before it was also sold to audiences around the world. Both book and movie—the GWTW phenomenon has usually circulated in a hybrid of both versions—continued to be widely appreciated everywhere in the next half century. The book was enjoyed even surreptitiously in Nazi Germany after 1942 and in the Soviet Union after World War II, where it and other American books were banned. *Gone with the Wind* was praised as an example of "people's literature" by authorities in China during the trial of the Gang of Four. It was so popular in Russia during *perestroika* that it went through at least ten editions in the 1980s; two million copies were published of an edition issued by the publishing house Pravda in 1991. One of the Russian fans of the novel, Alexandra Alekseevna Krupoder, was so moved by the plight of the characters that she wrote a thousand-page sequel that brought to a happy conclusion the sentimental yet unhappy closing of the original. Elsewhere, the story also landed on fertile cultural soil, and foreign-language editions were published in places that had relatively small markets for the book. One collector of "Windiana" that Tony Horwitz encountered in Georgia possessed copies of the book from Czechoslovakia, Bulgaria, Ethiopia, and even one from Latvia, published in 1938, just before Latvia disappeared as an independent country for a half century.[2]

And there was also one from Vietnam. The book was available in the south of Vietnam in the 1960s and widely read there in the 1980s; the film version was available in the 1960s and again in the 1990s. Alexandra Ripley's massive *Wind*-inspired novel, *Scarlett: The Sequel to Margaret Mitchell's "Gone with the Wind,"* arrived in Vietnam at a propitious time in 1991, when it could feed on the rediscovery of GWTW, as well as benefit from the 1986 market reforms of the Sixth Party Congress and a liberalized book publishing industry that began, at least in Hanoi, churning out translations of American bestsellers. Though the Vietnamese version of *Scarlett* was a bumpy one—a Vietnamese translation of a French translation of the English original—it was an instant hit, along with several other novels new to Vietnam by the likes of Harold Robbins, Danielle Steel, and Stephen King. A new Vietnamese edition of GWTW also appeared in the 1990s and was again widely read. The sequel has since largely disappeared from the shelves of bookstores, while the original experienced renewed interest in the late 1990s among another generation of younger readers.[3]

Vietnam was mainly closed to American novels and films between the end of what the Vietnamese call the American War in 1975 and the normalization of relations between the United States and Vietnam in 1995. It was with some awareness of the currency of *Gone with the Wind* and its progeny in this relatively closed culture that I developed a series of seminars on the book and the film, as well as on Alice Randall's 2001 parody of Mitchell's classic, *The Wind Done Gone*, while teaching in Ho Chi Minh City (formerly Saigon) as a Fulbright Senior Scholar in 2001. I had distributed a questionnaire about American novels in Vietnam to undergraduate students who attended an earlier lecture series and to university faculty who had participated in several training seminars in American studies. They had identified a fairly short shelf—especially when the relatively ephemeral potboilers were eliminated—that had been commonly read and studied in Vietnam in the previous twenty-five years. Several readers had very recently worked their way through some of *Beloved* with a teacher who had learned about Toni Morrison's novels from a visiting American professor. Another was translating two of Amy

Tan's novels into Vietnamese (now in print); respondents to the questionnaire also recognized that young readers, who now have far more contacts with Americans and American literature than did their elders, were revising the canon of American literature in Vietnam by voting with their feet. These are recent introductions, however.

Other colleagues or students had had a serendipitous encounter with one American novelist or another in the years since 1975: one colleague had acquired a copy of *Look Homeward, Angel* from a heap of books and papers left on the street after the fall of the Saigon regime, when most Saigon residents were hurriedly shedding any evidence of connections to the United States (a flood of American literature of all types was translated into Vietnamese and published in the south of Vietnam before 1975); another had read some of the American and French novels and plays left to her by her late father just after 1975, before she ripped out clutches of pages—from *For Whom the Bell Tolls* and *No Exit*, for example—to cook her daily rice during the very hard years of the late 1970s and early 1980s. The standard serious reads in American literature during the time Vietnam was closed to the United States made up a very small canon and favored American writers who could be imported under the rubric of socialist realism: the novels of Ernest Hemingway were studied most often, but works by Jack London and John Steinbeck, Faulkner's "A Rose for Emily," several short stories by O. Henry, *Tom Sawyer* and *Huckleberry Finn*, and *Uncle Tom's Cabin* were read as well. And so, though it verged into the sentimental borderlands of socialist realism and was never studied in universities or allotted the status of "serious" literature, was *Gone with the Wind*.[4]

A second questionnaire dealt more directly with GWTW itself and sought respondents' impressions of the United States and the American South gained from their reading of the novel or viewing of the film, as well as anecdotes from discussions with friends and colleagues about the meanings of the novel and film to Vietnamese readers and viewers. The responses I received from both questionnaires informed the six-seminar series I eventually developed titled "How American Culture(s) is Made and Re-Made: Regionalism, the American South, and Collective Memory." We used Mitchell's book, the 1939 movie, and Randall's parody as "texts" to examine larger themes of the construction of collective memory and the relationship between cultural expressions and regionalism that are important to Vietnamese as well as American readers. The seminar series was part of my Fulbright appointment's larger project: to teach methods in cultural studies and to identify themes and areas of interest in American studies that are important to Vietnamese students and teachers.[5]

In the first seminar in the series, we looked at cultural strategies for creating meaning and identity and how history and literature are employed as both markers of identity and as part of the process of making it. Since most of the participants had experienced the American Civil War only through *Gone with the Wind*, I gave a brief lecture on the war, on the reinvention of the antebellum South for a segregated South through the plantation myth, and on Mitchell's appropriation and retelling of this myth for a 1930s American audience. We focused on the book and the movie in the next session, and then on "what's wrong with GWTW" by way of a discussion of *The Wind Done Gone*. In another session, we examined the making and the remaking of collective memory, using historian Fitzhugh Brundage's essay "No Deed but Memory: Historical Memory and Southern Identity," and in the final session we looked at the geography of collective memory and regional, national, and global identities—which allowed us to talk again about GWTW and how the same novel had been enlisted differently in different places for different cultural purposes.[6]

In all of the seminars, my Vietnamese colleagues talked in code about issues—especially those having to do with regionalism and cultural conflict—that had meaning to them but that they could rarely discuss openly. I had been instructed by my hosts at the outset of my appointment that teaching the American Civil War was potentially politically volatile because it could too easily lead to a discussion of a "civil war" closer to home, which went against the official construction of the history of the Vietnamese national struggle against colonial and imperial powers and the creation of an independent Socialist Republic of Vietnam. The master narrative of nation-building in Vietnam does not yet admit the history of regional struggles, yet many conversations about cultural differences between the country's north and south with colleagues both in Ho Chi Minh City and Hanoi often reminded me of Winston Churchill's famous remark about Italy—that it was "entirely too long to be a country." Our discussion of the American South by way of GWTW, a book that many of the middle-aged teachers in the seminar had retreated into repeatedly in the 1980s, was as much about Vietnam as about Dixie and its discontents—but largely in code.

For most readers in the seminar, the characters of the novel were the main attraction. Though they recognized that the characters were at times thinly drawn, and only Rhett and Scarlett had much more than cardboard to them, they pointed to what they believed to be universal tendencies in human behavior that were represented in the whole by the quartet of Scarlett, Melanie, Rhett, and Ashley. In general, rather than exalting the qualities of individual characters, participants in my American studies seminars looked for relational qualities when analyzing voice and character in stories and novels. They recognized qualities in the main characters that all readers recognize, but their understanding of these qualities came from their own cultural backgrounds. Scarlett's behavior and qualities were illuminated by Melanie's, and vice versa, and Rhett's by Ashley's, and vice versa; all four represented different combinations and exchanges of fundamental human virtues and their concomitant vices. The taxonomy they developed is familiar to most readers: Melanie was the flawless female, the embodiment of selfless "love" and sympathy for others, who was willing to fight for her kin but was easily oppressed by difficulties; she was "what women would like to be," my students said. Scarlett was the "bad girl," the readers said, selfish, ruthless, unkind, "not well-educated," but practical, vigorous, "active" (as opposed to Melanie's passivity) and able to overcome difficulties through shrewdness and sheer force of will; she was "what a woman had to be." Ashley to these readers was the embodiment of honor, moral courage, the consequences of a good education (though not up to mandarin standards in its training in character), and aristocratic ideals, though he needed Melanie to express these ideals with warmth and humanity; Rhett, of course, was the archetypical rascal —adaptable, flexible, charming, unscrupulous, strong, cunning, masculine, self-confident—who saw the world as it is rather than as he would like it to be. What was most important to these readers, though, was that the emotional principles the characters in GWTW represented had to be regarded as an organic social whole in order for any of it to make sense.

Though any attempt to identify the essential qualities of a group of people is always fraught with error, it's appropriate here to make a claim about the "relational" quality of Vietnamese society. This quality is, first of all, preserved in the Vietnamese language in part by a symmetrical array of pronouns and terms of address that identify others and the speaker by their relationship to each other. Individualism arrived late in Vietnam—not until the second quarter of the twentieth century—and then, as perhaps now, it was an individualism that attempted to make sense of the individual in terms of family and tradition and at first was also employed as a weapon of resistance against the coercive lumping of colonialism. When readers explained Melanie, Ashley, Rhett, and Scarlett as characters in terms that related them to each other, they expressed at the same time the profoundly relational character of Vietnamese society.[7]

Not that at least two of the characters did not register as individuals. Rhett caught the attention of several women readers, who concluded from his example and their experience with Vietnamese men that attractiveness and rascality were a universal combination in certain kinds of men; he was the "ideal lover," they said, but Scarlett was a fool to marry him. Scarlett resonated most powerfully with most of my Vietnamese colleagues and students. The majority of the seminar participants were women, but Scarlett appealed to the male readers as well; in our discussions, certain of her actions and qualities were "Vietnamized" across gender lines and then amplified. For example, one respondent to the questionnaires summarized Scarlett's importance this way: "Though she is said to be selfish, reckless, and even immoral, we still admire her because of her great love for her family, home place, and the people she cares about. She strove, even going against tradition, to survive and to protect her family and her home place, Tara." Vietnamese women, especially those on the losing side in the complicated struggle of the American War, know a great deal about tenacity and survival both before and after 1975. They know the difficulties of eking out a living from a war-devastated landscape and an unpredictable economy, and the uncertainty that accompanies the cycles of reform and reaction that occur at the end of a war. Some of them know about the perils of living under thunderous bombardments or in a territory where enemies could materialize without warning. And every one of them has a story about it. They also understand what historian Grace Elizabeth Hale identifies as one of the central political ploys of the novel: that it's a story of the main characters' "desperate struggle for survival with their own values, with the identities that alone ground their sense of themselves." At the same time, these Vietnamese readers acknowledged that the novel opens up the possibility of survival in a new economic and political order for those who are able to cut loose the past and move deliberately into the future. For most readers, the pivotal point in GWTW—and an experience in the novel that strongly resonated with their own—is Scarlett's vow, after grubbing in Tara's garden at the end of the war for a mere turnip, never to go hungry again. As one student explained, "There were a lot of Scarletts in Vietnam after 1975."[8]

Finding a way to think and talk about Mammy and Prissy and the other African American characters required much more in the way of introduction. Very few university teachers and students in Vietnam have had any experience at all with African American culture and history. For most, the only literary window to the complicated relationships of blacks and whites in American history that has been available in Vietnam is *Uncle Tom's Cabin*, *Huckleberry Finn*, and *Gone with the Wind*. A couple of the participants had just completed a careful reading of *Beloved* but were still working to make sense of it. Slavery as presented in Mitchell's book and the Hollywood film made from it was not a "cultural representation" for most Vietnamese readers and viewers; instead, it was almost the only history they knew about it—a history that was a hybrid of the brutal institution that would tear a child from his mother's bosom, as in *Uncle Tom's Cabin*, and the benevolent one in which slaves and masters sunnily looked out for each other, even after Emancipation, in GWTW.

Rather than attempt the impossible task of summarizing in a meaningful manner in a single lecture the profound and rich literature on the complex history of slavery, Emancipation, and Jim Crow, I chose to give a short information lecture on slavery and segregation. This was followed by a slide presentation of the early history of African Americans in the movies to show that Mammy and Prissy did not come out of the American South of the 1850s but were invented for Americans in the 1930s. And then, with this in mind, we looked at Alice Randall's *The Wind Done Gone* as a way to explore further the African American characters introduced in GWTW. I showed them slides of posters of *The Jazz Singer*, of Al Jolson in blackface, and explained Stepin' Fetchit's characters in 1930s American films made for whites. We examined slides of posters advertising films made for African Americans to illustrate a parallel trajectory of representations of African Americans in cinema previous to the film version of GWTW. (Hattie McDaniel's Oscar-winning performance was in fact a breakthrough one, they agreed.) Just as large household staffs once gave French colonialists and rich mandarins credibility, the readers noted, so were Mammy and her class essential to the illusions white southerners had about racial superiority. Despite their limited knowledge of African American history, they understood the social dynamic represented by Mammy and the other slaves among the O'Haras and their class. They also quickly grasped that the conditions of production on the plantation were nearly invisible in the novel and movie—knowing as they did the full range of struggles faced by the Vietnamese peasantry in their historic efforts to eke out a livelihood under the control of a succession of landlords and commissars. At the same time that they Vietnamized Scarlett and emphasized her central importance to the novel, they also understood, from their experience with the history of colonization, that it was Mammy's labors, as well as the image of her as Scarlett's coarse but practical and indefatigably loyal retainer, that illuminated Scarlett's class privilege, her whiteness, and her femininity.[9]

Though the readers found portions of *The Wind Done Gone* utterly inaccessible, they agreed that this parody of the original gave "Mammy" and other African American characters a humanity and a "realism" that was not evident in both the novel and the movie versions of GWTW. Although they connected with these characters, they greeted with a quiet uneasiness my question that, if Scarlett could be Vietnamese, why not Mammy? While it would have been interesting to explore this silence, responses to similar questions in other seminars revealed that American race matters were as strange to Vietnamese students as was African American history. Pushing students to explore their own views of "race" risked sounding accusatory—and forgetting that it was the Americans, not the Vietnamese, who enslaved Africans and that the history of American relations with the Vietnamese has hardly been free of racism.

Though the participants side-stepped questions about race in *The Wind Done Gone*, they connected energetically with the intimate and complicated relationship between subalterns and those who have power over them. This was as familiar to them as Scarlett's tough-minded will to survive. They understood the complexities of resistance—the Vietnamese have a two-thousand-year history of it. They were especially interested in the ideas about identity suggested by the use of names in *The Wind Done Gone*. Some readers, as did Ho Chi Minh himself, who according to historian David Marr, used over a hundred aliases between 1911 and his death in 1969, had also had to move about under assumed identities. They understood why slaves had different names for themselves than those given to them by their masters, and they understood the dual identity embodied in the mode of existence W. E. B. DuBois called "double-consciousness." At the same time, they could understand how everyone was related to everyone else, if not through blood, through blood-and-struggle. It was a stretch to identify a political kinship between Mammy, Peter, Cynara (Scarlett's half-sister, Rhett's lover, and the narrator of *The Wind Done Gone*), and Ho Chi Minh, but the Vietnamese struggle for national liberation against first the French and then the Americans could be easily represented as having something in common with the African American struggle for freedom. And if GWTW, both the novel and the film, was more popular with seminar participants from the south of Vietnam, who understood intimately the experience of survival in the cauldron of defeat, then the "parody" of the novel in *The Wind Done Gone*, which adds a patina of character and complexity to the relationships between the oppressed and the oppressors at Tara, was more attractive to those of the same generation who had been on the winning side during the American War and the hard twenty years after 1975.[10]

How did all of this add up in a discussion of reading GWTW as "collective memory" and how collective memory informed a sense of place—and in this case, a sense of a couple of "Souths"? Discussions of culture in the half-dozen classes and seminar series I taught in Vietnam usually quickly diverged into two discussions: one that reflected official versions of the country's past that were well established within the classrooms of Vietnamese universities; the other springing from the sublime chaos of Saigon streets. In university classrooms, "culture" was high culture, the best that has been produced by a group of people; on the streets, everything was negotiable, everything meant something, and culture was the stories we told about it. "History" has a kindred existence in Vietnam: students learn and then learn some more the official history of the creation of the Vietnamese Fatherland, but then they talk about another history outside of official contexts when they tell stories about themselves as Vietnamese. In our seminars we were in class but talking out of it at the same time, in a sometimes fragile negotiation between a history of Vietnam that was prescribed and the history various participants believed they had experienced and now remembered. The participants were willing to discuss the idea that history was constructed—and that we all create collective memories that reflect unique perspectives, are employed for political purposes, and connect with deeply felt experiences at the same time that they purify, simplify, and sanitize them. Everyone in Vietnam knows Ho Chi Minh operated under a variety of assumed identities—but, at the same time, they'll tell you he had only one, and this can be found in statues to his memory everywhere in Vietnam and especially in the mausoleum where his body is preserved for a daily pageant of homage in Hanoi. Our discussion of collective memory traveled the same ground, inside and outside of class, hewing to the official history of the

Fatherland and at the same time circuitously interrogating it, exploring several ways of being "Vietnamese" all the while assuming that there is only one way.[11]

In these ways, the group tested as well as explored current ideas about the workings of collective memory in the history of the American South. Collective memory, whether worked out in a significant dialogue between readers and the text of *Gone with the Wind* or in some other way, is the shared recollections that consolidate a group's sense of itself in relationship to both the past and the future and that become "an essential component of [a group's] social identity." It is always the product of negotiation—and implicitly an answer to the question about history: "Who gets to say?" Vietnamese students receive a steady serving of the official history of Vietnam, a history that is also memorialized in war monuments, museums, and national political rituals, and one that has been usefully employed by the Communist Party to build a unified nation after the long divisive struggle against the French and then the Americans. The face of this history is effectively presented even to visitors to Vietnam, especially in several war memorials and museums, in the "Hanoi Hilton" (where American POWs were held), and in an American War theme park at the Cu Chi Tunnels just north of Ho Chi Minh City. At Cu Chi, tourists are first treated to a brief lecture on the extensive tunnel system (250 kilometers in Cu Chi District alone) constructed by the National Liberation Front during the American War and a video that explains the tunnels in terms of a peasant nationalist revolution against an imperialist invader—and also as a triumph for grassroots solidarity. Guides then show visitors around a few tunnels that have been widened to accommodate broad-beamed Westerners, give them a hands-on demonstration of various booby traps, and escort them to a firing range—where tourists can choose to fire at targets with an M-15, an AK-47, or a Russian carbine, at a buck a bullet.[12]

Of course, the official history of the struggle of Vietnam for nationhood is modified by the context in which it is presented—whether to students in schools, at war memorials that are visited almost exclusively by Vietnamese, or at these sites for Western tourists. But as "collective memory" in general, the similarities between the performances of history in these different places are more significant than the differences. The official (and lucrative) history that is presented and reenacted at the Cu Chi Tunnels does not admit divisions, geographical or otherwise, in the struggle of the Vietnamese against outside forces. Another history percolates on the streets and in households, however, especially in the south of Vietnam, and also showed up in this seminar when we began talking about "collective memory" and GWTW. This other history acknowledges not just divisions but a staggering complexity of alignments and realignments, especially for those whose first aim was simply to survive the violence and disorder all around them. This unofficial collective memory has a geography—kindred to the mental geography that has historically been a part of identity in the American South. Just what the "South" was or is in Vietnam cannot really be marked on the map, though several political agreements and a clearly marked demilitarized zone between 1954 and 1975 presented the illusion of a boundary. Numerous political events in the last half century, the seminar participants explained, produced a great deal of migration within Vietnam. "Factors related to everyday life"—the precariousness and changing contingencies of livelihoods, scant resources in one place and more plentiful ones in another—have also produced large-scale migrations, especially from the countryside to the major urban areas of Vietnam. In Vietnam, as in the American South, identity is also connected to place. *Everyone* in Vietnam is from someplace, and for many that place still has a powerful hold on their memories and is also experienced as a *loss*; the history of migration is also a vast lament. The history of postcolonial Vietnam and at least of the "South" is really a kaleidoscope of migrations and nostalgia—regions in Vietnam are vaguely defined by geography but sharply illuminated by what people have made of them.

Here is where the readers in the seminars found a point of contact between their own memories—and to the extent that they could be defined, the memories of their groups—and the process of "collective remembering" that was represented by Mitchell's iconic novel. At the same time, they Vietnamized the novel still further. They appreciated the sense of loyalty to home that was represented by the efforts of the O'Haras to keep Tara in the family and by Scarlett's desire to return to it, but they also understood that Mitchell did not require Scarlett to break entirely with the "South" and the plantation past represented by Tara. They explained that the "South" and, more specifically, Tara, as a homeplace, was like the "South" of Vietnam, but that they had genuinely lost, there in the mushrooming urbanity of Ho Chi Minh City, the place they had come from and were energetically creating a new one. The "South" they identified with and embraced in GWTW was the one that Scarlett pined for, not the refashioned version to which she was able to return. Like Scarlett, they longed for a place they had lost, but they acknowledged that what was gone was gone. Scarlett's loyalty to Tara and the South it represented was akin to the geography of fierce loyalties to place many of the readers understood as part of the Vietnamese experience. The persistent nostalgia these readers felt about the places from whence they came had not been underpinned by a camouflaged return, however, but came from a profound experience of loss; in other words, their feelings were not mere sentimentality. These Vietnamese readers found their own "South" in GWTW and subverted the "South" of the book at the same time. They also made it clear that the history of *their* South had yet to be recovered in its complexity.[13]

Gone with the Wind, still widely available in Vietnamese bookstores, has found another generation of readers in the enormous population of young people in Vietnam—60 percent of Vietnam's eighty-one million people have been born since 1975. *Gone with the Wind*—the book and the movie, which many young people saw for the first time when it was shown on VTTV in 1999—does not appear to carry the same freight of meanings for young readers and viewers as it held for older ones. Scarlett is still beautiful to them, and some of the younger ones, fresh out of schools where *ao dais* are still the uniform, marvel at her "17-inch waist." She still represents a model of womanly willfulness that many of the women students find attractive. But the remark of one student was telling, that "the United States in modern times is more attractive and thrilling than it was in *Gone with the Wind*." Many of them have looked to America—though with qualified appreciation since the beginning of the Iraq War—as an embodiment of aspirations of affluence and a certain kind of youthful freedom. The attention of many urban youth is also more likely to be affixed to the text messages on their cell phones than to whatever they have in their book bags. If Vietnam taught Americans the pain of defeat and made all of America more reflective, more aware of cultural complexity, and more "southern," and if the history of America in Vietnam gave Americans a past they have struggled to forget, ideas about America have given young people in Vietnam a future they would like to acquire. Many of them chafe against the stories of suffering their parents tell them at the same time that they respect their parents and what their parents have suffered. For these young readers, GWTW may be good escapist fare, but it also reminds them of a past that they are ready to leave behind as Vietnam opens up to the world and engages in the complicated process of accepting but also modulating the cultural artifacts and influences that are bombarding it from the United States and the West.

It is unlikely that young Vietnamese will ever become as enamored of GWTW as were their parents, especially their mothers, or if they'll need GWTW's "South" to talk about their own. As Vietnam continues to open up to the world and levels of affluence for some Vietnamese increase, it is also very unlikely that any of them will ever flock to Georgia to see Melly Meadows or her kind flash their red pantalets. Nor will Melly find it profitable to learn a few words of Vietnamese. But this American and southern cultural icon, which at one time resonated with Vietnamese who themselves had stories to tell of love—of each other and of home place—and the struggle for survival against the background of war, has now had a long history of showing up in surprising guises with surprising cultural force in places very far away from Tara. Even if *Gone with the Wind*'s popularity is waning in Vietnam, tomorrow is another day.

NOTES

My thanks to Fitzhugh Brundage, Robert Ogburn, Dan Duffy, and the two anonymous reviewers of this journal for helpful comments and to my Vietnamese colleagues—if they were "students," they taught the teacher—who collaborated in this exploration with me.

1. Tony Horwitz, *Confederates in the Attic: Dispatches from the Unfinished Civil War* (Vintage, 1999), 296–300.

2. Tara McPherson, *Reconstructing Dixie: Race, Gender, and Nostalgia in the Imagined South* (Duke University Press, 2003), 47. A richly textured discussion of the receptions of the initial edition of *GWTW* and of the 1939 movie and Mitchell's reaction to these can be found in Darden Asbury Pyron's superb biography of Margaret Mitchell: *Southern Daughter: The Life of Margaret Mitchell* (Oxford University Press, 1991), 328–50, 373–93. Pyron's study also includes an account of the foreign reception, 418–35. On *GWTW* in China, see Moody L. Simms, "Gone with the Wind: The View from China," *Southern Studies: An Interdisciplinary Journal of the South* (Spring 1984): 5–7. On *GWTW* in Russia, Nazi Germany, and several other places outside the American South, see Irina M. Suponitskaya (Samuel Ramer, trans.), "The American South as Depicted in *Gone with the Wind*: A Russian Historian's Observations," *Georgia Historical Quarterly* 86 (Winter 1992): 877–79; John Haag, "*Gone with the Wind* in Nazi Germany," *Georgia Historical Quarterly* 73 (Summer 1989): 279–304; and Horwitz, *Confederates in the Attic*, 304–

5. My thanks to John Inscoe for sending copies of the Suponitskaya and Haag articles and of several news items about the copyright flap over *The Wind Done Gone* to me in Ho Chi Minh City.

3. A. Carey Zesiger, "A Long Way from Tara," *Vietnam Generation Journal* 4 (November 1992), http://lists.village.virginia.edu/sixties/HTML_docs/Texts/Reviews/Zesiger_Scarlett.html (accessed 13 April 2005); conversation with Vietnamese writer Ly Lan, 15 June 2004.

4. See also Zesiger, "Long Way," 2–4. Curiously, the first American writer translated into Vietnamese was Edgar Allan Poe, in the 1930s. According to Hanoi scholar Nguyen Lien, only the works of Mark Twain, Jack London, and Ernest Hemingway were taught at the universities between 1975 until the mid-1990s in Vietnam: Nguyen Lien, "Some Theoretical and Practical Problems Regarding the Teaching of American Literature in Vietnam," in Nguyen Lien and Jonathan Auerbach, eds., *Contemporary Approaches to American Culture* (Nha Xuat Ban Van Hoa—Thong Tin, 2001), 465–76. See also Buu Nam, "The Introduction, Research, and Teaching of American Literature in Vietnam," and Bui Viet Thang, "Influence of American Short Stories on Vietnamese Writers," in the same volume: 477–94, 543–54; and Hoang Hung, ed., *15 American Poets of the XXth Century* (Publishing House of the Vietnam Writers' Association, 2004). My effort to teach American Studies as an American Fulbright scholar was itself something relatively new in Vietnam, and the task of finding common ground that was also politically acceptable—in collaborative efforts with my Vietnamese colleagues and on the streets as well as in the university—is a backdrop to the teaching experience I analyze here.

5. Questionnaires are a common form of doing otherwise informal surveys by teachers in Vietnam. Because of habits of deference, students do not readily volunteer their opinions in discussions until they are quite comfortable with the teacher (though this is changing). I distributed fifty copies of each questionnaire and received twenty-three responses to the first one and fourteen from undergraduates (ages nineteen to twenty-one) and eighteen from university teachers (ages thirty-eight to fifty-two) to the second one. Quotations from seminar participants in this essay are from the second set of questionnaires.

6. Fitzhugh Brundage, "No Deed but Memory: Historical Memory and Southern Identity," in Brundage, ed., *Where These Memories Grow: History, Memory, and Southern Identity* (University of North Carolina Press, 2000). My thanks to Professor Brundage for making an electronic copy of this essay available to me on short notice in Ho Chi Minh City. We used whatever editions of the English version of *GWTW* we could rustle up; my edition was a battered 1964 Macmillan hardcover edition; several of my students also had Vietnamese translations of the novel, which they used side-by-side with the original. The edition of the "unauthorized parody" of *GWTW* was Alice Randall, *The Wind Done Gone* (Houghton Mifflin, 2001).

7. See Neil L. Jamieson, *Understanding Vietnam* (University of California Press, 1995), especially 111–69. We devoted little attention to minor characters in the novel that are also important in establishing the authority of the main characters: see Jim Cullen, *The Civil War in Popular Culture: A Reusable Past* (Smithsonian Institution Press, 1995), 65–107.

8. Grace Elizabeth Hale, *Making Whiteness: The Culture of Segregation in the South, 1890–1940* (Pantheon, 1998), 264–67. The set of attributes commonly associated with the color suggested by the heroine's name means something different to Vietnamese readers; red and related colors signify good luck in Vietnam, and also suggest vitality and good health. For "scarlet" and "Scarlett" in the book and film, see Helen Taylor, *Scarlett's Women: Gone with the Wind and Its Female Fans* (Rutgers University Press, 1989), 79–81. This study by a British scholar also parses out the enormous popularity of *GWTW* and Scarlett with women readers; she reveals a bevy of "different Scarletts" discovered by different readers—see especially 78–108. Though the discussion of *GWTW* by the teachers in the Vietnam seminar, the majority of whom were women, revealed some telling gender distinctions in how the book was read in Vietnam, this was one of several possible directions for discussion that we had little time to pursue. For how women readers elsewhere have read Scarlett as survivor, see Taylor, *Scarlett's Women*, 98–100.

9. See McPherson, *Reconstructing Dixie*, 55, for an examination of this idea in general.

10. I shared with the seminar participants Grace Hale's analysis of Mammy and of *GWTW*, in *Making Whiteness*, 105–14, 259–68. For the general history of images of African Americans in films, see Donald Bogle, *Toms, Coons, Mulattoes, Mammies, and Bucks: An Interpretive History of Blacks in American Film* (Penguin, 1973); and Ed Guerrero, *Framing Blackness: The African American Image in Film* (Temple University Press, 1993). The background of the participants in this seminar ranged across the full spectrum of experiences with the politics of revolution and nationalism in Vietnam.

11. David Marr, *Vietnam, 1945: The Quest for Power* (University of California Press, 1995), xxiii–xxiv.

12. Quotations from James Fentress and Chris Wickham, *Social Memory* (Blackwell, 1992), quoted in Brundage, "No Deed but Memory," and from Brundage, 2. A collection of path-breaking essays that examine different ways the Vietnam/ American War is commemorated by the Vietnamese is Hue-Tam Ho Tai and John Bodnar, eds., *The Country of Memory: Remaking the Past in Late Socialist Vietnam* (University of California Press, 2001); see especially Laurel B. Kennedy and Mary Rose Williams, "The Past Without the Pain: The Manufacture of Nostalgia in Vietnam's Tourism Industry." For an analysis of the anticolonial "construction" of history in postcolonial Vietnam, see Patricia Pelley, *Postcolonial Vietnam: New Histories of the National Past* (Duke University Press, 2002). Any judgment of the

Vietnamese government's efforts to employ a specific version of the history of the American War for political purposes should be conditioned by an acknowledgement of the persistent tendency of Americans (especially those running for national political office), in their reflections on the Vietnam War, to use it to serve their own needs and purposes.

13. Vietnamese readers here read the book literally at the same time that they Vietnamized it. A full study, or at least a critical appreciation, of the different "Souths" that different readers have found in the book might be as useful to *GWTW* scholars as Helen Taylor's discovery of a bevy of Scarletts. For an insightful argument about the mental geography of *GWTW* that nonetheless does not acknowledge the possibility of pluralistic readings of the book's "South," see McPherson, *Reconstructing Dixie*, 49.

Haiku

C. Vann Woodward

Renowned historian C. Vann Woodward. Courtesy of Billy Howard.

arly in 1953, while I was at Johns Hopkins, I received an invitation from the University of Tokyo to teach a class on the South during Reconstruction in the following summer term. I replied that I would like to accept their invitation, but added that in view of their students' probable lack of background, I thought it better to make my course treat the South in the nineteenth century. Their reply was extremely polite but quite firm in asking that my subject be confined to the South during Reconstruction. With some puzzlement I agreed.

The puzzlement was cleared up shortly after I arrived and reported for duty. By far the most popular movie in town was *Gone with the Wind*, Japan was under reconstruction by Yankees, and the Japanese identified with the defeated South. Facing a room full of rapt and attentive students, who seemed to understand my American English with southern accent, I held forth for the term. It was agreed that I give no examination and no grades, but I was asked to wind up with an address to a university-wide audience, which seemed to go off well.

During the term I lunched daily with Japanese colleagues at their faculty dining hall. At lunch toward the end of the term, I remarked that I had read a lot in an English newspaper about anti-American feeling and demonstrations in Tokyo but had not witnessed any and asked where I could find it. Silence was followed by the customary titter covering embarrassment. Then one friend, who later visited me in the States, smiled slowly and said, "My dear colleague, you have been living at the center of it since you have been with us."

Intractable Identity

In an ever-evolving region, potent markers of southern pride and identification remain.

Landmarks of Power

Building a Southern Past, 1885–1915

Catherine W. Bishir

*The creation of symbolic sculpture and architecture by the southern elite functioned
as part of their reclamation of regional and national power. The Vance monument, by
Henry J. Ellicott, and the State Capitol, looking west from New Bern Avenue, Raleigh,
North Carolina, 1911, courtesy of the Collections of the Library of Congress.*

n 1901, the speaker at the dedication of the Olivia Raney Library in Raleigh, North Carolina, compared the city's landmarks with those of Washington, D.C. In the national capital, "three great architectural monuments" possessed "symbolic significance": the United States Capitol, the Washington Monument, and the Library of Congress. "So in our smaller sphere," three landmarks of Raleigh stood out. First was the old State Capitol, "symbolizing the commonwealth's loyalty to constitutional liberty." Near it stood two newer landmarks. "Our handsome Confederate monument" on the Capitol grounds offered "a token of our loyalty to the memory of our fallen heroes who laid down their lives in defense of those principles for which Washington so successfully fought." And the library, given by local businessman Richard Beverly Raney in memory of his wife, provided "a memorial of the highest type of our cultured Christian womanhood"—a classically detailed building in which "the simplicity and elegance of its graceful proportions and unpretentious appearance" evoked its namesake's exemplary character, while its proximity to the war memorial recalled "that noble band of women" (including Mrs. Raney) "to whose untiring efforts we are chiefly indebted for our Confederate monument."[1]

In this address, the Reverend M. M. Marshall of Christ Episcopal Church in Raleigh identified three important types of landmarks that gained dominion throughout the turn-of-the-century South. In addition to revering antebellum buildings as survivors from a glorious past, leaders of his generation employed the twin arts of sculpture and architecture to assert their own definition of the past and its relationship to the present and the future. As Marshall's ceremonial comments illuminated, these new landmarks represented a set of interlocking beliefs, including the renewed place of the vindicated South in the American mainstream, the rightness and patriotism of the Confederate cause, and the association of classical architecture with idealized southern virtues.

Seen in the context of contemporary cultural and political events, the creation of symbolic sculpture and architecture by the southern elite functioned as part of their reclamation of regional and national power. As they placed monuments in prime civic spaces, whether commemorating the heroes of the Confederacy, the patriotic women of colonial Edenton, or the Revolutionary fighters of the Cape Fear region, these leaders spelled out chapter after chapter of a saga of patrician Anglo-Saxon continuity, of order, stability, and harmony. The location of monuments in the state's principal civic places lent authority to the version of history they represented, while at the same time the monuments claimed those public spaces and thereby defined the setting for public life. And, just as monuments commemorated specific heroes and events, so architecture commemorated and asserted the renewed continuity of the values and way of life those heroes represented. In public and institutional buildings, classicism universally reiterated the ideal of a venerable and stable hierarchy, while in residential architecture the Colonial Revival symbolizing "the big-heartedness and hospitality which are the rightful heritage of the southern people" recreated in modern terms the deferential social relations the antebellum plantation represented.

Thus, just as they took control of the political process during the decades spanning the turn of the century, the southern elite also codified a view of history that fortified their position in the present and their vision of the future. By erecting public landmarks celebrating that history and proclaiming a legitimizing continuum from the Old South to the New South, they shaped both public memory and public life. Raleigh and Wilmington, North Carolina's largest cities in 1890 and its main centers of political and cultural activity, provide case studies of this process during a defining period of crisis.[2]

THE SOUTHERN ELITE AS SHAPERS OF PUBLIC MEMORY

Throughout America in the decades just before and after 1900, political and cultural elites drew upon the imagery of past golden ages to shape public memory in ways that supported their own authority. By commissioning monumental sculpture that depicted American heroes and American virtues in classical terms, and by reviving architectural themes from colonial America as well as from classical Roman and Renaissance sources, cultural leaders affirmed the virtues of stability, harmony, and patriotism. They were responding to sweeping changes in the nation's fabric, including national reunification after the Civil War, industrial modernization, growing immigration and social tensions, and rising American nativism, nationalism, and imperialism. Leading patrons ranged from the new princes of industry, who saw America as the site of a second Renaissance, to the embattled "native" aristocrats of various regions; they worked in concert with Beaux-Arts-educated architects and artists who brought European training and ideas to their practices in burgeoning American cities. In 1893, the World's Columbian Exposition in Chicago presented a spectacular display of a set of official American ideals. An ensemble of heroic sculpture and classical architecture, laid out in the formal plan and rationally divided sectors promoted by the City Beautiful movement, offered an image of a unified, stable, hierarchical Anglo-Saxon nation asserting its place in the world, an image that soon reached into communities of the North and South.[3]

The principal shapers of public memory and patrons of public sculpture and architecture in Raleigh and Wilmington were likewise members of an established elite. They were akin to aristocrats throughout the nation, and (as Marshall's remarks at the library dedication revealed) they were well acquainted with national cultural trends and their relationship to them. They also shared among themselves certain backgrounds, experiences, and values. All were Democrats, and, with a few notable exceptions, they were members of families of long-established social and economic prominence, who had customarily participated in national and international currents of trade and taste. Many boasted colonial ancestry and had traditions of service in the Revolutionary and Confederate causes. Their families were interlaced by ties of ancestry and marriage, as well as by education—typically at the University of North Carolina at Chapel Hill for men and St. Mary's, an Episcopal school in Raleigh, for women—and by religion, for most of this group were members of the Episcopal church, a denomination long associated with the state's upper class and with the values of hierarchy and social stability.

Although they had much in common with patricians elsewhere in the nation, these North Carolinians had their own special concerns as well as their own version of history, for as southerners they alone among American elites had experienced devastating military and political defeat along with jolting impoverishment. Yet, in contrast to blue bloods in many northern cities, they managed to regain their political as well as social and cultural clout. In the last decades of the nineteenth century, they were in the process of consolidating their reclamation of power and position and reasserting their status as vindicated patriots in a reunified America. They recalled a golden age before the Civil War, when "Southern statesmen directed the policies of the nation," when "aristocratic" southern society was led by "the wisest, the strongest, the most learned," and when their families had constituted the upper tier in a hierarchical society and slavery-based economy. Although many of them had opposed secession, they nevertheless had sacrificed family members and fortunes to the southern cause. During Reconstruction, they had seen their world turned upside down and their political power and wealth shrivel, as "democracy" replaced "aristocracy," and power passed into the hands of black and ordinary white citizens who were "not so able or cultured." In the mid-1870s, white Conservatives regained political power and soon revived the Democratic party label in North Carolina. Calling themselves "Redeemers" and led by Civil War governor Zebulon Vance, who retook the governor's office in 1876, they considered themselves saviors of the state. With a series of constitutional amendments, the Democratic legislature rolled back many of the egalitarian measures of Reconstruction and took control of local government. As one of their number recalled, "For twenty years this new system remained in force and quiet reigned."[4]

Along with recapturing political dominance, members of the old aristocracy gradually adjusted to a new economy. Some remained agriculturalists and renegotiated farm labor arrangements, while many moved to town to engage in business and professions, where their prospects were tied increasingly to national corporate networks. Even as they adapted economically, the leading families perpetuated their customary social networks. Almost in inverse relationship to their threadbare circumstances, they revitalized elaborate social rituals and public rhetoric, which they adorned with carefully polished silver and phrases. And, like their compatriots throughout the nation, they entered into cultural and patriotic pursuits that asserted their accustomed political, economic, and social dominance.

In their hands, the creation of symbolic landmarks unfolded in two principal phases, punctuated by political events. In the 1880s and early 1890s, patrician Democrats began to call for a rehabilitation of state and southern history and the erection of civic monuments dedicated to that history, transforming the cult of defeat into the dominant culture of power regained. At the end of the century, the turbulent political campaigns of 1898 and 1900 riveted public attention and generated new themes in the Democrats' use of history. After 1900 the re-entrenched elite turned with unprecedented energy and conviction to the shaping of public memory and the creation of official symbols, which quickly established a codified tradition and transformed the setting of public life.

THE CONFEDERATE MONUMENT AND SOUTHERN PATRIOTISM

In 1883, Samuel A'Court Ashe, a Raleigh newspaper publisher, politician, and historian, returned from a trip to Boston fired up by New

Englanders' commemorative zeal. As a Confederate veteran, a native of the Wilmington area, and descendant of colonists and Revolutionary heroes of the Cape Fear region, Ashe typified North Carolina's early leaders in collecting and publishing state history. Upon his return to Raleigh, he immediately began a series of articles in his *News and Observer* urging North Carolinians to celebrate their own history and patriotic shrines.[5]

In the same spirit, and probably influenced by Ashe, Alfred Moore Waddell addressed the Raleigh Ladies Memorial Association on Confederate Memorial Day, 10 May 1885. Waddell, likewise a former Confederate officer and a descendant of Cape Fear colonists and Revolutionary War officers, was a Wilmington resident and former congressman who had become one of the state's most popular public speakers. The sponsor of the occasion was one of the many local Ladies Memorial Associations established throughout the South in the 1860s to assure the proper burial of Confederate soldiers and the marking and decoration of their graves. Through participation in Ladies Memorial Associations, many genteel southern women first stepped into public roles as guardians of regional memory and history. For certain tasks, they enlisted the aid of male relatives, friends, and political figures, especially for speeches on Confederate Memorial Day.[6] In his oration of 1885, Waddell issued a call to memorialize the state's heroes and laid out an agenda for action.

He proclaimed that the period of mourning after the war was over, as was the era of poverty that excused failure to build monuments to the state's heroes. The state, "though stripped of the sovereignty in which, with her sisters, she once robed herself, has long since put off the habiliments of mourning, and, clad in a new vesture, with renewed hope and courage, is moving majestically onward to a grand destiny." He pointed out that whereas "every civilized land" had monuments to its greatest sons to inspire and instruct natives and visitors, North Carolina had never erected memorials to her heroes and statesmen. Waddell challenged his audience:

> Go to the Capitol at Washington and enter the . . . Hall of Statuary. There is a place reserved in it for two statues from each State, and these places are being rapidly filled by the marble and bronze images of distinguished soldiers and statesmen. Look around for North Carolina's contribution. It is not there. Go to any other State Capitol, and if its public grounds do not contain some statue or monument in com-

memoration of its great men, its legislative halls at least are hung with portraits of its Governors. Then come back here to Raleigh—go into your own State Capitol—see at the base of the rotunda those four empty niches—pass through the corridors—enter the Legislative Halls and look around! No monument, no statue, no bust, not even a portrait to remind you that North Carolina ever produced one man that she thought worthy of remembrance. Surely if her gratitude to or appreciation of her dead soldiers and statesmen is to be measured by the number of memorials which she has established in honor of them then it is safe to say that such a sentiment does not exist.

Addressing first the heroes of the recent war, Waddell acknowledged the importance of Confederate monuments already standing in cemeteries across the state, but he insisted that the memory of the Confederate dead "deserve[d] to be perpetuated otherwise than by such memorial marbles as private affection may erect." He called for public support of civic monuments to the Confederate soldier to reflect "a sentiment alike jealous of the honor of North Carolina, and tenderly grateful to her heroic sons."[7]

In the next three decades, the civic memorial movement Waddell envisioned followed precisely the course he laid out. In the 1890s, Civil War memorializing shifted from funereal markers placed in cemeteries to monuments of southern patriotism located in such civic spaces as courthouse greens and town squares. The North Carolina Confederate Monument, on Union Square at the State Capitol, was one of the state's earliest and certainly its most imposing monument of this new type. It was the project of the North Carolina Monumental Association, led by socially prominent women with links with the older Ladies Memorial Association. Proclaiming that "a land without monuments is a land without memories," the Monumental Association organized a statewide fundraising campaign. By 1895 these women, with assistance on practical matters from "experienced gentlemen," oversaw the completion of the state's official monument to the Confederate soldier.[8]

On 20 May 1895, some thirty thousand people gathered from across the state for the unveiling of the seventy-five-foot monument that rose at the west end of Union Square, the most prominent public site in the state. The granite column, flanked by bronze figures of a North Carolina cavalryman and artilleryman, and topped by a bronze infantryman, stood on axis with the western portico of the Capitol and faced Hillsborough

Street, the premier residential avenue and one of four axial streets that defined the city plan. The Monumental Association's president, Nancy Haywood Branch Jones, and other dignitaries presided over elaborate ceremonies in which the seven-year-old granddaughter of Gen. Stonewall Jackson pulled the cord that let the draperies slide from the monument like "the garments of Elijah." The orator of the day was Alfred Moore Waddell.[9]

Again Waddell set forth an emerging agenda—the "true" history of the Confederate cause and North Carolina's role in that story. His hour-long oration was headlined in the *News and Observer* as "A Masterly Defence of the Cause for Which They Fought—In History's Clear Light." It featured the retelling of southern history then sweeping the region—a southern interpretation that played an essential role in the gradual reunion between North and South on southern Democrats' terms. Waddell began by observing that a southerner reading history written by northern men could not but recall "what Froude said about history generally, namely that it seemed to him 'like a child's box of letters with which we can spell any word we please. We have only to select such letters as we want, arrange them as we like, and say nothing about those which do not suit our purpose.'"

He then set forth "the plain unvarnished truth concerning the causes of and the responsibility for the war in which men to whose memory this monument is erected, were sacrificed." This was necessary because

> for thirty years past, my countrymen, kinsmen and my friends have been pilloried before the world as ignorant, barbarous, cruel traitors and rebels, who, without the slightest justification or excuse, sought to destroy the best government under the sun, and deluged a continent in blood. The charge is still made and reiterated in conversation, in school books, in magazine articles, in public speeches, in public records, and in published history.

To counter this "monstrous perversion of the truth," Waddell insisted, "self respect and a decent regard for the memory of our heroic dead" required a statement of "the facts and the proof."[10]

Waddell presented the southern cause as part of the heroic tradition of American patriotism. For the throng gathered around the monument, the message was illustrated by the inscriptions, symbols, and figures on the monument itself, and Waddell's speech reinforced the meaning of those emblems. Drawing first upon the North Carolina state seal on the monument, with its date of 20 May 1775, he lauded "the men of Mecklenburg" who "on this day one hundred twenty years ago" declared their independence from British tyranny: "[F]irst of all Americans, despite the doubting Thomases—[they] renounced allegiance to the British crown, declared themselves a free and independent people." With this Waddell invoked belief in the 20 May 1775 "Mecklenburg Declaration of Independence," an alleged event disputed by historians but popularly revered. When North Carolina seceded from the Union on 20 May 1861, the secession convention authorized a state flag emblazoned with the two dates to glorify the parallel between the two declarations of independence.[11] Amid the turn-of-the-century passion for southern vindication, selection of 20 May 1895 as the day to unveil the state's Confederate monument reaffirmed the linkage of the Confederate and Revolutionary causes.

Next, Waddell traced the nation's early history from a southern perspective, stressing the retention of states' rights, including secession, under the Constitution—a theme emphasized on the monument by the seal of the Confederate States with its image of George Washington. He defended the southern people—"Deo Vindice," said the Confederate motto on the monument—who had "sought peace and not a quarrel" and were "forced to defend their liberties and their homes." And, sharing in an ongoing process of affirming North Carolina's contribution to the Confederacy, he recited the saga of North Carolina's long and valiant soldiering as a source of state pride. Her men had proved themselves "worthy of their Revolutionary sires" in battles from the first to the last of the war: their motto "First at Bethel, Last at Appomattox" is writ large on the monument. He ended with an encomium to the Confederate soldier, loyal like his fathers to the Union, but compelled by love of his state to come to her defense. Surely gesturing to the bronze infantryman outlined against the sky, Waddell declaimed, "Stand then, bronze image of him who wore the gray! Thou art a triumph of Art; he was God's gift to his country. Thou shalt perish, but he shall live forever in the hearts of his people."

Waddell's oration struck sympathetic chords. Fellow Wilmingtonian and business leader James Sprunt wrote, "You were first in the hearts of your countrymen yesterday. . . . [O]n all sides the speech is said to be the best ever delivered in North Carolina." Little anticipating the direction of the future, Sprunt predicted that "the eloquent words of your masterful address on probably the last occasion of such public honours to the

Lost Cause will be repeated from generation to generation by those who look with reverence and admiration upon the beautiful shaft in Raleigh." Democratic spokesman Henry Groves Connor of Wilson praised Waddell for his "setting forth of our side of the question," noting that "we must preserve our integrity and make our fight in the struggle now confronting us. It behooves us to purify our hearts and educate our minds to meet the common enemy."[12]

THE WHITE SUPREMACY CRUSADE

Connor alluded to political developments then gaining momentum in the state, which in the mid- and late 1890s absorbed the energy of the state's cultural and business as well as political leaders. Throughout the South, Democrats faced challenges from Populists and Republicans, but only in North Carolina did they lose control of the state. After "Redemption" in the 1870s, despite strong, steady opposition from the Republicans (who included both upland, ex-Union whites and nearly all of the state's black voters), the state's Democrats had narrowly retained power by evoking race fears and the specter of Reconstruction.

By the 1890s, however, the "Bourbon" Democrats were perceived increasingly as the allies of moneyed interests and railroad magnates, at the expense of small farmers and workers. Amid nationwide economic woes, especially the worsening poverty among farmers, the Populist movement gained strength from eastern as well as western white farmers disillusioned with Democratic policies. In 1894, after their efforts at reform were rebuffed by the Democrats, North Carolina's Populists forged a "Fusion" ticket with the Republicans. Democrats were stunned when the Fusionists, drawing support from both white and black voters, swept the state and took a majority of seats both in the state legislature and in Congress. In 1896 the Fusionists repeated their success with the electorate, maintaining a majority in the legislature while Republican candidate Daniel Russell won the governor's office. The Fusionist government enacted many reforms beneficial to farmers and to public education, and, reversing a "Redeemer" policy, returned control of local government to the local electorate. As a result, more Republicans (including some blacks in heavily black counties of the eastern plantation region) and Populists took office in local and state government.[13]

To recapture political power by splitting the opposition, the Democrats, long known as "the white man's party," set upon a "White Supremacy Crusade." Such campaigns swept across the South, but the one in North Carolina was especially vicious, in part because the Democrats had lost more ground than in other states. The crusade tore aside the veil of gentility that normally inhibited public discourse and presented the specter and actuality of violence involved in an all-out fight for power. In addition to the customary ballot fraud, Democrats played upon fears of "Negro domination" to pull white voters away from the Fusionist ticket, and they sent gangs of "Red Shirt" riders to silence opposition speakers and intimidate voters. Organized by Furnifold M. Simmons, chairman of the Democratic party, and led by Charles B. Aycock, Robert Glenn, and Francis Winston, the crusade inspired Democrats across the state to put aside old intraparty differences. Josephus Daniels made his recently acquired Raleigh *News and Observer* "the militant voice of White Supremacy" and "the printed voice of the campaign." Swept along by the savage rhetoric of these leaders, many whites came to believe that their way of life and indeed civilization itself were at stake. The election of 1898 proved to be so violent that, as Josephus Daniels later commented, it was "sometimes difficult for readers of *The News and Observer* to tell which was the bloodier, the war against Spain or the war to drive the Fusionists from power."[14]

The epicenter of violence was in Wilmington. Businessman James Sprunt later recalled that the port city had a growing number of black citizens "whose attitude towards the whites had become unbearable," and, since the Fusionist victory, a city council that included black and white Republicans who were "not at all responsive to enlightened opinion." Repeatedly, as the city's Democratic leaders and prominent businessmen strove to regain control of city government, they drew upon the heroic actions of their ancestors as precedent. As early as 1897, when Democrats sought unsuccessfully to have the city council removed, their attorney, John D. Bellamy Jr., declared that "it was quite in the order of things for Wilmington to be resisting the infamous legislation by which her citizens are deprived of local self-government, for it was the citizens of this city who first resisted the odious British Stamp Act."[15]

In August 1898, an editorial in the city's black newspaper, the *Wilmington Record*, on the inflammable topic of interracial sex became a rallying point for the state's white supremacist campaign, whose leaders fanned the flames of racial and sexual fears. In Wilmington this editorial supplied the catalyst for action. As Sprunt remembered, "Hope of better days had almost faded away when a vile publication in a negro newspaper aroused the whites to action and determined them to rid the city of the pests that had been a menace to its peace and an incubus on its prosperity. It was resolved to purge the city and to displace the inefficient government."[16]

In late October 1898, as Wilmington seethed with tension and election day neared, again the precedent of history was sounded, when Alfred Moore Waddell gave a "sizzling talk" to a packed house of white men and women at the municipal theater. As a contemporary recalled, "In ordinary times Waddell was one of the most graceful and classical of speakers," but in this campaign "he was an American Robespierre." After a fiery oration blasting the evils of Negro domination and asserting Anglo-Saxon supremacy in the South, the nation, and the world, Waddell looked to history as he invoked the spirit of the "men of the Cape Fear" to move his compatriots to action instead of talk. "We are the sons of the men who won the first victory of the American Revolution at Moore's Creek, who stormed at midnight the rocky face of Stony Point. . . . We are the brothers of the men who wrote with their swords from Bethel to Bentonsville [sic] the most heroic chapters in American annals." Proclaiming that "we ourselves are men who, inspired by these memories, intend to preserve, at the cost of our lives, if necessary, the heritage that is ours," he stated that the men of the Cape Fear could no longer abide "intolerable conditions" in Wilmington: "We are resolved to change them if we have to choke the current of the Cape Fear with carcasses."[17]

Waddell's speech captured attention throughout the state. A friend in the northeastern part of the state called it "the equal of Patrick Henry's famous oration." Responding most passionately was his cousin, Rebecca Cameron of Hillsborough, a patriotic leader and Episcopal churchwoman. Receiving a copy of the speech, she wrote, "did me good 'down to the ground.'" She and others had been "amazed, confounded and bitterly ashamed of the acquiescence and quiescence of the men of North Carolina at the existing conditions, and more than once have asked wonderingly, Where are the white men and the shotguns?" Continuing her cousin's theme, she wrote, "We applaud to the echo your determination that our old historic river shall be choked with the bodies of our enemies, white and black, but what this state shall be redeemed. It has reached the point where bloodletting is needed for the health of the commonwealth, and when the depletion commences let it be thorough!" Sharing Waddell's history, she recalled that "the men of the Cape Fear were the first to stay . . . English aggression when your greatgrandfather was one of a goodly company in the proud light of day who said to the Magistry of

England 'no farther.' And I am glad that it is once more our colony and our family who catch up the far back echo, and bugle forth the story." She added, "We are aflame with anger here. I wish you could see Anna, she is fairly rampant and blood thirsty. These blond women are terrible when the fighting blood is up. I hope it will not come to the last resort but when it does let it be Winchesters and buckshot at close range."[18]

In Wilmington, the election day of 8 November was peaceful. There, as throughout the state, the Democratic ticket triumphed. But in Wilmington the story had not ended. The next day, several groups of "prominent businessmen" assembled to make plans to oust the city council (which was not up for election) and rid the community of certain blacks and other Republicans. Then, on 10 November, Waddell led a group to the *Wilmington Record* office, where he forced open the door, and the group destroyed the press and burned the building. In a confusing sequence of events, threats and rumors of violence sped through the city, and white men shouldered their Winchesters and shotguns and moved into the streets. The Wilmington Light Infantry, recently returned from service during the Spanish-American War, turned out in force in support of the Democrats. Sporadic violence broke out. At day's end, the conflict ceased, leaving an unconfirmed number of black men dead—Waddell put the number at twenty—and several whites and blacks wounded. That evening, Waddell and others forced the resignation of the city council and took control of the government with Waddell as mayor. The Wilmington Light Infantry patrolled the city on horseback to round up and imprison overnight those black and white Republicans whom the Democrats planned to banish from Wilmington. Some were found and put on northbound trains the next day. Others had already left town, beginning an exodus of blacks who left Wilmington forever.[19]

Although the Wilmington "race riot" was widely condemned in northern newspapers, and although many North Carolinians cringed at the violence it had unleashed, the Democrats who had led what they called the "Revolution of 1898" became heroic figures to many others. On 13 November Bennehan Cameron, a wealthy and wellborn Hillsborough planter and businessman who had been active in the white supremacy campaign, wrote to his kinsman Waddell, "As you well know, I have always admired you; & now, I am almost a hero worshiper. God bless you! for your deliverance of your good people." On the local scene, James Sprunt later recalled that "while some of the incidents were deplored by whites generally, yet when we consider the peaceful and amicable relations that have since existed, the good government established and maintained, and the prosperous, happy conditions that have marked the succeeding years, we realize that the results of the Revolution of 1898 have indeed been a blessing to the community." For his part, Waddell characterized the event as "a radical revolution accompanied by bloodshed and a thorough reorganization of social and political conditions," which "set the pace for the whole South on the question of white supremacy, and assured beyond further controversy the adoption of the Constitutional amendment in regard to negro suffrage in the state."[20]

In the next election, held on 2 August 1900, the Democrats aimed at total victory. The governorship was at stake as well as legislative seats, but the central issue was an amendment to the state constitution designed to disfranchise blacks and eliminate them from political participation. The newly Democratic legislature devised a suffrage amendment carefully adapted from those in other southern states so as to avoid federal challenges of unconstitutionality. After altering state election procedures to assure a Democratic victory, they submitted the amendment to the electorate. Again Democrats employed violence and intimidation to keep blacks from the polls. "You are Anglo-Saxons. You are armed and prepared and you will do your duty. . . . Go to the polls tomorrow, and if you find the negro out voting, tell him to leave the polls and if he refuses, kill him, shoot him down in his tracks. We shall win tomorrow if we have to do it with guns," proclaimed Waddell in a "fighting speech."[21]

By winning an overwhelming victory in 1900, North Carolina's Democrats, like their compatriots throughout the South, gained control of the political process itself. To many of them it seemed that a long chapter that began in defeat had finally ended in triumph; for some, the very violence of their victory was an essential catharsis of old defeat. As promised in the campaign, young Democratic leaders inaugurated an era of economic progressivism that emphasized public education, transportation, and encouragement of business. They also passed "Jim Crow" laws to legalize racial segregation in more and more sectors of public and private life. They promoted segregation, along with disfranchisement, as a modern, rational remedy to past ills, a reform essential to "cleanse" public life and promote peaceful social and economic advancement.[22]

Once again the vindicating muse of history was invoked, this time by Gov. Charles B. Aycock in his inaugural address of January 1901. As he proclaimed the bright new age for a new century, the young leader looked back briefly to link recent events with the heroic past. First he compared the Democrats who had waged the "combat" of 1898 with North Carolina's early heroes of the American Revolutionary cause—"that people who fought the first fight in Alamance against bad government and wrote the first Declaration of Independence in Mecklenburg." He then likened the "revolutionary" suffrage amendment to "the war for Independence . . . known as the Revolution," and tied the spirit of the disfranchisement movement to "the revolutionary spirit of 1776," which "still lives in the hearts of North Carolinians . . . a glorious part of their heritage."[23]

THE CODIFICATION AND COMMEMORATION OF SOUTHERN HISTORY

It was in this highly charged context that in 1900 the state's Democratic leaders inaugurated an era of "historical awakening." Many felt that North Carolina had lagged behind while other states had progressed in historical activities; now they proceeded to remedy the situation. In the fall of 1900, in the auditorium of Raleigh's new Olivia Raney Library, prominent Democrats organized the State Literary and Historical Association. This group worked in affiliation with kindred organizations: its published reports included news from the recently formed North Carolina chapters of such hereditary and patriotic groups as the Colonial Dames of America, the Daughters of the Revolution, the Daughters of the American Revolution, the Order of the Cincinnati, the Sons of the Revolution, the United Confederate Veterans, and the United Daughters of the Confederacy. Many people belonged to more than one of these organizations. They constituted a statewide network of men and women interested in the histories of their own patrician families and of the state at large, which they usually perceived as one and the same.[24]

These men and women led a surge of patriotic, cultural, and historical activity. They collected and published historical records; published state histories and school textbooks; initiated "North Carolina Day" in the public schools; established and expanded historical museum collections; and, with equal fervor, marked and memorialized historic sites, events, and personages. These endeavors had less to do with an obsession with the past than with the belief that a proper understanding of history and state pride, like educational reform and literary production, were necessary components of a modern American state. A remarkable sense of shared purpose threaded through these pursuits. Just as members of ancestral patriotic groups traced their family lineages to colonial and Revolutionary forebears in order to affirm their place in contemporary society, so like-minded politicians and historians traced political lineage back to those heroic ancestors to affirm political legitimacy.[25]

With competing visions of the state's past, present, and future all but silenced in official discourse, these leaders shared a powerful sense that both in politics and in the culture at large, matters had been returned to their correct alignment. Again they occupied their unquestioned and proper place in a stable, racially tiered society.[26] From this perspective they codified a lasting version of the state's history that tied Old South to New, interweaving old family heritage, Anglo-Saxon supremacy, and military and political heroism. The saga began with the establishment of the "first Anglo-Saxon settlement" in the New World at Roanoke in the 1580s, focused on aristocratic families and the plantation culture they established in the colonial period, and glorified Revolutionary North Carolinians' early resistance to British tyranny. It lauded the progress of the antebellum era, sanctified the sacrifices and patriotism of North Carolina Confederates, and insisted that their cause had engaged the unified support of the populace. Finally, the story demonized the era of Reconstruction, ennobled the Democratic redemption of the state, and asserted the present era as a rebirth of southern progress and leadership in the nation.[27] As they erected memorials to the events and heroes of this narrative, Democratic leaders transformed principal civic spaces into visual illustrations of their saga. In both Wilmington and Raleigh, their memorial work moved beyond commemoration of the Confederacy to mark a continuum of patrician patriotism that wove each chapter into a single epic stretching from the colonial past to the redeemed present.

Immediately after the election of 1900, the Democrats triumphantly unveiled a giant bronze figure of their hero Zebulon Baird Vance. Sculptor Henry J. Ellicott's lifelike portrait captured Vance in a characteristic gesture of debate, a Beaux-Arts sculptural technique of depicting the subject in mid-gesture to intensify the emotional impact of the work. Standing on a base that raised the eight-and-a-half-foot statue to a height of more than twenty-five feet, the powerful monument took command of the eastward axis of Raleigh's Union Square. Acclaimed by Democrats as the perfect ideal of North Carolina, Vance had governed the state during the Civil War, led Redemption and won the governorship in 1876, and served in the United States Senate from 1879 until his death in 1894. Soon after his death, friends had proposed a memorial, but funding was not forthcoming, nor was the racially and politically divided legislature likely to support such a project. When Democrats again "redeemed" the legislature in 1898, they promptly appropriated funds to memorialize the heroic figure of the earlier Redemption. The unveiling on 22 August 1900 was "a fitting time," as Josephus Daniels happily observed, "for Aycock, the new Governor was to receive it." In lauding the "immortal Vance" as the ideal subject for the first memorial to a North Carolina leader on Union Square, the speaker at the unveiling also advocated another in Statuary Hall in Washington, D.C. Within a few years, Vance's marble likeness filled that long-empty niche, where in due course it was joined by a statue of Aycock in the other niche.[28]

On 20 May 1907, a bronze figure of Worth Bagley, unveiled before a huge throng on Union Square, provided a new chapter in the saga of heroic southern vindication. The monument, made by popular New York sculptor Francis H. Packer, memorialized the young North Carolinian who had been the first American officer killed in the Spanish-American War. Bagley was a member of a prominent eastern North Carolina family, and his sister Adelaide was the wife of *News and Observer* publisher Josephus Daniels. The Spanish-American War, in which northern and southern soldiers fought together under a single flag, fostered sectional reunification in the cause of American nationalism. The young southerner's death in Cuba on 11 May 1898 was hailed in the national press as sealing the "covenant of brotherhood between the north and south," for now "we are all Worth Bagley's countrymen."[29]

The 1907 commemoration further expanded the meaning of Bagley's death. On the base of his monument, the inscription—"First Fallen, 1898"—linked his heroism to the nearby Confederate monument with its motto, "First at Bethel, Last at Appomattox." And the unveiling date of 20 May, as speaker Gov. Robert Glenn explained, deepened the sense of continuity: already sacred as "first marking the Declaration of Independence, second as the day on which North Carolina had turned to fight for friends and kindred," 20 May now had a third significance as "the day on which the breach of sectionalism had been healed and union had been cemented in the blood of Worth Bagley." Thus, claimed another speaker, Bagley's death signaled "a new era of Union" in which "the logical adjustment of history would again give the leadership of the nation to the South."[30]

In Wilmington as well, memorializing focused upon heroes central to city leaders' interpretation of the past and present. The Wilmington

Ladies Memorial Association had already given the city its Confederate memorial at Oakdale Cemetery in 1872. Now Wilmington women led state patriotic organizations to commemorate other heroes of the Cape Fear. The city's first civic monument—the Cornelius Harnett Monument—was presented by the North Carolina Society of the Colonial Dames of America, whose officers were mainly patrician Wilmington women, including Luola Murchison Sprunt (wife of James Sprunt), Gabrielle DeRosset Waddell (wife of Alfred Moore Waddell), and her aunt, Catherine DeRosset Meares. The Dames selected a prime site, a "commanding and beautiful position" in the central plaza of Market Street.[31]

The cornerstone laying ceremony in 1906 drew a large and festive crowd that reflected the overlapping circles of political and cultural leadership. The Colonial Dames invited the North Carolina chapter of the Society of the Cincinnati to participate, and requested that the Wilmington Light Infantry, "the flower of Wilmington for more than a half-century," provide a military feature. They asked Francis Winston, Masonic as well as political leader, to lay the cornerstone, and Wilmington mayor Alfred Moore Waddell to deliver an address. Waddell extolled the "heroes and patriots of the Lower Cape Fear" and assured his listeners that despite the previous absence of monuments as "material evidence of such loyalty of sentiment," the descendants of those heroes "cling with tenacity to their traditions." The following spring the Colonial Dames presented the classical granite obelisk to Mayor Waddell. As the inscription showed, the thirty-foot memorial commemorated both Cornelius Harnett and "the memory of the colonial heroes of the lower Cape Fear," especially the 150 men "who made the first armed resistance in the American Colonies to the oppressive stamp act of the British Parliament February 19, 1766."[32]

At one level, this first civic monument in Wilmington simply commemorated local colonists who resisted the Stamp Act and led the Revolutionary cause; since the leaders of the Colonial Dames were Wilmington residents and descendants of colonial Cape Fear planters, the subject was a natural choice. Yet for these women as for most members of the audience, the recent "Revolution" in Wilmington was fresh in memory. Indeed, in 1906 a reporter from Raleigh observed that the residents of Wilmington who "participated in or who flourished at the time of the post-election burning of the negro newspaper office and in the suppression of black supremacy in the city [still] date events from the 'Revolution.' That now is heard a good many times here in the course of a day." The rhetoric of the "Revolution of 1898" repeatedly linked that event with the "heroes of the lower Cape Fear" and their resistance to the Stamp Act. By erecting this obelisk, the women marked the center of the city with a monument that evoked a continuity of heroism from their colonial ancestors to their own men of the Cape Fear. Perhaps, too, the obelisk in its commanding position also served as an inspiration or a warning that the old "tenacity to their traditions" yet lived on.[33]

Four years later a second monument on Market Street honored George Davis, a brilliant aristocrat who had served as attorney general of the Confederacy. The Cape Fear chapter of the Daughters of the Confederacy (which shared many members with the Colonial Dames) had conceived the idea of a memorial to Davis soon after his death in 1896, but was at the time devoting its energies to creating a Confederate museum, which it opened in 1898 in the Wilmington Light Infantry Armory. In 1904 the Daughters began fundraising for the monument, but donations came slowly until 1909, when their president recruited James Sprunt to spearhead a quick and effective financial campaign. In 1911 they presented to the city a life-size bronze figure sculpted by Francis H. Packer. Like the Vance memorial in Raleigh, the statue of Davis showed its subject in mid-gesture, "reaching forward in a characteristic gesture of the right hand, while the left rests lightly upon the flag to which he was true to the end of his life." After the unveiling by Davis's grandsons and a historical address by Democratic leader and judge H. G. Connor, a stirring rendition of Davis's poem, "Carolina's Sons Are Ready," tied the Confederate cause to the Revolutionary War and "Mecklenburg! the proud old story!" On the base of the monument, paired seals of North Carolina and the Confederacy, the latter with its figure of George Washington, reiterated the vindication of Confederate leadership as noble and patriotic service.[34]

Memorializing continued in Wilmington and Raleigh after 1911, expanding on the intertwined themes of patriotic heroism and Democratic political accomplishments. It took several years before the impulse to glorify the Confederacy was fully satisfied. As late as 1924 a private bequest funded a Confederate memorial in downtown Wilmington, designed by architect Henry Bacon with expressive figures representing courage and sacrifice, again sculpted by Francis H. Packer. In Raleigh, where Union Square had become the focus of statewide commemorative interest, two new memorials filled out the Confederate story. On 10 June 1912, the North Carolina Division of United Daughters of the Confederacy unveiled sculptor Gutzon Borglum's dramatic bronze of Henry

Lawson Wyatt (1842–61), the North Carolina private who had been the "First Confederate Soldier to Fall in Battle in the War Between the States," at Bethel Church on 10 June 1861. Two years later, again on 10 June, a memorial to the North Carolina Women of the Confederacy was unveiled, the result of another private donation by a Confederate veteran. The architect for the project was Henry Bacon and the sculptor was New Yorker Augustus Lukeman. The donor, Ashley Horne, appointed a committee consisting mostly of prominent veterans to direct the project. The sculptor presented two designs for the principal figures —one "an elderly woman seated, reciting to a young girl . . . the story of the War Between the States, representing the activities of the Women of the South in perpetuating the memories of the Confederacy," the other showing the same woman telling the story to her grandson at her side, "inciting him to emulate the deeds of his fathers." The committee unanimously chose the latter.[35]

Inside the State Capitol, commemoration also proceeded. In 1908 the Daughters of the Revolution dedicated the first memorial in the long-naked rotunda—a bronze plaque commemorating "Fifty-one Ladies of Edenton" who, on 25 October 1774, had signed a resolution supporting the patriot cause. This early political act by American women, which became popularly known as the "Edenton Tea Party," was especially inspiring to the Daughters as an example of feminine "patriotism and zeal." The Daughters initially planned to place their memorial in Edenton, but after Edentonian Frank Wood erected a cannon topped by a teapot on the alleged site of the "tea party," the group decided to install their memorial in the Capitol. To raise money for the plaque, in 1901 the Daughters inaugurated a popular historical series, *The North Carolina Booklet*, which featured works by political and cultural leaders and prominent historians. Leaders in planning the memorial and editing the *Booklet* were two local women, Mary Hilliard Hinton and Elvira Worth Moffitt, both members of elite political families and both deeply involved in the era's full range of patriotic and cultural work.[36]

The unveiling of the plaque drew together the overlapping circles of aristocratic families and Democratic leaders: Lt. Gov. Francis Winston and Chief Justice Walter Clark gave addresses, Bennehan Cameron represented the Society of the Cincinnati, Marshall DeLancey Haywood represented the Sons of the Revolution, and, in a typical involvement of the rising generation in the ceremony, several children of "Revolutionary Patriots" unveiled the tablet. Within four years, the long-empty niches in the rotunda were filled with marble busts of political leaders, and these were soon followed by plaques celebrating colonial and Revolutionary heroism, and by various portraits throughout the building.[37]

Surely the most powerful recitation of the history that took form in these years resounded through the Capitol when historian, editor, and political leader Samuel A'Court Ashe—who had sparked the commemorative movement back in 1883—delivered the dedicatory address in 1909 for a portrait of the building's architect, David Paton. Speaking in the Senate chamber, Ashe used the Capitol itself as a text by evoking the "undying memories" that pervaded its halls. He began with the accomplishments of antebellum days, then recalled the trials of the Civil War and the leadership of "the mighty Vance" before turning to the years that followed: "[T]hese mute walls are witnesses of the saturnalia of Reconstruction still awaiting some Dante to portray the scenes with realistic power." As to the recent past,

> these walls have witnessed the reversal of that State policy forced on an unwilling people by the mailed hand of the conquering power, and the full restoration of Angli-Saxon [sic] control. Never in history has a people been so clearly and effectually vindicated as those gallant souls of North Carolina, who, emulating the constancy of Hamilcar, swore their children to undying opposition to those who would destroy their civilization. Let the oppressed of future ages gaze on the scene and take courage. Already hallowed are the memories that these chambers evoke. What grand occasions yet await them![38]

THE ARCHITECTURE OF THE NEW OLD SOUTH

Ashe recognized that buildings possessed the power to evoke hallowed memories and to inspire future ages. For his generation of southern leaders, the architecture of the colonial and antebellum past had special meaning, as did the construction of new buildings whose form and imagery captured in modern terms the symbols of that glorious past. The South's revival of classicism in public architecture and its embrace of the closely related Colonial Revival in residential architecture paralleled national trends, but with a distinctively southern face and meaning. Just as the monuments they erected in civic spaces commemorated past heroes and events, so in block after block of downtown buildings and in the premier residential neighborhoods where they had their homes, the southern elite's revival of classical and colonial architecture commemorated an entire way of life: the "golden age" before the war. This architecture shaped public memory of the past and defined the life of the present by asserting in ubiquitous physical form "the southern aristocracy's continuing legitimate authority as the dominant force in the region's political, social, and economic life."[39] And, moving beyond mere glorification of a past epoch, this architecture perpetuated and revitalized for modern daily use the deferential social values of the heirs and heiresses of the glorified tradition.

A vivid local explication of the new architecture appeared in a 1907 article in Josephus Daniels's *News and Observer*. The story was entitled, "A People Known by Way They Build: How Raleigh Has 'Found Herself' Architecturally and the Building That is Replacing Mistakes and Fixing Permanent Standards." Superficially, the article simply reported changing taste in Raleigh architecture. But just beneath the surface was the story of architecture as a marker of political and social events and values. Asserting that "Beauty in architecture sounds the signal in a community of stability," the writer presented a brief history of architectural evolution in terms that paralleled the publisher's own sense of recent history. Condemning previous decades' architectural "atrocities," the writer blasted that era's "pretentious frames, garbled ideas put together for the purpose of display." He contrasted these errors with recent improvements that defined a time when "the community has found itself, when the frightful begins to be pulled down; when the pretentious becomes an eyesore, when the notion is that of harmony, of fitness to use and right to be. Each has its place." He pointed to the present desire for "simplicity and timeliness" as evidence that "the callow period has passed, that the bumptious period of uncertainty has been weathered, and that there is experience as well as confidence in the air."

The city's admirable models of architecture were either antebellum landmarks or newly constructed works of classical mien. The writer praised the State Capitol—"an anomaly of beauty [which] stood as a protest against bad taste, over-pretension, under-estimation"—and admired Christ Episcopal Church as a spiritually inspiring edifice in English Gothic style. "These two early triumphs of city-building," he asserted, "stand as the case may be as a reproach or congratulation to the city that is building about them. And in recent years there has been an effort towards the symetry [*sic*] which they speak and the form which they glorify." The writer saw evidence of "the progress of the new thoughts in the homes of the people, in the buildings that exactly or by relation speak the public mind." He singled out a new state college building "in the Greek style" as "a triumph of proportion and taste," praised the "Colonial design" of buildings at Peace and St. Mary's (schools for young women), and admired a number of churches and businesses affiliated with the local elite. "It is in the homes of Raleigh," he concluded, "that the significance of the building and architectural spirit may be best observed," for new homes showed "a notable taste and an evident building for permanency. Whether the new homes be simple cottages or, as in many cases, real mansions the note is the same, a regard for art with comfort."[40]

The architecture the *News and Observer* writer so admired shared in the national revival of symmetry and classical themes. In the late nineteenth century, most southern cities had built more or less ornate versions of the eclectic, picturesque styles popular throughout the nation, characterized by irregular outlines, exuberant machine-made ornament, and rich textures and colors. As these variegated styles faded from fashion, and tastes turned toward balance, classical motifs, and smooth pale surfaces, the southern elite went beyond the usual rejection of recent styles, vehemently demonizing the architecture of the late nineteenth century along with the political and social conditions it seemed to represent. They embraced a new architecture that blended modern technological convenience with a revival of classical imagery akin to antebellum landmarks. This architecture provided a compelling metaphor for southern leaders promoting their region as offering the best of modern reform and race relations combined with the stable social hierarchy modeled by the Old South. Thus the new classically detailed skyscrapers and columned public buildings of southern cities represented both the South's renewed prosperity and participation in the urban American mainstream, and the region's preoccupation with "harmony, fitness to use and right to be."

In residential architecture a more specifically southern image emerged, both in the nationally popular Colonial Revival style and especially in the "Southern Colonial" style. Introduced to the region in the 1890s in homes of the elite, the Colonial Revival style swiftly gained broad and lasting acceptance. Besides its appeal as a national fashion with a certain regional flavor, the strength of the Colonial Revival was also rooted in deeper impulses in society.

The American Colonial Revival gained momentum when the 1876 Centennial Exposition sparked national enthusiasm for the American past and for "Old Colonial" (especially New England) architecture. American architects recorded colonial buildings of both the North and the South and used colonial motifs in their designs. In 1893, the grandiloquent Beaux-Arts architecture of the White City of the Chicago World Exposition encouraged the shift in popular taste toward imperial classical styles, while the exposition's individual state buildings showed visitors myriad "Colonial" styles. A few, such as Virginia's Mt. Vernon, were meant as replicas (North Carolina planned but could not fund a copy of Tryon Palace), but most, such as the Connecticut, West Virginia, and Kentucky buildings, were creative assemblages of motifs inspired by colonial architecture. Initially the Colonial Revival cast a broad net, drawing upon a heritage that reached from initial white settlement to the mid-nineteenth century's industrial and picturesque architecture. "The term Old Colonial is applied to a certain style of work, a free, and in many instances a refined, treatment of Classical details rather than to any fixed period," explained one early practitioner. Increasingly after about 1915 the focus narrowed to more literal use of seventeenth- and eighteenth-century precedents. The ascendancy of the Colonial Revival was linked to rising American nationalism and Anglo-Saxon nativism in the face of labor and class turbulence and massive immigration. Popular architectural literature, especially from the 1890s through the 1910s, presented the Colonial Revival as the architecture of Americanness; of patriotism, stability, and longevity; and specifically as "the architecture of our Anglo-Saxon heritage."[41]

In the South, identification of the colonial style with Anglo-Saxon American culture appealed not only to nativist pride but also to white supremacy. Southern bonding of colonial architecture with Anglo-Saxon elite culture likewise extended from the first settlement to the Civil War, particularly emphasizing the flowering of plantation culture just before the war. Within the broader colonial style, a specific "Southern Colonial" style emerged in the form of a large and symmetrical house characterized by a portico of great white columns. The Kentucky Building at the Chicago World's Fair in 1893 presented an early use of the type and term. National architectural writers eagerly embraced the term Southern Colonial along with the ideal of southern life it symbolized. In 1895, *American Architect and Building News* described a new house in St. Louis whose massive columned portico made it "more of the southern Colonial architecture than its sister style of the Northeastern States," and "somewhat of a relief from the ordinary run of Colonial houses." The columns were "part and parcel of the southern Colonial, [which] somehow or another bear with them a certain tinge of the big-heartedness and hospitality which are the rightful heritage of the southern people." The Southern Colonial house also incorporated modern conveniences of plumbing, heating, and lighting, an apt parallel to the Democrats' carefully devised amalgam of tradition and modern reform. That the Southern Colonial house was built more often for an urban businessman than for a cotton planter only confirmed its power. Modeled around 1900 chiefly in residences of prosperous members of old families, by 1910 it gained sway among wealthy citizens of various backgrounds.[42]

In a 1903 article entitled "Revival of the Colonial Style—A Simple, Dignified Home after the Old Fashion," Charlotte architects Charles Christian Hook and Stewart Rogers laid out the meaning of the style by way of a "resume of architecture in this country in the last fifty years" on southern terms: "The civil war marked the change from good to bad architecture in the South, the reason for which is apparent. In antebellum days when a home was built of any pretensions the owner and designer as a rule was an educated gentleman of refinement," who, "familiar with the classics and having other colonial work as models took pains to preserve the proper proportions." But "after the great conflict and things being reversed in general, we find a greater reversal in architecture than any other sign of the times. Why was it? Because the illiterate and unrefined being new to wealth desired it more than purity, and the cultured and once wealthy were either too poor to build or were so busy during the reconstruction period they had no time to devote to art." In those evil times, architecture was handed over to "the most ignorant class of men, in fact, any jack-leg who could wield a hatchet and saw. All colonial details and proportions were discarded as being 'old timey' [and] the jack-leg-carpenter with the deadly jigsaw ran riot in the land." But now, they affirmed, "out of all this chaos we again have a revival of the colonial, [which] in its purity expresses more real refined sentiment and more intimate associations with our history than any [other style], for it is not only an association of English history with our own but also expresses the authentic memoirs of the American people." In this framework the architects presented their design for a colonial style house, symmetrical and pure white, with a "stately portico." The interior as well as the exterior was "strictly colonial in detail," with a paneled den, a mahogany staircase, polished hardwood floors, and white enameled walls.[43]

In both Raleigh and Wilmington, the first major residential projects in the Southern Colonial style were for patrician families for whom the architectural reclamation of continuity from glorious past to redeemed present had deep associations. Such houses reinforced a way of life in which, as one resident remembered of Raleigh in 1905, "the women were fine hostesses, not only abounding in wit and delightful chit-chat but in well-ordered households" where "the relation between old Raleighites and their black friends was beautiful," for many of the servants "never left the premises and scarcely knew they had been set free." And, as the feminine domain in an era of elaborate, large-scale entertaining, the magnified version of the antebellum plantation house offered the perfect setting for hospitality, patriotism, and ancestral distinction—all in an urban residence larger and vastly more convenient than most plantation houses had ever been.[44]

Continuity with the past was literal in some of the earliest Colonial Revival projects, in which elite couples aggrandized existing antebellum mansions. An important early example came when Wilmington civic leaders James and Luola Sprunt remodeled the downtown residence of antebellum governor Edward Dudley. James Sprunt, a Scots-born businessman and Confederate veteran, wrote local history and endowed a series of historical monographs at the University of North Carolina. As president of the North Carolina Society of Colonial Dames, Luola Murchison Sprunt led in local and state efforts to mark important colonial sites. Soon after the Sprunts bought the house in 1895, they expanded it and transformed its public visage with a monumental Corinthian portico flanked by broad porches. The resulting "handsome Colonial residence" instantly gained acclaim as one of the city's principal landmarks and the setting for Mrs. Sprunt's Colonial Dames meetings and celebrated hospitality.[45]

In Raleigh, too, the first major statement in the Southern Colonial style appeared in the refashioning of an antebellum residence. In 1901 Bennehan and Sallie Cameron undertook an expansion of his grandfather's house on Hillsborough Street. Bennehan Cameron, whose father and grandfather had been among the richest men in the state before the Civil War, was a free-spending and progressive planter active in the 1898 and 1900 Democratic campaigns and later in promotion of better highways. Tracing lineage from Revolutionary heroes, he enthusiastically supported patriotic groups and commemorative pursuits. Sallie Taliaferro Mayo Cameron, a descendant of old Virginia families, was the daughter of Peter H. Mayo, a wealthy Richmond businessman who had been on Gen.

Robert E. Lee's staff.[46] With her father's help, Sallie and Bennehan Cameron obtained remodeling plans from Richmond architect William G. Noland, a prominent practitioner of revival styles. To the rear they built a large addition with bedrooms, modern bathrooms, and a new kitchen. Sallie was especially interested in transforming the public face of the residence: her father reported that Noland was "working up the front porch drawing . . . after getting your first letter about it last week. We think we can carry out your wishes." With its towering portico of Ionic columns and curved porches at each end, the Cameron mansion impressed Raleigh as "a fine old colonial-type residence" that "carried one's thoughts back to the days of large plantations and baronial rule."[47]

The same architectural themes also appeared in new residences. The epitome of the Southern Colonial house and Raleigh's first and grandest example was built in 1902 for Richard Beverly Raney. The wealthy widower Raney had previously erected the Olivia Raney Library as a memorial to his first wife; in 1902, in preparation for his marriage to Kate Whiting Denson, he constructed a new house on Hillsborough Street across from the library, thus completing a symmetrical relationship with the Confederate monument. The couple both came from old planter families that had suffered losses during the war and endured years of poverty afterward. R. Beverly Raney, son of a Granville County planter, had come to Raleigh at age eighteen in 1868 to work as a hotel clerk, had moved up rapidly, and had soon become general agent for a national life insurance company. Kate Denson came from an aristocratic Cape Fear planter family that had "lost everything" after the war; her parents had moved to Raleigh, where her father was a teacher and a leader in Confederate veterans' affairs. Although not involved in political activities, Beverly and Kate Raney moved in the city's highest social circles, in which Raney's business success enabled them to enjoy the fruits of prosperity regained.[48]

To design their house, Raney turned to Raleigh architect Charles Barrett. Barrett was an early proponent of the Southern Colonial style, who, with his former partner William P. Rose, had published an example of "a complete modern southern home" in the *Southern Architect* in 1899. Now working on his own, Barrett designed the Raney mansion as a full-fledged exemplar of the style and immediately published it as the centerpiece of his *Colonial Southern Homes* (1903). Carrying forward many aspects of antebellum plantation houses, the symmetrically planned residence had a central hallway and flanking formal rooms—all rendered on a vaster scale and with more rooms than its antebellum predecessors. Its modern amenities included "sanitary, scientific" plumbing, heating, and electric lighting. The exterior presented the Southern Colonial at its most spectacular, with two massive Ionic porticoes addressing Hillsborough Street and the Capitol. In such a house, the imagery of the old plantation evoked family histories of lost grandeur, while its modern luxury and prominent location expressed the Raneys' position in the city where they and other children of planter families had created a new urban version of the old way of life.[49]

More and more columned residences appeared as other members of the cities' elites followed suit. Raleigh's Hillsborough Street was soon lined by a parade of pillared porticoes on both old and new houses. A mile down the street, opposite the Cameron mansion, St. Mary's School, the old Episcopal girls' school, refurbished its campus in Southern Colonial style.[50] In Wilmington, too, local reporters rhapsodized reliably over the "modern," "convenient," "Colonial" residences wealthy citizens were building. The most flamboyant example rose in 1905 when Elizabeth Eagles Haywood Bridgers—descendant of ancient North Carolina families, and the recent widow of Preston L. Bridgers, a local businessman who had been among the leaders of the 1898 "Revolution"—built a massive stone townhouse dominated by a curved portico of colossal Ionic columns and filled with the latest in luxurious modern amenities.[51] As the popularity of the style continued, an especially powerful rendition appeared in 1913 when the Cape Fear Club, bastion of the city's business and professional men, erected its new clubhouse in the form of a red brick mansion trimmed in white marble, "patterned closely after the Colonial style of architecture," and featuring "long commodious verandas, with large white columns" and reception rooms "arranged and decorated after the Colonial style of the Adams period."[52]

The Southern Colonial image also reached beyond the city into suburban enclaves. Between 1907 and 1910, Mary Bridgers, Preston Bridgers's sister, developed Carolina Heights east of Wilmington for leading industrialists and merchants, building the most imposing residences in "Colonial" style with porticoes in every classical order.[53] At the same time, on their Orton Plantation on the Cape Fear River, James and Luola Sprunt transformed another antebellum mansion into a hybrid Colonial Revival composition, keeping the classical, temple-form plantation house with its grand portico as the central element to which they added conveniently appointed wings on either side. Sprunt regarded Orton as "the most attractive of all the old colonial estates on the Cape Fear," which "still maintains its reputation of colonial days for a refined and generous hospitality" and presents "one of the finest examples of pure Colonial architecture in America . . . with its stately white columns gleaming in the sunshine."[54] These landmarks inaugurated a lasting pattern. As cities' changing residential trends and the proliferation of suburbs embodied growing separation among races and classes, the Colonial Revival in its myriad forms came to dominate upper- and middle-class housing throughout the South, and to be identified simply and universally with traditional domesticity, respectability, and continuity.

THE EPITOME OF THE NEW SOUTHERN ORDER

When North Carolina Democratic leaders organized the state's official presentation at the Jamestown Tercentennial Exposition of 1907, they recapitulated themes that had recently emerged in the state's life. The exposition combined a celebration of the oldest (1607) establishment of Anglo-Saxon culture in America with a southern-sponsored reunion of blue and gray, a presentation of modern southern race relations, and a certain amount of economic boosterism. Led by Gov. Robert Glenn, North Carolina set out to put on an exhibit "first-class in every respect" to attract investors and "desirable" immigrants. Business leaders presented displays touting the state's economic progress and opportunities.

Charged with creating a state history exhibit, Mary Hilliard Hinton, editor of the Daughters of the Revolution's thriving *North Carolina Booklet*, worked with other prominent women to assemble a dazzling display of the recent "historical awakening in the Old North State." The exhibit began with depictions of America's first Anglo-Saxon settlement, the Lost Colony at Roanoke, illustrated by paintings funded by Bennehan Cameron and copied from John White's 1585 and 1588 drawings of native Indian life. (Miss Hinton noted that this feature was presented simply "to start with the beginning of our state's history, and not with an ambition to antedate the first permanent English settlement at Jamestown by twenty-two years.") Displays included photographs of James Sprunt's collection of portraits of the Lords Proprietors; silver from various "aristocratic" families; pictures of celebrated plantation homes and furniture from a few of them; and a depiction of the Edenton Tea Party scene together with possessions of those patriotic colonial ladies.[55]

North Carolina's chief expenditure was on its state building. With each participating state constructing an example of its "typical Colonial" architecture, the exposition managers hoped to create a "Colonial acropolis restful to the eye and satisfying to sentiment," which would "result in a revival of interest in Colonial architecture, which is really the only distinctive American order of building." Virginia erected a brick and marble colonial mansion 116 feet long, while Georgia offered a Greek Revival temple modeled on President Roosevelt's mother's ancestral home as "a splendid specimen of the old colonial home." North Carolina leaders chose the Southern Colonial style that had become so popular in the state, a house built of North Carolina pine and "of large colonial design with immense columns and porches." The North Carolina Building further promoted the style back home by inspiring citizens who visited the exposition to copy it in their own houses. And the North Carolina Architectural Association, which included many of the state's chief practitioners of the Colonial Revival, held its summer 1907 meeting at the exposition amidst the seaside "Colonial acropolis."[56]

In this official display of the state's self-image, as in the Colonial Revival architecture and commemorative monuments back home, Democratic leaders set forth the values and heritage they intended to shape the state in the new century. Miss Hinton summed up their accomplishment:

> The keynote of American life is progress—an excellent and most powerful characteristic; yet harm and ultimate ruin will surely follow in its trail unless safeguarded by conservatism. No study so engenders and promotes the cultivation of this check to vandalism as does History. At last the dominant trait of the Anglo-Saxon race is asserting itself and we are becoming more like our relatives overseas, who guard sacredly whatever bears on their glorious past.[57]

For the Democratic elite, the book had opened on a redeemed and progressive South that reaffirmed the social order of their antebellum heyday, while embracing a program of modern economic progress. Just as they had taken control of the political process with strategies devised to dictate the present and the future, so at the same time they took control of the region's history and defined the meaning of the past in a fashion that explained and vindicated the present. By molding public memory of the past, they also shaped the direction of the future. They engaged in a process that, while sharing some features with what has been called the "invention of tradition," might best be termed the "arranging of tradition."[58] Rather than concocting a history to undergird their position, they employed precisely the same tactic that Alfred Moore Waddell had described in 1895, using the events of the past "like a child's box of letters with which we can spell any word we please. We have only to select such letters as we want, arrange them as we like, and say nothing about those which do not suit our purpose." Vital to this spelling out of the past was the creation of public, visible, lasting symbols of that past.

Thus between 1890 and 1910 elite Democratic leaders succeeded in forging a symbolic ensemble that defined North Carolina history and public life in accord with their vision of society. Within a short time, both the history they spelled out and the social and political system they had established took on an aura of permanence, which was reinforced in the form of monuments and architecture. So effective was the combined effect of cultural and political control that for many it seemed that the hierarchical, racially segregated South had always been thus, except for the brief aberration of Reconstruction, and presumably would always remain so.

In the mid-twentieth century, challenges to the racial and political structure created by the Democrats in 1900 began to change the South. Far more lasting, however, was the definition of history they had established. Although historians in the middle and late years of the twentieth century have begun to reexamine old assumptions, public memory has been slow to change. In the sagas told by memorials and by the seemingly unbroken continuity of colonial architecture, the old story persists. Through the powerful and lasting language of monuments and architecture, the guardians of the glorious past have continued to guard the past, the present, and the future.

NOTES

The author acknowledges with thanks a 1987 Henry Francis du Pont fellowship at the Winterthur Museum for initial research on this topic. The author also thanks, for critical readings and suggestions, John Bishir, Jerry Cashion, Jeffrey Crow, Catherine Hutchins, James Leloudis, Carl Lounsbury, William Price, Janet Seapker, Dell Upton, Harry Watson, Camille Wells, and Chris Wilson; and for encouragement and assistance in obtaining illustrations and information, Claudia Brown, Ned Cooke, Michael Hill, Elizabeth Reid Murray, Beverly Tetterton, Edward Turberg, Abigail Van Slyck, Harry Warren, and R. Beverly R. Webb.

1. Rev. M. M. Marshall, "Address," in *Exercises at the Opening of the Olivia Raney Library, Held in the Library Hall on the Evening of Thursday, January Twenty-Fourth, 1901* (Capital Printing Co., 1901), 14–15.

2. Wilmington, the Cape Fear River port settled in the early eighteenth century, was from 1850 through 1900 North Carolina's largest city, with about 20,000 people (56 percent of whom were black) in 1890. Raleigh, the inland capital established in 1792, had in 1890 nearly 13,000 people (50 percent black and 50 percent white). In subsequent decades the Piedmont industrial cities of Charlotte and Winston-Salem drew ahead in population.

3. This summary derives primarily from the following works: Kenneth Ames, "Introduction," in *The Colonial Revival in America*, ed. Alan Axelrod (W. W. Norton and Co., 1985); Edward L. Ayers, *The Promise of the New South: Life After Reconstruction* (Oxford University Press, 1992); John Bodnar, *Remaking America: Public Memory, Commemoration, and Patriotism in the Twentieth Century* (Princeton University Press, 1992); Michele H. Bogart, *Public Sculpture and the Civil Ideal in New York City, 1890–1930* (University of Chicago Press, 1989); Gaines M. Foster, *Ghosts of the Confederacy: Defeat, the Lost Cause, and the Emergence of the New South, 1865 to 1913* (Oxford University Press, 1987); Michael Kammen, *Mystic Chords of Memory: The Transformation of Tradition in American Culture* (Alfred A. Knopf, 1991); Robert W. Rydell, *All the World's a Fair: Visions of Empire at American International Expositions, 1876–1916* (University of Chicago Press, 1984); Christopher Wilson, *The Myth of Santa Fe: Creating a Modern Regional Tradition* (University of New Mexico Press, 1997); Richard Guy Wilson et al., *The American Renaissance, 1876–1917* (Pantheon, 1979); and Richard Guy Wilson, "Architecture and the Reinterpretation of the Past in the American Renaissance," *Winterthur Portfolio* 18 (Spring 1983): 69–87.

4. Quotes from Charles B. Aycock, "The South Regaining Its Prestige," in *Literary and Historical Activities in North Carolina, 1900–1905* (Raleigh Publications of the Historical Commission, 1907), 1:120; and *The Biographical History of North Carolina from Colonial Times to the Present*, ed. Samuel A. Ashe (Charles L. Van Noppen, 1905), 1:36.

5. Harry S. Warren, "Colonel Frederick Augustus Olds and the Founding of the North Carolina Museum of History" (M.A. thesis, East Carolina University, 1988), 20–21. Samuel A'Court Ashe (1840–1938), a graduate of the U.S. Naval Academy and an Episcopalian, engaged in several occupations, founded the *News and Observer* in 1881, and produced *The Biographical History of North Carolina*. See *The Dictionary of North Carolina Biography*, ed. William S. Powell (University of North Carolina Press, 1979–).

6. The Raleigh Ladies Memorial Association was organized in 1866 with Mrs. General L. O'B. Branch (née Nancy Haywood Blount) as president ("Ladies Memorial Association," the *News and Observer*, 10 May 1903). North and South Carolina and some of Virginia used 10 May as Memorial Day, the anniversary of Stonewall Jackson's death (Foster, *Ghosts of the Confederacy*, 42). Alfred Moore Waddell (1834–1912), a descendant of colonial general Hugh Waddell and Revolutionary general Francis Nash, practiced law, edited newspapers in Charlotte

and Wilmington, and though opposing secession, served as an officer in the war. As a "Redeemer" Conservative and Democrat, he was elected to Congress (1870–79); he wrote *Some Memories of My Life* and works of Cape Fear history (Powell, ed., *Dictionary of North Carolina Biography*).

7. Ladies Memorial Association Records, North Carolina State Archives, Division of Archives and History, Raleigh. As Waddell noted, the state had previously (1857) erected a bronze cast of Houdon's statue of George Washington on the Capitol grounds. Still earlier (1816), the state had commissioned a marble figure of Washington from the celebrated Italian sculptor Antonio Canova, which stood in the rotunda of the State House until a fire in 1831 destroyed both the building and the statue.

8. See Foster, *Ghosts of the Confederacy*, on the shift from funereal to civic memorials. Similar trends took place in the North. According to Ralph W. Widener Jr.'s *Confederate Monuments* (privately published, 1982), in North Carolina only the Concord monument (1892) predates the Raleigh monument on a civic site. On the North Carolina Monumental Association, see Branch Papers, North Carolina Division of Archives and History. Officers included Mrs. Armistead Jones (president), Mrs. Garland Jones, and Mrs. John W. Hinsdale. Mrs. Armistead Jones (née Nancy Haywood Branch) was the daughter of Gen. Lawrence O'Bryan Branch (railroad president and Confederate officer) and Nancy Haywood Blount Branch, founding president of the Ladies Memorial Association. Her husband, Armistead Jones, was a Confederate officer, Raleigh attorney, and Democratic party leader; the couple belonged to Christ Episcopal Church (see "Armistead Jones" in Powell, ed., *Dictionary of North Carolina Biography*). Among the couple's best-known descendants is novelist Armistead Maupin. First quote, undated (February 1895) clipping, Scrapbook, Branch Papers, North Carolina Division of Archives and History.

9. *News and Observer*, 20, 21 May 1895. The granite came from Mount Airy, N.C., quarries. In contrast to the popular mass-produced soldier figures, the figures were modeled on North Carolina regiments and fashioned by Bavarian sculptor Ferdinand Von Miller. Prominent on the dais were Mrs. Armistead Jones, Mrs. Gen. Branch, Mrs. Gen. Stonewall Jackson, and Mrs. Gen. D. H. Hill. Rev. Aldert Smedes, principal of St. Mary's School, offered the prayer. Julia Jackson Christian unveiled the monument.

10. See Fred Arthur Bailey, "The Textbooks of the 'Lost Cause': Censorship and the Creation of Southern State Histories," *Georgia Historical Quarterly* 75 (Fall 1991): 507–33, for a similar 1895 speech by Stephen D. Lee to the United Confederate Veterans in Houston, part of the effort of the "South's aristocrats" to defend "not merely the South, but, more importantly, the embattled status of southern patricians" (508).

11. Richard N. Current, "That Other Declaration, May 20, 1775–May 20, 1975," *North Carolina Historical Review* 54 (April 1977): 169–91. North Carolina

Confederate leaders' usage of the symbolic date paralleled the Confederate government's choice of 22 February as its founding date and the use of Washington's image on its official seal.

12. James Sprunt to Alfred Moore Waddell, 21 May 1895, and H. G. Connor to Alfred Moore Waddell, 23 May 1895, Alfred Moore Waddell Papers, Southern Historical Collection, Library of the University of North Carolina at Chapel Hill. (See political leader Henry Groves Connor and his son, historian and archivist Robert D. W. Connor, in Powell, ed., *Dictionary of North Carolina Biography*.)

13. J. Morgan Kousser, *The Shaping of Southern Politics: Suffrage Restriction and the Establishment of the One-Party South, 1880–1910* (Yale University Press, 1974); C. Vann Woodward, *Origins of the New South, 1877–1913* (Louisiana State University Press, 1971); and Paul Escott, *Many Excellent People: Power and Privilege in North Carolina, 1850–1900* (University of North Carolina Press, 1985).

14. Quotes from Josephus Daniels, *Editor in Politics* (University of North Carolina Press, 1941), 295, 283. Other first-hand accounts that capture even in retrospect the spirit of the times include Alfred Moore Waddell, *Some Memories of My Life* (Edwards and Broughton, 1908), and a 1933 interview with Furnifold Simmons in Carl Goerch, *Down Home* (Edwards and Broughton, 1943), 131–58. Charles B. Aycock and Robert Glenn later served as governors, and Francis Winston, organizer of the "White Supremacy Club" system, became lieutenant governor. Glenn and Winston came from old plantation families; Aycock came from a small farming family. As in other southern states, the Democrats who initiated the white supremacy crusade came from heavily black plantation counties where black voters challenged their candidacies; these men spread Negrophobia westward to bring white voters of the heavily Populist and Republican counties of the Piedmont into their camp.

15. James Sprunt, *Chronicles of the Cape Fear River* (Edwards and Broughton, 1916), 554–55; and H. Leon Prather, *We Have Taken a City: The Wilmington Racial Massacre and Coup of 1898* (Associated University Presses, 1984), 45. In 1898 Bellamy was the successful Democratic candidate for Congress.

16. Alex Manly, publisher of the *Wilmington Record*, wrote the editorial in response to Atlanta writer Rebecca Felton's article on lynching black men for raping white women. Portions of his editorial were taken out of context and widely reprinted to exacerbate white fears. Prather, *We Have Taken a City*; and Sprunt, *Chronicles*, 554–55.

17. *Wilmington Messenger*, 25 October 1898. On 28 October 1898, at the "White Supremacy Convention" at Goldsboro, Waddell used similar language. Following a speech by William A. Guthrie of Durham (a former Populist)—who led off with an assertion of Anglo-Saxon supremacy: "Resist our march of progress and civilization and we will wipe you off the face of the earth"—Waddell described white Wilmingtonians' problems and their determination to drive out Manly, Russell, and others "if they have to throw enough dead Negro bodies in the Cape

Fear to choke up its passage to the sea." This speech "electrified" the convention and, quoted across the state, made Wilmington's cause "the cause of all" (Daniels, *Editor in Politics*, 301).

18. George M. Tolson, Hertford, N.C., 27 October 1898, to Alfred Moore Waddell; and Rebecca Cameron to Alfred Moore Waddell, 26 October 1898, Waddell Papers. Miss Cameron, a cousin of both Waddell and Bennehan Cameron, was a leader in the United Daughters of the Confederacy and a founder in 1900 of the State Literary and Historical Society. "Anna" was her sister (see genealogical chart, Jean Bradley Anderson, *Piedmont Plantation: The Bennehan-Cameron Family and Lands in North Carolina* [Historic Preservation Society of Durham, 1985]).

19. Prather, *We Have Taken a City*; and Waddell, *Some Memories of My Life*.

20. Bennehan Cameron to Alfred Moore Waddell, 13 November 1898, Waddell Papers. Sprunt, *Chronicles*, 555; and Waddell, *Some Memories of My Life*, 243.

21. Waddell is quoted in Daniels, *Editor in Politics*, 368. Chief "engineers" of the state's suffrage amendment were George Rountree of Wilmington, Francis Winston of Bertie County, and Josephus Daniels. The election of 1900 was held in August rather than November to prevent possible Federal interference (Kousser, *Shaping of Southern Politics*, 190–91).

22. With the disfranchisement of blacks, the Republican party also wrote off the Negro vote and became "lily white," and factionalism promptly returned to the Democratic party. These events were entwined with such national trends as dwindling northern concern over the fate of southern blacks (as epitomized in the acceptance of separate but equal facilities in *Plessy vs. Ferguson*); mounting Anglo-American nativism in the face of growing immigration from eastern and southern Europe; and expanding American imperialism in lands with non-Anglo-Saxon populations. Amidst these trends, the New South used its white supremacist "solution" to the "Negro problem" and its predominantly native-born white population to undergird a position of national leadership.

23. *Public Documents of the State of North Carolina* (Edwards and Broughton and E. M. Uzzell, 1901), vol. 1, document 1a, pp. 2, 4, 12.

24. The qualification for membership read "any white resident of the State, or North Carolinian residing out of the State, who subscribes to the purposes of the Association" (*Literary and Historical Activities in North Carolina*, 1–3, 6).

25. From these roots also emerged the state's tradition of distinguished historians as well as the fruitful relationship between historical pursuits and civic and political leaders. See William S. Price Jr., "Plowing Virgin Fields: State Support for Southern Archives, Particularly North Carolina," *Carolina Comments* 29 (March 1991): 41–47.

26. An important dimension of this story is to be explored in dissenting views of other groups both black and white, whose stories were omitted or denied in the official codified saga written and symbolic. In Virginia, as Kirk Savage de-

scribes in "Race, Memory and Identity: The National Monuments of the Union and the Confederacy" (Ph.D. diss., University of California, Berkeley, 1990), blacks' dissenting views took a variety of forms, including both nonparticipation and pointed commentary. For example, concerning the monument to Robert E. Lee in Richmond, a local black newspaper, the *Richmond Planet*, observed on 7 June 1890 that "[t]he Negro . . . put up the Lee Monument, and should the time come, will be there to take it down" (Savage, 150).

27. See *Literary and Historical Activities in North Carolina* for representative rhetoric on these topics and such activities as Francis Winston's report (29–35) on the first "North Carolina Day" celebrations in the public schools, a project assisted by the Daughters of the Revolution and the North Carolina Literary and Historical Society. The first "North Carolina Day" program in 1901 was on "The First Anglo-Saxon Settlement in America," followed in 1902 and 1903 by studies of the Albemarle and Cape Fear settlements and their "distinguished citizens." See also *The North Carolina Booklet* (North Carolina Society of the Daughters of the Revolution, 1901–1926); Daniel Harvey Hill, *Young People's History of North Carolina* (Alfred Williams, 1916); and Ashe, ed., *Biographical History of North Carolina*.

28. *News and Observer*, 16, 18, 19 August 1900; *Heroes and Heroines on Union Square* (State Capitol Foundation, Inc., 1983); Daniels, *Editor in Politics*, 369; and *Literary and Historical Activities in North Carolina*. See Bogart, *Public Sculpture and the Civic Ideal*, 32, on Beaux-Arts sculptor Augustus Saint-Gaudens's influential use of gesture in his celebrated *Farragut* (1881).

29. Quotes from the *Atlanta Constitution* and *New York Tribune*, Ayers, *Promise of the New South*, 331–32. Francis H. Packer was a New York sculptor who worked with the prominent Beaux-Arts sculptor Daniel Chester French on such projects as the figure of Lincoln in Henry Bacon's Lincoln Memorial in Washington, D.C. (Tony P. Wrenn, *Wilmington, North Carolina: An Architectural and Historical Portrait* [University Press of Virginia, 1984], 203).

30. *News and Observer*, 19, 20, 21 May 1907.

31. Wrenn, *Wilmington*, 295–97; *Wilmington Star*, 2, 3 May 1907; and Rosa Chiles, "North Carolina Society of Colonial Dames in America," in Sprunt, *Chronicles*, 578–79.

32. *Wilmington Messenger*, 20, 21 April 1906, and 3 May 1907; and *Wilmington Star*, 2, 3 May 1907.

33. Fred Olds, *Wilmington Morning Star*, 28 January 1906, reprinted from the 27 January 1906 *Charlotte Observer*; courtesy of Harry Warren. In 1909 the Colonial Dames erected a second marker to the "Men of the Cape Fear" at Brunswick, a ruined town that was the actual site of the Stamp Act resistance, citing the 150 "armed men of the Cape Fear," led by George Moore of Orton and Cornelius Harnett. The site was part of the Murchison and Sprunt holdings; in 1952 James

Laurence Sprunt donated the Brunswick Town site to the state (James Sprunt, *The Story of Orton Plantation* [published privately in Wilmington, 1958]).

34. *Presentation of the Statue Hon. George Davis to the City of Wilmington by the Daughters of the Confederacy*, 20 April 1911. The address at the cornerstone laying was by Alfred Moore Waddell; that at the unveiling by Judge H. G. Connor (Mrs. William M. Parsley, "The George Davis Monument," in Sprunt, *Chronicles*, 572–73). On Sprunt's role see Mrs. William M. Parsley to James Sprunt, 9 January and 27 March 1909. Sprunt promised to donate $1,000 and persuaded two businessmen to match his sum (Sprunt to H. Walters, 2 February 1909; Sprunt to S. P. Shotter, 4 March 1909), and others to donate smaller amounts (Sprunt to various recipients, March 1909); he also worked out arrangements with the sculptor (correspondence from the Alexander Sprunt and Sons Papers, Special Collections Library, Duke University, Durham).

35. Architect Henry Bacon had lived in Wilmington and maintained ties during an illustrious career that included the Lincoln Memorial. Horne Committee Papers, North Carolina Division of Archives and History. Other monuments on Union Square commemorate Democratic educator Charles McIver (1912); Charles B. Aycock (1924); Samuel A'Court Ashe (1940); three presidents North Carolina "gave the nation" (1948); Vietnam veterans (1987); and World Wars I and II and the Korean Conflict (1990).

36. The *Booklet* began in May 1901 under Miss Martha Helen Haywood and Mrs. Hubert Haywood; they were soon succeeded by Miss Hinton and Mrs. Moffitt. These women made the *Booklet* a long-lived success that helped define the emerging canon of state history. Mary Hilliard Hinton (1869–1961), daughter of planter David Hinton and Mary Boddie Carr (sister of Gov. Elias Carr), was active in Christ Episcopal Church, the Daughters of the Confederacy, the Literary and Historical Association, the Association for the Preservation of Virginia Antiquities (APVA), the Daughters of the Revolution, the Colonial Dames, the Daughters of the Barons of Runnymede, the Woman's Club of Raleigh, and the Anti-Suffrage League. Elvira Worth Moffitt (1836–1930), daughter of a governor and aunt of Worth Bagley and Adelaide Bagley Daniels, led in patriotic and reform causes including the Daughters of the Confederacy, the Daughters of the Revolution, the Literary and Historical Association, the Wake County School Betterment Association, the Woman's Club of Raleigh, the North Carolina Peace Society, the Virginia Dare School, and the APVA (Powell, ed., *Dictionary of North Carolina Biography*; Mary Hilliard Hinton Papers, Southern Historical Collection; and Elvira Worth Moffitt Papers, Southern Historical Collection).

37. *News and Observer*, 24 October 1908; *Charlotte Evening Chronicle*, 24 October 1908; and *Greensboro Daily Industrial News*, 25 October 1908.

38. *David Paton: Architect of the North Carolina State Capitol, An Address by Samuel A. Ashe* (Edwards and Broughton, 1916), 15.

39. Quoted in Bailey, "Textbooks of the 'Lost Cause,'" 508.

40. *News and Observer*, 6 June 1907. See also Charlotte V. Brown, "The Day of the Great Cities," in Catherine W. Bishir, Charlotte V. Brown, Ernest H. Wood, and Carl R. Lounsbury, *Architects and Builders in North Carolina: A History of the Practice of Building* (University of North Carolina Press, 1990), 298.

41. Glenn Brown, in "Old Colonial Work in Virginia and Maryland," *American Architect and Building News*, 22 October 1887, 198. Joy Wheeler Dow, *American Renaissance: A Review of Domestic Architecture* (William T. Comstock, 1904). See also Axelrod, ed., *Colonial Revival in America*, 11–12. Nationally the Colonial Revival was related to the creation of American period rooms in museums, the establishment of many national patriotic and ancestral organizations, and the passage of the National Origins Act in 1924; see William B. Rhoads, *The Colonial Revival* (Garland Publishing, Inc., 1977), and William B. Rhoads, "The Colonial Revival and American Nationalism," *Journal of the Society of Architectural Historians* 35 (December 1976): 239–54.

42. *American Architect and Building News*, 6 April 1895. Issues of *Southern Architect* show the incorporation of Colonial motifs into houses of a variety of forms in the late 1890s and a shift to the symmetrical house with a dominant portico in 1899. Many local and regional architects worked in this style, including mail-order architect George F. Barber of Knoxville, Frank Milburn, William P. Rose, Herbert W. Simpson, and others. For examples, see Catherine W. Bishir, *North Carolina Architecture* (University of North Carolina Press, 1990), 365, 416–25. On the "Southern Colonial" in Virginia see Richard Guy Wilson, "Building on the Foundations," in Charles E. Brownell, Calder Loth, William M. S. Rasmussen, and Richard Guy Wilson, *The Making of Virginia Architecture* (Virginia Museum of Fine Arts, 1992), 116–23.

43. *Charlotte Observer*, 20 December 1903. Similar ideas were repeated in national literature, as, for example, J. Robie Kennedy Jr., "Examples of Georgian and Greek Revival Work in the Far South," *Architectural Record* 21 (March 1907); and Russell F. Whitehead, "The Old and the New South," *Architectural Record* 30 (July 1911).

44. Robert W. Winston, *It's a Far Cry* (Henry Holt and Co., 1937), 262–63.

45. Wrenn, *Wilmington*, 53–55. See also the *Wilmington Star*, 2 May 1902 and 4 May 1907. After James Sprunt's death his son, J. Laurence Sprunt, replaced the portico and porches with a small, Georgian Revival entrance portico. James Sprunt (1846–1924) came as a child with his parents from Scotland to Wilmington, served as purser on Confederate blockade runners, and then formed Alexander Sprunt & Son, a successful cotton and naval stores export firm. A Presbyterian, he was a philanthropist to hospitals, churches, and historical projects. He published *Tales and Traditions of the Lower Cape Fear, 1661–1896* (1896) and *Chronicles of the Cape Fear River, 1666–1914* (1914, 1916), and endowed the *James Sprunt Historical Monographs*, begun by the University of North Carolina in 1900. Luola

Murchison was the descendant of Cape Fear colonists and the daughter of Kenneth Murchison, a Confederate officer born of Scots ancestry near Fayetteville who engaged in business in Wilmington and New York before and after the Civil War. As Colonial Dames president, she developed a systematic list of colonial sites to mark, which formed a basis for subsequent state programs (Sprunt, *Chronicles*, 578–85, and Sprunt, *Story of Orton Plantation*).

46. Bennehan Cameron (1854–1925), son of Paul and Anne Ruffin Cameron, and grandson of Duncan Cameron and of North Carolina Supreme Court Justice Thomas Ruffin, belonged to the Episcopal Church, the Society of the Cincinnati, and the North Carolina Literary and Historical Association. He led in erecting monuments to Revolutionary generals Francis Nash and Nathanael Greene, and, though too young to serve in the war, took part in Confederate commemorative activities (Powell, ed., *Dictionary of North Carolina Biography*; Jean Anderson, *Piedmont Plantations*; and Bennehan Cameron Papers, Southern Historical Collection).

47. P. H. Mayo to Sallie Cameron, 17 June 1901; Sallie Cameron to Bennehan Cameron, July–October 1901; and "Alterations & Additions to Residence of Col. Bennehan Cameron," September 1901, Noland & Baskervill, Architects, Richmond (blueprints for rear extension and porch details), Bennehan Cameron Papers, Southern Historical Collection. Last quote is from Virgil St. Cloud, *Pioneer Blood* (Edwards and Broughton, 1948). Bennehan Cameron was a friend of Thomas Dixon, and unsubstantiated local tradition claims the house was the setting for Dixon's novel *The Clansman*.

48. Culled from clippings and family memorabilia, courtesy of R. Beverly R. Webb. See Richard Beverly Raney in *Who's Who in America*, 1903 (1215). Kate's parents were Capt. Claudius B. and Mary Matilda Cowan Denson (see "Claudius Denson" in Powell, ed., *Dictionary of North Carolina Biography*). Mary Matilda was the daughter of Thomas and Mary Ashe London Cowan of Old Town Plantation on the Cape Fear. After the war, the Densons lived in reduced circumstances in Pittsboro, then moved to Raleigh in 1887 when Denson became co-principal with Hugh Morson of the Raleigh Male Academy. On the day of the unveiling of the Confederate monument, the Densons hosted a lawn party for the Wilmington Light Infantry. Kate Denson pursued church, patriotic, and artistic interests: in 1899 when the city adopted a coat of arms and city flag to give to the U.S.S. Raleigh, which had distinguished itself in the Spanish-American War, she sewed the flag, and in 1900 she helped organize a Confederate lawn party for veterans on the occasion of the unveiling of the Vance Memorial (*News and Observer*, 16 August 1900). Kate and Beverly Raney were also members of Christ Church.

49. *Southern Architect* 10 (March 1899): 684–85; and Charles Barrett, *Colonial Southern Homes* (privately printed in Raleigh, 1903).

50. Next to the Raney House, the Johnson residence gained a tall Corinthian portico. Nearby, the Rogers family built a big new columned brick house fronted

by a tall Ionic portico. In the next block rose Dr. Andrew Goodwin's frame house with an Ionic portico by William P. Rose. Across the street the antebellum residence of Gen. Lawrence O'Bryan Branch received a bowed Corinthian portico (Survey and Planning Branch Files, North Carolina Division of Archives and History). At St. Mary's, the Episcopal diocese bought the campus from its long-time owners, the Cameron family, in 1897, and soon began a building campaign. In 1903–4 a brick residence for Bishop Joseph Blount Cheshire Jr. was built on the campus from designs by Charles Barrett. It was followed by the neoclassically detailed Eliza Battle Pittman Auditorium of 1907 and the 1910 expansion and remodeling of the main building by architect Charles E. Hartge, with a towering portico facing Hillsborough Street (Martha Stoops, *The Heritage: The Education of Women at St. Mary's College, Raleigh, North Carolina, 1842–1982* [St. Mary's College, 1984]).

51. Preston Bridgers, son of leading railroader Robert R. Bridgers, was "a merchant, manufacturer, banker, capitalist" who was "prominently identified with the 'Revolution of 1898,' when the best citizenship of the city banded together to suppress negroes and substrata agitators" and "cleans[e] the community of its viciously undesirable riff-raff" (R. H. Fisher, *Biographical Sketches of Wilmington Citizens* [Wilmington Stamp and Printing Co., 1929], 85). On the Bridgers mansion see the *Wilmington News*, 23 July 1971; Wrenn, *Wilmington*, 87; and McMillan's blueprints in the Bridgers Mansion File, Survey and Planning Branch, North Carolina Division of Archives and History.

52. Leslie N. Boney Jr., *The Cape Fear Club, 1967–1983* (Wilmington Printing Co., 1984), 1–7. The Cape Fear Club was organized in 1866, mainly by former Confederate officers, to "promote literary and social intercourse among its members" and to reassert old social patterns in the turbulent postwar years. After accepting a $70,000 offer for their lot in 1912, they built a clubhouse on a new site from designs by New York architect Charles Pierrepont H. Gilbert (*Wilmington Evening Dispatch*, 3 November 1913). Prominent among the club's members were men who "redeemed" government at the end of Reconstruction and who led in the "Revolution of 1898." See George Rountree, "Memorandum of My Personal Recollection of the Election of 1898," Henry G. Connor Papers, Southern Historical Collection; and "Wilmington Light Infantry Meeting at Lumina, Memories of the Wilmington Race Riot," 1905, North Carolina Collection, Library of the University of North Carolina at Chapel Hill.

53. Mary Bridgers (1871–1910), heiress of railroader Robert Bridgers, led in establishing the Christian Science church in Wilmington. Architect Burett Stephens, who came from Chicago in 1905, planned the Carolina Heights development and designed its principal houses. These were the homes of Atlantic coastline railroad president Thomas Emerson, Delgado Cotton Mill president Edwin C. Holt, and wholesale grocer J. W. Brooks (S. Carol Gunter, *Carolina Heights:*

The Preservation of an Urban Neighborhood in Wilmington [Wilmington Department of Planning, 1982], 15; and Wrenn, *Wilmington*, 280–84).

54. Orton began as the early-eighteenth-century home of "King" Roger Moore of the powerful Moore family; it was incorporated into an imposing temple-form Greek Revival mansion in about 1840. After the war, Orton Plantation was the winter home of Col. Kenneth Murchison; after his death in 1904, his son-in-law Sprunt bought Orton and encouraged his wife to restore and expand the house (Sprunt, *Story of Orton Plantation*). Sprunt, *Chronicles*, 57–58.

55. Mary Hilliard Hinton, *The North Carolina Historical Exhibit at the Jamestown Ter-Centennial Exposition* (Edwards and Broughton, 1916), 7, 9.

56. *The Official Blue Book of the Jamestown Ter-Centennial Exposition*, ed. Charles Russell Kelley (Colonial Publishing Co., Inc., 1909), 367–68. Lumber merchant Kenneth Howard in Dunn, North Carolina, was one who copied the North Carolina building in his residence (Davyd Foard Hood, "Kenneth L. Howard House National Register Nomination," Survey and Planning Branch, North Carolina Division of Archives and History). On the NCAA meeting see *Southern Architect and Building News*, 28 December 1907. Predecessor and later contemporary of the North Carolina chapter of the American Institute of Architects, the group included as founding leaders Charles Barrett (vice president), Charles McMillan, C. E. Hartge, and C. C. Hook. On the NCAA and the North Carolina American Institute of Architects, see Brown, "The Day of the Great Cities," in Bishir et al., *Architects and Builders in North Carolina*, 337–40.

57. Hinton, *North Carolina Historical Exhibit*, 7.

58. See *The Invention of Tradition*, ed. Eric Hobsbawm and Terence Ranger (Cambridge University Press, 1983).

The Southern Accent—
Alive and Well

Michael Montgomery

Sociologists and linguists say that as long as southerners maintain their regional consciousness and accentuate the regional qualities of their culture, the southern accent will not be lost. President Gerald Ford and First Lady Betty Ford at a campaign stop in the South, courtesy of the Collections of the Library of Congress.

n May of 1986, newspapers throughout the South ran a feature story about a southern linguist who'd been researching the region's speech. Local papers topped the story with catchy headlines like "Southern Accent Here to Stay," "Ain't No Cause fuh Alahm, Y'all," "Don't Fret Y'all—The Drawl Isn't Dying," and "Southern Drawl Still Going Strong."

This was not an isolated case. Other stories with the same slant have run from time to time, and at least four wire-service pieces on the same topic have appeared throughout the region's press since the 1986 account, not to mention stories in magazines and on radio and television (at this writing, the most recent was a December 1991 *Atlanta Journal-Constitution* story focusing on which of several current southern accents Scarlett O'Hara should adopt in the movie sequel). The southern way of using the English language seems to be a perennial issue. For some reason, there's a widespread notion that it's dying, being wiped out by television or drowned out by a horde of northern migrants or some other force. So the media check up on its health.

Are the days of the southern accent or the southern dialect in fact numbered? (I'll use "dialect" and "accent" interchangeably, applying both to southern speech patterns in their broadest sense; linguists do make a distinction between the terms, but one that's unimportant here.) For over a century scholars and researchers have rallied to the cry to get out and collect the dialect and old expressions because these were "dying and just about gone." Indeed, it seems like common sense to believe that the southern accent is disappearing—after all, the country is changing, people are changing, lots of things that are regionally distinctive are changing, and things just aren't what they used to be (well, but are they ever?). Of course, patterns of speech are continually changing as well. However that may be, a gloomy prognosis for southern English would be at the least premature. Writers on southern speech have long predicted its demise by the next generation, and yet, here we are within a few short years of the twenty-first century, with newspapers and scholars still addressing this same question, which implies that the accent is still indisputably with us. If I had any Confederate money, I'd bet it all on the proposition that the health of southern ways of using the language will still be discussed a century from now.

Southerners might differ in whether they think the persistence of the southern accent is entirely a good thing. But there must certainly be something amiss when southerners with a pretense to common sense have somehow accepted as an article of faith, or even promoted the idea, that the region's distinctive language is on its deathbed. Such was the case not long ago with the head of the speech department at Auburn University, an Alabamian himself. After years of telling his students that southern English was terminally ill and soon to be a thing of the past, he was finally challenged by a linguist from the English department, and these two squared off in a one-hour debate on the proposition that "the Southern dialect will disappear sometime in the future." The speech professor offered four arguments in favor of this proposition—arguments that are not very surprising, in that they reveal widely held beliefs about how language changes (but widely held beliefs are not always true, as we'll see):

(1) Radio and television, those supposedly dialectless, accentless media, are homogenizing the speech of the South. This influence has sometimes been referred to as "the Walter Cronkite Factor."

(2) World War II and the armed forces have created a melting pot by mixing young men (and women) from towns and neighborhoods throughout the country and by building dozens of military bases in the South that have drawn thousands of people from outside the region. This is what I'll call "the Homogenization Factor."

(3) Immigrants from the Midwest and the Northeast have been arriving in the last generation or two on such a scale that they are diluting the South's speech patterns. I'll call this "the Snowbird Factor."

(4) More and more southerners are getting college-educated and even going outside the region for their education. This we will term "the Special Education Factor."

These may seem like plausible reasons *aplenty* to think that the southern accent is disappearing, and they may all seem to make self-evident sense; but we need, to paraphrase Jack Webb, to "look at the facts." And those facts, gathered by a good deal of linguistic and cultural research, tell us that none of these factors has had much influence: southern speech is changing in some ways, but this doesn't mean it's disappearing, being swallowed up by some kind of generalized "American" speech. In some cases, in fact, the rest of the country is talking in a more and more southern fashion; and in others, the South's speech is becoming less like that of the country at large. One important factor that may well override all the influences toward homogenization is that most southerners like the way they talk just fine, thanks.

Sociologists and linguists say that as long as there is regional consciousness in the South, as long as southerners don't care to be like the rest of the country, and as long as there are efforts to accentuate the regional qualities of their culture, southerners will use varieties of speech that express and embody this regional consciousness, and the southern accent will not be lost. Anyone who doubts that the regional loyalties of southerners are still pretty strong need only be reminded of the college football bowl season, when even the most die-hard fans of the bitterest foes like Alabama and Auburn root for one another's teams when they play a school from outside Dixie.

Few traits identify southerners, or express their attachments to the region, as readily as their speech. For better or for worse, it's the way southerners talk that nonsoutherners so often notice and that draws the most comment. When Lyndon Johnson and Jimmy Carter made the run for president in recent years, the country was acutely conscious of their speech patterns. The national media drew considerable attention to their accents in their reporting as well as in their editorial cartoons. Often, the way southerners talk draws admiration. When Sam Ervin ran the Watergate hearings in 1973, the nation was spellbound by this North Carolinian's adroit handling of the English tongue, as well as by his ability to quote apt Scripture to uncomfortable witnesses. Southerners have long been well-reputed for their able use of language in politicking, in preaching, and in storytelling.

For many southerners, their speech is a kind of badge that signifies their self-identification as southerners. It represents their upbringing, their loyalties, their education, and their roots. It's as much a part of them and their heritage as the verities of grits, football, and barbecue, and they can sometimes get just as contentious about it. Their speech is inseparable from pride in their region and in their cultural traditions.

On the other hand, there's no wonder why some southerners are insecure about the way they talk. They know how conspicuous their speech is to nonsoutherners (after all, Tennessee Williams got his nickname from fraternity brothers at a Midwestern college because of his thick southern accent—he was actually from Mississippi), and they know very well that their speech is often caricatured by people elsewhere. All this is enough to make some southerners worry, especially those of us who are parents, as we watch our children come up and develop their accents. A lot of class-conscious southern parents have worked to modify or even "correct" their children's speech, and the same goal has been energetically adopted as their mission by legions of schoolteachers. Thus southerners are often of two minds about themselves and their speech, proud of who they are and how they talk, but not always sure how—or if—they want to be set off from the rest of the country.

Ambivalence sometimes leads to defensiveness, and southerners can get pretty defensive about their speech. In 1984, a community college in Chattanooga offered a course entitled "Success without the Southern Accent" for local residents wanting to change their accents, particularly those aspiring to traffic in the business world with nonsoutherners. The instructor was a speech pathologist from Ohio, and according to press reports the course "drew about sixteen locals—housewives, insurance sales reps, secretaries, a businessman or two—who paid $95 each for help in untwisting their native tongues." Outside the classroom, the instructor was publicly harassed and vilified.

Now, there's nothing particularly unusual about a speech alteration (more often called a speech *improvement*) course; you can find them at colleges and institutes throughout the country. For many years a school in New York City has regularly offered a four-week course called "How to Lose Your New York/Foreign Accent" that promises to teach self-conscious Yankees how to "minimize your New York accent" and "eliminate undesirable speech patterns by correcting articulation, and enhancing your vocal quality and diction." Mentioned on television more recently have been a speech-change·course in Los Angeles for New Yorkers recently settled on the West Coast and a course in Philadelphia for southerners who have moved north. But apparently none of these aroused a storm of protest, as did the dialect-fixing course in Chattanooga and several others that were reported at about the same time in the Atlanta area.

The entrepreneurial Yankee instructor in the Chattanooga course cited a kind of drawl discrimination as the motivation for business people taking her course; her philosophy was that "the perfect accent is no accent" and that "people should be able to choose the way they sound, just as they choose the way they dress. . . . Speech is a habit, so you have to unlearn. But with guidance and motivation, people can accomplish anything they want." But because of this philosophy, her mailbox was demolished, her yard was rolled with toilet paper, and she started getting hate mail. Lewis Grizzard, the feisty Atlanta columnist, called the course subversive. He allowed as how while "Yankees think we talk funny . . . God talks like we do." Another journalist feared what would happen when a graduate of the course got pulled over by a local cop and his accent didn't match up with his Tennessee state tags—would he get arrested for car theft?

Obviously many southerners had little use for this self-promoting intruder from beyond the Ohio. But they had even less use for the locals who submitted themselves to the treatment. One Tennessean called a Chattanooga radio station and threatened to kidnap all the students taking the course and "deprogram" them.

Why such a fierce reaction? What's the problem with these attempts to shuck one's native speech patterns? Well, one thing is that when people try to change their speech so that you can't detect their background, you begin to wonder what else they might be trying to hide. But more to the point, this effort to change their accents is evidence that a handful of southerners are trying to become citified and "yuppified" by giving up habits they consider rural or old-fashioned. And that's the main reason for the fierce reaction: most southerners take it as a personal insult when others look down on them for the way they speak, and they defy the notion that they have any reason to change the way they talk. A friend of mine, the English-curriculum consultant for a large South Carolina school district, puts it—typically—this way: "I don't want my speech to be viewed as nonstandard, but I don't want to change the way I talk, either."

So while the regional ties may be weakening for a few people, their numbers remain small. Therefore, it's doubtful that we who are attached to the southern way of speaking have any reason to get alarmed.

IS THERE AN IDENTIFIABLE "SOUTHERN DIALECT"?

The South is the most widely recognized speech region in the United States, but actually it's hardly more uniform than the nation as a whole. Outsiders tend to perceive much more uniformity than southerners themselves do. Research conducted by two linguistic atlas projects, the Linguistic Atlas of the Middle and South Atlantic States, covering Virginia, the Carolinas, and part of Georgia, and the Linguistic Atlas of the Gulf States, covering Georgia and Florida west to Texas, has identified two broad geographic speech areas in the South. These are established by correlating vocabulary, pronunciation, and grammar with settlement and cultural patterns. These are (1) the Lower South (also known as the

Coastal South or Lowland South), which covers the Atlantic coastal plain southward from Virginia and extends along the Gulf Coast to Texas; and (2) the Upper South (sometimes known as the Upland South or South Midland), which covers the Piedmont and the southern Appalachians from western Virginia and West Virginia southward and southwestward to South Carolina, Georgia, and Alabama. (It must be pointed out that this two-way geographical division of southern speech applies to the white population rather more than to blacks.) Lee Pederson, director of the massive Linguistic Atlas of the Gulf States Project at Emory University, has outlined as many as twenty-eight regional dialect subareas and has identified at least twelve urban dialects distinguished by their combinations of vocabulary, pronunciation, and grammar. Yet many who have written about southern speech and culture, including scholars, have viewed it as monolithic, ignoring the immense diversity within the South —regionally, ethnically, and otherwise. Many nonsoutherners have the firm idea that all natives in the region talk pretty much alike; this is an outlandish notion to southerners, who nevertheless do share the view that the South is a distinct place linguistically.

Here's another problem for those who wish to discuss the southern dialect: Just where does the South begin and end, linguistically speaking? Neither the Mason-Dixon line nor any other boundary has ever clearly set the region off from the rest of the country in terms of speech patterns. At least in the early days, the whites who brought English from the British Isles to the South were really no more homogeneous than those who came to other parts of North America, nor was the South as a whole more isolated. Yet all Americans, southerners and nonsoutherners alike, view it as a distinct speech region, even though linguistic research can identify only a very few words and linguistic features that are used throughout the South and nowhere else.

This last point means there's something of a gap between the linguistic facts and the popular conceptions about southern speech. Scholars and the general public have very different ideas about what makes southern dialect distinctive and what its sources might be. Take the so-called "southern drawl," the drawing out of vowels, for instance. Linguists have hardly begun to describe this best-known but quite complex feature of southern pronunciation, and are now relying on technical measurements —acoustic and spectrographic analyses—to do so. To linguists, the term "drawl" refers to the lengthening and raising of accented vowels, which is normally accompanied by a change in the pitch of the voice. It involves adding a second vowel (the "UH" in DAY-UHM for *damn* or WAY-UHLL for *well*) or even a third vowel (pronouncing WAY-EE-ULL for *well*), but the drawing out of vowels doesn't necessarily result in a slower overall rate of speech, which is what most people on the street mean by "drawl." The slower pace of southern speech is actually a figment: studies have shown that, although their vowels may be longer, southerners speak just about as many words per minute as their counterparts elsewhere.[1]

HISTORICAL DERIVATION

What factors account for why English is used in the South in a distinctive fashion? Here are some of the things that have been proposed.[2]

Climate and Pace of Life. The notion that the weather is responsible for some southern speech habits has long been prevalent. For instance, the nasality or so-called twang of Upper Southern speech is sometimes attributed to heavy rainfall and humidity. Likewise, the more pronounced "drawl" of the Coastal and Lower South has been attributed to the long, hot summers, which supposedly retard the pace of life and the tempo of speech. Advanced by early social scientists (such as Clarence Cason a half century ago in his book *Ninety Degrees in the Shade*) and still widespread, the idea that weather affects speech is easily refuted: natives of Charleston and the South Carolina Low Country, among the hottest parts of the region, normally speak with shortened vowels, not with the elongated vowels of the "drawl" (just listen to South Carolina senator Fritz Hollings); and besides, southerners aren't known to talk faster in the winter! Those who assert that southerners talk more slowly because they have less to say show that they just haven't been to the right social occasions, when southerners will talk their ears off.

Temperament of the People. That southern speech is distinctive because southerners are more polite and genteel is another folk notion—attractive and maybe romantic, but not valid. while such qualities may play a role in the use of certain common expressions like "ma'am" and "sir" as modes of address in the South, the case for a close connection between southern hospitality and the way southerners use the English language can hardly be carried very far.

Historical, Demographic, and Social Factors. These factors are the most valid—original settlement patterns, migration, urbanization, education, the interaction of different social groups, and the influence of topography and geographical boundaries. But even these are often very difficult to pin down.

To begin with, let's look at the roots of southern speech in the Old World. We know a lot about the early comers to the South—historians have done their work well—but there are several reasons why we can't firmly pinpoint the area(s) of the British Isles from which southern speech derives and why we can't trace speech patterns as we can ancestors: (1) the early English-speaking settlers in most of the South were heterogeneous, coming from many parts of Britain and Ireland; (2) we don't know much about the intimate social dynamics of seventeenth-, eighteenth-, and nineteenth-century southern society, which would tell us about the speech of which group(s) served as models for which others; and (3) there are inherent problems in "proving" how a linguistic or cultural feature migrated from one area of the Old World to one area of the New World beyond a reasonable doubt. Diffusion is very hard to establish. Suppose, for instance, that someone finds a version of the ballad "Barbara Allen" in the mountains of North Carolina that is almost identical to a version still known in a certain district of Lowland Scotland. Can we "prove" or assume that the North Carolina version is a descendant of the Scottish one or say that the people who settled that community in North Carolina descended from Lowland Scots of that district? This would be very iffy. The ballad may have been known at one time in many southern Appalachian communities, and in many Scottish and English ones as well. So it is for words and pronunciation.

Though we know that many early whites who settled in the Lower South derived from London and nearby counties, Lower Southern speech is not just a transplant from southern England. No doubt when dialects (and languages too) competed with each other during the settlement days, this involved a leveling and a merging of patterns, producing a middle ground between dialects. Scholars therefore have not progressed much beyond very general conclusions like those mentioned on the recent PBS television series *The Story of English*: (1) the speech of the coastal areas like the South Carolina Low Country and the Virginia Tidewater resembles that of southeastern England in some ways; (2) the speech of the Lower South resembles in part that of London and southern counties of England; and (3) the speech of the Upper South is akin to that of northern England, and of Scotland and Northern Ireland.[3] These are broad tendencies, so southerners who would like to trace speech patterns and usages as if they were members of a family tree are inevitably disappointed.

Loose connections with British speech patterns can be made because far fewer non-English-speaking Europeans settled in the South than elsewhere in the United States. But the influx of millions of Africans, speaking scores of languages and brought against their will, made the linguistic mix in much of the South quite complex in another way and has had profound effects on southern English that have only recently been recognized. No community of the South was transplanted from only one area of the Old World. Dialects and languages competed everywhere, even in remote locations, so popular statements about isolated areas like the Outer Banks, the Chesapeake Bay islands, or the southern Appalachians preserving "pure" Scotch-Irish or Elizabethan English are pretty much complete exaggerations.

We can speak with more certainty about how dialects developed in this country than about how they were transplanted from the British Isles. The speech of the Upper South, particularly the southern hills and mountains, derives largely from the colonial settlements in Pennsylvania. It was carried, by the Scotch-Irish, English, and Germans, westward across Pennsylvania, then southwestward down into Virginia, North Carolina, South Carolina, Tennessee, and Kentucky, and then in the nineteenth century across the northern parts of Georgia, Alabama, and Mississippi and also across Tennessee, Kentucky, and Arkansas into east Texas, and up into the Midwest. Lower Southern speech was also carried southwestward from the colonial settlements on the coastal plain of Virginia and the Carolinas, along with cotton and the plantation economy, into southern Georgia, Alabama, and Mississippi and then northward into Arkansas, western Tennessee, and Kentucky, into Louisiana and east Texas, and into Florida. Crossing migration patterns have blended these two general varieties of speech in the interior South, so that the more clear-cut dialect differences in the Atlantic states diminish as one travels west. Contact with non-English speakers—French, Mexican, and Indian—distinguishes the speech of the interior South and gives special flavor to the English spoken in Texas and Louisiana. And contact with African languages in much of the South was not only the deepest and most persistent influence of all—in fact, it was as responsible as any other formative factor for the developing distinctiveness of southern speech.

What I've said earlier about identifying with the South and its speech no doubt applies more strongly to whites than to blacks, for the reality of social grouping is that southern whites often associate themselves primarily with the region or a state, while blacks do so primarily with their race, then secondarily with the region. However, what is said about linguistic features themselves (pronunciation, grammar, and vocabulary) and about how they are changing today applies for both white and black southerners. There can be no doubt that the vocabulary, pronunciation, and grammar of blacks and whites in the South are far more alike than different, particularly in the Lower South. While the existence of "black English," encompassing linguistic features associated with, and more or less restricted to, American blacks is now beyond dispute, there is still considerable debate over its dimensions and elements.[4] Relatively few southern words have been contributed from African languages (e.g., *cooter*, *goober*, *gumbo*, *chigger*), but Africans who were brought to the South profoundly affected the pronunciation of southern whites, influencing or contributing many features now characteristic of many types of southern accent: the southern drawl (the stretching of vowels), the lack of "r" in words like *farther*, the simplification of final consonant clusters (*des* and *tes* for *desk* and *test*), the deletion of "l" (in words like *fall* and *Elvis*), etc.[5]

Since settlement days, the South has been rather conservative in its cultural institutions and agrarian habits, and so has southern speech in general (not only in isolated areas like the mountains) been more conservative than other regional types of American English. Southern English thus retains some features of earlier British speech hardly found today either in Great Britain or elsewhere in the U.S., like the pronunciation of *get* as *git* and the suffix *ing* as *in* (the so-called "dropping of the g") in words like *hunting* and *fishing*—both of these were quite fashionable British usage two hundred years ago. With some justice, Cleanth Brooks, the eminent literary scholar, has claimed that eighteenth-century pronunciations like those just mentioned survived in the South, as opposed to New England, because of a strong oral tradition—an emphasis on the spoken word— that has resisted the admonitions of schoolteachers who instruct pupils to pronounce words as they are spelled, not as they are used to saying them.[6] So, when southerners say *git*, they're speaking a general old-fashioned type of English, and on this basis, they can with some justice claim that their speech is older than that of the rest of the country— though whether it can be justifiably labeled the "Queen's English" or the "King's English" is doubtful: it certainly can't be called "Elizabethan."

But southern speech isn't just made up of holdovers that the rest of the country has lost. Around the mid-1800s, about the time that the region was developing strong self-consciousness, travelers and journalists began commenting on the South's speech as being different, and literary traditions began portraying both white and black southern speech in dialogue. Brief statements by Noah Webster and Reverend John Witherspoon in the late eighteenth century noted (and condemned) some southern usages as contrary to the national ideal, but the middle third of the nineteenth century was apparently when southern speech developed a distinct cast—not just as a condition of regional identity, but also because of internal factors like the assimilation of blacks and whites in the region. There is much less speculation about this timing than there was a few years ago because of two recent studies that analyzed the speech of descendants of ex-Confederates who migrated five thousand miles to southern Brazil in the 1860s.[7] Now bilingual, these Brazilians retain a variety of English that sounds remarkably like old-fashioned southern American speech today. Even so, they lack some characteristic southern pronunciations, like the homophony of *pen* and *pin*, which apparently spread throughout the South at the turn of this century, evidence that southern speech continued to diverge from that of the rest of the country after the Civil War.

WHAT IS ACTUALLY CHANGING IN SOUTHERN SPEECH?

One thing is sure—southern speech has been experiencing major changes during the second half of the twentieth century. Change is the natural state of affairs for any language or dialect. All dialects of English are changing in our highly mobile and increasingly urbanized, industrialized society. Many people besides the Auburn professor mentioned earlier seem to think that southern English is passing away, becoming more and more like the speech of the rest of the country. Yet linguistic research shows that southern English is neither merging with other kinds of American English nor losing its distinctiveness (much less dying) as it evolves.

Changes in vocabulary, which are the most noticeable, are indeed moving primarily in the direction of the national mainstream—toward homogeneity with the rest of the country (most younger southerners say *wishbone* nowadays, for instance, not *pullybone*). These changes largely reflect the shift from a rural, more agriculturally oriented society to a more urban one. But grammar and especially pronunciation, while evolving, are by no means following suit with vocabulary. One recent study has shown, for instance, that young women in a city in northern Alabama continue to "drawl" at least as much as older women.[8] Young men, while using the drawl less than young women, also employ it as much as older men. This is important evidence that southerners want to preserve their distinct speech. In some ways, southern pronunciation is actually diverging from that of the rest of the country. Throughout the South, pairs of words like *pin/pen* and *hem/him* are pronounced alike by middle-aged and especially younger speakers—more and more people as one goes down the age scale.[9] Also, words with long vowels like *steal* and *stale* are changing, *steal* being pronounced more like *stale*, and *stale* more like *style*. Both of these changes have spread during this century from the Upper South into and throughout the Lower South. This has nothing to do with educational attainment. Bill Clinton and Al Gore, both with Ivy League credentials, do not distinguish *ten* from *tin*, thus showing their regional ID, even if their southern tones have been smoothed away in other ways. And when southern politicians, especially Texans, talk about "tax rates," many nonsoutherners think they're saying "tax rights."

DEBUNKING THE MYTHS ABOUT CHANGE

But if southern English is becoming more like the English spoken in the rest of the country in some ways, especially vocabulary, what's bringing this about? A common claim is that it's the standardized, nondescript network speech of the national media, news readers and news commentators in particular, that is homogenizing speech in our television-addicted society. Because of the media's irresistible influence, the Auburn professor cited earlier argued, the days of regional dialects in this country are definitely numbered, whether one accepts this as the price for progress or holds out against it.

Well, it ain't necessarily so. The "Walter Cronkite Factor" isn't much more than an impression. There is scant scientific evidence for it, and it assumes what is unlikely to be true: first, that newscasters themselves have enough prestige for people to mimic their speech; and second, that Americans talk back to their televisions and radios (linguists say that we usually pattern our speech after real-life models). Television is the most easily identifiable influence on the nation's evolving speech patterns, but it's not the most powerful. And there is considerable diversity among the newscasters at the top; Texan Jim Lehrer of PBS often uses *y'all* and other southernisms, while Canadian Peter Jennings of ABC has the distinctive pronunciation of *out* and *about* that Tidewater Virginians also employ.

Every type of modern-day American English, including southern English, is changing. The main forces of change are social—mobility (geographical mobility, of course, but especially social mobility of the upward kind), mass education, and urbanization (the massive shifts of the population to urban areas since World War II). In the South, these forces have smoothed many of the edges off older, rural-based geographical dialects and blurred many traditional habits of speech lingering from the days of greater social stratification. The result is that the speech, even of natives, in the urban South of Atlanta or Memphis today is significantly different from that of a generation ago.

But just down the road from Atlanta and Memphis in the small-town South of Milledgeville, Georgia, or Brownsville, Tennessee, the speech of successive generations is not nearly so divergent. In other words, young, middle-class speakers of the urban and suburban South today are often closer to their urban counterparts elsewhere in the South than to their rural peers living just a county or two away. This can't be because of television. It's doubtful that urbanites watch it any more than their country cousins. To the extent that speech in the urban/suburban South, and in some respects throughout the country, is converging, this reflects common social forces, not the influence of television.

In addition to urbanization, one thing that is currently happening is that the speech patterns of the Upper South are expanding. The older type of "elegant" Lower Southern speech—characterized most strongly by the lack of an "r" after a vowel and spoken in the former plantation belt (a territory dominated by such important cultural centers as Charleston and Richmond)—has been losing the prestige it has held since colonial days, even though it was still strong and spreading two generations ago.[10] Nowadays, it's the newer metropolises in the Piedmont and Upper South, such as Charlotte, Nashville, and Atlanta, that are the dynamic centers of activity and linguistic change.

We see, then, that the picture is also far too complex to be accounted for by the influx of northerners into the South, or by military personnel creating a melting pot. Our "Snowbird Factor" claims that the recent settlement of northern migrants in the South is prompting natives to speak more like the new arrivals. There's little evidence for this either, though it may be too early to expect much. Even though a few of these immigrants to the Sun Belt have climbed to positions of some prominence, the escape from the Frost Belt is too recent a population shift for linguists to have explored yet. What's obvious, however, is that many of these immigrants are retirees who live in enclaves and have little contact with the members of the local population, especially the younger members whose speech patterns are still formative. Meanwhile, many recently arrived northern parents find it's their kids who are bringing home unfamiliar speech patterns from native southern peers, not vice versa.

The "Homogenization Factor" mentioned by our Auburn professor seems even more unlikely to be a real influence. In fact, it seems improbable that the military has been the catalyst for much permanent shifting of speech of any kind. Not only are most recruits in the service for only a couple of years, but this factor applies almost entirely to men. Linguists have shown convincingly that it's not men, but women, who normally bring about linguistic change.

As I stated earlier, the regional consciousness of southerners accounts in large part for the staying power of the region's distinctive speech patterns. One's speech, and much of the rest of one's social behavior, expresses one's identity—local, regional, and national—and indicates the speakers that one prefers to be identified with. The attachments of most southerners to their communities and to their region are pretty strong, and they express this in their speech. These attachments are perhaps the strongest buffer against the disappearance of southern English.

But do southerners outgrow these attachments by attending college or living outside the region? Apparently not. Often they learn an additional, somewhat modified way of speaking when they go away to school, but this hardly confirms the "Special Education Factor," which, according to the Auburn prof, is the final factor in the putative disappearance of the southern dialect. Southerners may *add* a second (or even a third) variety of English, but, with few exceptions, they don't lose their native speech patterns, which they use with their relatives and friends as soon as they step in the front door back home. Perhaps a handful of southerners who patronize universities outside the region permanently shift their accent, to the point where they startle relatives at holiday time into comments like "You sound like a Yankee"; but very few won't shift their speech back toward the "less-educated" down-home variety after a few days of southern cooking. And northerners who come South for college? At least at my school (the University of South Carolina), northerners usually shift their speech to fit in with the locals, quickly adopting *y'all* and other southernisms.

Many southerners have long had the ability to shift styles. A Tennessean who has moved to New York City may alter his speech for the locals, but get him together with half a dozen other Volunteers who have migrated to the city and he will shift his speech markedly, immediately, and quite naturally. (Rumor has it that some folks have organized a group in New York called Tennesseans Anonymous or some such, but I haven't been able to track them down yet.)

THE SOUTHERN ACCENT AND SOCIAL STATUS

Southerners are embarrassed and annoyed by the stereotypes of slow-witted rustics, mountain denizens, hayseed bumpkins, country sheriffs, and stock-car addicts that TV programs present, even though such shows often portray southerners using their country wit to thoroughly outsmart their city counterparts. Not many things rile southerners so much as why the South is singled out as a region whose speech and behavior is given such attention, and often not very accurate representation. Maybe it will help southerners to recall that *The Waltons* and other "wholesome" programs (like the *Andy Griffith Show*) that are strong on down-home, traditional values feature a cast of characters with southern accents. But lest we take them too seriously, we should all remind ourselves that these characters, these stereotypes, aren't from the South—they're from Hollywood. Who in the world would imagine that Eva Gabor, the Mrs. Douglas of *Green Acres*, or any of the cast of *Petticoat Junction*, accurately represented people from Tennessee?

While most Hollywood stereotypes do seem to be negative ones, what does this have to do with the prestige of southern speech? Very little, actually. We don't need to look far for evidence that southern speech patterns are spreading and gaining increasing status. The southern drawl has recently been reported to be spreading into the Midwest; double modals (expressions like *might could* and *may can*) are spreading northward in the Atlantic states, and other features of southern speech have recently been reported as fashionable among younger speakers north of the Mason-Dixon line.[11] And this is in addition to the massive exportation of southern speech patterns north and west by black southerners who have migrated into large urban areas over the past three generations.

This positive evaluation and trendiness of southern speech goes not only for "southern chic," or for the "Nashville chic" pursued with such determination by both country-and-western and pop singers (which is why Bob Dylan, from Minnesota, and Olivia Newton-John, from Down Under, do their best to "sound" southern). It goes for sportscasters as well. Answer this question: Where is Joe Willie Namath from—Alabama? He's got a southern-sounding name, but he's from Beaver Falls, Pennsylvania. Some time back, Joe Willie wanted to sound more knowledgeable about football, especially on television, so he shifted his speech to sound like a southerner. This southern inclination of sportscasters is nothing new, either. In 1957, W. Cabell Greet, the long-time consultant to CBS on matters of pronunciation, remarked that "for baseball and other sports announcers a southern accent has lately become almost de rigueur: Red Barber, Mel Allen. The latter, a native of Alabama, has reverted to and even intensified his original southern pronunciation (deliberately)."[12] Not long ago Mike Royko, the *Chicago Tribune* columnist, recognized part of this phenomenon. He wrote that

> a dialect . . . has crept into American speech. I call it yuppabilly, because it is often spoken by white Northern yuppies who, for whatever reason, want to sound like Southerners or blacks. I first noticed the yuppabilly dialect when I heard a former yuppie coworker of mine speaking it. If you didn't know him, you would have thought he was from Arkansas or some such rustic place.
>
> In fact, he was from a wealthy New England suburb and had attended Ivy League schools.
>
> But he developed his yuppabilly dialect because he was single and discovered that he could impress more females in singles bars if he spoke with a drawl. It provided him with a more rakish, macho, good old boy personality than did his Yale background.[13]

The greater prominence of southern politicians in national races in recent years has also had an impact. When a southern politician gets attention, the national media is inclined to focus on his or her accent. This alternately pleases and pains southerners. An important year in this regard was 1976, when a peanut farmer from south Georgia with a soft, high-pitched voice ran for the White House. Jimmy Carter's presidential campaign in the Bicentennial year sparked inordinate attention to the candidate's regional accent and countless newspaper stories, as the campaign intensified, by glib Washington journalists who claimed to fear that they would have to learn a second dialect. It also produced a rash of miniature, bookstore-counter primers, one or two still in print, on how to talk like a southerner. Many southerners were justifiably proud that one of their own, a political outsider, had garnered so much national interest, but much of the attention made southerners squirm because the media was full of cornpone jokes, often with the candidate's brother Billy and the all-too-familiar collection of regional stereotypes.

After Carter's victory, a writer for the UPI reported that a couple of Washington language schools specializing in crash study techniques were fixing to offer emergency courses in conversational southern speech, to get bureaucrats ready by inauguration day. He quoted the manager of one of them as saying that the students obviously "won't have time to master more than a rudimentary vocabulary. But I'll guarantee that if a bureaucrat's new boss turns out to be a southerner, he'll be able to carry on a limited conversation." And just how does one teach a cram course in Southern? Said one instructor, "We lock our students in a room and make them listen for three hours to a tape recording of Sen[ator] Strom Thurmond reciting Jefferson Davis' inaugural address."

In 1984 the country was treated to two southerners, both South Carolinians, making a run at the Democratic nomination for president—Ernest Hollings and Jesse Jackson. If the plantation-belt tones of Jimmy Carter had pricked the nation's ears, then the speech of these two gentlemen assaulted them, to judge from the media reaction. The media presented the public with such a caricature of Hollings's accent during the campaign that few knew his positions on issues or took him seriously as a candidate. One national columnist claimed that Hollings's "lockjaw Southern drawl is almost unintelligible." But the Carolina Low Country accent was also strange to many southerners: one syndicated columnist, a southerner, complained that Hollings's voice "could call the cows home four counties away. Fritz has a Charleston, S.C., accent so thick, he sounds like a grits-and-magnolia parody of a Southern politician."

But behind all the media attention lies an interesting truism: that southern politicos are often recognized as having superior linguistic and rhetorical skills—an ability to speak off the cuff, to use the apt turn of phrase and down-home proverbial quips, to keep an audience lively and keen. Sam Ervin captured the country's imagination with his down-home quips and anecdotes when chairing the Watergate investigation. The few newspapers that did listen closely to Hollings confessed that he had more to say on the issues than any of the other candidates. Thank heavens we had Fritz and Jesse in 1984 and Jesse again in 1988; the latter especially enlivened the Democratic presidential primaries and the convention with his animated rhetoric and wordplay. Can we imagine how utterly dull the campaign would have been without these two? Both Lloyd Bentsen in 1988 and Bill Clinton in 1992 drew media comments about their accents, but the comments were quieter and began to include political statements about the possible advantage of having a southern accent. Bentsen, in a campaign swing throughout the South, was touted by Georgia Senator Sam Nunn: "Lloyd Bentsen speaks three languages. He speaks Spanish, he speaks English, and he speaks Southern."

In summary, even if the southern accent is changing, it's certainly not disappearing. As long as there is regional consciousness in the South, as long as southerners don't care to be like the rest of the country, and as long as there are efforts to accentuate the regional qualities of the culture, southerners will use a clearly discernible variety of speech that expresses and embodies this regional consciousness, and (though it will surely evolve) the southern accent will remain alive and well. In 1990, Hodding Carter III, in an essay for *Time* titled "The End of the South," regretted that the "distinctive personality" of the South is now "so hard to find in the vital centers of the region's daily life." That may be true for some things, but not for southern speech patterns yet—their death, as Mr. Twain would say, has been greatly exaggerated.

NOTES

1. Howard A. Freeman, "Speech Rate as a Function of Dialect Geography," in *Applied Sociolinguistics*, ed. Robert N. St. Clair (Coronado, 1979), 128–36.

2. Raven I. McDavid Jr., "Changing Patterns of Southern Dialects," in *Varieties of American English: Essays by Raven I. McDavid, Jr.* (Stanford University Press, 1980), 34–50.

3. See Robert McCrum, William Cran, and Robert MacNeil, *The Story of English* (Viking, 1986).

4. See the essays in *Language Variety in the South: Perspectives in Black and White*, ed. Michael Montgomery and Guy Bailey (University of Alabama Press, 1986).

5. Lee Pederson, "Contributions from the African Languages," in *The American Heritage Dictionary* (Houghton Mifflin, 1982), 27–28.

6. Cleanth Brooks Jr., "The English Language in the South," in *A Southern Treasury of Life and Literature*, ed. Stark Young (Scribners, 1937), 350–58.

7. Michael Montgomery and Cecil Melo, "The Phonology of the Lost Cause," *English World-Wide* 11 (1990): 195–216; and Guy Bailey and Clyde Smith, "Southern English in Brazil, No?" *SECOL Review* 16 (1991): 71–89.

8. See Crawford Feagin, "A Closer Look at the Southern Drawl: Variation

Taken to Extremes," in *Variation in Language NWAV-XV at Stanford*, ed. Keith M. Denning et al. (Stanford Department of Linguistics, 1987).

9. Vivian Brown, "Evolution of the Merger of/and before Nasals in Tennessee," *American Speech* 66 (1991): 303–15.

10. Raven I. McDavid Jr., "Postvocalic /-r/ in South Carolina: A Social Analysis," *American Speech* 23 (1948): 194–203.

11. Timothy Habick, *Sound Change in Farmer City: A Sociolinguistic Study Based on Acoustic Data* (Ph.D. diss., University of Illinois, 1980).

12. W. Cabell Greet Papers, Columbia University Library Special Collections.

13. Mike Royko, "Yuppabilly Fad Explains Why Joe Willie Namath Ste-uhl A-talks Thet-away," *Atlanta Journal-Constitution*, 29 September 1985.

The Banner That Won't Stay Furled

John Shelton Reed

To alter the Mississippi flag, said one opponent of the 2001 proposal to change it, would be "a slap in the face of the brave men who fought and died for the Confederacy." Civil War veteran, ca. 1913, courtesy of the Collections of the Library of Congress.

Furl that Banner, for 'tis weary;
Round its staff 'tis drooping dreary;
Furl it, fold it, it is best:
For there's not a man to wave it,
And there's not a sword to save it,
And there is not one left to lave it
In the blood which heroes gave it;
And its foes now scorn and brave it;
Furl it, hide it—let it rest.
—Father Abram Ryan, "The Conquered Banner"

In April of 2001, 750,000 Mississippians went to the polls to decide whether to change their state flag. The old flag, adopted in 1894, prominently incorporates the Confederate battle flag, and a committee set up by the governor had proposed to replace it with a pattern of twenty stars on a blue field. The stars were apparently to represent the thirteen original colonies, the six nations and Indian tribes associated with the state, and the state of Mississippi itself, although it was also said that they represent Mississippi's status as the twentieth state. The important point was that they were *not* the Confederate flag.

The summer before in South Carolina, where the battle flag had flown for nearly a half-century over the statehouse, legislators from both parties, black and white, faced with an economic boycott of the state by the National Association for the Advancement of Colored People (NAACP), agreed to move the flag to a new location next to a Confederate memorial on the statehouse grounds. Nobody was really happy with that arrangement, but most parties to the dispute seemed to take some satisfaction from the fact that their opponents were unhappy, too.

And in January 2001, after a running battle that had begun well before the 1996 Atlanta Olympic Games, the Georgia legislature voted to remove the Confederate emblem from its prominent place on the Georgia state flag, adopting a new, compromise flag that includes the former flag in a sort of catalog of historic flags. It looks like—well, it looks like a flag designed by a committee, and cartoonists have had fun with it. But it, too, seems to have done the job of imposing a sort of grumpy stalemate.

These three events were only the latest in a string of conflicts over Confederate symbols. Beginning seriously in the early 1990s, we have seen controversy over high school and university emblems, names, and mascots; police and National Guard and Boy Scout and Little League baseball insignia; flags flown by parks, cemeteries, historical sites, businesses, hotels, and college fraternities; seals of towns and organizations; customized automobile license plates; Confederate holidays and monuments; junior-high-school dress codes; workers' lunch-boxes; and no doubt other things I've missed. Up to a point, the Mississippi conflict was virtually a replay of the South Carolina and Georgia disputes, and—except for its statewide scale and the national attention it received—a replay of most of the others as well. As franklin forts points out in "Living with Confederate Symbols," the players, the line-up, the arguments pro and con tend to be pretty much the same, again and again.

The new flag was endorsed by nearly every Mississippian that anyone ever heard of: the present governor and five other statewide elected officials; the former governor who headed the panel that proposed the new flag; the state conference of the NAACP; the bishops of the Roman Catholic, Episcopal, and Methodist churches, leaders of the Presbyterian Church, and the Reverend Donald Wildmon, a nationally influential leader of the Christian Right; the Jackson *Clarion-Ledger* (Mississippi's major newspaper), all the other daily papers in the state that I was able to track down, the student newspaper at the University of Mississippi, and the *Mississippi Business Journal*; the Mississippi Tourism Association, the Mississippi Economic Council, and the Chambers of Commerce in most of the state's major towns; the Mississippi Manufacturers Association and other trade and professional associations; the management of the Grand Casino in Gulfport; the city council of Jackson (the capital); the presidents of the eight state universities, the faculty senate at Mississippi State, eighty-seven historians from colleges in the state, thirteen head coaches in football, basketball, and baseball at the four largest universities; Myrlie Evers-Williams, widow of civil rights martyr Medgar Evers and former national chairman of the NAACP; actors Morgan Freeman and Gerald McRaney; authors Ellen Douglas, Barry Hannah, and John Grisham; Jim Barksdale, former CEO of Netscape; football hero Archie Manning; and Mary Ann Mobley, Miss America 1959. (Anyone who knows Mississippi will recognize the significance of those last two names.)

This was a truly remarkable coalition of historic adversaries: civil rights activists and country-club Republicans; student newspapers and university presidents; casino managers and fundamentalist ministers; trial lawyers and industrialists; college professors and football coaches. According to a highly decorated Vietnam war veteran who wrote the *Clarion-Ledger*, as devout Christians even Robert E. Lee and Stonewall Jackson would have supported changing the flag, and at a conference on Christian unity one minister asked the rhetorical question "What Would Jesus Do?" about the flag.

On the other side a ragtag assortment of old-flag loyalists also made up an uneasy, if not so unlikely, alliance. The most vocal were "heritage" organizations like the Sons of Confederate Veterans (SCV), an ostensibly nonpolitical group who nevertheless ran spot television ads in several markets around the state, defending the flag—and, by implication, the honor—of their ancestors. Sharing their views was the only supporter of the old flag widely known outside Mississippi, the novelist and historian Shelby Foote.

Although Foote and many other defenders of the Confederate heritage took pains to distance themselves from white supremacists, they found themselves allied, willy nilly, with folks like a white "Nationalist" named Richard Barrett, who argued that "Negroes, communists and Japanese" are trying to take over Mississippi and "the Confederate flag is there to signify defiance of oppression." (Barrett also claimed that the new flag was modeled after that of Communist China, although the Southern Christian Leadership Conference, an old-time civil rights organization, protested, more plausibly, that the new flag resembled the first national flag of the Confederacy.)

The proponents of the new flag plainly won the endorsement battle. They also won the money battle. They raised over $700,000—nearly a dollar per voter—and spent much of it on a sophisticated phone bank and direct-mail campaign. Their opponents reported expenditures of less than $20,000, or about two and a half cents per voter, some of which apparently went to buy old-flag Mardi Gras beads for the Catholic Gulf Coast.

As I said, pretty much the same story could be written about the earlier controversies in South Carolina and Georgia, which also saw a broad coalition in favor of change, collectively well-heeled, well-connected, and seemingly unstoppable. And in South Carolina and Georgia, they *were* unstoppable. They didn't get everything they wanted, but they got the flag off the South Carolina statehouse dome, and they got it relegated to obscurity on the new Georgia flag.

But in Mississippi the outcome was different. The pro-change forces' campaign seems to have turned out a substantially higher percentage of those who agreed with them. But the polls suggest that there simply weren't many such people in the first place, and the campaign didn't change many minds. By a margin of 65 percent to 35 percent Mississippians voted against the change. Mississippi will remain for now the only state with the Confederate battle standard as a legible component of its flag.

This raises a couple of interesting questions. First of all, what is it with Mississippi? Why was the outcome there different from those in Georgia and South Carolina?

That one's easy. The outcome was different because the question was put to a popular vote. In Mississippi the forces for change were strong enough to get the question of the flag on the table (as they could not have done even a decade ago), but they weren't strong enough just to tell legislators to fix it. In the other states, more urban and economically developed, legislators were persuaded to work out compromises that surveys showed would almost certainly not have won a majority in a referendum. Maybe legislators are more far-sighted than ordinary citizens; certainly they're more responsive to organized interest-group pressure. You can argue either that Georgia and South Carolina legislators betrayed their constituents or that they showed the sort of leadership that is all too rare in democratic polities—or quite possibly both.

Another, harder, question is why so many southerners are attached to the Confederate flag. Again, let's take Mississippi as an example and look at why the numbers worked out the way they did.

Since whites outnumber blacks in Mississippi by about the same ratio as anti-change voters outnumbered pro-change ones—that is, by about two to one—it's tempting just to conclude that whites want to keep the old flag and blacks don't, and certainly that's a large part of the story. A *Clarion-Ledger* pre-referendum poll showed that something like 80 percent of whites who had an opinion were in favor of the old flag and almost as high a percentage of blacks were against it. But that just raises another question. Why did an overwhelming majority of white Mississippians and a significant minority of black ones want to keep the Confederate emblem on their state flag? What does that flag *mean* to southerners?

It's hard to talk about this without sounding like some sort of postmodernist twit, but we need to recognize that there is no intrinsic meaning to colors on a cloth. A flag is a "text" to which different "interpretive communities" bring their own meanings. Some of these communities insist on the unique validity of their own understandings and seem incapable of recognizing other points of view. Some folks, in other words, are simply talking past each other. Others, however, understand each other all too well. Let's try to sort this out.

The proponents of change were often eloquent about what the old flag meant to them. Most African Americans and some white liberals agreed with the black minister from Raymond, Mississippi, who told an AP reporter that the Confederate flag evokes "bad memories"—in particular, memories of its use by supporters of white supremacy.

Look at the old films of George Wallace rallies, for example. There's the governor of Alabama standing tall (or as tall as he could) for segregation. And those who stood with him waved the flag as they did it. These white folks identified the "southern way of life" with white supremacy, and they weren't the least bit hesitant to say so. When Wallace pledged to "Keep Alabama Southern" and then to "Southernize America," those promises had an unabashed racial component. The days when overwhelming majorities of white southerners felt that way are gone, but it's simply ahistorical to deny that the flag's principal use in the 1960s was as a segregationist symbol—and black southerners haven't forgotten that.

Unita Blackwell, the mayor of Mayersville, Mississippi, said, "When I think about the flag I think about the Ku Klux Klan and when they came along here burning crosses in my yard—they had that flag." Others who remember that era have the same associations. Hezekiah Watkins, a Jackson grocery store owner, told the *New York Times*: "I was a freedom rider. The other side would hold the rebel flag. It was always a sign of segregation and hatred." No wonder that, as black columnist Donna Britt put it, "For many African Americans just seeing the battle flag—on a T-shirt or a coffee mug—is a stab to the heart." Kweisi Mfume, president of the national NAACP, said the old Mississippi flag "celebrate[s] the twisted philosophy of bigotry and hatred in this country." And the NAACP's state president interpreted the vote to retain it as a sign that "Mississippi wants to remain in the eyes of the world a racist state."

Even many black Mississippians who took a more sympathetic view of their white neighbors' attitudes felt, understandably, that the battle flag is a symbol of the *white* South, a symbol that excludes them and denies them respect. As Harrison County supervisor William Martin told the AP, "I want to be counted. I'm a citizen in this state. I want a flag that represents me, too."

Some white Mississippians agreed that the state flag should not be divisive and recognized that the existing one inevitably is. This was the line taken by the religious leaders and most of the academics who spoke out on the matter. One letter-writer in the *Clarion-Ledger* asked his fellow white Mississippians to "consider the fact that our present flag is offensive to a large percent of our population" and implored them, "in a spirit of good will, [to] take a positive step, make the change and show the people it offends we care and are willing to do something about it." Others put it as just a matter of good manners. One white man argued at a public meeting in Jackson that "a state flag should not cause pain to its own people," and the author John Grisham made the same case, arguing that the flag should be changed to "something not offensive to 35 percent of our population."

Many white Mississippians who made this argument made it clear that *they* didn't see the flag as racist and regretted that others did. Author Barry Hannah, for example, said that he never saw the battle flag "as the flag of hostility and hate" and that he "still feel[s] reverence to the troops who fought the war." He said it is "a damn crying shame we can't celebrate them because of the Klan and idiots that began grabbing the flag," but "if [the new flag]'s what times call for, so be it." And Mary Ann Mobley, the former Miss America, said simply, "I've never thought of that flag as racist, but I'm also not African American."

The most common argument against the old flag, however, at least in the published record, was that it was bad for Mississippi's public relations and ultimately for tourism and industrial recruitment. (The fact that business interests largely funded the campaign for change may have something to do with that.) A spokesman for the Mississippi Economic Council (the state chamber of commerce) said that organization's support for changing the flag was "a strategic business decision," adding that "it can help create a more positive business climate for our state." The president of the Mississippi Tourism Association concurred: Changing the flag "will enhance our state's economic development efforts," he said. And the *Mississippi Business Journal* ran an editorial headlined simply, "*Bad for business.*"

The largest donor to the campaign for change was Jim Barksdale, a Jackson native and Internet millionaire who made it clear that he is kin to Mississippi's best-known Confederate general. Barksdale gave $185,000 to the Mississippi Legacy Fund, the major pro-change PAC, remarking that the old flag "doesn't send a positive signal outside the state." (It didn't escape notice that he made this observation from his home in

California.) Barksdale argued that the flag "prompts some businesses to steer clear of Mississippi," and his money went to pay for fliers stating that "The current flag is . . . discouraging companies from bringing good paying jobs to our people" and radio spots in which a man's voice said "Changing Mississippi's flag tells companies that we're ready to work."

In retrospect, it might have been better to emphasize the argument from good manners, or from Christian charity, rather than the pocketbook case for change, which put a new spin on Jefferson's remark that "merchants have no country" (or, as Pat Buchanan put it, "Money has no flag"). Shelby Foote dismissed the economic argument with aristocratic contempt. "I think the people who want a new flag are worried about tourists," he said. "I never cared much for tourists myself." A few defenders of the old flag pointed out the absence of any actual *evidence* for the proposition that it discouraged outside investment in the state. "Industry's going to come here because of the deal they get, not because of the flag," one said. Another even wrote the *Clarion-Ledger* to point out— and regret—that the flag hadn't kept the national Gannett newspaper chain from buying the *Clarion-Ledger*. And a Vicksburg woman told pollsters, "I don't see that many companies looking to come to Mississippi anyway."

My guess is that most nonsoutherners at least understand the arguments for changing the flag, but what could the other two-thirds of Mississippi voters have been thinking? Why did they turn out in such numbers to crush the proposal for change? And I don't want to pick on Mississippi: Why would so many Georgians and South Carolinians and other southerners have done the same, given the chance?

Some—a dwindling, if not insignificant number—like the flag for the same reason the NAACP despises it: because they see it as a symbol of white supremacy. There is a strange sort of agreement here. In fact, a couple of years ago, a black man suing to change the Georgia state flag called the leader of the Southern White Knights of the Ku Klux Klan as a friendly witness to testify that the battle flag does indeed stand for "segregation, white supremacy and states' rights."

I don't want to belabor this point, but when skinheads turned out to decorate Confederate graves with battle flags, as they did not long ago in Alabama, when Byron de la Beckwith wore a flag pin in his lapel at his trial for the murder of Medgar Evers, when a householder in my town flies the flag on Martin Luther King's birthday—well, there's no question that they mean by the flag the same thing that the opponents of the civil rights movement meant by it forty years ago, and that message is understood by their adversaries, as it's meant to be.

Such outspoken white racists were, in fact, rarely heard from in the referendum debate, but even if such folks are now relegated to the lunatic fringe, they're still there, and they have websites where they make their views known. And you can make what you will of the fact that some of the old flag's supporters had ties to the Council of Conservative Citizens, the successor group to the old, segregationist White Citizens' Council. The upshot is that when defenders of the old flag argued that the Confederate flag isn't a racist symbol, their argument was less effectively refuted by their adversaries than by some of their allies, like the woman who told a meeting at Millsaps College that blacks should be grateful for slavery because they're better off in America than in Africa.

My guess is that overtly racist support cost the old flag votes, on balance. It's clearly no longer quite respectable to express such views in public: When the *Clarion-Ledger* poll asked people why they supported the old flag, the only response that even suggested racial animus was "[We] have given too many concessions already." As one woman said, "If we change this, they won't be happy. They'll want to change the state flower next because they don't like the smell." Although she didn't say who "they" were, she might have had the NAACP in mind. But that kind of response was given by only two percent of the flag's supporters. Clearly something else was at work here.

By far the bulk of the verbiage in defense of the old flag came from Mississippians like those who told the *Clarion-Ledger* that their reasons had to do with "history" and "heritage." To change the Mississippi flag, one opponent of the change said, would be "a slap in the face to the brave men who fought and died for the Confederacy," a phrase that seems to have been a popular metaphor. Another white Mississippian observed at a public meeting that keeping the old flag would be "a deliberate slap in the face to the black people of Mississippi." Obviously, whatever the outcome, there was going to be some face-slapping going on in Mississippi.

In any case, for the Sons of Confederate Veterans, for many other historically minded white folks and even a few black ones, the battle flag remains what it was originally: a symbol of the southern Confederacy, and (some) aspects of that nation, its cause, and experience. In particular, it serves as an emblem of the courage, honor, and devotion to duty of those who suffered and died for that cause. That rhetoric figures in all of the many flag disputes. Consider these few examples, chosen more or less at random from literally hundreds:

From the *Southern Partisan* magazine: "The Confederate flag is a symbol, recognized around the world, of heroism, dedication, sacrifice, and high political ideals. It serves as a symbol not only for southerners but for all Americans."

From South Carolina state senator Glenn McConnell: "The flag is the emblem of our ancestors. It's the flag they saw across the battlefield and is an emblem of unity and now it flies as a war memorial for those folks who went off to battle."

From the commander of the North Carolina Division of the SCV: "[The flag represents] the honor of all who willingly made a sacrifice for their state and nation that few today could even imagine, much less emulate. . . . The blood-stained banner helps us remember [those] who made the ultimate sacrifice, many still buried in long-forgotten, unmarked graves."

And, in Mississippi, from the ever-quotable Shelby Foote: "I'm for the Confederate flag always and forever. Many among the finest people this country has ever produced died in that war. To take it and call it a symbol of evil is a misrepresentation."

This has been a consistent interpretation of the flag since at least 1889, when the United Confederate Veterans adopted it as their emblem. (I for one find it worthy of respect and, in fact, largely share that view, if not the desire to impose it on others.)

Only recently has this attitude become at all controversial. The online magazine *Slate* got it exactly backwards in January 2001 when, in an article called "Tricky Dixie," it argued that "Confederate ideology" was being "mainstreamed." Observing that two of President Bush's cabinet nominees, Attorney General–designate John Ashcroft and Secretary of the Interior nominee Gale Norton, had both "expressed a measure of sympathy for the ideals of the Old South," *Slate* remarked that "defending Dixie [has] become suddenly fashionable" and asked, "Is this the onset of reactionary chic?" But Norton and Ashcroft were not on the cutting edge of fashion at all: The views they expressed were decidedly old-fashioned, reflecting what was virtually a national consensus for over a hundred years about how the Confederacy should be viewed. The conflict over how Confederate symbols should be deployed reflects the breakdown of that consensus.

This understanding, which reached full flower in the 1890s and the early years of the last century, required that ex-Confederates and their families acknowledge that the preservation of the Union and the abolition of slavery were good things, even providential. As Joel Chandler Harris, Uncle Remus's amanuensis, put it: "I am keenly alive to the happier results of the war, and I hope I appreciate at their full value the emancipation of both whites and blacks from the deadly effects of negro slavery, and the wonderful development of our material resources that the war has rendered possible." As an Atlanta booster he would of course mention economic development.

In return for these concessions, former Confederates were allowed to fly their flags, sing their songs, honor their heroes, and celebrate their holidays. And not just as a private devotion: Confederate Memorial Day and the birthdays of Confederate leaders became state holidays in the South, and state flags, including Mississippi's, began to incorporate or otherwise refer to the Confederate flag. (The Alabama, Arkansas, and Florida flags also contain explicit symbols of the Confederacy: We may hear about them next.) But there was more to this than simple toleration. An important step on what has been called the "road to reunion" was that "everyone" (note the quotation marks) agreed that Unionists and Confederates alike were answering the call of duty, that both sides were courageous and acted in good faith. Innumerable works of popular fiction were written, as one scholar has put it, "to show both North and South that the adversaries were people who were kind and honorable and had fought for what they thought was right."

This agreement even allowed former rebels to put on blue uniforms and join their recent enemies in pursuing America's imperial destiny overseas. A popular song of 1898 delighted in the fact that:

> Old Virginia's heart is happy,
> And the Southlands fill'd with glee—
> They are goin' to march to Cuba
> Under Major General Lee!

(That was Fitzhugh Lee, who had last seen action as a major general in the *Confederate* army and whose late uncle Robert was well on his way to becoming a national hero, not just a southern one.) But southerners' renewed American nationalism did not come at the expense of their sectional loyalties. In 1898 and again during World War I, southern boys were fighting, as another Tin Pan Alley song put it, "For Dixie and Uncle Sam." That was part of the deal, and by the turn of the century it was acceptable to virtually all Americans whose opinions signified.

The former adversaries even agreed, in principle, to honor one another. When the composer Dan Emmett died in 1904, he was buried near his home in Mount Vernon, Ohio, under a tombstone that says his song " 'Dixie Land' inspired the courage and devotion of the southern people and now thrills the hearts of a united nation." And a significant milestone was the 1913 joint reunion of the Union and Confederate veterans' organizations, funded in part by the federal government, which brought over fifty thousand old soldiers from both sides to Gettysburg for four days of reminiscence and reenactment.

Another part of the deal was that the role of slavery in precipitating the conflict was downplayed. Let me be clear here: To say that the Confederate states seceded to protect their peculiar institution says nothing about the motives of individual Confederate soldiers. But on the road to reunion ex-Confederates not only agreed that they were better off without slavery, they almost denied that it had anything to do with the war. As Basil Lanneau Gildersleeve, distinguished classical philologist and veteran of the Confederate cavalry, wrote forty years after the war, "That the cause we fought for and our brothers died for was the cause of civil liberty and not the cause of human slavery, is a thesis which we feel ourselves bound to maintain whenever our motives are challenged or misunderstood, if only for our children's sake."

And to repudiate slavery was not to reject white supremacy. Quite the contrary. The ideology of the Lost Cause included a rose-colored view of life in the Old South, a frightening account of the horrors of black rule after the war, and a forthright racism that not only justified but also virtually required white domination. White southerners successfully exported most of this to the rest of white America, which was more than ready to hear it. In 1915 the movie *Birth of a Nation* presented a heroic view of the Confederacy and a distinctly unreconstructed view of Reconstruction, celebrated the Ku Klux Klan as saviors of white civilization, and attracted record-breaking and appreciative audiences nationwide. President Wilson watched it in the White House and said it was "like writing history with lightning" and "all so terribly true."

This rapprochement held for decades; several generations of Americans, including mine, grew up under it. (My Tennessee hometown had public schools named for both Abraham Lincoln and Robert E. Lee.) The federal government commemorated Lee and Jackson on a postage stamp in the 1930s, and in the 1950s it honored the United Confederate Veterans with a stamp on the occasion of their last encampment. A few years later President Eisenhower's proclamation marking the centennial of the war praised the "heroism and sacrifice by men and women of both sides, who valued principles above life itself and whose devotion to duty is a proud part of our national inheritance." Soldiers of both sides, he said, were "as good as any who ever fought under any flag," and the war was a "great chapter in our Nation's history."

But even as the Civil War centennial was being celebrated, with compliments all around, what I've taken to calling the "old settlement" was beginning to unravel. When I said that "everyone" had signed off on it, I meant everyone whose opinion mattered. Black Americans, in particular, were not consulted. Had they been, of course, it would have been a different story. Most African Americans' views of the Old South and of Reconstruction have differed radically from the Authorized Version.

African Americans tried to dissent—in 1915 the fledgling NAACP organized protests in several (northern) cities against *The Birth of a Nation*—but no one was listening. No one had to listen. Especially in the South, where blacks were effectively disfranchised, no one in authority had to pay any attention to their opinions on any subject. But a hundred years after Appomattox the Voting Rights Act of 1965 profoundly changed the public opinion calculus in the South, and nowhere more than in Mississippi. These days there are roughly eight thousand black elected officials in the United States, five thousand of whom are in the South, and fifteen hundred in Mississippi. In contemporary southern politics, the interests of black southerners may not prevail, but their opinions cannot simply be ignored. And, as we've seen, African Americans do have opinions about the Confederate battle flag.

Thirty years ago, in a small-town southern hamburger joint, I saw a group of high-school girls in battle-flag T-shirts with the legend "Proud to Be a Rebel." They were cheerleaders, and the Rebels were their team. One of the girls was black, and at the time I took great satisfaction in that. I saw it as a universalizing of these southern symbols (the most obvious ones available), an expansion of the southern community to include the South's largest and most mistreated minority. But of course I hadn't really thought it through. Including folks in your community means they get to have a voice in it, including a voice about what the symbols of that community are to be. And when it comes to the Confederate flag, by far the most common view among black southerners seems to be the one we've already examined: that it has been irremediably tainted by its use as a symbol of opposition to the civil rights movement.

In response, both the national Sons of Confederate Veterans and innumerable local "camps" have passed resolutions denouncing, as one put it, anyone "whose actions tarnish or bring dishonor upon the Confederate soldier or his reason for fighting," especially those "using our cherished flag as a symbol of hatred." Another says plainly that "Philosophies, attitudes and activities advanced by white supremacist organizations and other groups designed to subordinate the lives, intrinsic value and contributions of people because of their race are both morally repugnant and inconsistent with the purpose of the Sons of Confederate Veterans." But these resolutions are apparently too little, too late. Most African American voters in Mississippi were having none of it. They know what they know and don't like being told they are mistaken any more than Sons of Confederate Veterans do.

Now, for the record, it should be said that a handful of black Mississippians expressed essentially the same views as the Sons of Confederate Veterans. Some in fact *were* Sons of Confederate Veterans: an estimated two-dozen members of that organization, nationwide, are African American. Anthony Hervey, a young Mississippian, has started something called the Black Confederate Soldier Foundation to memorialize blacks who fought for the Confederacy. Hervey said the battle flag "stands for freedom and states' rights." The Reverend Walter Bowie of Jackson's Koinonia Baptist Church more or less agreed: "The so-called Rebel flag is the flag of the South," he said, "the symbol of many good things about our culture and history that are dear to the hearts of southerners, white, black and red. It becomes racist only in the hands of a racist." But this was decidedly a minority view among black Mississippians: in fact, these are the only two examples I found. And their opinions were, to say the least, unpopular. The mildest epithet directed at blacks who felt that way came from the president of the Columbia County branch of the NAACP who called them "house Negroes." Anthony Hervey even claims that somebody took a shot at him.

Both the poll data and the written record suggest that far more common among black Mississippians was the sort of workaday pluralism expressed by the actor Morgan Freeman, who said, "Personally, I have every appreciation for those Mississippians who say the flag represents their heritage. But it's not everybody's heritage." Or the black cab driver in Jackson, who told a *Washington Post* reporter, "You don't need to have this flag flying over all the state office buildings and everything. . . . Just put one in your yard or your house or your bedroom, and you'll have all your heritage right there in your house." In other words: Go ahead and celebrate your heritage. Just don't make everybody do it.

But to this the scv and other "heritage" groups respond that the Confederate heritage *is* the heritage of all Mississippians, black as well as white. In the last few years some members of these groups have taken the argument that the Lost Cause was not about slavery a giant step farther. Read their literature, go to their websites, and you will find them arguing that scores of thousands of black men actually took up arms for the Confederacy. We're not talking just about enslaved teamsters and cooks and laborers, not just about the odd body servant who took a few pot-shots at the Yankees, or the handful of blacks who were enlisted in the last desperate days of the war, but regular combat troops, fighting for their homeland. Black and white together, they were overcome.

As history—well, let's just say that the legend of black Confederates is not quite in the same genus as tales of alien abduction and Satanic ritual abuse, but the numbers have been greatly exaggerated. Mississippi historian Robert McElvaine pointed out in the *New York Times* that this kind of "feel-good history" has a lot in common with Afrocentrism, but he argues that it's a sign of progress that slavery and racism are no longer "honored as part of the Southern heritage," even if it means that "it has left a sizable number of people clinging to a pseudo-historical mythology." I agree that it's progress, but I don't think many black southerners are going to be persuaded that their ancestors were on the Confederacy's side, or vice versa. Even if it were true, it would be a hard sell. No, for the foreseeable future, as Rip Daniels, a black businessman from Gulfport, said during the Mississippi debate, "You leave me no choice but to be your enemy as long as you wave a battle flag. If it is your heritage, then it is my heritage to resist it with every fiber of my being."

Notice that, on both sides, the argument has turned increasingly historical. Some of the flag's defenders are now saying not just that it *should* be a symbol of transracial southern unity and that its deployment by racists in the 1950s and 1960s was a regrettable aberration, but that it has *always* been a symbol of unity. On the other side, although the most common objection is still to the flag's use by twentieth-century segrega-

tionists, lately we've heard more and more about its use by the Confederate States of America. At last, and predictably, the entire post–Civil War
settlement is being challenged, primarily by African Americans whose
forebears were not parties to it.

To be sure, the old settlement, the old deal, still prevails in some
circles. Last year the Sons of *Union* Veterans passed a resolution noting
that their ancestors "met in joint reunions with the confederate veterans
under both flags in . . . bonds of Fraternal Friendship" and expressing
their "support and admiration for those gallant soldiers and of their
respective flags." But compare that, or President Eisenhower's words
about the Civil War as "a great chapter in our Nation's history," to
Congressman John Lewis's recent remark that "It is unfortunate and
somewhat tragic that after all these many years, people are still looking to
this part of our history as some glorious time. It's not something we can
be very proud of." Or consider the legislation recently introduced by
Mississippi congressman Bennie Thompson condemning the use of the
Confederate flag for "any reason other than as a historic reminder of the
secession of the Confederate States, which prompted the violent, bloody,
and divisive Civil War, and of the Confederacy's flagrant disregard for the
equality of all Americans in accordance with the United States Constitution and in the eyes of God." Thompson, the only member of Congress
who doesn't have a state flag outside his office, says his bill "is intended to
set the record straight. The leaders of the Confederate States of America
were traitors."

And it's not only African Americans who are challenging the old
settlement. I had a letter recently from a former student, in Chatham
County, North Carolina, who wrote that a Yankee couple who attended
an scv meeting to hear a historical lecture had written to complain about
the scv's practice of saluting the state and Confederate flags, after the
Pledge of Allegiance to the Stars and Stripes. "I can see myself one day,"
my friend wrote, "belly down on the west bank of Jordan Lake, picking
off Yankee cars as they cross over the Highway 64 bridge. Even better on
the northern front, where we have the high ground overlooking the two-
lane Haw River bridge." "John, I was at that meeting," he continued, "and
nobody was mean or ugly. Everybody, in fact, was nice and friendly."

The former commander of the Mississippi scv echoed this frustration
when he told the *Washington Post* that people "label us and malign us and
abuse us just because we want to protect our Confederate emblems,"
which are, after all, symbols of "courage, devotion to duty, devotion to

family, honor, valor, and a lot of other qualities that we should aspire to in life." If Sons of Confederate Veterans sound a little aggrieved these days, it's because they feel betrayed. They've kept *their* side of the bargain: Their meetings begin with the Pledge of Allegiance. Many honestly don't understand why the old settlement doesn't work anymore. I think others do understand—but, after all, lost causes are what they're all about.

We're going to hear a lot more about heritage and hate—pride and prejudice—in Mississippi and elsewhere for years to come. But there was another factor—perhaps the determining factor—in the Mississippi vote that we heard much less about. Consider that a half-million Mississippians, including what had to be tens of thousands of black Mississippians, voted to keep the old flag. This is vastly greater than the membership of all the "heritage" groups put together. (The largest, the SCV, has only 1639 members in the state.) Many of these voters were expressing rebel pride, certainly, but of a less historical sort.

Sometime around the middle of the last century, the Confederate battle flag took on yet another meaning: Especially in the South, but not only there, it began to send a message of generalized defiance directed at authority and to some extent at respectability. People who use the flag this way may not care if it offends black folks or Yankees, but those groups are somewhere behind high-school principals on the list of targets.

You can see this use of the flag in the world of popular music, where it came to stand for a hell-raising, good-timing, boogie-til-you-puke spirit associated with southern rock and country musicians like Alabama, Hank Williams Jr., Charlie Daniels, and Lynyrd Skynyrd. Similarly, on the television program *The Dukes of Hazzard* in the early 1980s, Bo and Luke Duke had a car called the General Lee: Its horn played "Dixie" and it had a battle flag painted on the roof, but there was never any indication that Bo and Luke were acquainted with their heritage—although they'd probably be ready to fight about it.

In short, for many southerners the flag represents a don't-tread-on-me attitude that I suspect had a lot to do with the Mississippi vote, an attitude displayed by the woman who was cheered at a public meeting when she said, "If you don't like the state flag, there are forty-nine other states you can move to!" Americans don't have that marvelous British phrase "bloody-minded," but we certainly have the behavior it describes—perhaps especially in the South. In fact, a reporter for *The Irish Times* found the whole Mississippi controversy eerily reminiscent of Ulster, where they also "do battle over the right to flaunt symbols of division in the name of irreconcilable versions of history." Certainly many in Northern Ireland share the ornery streak that Donald Wildmon, the Christian Right leader, said he feared would lead Mississippians to vote for the old flag "not because they are opposed to a new flag, but because they feel that someone is trying to force them to do something."

And who might this "someone" be? Well, recall that list of endorsements. It included the NAACP, to be sure, but it also included nearly all of the Great and the Good in Mississippi. My bet is that many Mississippians who are neither great nor good (in the sense of that phrase) suspect that there's an element of social-class prejudice at work—and they are not wholly wrong about that. When I interviewed upper-middle-class college students about the flag a few years ago, many of them saw it as a "redneck" symbol. Not without reason, they associated it with trailer parks, tattoo parlors, and outlaw bikers. As one girl said, "When I see the Confederate flag I think of a pickup truck with a gun rack and a bumper sticker that says I DON'T BRAKE FOR SMALL ANIMALS." In other words, to at least some cosmopolitan southerners the flag symbolizes not race but social class—not to put too fine a point on it, they're snobs—and nobody likes being told what to do by people they suspect of looking down on them.

Of course, even worse, Mississippians were being told what to do by the *national* elite, whose opinion that *all* Mississippians are ignorant yahoos could have gone without saying—but didn't. One columnist said, for instance, that he found the flag debate "encouraging" because "it's always nice to see states worry about entering the twentieth century."

As Kirk Fordice, Mississippi's Republican former governor, explained, "people have to understand . . . that Mississippians resent the heck" out of that sort of thing. Is it surprising that a great many of them seized the chance to cock a snoot at the agents of enlightened opinion and tell them to go to hell? Keeping their old flag may cost Mississippians in the end, both financially and otherwise. But southerners like to joke that the most common last words in our region are "Hey, y'all! Watch this!"

NOTE

Originally presented as the John M. Olin Lecture on Politics, Morality, and Citizenship at the Institute of United States Studies, University of London, 2001. I thank Professor Gary McDowell and his staff for their hospitality.

Living with Confederate Symbols

franklin forts

"When General Robert E. Lee is commemorated, what do we do with the fact that he was a racist?" The Robert E. Lee Statue on Monument Avenue in Richmond, Virginia, courtesy of the Richmond Convention & Visitors Bureau.

ragg Bowlin and I are talking as we sit in the living room of his home, a 1920s-era row house two blocks from the famous Monument Avenue historic district in Richmond, Virginia. The room is furnished in dark mahogany and cherry, with impressive overstuffed chairs and sofa. Antique lamps and rugs join with the heavy wood furniture to give the room a turn-of-the-century feel. In these formal surroundings, Bragg's bare feet, blue jeans, and white T-shirt look out of place. The room's most prominent features, however, are its numerous images of the Confederacy and antebellum South. On a bookshelf is a bust of Confederate general Robert E. Lee. Above the fireplace are framed prints of figures on horseback, generals Robert E. Lee and Thomas "Stonewall" Jackson. A Confederate battle flag hangs limp in one corner of the room. But the icon of the Old South that keeps drawing my attention is a striking collection of figurines, men in minstrel-style black face. Their pitch-black faces, stark white lips, and bulging eyes are contorted and twisted into expressions meant to convey lightheartedness and contentment. Whether these are antiques, the objects of a collector's curious fancy, or the wistful longings for the good-old days purchased by a middle-aged white southerner at a tourist shop, I do not know. I did not ask.

Bragg is a self-assured member of the Richmond chapter of the Sons of Confederate Veterans. He and I are both southerners, proud of that designation and heritage. Yet Bragg's shrine to "our" shared past leaves me uneasy for many reasons. I am an African American descendant of slaves, and, save for a few ancestors who were Cherokee and a small number who were white, I consider myself fully African American and fully southern. As I sit in the middle of Bragg's Confederate sanctuary, I wonder whose interpretation of these images is more accurate. Bragg reveres those gray-clad men of honor, courage, and love of country— men he would claim fought to uphold the independence and rights of a sovereign people. I do not see that. I see men who hoped to sustain a society based on chattel slavery and an ideology of white supremacy, a society that held that some men were by right born "booted and spurred" to ride the saddles placed on the backs of Negroes by providence itself. Looking around the room I see images that degrade the memory of my ancestors. Which of our interpretations is more faithful to the historical reality? Who is the true southerner?

Examine any newspaper in the American South during any week and you will undoubtedly find an article detailing yet another storm over a Confederate image. The principal actors are by now clichés—vocal black southerners and their liberal white southern allies on one side, demanding justice, calling for an end to bigotry and the consignment of all things Confederate to the nearest museum. Facing down this group is the needed adversary, the other half of the cliché—the conservative white southerners, usually stressing heritage, history, and the undeniable truth that their great-great-granddaddies did not own slaves. They were men, in fact, who fought for their homes, hearths, and independence. Whatever the source of the conflict—the Confederate battle flag, an image of a Confederate general, the portrayal of the Confederacy in print or film— the rhetoric from both sides is so familiar that it has taken on the characteristics of a refrain from a worn-out song heard once too often at too high a volume.

I believe that for most Americans this debate is a nonissue. It's an old dog that won't hunt. This third group is guided by the principle of "The war is over, you lost (or slavery is over, you're free). Get over it! Move on!" In spite of this shortsighted majority sentiment, something important *is* going on in this debate. This argument is a dispute that goes to the heart of southern collective memory, a struggle over shared history and contested identity. In other words, who is really a southerner, Bragg or myself? Which one of us gets to define the region of our birth?

Recent scholarship in history, sociology, anthropology, and psychology suggests an answer to this question of southern identity and the place of memory in shaping our understanding of the past. The ways in which societies and individuals assemble their identities through the complex interaction of history, national myths, images, and folklore provide a framework to approach the question of southern identity that could steer southerners, both black and white, beyond the language of clichés and towards the possibility of new ways of understanding the South's relationship to its troubled past and its problematic symbols.

It is true, as sociologist John Shelton Reed has asserted, that "the South needs and deserves some sort of symbols."[1] Individuals and groups partially understand themselves and locate their place in the world through their symbols, icons, and myths. Symbols, however, are not created ex nihilo or artificially constructed. They spring from the history of the people they represent and for whom they have meaning. Because of their complexity, however, the images and symbols of the Old South and Confederacy stand in an awkward relationship with present-day southerners. White southerners have a right to commemorate their Confederate ancestors, but African Americans also have the right to remind their fellow southerners that the southern past is not just Chancellorsville, Gettysburg, or the Wilderness. The southern past is also the Middle Passage, the break-up of families, and the perseverance of a people who through their collective strength feel "no ways tired." Understanding this elemental point would help all southerners in constructing an identity that incorporates the complexity of the region's racial interactions over the last four centuries.

The late Madan Sarup, cultural critic and philosopher, begins his description of how individuals and societies construct identity with the assertion that identity is a process, "not something we find, or have once and for all."[2] He points out that a traditional position on the formation of collective and individual identity sees "all [personal and communal] dynamics, such as class, gender, race, nationality, etc. . . . operating simultaneously to produce a coherent, unified and fixed identity." Sarup argues that much of the world's population understands identity in these terms. Bragg Bowlin, then, is now and forever only a middle-class white southerner with a Confederate past living at this particular moment of history, and I am now and forever only a middle-class African American. This understanding locks us both into identities rooted in biology and history, forever static and fixed. Sarup, however, outlines a postmodern understanding of identity as "fabricated, constructed, in process" and influenced by both psychological and sociological factors. This view of identity would claim that Bragg and I have constructed the way we present ourselves to the world. Through the socialization process, which involves interactions with various institutions—childhood influences, state ideology, religion, etc.—we both are "fabricated beings." But fabricated isn't the same as counterfeit. Rather, Sarup argues, the longstanding view that some categories are "natural" and bear no trace of human invention is erroneous and intellectually naïve. He suggests, rather, a fluid process in which we select and choose those things that will identify us, a process that "is carried-out in the interests of constituting a story of a particular kind."[3]

People often live, think, and argue as if categories were independent of human activity. Many see their "particular kind" of story and identity as grounded in an extra-human reality, immutable, unalterable and forever true. Yet, Sarup would claim that all categories of human identity are products of the human capacity for thought and, consequently, are subject to change and variability. We are not locked into an external, prescriptive understanding of the self.

Historian Gaines Foster offers one example of constructed identity in his scholarship on the South and the myth of the Lost Cause. In the late nineteenth and early twentieth centuries, Foster argues, the high priests and priestesses of Confederate memory—memorial associations like the Southern Historical Society, the United Confederate Veterans, and the United Daughters of the Confederacy—helped develop traditions that became the building blocks of subsequent white southern culture.[4] During the post-Reconstruction era, the white South perceived Confederate soldiers as gallant heroes, courageous men fighting for constitutional principles, who, after four brave and glorious years of fighting, only succumbed to superior numbers and resources. In this myth of the Lost Cause, certain information is emphasized while other information is forgotten or simply not discussed. This omission is not a conscious effort to falsify history but an attempt to meet a particular need at a unique time in a society's history. Foster argues that southerners used the Lost Cause myth to make the transition from an Old South defeated in war to a New South of growing industrial development and rising social and political unrest. As numerous historians have pointed out, the South's pre–Civil War ruling class used a particular understanding of the war to help reestablish its political, social, and economic hegemony within the region. There is no room in this narrative for the horrors of slavery or the ideology of white supremacy that was part and parcel of both the Old South and the New South. Could one really expect any other interpretation of the war from the white South at this particular time?

What, then, do we make of the claim that the South fought the war to preserve slavery? As historians of the Civil War tell us, it is important to make the distinction between what led the sections to wage war and why men subsequently fought the war. The war began over the issue of slavery and its expansion into the West. But did the men of the South leave their homes and fields to give their lives for chattel slavery? I do not think so. Southern men fought because they believed it their duty and because their homeland was invaded. Competing camps in the debate over Confederate symbols fail to understand this crucial distinction. Far too often the complexity and conflicted nature of individual and collective actions and their motivations are overlooked in the heat of debate.

A white man in the American South during the nineteenth century could be a person of honor, courage, and kindness. Yet that very same person could be a man who was racist and a firm believer in the inferiority of blacks. In fact, this description applies to most white men and women in this nation during much of its existence. When General Robert E. Lee is commemorated, what do we do with the fact that he was a racist? He believed in a social hierarchy with the Irish and blacks at the bottom of the ladder, but within the context of his time, Lee was at worst a moderate on the race issue. He detested slavery, yet he thought blacks less than fully human. I do not know if Bragg Bowlin and I would agree on this point, but the current historical scholarship supports this interpretation.[5] This moral and ethical dissonance within the life of a man many revere as a hero is not unusual. Throughout much of this nation's history, many of the men and women whom we hold in high regard were complex and often not consistent ethically or politically with their heroic status. Does the term hero connote perfection? By celebrating Abraham Lincoln's birthday, does the nation at the same time celebrate his views on race? I think not. We humans are complicated beings, a jumble of psychological and social contradictions, and more often than not one identity does not fully capture our lived reality. What seems obvious to Americans at the start of the twenty-first century surely was less clear to our ancestors. I am not an apologist for the slave regime of the Old South, but I do believe the issue is more complicated than black and white southerners often realize. But the unique role that the past plays in shaping identity can't really be understood without looking at the relationship between individual identity and the larger national culture.

"Nationalism," wrote political scientist Benedict Anderson, "is not a political ideology, like Socialism, Marxism, or Liberalism, but rather it is a belief system."[6] Belief systems—unlike rational, logically held views, which with effective argumentation can be altered—resist change. Most Americans possess the traditional understanding of identity as fixed and unchanging, and in that sense they are identity fundamentalists. Anderson's association of nationalism with religion can help us to understand the importance and persistence of personal and collective identities over time and the power that Confederate imagery holds over many in this nation.

Anderson reminds us of the enduring appeal of religious language and ritual, which seeks "to respond to the overwhelming burden of human suffering, locating humans in the cosmos and in coping with the inevitability of death." He goes on to argue that with the waning of Church power and other religious institutions during the seventeenth and eighteenth centuries, the ideal of finding one's identity within the nation was born. Nationalism became a "social religion" of sorts. Commenting on the declining organizational influence of religion, Anderson observes that "what was then required was a secular transformation of fatality into continuity, contingency into meaning . . . few things are better suited to this end than [the] ideal of nation."[7] Consider, for example, the popularity of Washington, D.C., as a tourist attraction. Although many Americans heap ridicule on the occupants of both houses of Congress and the resident of 1600 Pennsylvania Avenue, each year millions of these very same citizens flock to our nation's capital to connect with the American past and secure their place in the larger narrative of this nation. In the shrines of American identity—the Lincoln Memorial, the Jefferson Memorial, and the White House, to name a few—we find affirmation of our American selves and the hope that as long as the nation lives and endures, we live and endure.

Writing on the place of myths in national identity, J. F. Bierlein, a scholar of classical studies, asserts that "myths of states are really collective hero myths, with the heroic character shared by a people, for our identity in the cosmos has a great deal to do with our [sense of place within the] national or ethnic identity."[8] The same sentiment that draws Americans to Washington is at work in what has become known as the neo-Confederate movement. The popularity of Civil War literature, battlefield tours, and reenactment groups points to a religious-like devotion to the conflict. White southerners always try to make sense of their Confederate past, to touch it, to locate themselves somewhere within the "heroic rebel" narrative. Yet, as historian George Tindall has warned, idealized notions of the past can be dangerous because "the myth may predetermine the categories of perception, rendering one blind to things that do not fit into the mental image."[9] I perceive this "blindness" to be at the heart of many of the controversies surrounding Confederate imagery. Both sides are blinded by their sense of an idealized notion of identity rooted in the Old South. White southerners claim a heritage of honorable and brave service in the protection of home and hearth while denying their ancestors' complicity in upholding a slave society. Black southerners claim the horrors of bondage and the resilience of a noble and resourceful people during "dem dark days" while often refusing to acknowledge the possibility of bonds of affection that undoubtedly existed at times between slaves and masters. Each group's predetermined category locks out the possibility of other interpretations. Neither group is willing to compromise its particular understanding of the past.

Why is this the case? The answer lies in the role identity plays in anchoring and stabilizing us in a modern world that is often confusing and in an existence that at times seems capricious and fleeting. Few, if any, believers will give up a faith simply because contrary evidence has been presented. In fact, as the early Christian martyrs demonstrated, the greater the tenacity in holding on to the "faith" in the face of adversity, the greater the display of faithfulness to the cause. Such is the case with those involved in debating Confederate symbols. There is, however, a way out of this intellectual straitjacket. The work of Polish philosopher Zygmunt Bauman offers an intellectual framework that could end the "religious war" besieging the symbols of the Confederacy.

Exiled from Poland in 1968, Bauman was influenced primarily by the Italian Marxist Antonio Gramsci and twentieth-century continental philosophy. Bauman follows Gramsci's understanding of the hegemonic tendency and inherent coercive forces at work in the modern nation-state. Echoing the contributions of Benedict Anderson, Bauman analyzes the ability of the state to establish an artificial reality where none existed before. Specifically, he examines the development of culture and society, both of which are key in constructing personal identity. He goes on to present the idea of ambivalence, which can be used as a saber to cut the Gordian knot of misunderstanding between those disagreeing over Confederate imagery. Bauman's thesis on ambivalence can be simply stated: twentieth-century western men and women, shaped by the intellectual, social, and political order born in the Enlightenment, seek a rational, perfect, and neat human order, "with rigid boundaries and identities."[10] In the context of this discussion, Robert E. Lee is either a man of honor and a patriot or a racist and defender of slavery. The Confederate battle flag is either a symbol of pride and heritage or an icon of hate and intolerance. According to Bauman, the problem with this modern project of binary classification is that most of our experiences do not neatly conform to these boundaries and typologies. He suggests the category of ambivalence for those parts of human experience that do not neatly fit into the rigid categories wished for by the modern mind.

Using the Gramscian idea of hegemony, Bauman argues for the coercive power of the Enlightenment in shaping modern thought. He pictures the modern person as blending the need for order and security in national and personal identity, which he or she perceives to be grounded in truth and based on certainty. There is no contingency or ambivalence in this structuring of collective or personal identity. The Enlightenment view of rational classification and order in the physical world spawned a concomitant desire for classification and order within all realms of knowledge and experience. Bauman sees this desire for order in the modern-day assumption that the "seed of future universality has been planted in the world and is destined to replace most, if not all, differences between people."[11] A perfect example of this is the current concept of the global market, the hope of a growing interdependence among nations based on mutual economic interests. Proponents of the global market predict the domination of international capitalism as it spreads prosperity throughout the world. It is no accident that many of the leading reformers demanding an end to the use of Confederate symbols in the American South are the region's business leaders fearful of the adverse economic consequences of perceived intolerance. For these "New Whigs," the South's Confederate distinctiveness stands in the way of integrating the region into the global market.

Bauman's discussion of the social construction of binary classification begins with the observation that people typically categorize others in terms of friend, enemy, or stranger. He interprets this friend/enemy opposition as a template for much of our classification of knowledge and experience. Like the stranger, who will always be subject to suspicious stares until he or she can be classified as friend or enemy, knowledge that does not fit into neat categories is viewed with mistrust. This binary opposition separates truth from falsity, good from evil, beauty from ugliness, and is the basis for our notions of what is proper and improper, right and wrong, tasteful and unbecoming. This either/or approach is often used in the debates surrounding the use of Confederate images, and, according to this view, the Confederate battle flag means either hate or heritage.

In June of 1999, the city of Richmond decided to refurbish its riverfront area near the James River. City leaders designated a large, white concrete floodwall to be covered with murals of people and events important to the history of the city. Among these were Bill "Bojangles" Robinson, Native American chief Powhatan, and Confederate general Robert E. Lee. Richmond has a majority African American population, and once word of the Lee mural became public, black political leaders began protesting the use of Lee's image in a city project. He was a racist and a slaveholder, some vocal members of the African American community claimed. The Sons of the Confederate Veterans and other like-minded groups upheld Lee as a gentleman of honor who fought for his homeland. As in all of the disagreements over Confederate icons, neither side could imagine itself being wrong. Each side pointed to history books to support its case.[12]

Bauman would use the analogy of a person arriving in a foreign country, unable to understand the native language, to describe this deadlock. The discomfort and fear experienced by this visitor is the same discomfort and fear that either side of the Lee debate would experience if ever it entertained the notion that the other side could possibly be correct. Like the stranger who makes us uneasy until he or she is known, situations that are not yet grouped are disturbing until we categorize them. Bauman would challenge both sides of the debate to make room for the idea of ambivalence.[13]

Ambivalence is the possibility of assigning an object, action, or person to more than one category. Unlike many who would object to ambivalence as a temporary reality or a defect in language or knowledge, Bauman sees ambivalence as simply the manifestation of life's randomness and contingency. These postmodern views fly in the face of Enlightenment notions of an ordered and rational universe. Recall, for example, the minstrel figures in Bragg Bowlin's home. They made me uncomfortable. Bragg did not see my discomfort. This circumstance raises the question of whether Bragg is open to the possibility that his symbols could be offensive to me. Would he say I am interpreting them incorrectly? Both of us are dominated by the desire for binary classification, and until we come to grips with that desire we will never be able to come to a joint understanding of our mutual past. But what is the ground for truth in Bauman's system of ambivalence? How can southerners use this idea to understand their complex past?

Bauman sees truth much as his intellectual ancestor Antonio Gramsci saw it: as a structuring force used by the few to dominate and humiliate the many. He calls for abandoning the rigid adherence to one perspective and writes of the need for kindness and acceptance, the need "to honor the otherness in the other, the strangeness in the stranger."[14] Truth does not reside outside of human experience in some realm of immutable and eternal essences. Rather, it arises gradually from the messiness of human interactions and contestation, ever contingent and provisional, always ready to be refined, updated, and influenced by new insights and discoveries.

Achieving this goal, Bauman acknowledges, is a great challenge requiring "nerves of steel." To live a life of contingency and ambivalence is to experience uncertainty and spiritual discomfort. He asks us to give up our ideal that our truth must be truth for others. For southerners to begin a new dialogue on their symbols will require openness to the other—in a word, tolerance. This is not the tolerance that right or truth extends to ignorance, for that tolerance between superior and inferior is still within a system of domination and humiliation. What Bauman calls for is a tolerance that leads to solidarity with the other, a common acknowledgement that absolute truth escapes us all. When descendants of slaves can defend descendants of slaveholders and Confederate soldiers in their right to commemorate their ancestors, then solidarity is present. A readiness to fight and join the battle for the sake of the other's difference is at the heart of solidarity.

Where does this leave us? Black and white southerners have produced a culture that has given this nation and the world contributions that range from unique foods to the musical influences of gospel, jazz, and the blues. In a world that grows increasingly fractured along ethnic lines, the American South has the opportunity to demonstrate that a diverse population can live in solidarity with its differences, differences that stem from a troubled and at times harsh past, but that nonetheless point to the possibility of a bright future.

NOTES

1. John Shelton Reed, "Capture the Flag," in *Kicking Back: Further Dispatches from the South* (University of Missouri Press, 1995), 42.

2. Madan Sarup, *Identity, Culture, and the Postmodern World* (University of Georgia Press, 1996), 194.

3. Ibid., 14–17.

4. Gaines M. Foster, *Ghosts of the Confederacy: Defeat, the Lost Cause, and the Emergence of the New South* (Oxford University Press, 1987), 89.

5. For Lee's racial views see Emory Thomas, *Robert E. Lee: A Biography* (Norton, 1995), 173, 371–72, 382.

6. Benedict Anderson, *Imagined Communities: The Origins and Spread of Nationalism* (Verso, 1983), 12.

7. Ibid., 10–11.

8. J. F. Bierlein, *Living Myths: How Myth Gives Meaning to Human Experience* (Ballantine, 1999), 203.

9. George Tindall, "Mythology: A New Frontier," in *Myth and Southern History*, vol. 1, *The Old South*, ed. Patrick Gerster and Nicholas Cords (University of Illinois Press, 1989), 3.

10. Zygmunt Bauman, *Modernity and Ambivalence* (Polity Press, 1991), 1.

11. Ibid., 233.

12. Gordon Hickey, "Lee Absent from Canal Walk Opening," *Richmond Times-Dispatch*, 4 June 1999, A-1.

13. Bauman, *Modernity and Ambivalence*, 56.

14. Ibid., 235.

The New Days of Yore

Country music, the blues, Atticus Finch, and southern childhoods aren't what they used to be—and perhaps never really were.

Rednecks, White Socks, and Piña Coladas?

Country Music Ain't What It Used to Be . . .
And It Really Never Was

James C. Cobb

Hank Williams's emotional songs and tragic life seem most quintessentially
"country" today. Courtesy of BMI Archives.

*J*ust the other day, I read a lengthy piece suggesting that the Grand Ole Opry is about to fade away. Fans of "contemporary" country apparently don't find Little Jimmy Dickens or Porter Waggoner terribly relevant, and the current chartbusters among the younger generation of artists are loath to forgo the big bucks from lucrative road gigs for the paltry $500 or so that the Opry pays. Such news is certain to set off a new season of wailing and hand-wringing from those who fear the imminent demise of so-called "traditional" country music. Before we get too lathered up, however, let me point out that we've heard all this before. Actually, every time Garth Brooks or one of his big-hatted buddies kicks off another over-hyped mega-tour or cuts a new CD, somebody tells us that if ol' Hank were alive today, he'd be spinning in his grave.

Now, don't get me wrong. The more "old fashioned" or "down home" a country song is, the better I like it. They simply don't come too maudlin or twangy for this boy. Still, I'm not ready to throw in with those who reject everything they hear on the radio these days as nothing but over-produced, pop-oriented drivel and long for the good old days when times were bad and country music was a pure, unadulterated reflection of the life experiences of rural southern whites. As is often the case, these self-described "purists" are actually worshiping something that was never pure in the first place.

In fact, as I see it, the entire history of country music reflects the manner in which southern culture at large has survived by accommodating rather than resisting the forces of change.

Technology, especially the advent of the phonograph and the radio, seemed to pose a formidable threat to the region's traditions and values, yet these contraptions also served as vehicles by which southern music would reach listeners around the nation and ultimately the world. Likewise, technology brought other musical forms into the South and encouraged the lyric and stylistic intermingling and cross-fertilization that marked southern music from the beginning.

As early as the turn of the century, Harvard archaeologist Charles Peabody was dismayed to find black southern workers singing not only hymns but "ragtime" tunes that were "undoubtedly picked up from some passing theatrical troupes." By the time folklorists began their early field recordings in the South, as Francis Davis put it, "a supposedly authorless and uncopyrighted song learned by ear for generations might be in reality a song once featured in a vaudeville revue or written or recorded by some long-forgotten professional entertainer." Historian Edward L. Ayers clearly had both early country music and the blues in mind when he observed that "what the twentieth century would see as some of the most distinctly southern facets of southern culture developed in a process of constant appropriation and negotiation. Much of southern culture was invented, not inherited."[1]

For southern whites, the nostalgic and weepy Victorian parlor songs popular throughout the nation at the turn of the century were particularly appealing, and songs such as "Pale Amaranthus" were soon southernized into the famous Carter Family classic "Wildwood Flower." Early recordings of southern rural musicians, black and white, proved so commercially successful that recording companies quickly dispatched talent scouts who fanned out across the region in search of new singers and new songs. The quest for fresh material soon exhausted the available reservoir of folk, spiritual, gospel, and dance tunes and encouraged performers such as Fiddlin' John Carson and Ernest V. "Pop" Stoneman to try their hand at songwriting. Although these early country composers frequently retained the old Anglo-Saxon ballad format, they often lifted their subject matter directly from recent headlines. Not surprisingly, many of their songs expressed some significant misgivings about the impact of modernization. Stoneman's "Sinking of the *Titanic*" deplored the sin of human arrogance and stressed the limits of human capability by pointing out that although the *Titanic* was billed as an unsinkable ship, "God, with his mighty hand, showed the world it could not stand."

Country music pioneer Uncle Dave Macon seemed to be making a similar statement when he vowed, "I'd rather ride a wagon and go to heaven / Than go to hell in an automobile." (It is worth noting in passing that at this point Uncle Dave's wagon-freight company had recently been driven out of business by a trucking line.) As Charles Wolfe pointed out, however, "Uncle Dave was able to make his peace with technology" once "he was able to integrate it into his life." As soon as traveling by auto became vital to Macon's performing career, he began to sing the praises of the "Model T" in "On the Dixie Bee Line (In That Henry Ford of Mine)." Uncle Dave kept abreast of later developments by recording "New Ford Car," a tribute to the newer, more comfortable "Model A" that succeeded the Model T.[2]

As time passed southern songwriters soon managed to harness the imagery of modern technology to moralist-traditionalist ends. The radio, which provided an ever-widening invasion route for the influences of mass society, also became an agent for indoctrination in Protestant fundamentalism. If you missed church on Sunday, all you had to do, as the title of Albert Brumley's 1937 gospel composition insisted, was "Turn Your Radio On" and "get in touch with God" by listening to "the songs of Zion coming from the land of endless Spring."

The same adjustment to new technology was playing out on the other side of the color line. This is apparent in the lines of songs popular among black sharecroppers in the Mississippi Delta:

> Friend, I'm married unto Jesus
> And we's never been apart
> I've a telephone in my bosom
> I can ring him up from my heart
> I can get him on the air [radio]
> Down on my knees in prayer.[3]

Finally, the "trucker" songs of the post–World War II era suggest a growing belief in humanity's inherent ability to win not just a stalemate with technology but a victory over it. In the hands of a hard-drivin', pill-poppin', bed-hoppin', smokey-baitin', "Truck Drivin' Son of a Gun," an eighteen-wheel diesel behemoth became as docile as a dutiful and pampered cowpony. Whereas the mysterious but tragic hobo of yesteryear romanticized by Jimmie Rodgers was forever "Waitin' for a Train," the truck driver was always in motion and firmly in control, confident that he was "gonna make it home tonight." "Six Days on the Road" was little more than a joyride, especially if you were perpetually "ratchet-jawing" on your CB radio. The latter activity presented a prime example of high technology—harnessed and humanized, southern style. A classic illustration was "Teddy Bear," a phenomenally popular ballad that told the story of a disabled but ever-chipper orphan lad whose deceased trucker father's old CB was his only link to the outside world.

The pursuit of larger commercial markets intensified in the 1920s, and the more rustic country performers like Fiddlin' John Carson gradually gave way to the decidedly more "modern" and innovative Jimmie Rodgers, who took hillbilly music into areas undreamed of a decade earlier, yodeling melodically, incorporating Hawaiian-style steel guitars and even the jazz stylings of Louis Armstrong into his songs. Before he died of tuberculosis in 1933, Rodgers sold twelve million records and at one point was earning more money than Babe Ruth. A slick-talking, black-sounding hipster, Rodgers was a romantic, if ultimately tragic figure, and also one of the first hillbilly performers to don a cowboy costume.

As performers in the Depression-ravaged South realized that their audiences preferred the carefree cowboy to the down-and-out plowboy, the Southwest was busily producing yet another strain of country music, "western swing," a marvelous synthesis of jazz and hillbilly with a little Cajun, Mexican mariachi, and polka thrown in as well. Almost solely the creation of Bob Wills, western swing stood out as a musical melange, blending the "big band" sound with the folk tradition. Wills's signature song, "San Antonio Rose," was also recorded by Bing Crosby, suggesting that the possibility of taking country music into the mainstream market was not as remote as it once had seemed.

Like western swing, World War II–era "honky tonk" was a music born in the midst of drinking, dancing, and often brawling. The sinful practices associated with honky-tonk music suggested the morally ruinous potential of modernization, and the lyric content seemed a radical departure from the moralism and Victorian restraint that marked the songs of the Carter Family, Roy Acuff, and many others who are viewed as country-music pioneers. Yet, as Tony Scherman rightly notes, "In its sounds and lyrics honky tonk embodies country's great complex of themes: the opposing tugs of country and city; the collapse of traditional supports like family, community, church; rural Americans' hard adjustment to urban life." Despite its controversial beginnings as a threat to the values traditionally upheld in country music, most of today's fans would probably identify honky tonk as the pure essence of country music.[4]

Shortly after World War II the legendary Bill Monroe, revered by subsequent generations of fans as the personification of traditional, folk-derived music, actually revolutionized the old string-band sound by building his band's offerings around the new three-finger banjo stylings of Earl Scruggs. The result was "bluegrass," a decidedly jazzed up version of the old "high lonesome" sound that one scholar described as "folk music with overdrive."[5]

Actually, the performer whose emotional songs and tragic life seem most quintessentially "country" today is Hank Williams. Yet in its day, Williams's style was both innovative and controversial. It combined country, honky tonk, and black instrumental and vocal influences to develop a distinctive sound whose appeal shows remarkable endurance. Though Williams's music now seems country through and through, his frequent reliance on a heavy beat and his physical gestures and gyrations onstage clearly made him controversial in more conventional circles and foreshadowed the style of Elvis Presley, the "King of Rock 'n' Roll."

Some observers foresaw rock 'n' roll actually killing off its country-music ancestor. Country did suffer greatly in the 1950s, but the 1960s saw a resurgence as the "Nashville Sound," or "country pop," offered the easy-listening sounds of artists such as Eddy Arnold and Jim Reeves. Patsy Cline, who is widely regarded today as the classic female country vocalist, actually made her enduring reputation as a country pop star who "crossed over" into the popular mass market with hits such as "Walking After Midnight" and "I Fall to Pieces." The Nashville Sound sold big, but the so-called traditionalists despised it. It elicited a sort of "neo-honky-tonk" reaction (the once suspect honky tonk had already become "traditional") personified first by "The Possum" George Jones and later by the "Bakersfield Sound" of the great Merle Haggard, the "poet of the common man" whose "Okie from Muskogee" did so much to suggest the southernization of America.

And so it goes in a recurring dialectic wherein country music seems ready to fade completely into the enveloping blandness of the pop-music scene only to have a "new traditionalist" movement emerge. Current favorites Emmylou Harris, Ricky Skaggs, Dwight Yoakam, and Randy Travis have at one time or another worn the "new traditionalist" collar. Meanwhile, contemporary critics regularly heap waves of abuse on Garth Brooks for his relentless pursuit of the mass market with songs that substitute piña coladas for longnecks and stage shows that make the halftime extravaganza at the Super Bowl look like a third-grade Christmas pageant. Elsewhere, Shania Twain, whose husband once produced Def Leppard, juxtaposes fiddles and twangy pedal steel guitars with emphatic rock beats and stylings featured in songs by artists ranging from the Rolling Stones to The Police.

Certainly, liberal America's lamentations about country music's ascendance in the 1970s seem ironic indeed in retrospect as the twentieth century draws to a close amid a flood of concerns about the South's—and country music's—loss of identity. For more than three quarters of a century, both those who listened to country music (many of whom also pretty much lived it) and those who performed it have struggled to reach the mainstream of American life. Having arrived, they must face up to the cultural consequences of their accomplishment, especially the loss of identity that total immersion may bring.

Social critics in the 1970s had fretted about country music's soaring popularity because of its ostensibly reactionary ideological agenda, but music critics of the 1990s complain that the music has no agenda at all, ideological or otherwise. Their argument goes something like this: Settled into a comfortable suburban existence, its traditional core constituency, or at least the heirs thereof, no longer needs or wants to hear songs about suffering, struggle, tragedy, death, and damnation. Consequently, the once unapologetically candid and gritty idiom that expressed real struggle and genuine alienation from the unfamiliar urban-industrial environment now serves up little more than mass-produced, smoothed-out suburban escapism. When detractors dismiss Garth Brooks as the evil "anti-Hank," however, they fail to realize that, like Brooks, Williams and a number of the other "pioneers" who are now enshrined in the Hall of Fame were also seen in their own day as threats to country music's identity and integrity.

When Tony Scherman asks, "How far from its social origins can an art form grow before it simply loses meaning?" he ignores the fact that country music's "social origins" are in a South that was anything but static as it adapted to a slew of changes, including industrialization, urbanization, and the cultural fallout from technological advances such as the phonograph, the radio, and the automobile.[6] As time passed, the changes in country music have reflected the Americanization of Dixie just as its soaring popularity nationwide has documented the southernization of America. Before we offer up any more premature obituaries, let's remember that, to paraphrase Hank Jr., for country music, change is actually a family tradition.

NOTES

This article was adapted from "Modernization and the Mind of the South" in James C. Cobb's *Redefining Southern Culture: Mind and Identity in the Modern South* (University of Georgia Press, 1999).

1. Edward L. Ayers, *The Promise of the New South: Life after Reconstruction* (Oxford University Press, 1992), 385, 377, 373; Francis Davis, *The History of the Blues: The Roots, the Music, the People from Charley Patton to Robert Cray* (Hyperion, 1995), 169.

2. Charles Wolfe, "Uncle Dave Macon," ed. Bill C. Malone and Judith McCulloh, *Stars of Country Music: Uncle Dave Macon to Johnny Rodrigues* (University of Illinois Press, 1975), 42, 59–62.

3. Anonymous song citation, Samuel C. Adams Jr., "The Acculturation of the Delta Negro," *Social Forces*, 76 (December 1997): 203.

4. Tony Scherman, "Country," *American Heritage* 45 (November 1994): 47–48.

5. Alan Lomax, "Bluegrass Background: Folk Music with Over Drive," *Esquire* 52 (October 1959): 103–9.

6. Scherman, "Country," 57.

"Where Is the Love?"

Racial Violence, Racial Healing, and Blues Communities

Adam Gussow

It may not quite qualify as the *home of the blues, but Mississippi—birthplace of such greats as John Lee Hooker (here)—has blessed the blues world with many of its greatest musicians. Courtesy of the Fantasy Archives.*

"here Is the Love?" is the title of a memorably wistful duet recorded in the early seventies by Roberta Flack and Donny Hathaway; a lament for the way in which Martin Luther King Jr.'s dream of redemptive interracial brotherhood or "beloved community," which animated the civil rights movement, seemed to have dissolved in the aftermath of King's assassination, the riots that ravaged black urban communities, the militancy of the Black Power movement, and the war in Vietnam. The title's question might also serve as a touchstone for a reconsideration of the blues. What role does love, and the absence of love, play in the emergence of blues music and the creation of blues communities? Does love have the power to heal our blues, particularly the blues inculcated by racial violence and the persistence of what W. E. B. DuBois called the color line, the socioeconomic and attitudinal boundary separating white from black? Finally, is it possible to understand the contemporary blues scene, or elements of it, as an incarnation of King's beloved community—which is to say, as a brotherhood of equals, animated by love in the service of racial healing?

A New Yorker by birth, I currently make my home in Mississippi, a state fond of proclaiming that it is the home of the blues. Certainly, Mississippi is *a* home of the blues, if not perhaps *the* home, since it is the birthplace of Charley Patton, B.B. King, Muddy Waters, Robert Johnson, John Lee Hooker, Howlin' Wolf, Sonny Boy Williamson, and countless other foundational blues performers whose names are familiar to blues fans around the world. Mississippi was also unparalleled between 1890 and 1965 for the violence and humiliation that its white citizens routinely inflicted on its black citizens as a way of keeping an exploitative cotton sharecropping economy in place. In this respect, Mississippi was indeed the home of the blues: it was the wellspring not just of blues *music* but of blues *feeling*, a whole complex of emotions and attitudes engendered in its African American residents—a swirling mixture of fear, despair, fury, heartache, extreme restlessness, freely ranging sexual desire, and a stubborn determination to persist against all odds and sing the bittersweet song of that persistence. One of the most evocative descriptions of this Mississippi, the Mississippi that produced blues feeling in its terrorized and survival-oriented black residents, can be found in the autobiography of Danny Barker, a black New Orleans jazzman. "Just the mention of the word *Mississippi* amongst a group of New Orleans people," insisted Barker in 1986, would cause complete silence and attention. The word was so very powerful that it carried the impact of catastrophes, destruction, death, hell, earthquakes, cyclones, murder, hanging, lynching, all sorts of slaughter. It was the earnest and general feeling that any Negro who left New Orleans and journeyed across the state border and entered the hell-hole called the state of Mississippi for any reason other than to attend the funeral of a very close relative—mother, father, sister, brother, wife, or husband—was well on the way to losing his mentality, or had already lost it.[1]

Mississippi has changed a great deal since the dark, bluesy days evoked by Barker—orchestrated "massive resistance" to the civil rights movement finally dissolving in the wary, anxious, exhausted, but also exhilarating rapprochement described by Willie Morris in *Yazoo: Integration in a Deep-Southern Town* (1971). My own institution, "Ole Miss," the state's flagship university, has been transformed from a bastion of white supremacy, where students and others rioted in 1962 to keep James Meredith from enrolling, into a comprehensively integrated campus (albeit with separate black and white Greek organizations) that features an activist Institute for Racial Reconciliation named for William Winter, a former governor (1982–1986) who made equal funding for public education the mission of his administration.

Blues music, once strictly the province of Mississippi's African American community, has become a mainstream enterprise in the state—a so-called cultural resource rather than a disreputable subculture and a conspicuous source of civic pride for black and white Mississippians alike. There are tourist dollars to be made from the Mississippi blues; everybody is hungry for a piece of the action.[2] Since economic power here continues to be wielded primarily by whites, even as African American political power has markedly expanded since the end of segregation, the nascent blues-tourism business may of course turn out to be one more way in which white capital extracts profit from black artistry without truly sharing in the wealth. Blues tourism may yet end up reinscribing the same old blues on Mississippi's black citizens, the blues of economic expropriation that generations of black sharecroppers knew so well.

That's a cynical way of looking at the blues in twenty-first-century Mississippi and not an unreasonable one: the law of unintended consequences in the service of longstanding and retrograde racial dynamics. But there are other, more hope-inspiring ways. Morgan Freeman and Bill

Luckett—a black actor and a white businessman, both native Mississippians—recently joined together to help revitalize Muddy Waters's old hometown of Clarksdale by opening the Ground Zero Blues Club. This sort of interracial partnership would have been unimaginable fifty years ago, when the White Citizens' Council was fostering separatist hysteria on the heels of *Brown v. Board of Education*. There is also the American Blues Network, a forty-station chain based in Jackson that is the brainchild of Rip Daniels, a Mississippi native and African American entrepreneur. The great-great grandson of a black Civil War veteran who fought against the Confederacy, an outspoken opponent of Confederate flag displays on public property, Daniels presides over a broadcast operation that features African American on-air personalities who play the blues for a largely but not exclusively black audience across the South. "The country has rediscovered what we call soul blues, because we'll play Aretha Franklin as well as Muddy Waters," Daniels told an interviewer in 2003. "It's just salt-of-the-earth, working-class music."[3]

If one wants more evidence that the blues can be a force for economic justice and interracial fraternity in contemporary Mississippi, consider that my own University of Mississippi not only paid B.B. King $50,000 last year—his standard fee—to play a ninety-minute concert at the new performing arts center, but also made him an honorary professor of southern studies. Both acts were, by any measure, outpourings of admiration and respect, symbolic rituals of atonement whose healing moment was evident to all. King, who came of age in a state scarred by lynching, disenfranchisement, racialized poverty, and routinized racial humiliation, is a revered elder in the new Mississippi. In June 2004, fifty-one years after the founding of the invidious White Citizens' Council in Indianola, groundbreaking ceremonies were held in that cotton-and-catfish capital for the new B.B. King Museum and Delta Interpretive Center, an institution that plans to tell King's "life's story of hardship, perseverance, talent and humility as a way to further the arts, youth development, and racial reconciliation in the Mississippi Delta and beyond."[4]

There's paradox at work here, plainly. Blues music, a form of cultural expression whose very ground was the unjust and painful relationship between blacks and whites in the segregated South, is also a music that has helped minister to the lingering wounds of segregation during the post–civil rights era. Not only has it granted its best-known African American performers a measure of wealth and mainstream acceptance, but it has helped erode what remains of the color line by bringing black and white musicians and audiences together into a series of local sub-cultural communities—"blues scenes" governed, at their best, by mutual admiration, economic partnership, and the spirit of shared aesthetic creation. Subcultural life in postmodern, media-savvy America is, of course, not always at its best; as sociologist David Grazian makes clear in *Blue Chicago* (2003), the Windy City's nocturnal blues scene is pressured by the hunger of white tourists for a stylized African American exoticism it misreads as authenticity. Literary critic and cultural theorist Vincent B. Leitch sees more promising social dynamics at work in Oklahoma City's blues subculture, a view that resonates with my own experience in New York. "It is a realm of freedom, comparatively speaking," Leitch insists, "and of entertainment and art." It is both critical of, and an antidote to, such social problems as racism and class segregation. The music and the dancing of the blues subculture regularly bring different groups together who wouldn't normally interact. Although social, artistic, and business conventions and restrictions remain in place, blues culture nonetheless "subverts key social barriers."[5]

One outgrowth of what might be called the mainstreaming of blues subculture is a desire, particularly on the part of younger whites, to transcend spectatorship through a progressive social activism that engages race-based inequalities. The civil rights movement may have ended decades ago, but the spirit of the movement is renascent in the volunteer-ist, ameliorative tenor of certain prominent sectors of the contemporary blues world. The Music Maker Relief Foundation, based in Durham, North Carolina, for example, describes itself as "a nonprofit organization dedicated to helping the true pioneers and forgotten heroes of Southern musical traditions gain recognition and meet their day to day needs." "Keeping the bluest of the blues alive" is the Music Maker creed. The organization's advisory board is a Who's Who of the contemporary black-and-white American blues scene: Taj Mahal, Bonnie Raitt, B.B. King, Kenny Wayne Shepherd, Dickey Betts. "Today," proclaims the organization's website, "many [blues] musicians are living in extreme poverty and need food, shelter, medical care, and other assistance. Music Maker's aid and service programs improve the quality of recipient's lives. Our work affirms to these artists that we value the gifts of music and inspiration they have delivered to the world. Our mission is to give back to the roots of American music."[6]

Decades of overseas tours by American blues artists, beginning with Big Bill Broonzy in the 1950s and numerous incarnations of the American Folk Blues Festival in the 1960s, have sowed a great deal of enthusiasm for those roots on foreign soil, a notable exception to the world's ambivalence towards many other overseas projections of American cultural might. An Israeli organization called "Blues for Peace" declares on its website that it was founded "to honor the roots of blues music and promote peace and the understanding that ALL peoples have had their share of the blues. 'Isn't it time people stopped fighting and learned to play twelve-bar shuffles instead?'" asks the website. French blues fans who want to endorse this bluesy version of "We Are the World" can purchase attractive cotton T-shirts with the logo "Blues Pour La Paix." German blues fans can order trucker's caps with "Blues fur Frieden" over the bill. Italian blues fans can order hooded T-shirts with "Blues per la pace" across the front.[7] Anyone who begins to investigate the blues in an international context is forced into an unexpected conclusion: Once the soundtrack of segregated black American life, the blues today are at many points around the globe the musical backdrop for a multiracial utopia grounded in the gospel of racial and ethnic healing. It is as though the blues themselves, through the medium of music, have transmuted the mixture of fear, despair, fury, heartache, and restlessness that were their founding racial impulse into a powerful urge toward compassionate brotherhood, a brotherhood that yearns, in however partial and compromised a way, to undo the spiritual and material conditions responsible for precipitating those blues-feelings in the first place.

"We are tied together," Martin Luther King famously insisted, "in the single garment of destiny, caught in an inescapable network of mutuality." King's prophetic words seem to speak the condition of beloved community, or at least friendly, enthusiastic, and mutually profitable interwovenness, that the blues have helped birth in recent decades. It is worth remembering that when King spoke of love, he carefully distinguished between *eros*, *philia*, and *agape*. "The word *eros*," he wrote, "is a sort of aesthetic or romantic love. In the Platonic dialogues *eros* is a yearning of the soul for the realm of the divine." Blues singers know from *eros*, but their conception of romantic love owes little to Plato. Every time a bluesman cries, "Hey baby, won't you take a walk with me," he is dallying in the fields of *eros*. "The second word [for love]," writes King, "is *philia*, a reciprocal love and the intimate affection and friendship between friends. We love those whom we like, and we love because we are loved." The enthusiast's passion that binds blues performers and blues fans into a blues scene arguably falls into this second category of love, the "friendship between friends" category. *Philia* is not trivial; it has the power to break down social barriers and create new forms of civil society. If the contemporary blues scene is animated by a large helping of multiracial *philia*, if it creates intimate affection and friendship between friends who hail from different locations on the social spectrum, then it is, by that criterion alone, a force for racial healing. Yet mere *philia* by itself is not, according to King, enough to constitute beloved community. Another kind of love is needed, wider and more comprehensive than the first two. "The third word [for love]," writes King, "is *agape*, understanding and creative, redemptive goodwill for all men. An overflowing love which seeks nothing in return, *agape* is the love of God operating in the human heart."[8]

King's *agape* is the love-your-enemies ethos that was cultivated by civil rights workers in the early 1960s as they confronted the most intransigent forms of white southern racism in Mississippi and elsewhere. It is also, arguably, the kind of redemptive, world-serving love that is striving to make itself visible through the instrumentality of bluesy service organizations like the Music Maker Relief Foundation and Blues for Peace. Such love sometimes leads to unlikely pairings, grounded in a familiar blues dialectic of individual pain transcended with the community's help: the annual "Childhood Cancer Lifeline Day and Blues Night" at the Pat's Peak ski resort in New Hampshire, for example, featuring the A & B Wrecking Company, Big Boy Guitar, and Roxanne and the Voodoo Rockers. More familiar is the sort of example provided by Rhino Records, a leading member of the Social Venture Network (www.svn.org) and Businesses for Social Responsibility (www.bsr.org). "A portion of the proceeds from each volume (eighteen to date) of Rhino's popular *Blues Masters: The Essential Collection* series," reports the company website, "have been donated to the Rhythm & Blues Foundation," an organization dedicated to undoing a legacy of white exploitation of black blues and soul artists—not least at the hands of unscrupulous record companies—by assisting ageing musicians and songwriters in various ways. In the aftermath of Hurricane Katrina, the Oregon Food Bank and the Waterfront Blues Festival in Portland teamed up to host "Blues for Katrina," an all-day concert intended to help New Orleans's many refugees. The Portsmouth (New Hampshire) Blues Bank Collective, a twenty-year-old educational organization, states in its creed that it intends "[t]o use the music as a means of positive social change. And, whenever possible, to eliminate all forms of racism, intolerance, and prejudice"; its activities, along with an annual Portsmouth Blues Festival, a local Black Heritage Trail, and a multicultural studies program called "Hope, Heroes, and the Blues," include "Random acts of BLUENESS on the streets of the world."[9] *Agape* does indeed show up in the contemporary blues scene—allied with more conventional forms of volunteerism and commodity capitalism, to be sure, but with a determination to engineer social justice and create beloved community nonetheless.

Endlessly malleable yet hewing with surprising tensile strength to their distinctive AAB stanzaic form and sweet-sour tonality, the blues have evolved during the past century from a black southern subculture (1890–1920) into a black American pop music with a minority white audience (1920–1960), a white Anglo-American folk-and-electric subculture (1960–1990), and a worldwide roots music aligned in significant ways with the spirit of beloved community (1990–present). This curious trajectory might lead us to probe the music's origins a little more deeply. Where, if at all, does *agape* show up in the harsh, brutal, segregated world in which the blues were born—Mississippi in the pre–civil rights era, for example? It's certainly tempting to see that world reductively, as a place ruled by hardhearted white overlords and less advantaged but grimly prideful poor whites, both groups utterly deaf to the call of beloved community.

"WOUNDED IN THE PLACE WHERE WE WOULD KNOW LOVE"

A particularly suggestive meditation on love and lovelessness can be found in *All About Love* (2000), a collection of essays authored by bell hooks, an African American cultural critic who grew up in segregated Kentucky during the 1950s. A prolific and uncompromising advocate for working-class black feminism, whose previous books engage in a sustained critique of what she terms "white supremacist capitalist patriarchy," hooks surprised many with her turn towards New Age soulministry in the late 1990s. The word "love" shows up in virtually every sentence of *All About Love*; the words "black" and "white" are entirely absent from the first several chapters, although epigraphs from white male transformational psychologists such as M. Scott Peck and John Welwood proliferate. If we define *agape*, with King, as "the love of God operating in the human heart," then *agape* is indisputably hooks's subject: the power of God's grace working through the human heart to transform blues-bearing wounds into a world-embracing love that bespeaks psychological and spiritual wholeness. "Love heals," writes hooks.

When we are wounded in the place where we would know love, it is difficult to imagine that love really has the power to change everything. No matter what has happened in our past, when we open our hearts to love we can live as if born again, not forgetting the past but seeing it in a new way, letting it live inside us in a new way. . . . Mindful remembering lets us put the broken bits and pieces of our hearts together again. This is the way healing begins.[10]

hooks's invocation of love's transformative power implicitly challenges our familiar ways of talking about the blues. If our mission, according to hooks, is not to forget the past but to see it in a new way, then it may be possible for us to see blues song, and the literature and culture that embrace it, as sites of trauma and recovery, racial wounding and racial healing, love denied and love extended. We might come to see blues communities of all kinds, for example, as healing alternatives or antidotes to the radical isolation of the love-deprived, blues-suffused individual. I know fifty different definitions of the blues, but hooks has inadvertently provided us with the master key: *to have the blues is to be wounded in the place where we would know—or have known—love*. This definition might enable us to understand blues as both a universal feeling—since virtually all of us, at one time or another, have been wounded in that place—and a more narrowly racial feeling, a "black thing"; any honest reappraisal of the Jim Crow South in which blues song rapidly consolidated as a folk form between 1895 and 1915 would acknowledge the humiliations inflicted by new segregation statutes, the fears engendered by spectacle lynching, the rages and despairs prompted by disenfranchisement and economic exploitation for the uniquely heart-ravaging wounds they were. What is lynching, with its bodily tortures and ritual castration, if not the white South's loveless attempt to wound black folk, literally and metaphorically, in the place where they would know love? It may seem fatuous to speak of the "blues South" as a land traumatized by the loss of interracial *agape*, of embracing brotherly love. Yet what is blues song, with its thousand and one ways of saying, "Baby, you don't love me," if not the profoundest kind of lament for just such a loss?

At the dawn of the twentieth century, as angry, young white and black generations segregated and violently collided across the South, and residual paternalist sympathies dissipated and spectacle lynching flared out of control, the blues line "Baby you don't love me" spoke not just to romantic desertion but to black sociopolitical despair, the utter failure of white America to deliver on the promise of full citizenship for its African American residents. As cultural historian Ann Douglas suggests, such lyricized complaint may also have expressed powerful but furtive *white* despair at a moment when Americans were notably obsessed by their country's "massive, painfully failed and unsolved racial experiment." The fact that most Americans, according to Douglas, "were trying to ignore this failure—by banning blacks from their lives and facilities, theorizing them into pseudo-scientific inferiority, lynching and disenfranchising them—necessitated and guaranteed a reaction that inevitably incorporated not just black thoughts and feelings but white ones; the blues were the fullest expression of this phenomenon." White men may, as journalist Whitelaw Reid of the *New York Tribune* wrote after a visit to Mississippi in 1866, have been "virulently vindictive against a property that had escaped from their control," but many white southerners were also quietly broken-hearted at the loss of "their" previously compliant and apparently happy Negroes—a loss that only intensified as the old order gave way to the new.[11] That white perceptions of a loss of interracial community were predicated on white ethical blindness during the antebellum period and the decades that followed made the sense of loss no less profound; white disillusion during Reconstruction, the nadir of American race relations, shadowed black disillusion, even as white repression spurred the latter. "Baby, you don't love me" bespoke a region's dismay, not just a race's.

Yet it has never been difficult for African American blues people—or whites moved by their songs—to imagine, in bell hooks's words, "that love really has the power to change everything." Quite the opposite: blues lyricism is grounded in a desperate faith that one good lover entering your life, one transcendent burst of *eros*, has the power to change everything, healing all the wounds inflicted by the white world's manifest lovelessness, if only for the moment. Marvin Gaye sang of sexual healing; so did virtually every blues singer who came of age in pre–civil rights Mississippi. In this respect, *eros* plainly trumped *agape*, at least among early blues people; an ethos of open-hearted, world-redemptive love was something only God's people, and suckers, could afford. "I had three ways of making it," Delta bluesman David Honeyboy Edwards proudly insists in his autobiography. "The women and my guitar and the dice." B.B. King, a better-capitalized performer but less sanguine lover than Honeyboy, fathered fifteen children by fifteen different women. "I felt starved . . . for love and affection," he confesses in his own autobiography.

"I couldn't—and still can't—get enough of both."[12] "Can't Be Satisfied," the song Muddy Waters sang for Alan Lomax at Stovall Plantation in the early 1940s, is both a comprehensive and representative complaint, a touchstone of the blues South. No one lover, of course, could finally fill the aching void left by so much willfully inflicted spiritual damage, which is why blues song is a never-ending dance of immoderate hungers—for love, for money, for a fresh start in a friendly town—and bitterly dashed promises. *"Well bye bye babe, if I . . . never see you no more. . . . You know I love you girl. . . . I can't stand to see you go."*

Blues literature, both autobiographies by elder bluesmen and creative works by contemporary black writers, offers memorable inscriptions of this blues-heroic dance of desire and disillusionment, love extended and love denied, trauma suffered and trauma overcome. Sometimes the spiritual wounds inflicted by loveless white folk are an insurmountable burden, destabilizing and defeating would-be blues heroes. In *Ma Rainey's Black Bottom* (1985), by August Wilson, the Mississippi-born blues trumpeter, Levee, erupts twice in the course of the play. The first outburst reveals the scars that white racial violence has carved into his body and spirit; the second eruption, in which he succumbs to murderous fraternal rage, shows us what happens when unhealed trauma is left to fester for decades without love's transformative intercession. Levee explodes after his fellow band mates tease him about how he is "spooked up by the white man." "Levee got to be Levee!" he yells. "And he don't need nobody messing with him about the white man—cause you don't know nothing about me. You don't know Levee. You don't know nothing about what kind of blood I got! What kind of heart I got beating here! I was eight years old when I watched a gang of white mens come into my daddy's house and have do with my mama any way they wanted." Levee continues his impassioned narration: he interrupted the rape of his mother by attacking one of the men with his father's hunting knife, suffering a deep gash across his own chest. His father later managed to kill four members of the gang before the rest "caught up with him and hung him and set him afire."[13] "Mindful remembering," to repeat bell hooks, "lets us put the broken bits and pieces of our hearts together again. This is the way healing begins." Levee's tragedy is that he begins the healing process hooks describes—centering himself in his rage-filled heart, engaging in a kind of mindful remembering—but he's never graced by his fickle female lover or his fractious male band mates with the kind of compassionate audience that might enable him to reassemble the "bits and pieces" of his broken heart and make peace with his past. His blues-filled life lacks redemptive love. When his dream of fame and fortune as a blues songwriter is shattered by a manipulative white record executive who has been playing him for a fool, Levee's unhealed "white man" blues are reanimated. They possess him, overpower him, and lead him to stab his black band mate Toledo to death for no good reason. His blues community wounds him with callousness rather than heals him with love; he, in response, violently shatters that community, highlighting its greed and divisiveness as he does so.

I argued earlier that blues music now functions at many sites in the contemporary world as an adjunct to *inter*-racial healing, an instrument for addressing and transcending the continuing aftereffects of segregation and racial violence. The truth is, however, that not all African Americans are happy about the surge of white interest in blues music and black blues people over the past several decades. Some are disturbed by the dizzying proliferation of white claims on a music that has been for most of its lifespan an indisputably African American cultural practice, one grounded in a continuing legacy of violent, impoverishing, and humiliating actions inflicted on black folk by white folk.

For African American novelist Bebe Moore Campbell and photographer, poet, and activist Roland L. Freeman, the modern blues scene is a terrain on which new versions of familiar and retrograde scenarios are played out. "Do you see 'em, here they come," writes Freeman at the beginning of his 1997 poem, "Don't Forget the Blues,"

> Easing into our communities
> In their big fancy cars,
> Looking like alien carpetbaggers
> Straight from Mars.
> They slide in from the East,
> North, South, and West,
> And when they leave,
> You can bet they've taken the best.
>
> Listen to me,
>
> I've been drunk a long time
> And I'm still drinking.
> I take a bath every Saturday night,
> But I'm still stinking.

This world's been whipping me upside my head,
But it hasn't stopped me from thinking.
I know they've been doing anything they choose,
I just want 'em to keep their darn hands off 'a my blues.[14]

It's not clear whether Freeman is complaining about white blues fans who swarm into black communities and party down, exoticizing the locals in a way that highlights their own ethical cluelessness, or about white executives who record black blues artists and squirrel away the profits. Perhaps he's complaining about both. What is clear is that white blues fans who cross the color line in search of "real blues" aren't necessarily propagating the ideal of beloved community—at least in the eyes of some African Americans—and may in fact be wounding their hosts in various ways.

In her 1992 novel *Your Blues Ain't Like Mine*, Bebe Moore Campbell critiques the contemporary blues scene for precisely this reason, depicting a conversation between several older black regulars of a Chicago blues bar called the Down Home. The Down Home has recently been renamed "The All-New Down Home Bar and Grill" after being overrun by white college kids. " 'The white kids done discovered us. That's what's new,' " complains the bartender. " 'That's why I don't hang out here on the weekend nights no more,' " volunteers an older black patron. " 'Ain't nothing worse,' " complains a third man,

than drinking with white college kids. While it's early, they all educated. By midnight, they done turned into the damn Klan and shit. They get drunk, they liable to say or do anything. Next thing you know, one of 'em done called you a nigger. If I'm in a situation where white folks is drinking, I be watching them. Soon as they faces turn red, shade number three, I'm gone. Shades number one and two are manageable. Number three is the turning point. They start looking like beets and shit. That's when the devil commence to possessing they souls. You know what I mean? What they want to come in here for anyway? They got they own music."

"But they ain't got no blues," said a light-skinned man, so thin that the veins in his temples seemed to bulge out of the sides of his skull.

"Yeah, they do," the man in the [Chicago] Bulls cap said. "That yahoo music. Loretta Lynn. Hank Williams. Willie Nelson. That's they blues."

"That ain't no blues," the light-skinned man said. He slammed his fist against the counter, and the ice in his drink tinkled. "White people don't sing no blues, 'cause they ain't got no blues. But they indirectly responsible for the music, 'cause they sure be giving black folks the blues."[15]

The vision of race relations offered by Freeman and Campbell is a blues song of its own, a kind of interracial blues-scene blues that offers us vital but partial truths about contemporary blues culture. The spiritual lesson it conveys is undeniable: both Freeman's poetic speaker and the aggrieved patrons of the Down Home blues bar are, to paraphrase bell hooks, wounded in the place where they would know love. They are traumatized by painful histories of cultural and economic expropriation, sensitive to perceived signs of racial disrespect, and leery of white violence erupting out of the rebel yell of blues-stoked white euphoria. As far as they're concerned, a form of interracial sociality organized around blues consumption and imposed on them by white people reinflicts familiar wounds in a grievous way rather than heals them.

Yet there is a very different vision of blues music as a terrain of interracial contact put forward by another set of contemporary African American writers, a vision that accords with Reverend King's dream of redemptive brotherhood. In this vision, white American blues musicians and blues fans are not cultural thieves and callous exploiters of African American blues people but supportive audiences, committed musical apprentices, and even, on occasion, blues masters in their own right, equal partners in the shared task of aesthetic creation. Such a vision animates Stanley Crouch's novel *Don't the Moon Look Lonesome* (2000), the story of an interracial romance between Carla, a white jazz and blues singer from South Dakota, and Maxwell, a black sax player from Texas. Crouch audaciously imagines himself into the soul of his white female protagonist at the moment of her triumphant vocal showcase at a Manhattan party given by Celestine, a New Orleans trumpeter modeled on Wynton Marsalis. There are no familiar white rip-offs of black music in Crouch's telling. Rather, Celestine and his band back up Carla as a kind of teaching ministry, cradling and prodding her talent, drawing her—a cultural pilgrim on the cusp of musical mastery—into a call-and-response dialogue. "This time," Crouch writes,

> . . . right in the middle of the blues, everybody was equal to the action— no room for squares—and [Carla] was the quarterback, calling the plays and throwing the passes out of her throat, which was, like her heart, all the way open. . . . Her classical training allowed for a sound of

such magnitude that the guys didn't have to back away in order to allow this woman the freedom of space that keeps a singer without a microphone from being smothered. She was meeting them, and as they touched in the invisible huddle of the rhythm, Carla called some gutbucket verities into the room, hitting the next to last word of the third line with a correct and saucy illiteracy that inspired calls of approval from the dancers: "All right now, get below sea level."[16]

Carla may be a white girl singing the blues here—and thus culturally suspect—but Crouch demands that we forget what we *think* we know about white and black interchange under the sign of the blues and acknowledge what is actually transpiring: Carla is *getting down*, engaging in a deep, playful, and joyous dialogue with her black musical peers. Far from diluting somebody's occulted version of "black culture" with her pale-faced presence, she brings her own cultural gifts to the table—a powerful vocal instrument she's been graced with thanks to her "classical training" —and deploys them in the service of "gutbucket verities" for everyone's benefit. Whereas August Wilson's Levee accuses his band mates of "not knowing what kind of heart I got beating here," Crouch shows us Carla singing from her "all the way open" heart, sharing what and who she is with her black band mates, amalgamating her own distinctive blues with the common stock. Buoyed and supported by her blues community, musicians and dancers alike, Carla has opened her heart to love in a way that Levee, mocked by his band mates and exploited by his white bosses, simply could not.

Since the so-called "usual crime" that led to lynching in the blues South was sexual intimacy—indeed, *any* sort of suspected intimacy— between black men and white women, an intimacy figured invariably as rape, Crouch is treading on haunted terrain. The point he makes is bold, witty, and necessary: Carla's husband is a black man, her band mates are black men, her familial and creative life is defined by sexual and musical intimacies with black men, and she's . . . *okay!* In fact, she's flourishing. And she's doing so under the sign of the blues.

It's instructive to compare the fictional vision of blues-healing offered by Stanley Crouch with the autobiographical vision offered by B.B. King in *Blues All Around Me* (1996). The world in which King came of age, Mississippi of the bad old days, is a long way from the contemporary Manhattan of Carla and Celestine—something young B.B. discovers one afternoon when he wanders into the village square of Lexington, a small town in the Delta: "There were . . . moments . . . of shock and pain that can't be erased from my memory," confesses King.

> Suddenly I see there's a commotion around the courthouse. Something's happening that I don't understand. People crowded around. People creating a buzz. Mainly white folk. I'm curious and want to get closer, but my instinct has me staying away. From the far side of the square, I see them carrying a black body, a man's body, to the front of the courthouse. A half-dozen white guys are hoisting the body up on a rope hanging from a makeshift platform. Someone cheers. The black body is a dead body. The dead man is young, nineteen or twenty, and his mouth and his eyes are open, his face contorted. It's horrible to look at but I look anyway. I sneak looks. I hear someone say something about the dead man touching a white woman and how he got what he deserves. Deep inside, I'm hurt, sad, and mad. But I stay silent. What do I have to say and who's gonna listen to me? This is another secret matter; my anger is a secret that stays away from the light of day because the square is bright with the smiles of white people passing by as they view the dead man on display. I feel disgust and disgrace and rage and every emotion that makes me cry without tears and scream without sound. I don't make a sound.[17]

King starkly evokes the lovelessness of the blues South. We have become so used to his mellow, avuncular presence as a mainstream-culture hero and commercial spokesman that it shocks us to envision him as a helpless ten-year old: furious, grieving, and humiliated, but also silenced by the aftermath of a lynching that, by design, threatens everything that he is about. The witness that King bears in this confession, years after the incident, is one way racial healing proceeds, for it is we, his readers, whose compassionate audience he requests. Like all blues performers, he needs listeners; he opens his heart, sings his song, and trusts that we'll feel him. "Mindful remembering"—bell hooks's observation again comes to mind—"lets us put the broken bits and pieces of our hearts together again. This is the way healing begins." Mindfully remembering his youthful blues feelings in all their debilitating intensity, King asks his imagined blues community—we who read his words—to participate in his unburdening.

But King depicts an earlier scene of racial healing in his autobiography that is a locus of interracial communion in which blues music itself plays a crucial role. In 1969 King played a concert at the Fillmore West auditorium in San Francisco in which, for the first time, he found himself playing for a large white audience, a sellout crowd of flower-children. "At the microphone," King remembers,

> Bill Graham gave me a straight-to-the-point introduction. "Ladies and gentlemen," he said, "the Chairman of the Board, B.B. King." By the time I strapped on Lucille, every single person in the place was standing up and cheering like crazy. For the first time in my career I got a standing ovation *before* I played. Couldn't help but cry. With tears streaming down, I thought to myself, *These kids love me before I've hit a note. How can I repay them for this love?* The answer came in my music. I played that night like I've never played before. Played "Rock Me Baby" and "Sweet Little Angel" and "You Upset Me Baby" and "How Blue Can You Get," played all my stuff with all my heart while they stayed on their feet, screaming and stomping for nearly three hours. It was hard for me to believe that this was happening, that the communication between me and the flower children was so tight and right. But it was true, it was probably the best performance of my life.[18]

In its own way, this passage is as astonishing as King's description of a Mississippi lynching. King's triumphant night at the Fillmore West *is* such a triumph because it represents a point-by-point redress of that earlier traumatic occasion. In the earlier scene, violence and hatred structure the relationship between the white lynchers and their black victim as King watches from the sidelines; here, loving approval shines down from the enthusiastic white audience onto the now-centered King, a celebrated rather than reviled black subject. In the earlier scene, King felt silenced, annihilated by the dead black body and the leering white looks; he wanted to cry but couldn't. Here, by contrast, he is blown wide open by love, and he can't *help* but cry—freely, gloriously—before returning the gift of the audience's love with his own inspired playing. Again, bell hooks: "When we are wounded in the place where we would know love, it is difficult to imagine that love really has the power to change everything." In this extraordinary pair of scenes, King mindfully reenters the disgust, disgrace, and rage that lynching engendered in him, but he also opens his heart to love, receiving it and reciprocating it across a color line that blues music seems temporarily to have liquidated. The result, as hooks prophesies, is that he thrives onstage "as if born again." He offers us a striking example of the way in which blues communities, under the right circumstances, can embody the ideals of Martin Luther King's beloved community, healing old wounds and enlivening our social imaginations.

King's example returns us to the paradox that the blues, the soundtrack of segregation and the witness to racial violence, has in our own day become the instrument through which so many are pursuing the project of racial healing. Blues performers, blues writers, and blues-based activists challenge us to throw off our reflexive cynicism and unconscious despair about American race relations. They ask us not merely to groove to the music and celebrate its makers, but to respond to the music's call in a way that serves both *philia* and *agape*. Bebe Moore Campbell's vision of contemporary white investments in the blues, a vision in which "your blues ain't like mine," is one possible articulation of where we are these days, and it has its merits. The blues do live on in black communities, not just as music but as age-old disparities between white and black, in ways that demand articulation and redress. But there are other blues-based visions at large in the new millennium that deserve our attention, too. bell hooks offers a useful guideline drawn from her own therapeutic journey that might be enlarged into a national imperative: if we're serious about healing old wounds and moving on, we don't need to forget about the past, but we do need to let it live inside us in a new way. Slavery and segregation did happen: the blues bear deep and eloquent testimony to that history, as do continuing socioeconomic inequalities and attitudinal divergences that parse along racial lines. If we party down with B.B. King and think that's enough to salve our uneasy consciences, we're making a mistake. But the blues also challenge us to push beyond the traumatic histories that helped generate them—to keep on moving down the road, looking for love, extending ourselves in the direction of beloved community, singing the song we were put here to sing. That, with luck, is how healing begins.

NOTES

1. The claim that Mississippi is the home of the blues is made, for example, by the Delta Blues Museum in Clarksdale, http://www.deltabluesmuseum.org/index.cfm?page=AboutTheDelta&subID=22, and by Ted Ownby in "Jimmie Rodgers: The Father of Country Music," *Mississippi History Now*, an online publication of the Mississippi Historical Society, http://mshistory.k12.ms.us/fea

tures/feature54/rodgers.htm. Danny Barker, *A Life in Jazz*, ed. Alyn Shipton (Macmillan, 1986), 71.

2. The Blues Highway Association and the Mississippi Blues Commission (http://www.blueshighway.org/synergies.htm) currently orchestrate and oversee much of this activity. For more on the subject of blues and economic development, see Stephen A. King, "Blues Tourism in the Mississippi Delta: The Functions of Blues Festivals," *Popular Music and Society* 27.4 (December 2004): 455–76.

3. Arnold Lindsay, "Radio Network Owner Recognized," (Jackson, Miss.) *Clarion-Ledger*, 18 September 2003, http://www.clarionledger.com/news/03 09/18/b04.html.

4. B.B. King Museum and Delta Interpretive Center, http://www.bbking museum.org/html-site/the-museum-mission.html.

5. David Grazian, *Blue Chicago: The Search for Authenticity in Urban Blues Culture* (University of Chicago Press, 2003); Vincent B. Leitch, "Blues Southwestern Style," *Theory Matters* (Routledge, 2003), 137–64. I describe my journey into New York's blues scene—clubs and streets, downtown and Harlem—in *Mister Satan's Apprentice: A Blues Memoir* (Pantheon Books, 1998).

6. Music Maker Relief Foundation, http://www.musicmaker.org/mission.html.

7. Blues for Peace, http://www.bluesforpeace.com/, http://www.cafepress.com/bluesforpeace.

8. Martin Luther King Jr., "Remaining Awake through a Great Revolution," a sermon delivered at the National Cathedral, Washington, on 31 March 1968, http://www.stanford.edu/group/King/publications/sermons/680331.000_Remaining_Awake.html; an earlier transposed version of this homiletic epigram appears in "Letter From Birmingham Jail" (1964). Martin Luther King, "Loving Your Enemies," *Strength to Love* (1963; rprt. Fortress Press, 1981), 52.

9. The fifth annual Childhood Cancer Lifeline Day and Blues Night took place on 19 March 2005, http://www.snocountry.com/article.php/20050226104549927; Rhino Entertainment, http://www.rhino.com/about/about_ourmission.lasso; "Blues For Katrina: A Benefit for Gulf Coast Hurricane Relief" took place on 25 September 2005 at Tom McCall Waterfront Park in Portland, Oregon; Safeway Waterfront Blues Festival, http://www.waterfrontbluesfest.com; Blues Bank Collective, http://www.bluesbankcollective.org/index.shtml.

10. bell hooks, Answers.com, http://www.answers.com/topic/bell-hooks; bell hooks, *All about Love: New Visions* (William Morrow, 2000), 209.

11. Ann Douglas, *Terrible Honesty: Mongrel Manhattan in the 1920s* (Farrar, Straux and Giroux, 1995), 401–2; David M. Oshinsky, *"Worse Than Slavery": Parchman Farm and the Ordeal of Jim Crow Justice* (The Free Press, 1996), 15.

12. David Honeyboy Edwards, *The World Don't Owe Me Nothing: The Life and Times of Bluesman Honeyboy Edwards*, as told to Janis Martinson and Michael

Robert Frank (Chicago Review Press, 1997), 77; B.B. King with David Ritz, *Blues All Around Me: The Autobiography of B.B. King* (1996; rprt. Avon Books, 1997), 88.

13. August Wilson, *Ma Rainey's Black Bottom* (Plume, 1985), 68, 70.

14. Roland L. Freeman, "Don't Forget the Blues," *Obsidian II: Black Literature in Review* 13.1 and 2 (Spring–Summer 1998/Fall–Winter 1998): 63–65.

15. BeBe Moore Campbell, *Your Blues Ain't Like Mine* (Ballantine Books, 1992), 408–10.

16. Stanley Crouch, *Don't the Moon Look Lonesome* (Pantheon Books, 2000), 238–41.

17. King, *Blues All Around Me*, 53–54.

18. Ibid., 242.

The Strange Career
of Atticus Finch

Joseph Crespino

Atticus Finch remains a touchstone figure of decency and respect. Gregory Peck's portrayal of the lawyer in the Universal Pictures adaptation of To Kill a Mockingbird *merited the cover of the Summer 2000 issue of* Southern Cultures. *Courtesy of the Museum of Modern Art Film Stills Archive.*

*C*ontemporary debates concerning race in America owe much to the 1960s when African Americans and other minority groups gained basic legal protections and rights of citizenship denied them in the century following Reconstruction. The current offspring of this movement is multiculturalism, a term that encompasses a range of progressive educational techniques, policy recommendations, and social movements that celebrate racial and ethnic differences and seek to empower people to pursue goals of personal and communal freedom. One of the basic questions raised in the 1960s that reverberates in multiculturalism today is who in our society is allowed to speak authoritatively on racial issues. Over the course of the twentieth century, but particularly with the flowering of African American studies, the era in which white intellectuals debated the "Negro problem" among themselves has ended once and for all. In countless cultural productions and scholarly works from the civil rights era and more recent decades, African Americans are the subjects in the exploration of racial inequality in American history and life. And yet looming among the most popular and enduring works on racial matters since the 1960s is Harper Lee's *To Kill a Mockingbird*, the Depression-era account of Atticus Finch's legal defense of a black man wrongly accused of raping a white woman, told through the eyes of Finch's nine-year-old daughter, Scout.

In the twentieth century, *To Kill a Mockingbird* is probably the most widely read book dealing with race in America, and its protagonist, Atticus Finch, the most enduring fictional image of racial heroism. Published in the fall of 1960, the novel had already sold five hundred thousand copies and been translated into ten languages by the time it received the Pulitzer Prize in 1961. The story was almost immediately snatched up by Hollywood, and the Alan Pakula–directed film had the double distinction of landing Gregory Peck an Oscar for his portrayal of Finch and giving Robert Duvall, with a brief role as the mysterious Boo Radley, the first of his seemingly countless screen appearances. It is estimated that by 1982 *To Kill a Mockingbird* had sold over fifteen million copies, and a 1991 American "Survey of Lifetime Reading Habits" by the Book-of-the-Month Club and the Library of Congress revealed that next to the Bible the book was "most often cited in making a difference" in people's lives.[1]

The novel influenced a generation of Americans raised during the turbulent years of the 1960s and 1970s. Former Clinton adviser James Carville, who spent his formative years in the 1960s South, reflected on

Harper Lee's achievement: "I just knew, the minute I read it, that she was right and I had been wrong. I don't want to make it noble, or anything. I was just bored with all the talk of race." Evidence of the novel's continuing influence on rising generations can be found on the Internet, where dozens of high school and college chat groups discuss the adventures of the Finch children or debate the meaning of the Radley neighbors. Atticus Finch himself remains a touchstone figure of decency and respect. In the recent Democratic primary campaign in New Hampshire, Bill Bradley, in an effort to appear above ordinary political wrangling, posed in a rocking chair on the set of a theatrical production of *To Kill a Mockingbird*; one of his speech writers told reporters later that Bradley had been in his best "Atticus Finch" mode. Given this legacy, the dearth of critical commentary on the novel is surprising. Literary critic Eric Sundquist writes, "It is something of a mystery that the book has failed to arouse the antagonism now often prompted by another great novelistic depiction of the South . . . *Adventures of Huckleberry Finn*, which arguably uses the word nigger with more conscious irony than does *To Kill a Mockingbird* and whose antebellum framework and moral complexity ought to be a far greater bulwark against revisionist denunciation."[2] A critique as basic as noting Atticus Finch's paternalism did not emerge until recently, and even then such a reading has been contested by Finch defenders.

The enduring career of *To Kill a Mockingbird* as a story of racial justice, and of Atticus Finch as a racial hero, reveals much about American racial politics in the second half of the twentieth century. From 1960s liberalism to 1990s multiculturalism, from the inchoate conservatism of Goldwater through that of the Reagan-Bush era, Atticus Finch has been both admired and scorned by liberals and conservatives alike. Tracing Atticus's place within the American imagination reveals some of the major fault lines in the struggle for racial equality over the past forty years and allows us to look again at how competing groups have framed racial issues in America.

ATTICUS FINCH AND THE LIBERAL CONSENSUS

The early success of *To Kill a Mockingbird* and Atticus Finch's warm reception can be explained in part by the way Finch embodies what historians have called the "liberal consensus" of mid-twentieth-century America. With the defeat of the Depression at home and fascism abroad, postwar Americans were confident that democracy and western capitalism could answer basic questions of material need and class inequality that plagued the nation in prior decades. Among American historians, the generational change away from the concerns of Progressive historians, who emphasized conflict and inequality in American history, to the new focus on the "liberal tradition" reflected this consensus. Consensus historians described an adventurous but fundamentally conservative America in which liberalism marked the continuity between past and present.[3]

By the time of *To Kill a Mockingbird*'s publication, civil rights had become an important part of the liberal consensus. The decades stretching from 1935, the year in which the novel was set, to 1960, the year in which it was published, witnessed several important modernizing trends that shaped the world in which Harper Lee wrote her first and only novel. By 1935 industrial expansion in northern cities, along with reduction in foreign immigration, had attracted a significant number of African Americans from rural areas of the South. This migration would expand in the years following World War II so that by 1960 as many African Americans lived outside the South as within it. Liberated from southern disenfranchisement, progressive, urban African Americans demanded that America address questions of racial inequality. African American representatives elected from these urban areas drew Congressional attention to racial issues, and legal battles in the Supreme Court laid the groundwork for later, more far-reaching decisions such as *Brown v. Board of Education*. With northern African Americans focusing attention on the South, northern whites could not continue to ignore the transgressions of southern segregation. The Scottsboro trial of the 1930s and the murder of Emmett Till in 1955 became *causes célèbres* that focused attention on southern discrimination. Undoubtedly, the Scottsboro trial's false accusations of rape influenced Harper Lee's depiction of Tom Robinson's trial.

Liberal trends within the American academy gave new attention to issues of race. In the 1930s and 1940s, southern racism was the focus of several prominent works echoed in Harper Lee's novel. Studies such as Charles Johnson's *Shadow of the Plantation* (1934), John Dollard's *Caste and Class in a Southern Town* (1937), and W. J. Cash's *The Mind of the South* (1941) exposed the indignities of southern racism. The most influential contribution to racial liberalism was Gunnar Myrdal's *An American Dilemma* (1944). An instant classic, Myrdal's 1,500-page study argued that the discrepancy between the egalitarian impulse of the "American Creed" and the oppressive treatment of African Americans presented a troubling dilemma for white America. Myrdal offered hope for an end to discrimination and predicted that the democratic rhetoric following World War II and the convergence of other social trends would force "fundamental changes in American race relations."[4]

The Cold War also held important implications for the rise of American racial liberalism. By the end of World War II, the United States emerged as capitalism's primary defender in the fight against Soviet Communism. As the two superpowers competed for influence in the decolonizing areas of the globe, the rhetoric of American democratic liberalism became an important ideological weapon in the battle against what Americans saw as a repressive totalitarian state. The continued presence of legalized racial discrimination in the South was, of course, the glaring contradiction to American egalitarian rhetoric. The geopolitical demands of international diplomacy necessitated that the country incorporate the South into the American ideal by eradicating all vestiges of southern segregation.[5]

Much of the American South was insulated from these liberal trends, yet there were a small number of southerners influenced by the dominant intellectual developments of the day. Harper Lee was among this tiny minority of southern liberals in the 1950s South. A native of Monroeville, Alabama, which became the inspiration for the novel's fictional town of Maycomb, Lee attended a small women's college in Montgomery, Alabama, and later transferred to the University of Alabama where she completed her undergraduate studies and, in 1947, enrolled in law school. In October 1946, she contributed a one-act play to a university humor magazine satirizing a fundamentalist, racist politician of the kind who came to dominate southern political rhetoric in the age of massive resistance: "Our very lives are being threatened by the hordes of evildoers full of sin . . . SIN, my friends . . . who want to tear down all barriers of any kind between ourselves and our colored friends." In the February 1947 issue she parodied country newspapers by creating the fictional *Jacksassonian Democrat*, whose logo included two white-sheeted figures carrying burning crosses. Lee's budding liberalism undoubtedly grew after she moved to New York, where she was active in the city's literary circles along with fellow aspiring writer and childhood friend, Truman Capote.[6]

Lee's characters and choice of narrative strategies in *To Kill a Mockingbird* reflect the moral tensions that all liberals faced in the Jim Crow South. They combine the passion and ambivalence characteristic of southerners drawn to the South's agrarian tradition and heritage but frustrated by the South's ugly racial history. Lee places Atticus Finch within the tradition of southern progressivism by linking him with the turn-of-the-century New South booster Henry Grady. Atticus advises Jem to read the speeches of Grady, who, if not a believer in the absolute equality of the races, was enough of a racial progressive to be despised by many white southerners of his day. Lee's political consciousness was formed during a period when the Georgia novelist Lillian Smith emerged as the most acerbic and out-spoken liberal southerner. Smith's nonfiction work *Killers of the Dream* (1949) explored the deleterious effects of segregation on children and, like antilynching reformer Jessie Daniel Ames, exposed the links between racial and gender inequality.

Critical of the "paternalism" of liberals and their confusion of "the public rights of men with their private right to control their own personal relationships," Smith was deeply committed to the liberal vision of racial change. She could well have been describing Atticus Finch when she wrote of liberals, "They are the carriers of the dream. They will make the future, or the human being will have none. For they and only they have held on to a belief that man is more than his institutions. It is they who refuse to let him become a slave to his own logic; who know that though he is his own end he never arrives there. And it is they who value his life." Smith believed that racism was a moral and logical aberration, the glaring contradiction to the American egalitarian spirit. Optimistic that the South "can change quickly if given convincing reasons," she was confident that liberalism would provide them.[7]

Smith and Lee shared similar visions of the southern racial landscape and its prospects for social change. Lee sardonically critiqued southern white womanhood through Scout's unwitting observations of the wom-en's missionary circle, who discuss over tea the horrible plight of the Mruna tribe in Africa while remaining blind to the racial injustice in their own community. Similarly, Smith condemned southern white women who willingly participated in a society that glorified white womanhood at the expense of African Americans. Both writers shared similar limitations as well. Tom Robinson is sweetly innocent and naïve; Atticus feels a moral responsibility to defend him, as the novel's title attests, because a black man accused in the Jim Crow South was as helpless as a mocking-bird. In the same way, Smith saw African Americans as innocent and helpless victims of rabid racism. Smith wrote that African Americans "were brought into our backyards and left there for generations"; she never conceived an active role for African Americans either in the cre-ation of the modern South or in the abolition of racial segregation.[8] Lee and Smith imagined a form of racial change that would occur through the leadership of people like Atticus Finch—in other words, through elite southern white liberals.

Though these limitations may seem obvious to readers today, if the northern press recognized *To Kill a Mockingbird*'s paternalism they did not note it in their reviews. The book received widespread critical acclaim; reviewers praised the novel's liberal racial politics. The *New York Times* called the book a "level-headed plea for interracial understanding" and singled out Atticus Finch as "a highly esteemed lawyer and legislator and the embodiment of fearless integrity, magnanimity and common sense." *Harper's* called Atticus Finch "an old-fashioned 'hero' if there ever was one," adding that "Miss Lee has written a first novel which will satisfy all those . . . who are interested in the problems of the South to which there are no easy solutions." While reviews in the *Saturday Review* and the *Atlantic Monthly* noted Lee's evident difficulty in telling a complex story while maintaining the narrative voice of a child, they praised Atticus Finch's "determination as a lawyer, liberal, and honest man, to defend a Negro accused of raping a white girl." The *Review* wrote that Lee's "insight into Southern mores is impressive, and in Atticus she has done a notable portrait of a Southern liberal."[9]

Reviews of the 1962 film version of the novel were similarly laudatory. The *New York Times*, though disappointed that the film did not capture more fully the range of emotions experienced by Scout and Jem, praised the role of Atticus, "played superbly by Gregory Peck." *Variety* called the film "a significant, captivating and memorable picture that ranks with the best of recent years." Peck's performance stood out in particular, especially for the *Variety* reviewer who praised his powers of transformation: "For Peck, it is an especially challenging role, requiring him to conceal his natural physical attractiveness yet project through a veneer of civilized restraint and resigned, rational compromise the fires of social indignation and humanitarian concern that burn within the character." Clearly, the transition from page to film did not dim Atticus's liberal charm.[10]

The lone negative review appeared several months after the novel received the Pulitzer Prize. Elizabeth Lee Haselden remained unimpressed with the novel on the grounds that it failed to offer characters with which the reader could identify. She noted Atticus Finch's "Olympian wisdom and calm" and argued that the novel "depicts on the part of no one involved in the trial any inner struggle for an ethical answer to injustice, and is lacking in real compassion for people." Haselden believed the book presented "character types" rather than real people with real struggles and suggested this quality as an explanation for the novel's success. "Acclaiming the merits of the book's theme, keeping the book on the bestseller list, soothes the public conscience," wrote Haselden. "Thus the reader can witness to his concern about injustice-in-general, in some removed place, at a distant time, without feeling any personal sense of guilt or involvement in the extensions of injustice into our own time and place." Haselden reveals the curious manner in which the novel succeeded in reducing complicated matters of regional difference, racial inequality, and social justice to simple moral tales of right versus wrong. Furthermore, her review provides evidence that at least one of the more perspicacious commentators of the early 1960s recognized the novel's place within the contemporary political moment. The very qualities that stretched Haselden's belief, such as Atticus's "Olympian calm," were the characteristics that liberal America embraced. Liberalism held that southern racism was an obvious blight on the nation's conscience and should be fought with the level-headedness, moral equanimity, and common sense exemplified by Atticus Finch.[11]

Atticus's liberal pedigree comes through most clearly in his concern for his children. In a conversation with his brother, Atticus worries about the effect Tom Robinson's trial and Maycomb's racism will have on Jem and Scout. "You know what's going to happen as well as I do, Jack, and I hope and pray I can get Jem and Scout through it without bitterness, and most of all, without catching Maycomb's usual disease. Why reasonable people go stark raving mad when anything involving a Negro comes up, is something I don't pretend to understand. . . . I just hope that Jem and Scout come to me for their answers instead of listening to the town. I hope they trust me enough."[12] Atticus's puzzling over why people go "mad" and his concern with "Maycomb's usual disease" foreshadows the following scene in which Jem and Scout watch from the porch as their father shoots and kills a mad dog running loose on the street in front of the Finch home. The dog seems a likely symbol of white racism in the South. Up to this point, Scout and Jim think of their father as "feeble" because he was "nearly fifty" and did not play in the church football games. By shooting the dog, Atticus confirms his virility both as a father protecting his children and as a southern liberal dealing with white racism.

It is significant that Calpurnia, the Finches' domestic servant and the lone African American in the scene, is the one who alerts Atticus to the dog's presence and warns the all-white neighborhood to stay off the streets. In Calpurnia, Lee recognizes the role African Americans played in exposing white racism; through her Lee acknowledges the working-class African American civil rights protestors in the South who revealed the ugly face of Jim Crow to liberal America. While Lee does not entirely deny African Americans a place in the destruction of southern racism, in this scene their role is limited to that of warning the liberal white hero of the danger to come. As Finch bravely stops the mad dog in his tracks, Calpurnia watches on the porch with the children. It is also significant that Heck Tate, the Maycomb County sheriff, arrives with Atticus to stop the dog. Finch expects Sheriff Tate to shoot the dog, but the sheriff hesitates and then anxiously hands the gun to Finch: "For God's sake, Mr. Finch, look where he is! . . . I can't shoot that well and you know it!"[13] Atticus, a crack shot as everyone in town but his children knows, finishes the responsibility. The figure of Heck Tate in this scene may well refer to the elected officials of the South, such as Arkansas governor Orval Faubus in Little Rock, who through fear, incompetence, or narrow-mindedness were unable to face down the mad dog of southern racism. Only Atticus possesses the skill and courage to put the rabid dog to rest.

Lee's vision of liberal racial change remained distinctly regional; Atticus Finch is not a wild-eyed reformer who rejects his southern heritage. Lee believed that racial change would come through liberalism refined by a certain understanding of how the world works—particularly how white southerners work when it comes to the explosive issue of race. When Jem, frustrated by Tom Robinson's conviction, suggests doing away with all juries, Atticus stops him. "Those are twelve reasonable men in everyday life, Tom's jury, but you saw something come between them and reason," Atticus tells Jem. "The one place where a man ought to get a square deal is in a courtroom, be he any color of the rainbow, but people have a way of carrying their resentments right into a jury box."[14] Atticus understands that America's historic claim to justice and equality could not be realized without racial justice in the South, but he recognizes as well the extreme difficulties involved, given the prejudices of his region.

Similarly, Scout's precocious literacy becomes a symbol of southern liberals' competence in dealing with racism. At Scout's first day of school she encounters a recent college graduate schooled in what Jem mistakenly calls "the Dewey Decimal system," Lee's reference it seems to pedagogical techniques developed by the northern, progressive educator John Dewey. In the first half of the twentieth century, Dewey had become one of the most prominent liberal members of the American academy. Lee's indirect reference to him here encapsulates her vision of the relationship between northern and southern liberalism. Scout does not need the new, "improved" pedagogical techniques of the young teacher; she knows how to read already. She was taught by her father, Atticus, the model of southern erudition. Scout's literacy here is a symbol of the South's ability to analyze its own problems, to deal with them in its own regionally specific way.

Part of Atticus Finch's heroic power lies in his ability to embrace the need and the moral imperative for racial change without rejecting his native South. He reminds Scout that though this time they were not fighting against "the Yankees, we're fighting our friends," she should hold no grudges because "no matter how bitter things get, they're still our friends and this is still our home." But in this scene Lee comforts white southerners fearful of the change that was imminent in the South. As Eric Sundquist writes, "Just as the South closed ranks against the nation at the outset of desegregation . . . so *To Kill a Mockingbird* carefully narrows the terms on which changed race relations are going to be brought about in the South." Through Atticus Finch, Lee reassured anxious white southerners that civil rights change could come to the South peacefully, without bitterness, and without dividing the white southern community. After all, the southern liberals leading the change were longtime friends and neighbors; they were, first and foremost, southerners.[15]

At the same time, for readers North and South who admired the book's racial mores, Atticus represented the continuity of American values of justice and equality. The novel tells us that even in the Depression-era Jim Crow South, the era of Scottsboro and Bilbo, there existed within the South men like Atticus Finch who would be the seeds of the transformation to come. Atticus is a modern hero who, while embodying the most noble aspects of the southern tradition, also transcended the limits of that tradition and attained a liberal, morally rational racial viewpoint that was seen as quintessentially American.

Above all, Atticus's morality drives the novel, a morality that is as evident in *To Kill a Mockingbird* as it is in one of American liberalism's signature documents, the Supreme Court's majority decision in *Brown v. Board of Education* (1954). Earl Warren's decision resonated with moral authority: "Such considerations apply with added force to children in grade and high schools. To separate them from others of similar age and qualifications solely because of their race generates a feeling of inferiority as to their status in the community that may affect their hearts and minds in a way unlikely ever to be undone." In *To Kill a Mockingbird* Lee's decision to report Atticus's heroics through the perspective of his nine-year-old daughter is crucial in reinforcing the moral impulse that it is children who ultimately have the most at risk in the nation's struggle to end racial segregation. The project was to be carried out by good liberals like Atticus, but even then it was most effective because it was backed by the moral weight of a child's voice. This is the meaning of one of the novel's most famous scenes, in which Scout faces down a lynch mob that is ready to lynch Tom Robinson. As Sundquist writes, scenes such as this "are calculated to substantiate the ethical authority driving *Brown*."[16]

ATTICUS FINCH IN THE AMERICAN RACIAL IMAGINATION

While *To Kill a Mockingbird* shows American racial liberalism in full flower, by the close of the 1960s the liberal assumptions of racial change had come under serious attack. With the signing of the 1964 Civil Rights Act and the 1965 Voting Rights Act, the last vestiges of southern segregation were legally destroyed and the civil rights movement moved north. Incidents of racial violence in Chicago suburbs and urban uprisings, like those in Los Angeles, Detroit, and Newark, exposed the fallacy that racism was the South's problem. At the 1964 Democratic National Convention, a committee headed by soon-to-be Vice-President Hubert Humphrey granted convention credentials to the traditional, all-white Mississippi state delegation over the racially integrated Mississippi Freedom Democratic Party. Leaders of the Black Power movement would later point to this incident as exposing the essential bankruptcy of American liberalism.

Social movements such as Black Power were the American version of a larger global moment in which the basic tenets of modernist development came under attack. Black Power advocates identified with decolonization movements around the globe, and throughout the 1960s they mounted a devastating attack on American racial liberalism. In the classic statement of the movement, *Black Power: The Politics of Liberation in America* (1967), Stokely Carmichael (who has since changed his name to Kwame Ture) and Charles V. Hamilton exposed the impotence of American racial liberalism in winning meaningful change for the vast majority of African Americans. They most likely had in mind as the object of their attack the most prominent southern liberal of their day, Lyndon Johnson, though their criticisms could be applied with equal force to Harper Lee's fictional southern lawyer. *Black Power* asked, "How fully can white people free themselves from the tug of the group position—free themselves not so much from overt racist attitudes in themselves as from a more subtle paternalism bred into them by the society, and perhaps more important, from the conditioned reaction of black people to their whiteness?"[17] *To Kill a Mockingbird* provided a classic scene of just this kind of black deference. The setting was the Maycomb County courtroom; as Atticus Finch passes below them, the segregated, all-black balcony stands in recognition of Atticus's efforts in defending Tom Robinson.

Black Power also questioned liberalism's assumption of American moral rectitude and its fundamentally bourgeois character. Invoking Myrdal, Carmichael and Hamilton wrote, "There is no 'American dilemma,' no moral hang-up . . . Black people should not base decisions on the assumption that a dilemma exists." The liberalism represented by Atticus Finch viewed integration as ultimate goal for the races, yet Black Power questioned whether such a goal could ever provide equality for a black minority: "The goal of black people must not be to assimilate into middle-class America, for the values of the middle class permit the perpetuation of the ravages of the black community. That class mouths its preference for a free, competitive society, while at the same time forcefully and even viciously denying to black people as a group the opportunity to compete."[18]

Atticus's elite class position within the small southern town of Maycomb is an essential part of his heroism. Atticus is a paternal figure not only for blacks but poor whites as well. In a telling passage, Jem explains to his sister Maycomb's four different classes: "There's four kinds of folks in the world. There's the ordinary kind like us and the neighbors, there's the kind like the Cunninghams out in the woods, the kind like the Ewells down at the dump, and the Negroes." While Scout denies these distinctions, she lives in a world clearly divided along class lines. Atticus explains to Jem, "You and Jean Louise . . . are not from run-of-the-mill people . . . you are the product of several generations' gentle breeding . . . and you should try to live up to your name." Though they are both members of the white working class, the novel distinguishes between the Cunninghams and the Ewells based on the degree to which they aspire to bourgeois values—the degree to which they accommodate themselves to the hegemony of the dominant class. The young Walter Cunningham goes hungry rather than borrow money from the teacher that he knows he cannot pay back. Mr. Cunningham diligently pays back his legal debt to Atticus Finch through subsistence crops from his farm. Although Mr. Cunningham is a member of Tom Robinson's potential lynch mob, he politely retreats when faced by Scout's authentic moral presence. In contrast, the Ewells place no value on education, showing up the first day and never coming to school again. Mr. Ewell breaks the law by hunting out of season, and Mayella Ewell breaks the fundamental code of middle-class southern womanhood by desiring the black body of Tom Robinson.[19]

In the context of Black Power politics, one of the book's peripheral characters—Lula, the black-separatist member of Calpurnia's church—becomes one of its most interesting. Lula challenges Calpurnia for bringing the Finch children to worship at the black church: "You ain't got no business bringin' white chillun here—they got their church, we got our'n. It is our church, ain't it, Miss Cal?" Lula reminds Cal that she is a servant to the Finches, not an equal: "Yeah, an' I reckon you's company at the Finch house durin' the week." Calpurnia verbally spars with Lula in front of the church, reverting to an African American dialect that the children had never heard from her before. Lula mysteriously disappears from the scene, and the rest of the church comforts the children, telling them they should ignore Lula: "She's a troublemaker from way back, got fancy ideas an' haughty ways—we're mighty glad to have you all." Lee uses this scene to reveal her expectations for what the proper African American response to the white presence should be. Lula objects to both the white children's freedom to enter the black world and the inordinate respect they receive once they are there. Lula's position in relation to Calpurnia reproduces Black Power's position toward African American liberals during the civil rights era. Lee removes all doubt as to which model white America prefers; as one critic observes, "Lee makes it clear that people like Lula are not what is expected in the Blacks who hope to be protected by the white law."[20]

Despite its cogent critique of liberalism, Black Power failed to mount an enduring political movement that could advance African American interests. Government repression, accusations of reverse racism, and internal conflicts over issues such as sexism undoubtedly played a part in this failure. The breakup of American liberalism in the late 1960s made room for the American right to maneuver into cultural and political dominance. One example of this in racial politics was the conservative shift in the Supreme Court that led to decisions that pulled back from earlier liberal mandates. In the *Bakke* case the Court limited the reach of affirmative-action programs, and, in combination with other decisions, the Justices greatly qualified liberal commitments made in the previous decade. By the time of Ronald Reagan's election in 1980, American racial liberalism could hardly be heard from in an American political and cultural arena dominated by conservative voices. In the 1990s, Bill Clinton's record remained mixed. While his presidential commission on race generated discussions of race in American life at the highest levels of government, his administration triangulated not so much between the right and left as the right and center; the welfare bill he signed into law stands as one of conservatism's greatest victories over 1960s liberalism.

Although *To Kill a Mockingbird* has maintained its popularity as a modern-day race tale, in the aftermath of Black Power and with conservative ascendancy, both liberals and conservatives have become markedly more ambivalent in their views of Atticus Finch as an American racial hero. Certain school districts across the country have censored the novel for its sexual content, and more recently some have banned it because of its depiction of societal racism.[21] *To Kill a Mockingbird* has increasingly become a battleground where cultural critics from the left and right debate their respective views of contemporary racial politics. For example, a 1992 debate among legal scholars amounted to a public trial of Atticus Finch. Monroe Freedman, a law professor at Hofstra University, wrote an article in *Legal Times* titled "Atticus Finch, Esq., R.I.P." that questioned Finch's role as a model of humanity and morality for the legal profession. Freedman argued that as a state legislator and community leader in a segregated society, Finch was the "passive participant in that pervasive injustice." Freedman would extend his comments later in a symposium at the University of Alabama: "Throughout his relatively comfortable and pleasant life in Maycomb, Atticus Finch knows about the grinding, ever-present humiliation and degradation of the black people of Maycomb; he tolerates it; and sometimes he even trivializes and condones it."[22] Freedman de-emphasizes the personal heroism of Finch to focus on the larger structural racism of which he was a part and which, in Freedman's estimation, he did little to combat.

Freedman's critique appalled many of his colleagues. One legal commentator attacked Freedman personally, pointing out the violence, abuse, and crime of Freedman's own hometown of New York and asking why he wasn't "putting [his] butt on the line for these people instead of criticizing Atticus Finch, who did put his butt on the line for an innocent black man."[23] In his eagerness to challenge notions of legal ethics, Freedman does ignore Finch's more commendable character traits, but the public outcry against his article suggests that something more was involved.

Many who objected argued that Freedman ignored Finch's individual act of racial heroism and its power to inspire similar acts today. In an article revealingly titled "Atticus Finch *De Novo*: In Defense of Gentlemen," Timothy J. Dunn charged that Freedman underestimated "the value to the human spirit of acts of heroic value." No less an authority than the president of the American Bar Association, Talbot D'Alemberte, rose in defense of Finch. "Sixty years after Judge Taylor appointed Atticus Finch to defend a poor black man in *To Kill a Mockingbird*, these . . . fictional heroes still inspire us," wrote D'Alemberte. "Finch rose above racism and injustice to defend the principle that all men and women deserve their day in court."[24]

Dunn and D'Alemberte defended Atticus Finch not just as a man ahead of his times, but as a model of decorum in the very sensitive arena of race relations. Yet their defense did not take into account the many differences between Atticus's era and the present. As Freedman pointed out, Atticus Finch acted heroically in 1930s segregated Alabama, but to a modern reader the limits of his heroism should be fairly evident. Racism today does not always rear its head in such blatant and perverse forms as it did in Depression-era Alabama. Even unreconstructed liberals, however, would admit that the discrimination of the Jim Crow South that American liberalism defeated in the 1950s and early 1960s did not end racism in America. Carmichael and Hamilton warned of liberal blindness to institutional racism, which "is less overt, far more subtle, less identifiable in terms of specific individuals committing the acts. But it is no less destructive of human life."[25] At its core, the debate is over the nature of the racism at work in the post–civil rights era. If institutional racism survived the civil rights struggles of the mid-1960s, as the Black Power movement maintained, to what degree does holding up the model of Atticus Finch as racial hero obscure structural forms of racial discrimination?

Of course, one need not look in legal journals to find contemporary defenses of Atticus Finch. White lawyers who buck racial hostility and heroically defend African Americans have become one of Hollywood's stock figures. Films such as *Mississippi Burning* (1988), *Ghosts of Mississippi* (1996), and John Grisham's *A Time to Kill* (1996) present updated versions of Atticus Finch–style white racial heroism. Mindlessly following in the tradition of earlier courtroom racial blockbusters, *Ghosts of Mississippi* is largely about white assistant district attorney Bobby DeLaughter's fight to reopen the Medgar Evers's assassination case. The movie is based on a book of the same name by Maryanne Vollers that focuses much more clearly on Evers's life and work (DeLaughter is not mentioned until the twenty-second chapter). But *Ghosts of Mississippi* is more than another example in a long line of films that fail to do justice to a companion book. Its decision to place Bobby DeLaughter rather than Medgar Evers at the narrative center of the story is an affront to those who have struggled and continue to struggle to serve as the subject of their own narratives of liberation. As *Variety* reviewer Godfrey Cheshire wrote of *Ghosts of Mississippi*, "When future generations turn to this era's movies for an account of the struggles for racial justice in America, they'll learn the surprising lesson that such battles were fought by square-jawed white guys."[26]

This is the strangeness of Atticus Finch's career: once a tool of liberal racial politics, Atticus has now become the pawn of racial conservatism. The right, in its insistence on focusing on racial bias on the personal level, glorifies Atticus Finch–style racial heroism. If racism exists only on an individual basis, then racial reform can occur only through individual moral reform—not through social or structural change that might challenge the legal, economic, or political status quo. As conservatives beatify the racial heroism of Atticus Finch, they fight the symptoms of the disease and fail to look for a cure that might get at the issue of white privilege.

How is it in a multicultural America that Atticus Finch and his various cinematic progeny continue to be held up as racial heroes? One explanation is that having a white racial hero at the center of the story allows the public to conceptualize race issues within an individual, moralistic framework. Movies traffic in stereotypes: racist rednecks, innocent black victims, white liberal heroes. Unfortunately, so do American politicians. White people solving the "American Dilemma" was the fundamental assumption of postwar racial liberalism; today application of the same principle underlies claims of reverse racism and forms the basis for conservative opposition to affirmative action and declarations of "the end of racism." Ultimately, it is the belief that even though racism exists it cannot last because it is an aberration from American ideals of equality. Freedman's critique highlighted the structural racism of segregation-era Alabama but failed to link Finch to the obfuscation of white privilege that persists in America today. It should come as no surprise that when we place Atticus Finch under the lens of contemporary multicultural politics, we see the same symptoms that Black Power initially diagnosed in the sickness of American liberalism—a paternalistic and hopelessly moderated view of social change.

If multiculturalism is about racial and ethnic minority groups finding and using their own voices within American politics, there is also a segment of multiculturalism influenced by postmodern cultural critiques that objects to the idea of an essentialized, racial subject that is at the heart of minority group mobilization. Scholar and activist Cornell West has prevailed upon Americans concerned with issues of race, whatever race they may be, to deconstruct traditional American narratives of individual advancement and racial emancipation, particularly those which to this day persist with white males as their heroic protagonists. As West writes, "The new cultural criticism exposes and explodes the exclusions, blindnesses and silences of this past, calling from it racial libertarian and democratic projects that will create a better present and future."[27] The difficulty lies in realizing the practical political manifestation the new "libertarian and democratic projects" should take. How do they differ from the freedom movements of the 1960s? In West's case, with a personal charisma rooted in the oratorical traditions of the African American church, his activism is often hard to distinguish from that of the 1960s Southern Christian Leadership Conference.

The question of where Atticus Finch fits into this movement remains. My initial reaction is that the American social commentators who still invoke Atticus Finch's image, and the secondary school teachers who assign *To Kill a Mockingbird* in their classes year after year, should let Atticus come down from his perch as an emblem of American racial heroism. Harper Lee described her novel as "a simple love story"; while this element of the book cannot be separated from the novel's racial politics, one should not necessarily swim against the tide of Atticus's continuing popularity. This is a difficult thing to do because what one person sees as Finch's gentlemanly demeanor towards women another might characterize as sexist patronizing; what is decorum and self-restraint in racial matters to some may well seem small-minded and compromising to others.

My suggestion is that we reassign *To Kill a Mockingbird* from English class to history class and that rather than dismissing Atticus we deconstruct him. Certainly, we can no longer simply hold him up as a racial hero, for in a multicultural society that honors the dignity and agency of all people it is not clear what one would actually look like. But we can place Atticus alongside other members of the white liberal establishment, fictional and real, such as Lyndon Johnson, Gavin Stevens, Lillian Smith, Ralph McGill, and Gunnar Myrdal to name just a few. Like any good historian, we should historicize this group, celebrating their courage and success, lamenting the limits of their vision. We should teach students that racial liberalism played a part in ending a system of Jim Crow discrimination that had developed in the aftermath of emancipation; it also helped provide for equal political participation for African Americans, a phenomenon that, aside from a brief period during Reconstruction, this nation had never known. For all of its successes, however, the assumptions of American racial liberalism do not function well in contemporary America. The job for us today is to reconceptualize the problems of race by recognizing the continuing presence of white racial privilege and devising means of addressing it.

NOTES

The author would like to thank Joel Beinin, Barton Bernstein, George Fredrickson, Ted Ownby, Amy Robinson, and Eric Sundquist for their help in preparing this paper.

1. Claudia D. Johnson, *To Kill a Mockingbird: Threatening Boundaries* (Twayne Publishers, 1994), xiii–xiv.

2. Louis Menard, "Opening Moves," *New York Review of Books*, 2 December 1999, 4; Garry Wills, "From the Campaign Trail: Clinton's Hell-Raiser," *New Yorker*, 12 October 1992, 93; Eric Sundquist, "Blues for Atticus Finch," in ed. Larry J. Griffin and Don H. Doyle, *The South as an American Problem* (University of Georgia Press, 1995), 181–209.

3. John Higham, "The Cult of the 'American Consensus': Homogenizing Our History," *Commentary* 27 (January 1959): 93–100. For a fuller definition of the liberal consensus, see Godfrey Hodgson, *America in Our Time* (Vintage Books, 1978), 67–98; for an opposing view, see Gary Gerstle, "Race and the Myth of the Liberal Consensus," *Journal of American History* (September 1995): 579–86.

4. Gunnar Myrdal, *An American Dilemma: The Negro Problem and Modern Democracy* (Harper & Brothers, 1944), xix.

5. See Harvard Sitkoff, *The Struggle for Black Equality, 1954–1992* (Hill and Wang, 1993), 3–60, and Numan V. Bartley, *The New South, 1945–1980* (Louisiana State University Press, 1995), 38–73.

6. Johnson, *Threatening Boundaries*, xii.

7. Lillian Smith, *Killers of the Dream* (W. W. Norton, 1949), 244, 240.

8. Harper Lee, *To Kill a Mockingbird* (Warner Books, 1960), 227–37, 112.

9. *New York Times Book Review*, 10 July 1960, 5; *Harper's*, August 1960, 101; *Atlantic Monthly*, August 1960, 98; *Saturday Review*, 23 July 1960, 15.

10. *New York Times Film Reviews*, 15 February 1963, 3374; *Variety*, 12 December 1962, 6.

11. *Christian Century*, 24 May 1961, 655.

12. Lee, *Mockingbird*, 88.

13. Ibid., 96.

14. Ibid., 220.

15. Ibid., 76; Sundquist, "Blues for Atticus Finch," 194.

16. *Brown v. Board of Education of Topeka et al.*, 347 U.S. 494; Sundquist, "Blues for Atticus Finch," 189.

17. Stokely Carmichael and Charles V. Hamilton, *Black Power: The Politics of Liberation in America* (Vintage, 1967), 28.

18. Ibid., 77, 40.

19. Lee, *Mockingbird*, 229, 135–36.

20. Ibid., 119; Teresa Godwin Phelps, "The Margins of Maycomb: A Rereading of *To Kill a Mockingbird*," *Alabama Law Review* 45 (1994): 529.

21. Johnson, *Threatening Boundaries*, 14–17.

22. Monroe Freedman, "Atticus Finch, Esq., R.I.P.," *Legal Times*, 24 February 1992, 20; Monroe Freedman, "Atticus Finch: Right and Wrong," *Alabama Law Review* 45 (1994): 479.

23. R. Mason Barge, "Fictional Characters, Fictional Ethics," *Legal Times*, 9 March 1992, 23.

24. Timothy J. Dunn, "Atticus Finch *De Novo*: In Defense of Gentlemen," *New Jersey Law Journal*, 27 April 1992, 24; Talbot D'Alemberte, "Remembering Atticus Finch's *Pro Bono* Legacy," *Legal Times*, 6 April 1992, 26.

25. Carmichael and Hamilton, *Black Power*, 4.

26. *Variety*, 16 December 1996, 78.

27. Cornell West, "The New Cultural Politics of Difference," in ed. Steven Seidman, *The Postmodern Turn: New Perspectives on Social Theory* (Cambridge University Press, 1994), 79.

Rituals of Initiation and Rebellion
Adolescent Responses to Segregation in Southern Autobiography

Melton McLaurin

Race is a theme encountered in practically every account of growing up southern in the era of segregation. Farm Security Administration photograph of a tenant farmer's daughter, Greene County, Georgia, 1941, courtesy of the Southern Historical Collection, University of North Carolina at Chapel Hill.

*I*n Lillian Smith's *Our Faces, Our Words*, a young northern-born and -educated African American come south to join the civil rights movement reflects upon his experiences in the field with southern youths, black and white. Young southerners of both races, he realizes, have so much in common that at times he feels segregated from them. The foundation for this relationship between young southerners of both races, he concludes, is their shared memories. "These southerners are tied and tangled in a web of common memories they can't escape and don't want to escape," he writes. They are bound by memories of common foods, hot southern summers, and shared activities. A more insightful observation follows this eloquently expressed, if not original, concept: The South's residents, the young man notes, are also bound by "common hurts; each [race] hurt in a different way by that old barbed wire of segregation but both hurt. And they know it."[1] The virtual wellspring of southern autobiography published since the outbreak of the Second World War strikingly supports the validity of this young northern black's observation. Practically all these autobiographies explore to some extent the seemingly intractable problem of race, an exploration that the national social and intellectual climate of the time supported, especially when it was limited to the South.[2]

This outpouring of southern autobiography includes some excellent accounts of childhood and adolescence, and some of the best of these can be found in works devoted solely to the author's preadult life. These "childhoods" constitute a specialization within autobiographical literature, one already explored in considerable detail by literary scholars.[3] In addition, any number of southern autobiographies devoted primarily to the author's adult years nevertheless contain excellent material on his or her childhood. These sources provide invaluable insight into the manner in which young southerners, black and white, responded to issues of race in the era of segregation. Their responses in turn reveal the pervasive power of race in southern society. They explore the forces that made, and continue to make, meaningful change in the area of race relations so difficult and acknowledge that such change was, and remains, both desirable and possible.[4]

Although race is a theme encountered in practically every account of growing up southern in the era of segregation, a few white autobiographers almost manage to avoid the issue. Sometimes the author briefly mentions the topic before brushing it aside to get on with what he or she considers to be more important issues. Politicians, for example, do this rather frequently, sometimes totally ignoring personal relationships with blacks.[5] More often, however, race is either the dominant theme, or among the dominant themes, of southern autobiographical accounts of childhood, white and black. In these narratives, the authors tend to record two specific reactions to the problem of race relations within their society. The first is their initial awareness of race and its social significance. The second is their acceptance of their racial community's attitudes toward segregation and the racial views upon which it rested; white youths signaled their acceptance of segregation, black youths denounced it.

ACQUIRING AN AWARENESS OF RACE . . .
UNDERSTANDING ITS SIGNIFICANCE

In southern autobiography the remembrance of acquiring an *awareness* of race differs somewhat from the remembrance of acquiring an understanding of the *significance* of race in the life of the autobiographer. Black and white authors alike recall the moment of first understanding that the skin color of the people with whom they came in contact differed. This initial awareness of race took place at an early age, usually between four and six. African American autobiographers record an almost immediate understanding that this perceived difference in skin color carried a pointed significance for them: the ability of race to affect their lives directly and adversely. White authors, however, usually fail to see racial differences as something personally significant until much later, often during early adolescence.[6]

In Richard Wright's *Black Boy*, which has influenced practically all subsequent African American autobiography, Richard is aware of color before he is six. But he is not aware merely of differences in skin color. In a vague, almost intuitive way, he is also aware that whites present a possible threat to his well being. This point is clear in a scene in which a white policeman confronts Richard after he becomes lost while attempting to escape from an orphanage. A few months later, while waiting with his mother for a train to Arkansas, Richard becomes more fully aware of the significance of his color. In a classic scene, Wright recounts that during a previous visit to his Granny's, who was white, "a sense of the two races had been born in me with a sharp concreteness that would never leave me until I died." His observation of the white and colored ticket lines leads him to explore the significance of his color in a conversation with his mother, after which Richard, at six years of age, concludes that if whites tried to kill him, "then I would kill them first."[7]

Other accounts of childhood by black autobiographers, male and female, exhibit this same pattern. Anne Moody, in *Coming of Age in Mississippi*, recalls that as a very young child she played with white children with little consciousness of race. But at age seven when she tried to enter the Centreville, Mississippi, movie theater with her white playmates, her mother dragged her from the white section and roughly lectured her on the etiquette of race. After the movie incident, she writes, the white children ceased to play with her, and she understood that "not only were they better than me because they were white, but everything they owned and everything connected with them was better than what was available to me."[8] In her poignant record of a Durham, North Carolina, childhood of the 1940s, Mary Mebane recalls that she learned the significance of race from a minor incident that happened to her older brother. He was playing with a pretty cup, far prettier than the mayonnaise jars the Mebane family used, and Mary wanted it. She learns that a white lady had given the brother the cup because he had asked for a drink of water and she insisted that he keep the cup from which he drank. The incident awakens young Mary's understanding of race and segregation. "I knew," she writes "that it was something wrong."[9] In less dramatic fashion, Chalmers Archer Jr., in *Growing up Black in Rural Mississippi*, writes of his growing awareness of race: "I became aware of feelings of white animosity toward me, while I was still at an early age. I also gradually realized that the situation was a lot more serious than what we young folk were led to 'know' out on the Place. There existed much more than whites' negative attitudes. Whites took direct action against black people. . . . I became increasingly hungry—no, starved—to learn more about this thing between black and white people."[10]

Maya Angelou's memories of childhood encounters with the significance of race fill the first twenty-five pages of *I Know Why the Caged Bird Sings*. Angelou begins with a childhood fantasy of being a blond-haired, blue-eyed child in a beautiful Easter dress, which in reality was "a plain ugly cut-down from a white woman's once-was purple throwaway." The accounts that follow demonstrate how acutely aware was Angelou as a child of the restrictions race placed upon her and her family. This introduction to her life constitutes a litany of insults and threats by whites directed at Maya and the family members closest to her—her brother, uncle, and grandmother.[11]

Not surprisingly, white autobiographers, male and female, differ from black autobiographers in their treatment of the subject of racial awareness. Race was not an immediate concern for them; it was not a factor that in any way constrained, though it certainly impinged upon, their lives. As young children whites were aware of race but rarely thought much about its significance, either for themselves or for others within their family, or even for their acquaintances, white or black. In *Born in the Delta*, Margaret Jones Bolsterli, who was raised in Arkansas's Mississippi River delta in the 1940s, gives a rather typical account of a white child's perceptions of race. As a child Bolsterli plays with black children, who she realizes were different and in some vague way less important. She recalls catching crayfish with a black girl called Little Frankie, the daughter of one of her father's sharecroppers. When school starts, Little Frankie goes to a different school, and their separation is merely another fact of life, nothing that concerns Bolsterli. As a child Bolsterli talks with maids, tenants, and other black children, aware of and unthinkingly accepting their different color and inferior status. Her awareness of the significance of race comes only when she reaches adolescence. When she is thirteen, her father refuses a black tenant a loan to provide medical aid for the tenant's premature baby. When Bolsterli questions her father about his decision, he replies, "Why, honey, I never even heard of putting a niggra baby in an incubator." The following year a high school English teacher ventures the opinion that "blacks might be as competent as whites if they had the chance to prove it." These two incidents, which Bolsterli recalls almost as one, changed the manner in which she viewed race relations, and her father.[12]

Katharine Du Pre Lumpkin, in her classic *The Making of a Southerner*, presents a similar account. As a young child, she is instructed by her father about blacks, about their inferiority, their uppityness, even their threat to the virtue of white women. Yet Lumpkin connects little of this with the blacks she knows as servants, although she expects blacks to treat her with the deference due whites. At eight, she witnesses her father thrash a black cook for impudence, an event that makes her "fully aware of myself as white, and of Negroes as Negroes." But it is not until she is an adolescent, on a farm outside Columbia, that she begins to understand what being black means for those who are. There she watches blacks toil in the fields, hurrying to eat lest they lose an opportunity for some small reward, and gradually begins to comprehend that it is their color that relegates them to their position in society, just as it is her color that provides her position of privilege.[13] The autobiographies of white males also exhibit this pattern of recognition of racial differences. As a child Reynolds Price realizes that he is "different" from his black playmates but only begins to comprehend the significance of that difference as an adolescent contemplating the friendship between his father and a black handy man named Grant Terry.[14]

ADOLESCENT RESPONSES TO RACE

If blacks and whites differed in the manner in which they became aware of color and its significance, they also differed in the manner in which they responded to that awareness. A common theme in the autobiographies of white southerners is the adolescent's acceptance of segregation and the belief in the inferiority of blacks upon which that institution rested. Frequently, that acceptance is both acknowledged by the adolescent and signaled to others by the deliberate, public provocation of one or more blacks. In *Separate Pasts* I recall such an incident involving Sam McNeil, a retarded, harmless, middle-aged black man who lived on the outskirts of my village. Several boyhood friends and I taunted Sam with racial epithets, attempting to provoke his anger. It was a relatively mild incident of race baiting, as such incidents go, but it held enormous significance for me.[15]

Harry Crews recalls a similar incident in *A Childhood*, an account of growing up in the 1930s on a cotton farm in rural Georgia and perhaps the best white southern childhood yet written. Crews and his brother Hoyet play a prank on Willalee Bookatee, a black child their age who lived just down the road from the Crews's farm. Crews admits that he and Hoyet used Willalee "like a toy" as a "surefire cure for boredom." In the episode recalled, Harry and Hoyet march Willalee to the middle of a fenced field. Knowing that Willalee is deathly afraid of bulls, they announce that a bull will attack him unless he carries a citron (the fruit of a vine the weight and appearance of which can approximate that of a good-sized watermelon) to and across the nearest fence. They then take great delight in watching a terrified, tearful Willalee desperately struggle to pull a huge citron down a cotton row to the fence in order to escape the imaginary bull.[16]

Robert Houston describes a more vicious version of this game in an essay in an issue of *Southern Exposure* devoted exclusively to the subject of childhood in the South. Titled "Nigger Knocking," the article describes the Sunday night exploits of white male members of a Methodist Youth Fellowship (MYF) in Birmingham. After the church service, MYFers would collect rocks, bottles, pots, and water balloons. They would then pile into their cars and cruise black areas looking for targets. They also used automobile aerials to whack black pedestrians across the back if they ventured close enough to the curb to be reached from the safety of a moving vehicle. "Nigger Knocking," Houston observed, had about it "the joy of the hunt" and was a part of the process of his conversion to Methodism.[17]

In *North Toward Home* Willie Morris tells how he and his friends taunted blacks who entered their neighborhood. "We would hide in the hedges in my backyard and shoot Negro men who were walking down the sidewalk, aiming BB's at their tails," writes Morris, also an MYFer. "We would throw dead snakes from trees into their paths, or dead rats and crawfish." "On Canal Street," he recalls, "across from the old Greyhound station at the Bayou, there was a concrete banister where the Negroes would sit waiting for buses. On Saturday nights we would cruise down the street in a car, and the driver would open his door, and drive close to the curb. We would watch while the Negroes, to avoid the car door, toppled backward off the banister like dominoes." Morris, something of an all-southern white boy, was also adept at individual acts of cruelty toward blacks, such as taunting them on the telephone.[18]

The novelist Tim McLaurin records a scene of adolescent racial cruelty in his autobiography, but with a twist. McLaurin acknowledges that "in rural North Carolina, white was king," but notes that being pure black was better than being considered a mixed blood. He recalls how he and a black playmate, LJ, denigrated a Native American boy. Both Tim and LJ believed the boy to be neither black nor white, but "all mixed up," a "jumble of blood and genes that constituted the members of the Croatan Indian tribe." Tim and LJ trick the boy into falling into a pit they have dug, and then the two of them urinate on the boy's head and flee to the safety of the deep woods.[19]

Women autobiographers, too, record an adolescent defense of white racist values, although their actions tend to be less violent. Katharine Lumpkin writes that at "club-forming age" she and her peers formed their version of the Ku Klux Klan, in which the "chief topic of business was the planning of pretended punitive expeditions against recalcitrant Negroes." Such activities, she notes "went far beyond pretense. . . . It was truly a serious game, and in a sense we were children bent on our ideals."[20] Writing forty years later about her experience as an adolescent in Mississippi, Melany Neilson observes that she and her peers "were prisoners . . . to our concern for others' opinion of us, our need for respect," joined especially "in our awareness of race." Even the words they used in their conversations with one another demonstrated their acceptance of racist values. "Every time we spoke the word 'nigger,'" Neilson recalls, "each time a little more in condescension, we began to feel some power in the word itself." Ultimately, merely hearing the word gave her "some kind of dim satisfaction."[21]

Most of these accounts also indicate clearly that white youths of the so called "better class," or from families that considered themselves "decent people," as all these white autobiographers did, were often told by their families not to treat blacks badly. I was so instructed, as were Morris and Crews. Melany Neilson was admonished by her parents never to use the word "nigger" ("It's so uncouth") and to treat blacks with respect.[22] Yet the cultural message received by those white autobiographers who have to date explored their southern childhoods was that the ritual of taunting and demeaning blacks was not only acceptable behavior, it was expected, indeed, practically demanded. In the segregated South, such acts, like counting coup and making one's bones, were an initiation rite, a sign of allegiance to the southern white racist ideal. It is no accident that they are remembered as a significant part of adolescence by so many white southern autobiographers.

Autobiographical accounts by African Americans, on the other hand, demonstrate that long before the Greensboro sit-ins, black adolescents frequently revealed in public their contempt for Jim Crowism and those whites who developed and enforced it. These acts of repudiation were also ritualistic, although acted out in a different setting from that of the white segregationist rituals. The public school, an experience common to most black autobiographers, is perhaps the most common setting found in black autobiographies. It is also highly significant that local whites controlled the segregated schools African Americans attended and often the teachers they encountered there. Again, Wright's *Black Boy* develops the theme beautifully. Wright was valedictorian of his graduating ninth grade class at a segregated Jackson, Mississippi, school. After he has prepared his valedictory speech, the principal calls him to his office and requests that he read a speech that the principal has written. Wright refuses to do so. The principal explains that Wright needs to be careful about what he says to an integrated audience and lacks the necessary experience to be certain that his remarks cause no harm. Still Wright refuses. The infuriated principal threatens to stop his graduation, then thinks better of such drastic action but threatens to withhold his recommendation for training as a teacher. Eventually, classmates, friends, and family members try to convince Wright to deliver the principal's speech, all to no avail. On graduation night Wright delivers his speech. But in doing so, he effectively sacrifices his entrée into the world of blacks who held positions in a segregated, white-controlled educational bureaucracy, a group that in Wright's time was considered among the elite of southern black society.[23]

In the special issue of *Southern Exposure* devoted to southern childhoods, Sara Brooks recalls a confrontation with whites and her parents as a result of participation in a school play in the 1920s. The "professor," as black school principals were frequently called, had invited a number of "white peoples," positioned in front row seats, to the activity. Despite her parents' expressed misgivings, Sara recites a poem to that mixed audience that asserts that God created and watched over both blacks and whites, and condemns the notion of Jim Crow. In 1980, at sixty-nine years of age, Sara Brooks recalled that night as one of the highlights of her life.[24]

One of the most moving and eloquent of autobiographical depictions of adolescent rebellion is Maya Angelou's account of her high school graduation found in *I Know Why the Caged Bird Sings*. Once again, the presence of local white dignitaries integrates the audience at the ceremony. A white politician promises to see that the school receive a paved basketball court and some new equipment for the home-economics and workshop classes. His promises to improve the training of young blacks as athletes and hewers of wood and drawers of water enrages the young Angelou and her classmates. Henry Reed, the valedictorian, follows the politician to the dais. Rather than give his prepared address, the proper, studious Henry leads the audience in singing "Lift Every Voice and Sing."[25]

Often these acts of adolescent rebellion were challenges to individual whites, a continuation of a pattern of individual resistance to white power that was a characteristic of slavery. Maya Angelou, for example, writes of deliberately breaking the china of a white woman for whom she worked as a maid because the woman would not use her correct given name.[26] In *Coming Up Down Home*, Cecil Brown recalls deliberating breaking "the porcelain statue of a grinning Negro servant that I hated so much. With its grotesque grinning face, its lips curled up in a perfect servile, bootlicking gesture . . ." The statue stood in the yard of a white family to whom his father sent him to borrow a disk, a type of plow. The white lady of the house refers to him as "Cuffy's boy," though she lends him the disk. Humiliated, Brown realizes he is being watched and decides to give "that ugly grinning nigger a push. I shoved my hands into his fat, ugly nose and the statue tumbled backward speechless as the famed tar baby, and hitting the hard cement driveway, shattered into a million pieces." Brown's fleeting moment of psychological triumph, however, quickly turns to defeat when the white woman informs his father of his actions. Furious, his father forces Brown, a high school senior, to ride with him to the nearest town, where they select a similar statue, which the father, apologizing for his son's actions, then presents to their white neighbor.[27]

The rise of the modern civil rights movement, with its mass demonstrations against segregation, did not end spontaneous acts of rebellion by adolescent black youths, as is indicated by an event recorded in Anne Moody's *Coming of Age in Mississippi*. Moody's act of public defiance came a year after the beginning of the sit-in movement, itself a product of adolescent rebellion, while she was a junior at Tougaloo College in Jackson, Mississippi. That summer she worked with both the NAACP and SNCC to encourage blacks in the Greenville area to register to vote. At summer's end, Moody and a friend named Rose go to the Greenville bus station to take a bus to Jackson. On the spur of the moment Moody convinces her friend to accompany her into the white waiting room, where they purchase tickets from a thoroughly confused agent. The scene quickly turns ugly, but Moody and Rose escape harm at the hands of an angry mob by fleeing in the automobile of a black man who fortunately happens by the bus station. Cecil Brown's autobiography contains an almost identical scene, and Mary Mebane records a similar incident that took place on a Durham bus.[28]

In his recently published autobiography, *Colored People*, Henry Louis Gates Jr. recalls another post–civil rights movement act of adolescent rebellion in his hometown of Piedmont, West Virginia. In 1969, as an eighteen-year-old freshman at a local state college, Gates and three buddies decided to integrate "a weekend hangout where all the (white) college kids went to listen to a live band." "We were scared to death," Gates writes, "but we just had to get on with it." They barge onto the club's dance floor, where they are first met with shouts of "nigger," then set upon by white youths, who injure one of Gates's friends. Gates and his compatriots retreat, "ducking bottles and cans as we sped away." The following Monday, Gates calls the State Human Rights Commission, which insists the club integrate or close. Given this choice, the owner shuts it down, and so, writes Gates, the club became a family restaurant "run by a very nice Filipino family."[29]

Yet Gates's victory, like Cecil Brown's, is not without its price. Gates ends his childhood autobiography with a description of the last colored mill picnic. For years, Westvaco paper mill, the town's largest employer, had sponsored segregated picnics for its workers. With the passage of civil rights legislation, mill management decided to discontinue the practice. Gates writes movingly of the last colored mill picnic, an institution with which Piedmont's black community hated to part. In the autobiography, he does not connect the last mill picnic with the closing of the white night spot. But in an interview in the Winter 1994 issue of *Southern Changes*, published by the Southern Regional Council, Gates writes that mill management abandoned the separate picnics because they "looked at this (the closing of the night spot) and they said these guys are going to raise hell because of this segregated mill picnic, but it never crossed our minds. . . . So they issued a directive that because of the Civil Rights Act and because of dangerous troublemakers in the community, we feel we should shut down this thing."[30]

These accounts of black adolescent rebellion have several things in common besides the obvious impatience of youth. First, and most significant, is the imperative felt by black youths to confront segregation publicly, especially in front of whites. Had there been no whites in attendance at Sara Brooks's graduation, her act would have been considered much less courageous. Indeed, it is probable that she would have felt no need to speak out against Jim Crow to an all black audience. Second, in most of the accounts, older blacks who became aware of planned acts of resistance expressed disapproval of such actions and often strongly pressured the adolescents to abandon their plans. In this regard, the actions of black youths appear to differ from those of their white counterparts. White youths tended to act in ways that indicated acceptance of segregation, even if they were troubled by the morality of the system or its impact upon the lives of specific African Americans they knew and liked. This pattern is clear in the behavior of adolescent whites, male and female, who later wrote accounts of their childhoods. Black adolescents, on the other hand, often had to defy their parents, or at least what parents and other authority figures said, in order to voice their protest. Wright makes this clear, and so do Ann Moody, whose mother never understood her involvement in the civil rights movement, and Sara Brooks, who remembered that her parents were upset with her about the poem she chose to recite.

Viewed from a slightly different perspective, however, this African American adolescent defiance of parents and authority figures is similar to the behavior of their white counterparts who ignored parental admonishments against behaving "badly" toward blacks and chose instead to participate in race baiting activities. Black adolescents understood that the warnings of parents and teachers against open resistance to white power were motivated by the fear of white retaliation rather than a respect for white segregationists, whom the adult members of the black community held in contempt. Black youths chose to act upon what they discerned to be the black community's true attitudes about white power and control. Similarly, white youths understood that the occasional admonitions from parents and "respectable" community leaders to "be good to" blacks did not express the attitudes of the larger white community concerning racial relationships. They understood, in other words, that such admonitions had more to do with style than with substance, with class divisions within white society than with white attitudes about black inferiority or the rights blacks possessed that whites were obliged to respect.

Consulting southern autobiographies reveals just how adept both white and black youths were at "reading" their cultural environment, especially in the area of racial prejudice. Richard Wright, for example, recalls that as a young boy he heard a tale "that rendered me speechless for nights." It was the tale of a black woman who "humbly" begs to be allowed to retrieve the body of her husband, who has been killed by a white mob. Her request granted, the woman moves to her husband's body, and from underneath a sheet she carries, pulls a shot gun and proceeds to gun down four whites. Wright understood that the story of the woman's revenge represented the true feelings of the black community about the wrongs they suffered under segregation. "I did not know," he recalls, "if the story was factually true or not but it was emotionally true because I had already grown to feel there existed men against whom I was powerless, men who could violate my life at will. I resolved that I would emulate the black woman."[31]

While scenes of adolescent response to segregation in southern autobiography are so common that they may be considered a convention of the genre, they do not result from the authors' deliberate efforts to follow a literary convention. Rather, they are indicative of the manner in which segregation permanently scarred the psyches of individual southerners. As an adult, each autobiographer recorded the emotional conflict encountered as a youth while attempting to determine how to respond to the institution of racial segregation, and to the social mores of white society that undergirded and perpetuated it. That they all chose to record their initial awareness of race, and of the significance it held for their lives, reveals that race, for whites and blacks, was an essential element in the creation of a concept of the self.

These autobiographies also reveal that the autobiographers' emotional responses to the problem of race have remained relatively constant for most of this century. Katharine Lumpkin's reactions to segregation in the early twentieth century, for example, are remarkably similar to those of Mary Bolsterli, a generation younger than Lumpkin, and to those of Melany Neilson, younger than Lumpkin by three generations. Richard Wright's emotional revelations are echoed by those of Chalmers Archer and Henry Louis Gates. Fred Hobson's suggestion that, at least for whites, the modern civil rights revolution tempered the significance of race, is not supported by the autobiographies of such younger white writers as Neilson and Tim McLaurin. This cross-generational similarity is not surprising, since all of these individuals came of age in the segregated South.[32] The autobiographies of southerners, black and white, to come of age in a South that conformed to national norms of race relations have yet to be written. When they do appear, they may provide some provocative insights into the degree to which the formerly segregated South has changed and to which the racial views of the segregated South were similar to national norms.

Together, the individual youthful responses to segregation recorded by southern autobiographers represent the collective memory of generations of southerners, white and black. It is hard to imagine how African Americans in the South during the era of segregation could have avoided the emotional burdens, detailed in the writings of black autobiographers, that system imposed. The impact of the system upon the psyche of southern whites is more problematic. Segregation may have caused many, perhaps even most, white southerners little emotional discomfort or damage, although the frequency with which white autobiographers writing of their adolescence have recorded their emotional responses to racial segregation suggests otherwise. The mosaic of memories created by southern autobiographers of both races is a somber one, filled with pain and anger, sadness and guilt. Such memories only underscore the high psychic price segregation extracted from generations of the region's residents.

NOTES

1. Lillian Smith, *Our Faces, Our Words* (W. W. Norton & Company, 1964), 66–67. For similar comments by a white autobiographer, see Willie Morris, *North Toward Home* (Houghton Mifflin Company, 1967), 384–85.

2. The publication history of Richard Wright's *Black Boy* illustrates the reluctance of publishers to explore segregation outside the South, as well as their political concerns. The original manuscript was divided into two parts, the first dealing with Wright's experience with segregation in the South, the second with the racism he encountered in the North and his experiences in the Communist Party. Only the first section was published in 1945 under the title *Black Boy*. Richard Wright, *Black Boy (American Hunger)* (HarperPerennial, 1993), xi–xxi, 487–89.

3. While a study of European childhoods, Richard N. Coe's *When the Grass was Greener, Autobiography and the Experience of Childhood* (Yale University Press, 1984), is an excellent introduction to the genre.

4. Most southern autobiographies, white and black, published by national and academic presses after 1940 rejected racism. Among the exceptions are Will Alexander Percy's eloquent defense of the paternalistic racism of the planter patricians, *Lanterns on the Levee* (Alfred A. Knopf, Inc., 1941), although even the unrepentantly racist Percy realized the old order was passing, and Ben Robertson's *Red Hills and Cotton, An Upcountry Memory* (University of South Carolina Press, 1942), which contends that southerners will solve their racial problems in time, if left alone by the federal government.

5. For examples see Albert Gore, *Let the Glory Out, My South and Its Politics* (Viking Press, 1972), and Frank E. Smith, *Congressman from Mississippi* (Pantheon Books, 1964).

6. Lynn Z. Bloom, "Coming of Age in the Segregated South, Autobiographies of Twentieth-Century Childhoods, Black and White," in J. Bill Berry, ed., *Home Ground, Southern Autobiography* (University of Missouri Press, 1991), 115–19.

7. Richard Wright, *Black Boy* (Harper & Brothers, 1945), 37, 54–57.

8. Anne Moody, *Coming of Age in Mississippi* (Dell Publishing Company, 1968), 37–38.

9. Mary Mebane, *Mary* (Viking Press, 1981), 51–52.

10. Chalmers Archer Jr., *Growing up Black in Rural Mississippi* (Walker and Company, 1992), 137.

11. Maya Angelou, *I Know Why the Caged Bird Sings* (Random House, 1970), 1–25.

12. Margaret Jones Bolsterli, *Born in the Delta, Reflections on the Making of a Southern White Sensibility* (University of Tennessee Press, 1991), 66–67, 73–75.

13. Katharine Du Pre Lumpkin, *The Making of a Southerner* (Alfred A. Knopf, Inc., 1947), 85–88, 133–34, 154–57.

14. Reynolds Price, *Clear Pictures, First Loves, First Guides* (Atheneum, 1989), 83–87, 90–101.

15. Melton McLaurin, *Separate Pasts, Growing up White in the Segregated South* (University of Georgia Press, 1987), 98–110.

16. Harry Crews, *A Childhood, a Biography of a Place* (William Morrow and Company, Inc., 1978), 59–60.

17. Robert Houston, "Nigger Knocking," *Southern Exposure* 8 (Fall 1980): 94–95.

18. Morris, *North Toward Home*, 84–90.

19. Tim McLaurin, *Keeper of the Moon* (W. W. Norton & Company, 1991), 121–24.

20. Lumpkin, *Making of a Southerner*, 136.

21. Melany Neilson, *Even in Mississippi* (University of Alabama Press, 1989), 38–39.

22. Ibid.

23. Wright, *Black Boy*, 206–11.

24. Sara Brooks and Thordis Simonsen, "You May Plow Here," *Southern Exposure* 8 (Fall 1980): 60.

25. Angelou, *Caged Bird*, 148–56.

26. Ibid., 91–93.

27. Cecil Brown, *Coming Up Down Home, A Memoir of Southern Childhood* (The Ecco Press, 1993), 203–7.

28. Moody, *Coming of Age*, 254–58.

29. Henry Louis Gates Jr., *Colored People: A Memoir* (Knopf, 1994), 198–99.

30. "Henry Louis Gates: *Colored People, A Memoir*," *Southern Changes* 16 (Winter 1994): 21.

31. Wright, *Black Boy*, 86.

32. Fred Hobson, *Tell about the South: The Southern Rage to Explain* (Louisiana State University Press, 1983), 304–7.

Colliding Cultures

Peoples and powers intersect, forging and reshaping the South and its southerners.

Columbus Meets Pocahontas
in the American South

Theda Perdue

Pocahontas, depicted here saving the life of Captain John Smith, has become the "mother of us all"—a nurturing, beckoning, seductive symbol of New World hospitality and opportunity. Henry Schile's lithograph, courtesy of the Collections of the Library of Congress.

As icons of the European colonization of the Americas, Columbus and Pocahontas represent opposite sides of the experience—European and Native, invader and defender, man and woman. Biographies and other scholarly writings document their lives and deeds, but these feats pale in comparison to the encounter these two legendary figures symbolize. Columbus embodies European discovery, invasion, and conquest while Pocahontas has become the "mother of us all," a nurturing, beckoning, seductive symbol of New World hospitality and opportunity.[1] The two never actually met in the American South, of course, except metaphorically, but this symbolic encounter involved a sexual dynamic that was inherent to the whole process of European colonization, particularly that of the American South.

John Smith's tale of succor and salvation fixed the Pocahontas image forever in the American mind, and his autobiographical account of peaceful relations with her people, the Powhatans, has exempted Englishmen from the tarring Columbus has received as an international symbol of aggression. The Columbian encounter with Native women seemed, in fact, to be radically different from Smith's. On his initial voyage of discovery, Columbus had relatively little to report about Native women except that they, like men, went "naked as the day they were born." The loss of one of his ships on this voyage forced Columbus to leave about a third of his crew on Hispaniola. When he returned, he found the burned ruins of his settlement and the decomposing corpses of his men. Local Natives related that "soon after the Admiral's departure those men began to quarrel among themselves, each taking as many women and as much gold as he could." They dispersed throughout the island, and local caciques killed them. The men on Columbus's expedition had their revenge: "Incapable of moderation in their acts of injustice, they carried off the women of the islanders under the very eyes of their brothers and their husbands." Columbus personally presented a young woman to one of his men, Michele de Cuneo, who later wrote that when she resisted him with her fingernails, he "thrashed her well, for which she raised such unheardof screams that you would not have believed your ears." In the accounts of the conquistadores, Spaniards seized women as they seized other spoils of war.[2] Such violence contributed to the "black legend" of Spanish inhumanity to Native peoples and stands in stark contrast to early English descriptions of their encounters with Native women.

John Smith, according to his own account, did not face the kind of resistance from Pocahontas and other Native women of the Virginia tidewater that the Spanish had met in the Caribbean. When Smith and a delegation from Jamestown called at the primary town of Powhatan, Pocahontas's father, they discovered that he was away, but the chief's daughter and other women invited the Englishmen to a "mascarado." "Thirtie young women," Smith wrote, "came naked out of the woods, only covered behind and before with a few green leaves, their bodies all painted." They sang and danced with "infernal passions" and then invited Smith to their lodgings. By his account, written with uncharacteristic modesty in the third person, "he was no sooner in the house, but all these Nymphes more tormented him then ever, with crowding, pressing, and hanging about him, most tediously crying, Love you not me? Love you not me?"[3]

The contrast is obvious—the Spanish supposedly raped and pillaged while the English nobly resisted seduction. By focusing merely on the colonizing Europeans, however, we lose sight of the Native women who are central actors in this drama: they are, after all, both the victims of Columbus's barbarity and the seductive sirens luring Smith's party. Despite differences in the ways these women are portrayed in historical sources, their experiences suggest that conquest and colonization had their own sexual dynamic. One of the facts of colonization that rarely surfaces in polite conversation or scholarly writing is sex, yet we know from the written records left by Europeans and from the more obscure cultural traditions of Native people that European men had sexual relations with Native American women. What can the Columbian voyages, the Jamestown colonists, and the experiences of subsequent European immigrants to the American South tell us about the ways in which men and women crossed cultural and racial bounds in their sexual relations? What do these relationships reveal about European views of female sexuality? And how did these views shape European expansion?

THE EUROPEAN VIEW OF NATIVE SEXUALITY

One thing seems fairly certain: Native women were never far from the conscious thought of European men, be they Spanish or English. Nudity insured that this was so. Accustomed to enveloping clothes, Europeans marveled at the remarkably scant clothing of the Natives. De Cuneo described the Carib woman whom he raped as "naked according to their custom," and Smith noted that except for a few strategically placed leaves, his hostesses were "naked." De Cuneo and Smith were not alone in commenting on Native women's lack of clothing. The Lord Admiral himself noticed not only that the Caribbean women he encountered wore little but that they had "very pretty bodies." The Jamestown colonists first encountered the prepubescent Pocahontas frolicking naked with the cabin boys. The combination of her youthful enthusiasm as well as her nudity led William Strachey, official chronicler of the colony, to describe Pocahontas as "a well featured, but wanton young girl." Other Europeans also tended to link the absence of clothing to sexuality: Amerigo Vespucci, for whom America was named, noted that "the women . . . go about naked and are very libidinous."[4]

While Native women frequently exposed breasts, particularly in warm weather, they normally kept pudenda covered. When women did bare all, Europeans had another shock in store: Native women in many societies plucked their pubic hair. While some evidence points to female singeing of pubic hair in ancient Greece and even early modern Spain, most Europeans recoiled from hairless female genitalia. Thomas Jefferson, whose interests extended far beyond politics, attempted to explain hair-plucking among Native Americans: "With them it is disgraceful to be hairy in the body. They say it likens them to hogs. They therefore pluck the hair as fast as it appears." Jefferson revealed both the reaction of non-Native men and the artificiality of the practice: "The traders who marry their women, and prevail on them to discontinue this practice say, that nature is the same with them as with whites."[5] However comfortable Euro-American men may have been with visible penises, depilation left female genitalia far more exposed than most could bear. Because women revealed their private parts intentionally, they seemed to be flaunting their sexuality.

Another cultural modification to the female physique also provoked comment. Among many Native peoples, women as well as men wore tattoos. While some Euro-Americans became so enamored of the practice that they adopted it, others regarded tattooing in the same light as make-up applied to make one more physically attractive. The late-eighteenth-century Philadelphia physician Benjamin Rush, for example, compared the body markings of Native peoples to cosmetics used by the French, a people whom he described as "strangers to what is called delicacy in the intercourse of the sexes with each other."[6] Unnatural markings on the body, to Europeans, signaled an enhanced sexuality.

As contact between Native peoples and Europeans grew, women gave up tattooing and hair plucking, and they adopted the blouses and long skirts common among non-Native women along the colonial frontier. Other features of Native culture, however, perpetuated the view of Native women as sexually uninhibited. Some Europeans found the humor of Native women to be terribly bawdy. Most women enjoyed teasing and joking, and pranks and jokes with sexual overtones were not necessarily taboo. The teasing Smith endured—"Love you not me? Love you not me?"—provides a good example. One Native woman even managed to shock a Frenchman. Louis-Philippe made a tour of the American West at the end of the eighteenth century, and during his visit to the Cherokees, his guide made sexual advances to several women. "They were so little embarrassed," wrote the future French king, "that one of them who was lying on a bed put her hand on his trousers before my very eyes and said scornfully, *Ah sick*."[7]

Directness characterized courtship as well as rejection. Smith clearly expressed amazement at the forwardness of the "thirtie young women." In *Notes on the State of Virginia*, Thomas Jefferson compared the "frigidity" of Native men with the assertiveness of women: "A celebrated warrior is oftener courted by the females, than he has occasion to court: and this is a point of honor which the men aim at. . . . Custom and manners reconcile them to modes of acting, which, judged by Europeans would be deemed inconsistent with the rules of female decorum and propriety."[8] When the epitome of the American Enlightenment attributed Native women with a more active libido than Native men, who could doubt that it was so?

The arrangement and use of domestic space seemed to confirm a lack of modesty on the part of Native women. Native housing afforded little privacy for bathing, changing what little clothes women did wear, or engaging in sexual intercourse. Several generations, as well as visitors, usually slept in the same lodge. The essayist Samuel Stanhope Smith admitted that Indians were unjustly "represented as licentious because they are seen to lie promiscuously in the same wigwam." Nevertheless, few Natives allowed the lack of privacy in their homes to become a barrier to sexual fulfillment. During early-eighteenth-century explorations in Carolina, one of John Lawson's companions took a Native "wife" for the night, and the newlyweds consummated their "marriage" in the same room in which other members of the expedition feasted and slept: "Our happy Couple went to Bed together before us all and with as little Blushing, as if they had been Man and Wife for 7 Years."[9]

Most European accounts of Native women in the South commented on their sexual freedom, particularly before they married. In the late eighteenth century, naturalist Bernard Romans observed: "Their women are handsome, well made, only wanting the colour and cleanliness of our ladies, to make them appear lovely in every eye; . . . they are lascivious, and have no idea of chastity in a girl, but in married women, incontinence is severely punished; a savage never forgives that crime." John Lawson suggested that even married women "sometimes bestow their Favours also to some or others in their Husbands Absence." And the trader James Adair maintained that "the Cherokees are an exception to all civilized or savage nations in having no law against adultery; they have been a considerable while under a petti-coat government, and allow their women full liberty to plant their brows with horns as oft as they please, without fear of punishment."[10]

Women in the Southeast sometimes openly solicited sex from Euro-Americans because sex gave women an opportunity to participate in the emerging market economy. Unlike men, who exchanged deerskins, beaver pelts, and buffalo hides with Europeans for manufactured goods, women often had to rely on "the soft passion" to obtain clothing, kettles, knives, hoes, and trinkets. Among some Native peoples a kind of specialization developed according to John Lawson, who claimed that coastal Carolina peoples designated "trading girls." Sometimes prostitution was more widespread. Louis-Philippe insisted that "all Cherokee women are public women in the full meaning of the phrase: dollars never fail to melt their hearts."[11]

Selling sex was one thing; the apparent gift of women by their husbands and fathers was quite another. To Europeans, sex was a kind of commodity, purchased from prostitutes with money and from respectable women with marriage. An honorable man protected the chastity of his wife and daughters as he would other property. Native men in many societies, however, seemed to condone or even encourage sexual relations between Europeans and women presumably "belonging" to them. Even husbands who might object to "secret infidelities" sometimes offered their wives to visitors.[12]

Europeans also viewed the widespread practice of polygyny, or a man taking more than one wife, as adulterous because they recognized only the first as the "real" wife. Many Native people favored sororal polygyny, the marriage of sisters to the same man, and the groom often took sisters as brides at the same time. Since this meant, in European terms, that a man married his sister-in-law, sororal polygamy was incest as well as adultery. Jedidiah Morse, in his *Universal Geography*, wrote: "When a man loves his wife, it is considered his duty to marry her sister, if she has one. Incest and bestiality are common among them."[13] Morse apparently regarded marriage to sisters as serious a violation of European sexual mores as human intercourse with animals; in his mind, both constituted perversion.

Polygynous, adulterous, and incestuous or not, marriage meant little to Indians in the estimation of many Euro-Americans. Lawson, for example, described the ease with which the Native peoples of coastal Carolina altered their marital status: "The marriages of these Indians are no further binding than the man and woman agree together. Either of them has the liberty to leave the other upon any frivolous excuse they can make." The trader Alexander Longe relayed a Cherokee priest's view of his people's lax attitude toward marriage: "They had better be asunder than together if they do not love one another but live for strife and confusion."[14] Europeans would have preferred that they stay together and, despite domestic turmoil, raise their children in an appropriately patriarchal household.[15]

When husband and wife parted, children normally remained with their mothers because Native peoples of the southeast were matrilineal, that is, they traced kinship solely through women. John Lawson attributed this very odd way of reckoning kin, in his view, to "fear of Impostors; the Savages knowing well, how much Frailty posseses *Indian* women, betwixt the Garters and the Girdle." While paternity might be questioned, maternity could not be. Despite the logic of such a system, Europeans had both intellectual and practical objections. Matrilineality seemed too close to the relationship between a cow and calf or a bitch and puppies: it was, the Iroquois historian Cadwallader Colden asserted, "according to the natural course of all animals." "Civilized" man presumably had moved beyond this "natural course" and had adopted laws, civil and religious, that bound fathers to children and husbands to wives. Europeans who married Native women of matrilineal societies nevertheless had difficulty exercising any control over their children and often abandoned them to their mothers' kin because men had no proprietary interest in their offspring. Thomas Nairne wrote of the Creeks: "A Girles Father has not the least hand or concern in matching her. . . . Sons never enjoy their fathers place and dignity."[16]

Blatant disregard of marital vows and paternal prerogatives was shocking enough, but many Native peoples exhibited little concern for the chastity of their daughters. Jean-Bernard Bossu reported that among

Native peoples on the lower Mississippi, "when an unmarried brave passes through a village, he hires a girl for a night or two, as he pleases, and her parents find nothing wrong with this. They are not at all worried about their daughter and explain that her body is hers to do with as she wishes." Furthermore, according to Lawson, "multiplicity of Gallants never [gave] . . . a Stain to a Female's reputation, or the least Hindrance of her Advancement . . . the more *Whorish*, the more *Honourable*."[17]

THE REALITIES OF NATIVE SEXUALITY

European men who traveled through the Native Southeast thought that they had stepped through the looking glass into a sexual wonderland. Actually, they had encountered only a fractured reflection of their own assumptions about appropriate sexual behavior. Native women were not as uninhibited as most whites thought. Europeans failed to realize that Native peoples did have rules regulating marriage and sexual intercourse, although the rules were sometimes quite different from their own. In the Southeast, unmarried people could engage freely in sex, but many factors other than marital status regulated and limited sexuality. A warrior preparing for or returning from battle (sometimes much of the summer), a ball player getting ready for a game, a man on the winter hunt (which could last three to four months), a pregnant woman, or a woman during her menstrual period abstained from sex. In other words, Native southerners had to forego sexual intercourse for a far greater percentage of their lives than Europeans.

Furthermore, there were inappropriate venues for sex. Although a Native couple might engage in sex in a room occupied by others, there were places, such as agricultural fields, where amorous encounters were forbidden. Violation of this rule could have serious consequences. According to the trader James Adair, the Cherokees blamed a devastating smallpox epidemic in 1738 on "the adulterous intercourses of their young married people, who the past year, had in a most notorious manner, violated their ancient laws of marriage in every thicket, and broke down and polluted many of their honest neighbours bean-plots, by their heinous crimes, which would cost a great deal of trouble to purify again."[18] For many Native southerners, therefore, a "toss in the hay" would have been a very serious offense.

Native peoples also had rules against incest, but they did not define incest in the same way Euro-Americans did. Intercourse or marriage with a member of a person's own clan, for example, was prohibited, and the penalty could be death. Clan membership, which included all individuals who could trace their ancestry back to a remote, perhaps mythical figure, often ran into the thousands and included many people whom Europeans would not have regarded as relatives. Consequently, the number of forbidden partners was far greater than the number under the European definition of incest. The Cherokees, for example, had seven clans. No one could marry into his or her own clan, nor was the father's clan an acceptable marriage pool. The result was that, for any given Cherokee, almost one third of all Cherokees were off-limits as sexual partners.

Each Native people had particular rules regarding marriage and incest. Many societies permitted men to have more than one wife and to marry sisters. The effect was not necessarily the devaluation of women, as European observers often claimed. Some cultural anthropologists suggest, in fact, that sororal polygamy correlates positively with high female status.[19] In the Southeast where husbands lived with their wives, the marriage of sisters to the same man reduced the number of men in the household and strengthened the control of the women over domestic life. As Morse suggested, sisters often wanted to share a husband just as they shared a house, fields, labor, and children.

Ignorant of Native rules, southern colonials tended to view Native women as wanton woodland nymphs over whose sexuality fathers, brothers, and husbands could exercise little control. Many colonists took full advantage of the situation as they perceived it. Some evidence, however, suggests that southeastern Native women were not as amenable to sexual encounters as Europeans suggested. Louis-Philippe's anecdote reveals a woman, however bold and uninhibited, rejecting a sexual advance. When women did engage in sexual activity, many of them probably succumbed to pressure or force rather than charm.

European culture at this time countenanced considerable violence against women. William Byrd's confidential account of surveying the boundary line between North Carolina and Virginia, for example, describes several episodes of sexual aggression. One young woman, he wrote, "wou'd certainly have been ravish't, if her timely consent had not prevented the violence." This cavalier attitude toward a woman's right to refuse sex characterized much interaction between Native women and Europeans. Race almost certainly exacerbated the situation. The records of the South Carolina Indian trade are replete with Native complaints of sexual abuse at the hands of Europeans. One trader "took a young Indian against her Will for his Wife," another severely beat three women including his pregnant wife whom he killed, and a third provided enough rum to a woman to get her drunk and then "used her ill."[20] Obviously, the women in these incidents were not the ones who were lascivious.

Some Native peoples came to regard sexual misbehavior as the most distinguishing feature of European culture. The Cherokee Booger Dance, in which participants imitated various peoples, portrayed Europeans as sexually aggressive, and the men playing that role chased screaming young women around the dance ground. As it turns out, from the Native perspective, the British colonists of the American South may not have been so terribly different from Columbus's men after all.

The people who do stand in stark contrast are Native men. James Adair, a resident of the Chickasaw Nation and a trader throughout the Southeast, perhaps knew the region's Native cultures better than any other European in the eighteenth century. As the husband of a Chickasaw woman and an occasional member of Chickasaw war parties against the Choctaws, he wrote with authority that "the Indians will not cohabitate with women while they are out at war; they religiously abstain from every kind of intercourse, even with their own wives." While Adair believed, perhaps correctly, that the reason for a period of abstinence was religious, the implications for female captives were clear. "The French Indians," he wrote, "are said not to have deflowered any of our young women they captivated, while at war with us." Even the most bloodthirsty Native warrior, according to Adair, "did not attempt the virtue of his female captives," although he did not hesitate to torture and kill them. Even the Choctaws, whom Adair described as "libidinous," had taken "several female prisoners without offering the least violence to thir virtue, till the time of purgation was expired." Adair could not, however, resist the temptation to slander the Choctaws, the Chickasaws' traditional enemy: "Then some of them forced their captives, notwithstanding their pressing entreaties and tears."[21]

Captivity narratives suggest Indian men raped very few, if any, women victims of colonial wars—"a very agreeable disappointment" in one woman's words.[22] Rules prohibiting intercourse immediately before and after going to war may have contributed to the absence of documented sexual violence, but Native views on female sexuality and autonomy may have been equally responsible. Indians apparently did not view sex as property or as one of the spoils of war.

Columbus's men do seem to have equated sex and material plunder.

The accounts of the destruction of the Hispaniola settlement link his men's desire for women with a desire for gold. In perhaps a more subtle way, British colonists also considered women to be a form of property and found the Native men's lack of proprietary interest in their wives and daughters incomprehensible. It called into question the Indians' concept of property in general and paved the way for Europeans to challenge Native people's ownership of land. From the second decade of colonization in the South, wealth depended on the cultivation of land, and southerners found the argument that Indians had no notion of absolute ownership particularly compelling.

While Native southerners forcefully maintained their right to inhabit the land of their fathers, they did not, in fact, regard land ownership in quite the same way as the Europeans who challenged their rights to it. They fought for revenge rather than for territory, they held land in common, and they permitted any tribal member to clear and cultivate unused tracts. Land did not represent an investment of capital, and Native southerners did not sell out and move on when other opportunities beckoned. Indeed, the land held such significance for most of them that they suffered severe economic, social, and political disruption rather than part with it. In the 1820s and 1830s, frontiersmen, land speculators, and politicians joined forces to divest Native peoples of their land, and southern state governments and ultimately the federal government took up the aggressors' cause. White southerners made a concerted effort to force their Indian neighbors to surrender their lands and move west of the Mississippi to new territory. What difference did it make, many whites asked, which lands the Indians occupied? With squatters encroaching on them, shysters defrauding them at every turn, and federal and state authorities unwilling to protect them, Native peoples in the South struggled desperately to retain their homelands. They did so for reasons as incomprehensible to Euro-Americans as the sexual behavior of Native women. People who objectified both land and sex had encountered people who did not.

Ultimately, Native southerners lost. Representatives of the large southern tribes—the Cherokees, Chickasaws, Choctaws, Creeks, and Seminoles —signed treaties in which they agreed to move west to what is today eastern Oklahoma. Remnants of some of those tribes as well as other isolated Native communities simply retreated into the shadows and eked out a living on marginal land while the cotton kingdom expanded onto the rich soil that Native peoples had surrendered. In the cotton kingdom, land was saleable rather than sacred, and power not parity characterized sexual relationships.

In recent years we have come to admire Native sensitivity to the natural world and to compare ourselves unfavorably to Indians on environmental issues and attitudes toward the land. Columbus and Pocahontas probably thought about sex at least as often as they did ecology, but we seem incapable of recognizing that their views on sex might have been as different as their ideas about land use. Disney's recent movie, *Pocahontas*, merely perpetuates the notion that romantic love is a universal concept that transcends cultural bounds and has little connection with specific aspects of a culture. The film depicts Pocahontas not as the autonomous person she probably was, but as a subservient young woman submissive to her father, betrothed to the warrior Kocoum, and won by Smith. Pocahontas's love for Smith (and vice versa) resolves conflicts with the Indians, and the English presumably set about the task at hand. "Oh, with all ya got in ya, boys," Governor Ratclife sings, "dig up Virginia, boys." True love, of course, characterized neither the real relationship between Pocahontas and John Smith nor the dealings of Native women and European men. Instead of Disney's John Smith, most Native women really met Columbus. Perhaps in the American South, where Columbus and Pocahontas metaphorically collided so forcefully, we should expand our comparison of Native Americans and Europeans beyond environmental issues and consider the interactions between men and women. Then we might begin to make connections between the materialism and exploitation that have characterized so much of southern history and sexual violence against women.

NOTES

1. Samuel Eliot Morison, *Admiral of the Ocean Sea* (Little Brown and Company, 1942); Grace Steele Woodward, *Pocahontas* (University of Oklahoma Press, 1969); J. A. Leo Lemay, *Did Pocahontas Save Captain John Smith?* (University of Georgia Press, 1993); Philip Young, "The Mother of Us All," *Kenyon Review* 24 (1962): 391–441. See also Rayna Green, "The Pocahontas Perplex: The Image of Indian Women in American Culture," *Massachusetts Review* 16 (1975): 698–714.

2. Marvin Lunenfeld, ed., *1492: Discovery, Invasion, Encounter* (D.C. Heath and Company, 1991), 133, 161–64; S. E. Morison, ed., *Journals and Other Documents in the Life and Voyages of Christopher Columbus* (The Heritage Press, 1963), 212.

3. John Smith, *The Generall Historie of Virginia, New England and the Summer Isles . . .* (London, 1624), Book 3:67.

4. Woodward, 5; Robert F. Berkhofer, *The White Man's Indian: The History of an Idea from Columbus to the Present* (Knopf, 1978), 7–9.

5. Paul Leicester Ford, ed., *The Writings of Thomas Jefferson*, 10 vols. (G. P. Putnam's Sons, 1892–99), 3:154–55.

6. George W. Corner, ed., *The Autobiography of Benjamin Rush: His Travels Through Life, Together with His Commonplace Book* [1789–1813], *Memoirs of the American Philosophical Society*, vol. 25 (Princeton University Press, 1948), 71.

7. Louis-Philippe, *Diary of My Travels in America*, tr. Stephen Becker (Delacorte Press, 1977), 84–85.

8. Thomas Jefferson, *Notes on the State of Virginia* (1787; reprt. Matthew Carey, 1794), 299.

9. Samuel Stanhope Smith, *An Essay on the Causes of the Variety of Complexion and Figure in the Human Species*, ed. Winthrop D. Jordan (1810; reprt. Harvard University Press, 1965), 128; John Lawson, *A New Voyage to Carolina*, ed. Hugh T. Lefler (University of North Carolina Press, 1967), 37–38.

10. Bernard Romans, *A Concise History of East and West Florida* (1775; reprt. University of Florida Press, 1962), 40–43; Lawson, 194; James Adair, *Adair's History of the North American Indians*, ed. Samuel Cole Williams (The Watauga Press, 1930), 152–53.

11. Lawson, 41; Louis-Philippe, 72.

12. Romans, 40–43.

13. Jedidiah Morse, *The American Universal Geography; or a View of the Present State of All the Kingdoms, States, and Colonies in the Known World* (Thomas and Andrews, 1812), 105.

14. Lawson, 193; Alexander Longe, "A Small Postscript of the Ways and Manners of the Indians Called Charikees," ed. D. H. Corkran, *Southern Indian Studies* 21 (1969): 30.

15. Morse, 575–76; Albert Gallatin, "Synopsis of the Indian Tribes Within the United States East of the Rocky Mountains," vol. 2 of *Archaeologia Americana: Transactions and Collections of the American Antiquarian Society* (Folson, Wells, and Thurston, 1836), 112–13.

16. Lawson, 57; Cadwallader Colden, *History of the Five Indian Nations of Canada which are Dependent on the Provinces of New York*, 2 vols. (1747; reprt. Allerton Books, 1922), 1: xxxiii; Alexander Moore, ed., *Nairne's Muskogean Journals: The 1708 Expedition to the Mississippi River* (University of Mississippi Press, 1988), 33, 45.

17. Seymour Feiler, ed., *Jean-Bernard Bossu's Travels in the Interior of North America, 1751–1762* (University of Oklahoma Press, 1962), 131–32; Lawson, 40.

18. Adair, 244.

19. Alice Schlegel, *Male Dominance and Female Autonomy: Domestic Authority in Matrilineal Societies* (Yale University Press, 1972), 87–88.

20. William K. Boyd, ed., *William Byrd's Histories of the Dividing Line Betwixt Virginia and North Carolina* (The North Carolina Historical Commission, 1929), 147–48; William L. McDowell, ed., *Journals of the Commissioners of the Indian Trade, Sept. 20, 1710–Aug. 29, 1718* (South Carolina Archives Department, 1955), 4, 37; McDowell, *Documents Relating to Indian Affairs, 1754–1765* (University of South Carolina Press, 1970), 231.

21. Adair, 171–72.

22. James Axtell, *The European and the Indian* (Oxford University Press), 183.

A Sense of Place
Jews, Blacks, and White Gentiles
in the American South

David Goldfield

*In a region where roots have meant a great deal, Jews were from nowhere—but the South
nonetheless has been a hospitable region for Jewish aspirations. Jewish-owned Rich and Bros.
Dry Goods Store, Atlanta, Georgia, ca. 1880, courtesy of the Atlanta History Center.*

s quintessential outsiders, Jews have developed a sixth sense in taking cues on public behavior from the host society. Over the centuries, their successful assimilation and at times even their survival have often depended on blending in with the Gentile population; they have had to balance the pursuit of their culture and religion with the necessity of maintaining a low profile. This tension between preservation and assimilation has lessened in recent decades in the United States, but it is still a part of Jewish life in the South. For the South remains the most conservative and evangelical Protestant region of the country, as well as the section in which rural culture has the strongest hold. Jewish religious, social, and settlement traditions are very different from those of the dominant culture, and Jewish success in the South prior to and even to some degree after the civil rights movement depended on minimizing these differences.

The Jewish "place" in southern life—their role as perceived by white and black Gentiles—has been a key factor in determining Jewish-Gentile relations in the South. As the historically dominant group in southern society, white Gentiles became accustomed to "placing" individuals as a way of ordering a chaotic and often violent region. Placing drew upon a long list of characteristics including race, family name, birthplace, religion, occupation, and education. Placing also depended on conformity to the customs of a given rural area, town, or city at a particular point in time. To know one's place and to act accordingly was important for getting along in the South, especially before the civil rights era.

Race remained a fundamental element in placing individuals. Although white southerners distinguished blacks by color, status, gender, and adherence to racial etiquette, African Americans occupied the lowest place in southern society regardless of other variables. White Gentiles usually viewed Jews as white, but Jews initially failed to meet most of the other criteria of placing. Once they established themselves, however, and proved their fealty to local customs, Jews began to move up on the place list, though seldom if ever to the topmost rung. Mobility for Jews was possible, even probable; for blacks, rare, if ever.

A caveat here: Jewish southerners were and are a diverse lot, despite their relatively small numbers. Sephardim in the colonial era, German Jews in the nineteenth century, and Eastern European (mainly Russian) Jews thereafter brought distinctive traditions that did not always blend into one happy community. Denominational preferences—Orthodox,

Conservative, and Reform—further divided southern Jewry. Southern white and black Gentiles also included distinct social, denominational, and ethnic groups. These variations qualify some of the generalizations in this essay. But, as journalists and historians have noted, although there are many Souths, there is also One South, a common set of assumptions revolving around race, religion, and, most important, history. An individual's place within southern society originates from those common assumptions.

AMBIVALENCE AND ASSIMILATION

At first glance, few groups seem more out of place in the South than Jews. Centuries of restrictions in Europe have made them an urban and mercantile people. Southerners have exalted rural life and looked with suspicion on cities and mercantile pursuits that they have associated with modernism, exploitation, and alien ideas. For the past century, the South has also been the nation's most evangelical Protestant region, and, consequently, southern Jews have been either prime targets for conversion or permanent outsiders. Finally, in a region where roots have meant a great deal, Jews were from nowhere. They were a people without a country, wandering the earth to find a home anywhere, yet at home nowhere, seemingly loyal only to themselves.

But in the South, things are seldom as they seem. While the South has not always been a promised land for the Jewish people, it has been a hospitable region for Jewish aspirations and security. Rarely comprising more than one percent of the region's population at any given time, Jewish southerners have attained economic and political influence far beyond their meager numbers. This positive state of affairs is a result of three factors. First, because of their small numbers, Jews rarely appeared threatening to other southerners. Second, the behavior of southern Jews has tended to mute their differences from the host society. Finally, race matters most in the South. The ethnic cleavages that defined northern cities were much less relevant in the South. Even if some southern Gentiles considered the Jews not quite white, they were not black either, and this fact was their greatest advantage in adapting to the region.

None of these moderating elements, however, has enabled Jewish southerners to overcome fully the distinctions between themselves and white Gentiles. Indeed, the South has always been ambivalent about Jews, sometimes embracing those in their midst but railing against "foreign" or Yankee Hebrews; at once exuding an almost embarrassing philo-Semitism while at the same time propagating the crudest stereotypes of Jews. The South is a land of great irony, and the place of Jews in that land reflects that characteristic very clearly.

Few elements of southern culture demonstrate this ambivalence, even contradiction, better than evangelical Protestantism. Consider, for example, the recent resolution passed by the Southern Baptist Convention to reconstitute the mission to the Jews. On the one hand, the resolution acknowledges the Jews' importance to evangelical prophecy; on the other, the thrust of the proposal is to obliterate the Jewish religion. Or, take Sunday school lessons. Children learn to respect and adhere to the lessons of the Old Testament, but although numerous qualifiers frame the story of the crucifixion, many southern Gentiles learn early in their lives that Jews are Christ-killers.

Despite these ambiguities, evangelical Protestantism shares a number of tenets with Judaism. Civic and religious leaders in the South have periodically acknowledged the Judaic roots of evangelical Protestantism. For two decades after the Civil War, three-term North Carolina governor Zebulon Vance toured the country giving a speech about Jews called "The Scattered Nation." He noted that "all Christian churches are but off-shoots from or grafts upon the old Jewish stock. Strike out all of Judaism from the Christian church and there remains nothing but an unmeaning superstition."[1] Both evangelical southerners and Jews have considered themselves "Chosen People," special groups anointed by God to carry his work forward and reap the benefits in the afterlife despite setbacks on earth. As W. J. Cash observed in *The Mind of the South*, the relationship is more than parallel; it is an acknowledged bond between the two religions. On southerners' belief that they will prevail, he wrote, "Did He not suffer the first Chosen People to languish in captivity, to bleed under the heel of Marduk and Ashur and Amon and Baal?"[2] Evangelical southerners were well-versed in the Old Testament, perhaps more so than other Protestant denominations. They have interpreted the Jewish State of Israel as the fulfillment of biblical prophecy on the in-gathering of Jews in the Holy Land. Also, southern Protestantism, like Judaism, is inextricably bound to the culture of the people.

There are numerous incidents throughout southern history that demonstrate the philo-Semitism of evangelicals: The close cooperation and proximity of Jewish and evangelical religious institutions in many southern towns and cities; how Gentile store owners closed on Saturday morning in early-twentieth-century Woodville, Mississippi, to hear the preaching of an itinerant rabbi; and, as historian Eli Evans narrated, how eastern North Carolina farmers came to his grandfather's store to be blessed in the "original Hebrew." Or how a Methodist in Port Gibson, Mississippi, purchased and restored an old synagogue in 1988 simply because, as he explained, "The Jewish heritage is deep rooted here, and that's where we all come from, after all, back to Abraham."[3]

Finally, both southern evangelical Protestantism and Judaism have been relatively immune to theological fads. In 1909 Harvard's Charles W. Eliot, in a speech called "The Religion of the Future," anticipated some of the religious trends of the late twentieth century, but not as practiced by Jews or southern evangelicals today. He predicted that the new religion would have "no worship, express or implied, of dead ancestors, teachers, or rulers" and that, above all, it would not "perpetuate the Hebrew anthropomorphic representations of God."[4]

Southerners and Jews have also shared a similar historical perspective that is different from the American view of history as the story of inevitable progress. Both groups conflate time zones: the past so defines the present and future that the three seem to merge together. Traditions, especially family traditions, are very important, and in the literature and music of both cultures the tension between traditions and the modern world is a prominent theme. For this reason, literary critic Lewis Simpson noted, "southern fiction and Jewish fiction have been the most complex and vital expressions of American fiction in this century. Both expressions derive from visions in which faith in the American's ability to make his own world has had an entangled confrontation with an experience of memory and history that tells him he cannot do it."[5]

Perhaps this is one reason for southern writers' fascination with Jewish themes and people, both professionally and personally. Will Percy's relationship with Caroline Stern and Thomas Wolfe's stormy affair with Aline Bernstein are two personal examples. The works of Walker Percy, Robert Penn Warren, Willie Morris, William Styron, and Pat Conroy indicate the literary attraction. On southerners and Jews, Willie Morris has written that "despite the most manifest disparities they have emerged from two similar cultures, buttressed by old traditions of anguish and the promise of justice." Both groups, Morris noted, have "an affinity in the historical disasters of our ancestral pasts."[6] These "ancestral pasts" contribute to a collective memory that is a key element in maintaining group solidarity and distinguishing the group from others. Journalist Ben Robertson's comment about his upbringing in rural upstate South Carolina pertains as much to Jews as to his kin: "All about me, on every side, was age, and history was continuous . . . I was Southern, I was old."[7]

Jews and southerners, especially southern writers, share a sense of loneliness. This feeling of enforced detachment or exile derives from their shared view of personal history as separate from the American experience. In Robert Penn Warren's *Flood*, a novel about the impending inundation of a small Tennessee town situated by a dam, Izzie Goldfarb, a long-deceased resident of Fiddlersburg, functions as a metaphor for southern loneliness. We first meet Izzie sitting in front of his shop on a summer evening, alternately reading and gazing out at the river, thinking we do not know what but enveloped in a centuries-old loneliness, a weariness of flight and exile. Later in the book, while lead character Brad Tolliver and his friend search for Izzie's grave before the river obliterates it and the town, Tolliver declares, "Hell, the whole South is lonesome. The shared experience . . . that makes the word South is lonesomeness."[8] To be a child of history is to be set apart, especially in America where the past is often seen as irrelevant. History has exiled both the southerner and the Jew. As Walker Percy wrote in *The Moviegoer*, "I am Jewish by instinct. We share the same exile." In an almost identical vein, journalist Jonathan Daniels asserted, "For good or for ill, being a southerner is like being a Jew. . . . There is, of course, the sense of exile."[9]

Exile implies homelessness, and Jews have been among the world's most mobile people just as southerners have been America's most migratory group. Perhaps because of this mutual itinerancy, the attachment to place has attained almost mythic proportions for both. When Eli Evans took a vial of North Carolina dirt into a New York City delivery room as his son was born, every southerner understood why. It was a gesture that no northerner, Jew or otherwise, would likely make. Thomas Wolfe's rootless character, George Webber, ironically finds his "place" among the world's most placeless people in the most transient neighborhood in the most placeless city. "*Place!*" Webber exclaims. "The East Side was a Place—and that was the thing that made it wonderful."

Considering the intersection of God and history in the cultures of both groups, it is not surprising that Jews found a welcome home in the South. The lure of the regional culture, so like their own in many ways, facilitated their acculturation and distinguished them from their coreligionists in the North. As Eli Evans flatly stated: "I believe that no one born and raised in the South, even if one moves away physically, can escape its hold on the imagination." Such affinity does not imply a loss of cultural identity. In fact, being southern reinforces Judaism as Jews have assumed the regional church-going habit, attending synagogues in much greater frequency and proportion than do their coreligionists in the North.[10]

The appreciation of and involvement in the regional culture occasionally results in some unusual combinations for southern Jews. Food has a strong ritual element for all southerners, Jew and Gentile. Some Jewish families ring in the New Year with hoppin' john, a mixture of black-eyed peas and hog jowls that brings good luck throughout the year. Children participate in public pageants that often have Christian overtones. Alfred Uhry, Atlanta-born author of *Driving Miss Daisy*, recalled that as a boy he enjoyed going on Easter-egg hunts and receiving Christmas gifts. As a member of the Atlanta Boy Choir, he participated in the annual Easter recital, belting out, "Lord, I want to be a Christian in my heart." In smaller communities, the integration has been more complete. As Alfred O. Hero noted in his survey of southern Jewry more than a generation ago, small-town Jews "played poker with the sheriff, fished with the county judge, hunted with the planters, and became leaders of the local Chamber of Commerce, Rotary, and other service groups."[11]

So thoroughly acclimated have Jews become that some Gentiles have regretted the assimilation. In the 1930s Will Percy complained to David Cohn, his Jewish neighbor in Greenville, Mississippi: "I have a great grievance against southern Jews. It is that they have fallen to the level of Gentiles." He recalled discussing music and literature with local Jews twenty years earlier, "but now," he said, "[they] are just like everybody else—nice people and rooters for the home team. I never did expect to be able to talk to many Gentiles, and now that I can't talk to the Jews, I sit here a lonely man."[12]

Part of the Jewish success in the South results from the place occupied by blacks, the third side of the triangular relationship between Jews and black and white Gentiles. The dividing line of race serves to push the Jewish place in the South much closer to that of white Gentiles and at some distance to that of blacks. As Jonathan Daniels noted, "The direction of racial prejudice at the Negro frees the Jew from prejudice altogether—or nearly altogether." In the 1950s the Little Rock White Citizens' Council expelled one of its leaders for anti-Semitism. A Council spokesman explained: "You see, we had to throw him out, because we can't afford to be seen as an anti-Jewish organization. Why, we are having trouble enough just being anti-Negro." As Hodding Carter put it, "It takes perseverance to hate Jews and Negroes and Catholics all at the same time." For white southerners, Jew and Gentile, the South, in short, has been the land of the ethnic meltdown. As historian George B. Tindall observed, "Over the years, all those southerners with names like Krutt-schnitt, Kolb, De Bardeleben, . . . Toledano, Moise, . . . or Cheros got melted down and poured back out in the mold of good old boys and girls, if not of the gentry."[13]

The meltdown, however, has not been complete for Jewish south-erners. The very factors that drew Jews and southerners together also pulled them apart and created ambivalent if not downright contradictory Jewish-Gentile relations. Evangelical Protestants may trace their theology to the ancient Hebrews, but they have also viewed Jews as "Christ-killers." They have clashed with Jews over issues such as Sunday-closing laws and school prayer. Also, Talmudic traditions are based on doubt: that is, Judaism is rife with interpretive differences and constant questioning of biblical meaning; debate, analysis, and reinterpretation are expected. Evangelical Protestantism, as often practiced in the South, abjures doubt and is uncomfortable with skeptical inquiry.

EXCLUSION AND PERSECUTION

Tempering factors in national religious life such as religious diversity and the strict separation of church and state have been less evident in the South. The religious monopoly of evangelical Protestantism and the his-torical resistance of Jews to conversion led to mutual distrust and sus-picion. During the PTL scandals of the late 1980s, when Jim Bakker and Jerry Falwell struggled for control of the ministry, the most telling ca-nard that the Bakker forces used against Falwell was that he might have Jewish blood.[14]

Some white southerners perceived Jews as sufficiently alien to place them on a par with blacks, or even worse. The lynching of Leo Frank in 1915 jolted Jewish southerners, and its memory hovered over Jewish life in the South through much of this century. More than any other event, the Frank lynching demonstrated that acceptance, however widespread, and success, however attainable, were qualified. The lynching reinforced the importance of vigilance and circumspection as the cost for maintain-ing a comfortable life in the region, and it also affected Jewish relations with African Americans.

Leo Frank, a New York Jew, managed a pencil factory in Atlanta. The plant employed many young white girls from surrounding farms and towns. The girls worked at low wages amid filthy conditions with little privacy, and rumors circulated that supervisors traded promotions and better pay for sexual favors. These working conditions were typical in the South at this time. The rapid urban and industrial growth of the South during the early twentieth century, coupled with declining farm income uprooted families, removed children to the workplace away from the supervision of parents and placed employers in positions of power over youngsters. Many working-class white families both feared and resented the new urban, industrial order and its implications for family life. Thirteen-year-old Mary Phagan typified many of the workers in the pencil factory. Her family had lost their farm and worked as tenants. She had moved to Atlanta to help support her family. On Confederate Memorial Day 1913, someone robbed and murdered Mary as she left the factory to attend the parade downtown. Frank, a northern urban Jew who employed poor, white Gentile southern girls, became the convenient focus of the investigation. He was arrested, charged, tried, and sentenced to death for the murder, largely on the testimony of a black janitor with a criminal record. Much of the evidence pointed to the janitor, and not to Frank, as the killer.

That a prosperous manager would rob and then kill a poor young employee made little sense, but rumors surfaced that Mary had been raped, a charge unsubstantiated by the medical examiner's report. The rumor, taken as fact, fueled a torrent of anti-Semitic rhetoric about lustful Jews ravishing young white Christian girls. Georgia politician Tom Watson described the pencil factory as "a Jewish convent as lascivious as a Catholic monastery."[15] What made the case more bizarre was that white public opinion ignored the mounting evidence against the black janitor at a time when the image of black fiends raping white women had spurred a frenzy of lynching in the South.

The whole affair embarrassed Atlanta's leading white citizens, and they supported a movement to convince the governor to at least commute Frank's death sentence. At great personal and political peril, Governor John Slaton did just that. But a group of twenty-five men, calling themselves the "Knights of Mary Phagan," pulled Frank from his cell in August 1915, drove to Marietta, Mary's home town, and lynched their prisoner.

The Leo Frank lynching reverberated throughout southern Jewry, par-

ticularly in Atlanta. Josephine Joel, a Jewish high school student in Atlanta in 1915, recalled that so great was the fear of anti-Semitic terrorism
when Governor Slaton commuted Frank's sentence that many Jewish
families packed children and women off to stay with relatives in other
parts of the country. Josephine's father sent his entire family to live with
relatives in Birmingham. When Josephine returned to Atlanta, she noted
in her diary that her French teacher took special care to make her welcome. The teacher was Mattie Slaton, the governor's sister.[16]

Although Josephine's life returned to normal, and Atlanta's Jews weathered the crisis without any diminution in their status or influence, the
Frank lynching served as a lesson that skin color did not give Jewish
southerners immunity from the fury of white supremacy. The Frank
lynching also reminded Jews that although they were not black, many
southerners did not consider them white. Almost like William Faulkner's
mulatto character, Joe Christmas in *Light in August*, Jewish southerners
sometimes wandered in a half life between the legitimacy of being white
and the outcast status of being black; being neither, they were suspect by
both. Invisibility, or blending in, proved the best defense; and in the
context of southern society prior to the 1960s, invisibility meant the
public acceptance of racial segregation, even if doing so tortured the
Jewish soul privately. For a Jew to publicly support desegregation was to
risk identification with blacks on the place ladder, and such identification
could be dangerous. The association of Jewish southerners with blacks in
Gentile perceptions heightened Jewish vigilance during periods of racial
tension. "It was always an axiom of Jewish life in the South," Eli Evans
explained, "that racial trouble meant heated passions and a dangerous
atmosphere that was 'bad for the Jews.'"[17]

White Gentile southerners used more subtle ways than violence, however, or its threat to exclude Jews or, more properly, to remind Jews that
they were not completely citizens of the South. As in the North, certain
clubs, resorts, and neighborhoods refused entry to Jews. Some universities, such as Emory in Atlanta and the University of North Carolina at
Chapel Hill, restricted Jewish admissions in a few graduate programs.[18]

More than specific instances, however, an atmosphere prevailed that
excluded Jews from full membership in the white southern brotherhood.
Louis D. Rubin Jr., whose southern credentials none would deny, told of a
recurring dream he had as a child in Charleston in which Confederate
soldiers are patrolling the gateway to Hampton Park. "The soldiers who
patrolled the gateway did not bar my passage through the gate," he

recalled, "but they were present, going about their business, unconcerned with who I was or what I might want. To get into the garden I should have to go through the Confederate soldiers." Rubin never made the attempt in his dreams, but it symbolized the Rubins' place in Charleston. As Rubin noted, "We were part of [Charleston's] community life. But we were Jewish."[19]

THE DELICATE DANCE BETWEEN JEWS AND BLACKS

An objective of Jewish existence in the South has been to minimize this "but" factor. White southerners have welcomed Jews warmly but conditionally. The Jewish adjustment to their place in southern life involved accepting southern traditions, especially racial customs, so as not to arouse suspicion or confirm prejudices while at the same time maintaining Jewish identity. Jewish life in the South proceeded in a particular cadence, a delicate dance between assimilation and distinctiveness.

Relations between Jewish southerners and blacks fit within the context of this dance. Blacks understood the dance because they had internalized many of the steps. They balanced humiliation with self-respect, adopting the appropriate subservient etiquette in public, while privately building a race-conscious community. Even partial assimilation was never a realistic objective for them as it was for Jewish southerners; southern blacks sought survival and accommodation. Yet there was a comparability between black and Jew in the act they played for the dominant white Protestant society. Their relationship reflected both the possibility of shared community and the bitter disappointment of missed opportunities.

Blacks generally perceived Jews as whites but different from Gentiles, and, in some cases, even as a different race. Keen to the ways of discrimination, they saw how some Gentiles treated and talked about Jews. In the early 1900s, when the Richmond YMCA accepted Jews as members but not as lodgers, the black *Richmond Planet* commented, "It may not be too much to say that in some sections of the country the antipathy to Jews in the hotels is almost as marked as it is to Negroes." Blacks often noted approvingly how Jews stuck together and married among themselves. "Only now and then," observed one black writer, "does a Jew cross the line and marry into another race."[20]

The affinity blacks perceived went beyond mere observation and extended into the same areas that connected Jewish southerners to white Gentiles. Jewish history in general and the Old Testament in particular provided sustenance and proof for the ultimate redemption and success of African Americans. Slaves sang out the lessons of Exodus: "Go Down, / Moses, way down, in Egypt land; / tell old Pharaoh, Let My People Go." One of the leaders of Gabriel's revolt in Virginia in 1800 inspired his followers by reminding them of the days "when the Israelites were in servitude to King Pharaoh and they were taken from him by the power of God."[21] Booker T. Washington found "the most fascinating portion of the Bible the story of the manner in which Moses led the Children of Israel out of the house of bondage, through the wilderness, into the promised land." Black novelist Zora Neale Hurston took Old Testament stories as inspiration for some of her early works, especially *Moses, Man of the Mountain*, a take-off on the Book of Exodus. Hurston admired the Jews for having "a God who laid about [them] when they needed Him." Most blacks took to the Hebrew Scriptures "as a duck to water," according to NAACP official and Howard University professor Kelly Miller.[22]

Black affinity for Jews reached into the southern secular world. Jewish merchants and black customers established a close relationship in the Jim Crow era, and most black neighborhoods in the urban South included at least one Jewish-owned store. Theodore Coleman, the son of Miss Daisy's chauffeur, recalled moving frequently within Atlanta's black neighborhoods before World War II, but no matter where "we lived, there seemed to be a Jewish store on the corner."[23] This mercantile relationship began during the Civil War era when Jewish peddlers—"rolling store men," as Alice Walker remembers her parents calling them—penetrated the rural South and provided black families with one of the few nonthreatening contacts with whites.[24] Some peddlers catered exclusively to a black clientele. Sometimes they "graduated" to a small store in the black section of a town where they provided services most white merchants refused to offer.

Jewish merchants occasionally, and always quietly, extended courtesies to black customers that white Gentile businessmen rarely offered. They allowed black customers to try on clothing and referred to them by "Mr." or "Mrs." Alex Haley noted how Jewish store owners in Henning, Tennessee, treated his parents with respect. Southern historian Bell Wiley related that the Jewish owner of a dry goods store in his small Tennessee hometown "got most of the black trade because he treated Negroes as human beings and was kindly to them, taking time to joke, inquire about their families and otherwise manifest interest in them." Kelly Miller praised the "tutelage" of Jewish merchants who hired black clerks.[25] The clerks often became fluent in Yiddish, a phenomenon northern and foreign travelers found amazing. Jewish businesses advertised heavily in the black press. Prior to 1960, before the chain stores gobbled up free enterprise in the urban South, scarcely a southern black existed who had not spent some time in a Jewish-owned store.

Witnessing Jewish business acumen first-hand, blacks often cited Jews as positive examples for their own race. In 1876 black Louisiana politician P. B. S. Pinchback offered the example of Jewish upward mobility to an audience of discouraged Mississippi blacks: "Like you they were once slaves and after they were emancipated they met with persecutions. Generation after generation they fought their oppressors, and backed by principles they believed were right they finally emerged victorious. Once despised, they are now leaders of education and princes of the commercial world."[26] Two decades later, Booker T. Washington picked up the refrain. He often presented the tale of a Jewish emigré who arrived in a small town near Tuskegee in 1890 with "all of his possessions in a single satchel." He built a store, and within four years his business grossed $50,000 annually. Investing some of his profits in land, he acquired a plantation of several hundred acres by the late 1890s. Washington concluded that blacks should emulate "the saving and economical qualities of the Jews."[27] Ironically, Washington continued to emphasize the type of vocational education that would preclude most blacks from following the Jewish example, yet the analogy persisted in southern black culture. In 1926 a black editor in Norfolk summarized the Jewish example for his readers:

> In many ways the Jews show us how to succeed. The Jews have taught the Afro-American people how to organize and stand together; how to make money and how to save and wisely spend it, and how to conquer prejudices, obstacles, by mastering for themselves a place in all of the thought and efforts of our tremendous civilization. . . . How do they do it? They do it by sticking together; by taking a commanding part in the trade and finance of the world and by going into all of the intellectual fields where money and influence are possible to be made.[28]

Although blacks acknowledged that Jewish southerners were different in some positive ways from other southern whites, the dividing lines of race, class, and culture tempered black perceptions. Black and white southern Gentiles shared a tradition of anti-Semitism that existed alongside a tradition of philo-Semitism. In some respects the origins of black anti-Semitism reflected the southern heritage of blacks more than their racial background; in others, it related directly to the Jewish response to blacks. Despite the religious and commercial affinities, blacks grew up with grave doubts about Jews. Black novelist Richard Wright acknowledged that growing up in Arkansas, "an attitude of antagonism or distrust toward Jews was bred in us from childhood; it was not merely racial prejudice, it was a part of our cultural heritage." In 1945 the Nashville-based *National Baptist Voice*, a black newspaper, conceded that "Negroes are filled with Anti-Semitism. In any group of Negroes, if the white people are not around, the mention of the Jew calls forth bitter tirades."[29]

Black hostility toward southern Jews focused on the issues of Judaism and economic exploitation. After 1800 many slaves converted to evangelical Christianity, and though black southerners derived much from the Old Testament for their purposes, they also imbibed the prevailing notion of Jews as Christ-killers. Richard Wright's initial distrust of Jews emerged, as he explained, "because we had been taught at home and in Sunday school that Jews were 'Christ killers.'" Although most slave spirituals exalted Old Testament prophets, one included the following lines: "The Jews killed poor Jesus, an' laid him in a tomb. / He 'rose, he 'rose, and went to heaven in a cloud."[30]

The familiar relationship between Jewish shopkeepers and black customers often bred contempt, reflecting differences of both class and race. Black leaders, such as Booker T. Washington who praised Jewish ambition publicly (many of his benefactors were Jewish), worried privately that "we are getting our trade too much centered in the hands of a few Jews." At the same time, black editor T. Thomas Fortune, who grew up in Florida, blamed Jewish merchants for squeezing white planters who, in turn, exploited black laborers. In the 1930s Kelly Miller traced the origins of exploitation to ancient Egypt, where "Jewish servant women borrowed earrings and finger rings of their Egyptian mistresses [and] set up their husbands in the jewelry business."[31] Some of these remarks were tinged with the bitterness of betrayal: the feeling that Jews had traded friendship for racial solidarity. As black educator Horace Mann Bond noted in 1965, "much of the sharpest feeling among Negroes about Jews arises from a feeling that this man has especially let you down; he, of all men, ought to know what it was like; and how it had been."[32]

The dance that Jewish southerners performed to keep their place in southern society precluded a close relationship with blacks. In the triangular relationship between Jew and black and white Gentile, southern cultural traditions, including religion and race, drew Jewish southerners closer to other whites. The dance required Jewish southerners to maintain a low profile, especially with respect to race, for to call attention to themselves meant to call attention to their differences. And to sympathize with blacks on racial matters would reinforce the white Gentiles' perceptions of the affinity of blacks and Jews. Eli Evans, who is generally positive about his family's life in the South, admitted that "the Jews in the South have internalized a deep lesson: that the best way to survive was to be quiet about their presence."[33] Silence even extended to not speaking out on anti-Semitism for fear of being linked in the Gentile mind with blacks.

Nowhere was this silence more evident than in the area of race relations. A survey of the Nashville Jewish newspaper between 1939 and 1949 revealed that the paper discussed racial discrimination just four times and briefly at that. And when editors commented on racial matters, they often repeated the views of the larger white community. In the process of wishing for a white hope to defeat black heavyweight champion Joe Louis, an editorial asserted, "The color line is one which the colored folk may never hope to cross as a race, but the colored folk have given us some whom we are proud to claim as citizens."[34] Even when Nashville Jews performed good deeds on behalf of the city's black community, they did not publicize them. During World War II, the Nashville chapter of the National Council of Jewish Women (NCJW) operated a day-care center for black children. Nashville's white Gentile community displayed no similar benevolence. The city's Jewish newspaper made no mention of the day-care center, although several major articles appeared on NCJW participation in funding a nonsectarian children's hospital. The latter demonstrated, as one NCJW member asserted, that Jews are "contributing agents to the community in which we live." The NCJW never commented on the day-care center.[35]

During the civil rights era many Jews remained on the sidelines, even if privately they cheered black protest. In smaller towns in the Deep South, Jews rarely spoke out. As one Meridian, Mississippi, Jew put it in the 1950s, "We have to work quietly, secretly. We have to play ball." Jews were so successful in maintaining their silence that white southerners had few clues about Jewish views on race relations. Although polls revealed that Jewish southerners supported civil rights initiatives more than other white southerners, only 15 percent of Gentiles polled in a 1959 survey believed that Jewish southerners favored integration; a whopping 67 percent replied that they had no idea about Jewish racial views.[36]

Equally as frustrating for blacks, some Jews seemed unconscious of black distress. David Cohn wrote of Greenville in the 1930s that bigots formed only "a tiny minority" of the town. Did Delta blacks feel that way? During the civil rights era, southern Jewish leaders often confronted their northern brethren and either warned them out of town or implored them to remain silent. A Jewish political leader in the Deep South advised northern coreligionists to stay away, assuring them that "there is no race problem here except when it is created from the outside."[37]

This is not to say that Jews failed to respond positively to black civil rights initiatives. Even before the civil rights era, prominent Jews moved to the liberal edge of community sentiment, especially in the larger cities of the South. Early in the century southern Jews played an important role in the Committee on Interracial Cooperation. Southern chapters of the NCJW supported Jessie Daniel Ames's Association of Southern Women for the Prevention of Lynching. And though Alfred Uhry's grandmother thought that blacks were like children at times, she supported their right for equal, though segregated, education, a rather advanced position in the 1930s. When Jews served on southern school boards in the Jim Crow era, they frequently advocated upgrading black public schools. Occasionally, southern Jews participated in NAACP lawsuits when their interests matched those of local blacks. In the 1920s, for example, the Savannah Jewish community supported an NAACP protest against housing discrimination. As the black *Savannah Tribune* noted, Jews were interested in the issue "because of the effect the case will have on similar lawsuits involving Jews."[38] And, when the civil rights movement emerged in the 1950s, some Jewish clerics joined their black brethren.

The post–civil rights era in the South has not brought about an appreciable improvement in black-Jewish relations. Although there are numerous examples of cooperation such as the Atlanta Black-Jewish Coalition and Jewish involvement in Habitat for Humanity, a gulf persists between Jewish southerners and blacks reflecting both the racial divisions in the larger society and the anomalous place of Jews in the South.

Jews still feel the need to dance the delicate line between assimilation and distinctiveness. The merging of the radical Christian right and Klan elements in the South concerns Jewish southerners, and the growing influence of the Christian Coalition also generates uneasiness. When Rabbi James Bennett of Charlotte spoke out against school prayer, an angry letter writer to the local newspaper ordered the rabbi to return to his own country since "America serves God" and the rabbi does not.[39] Rabbi Bennett, incidentally, is from Ft. Worth, Texas. Also in Charlotte, a proposal to move the city's two synagogues to a campus adjacent to the new Jewish Community Center touched off a bitter debate within the Jewish community. The essence of the controversy was whether the grouping would look too much like "clannishness" to the Gentiles and feed a perception that Jews were withdrawing from civic life into their historical ghetto. The plan went forward. Oddly enough, most Gentiles liked the concept, and today more than one-quarter of the center's membership is non-Jewish. Many of the Jewish members are newcomers from the North and their racial attitudes on the whole are little different from those of Jewish southerners; if anything, they are less liberal.

The point is that Jewish life in the South remains wonderful but conditional, and race relations still reflect that. W. J. Cash wrote in *The Mind of the South* that "the Jew, with his universal refusal to be assimilated, is everywhere the eternal Alien; and in the South, where any difference had always stood out with great vividness, he was especially so." A few years after Cash wrote, David Cohn recalled, "I was born and raised in a good world. It was far more Gentile than Jewish, but I never felt alien there, nor was any attempt made to make me feel alien." When Eli Evans undertook research for his book on southern Jews, he discovered that "Jews were not aliens in the promised land, but blood-and-bones part of southern history."[40]

So who is right, Cash, the Gentile, or Cohn and Evans, both of whom grew up as Jewish southerners? It may be that they are all correct and reflect the contradictions inherent in contemporary southern culture: Jews as indelibly part of the South, yet apart from it; as sharing a common culture with white Gentiles, yet often reminded of cultural differences; as historically and culturally sympathetic to black equality, yet distanced by the realities of race in the South and the Jewish instinct for self-preservation in a foreign land.

NOTES

1. Quoted in Maurice A. Weinstein, ed., *Zebulon B. Vance and "The Scattered Nation"* (Wildacres Press, 1995), 23.

2. W. J. Cash, *The Mind of the South* (Knopf, 1941), 132.

3. Eli Evans, *The Lonely Days Were Sundays: Reflections of a Jewish Southerner* (University Press of Mississippi, 1993), 59, 341; Peter Applebome, "Small-Town South Clings to Jewish History," *Charlotte Observer*, 29 September 1991.

4. Quoted in Marion Montgomery, "Solzhenitsyn as Southerner," *Why the South Will Survive* (University of Georgia Press, 1981), 184.

5. Lewis P. Simpson, "The Southern Recovery of Memory and History," *Sewanee Review* 45 (Winter 1974): 14.

6. Willie Morris, *The Last of the Southern Girls* (Knopf, 1973), 41–42, and *North Toward Home* (Houghton Mifflin, 1967), 410.

7. Ben Robertson, *Red Hills and Cotton: An Upcountry Memory* (University of South Carolina Press, 1942), 245.

8. Robert Penn Warren, *Flood* (Harper & Row, 1964), 171.

9. Walker Percy, *The Moviegoer* (Knopf, 1961), 89; Jonathan Daniels, *A Southerner Discovers the South* (Macmillan, 1938), 8.

10. Evans, *Lonely Days*, xxiii; John Shelton Reed makes this point in *One South: An Ethnic Approach to Regional Culture* (Louisiana State University Press, 1982), 111.

11. Quoted in Jim Auchmutey, "Daisy: The Long Drive to Hollywood," *Southpoint* 1 (December 1989): 43; Alfred O. Hero Jr., *The Southerner and World Affairs* (Louisiana State University Press, 1965), 482.

12. Quoted in James C. Cobb, ed., *The Mississippi Delta and the World: The Memoirs of David L. Cohn* (Louisiana State University Press, 1995), 171.

13. Daniels, *A Southerner Discovers the South*, 259; quoted in Thomas F. Pettigrew, "Parallel and Distinctive Changes in Anti-Semitic and Anti-Negro Attitudes," *Jews in the Mind of America*, ed. Charles H. Stember et al. (Harper & Row, 1966), 377; quoted in Howard N. Rabinowitz, "Nativism, Bigotry, and Anti-Semitism in the South and Nation," presented at Temple Beth Ahabah, Richmond, Virginia, 13 November 1986; George B. Tindall, "Beyond the Mainstream: The Ethnic Southerners," *Journal of Southern History* 40 (February 1974): 8.

14. See Hunter James, *Smile Pretty and Say Jesus: The Last Great Days of PTL* (University of Georgia Press, 1993), 151.

15. Quoted in Nancy MacLean, "The Leo Frank Case Reconsidered: Gender and Sexual Politics in the Making of Reactionary Populism," *Journal of American History* 78 (December 1991): 942. Although there are numerous accounts of the Frank lynching, MacLean is the best among the more recent studies in placing the event in a broader regional context.

16. Mark K. Bauman, "The Youthful Musings of a Jewish Community Activist: Josephine Joel Heyman," *Atlanta History* 39 (Summer 1995): 46–59.

17. Ibid., 110.

18. See Edward C. Halperin, "Frank Porter Graham, Isaac Hall Manning, and the Jewish Quota at the University of North Carolina Medical School," *North Carolina Historical Review* LXVII (October 1990): 385–410.

19. Louis D. Rubin Jr., "The Southern Martial Tradition: A Memory," *Southern Cultures* 1 (Winter 1995): 289.

20. Quoted in Arnold Shankman, *Ambivalent Friends: Afro-Americans View the Immigrant* (Greenwood Press, 1982), 129, 135.

21. Quoted in Joseph P. Weinberg, "Black-Jewish Tensions: Their Genesis," *CCAR Journal* 21 (Spring 1974): 32.

22. Quoted in Shankman, *Ambivalent Friends*, 115; quoted in Andrew Delbanco, "The Mark of Zora," *The New Republic* 213 (3 July 1995): 32; quoted in Shankman, *Ambivalent Friends*, 115.

23. Quoted in Auchmutey, "Daisy," 43.

24. Quoted in Evans, *Lonely Days*, 7.

25. Ibid., 11; quoted in Shankman, *Ambivalent Friends*, 114, 121.

26. Quoted in Shankman, *Ambivalent Friends*, 116.

27. Quoted in ibid., 118.

28. "The Jew Shows Us How In Many Ways," *Norfolk Journal and Guide*, 22 May 1926.

29. Richard Wright, *Black Boy* (New American Library, 1951), 71; quoted in Leonard Dinnerstein, *Uneasy at Home: Antisemitism and the American Jewish Experience* (Oxford University Press, 1987), 230–31.

30. Wright, *Black Boy*, 70; quoted in Shankman, *Ambivalent Friends*, 134.

31. Quoted in Leonard Dinnerstein, "The Origins of Black Anti-Semitism," *American Jewish Archives* 38 (November 1986): 118; David J. Hellwig, "Black Images of Jews: From Reconstruction to Depression," *Societas* 8 (Summer 1978): 218; quoted in Shankman, *Ambivalent Friends*, 122.

32. Horace Mann Bond, "Negro Attitudes Toward Jews," *Jewish Social Studies* 27 (January 1965): 9.

33. Evans, *Lonely Days*, 30.

34. *Nashville Observer*, 8 May 1942.

35. Nashville Council on Jewish Women 1942–43 Annual Report, Jewish Federation Archives, Nashville, Tennessee.

36. Quoted in Rabinowitz, "Nativism, Bigotry and Anti-Semitism"; Hero, *The Southerner and World Affairs*, 496.

37. Cobb, ed., *Cohn*, 197; Hero, *The Southerner and World Affairs*, 479.

38. Quoted in Shankman, *Ambivalent Friends*, 131.

39. *Charlotte Observer*, 12 October 1994.

40. Cash, *Mind of the South*, 334; Cobb, ed., *Cohn*, 197; Evans, *Lonely Days*, xxii.

Martin Luther King and the Southern Dream of Freedom

Timothy B. Tyson

"When we come together to celebrate Dr. Martin Luther King Jr., it is important to realize that the King holiday is just shorthand for honoring all of those local people who stood up for justice in the civil rights—era South." Doorway in New Bern, North Carolina, courtesy of Billy E. Barnes.

This essay was taken from a Martin Luther King Jr. Day address given by the author on January 17, 2005, in Columbus, Mississippi. The author would like to thank everyone on the Columbus Martin Luther King Jr. Legacy Committee, especially Wilbur Colom and Deborah Schumaker of the Colom Foundation. He would also like to thank his wife, Perri Morgan, his sister-in-law Hope Morgan Ward, who is the United Methodist Bishop of Mississippi, and her husband, Mike Ward, who knows a good bowl of butterbeans when he spills it in his lap.

My Grandmama Irene Hart's granddaddy was a preacher, and her daddy was a preacher, and when she was sixteen Irene ran off with a young preacher named Jack Tyson and got married in the back seat of a car. Lots of people still get engaged in the back seat of a car, but Jack and Irene actually got married right there in the back seat of a Model-T Ford on Middle Swamp Road near Greenville, North Carolina. Jack came from a preaching family, too. His Uncle Alonza Tyson, who pronounced them man and wife from the front seat, was a preacher, and his two brothers, Marl and Luther, were both preachers. After they ran off, Jack and Irene raised six sons, and all six of them grew up to be preachers, including my father. My sister Boo graduated from divinity school, as did my cousins by the dozens. My sister-in-law is the United Methodist bishop of Mississippi.

In summary, then, though I am a historian, my father, all five of my Tyson uncles, my grandfather, my great grandfather and my great-great-grandfather were all Free Will Baptist or Methodist preachers. And I just accepted a job as Visiting Professor of American Christianity and Southern Culture at Duke Divinity School. I say these things now so that you know the background I bring to this discussion of another southern preacher, Martin Luther King Jr., and the way that we remember him.

When we come together to celebrate Dr. Martin Luther King Jr., it is important to realize that the King holiday is just shorthand for honoring all of those local people who stood up for justice in the civil rights–era South. If King had never been born, there still would have been a black revolution in the American South in the decades that followed World War II. King himself would be the first person to acknowledge that he did not make the movement; instead, the patient local labors of thousands and thousands of black southerners lifted him up among the rulers of the world. He not only spoke on behalf of thousands of people he never met, but his voice depended almost entirely upon them. Martin Luther King's message was not unlike that of a gospel singer who goes from church to church, making a joyful noise unto the Lord, lifting people's hearts and giving them the strength to do what they know needs doing. Our mind's eye focuses on King, but what historians have learned is that the movement was really made by local people, working in their own communities, far from the television cameras and civil rights celebrities.

And yet there is much to learn from Martin Luther King, and he deserves our attention today. Like all those preachers I grew up around, I have three points to make in this "sermon." First, it may not seem very profound to you, but King was a southerner, and that indisputable fact colors everything he said and did. Second, King's memory has been distorted almost beyond recognition in the years since we lost him. And last, King's message—not the sanitized version we hear about every January but that profoundly challenging message that cannot be separated from his life and death—speaks to our own predicaments today just as clearly as it did to the dilemmas of his day.

When I say King was a southerner, I recognize that some people have hung an invisible "whites only" sign above our southern heritage. I've got a nephew, Bud, that I worry about right much, and a couple of years ago he came roaring up to Christmas dinner with two great big Confederate battle flags flapping from the back of his truck. I asked him how did he think our black neighbors would feel about his stars and bars. Bud said it didn't have nothing to do with that. I asked him how would he feel if they thought he didn't like them because they were black. Bud replied that he couldn't help it what they thought, and then he gave me a bumper-sticker rationale for his banner: "Heritage, not hate."

I will concede that Bud ain't much of a hater. But I can be a mean man, myself, so I pretended to change the subject and lay low. After awhile I said, "Bud, what's your favorite William Faulkner novel?" He allowed as how he hadn't really read any William Faulkner. I tried Richard Wright, Carson McCullers, Eudora Welty. I even tossed him Shelby Foote, trying to be fair, since he liked that Civil War paraphernalia, but Bud hadn't read any of them.

"Bud," I suggested, "why don't you run in that kitchen and whip us up some sweet potato biscuits?" He said he hadn't ever heard of sweet potato biscuits. I told him his grandmama made them all the time, but that was okay, maybe he could just make us some regular buttermilk biscuits. Bud said he didn't make no biscuits.

I asked him about blues and gospel. About Mississippi greats Robert Johnson, Muddy Waters, Sam Cooke, Elvis Presley. Did he know that

Thelonious Monk was from Rocky Mount? Nope. When I asked him about Hank Williams, he thought I meant Junior, the one that sings about Monday night football. He told me the name of his favorite country music singer, who, I happen to know, is from Illinois.

I said, "Well, Bud, I thought you were some kind of southern heritage nut, but you don't know William Faulkner, you can't make no biscuits, you don't know anything about the blues or gospel, and the only country musician you've come up with is a Yankee. It seems like the only thing about the South that matters is that damn flag." And it went sort of downhill from there. I'm afraid my joy bell just wasn't ringing too loud that day.

Sometimes I can get my joy bell ringing again if I think hard about what I *should* have said, repent, and try to do better. When banging my head against the world gets me dissonant and off key, I will turn to my friend and say, "You know what I *should* have told that guy?" And then we think a little bit and laugh a lot, and this little exercise not only helps me but, once in awhile, as a result of all this practice, I end up actually saying what I should have said. And what I should have said to Bud is this: the problem, old son, is that your mental South is still segregated, in fact, it is more segregated than the actual South ever was. You can't keep southern culture and history in a box. Jerry Lee Lewis and Little Richard were just working two different sides of the same street. Jimmie Rodgers, our very first country-music star, was a white man who learned to play guitar and banjo from black railroad workers and always traveled with a black band.

If you're really into southern pride, if you're a bone-deep southern chauvinist like myself, your new, fully integrated mental South will come with immense advantages. You get to keep Eudora Welty, but you get Richard Wright, too. You still have Faulkner and Thomas Wolfe, but you get Margaret Walker and Zora Neale Hurston, too. Elvis is still on the team, but you get Muddy Waters and James Brown and Sam Cooke. You hang on to Billy Graham, but you get Martin Luther King, too. You get to "Stand by Your Man" with Tammy Wynette and "Kiss an Angel Good Mornin'" with Charley Pride. You keep country music and NASCAR, but you also get spirituals, gospel, blues, jazz, rock and roll, and a whole lot of hip-hop. You get the picture. When you start adding it up, you realize that southern culture, properly considered, actually more or less rules the world. If we could manage to hang a meter on southern culture, we'd be as rich as Arab oil sheiks. So when these young white folks start talking about southern pride, don't just shush 'em up, school 'em up, and the

South WILL rise again, the right way, this time. We'll rise up like those biscuits Bud ain't learned to make yet.

Martin Luther King wasn't afraid of a biscuit. He clung to his roots down in Dixie and was proud of them. My favorite southern fact-snack is this: Dr. King had a lifelong habit of interrupting important meetings to say, "Brothers and sisters, I just don't believe the Lord's work can go forward unless we get some soul food in here," and they'd send out to his favorite restaurant for piles of chicken and greens and cornbread. He loved the pig's ear sandwiches at La Vase Restaurant in Birmingham. Tell me a man whose favorite food is fried pig's ear sandwiches is not a southerner.

Born in Atlanta, educated at Morehouse College before he went up north to graduate school, King came back to Alabama and Georgia to do most of his work and died in Memphis. But more than a southern biography, he had a southern sensibility. He gave voice to a vision rooted in the black South, a vision of liberty forged in slavery, a vision that would capture the moral imagination of the world. This was the homegrown intellectual, political, and theological vision that he skillfully blended with Gandhian nonviolent direct action, a cultural achievement that would change the course of world history.

It was more a prophetic than a liberal vision, as David Chappell notes. King raised money among white liberals in the North, but he did not really share their faith in the power of reason and education and enlightenment. Perhaps because of the South's history of slavery, civil war, defeat, poverty, and oppression, southerners have rarely succumbed much to the sweet elixir of empty optimism or the siren song of human perfectibility. King was keenly aware that, as human beings, we not only have problems, we *are* a problem. In fact, King was a pessimistic theologian with a Deep South sense of tragedy; he saw that humanity was mired in a sinful nature, that evil was "rampant" in the universe, concluding that "only the superficial optimist who refuses to face the realities of life fails to see this patent fact."

Yet despite the bleakness of this view, King had hope, and he knew the difference between optimism and hope. If you are feeling optimistic right now, don't let me interfere, brothers and sisters. But I'm a sinner, myself, and a weak reed in a strong wind, and I need more than optimism. Optimism is when you have weighed your prospects and considered the likely outcome, and things look good. I wouldn't know about that, myself. You can *have* the weak tea of optimism. I need the straight whiskey of hope, the more daring and irrational the better. Hope is more of a prophetic faith than a sunny assessment, and that's what King had in lush southern abundance.

We associate Martin Luther King with nonviolent direct action, which has few deep philosophical or historical roots in the South. And we're right to do so. But in a world so far fallen from grace, King's most crucial insight was not so much the power of nonviolence as his insistence that coercion was essential, that society would never change of its own accord, that the world would never choose to do right, would never respond merely to moral persuasion. He grew up in a place where folks knew that a two-by-four was sometimes necessary to get the mule's attention. King lived in the South, but he lives for the ages and became a world-historical figure not because he was a dreamer but because he was a realist.

Which brings me to my second point, that Martin Luther King's memory has been distorted almost beyond recognition. In the years since his murder, we have transformed King into a kind of innocuous black Santa Claus, genial and vacant, a benign vessel that can be filled with whatever generic good wishes the occasion may dictate. Politicians who oppose everything King worked for now jostle their way onto podiums to honor his memory.

Part of the distortion of King's memory is that we pay so much attention to one speech, his famous "I Have a Dream" oration. It's a great speech, one of the timeless moments in American history, and yet I'd like to consider a different speech, his very first political speech, one that is more revealing in some ways and shows him to be both the most realistic and the most radical political leader of his generation: King's speech at Holt Street Baptist Church, given on December 5, 1955, at the first mass meeting in Montgomery, four days after Rosa Parks had been arrested.

Rosa Parks did not call King when she got arrested. She called the most influential African American activist in Montgomery, E. D. Nixon, like most black people in town would have done. Nixon knew King but considered him sort of a smart shirt-tail boy, promising but not well known in town and certainly unseasoned. Nixon saw this as an advantage, since King clearly had not been bought. "The city fathers hadn't had time to put their hands on him," Nixon said later. King was only twenty-six years old, but he was immensely well-spoken and had no real enemies. Nixon selected King to lead the boycott. King himself said of his ascendance to leadership in the Montgomery Improvement Association (MIA): "It happened so quickly I hadn't had time to think it through."

The Holt Street Speech revealed not only King's extraordinary oratorical abilities but his expansive brilliant strategy of black liberation. His
first point was to underline the nonviolent and Christian wellsprings of
the movement. "We believe in the teachings of Jesus," he declared. "The
only weapon that we have in our hands this evening is the weapon of
protest." By articulating the movement in the explicit language of Christian redemption, King wedded the philosophy of nonviolent direct action, which did not have deep roots in the South, to the central institution
in the African American community, the church. It was a brilliant move.
King was deeply rooted in southern black culture, and he knew that
somehow it would work, even though his own understanding of nonviolent direct action was clearly rudimentary at that point; pacifist Glenn
Smiley, writing from King's house a few days later, reported that "this
place is an arsenal."

King's next rhetorical move in the Holt Street speech was to deploy
the rhetoric of American democracy and the reality of the Cold War. King
was a big-picture strategist, and he played the U.S.-Soviet rivalry like a
violin. He understood the central political reality of his day—that the
United States and the Soviet Union were engaged in a bitter struggle for
control of the world, a world that was mostly dark-skinned, and that
America's biggest weakness was its hypocrisy on the race question. He
addressed the Cold War directly at Holt Street Baptist Church that evening: "If we were incarcerated behind the Iron Curtain of a communistic
nation we couldn't do this, but the glory of American democracy is the
right to protest for right." King held America to its own standards, even
though he knew he did not have freedom of speech. He knew white
terrorists were likely to bomb his house, for example, and soon they
would.

But violence could not muzzle King. After embracing Christian love
and the language of American democracy, King then reminded his listeners that the black freedom movement could undermine as well as
affirm America's position in the world. God was not just the God of love,
he said, but also "the God that standeth before the nations and says, 'Be
still and know that I am God—and if you don't, I'm gonna cast you out of
the arms of your national and international relationships, and break the
backbone of your power.'" King's direct reference to the Cold War un-
derlined the threat that black Americans could play to that international
crusade: "Not only are we using the tools of persuasion, but we have got
to use the tools of coercion."

King knew, too, that the problem of white supremacy was not just an external problem. Ku Klux Klan terrorism, disfranchisement, all-white juries, menial, low-paying jobs—all those things were a problem—but there was also the terrible and crippling poison of an internalized white supremacy that black children learned from the world around them, a world set up to show them that they were inferior. He saw the ads in *Jet* and *Ebony* for skin-bleaching creams and hair-straightening agents; he knew what "good skin" and "good hair" meant in the black community. He knew that the revolution that he hoped for depended on changing not just the outward but the inward manifestations of white supremacy—and not just among whites. King sought to undermine internalized white supremacy and affirm black beauty and self-esteem: "Right here in Montgomery, when the history books are written in the future, somebody will have to say, 'There lived a race of people, black people, fleecy locks and black complexion, of people who had the moral courage to stand up for their rights and thereby they injected a new meaning into the veins of history and of civilization.'"

In that speech by a twenty-six-year-old, we already see everything that is to come in the thirteen years it took to get to Memphis: demands that American civic and religious traditions live up to their promises; efforts to instill in black Americans what he eventually called "a new sense of somebodiness"; and, most importantly, strategies rooted in a realistic assessment of political power—where it lay and how to wield it. He was a realist as well as a radical.

When I say King was a radical, I do not agree with Ronald Reagan and Jesse Helms that he was a Communist. King flatly rejected Marxism because of its authoritarianism and materialism, because of its rejection of spiritual things. At the same time, we easily forget the King who wrote in 1957, "I never intend to accommodate myself to the tragic inequalities of an economic system which takes necessities from the many in order to give luxuries to the few." He explained later, "You don't have to go to Karl Marx to be a revolutionary. I got it from a man named Jesus."

The radicalism of King's thought and the militancy of his methods have all given way to cartoons invented after his death. The real Martin Luther King Jr. went to Memphis and called for those who opposed America's war in Vietnam to join forces with the unemployed and the working poor, declaring that "the whole structure of American life must be changed." He avowed that "unarmed truth and unconditional love will have the final say in reality," and then somebody killed him. We don't know all that much about why King died; we still don't know from what corridors the order for his assassination may have issued, and we may never know.

But we do know this. In 1963, after King told the nation about his dream that "one day on the red hills of Georgia, the sons of former slaves and the sons of former slave owners will be able to sit down together at the table of brotherhood," William Sessions, the FBI agent covering the speech who later became the agency's director, wrote, "We must mark [King] now, if we have not done so before, as the most dangerous Negro of the future in this nation from the standpoint of communism, the Negro, and national security." The memo then lays out a plan to destroy King personally and politically, including exploiting King's bouts of deep depression to try and encourage him to commit suicide. It is a matter of public record that our government sought King's ruin and even his death in the years before he was killed. Although King believed that America was the last, best hope of freedom, he knew, too, that our government sometimes engaged in activities unworthy of our country, and he wasn't reluctant to say so. He denounced the war in Vietnam, and most black leaders in the country then denounced him.

King's antiwar message has never been more timely than it is today. And now our government is engaged in what appears to be a vast grab for imperial dominion, sanctified by words like "freedom," justified in the language of national security but fueled by the will to control the world's oil supply. Many people today are worried or grieving about somebody dear to them. Nearly two thousand American families have lost a loved one. Tens of thousands of other families have had someone come home missing an arm, a leg, their eyes, their face, their future in a cause that is not worthy of their patriotism and sacrifice. And there are more than a hundred thousand dead in Iraq.

We have been assured by the president of the United States that this Iraq war was a crusade to topple a bloody dictator, and we were also told that Saddam Hussein possessed, in the president's words, "more than 38,000 liters of botulinium toxin, enough to subject millions of people to death by respiratory failure," that he wielded "500 tons of sarin, mustard gas, vx nerve agent," that the dictator menaced us with "upwards of 30,000 munitions capable of delivering chemical agents," an "advanced nuclear weapons development program," and operational ties to Al Qaeda.

None of this is true. Worse still, the president used our grief about the thousands of Americans killed in New York City on 9/11 to take us into a fruitless quagmire. It is not hard to imagine exactly what King would say about all this. He said the same thing about Vietnam: that the bombs we drop abroad will eventually explode in the streets of America and that spending billions and billions of dollars on the machinery of death will ruin our hopes for a decent and democratic nation.

King's challenging words still speak to our world. Almost forty years after he tried to organize the Poor People's Campaign, the gap between rich and poor in America is wider than ever. Forty-five percent of African American children are born in poverty in a deindustrialized urban wasteland. The *New York Times* reported recently that when a young black man and a young white man go to court charged with the same crime and neither of them has a criminal record, the young black man is eight times more likely to go to prison. If the crime in question is a drug-related crime, the young black man is forty-nine times more likely to go to prison. There are still more young black men in prison than in college. In some ways, I guess, the question is not so much what King would think about these things but what we think.

The world tells us that this monumental injustice is all part of the natural order and urges us to hide in the suburbs of our own indifference. Even thoughtful people who care about what happens suggest that progress can only come by changing "attitudes" or making friends across the color line. I am not going to say that our attitudes don't need examination or that friendship is not a good thing. My attitudes certainly need examination, and I think we need about all the interracial friendship we can get. But Martin Luther King did not simply want white America to invite him to tea. Instead, King insisted that "the whole structure of American life must be changed." He demanded policies that would address the real history of our country, and our day demands no less.

King was a son of the South, rooted in the land of cotton, and he drew from that rich soil the wisdom that we celebrate today. His wisdom was homegrown stuff, and he believed it so deeply that he was willing to die for it. While many people would prefer to forget what King actually believed and instead celebrate a saint who never existed, his truth goes marching on. It demands that we follow his example and confront the world that actually exists rather than the things we wish were true. It demands that we work together, all God's children, for peace and freedom and a decent life for all.

Dianne Nash, a student leader from Nashville who did much to make the movement and was very close to King, told my own students: "If people today think it was Martin's movement, then they—young people today—are more likely to say, 'Gosh, I wish we had a Martin Luther King here today to lead us.' But if people knew how the movement really started, then the question they would ask is 'What can I do?'" King would be the first to say that this struggle does not rely upon towering leaders and great speeches. Instead, he learned from the mothers and grand-mothers of the South that the quilt of freedom is made of many patches and stitched by many hands, that the movement for which he spoke depended upon people working together in their own communities, turn-ing to each other instead of on each other and taking power in their hands to build a world big enough for all the people, a world that is fearless and loving and true.

Read More About It

Taylor Branch, *Parting the Waters: America in the King Years, 1954–63* (Simon and Schuster, 1989).

Taylor Branch, *Pillar of Fire: America in the King Years, 1963–65* (Simon and Schus-ter, 1998).

David Chappell, *A Stone of Hope: Prophetic Religion and the Death of Jim Crow* (UNC Press, 2004).

John Dittmer, *Local People: The Civil Rights Struggle in Mississippi* (University of Illinois Press, 1994).

Martin Luther King Jr., *Stride toward Freedom: The Montgomery Story* (Harper, 1958).

Martin Luther King Jr., *Why We Can't Wait* (Harper and Row, 1963).

Our Lady of Guadeloupe Visits the Confederate Memorial

Thomas A. Tweed

Different traditions continue to coexist in small southern towns. Our Lady of Guadeloupe, riding in the back of a pick-up, approaches the Confederate memorial on the Clinton, North Carolina, courthouse lawn. Courtesy of Thomas A. Tweed.

ruisms are sometimes true. And if anything has seemed self-evident to interpreters of the South, it's the religious homogeneity of the Bible Belt. With the exception of the Mormon cultural area in Utah and adjoining states, no U.S. region seems less diverse. Fervent revivalism, civil war, and minimal immigration allowed a southern evangelical Protestant establishment—mostly Baptist and Methodist—to form by the nineteenth century. Free of challenges from immigrants, that evangelical alliance has shaped the religious landscape. Some observers have trumpeted the South as the last stronghold of faithful Christian witness; others, like the Baltimore-born iconoclast H. L. Mencken, have dismissed it as "the bunghole of the United States, a cesspool of Baptists, a miasma of Methodism, snake-charmers, phony real-estate operators, and syphilitic evangelists." However the assessments diverge—and they still do—almost all interpreters have agreed on one point: the South looks more homogenous than the rest of the nation.[1]

There is much truth to the still standard interpretation: the South seems more uniformly Protestant and more institutionally pious. Surveys indicate that southerners join churches and attend services more than Americans do in other regions. Even the unchurched in the South admit to a lingering piety: in one 1978 poll nearly three-fourths believed that Jesus was the son of God and rose from the dead, and another survey a decade later found that almost two-thirds of the unaffiliated believed in life after death. Recent surveys reveal the same pattern of attendance, membership, and belief. For example, the spring 2000 Southern Focus Poll found that nearly a quarter of southerners (23 percent) attend services more than once a week, as compared to about 15 percent of nonsoutherners, and significantly more southerners than nonsoutherners (40 percent compared to 29 percent) say that religion is "extremely important" in their lives. According to the fall 1999 Southern Focus Poll, more southerners than nonsoutherners claim the Bible is their authority for daily life (31 percent compared with 19 percent), and more than six out of ten say they prefer the biblical creation account to Darwinian evolutionary theory to explain the universe's origins. And some geographers and sociologists have argued that this regional pattern of piety shows few signs of changing.[2]

The South is not just more pious, either; it is also still predominantly Protestant. The 2000 Southern Focus Poll found that 65 percent of southerners claim Protestant affiliation, while the rest of the nation was only 43 percent Protestant. Two sociologists who have conducted the most comprehensive telephone survey of the last decade came to similar conclusions. Barry A. Kosmin and Seymour P. Lachman have found that Baptists, both black and white, are concentrated south of the Mason-Dixon Line. They are the largest religious group in fourteen states, nearly all of which are in the South, and Baptists comprise more than half the residents of Mississippi, Alabama, and Georgia. Furthermore, Kosmin and Lachman suggest, a "relatively stable" southern Protestantism, evangelical and Pentecostal, persisted into the 1990s.[3]

Truisms, however, need nuancing. We need to qualify the claims about the continuing evangelical Protestant dominance in several ways. First of all, diversity has a long history in the South. Among the earliest settlers, West African religious practices mixed with Christian piety to produce new creole spiritual forms, and even the Christian faiths Europeans transplanted bore varied fruits. Roman Catholics built the first permanent settlement in the South (and in North America) at St. Augustine in 1565. They have a long history in Texas and Louisiana, and Catholics built churches in small towns and larger cities. Jews also found a place in some southern cities—Charleston, Wilmington, Savannah, and Miami Beach, for instance. Presbyterians, Episcopalians, Quakers, Lutherans, Adventists, Disciples, Unitarians, Universalists, and other Protestants also competed with Baptists and Methodists for the allegiance of the region's faithful. And long before the Europeans and Africans arrived, the South had been home to Native peoples who spoke multiple languages and cultivated divergent religions for more than ten thousand years. As historian Joel Martin points out, "Non-natives became the majority population only 180 years ago, or after ninety-eight percent of the region's history had passed." The South was multiethnic, multicultural, and multireligious before anyone crossed the Atlantic.[4]

Today, while Protestantism continues to be the majority faith, the longstanding southern evangelical alliance might not be as "stable" as the work of sociologists Kosmin and Lachman has suggested. By some measures, the South does not appear much more religiously conservative. For instance, the 1998 Southern Focus Poll asked respondents who identified themselves as Protestant how they would describe their own faith. Slightly more southerners said they were "pentecostal" than nonsoutherners (12 percent compared to 10 percent), but fewer below the Mason-Dixon line identified themselves as "evangelical" (only 8 percent). We do not know whether the South has become less evangelical or the rest of the country has become more so, although other evidence suggests that the latter is the case. Seven of ten southerners still affiliate with Protestantism, and the old Baptist dominance persists (nearly 47 percent), but there is evidence the region is less disproportionately "fundamentalist" and "evangelical" in its theological vision.[5]

Within the South itself, some places have been more religiously diverse than others. It still makes sense to talk about the South as a distinct religious and cultural region, but we should not minimize the intraregional variation, which existed before Europeans arrived and continues today. The U.S. Census in 1906, for example, revealed that Catholics formed a majority in Louisiana and showed significant strength in Kentucky. Even within states with a legacy of Baptist-Methodist predominance, religious outsiders congregated here and there: in the early twentieth century, Greek Orthodox Christians gathered in Atlanta, Jews built a synagogue in central Savannah, and Italian Catholics worshiped in St. Helena, North Carolina.[6]

And while some southern places are more diverse than others, diversity in general has been intensifying in the South since the 1970s. In 1999 over 15 percent of southerners claimed Catholic identity, and altogether more than one in five (21 percent) affiliated with some non-Protestant faith—Catholicism, Judaism, Hinduism, Islam, Buddhism, or another religious tradition. The Bible Belt has loosened a bit, even if its hold on the region still can be felt on Sunday mornings in white-wood and red-brick Protestant churches all across the South. Transregional and transnational migration has been changing the region's religious and ethnic character. Economic realignments—and a variety of social and technological changes, including the introduction of air conditioning—have lured migrants from the North and Midwest to the Sun Belt, including, for example, more Catholics from the Northeast and Lutherans from the Midwest.

In addition, temporary, circular, and permanent transnational migrants from Asia, the Caribbean, and Latin America have been changing the southern religious landscape. The national immigrant population almost doubled between 1970 and 1990, and by 1994, almost 23 million Americans—nearly one in eleven U.S. residents—were foreign born. Of course, Atlanta is not Los Angeles and Richmond isn't New York, but transnational migrants have found their way to the South, too. Even if some states, including Mississippi and Kentucky, show less demographic change, Latinos and Asians taken together now make up almost 14 percent of southerners, and the 2000 census counted just over 8 million southern immigrants, or almost 9 percent of the regional population. The South's foreign-born population more than quadrupled between 1960 and 2000. Texas's almost 3 million foreign-born residents formed 14 percent of the state's population, and almost 17 percent of Floridians were born outside the United States.[7]

These new migrants have come for varied reasons. Political crises have pushed refugees from their homelands, and some of those have settled in southern cities. The obvious example is Miami, which was a southern Protestant town when Fidel Castro's revolutionary army marched into Havana in January 1959. Fleeing the new socialist state, hundreds of thousands of Cuban exiles boarded planes, boats, and rafts to cross the warm waters of the Straits of Florida. Other refugees from Central America and the Caribbean joined them. By the 1990s, these recently arrived Latino Catholics had transformed Miami: Latinos formed the majority and Roman Catholicism had become the city's predominant faith. Other refugees have made their homes in other cities and towns all across the South, including the Hmong in Selma and the Vietnamese in New Orleans, and they have done their part to reconfigure the region's religious landscape, too.[8]

Political changes in the United States have also played a role: the 1965 immigration act altered the old national quota system and allowed larger numbers of voluntary migrants from Asia and Latin America to cross U.S. borders legally. These migrants have brought with them multiple religions, including Hinduism, Catholicism, Islam, Sikhism, Jainism, Vodou, Santería, and Buddhism. By 2000, when a new federal law allowed even more immigration visas, approximately 24,000 Vietnamese—Buddhist, Catholic, and Confucian—claimed residence in Louisiana. Approximately 46,000 Asian Indians, many of them Hindu or Sikh, found their way into Georgia, and over 47,000 Filipinos, the overwhelming majority of them Catholic, had settled in Virginia. Atlanta boasted approximately 10,000 Buddhists, 12,000 Hindus, and 30,000 Muslims, and followers had built temples and mosques in and around the city. Even in southern states with smaller Asian immigrant populations—such as Arkansas, Alabama, and Tennessee—observers could notice signs of the new religious diversity: Wat Buddhasamakeedham, a Theravada Buddhist temple in Fort Smith, Arkansas, for example, and Sri Ganesha Temple, an Indian-style Hindu building in the capital of country music, Nashville. And the new, and not so new, Latino presence is even harder to miss. It is obvious in Texas, where a quarter of the residents claim Hispanic heritage. But elsewhere in the South—defined as the Gallup Poll does it, as the eleven Confederate states plus Kentucky and Oklahoma—more recent Latino migrants have transformed some states, especially Florida with its 2000 Hispanic population of more than 2.7 million. And all across the region Latinos, both circulatory migrants who leave when the growing season ends and those who have made the South their home, have filled the pews of Catholic, and some Protestant, churches.[9]

ASIANS AND LATINOS IN CONTEMPORARY NORTH CAROLINA

We might expect to find ethnic and religious diversity in Texas, with its unbroken Hispanic heritage, and in Florida, with its influx of migrants since the sixties, but this new diversity is evident throughout the South. Consider North Carolina, which has traditionally been one of the region's Protestant strongholds and as recently as 1990 had foreign-born Hispanic and Asian populations of less than 2 percent. According to the 2000 Census, which did not count illegal migrants, 113,689 Asians and 378,963 Hispanics lived in North Carolina; together, the two groups make up more than 6 percent of the state's population. Between 1990 and 2000, every county saw an increase in Asians and Hispanics. The Asian population of Mecklenburg County (Charlotte) rose 197 percent (to 25,186), Guilford County (Greensboro) increased 226 percent (to 12,168), and Wake County (Raleigh) swelled 201 percent (to 24,622). The Hispanic increases between 1990 and 2000 were even more dramatic, as the number of Latinos grew from 77,000 in 1990 to more than 378,000 ten years later. Six counties boasted increases of more than 1,000 percent, and many others found themselves transformed by migration. Durham County's Hispanic population rose 729 percent in the decade, and the city of Durham became an "all-minority" municipality where no racial or ethnic group could claim a majority. In 2000, Durham was 48 percent white, 39 percent African American, 8 percent Hispanic, and 3 percent Asian.[10]

Those demographic changes are evident in public schools throughout the state. By 1993 school officials in Charlotte began to see the changes as children from sixty-seven nations, who spoke forty-four languages, showed up for school on the first day. The majority of those students were the children of Southeast Asian immigrants, especially Vietnamese.

And in 1999 hundreds of parents attended a school board meeting in Siler City, the largest town in rural Chatham County, to express their worries about the ethnic and linguistic shifts that their traditional southern community had witnessed in recent years. When schools opened in Siler City in fall 1994, 15 percent of the students were Latinos; five years later that proportion had grown to 41 percent. Hispanics had become the town's largest ethnic group, with a total increase of 741 percent during the 1990s.[11]

North Carolina's new migrants, young and old, have not always received a warm welcome. In June 1998 Durham's community leaders felt the need to organize the "Operation TRUCE Campaign," which was aimed at reducing the rising violence against Latinos. And consider events in McAdenville, which locals dubbed "Christmastown, USA" because it draws a million visitors every December to view the dazzling display of 425,000 Christmas lights. In summer 2001 the 616 residents of that small mill town did what so many other communities across the region and the nation have done: they used zoning codes to prevent Asian American Buddhists from transforming an existing building into a new temple. Officials and residents pointed to legitimate concerns—about traffic and parking—and they suggested "it wouldn't have been any different if they'd been Baptist or Methodist." But not far beneath the surface were other worries about the Lao and Thai migrants and their unfamiliar religion, as with a forty-nine-year-old neighbor who worried about "what it might bring into the neighborhood." Those same worries surfaced even more clearly in Siler City when four hundred people gathered on February 19, 2000, at the steps of city hall to hear David Duke, the former Louisiana state legislator and current director of the National Organization for European American Rights. A service station owner, whose license plate reads ARYAN, had invited Duke to condemn Siler City's new ethnic diversity at a public rally. The former Ku Klux Klan grand wizard did not disappoint the crowd: "Siler City is at a crossroads," said Duke. "Either you get your public officials to get the INS in here and get these illegal immigrants out or you'll lose your homes, you'll lose your schools, you'll lose your way of life." As some Latino migrants and their supporters stood by with signs that signaled their dissent, Duke ended by linking local and national developments: "Siler City is symbolic of what's happening in America. Your battle here is America's battle."[12]

And those on both sides of the battle lines could not fail to notice that the increase in the Asian and Latino populations has also affected religious life in North Carolina. Most of the state's 12,600 Koreans are Protestants, as are some of the 19,000 Chinese. Some Latinos converted to Pentecostal and evangelical Protestantism after they arrived, in response to vigorous missionary efforts by some congregations. But most of the newcomers have added to the spiritual heterogeneity of North Carolina. For example, they have dramatically increased the state's Catholic population. Across the nation Latinos are a growing presence in the Catholic Church, where they now constitute about one quarter of all U.S. Catholics. According to a 2000 report by the National Conference of Catholic Bishops, North Carolina included two of the four U.S. dioceses with the highest percentage of growth among Hispanic Catholics: Charlotte, which topped the list, and Raleigh, which was fourth. The Latino Catholics in North Carolina have continued their traditions of domestic devotion to Mary and the saints they learned in their homelands, but many also attend the local parish when they can find Spanish language masses. As recently as 1990, that was much more difficult than it might seem. Caught off guard by the rising migrant population, the Diocese of Raleigh scrambled to find Spanish-speaking priests. When the new priest discontinued the bilingual mass at Holy Cross Church in Durham in 1996, most of the Latinos literally walked out, led by a middle-aged Mexican migrant carrying the statue of Our Lady of Guadeloupe down the church's front steps. Those exiled Latinos found a spiritual home across town at Immaculate Conception parish, where the priest established a Spanish mass for the 284 Latinos, and more than 200 other unregistered Hispanic households. As at Immaculate Conception, the state's Catholic leaders have begun to respond to the new Latino presence. By 2000 fifty-four parishes in the Diocese of Raleigh had at least one Spanish-language mass, including Saint Julia's in Siler City, where parallel congregations of Anglos and Latinos meet on Sunday mornings in the small white church for the English mass at 9:00 and the Spanish celebration at 11:15. This would not be news in Florida or Texas, of course, but in the home of Billy Graham, a state traditionally dominated by Baptists and Methodists, it is noteworthy.[13]

It is noteworthy, too, that several dozen Buddhist, Muslim, Jain, and Hindu congregations now meet across the state, in converted homes and renovated churches, and even in new structures built according to traditional Asian architectural models. Approximately twenty thousand Asian Indian immigrants made their homes in North Carolina in 2000, and the Hindus and Jains among them meet for worship in centers across the state, including a Swaminaryan Temple in Charlotte, a Jain Study Center in Garner, and a Hindu temple in Morrisville. The latter is a modest structure dedicated in 1985 by the Hindu Society of North Carolina, whose members hail from different areas of India, north and south. To accommodate the variety of regional and devotional styles, the founding members turned democratic: they voted on which images to enshrine in their new worship center, a practice rarely used in India, where temples tend to install clusters of mythically related deities. This turn to democracy stalled but did not prevent intracommunity conflict. Recently, some Hindus who were born in south India decided that the eclecticism—and even the subtle north Indian bias—of the Morrisville temple did not meet their spiritual needs and began construction of a second temple in the Raleigh area, in suburban Cary. On September 3, 1999, five Hindu priests from across the United States presided at a four-day ceremony to install the south Indian temple's primary image, a statue of Sri Venkateswara, the god of wealth and well-being.[14]

By 2002 the state's Buddhists, both cradle Buddhists and converts, could practice their faith in fifteen temples and fifty-one centers across the state. Southern California's Hsi Lai Temple, the largest Buddhist temple in the Western Hemisphere, has an affiliated center in the Tar Heel state: the Buddha's Light International Association in Chapel Hill and Cary. Local leaders of a Taiwanese transnational movement founded in 1980 by the Mahayana Buddhist teacher, the Venerable Master Hsing Yun, aim to nurture the state's Chinese devotees and, more broadly, establish a Pure Land on earth, a peaceful and just world community. One hundred and fifty members with more modest goals worship on Sundays at Chua Van Hanh, an expanding Vietnamese temple in a north Raleigh neighborhood where devotees chant the Lotus Sutra in their native tongue and make sense of their exile in America. And the temple helps. "At first we were homesick and religion-sick," one middle-aged refugee told me in 1994, "but now it's better since we have the pagoda." Hundreds of Southeast Asian Buddhists practice at two temples in Greensboro: Chua Quan Am, a Vietnamese Mahayana Buddhist center, and Greensboro Buddhist Center, a ten-acre monastery where three resident monks guide Lao and Cambodian migrants. The state's first Buddhist temple, Wat Carolina Buddhajakra Vanaram, had two Thai monks in residence by 1988. That Theravada Buddhist monastery with its traditional red curved roof was built in Bolivia, a small Protestant town in eastern North Carolina, about a thirty-minute drive southwest of Wilmington. The founding president, a lay follower from Bangkok, explained that he began the effort to build the temple "to give people from Southeast Asia a place to worship." At first the local residents, and the congregation at nearby Antioch Baptist Church, did not know what to make of the saffron-robed Thai monks and the new Asian-style building. "This area never had to deal with internationals before," the Baptist pastor explained. "Then it was thrust into becoming an international town overnight."[15]

SYMBOLS OF THE EMERGING DIVERSITY

One symbol of the state's transnationalism, and its emerging religious diversity, can be found in an unlikely place, Raleigh's North Carolina Museum of History, founded in 1902 and dedicated to "preserving state, regional, and local history for future generations." This museum might be expected to sponsor exhibits like the popular 1999 "North Carolina and the Civil War," but it also installed a more surprising and revealing permanent exhibit on everyday religious practices of North Carolinians for the opening of its new building in 1994. Buddhists had become visible enough by 1994 that curator Sally Peterson felt compelled to include the Buddhist home altar along with Protestant, Jewish, Muslim, Hispanic Catholic, and Hindu artifacts in the folklife exhibit. On March 23, 1994, Phramana Somsak Sambimb, a Thai monk from Wat Greensboro, placed two white candles on either side of a twenty-inch bronze image of the Buddha, along with three sticks of incense and several paper Lotus flowers. He chanted and bowed before the Buddha, and after five minutes, the altar was consecrated. "That OK," Sambimb announced.[16]

It is hard to know if all visitors to the museum agree with the Thai monk, but this permanent exhibit signals the state's rising awareness of Asian religions. Peterson and other museum officials anticipated much more negative criticism than they received, and docents report that when they "take people through who happen to be Hindu or Buddhist or Jewish, they're really pleased to see something there." Still, some visitor comment cards are critical. One Raleigh resident, who was raised as a Buddhist by his Vietnamese mother and American father, wrote in 1994 that the "placement of [the Buddha] statue should be higher. It's sacrilegious to *look down* on an image of Lord Buddha." If that complaint from a local Buddhist only confirms the perceptions of the state's growing religious diversity, another comment card was somewhat more negative. A woman from Burgaw, North Carolina, reported in 1996 that she was "concerned about seeing the Hindu and Budhu [*sic*] being represented." "What percentage are there of these in N.C.?" she asked. In a written response to this visitor, the curator argued that "membership of [Hindus and Buddhists] numbers in the thousands," and "showing how these historic world religions are represented in North Carolina demonstrates how our state has become an international community." The museum archives do not include any record of the visitor's reaction to the letter, and it is difficult to know how most other North Carolinian visitors respond to the Buddhist home altar. Even if many who have not filled out comment cards are quietly troubled by the inclusion of Asian religious images—or the exhibit's implication that Protestantism is only one of many southern religions—it is still important to note that the exhibit would have been unthinkable at a North Carolina history museum three decades ago. The state's religious landscape is changing, and the varied home altars displayed in Raleigh represent those changes.[17]

Another site, southeast of the Raleigh museum, symbolizes the South's emerging religious diversity even more vividly. In most ways, Clinton, the Sampson County seat, is a typical southern town. Its economy has depended upon tobacco, vegetable, and hog farming, and it has one of the oldest cotton markets in the state. By 2000 the town included Catholic, Mormon, and Universalist churches, as well as three Methodist and four Pentecostal houses of worship. Most residents, however, still attend one of Clinton's many Baptist churches. Not far from a prominent Baptist church, in the center of town, is the Sampson County Courthouse, which was built in 1801. On the courthouse lawn stands a Confederate monument, erected in 1916 by the local chapter of the United Daughters of the Confederacy (UDC) to memorialize the town's Civil War dead. For its chiseled inscription Annie Graham Grady, at that time the local president of the UDC, chose lines from "March of the Deathless Dead," a poem by wartime Catholic chaplain Abram Joseph Ryan (1838–1886), widely recognized as the "Poet-Priest" of the Confederacy. The monument's inscription reads,

> In Honor of
> The Confederate Soldiers of Sampson County
> "Who bore the flag of a sacred trust
> And fell in a cause, though lost, still just
> And died for me and you."
> 1861–1865[18]

This monument to the Religion of the Lost Cause, the South's civil religion, stands only two blocks from Clinton's lone Catholic church, Immaculate Conception parish. Eighty years after local Protestants dedicated the Confederate memorial, the courthouse was the site of another public ritual, a celebration that symbolizes the emerging diversity.

Just after noon on the December feast day of Our Lady of Guadeloupe, the patroness of the Americas, several hundred Latinos gathered at Immaculate Conception church, an architecturally unspectacular, small brick and wood structure, to await the six-hour festival, which would include a procession, mass, and meal.[19] At one o'clock, cars that had become mobile shrines to Mary lined the streets outside the church. Mothers fussed with their children's traditional Mexican costumes, and men readied the red pick-up truck that would carry the image of Our Lady of Guadeloupe. Minutes later, a priest carrying incense blessed the truck, and the procession began. Led by three Anglo clergymen, Bishop Joseph Gossman of the Raleigh Diocese and Immaculate Conception's two priests, Latinos from all over eastern North Carolina wound their way through the streets. Men from the Mexican state of Zacatecas performed a traditional dance as they passed dry cleaners and drug stores. Young children, on their best behavior, sat in the rear of the Virgin's truck. The rest of the Latino devotees, many of whom work in nearby fields or the hog processing plants, marched behind. The women and girls sang hymns to the Virgin in their native Spanish. The cars decorated with streamers and images followed.

When the procession of about seven hundred devotees reached Sampson Middle School auditorium at around two o'clock, the mass began with more singing. Eliciting only polite applause, Bishop Gossman's sermon was not the center of the ritual for most participants, even if the clergy used the occasion to evangelize and apologize. His words translated into Spanish by an interpreter, Gossman exhorted the people to focus on Jesus and attend mass. "Mary," he told the crowd, "shows us how to live and follow her son, Jesus." Then the bishop noted the contemporary cultural context. "All of us have problems," he said, "and you who come from Latin America have many problems. . . . Mary, the Virgin of Guadeloupe, will always be present for you with a mother's love." The bishop continued by acknowledging that the Diocese had been unprepared for the migration of so many new Catholics: "My special hope is that you who have come recently to this country and our Diocese will feel welcome." These remarks drew the only spontaneous and loud applause of the afternoon and were the only time the people did not await the translation or the interpreter's encouragement. "You are not visitors," the Bishop continued. "You are our brothers and sisters." And then in closing Bishop Gossman got to the apology: "I wish we could serve you better. Please believe me when I tell you we are trying our best. We will try to do better and better. . . . Let us pray for each other and the happy fiesta of Our Lady of Guadeloupe."[20] After the mass, everyone walked to the cafeteria next door for a traditional meal of pork, tortillas, and beans.

That sermon and the rest of the public ritual have multiple meanings. For interpreters of American Catholicism, the bishop's homily is historically significant in that a leader of North Carolina's Catholics acknowledged the Church's slow response to the recent Latino migration. It says much about one of the most pressing challenges now facing U.S. Catholicism—a challenge made vivid by the Latino Pentecostal storefront church that stands only a few blocks from Immaculate Conception parish. For many of the Latino devotees, the sermon was merely an interruption in the half-day festival. They endured the bishop's talk but cared more about the singing, praying, and eating. They came to express their needs and their gratitude to the Virgin, to gather with others who speak their language, and to remember the practices of their Latin American homelands. One thirty-six-year-old Mexican-born man from Jacksonville, North Carolina, offered a common viewpoint. That immigrant, who plans to stay in the United States, came to the Clinton festival to keep Mexican, and Catholic, traditions alive for his children. "I want my seventeen-year-old daughter to know the culture."

And there are other meanings. For interpreters of southern religion, and perhaps for the local Protestants who were watching football at home or window-shopping at the mall, another moment in the day's celebrations might have best captured its significance. Near the start of the procession, with the December sun overhead, the Virgin of Guadeloupe approached the courthouse lawn. It was that ritual moment, as she rode past the Confederate memorial, that best symbolized North Carolina's, and the South's, emerging religious diversity. Even this traditional southern Protestant town—with more than its share of tobacco farmers, gun racks, and Baptists—had begun to feel the effects of the post-1965 immigration. Our Lady of Guadeloupe had visited the Confederate memorial in—of all places—Clinton, North Carolina. And by the turn of the twenty-first century, other visitations were taking place throughout the state and the region. The Buddha had found a home in Atlanta, the

Cuban Virgin had been exiled in Miami, and Lord Ganesha had settled in Nashville. The South was becoming more spiritually diverse. And if the region remained disproportionately pious and predominantly Protestant, the usual claims about southern religious homogeneity seemed less sure and more in need of qualification than ever.[21]

NOTES

I am grateful to Elizabeth Miller Buchanan and Chad Seales, my research assistants, who helped in numerous ways, as did those who attended the 1999 DuBose Lectures at the University of the South, where I first presented these ideas in a symposium on religion in the South. I also want to thank others who read earlier drafts, including Christine Heyrman, Charles Lippy, Donald Matthews, Christian Smith, and John Shelton Reed.

A revised and expanded version of this essay appears in *Religion in the Contemporary South* (University of Tennessee Press, 2005), edited by Corrie E. Norman and Don S. Armentrout.

1. On religious regions in the United States see, for example, Samuel S. Hill, "Religion and Region in America," *Annals of the American Academy of Political and Social Science* 480 (July 1985): 132–41. On the historical sources of the South's evangelical Protestant dominance see, for example, Christine Leigh Heyrman, *Southern Cross: The Beginnings of the Bible Belt* (Knopf, 1997). H. L. Mencken's dismissal of southern religion has been quoted often, including in John Shelton Reed, *The Enduring South: Subcultural Persistence in Mass Society* (University of North Carolina Press, 1986), 57.

2. Southern Focus Poll, spring 2000, conducted by the Odum Institute for Research in the Social Sciences at the University of North Carolina at Chapel Hill; Southern Focus Poll, spring 1999; Southern Focus Poll, fall 1999. To access these data online, see www.irss.unc.edu/irss/insidethetute/spfstories/frequencies/freqspring00.pdf. For all information from these polls see www.irss.unc.edu/data_archive/catsearch.html and type "Southern Focus Poll."

3. As many observers have noticed, evangelical Protestantism has shaped southern cultures in pronounced ways—in music, art, entertainment, dress, and literature. For example, see Susan Ketchin, *The Christ-Haunted Landscape: Faith and Doubt in Southern Fiction* (University Press of Mississippi, 1994); Barry A. Kosmin and Seymour P. Lachman, *One Nation Under God: Religion in Contemporary Society* (Harmony Books, 1993), 51–55.

4. Joel W. Martin, "Indians, Contact, and Colonialism in the Deep South: Themes for a Postcolonial History of American Religion," in *Retelling U.S. Religious History*, ed. Thomas A. Tweed (University of California Press, 1997), 154.

5. Question 39, Southern Focus Poll, spring 1998. As John Shelton Reed points out, "non-Southerners (Protestants, at least) are increasingly likely to have had the sort of religious experience that is theoretically central to Southern Protestantism." Reed, *The Enduring South*, 100.

6. U.S. Bureau of the Census, *Religious Bodies: 1906*, part 1, *Summary and General Tables* (Government Printing Office, 1910), 145–293; Edwin S. Gaustad, *Historical Atlas of Religion in America* (Harper and Row, 1962), 48–51.

7. U.S. Bureau of the Census, *U.S. Census of Population: 1960*, vol. 1, *Characteristics of the Population*, part 1, *United States Summary* (U.S. Government Printing Office, 1964). Here and throughout the essay all population statistics for 2000 are taken from U.S. Bureau of the Census, *U.S. Census of Population 2000: General Population Characteristics* (www.census.gov/population/www/socdemo/foreign.html released 2 April 2001).

8. On the early history of Miami, and its southern Protestant character, see Thomas A. Tweed, "An Emerging Protestant Establishment: Religious Affiliation and Public Power on the Urban Frontier in Miami, 1896–1904," *Church History* 64 (September 1995): 412–37; on the Cuban shrine see Thomas A. Tweed, *Our Lady of the Exile: Diasporic Religion at a Cuban Catholic Shrine in Miami* (Oxford University Press, 1997).

9. U.S. Bureau of the Census, 2000; a North Carolina newspaper ran a story about the Latino migrants, including Juan Salazar Cruz, the Mexican migrant in the illustration who was sleeping beneath the underpass. Joby Warrick, "For Latin Immigrants, Home Is a Bridge," Raleigh *News and Observer*, 23 November 1994, B1.

10. U.S. Bureau of the Census, 2000. For the county statistics about Hispanics and Asians see http://census.state.nc.us/hisp_map_table.html and http://census.state.nc.us/ahpi_map_table.html. For an estimate of the (documented and undocumented) Latino migrant farm workers in eastern North Carolina see Ned Glascock and Jen Gomez, "A Bitter Harvest for Hispanic Workers," Raleigh *News and Observer*, 24 September 1999, 19A.

11. For an overview of the history of religion in North Carolina see John R. Woodward, "North Carolina," in *Encyclopedia of Religion in the South*, ed. Samuel S. Hill (Mercer University Press, 1984), 535–50; "Teaching English as a Second Language," Raleigh *News and Observer*, 29 December 1993, 3A; Sumathi Reddy, "Parents Fear Ethnic Shift in Chatham," Raleigh *News and Observer*, 22 September 1999, 1A, 4A.

12. "What's Happening: Durham," Raleigh *News and Observer*, 5 June 1998, B2; Joe DePriest, "North Carolina: Zoning Rules Block Path to a New Temple: Buddhists Had Hoped to Build a Home in Town Known for Christmas," *Charlotte Observer*, 24 June 2001, 1 (Gaston regional section); Ned Glascock, "Rally Divides Siler City," Raleigh *News and Observer*, 20 February 2000, B1, B3.

13. Chester Gillis, *Roman Catholicism in America* (Columbia University Press,

1999), 267; Yonat Shimron, "N.C. Dioceses Accommodate Nation's Largest Rise in Hispanics," Raleigh *News and Observer*, 1 May 2000, 1A, 12A; Michael Kammie, "Catholic Church to Drop Bilingual Service," Durham *Herald-Sun*, 14 October 1996, 1A–2A. For a partial listing of the parishes with a Spanish-language mass see "Liturgias en Espanol," supplement to the *North Carolina Catholic*, 22 August 1999, 4A. I borrow the term "parallel congregations" from Paul David Numrich, *Old Wisdom in the New World: Americanization in Two Immigrant Theravada Buddhist Temples* (University of Tennessee Press, 1996), xxii.

14. Yonat Shimron, "Temple Blessings," Raleigh *News and Observer*, 3 September 1999, 1F.

15. For an overview of Buddhism in the state see Thomas A. Tweed, ed., *Buddhism and Barbecue: A Guide to Buddhist Temples in North Carolina* (The Buddhism in North Carolina Project, 2001). That volume profiled thirty-three Buddhist centers, but by spring 2002 our collaborative project had identified and profiled sixty-six centers: for those profiles, and other information, see www.unc .edu/ncbuddhism. The quotation from the devotee at the Raleigh temple is from my fieldwork: Interview with DCN, male, aged 49, Chua Van Hanh, Raleigh, North Carolina, 26 June 1994. Christopher L. Lombardi, "Buddhist Celebration at Wat Buddhajakra Vanaram," *Carolina Asian News*, December 1991, 15; Debbie Moore, "A Separate Peace: Burgeoning Belief Brings Buddhists to Bolivia," Raleigh *News and Observer*, 18 September 1988, 1C, 5C.

16. North Carolina Museum of History, http://nchistory.dcr.state.nc.us, 26 September 1999; Stephan Hoar, "Buddhist Exhibit Reflects Diversity," Raleigh *News and Observer*, 24 March 1994, 3B.

17. The comments about staff expectations and docent observations are taken from a taped interview in the author's files with Sally Peterson, curator, North Carolina Museum of History, by Elizabeth Miller Buchanan, North Carolina Museum of History, Raleigh, 8 November 1999. The visitor responses are recorded in R.B., Raleigh, North Carolina, comment card, 31 July 1994, North Carolina Museum of History archives, and P.O., Burgaw, North Carolina, comment card, 21 July 1996, North Carolina Museum of History Archives. I determined the religious affiliation of the cradle Buddhist who wrote a comment card in a telephone conversation on 15 November 1999. For the curator's response to the female visitor's comment card see Sally Peterson to P.O., 22 July 1996, North Carolina Museum of History Archives.

18. Cora Bass, *Sampson County Yearbook, 1956–57* (Bass Publishing Co., 1957), 84. On the Confederate memorial see S. L. Smith for the United Daughters of the Confederacy, North Carolina Division, *North Carolina's Confederate Monuments and Memorials* (Edwards and Broughton, 1941), 117–18; Abram Joseph Ryan, "The March of the Deathless Dead," *Poems: Patriotic, Religious, Miscellaneous* (P. J. Kennedy, 1898), 76–77.

19. My account of the Our Lady of Guadeloupe Festival is taken from Field-

notes, 8 December 1996, Immaculate Conception Church, Clinton, North Carolina. For a journalist's description see Ben Stocking, "Hispanic Culture Comes to Downtown Clinton," Raleigh *News and Observer*, 9 December 1996, 1A, 4A.

20. Fieldnotes, 8 December 1996, Festival Mass, Sampson Middle School, Clinton, North Carolina.

21. Fieldnotes, 8 December 1996, Immaculate Conception Church, Clinton, North Carolina.

And the Dead Shall Rise
An Overview

Steve Oney

The 1915 lynching of
Leo Frank (here), the
Jewish factory manager
convicted of murdering
thirteen-year-old Mary
Phagan, captivated the
public's imagination.
Courtesy of Georgia
Archives, Vanishing
Georgia Collection
(bal0751).

Journalist Steve Oney offers a first-person account of the research and writing of And the Dead Shall Rise: The Murder of Mary Phagan and the Lynching of Leo Frank *(2003), the definitive work on the sensational 1913 murder of a factory girl in Atlanta and the subsequent trial, conviction, and lynching of her accused killer.*

On April 26, 1913, a thirteen-year-old child laborer named Mary Phagan was brutally murdered in a downtown Atlanta pencil factory. The girl was strangled and probably raped, her body then dragged across the plant's coal-slag carpeted basement floor to a dark recess, blackening it beyond recognition. Not until responding officers pulled down one of her stockings did they determine that she was white. Near her corpse, the police discovered two cryptic notes that pointed to an unnamed "long tall black negro" as the culprit. The notes were written in such a way as to suggest that the victim composed them in her death throes, but from the outset, their strange wording ("i write while he play with me," read one) raised doubts. From this terrible and puzzling start, a bizarre and tragic sequence of events ensued.

In short order, Leo Max Frank, a Cornell-educated Jew who managed the factory where the murder occurred and Mary Phagan worked, was arrested and charged with the crime. Suspicion focused on Frank because he was the last person to admit seeing the girl alive and because he reacted with what seemed to be undue anxiety when officers informed him of the murder. He shook uncontrollably. He couldn't tie his necktie. He repeatedly demanded a cup of coffee.

The next day, the *Atlanta Georgian*, a flamboyant daily newspaper owned by William Randolph Hearst, deluged the city with extras. Atlanta had never seen anything like it—new editions every hour, gigantic red headlines. To put it in contemporary terms, it was as if jumbotron televisions stood on every downtown corner blaring one of the cable news networks twenty-four hours a day. In such an atmosphere, the police were under tremendous pressure to firm up what was initially a flimsy case against Frank.

Ultimately, officers found their salvation in the person of Jim Conley, a black janitor at the pencil factory. After weeks of professing ignorance of the murder and claiming illiteracy, Conley—upon being confronted with samples of his handwriting—confessed that he'd lied. The truth was he knew how to write. Leo Frank, he told the authorities, had killed Mary Phagan and then dictated those peculiar notes to him in an attempt to pin the crime on yet another black man.

And the Dead Shall Rise: *An Overview*   273

For a month during the summer of 1913, in a cramped and airless temporary courtroom, the best lawyers in Atlanta contested Frank's fate. Imagine it: No air conditioners, over 90 degrees *inside*, packed galleries, throngs of curiosity seekers gathered in the streets, the more aggressive among them peering through open windows at the proceedings. Representing the state was Fulton County Solicitor Hugh Dorsey. Standing up for the defense were Luther Rosser and Reuben Arnold. Day after day, the battle surged back and forth. Hundreds of witnesses testified about scores of topics, among them allegations that Frank had been guilty of what today would be called sexual harassment; from the first to the last, however, the fight was only about one thing—Frank's word versus Conley's, a white man's word versus a black man's. In the end, the all-white jury, following just two hours of deliberation, decided that it was the black man who had told the truth, convicting Frank of the murder of Mary Phagan. As news of the verdict spread, spontaneous celebrations erupted across Atlanta. The next day, Superior Court Judge Leonard Roan sentenced Frank to death.

In the 1913 South the novelty of a white jury convicting a white man largely on the word of a black man was enormous. Yet even so, it was only in the trial's aftermath that the deeper and more volatile issues came to the fore.

Shortly after Frank's conviction, Rabbi David Marx of Atlanta's reform synagogue, the Temple, journeyed to New York to enlist the most powerful figures in American Jewry to assist him in exonerating Frank. As Marx saw it, the Jewish factory boss had been a victim of anti-Semitism. He had been not so much prosecuted as persecuted.

The extent to which religious prejudice played a part in Frank's conviction has always been a matter of debate. Undoubtedly a surface level of anti-Semitism permeated the investigation, and Solicitor Dorsey played to the jury's worst instincts by frequently referring to the Frank family's wealth. But at the time of the Phagan murder, Atlanta was a philo-Semitic city. Its assimilated, German-Jewish elite were part of the financial and legal power structure. The Jewish community was centered in a neighborhood of substantial, two-story homes just south of Georgia's handsome, domed capitol. The area was dominated by the Temple and the Hebrew Orphan's Home, which boasted exotic, onion-domed spires. (Leo Frank and his wife, the former Lucille Selig, lived in this section near what today is the site of Turner Field, home of the Atlanta Braves.) Jews were accepted in the city, and the record does not substantiate subsequent reports that the crowd outside the courtroom shouted at the jurors: "Hang the Jew or we'll hang you."

Nonetheless, by early 1914 Frank's northern allies included Adolph Ochs, publisher of the *New York Times*; Louis Marshall, president of the American Jewish Committee; and Albert D. Lasker, chief executive of the Lord & Thomas ad agency, predecessor to Foote, Cone and Belding. These powerful Jews, along with a few Atlanta Gentiles, spent in contemporary dollars untold millions in an effort to overturn Frank's conviction. In the process, the case became a nationwide cause célèbre. From early 1914 through 1915, newspaper headlines from New York to San Francisco told the story. There were petition drives everywhere, and movie stars came to Atlanta to speak out for Frank.

The reaction among Georgians to all of this can be summed up in the phrase they used for it: "outside interference." For one thing, the consensus was that Frank was guilty. For another, the bitter memory of defeat in the Civil War was a palpable presence in the state. Finally, though, it was Tom Watson—the great lawyer, populist politician, orator, and future U.S. senator—who whipped up passions in the state to a dangerous pitch. Week after week in his tabloid paper, *The Jeffersonian*, Watson attacked the "lecherous Jew, Leo Frank" and the wealthy northerners who in his eyes were trying to subvert the authority of the local courts. Watson was a formidable adversary—red-headed, brilliant, and demagogic. To borrow a phrase Mark Twain once used about someone else, he wielded a pen that had been warmed up in hell. The common people of Georgia loved Watson, and through him anti-Semitism indeed entered the case.

Every passing month, as Frank's appeals failed first at the state level and then before the U.S. Supreme Court, the rhetoric intensified. The *New York Times* editorialized almost weekly in Frank's behalf. Watson shot back instantaneously.

In June of 1915, his appeals exhausted, Frank placed himself at the mercy of Georgia Governor John Slaton. After lengthy hearings at the capitol, Slaton commuted Frank's death sentence to life imprisonment, and Frank was transferred from the Fulton County Jail in Atlanta to the Georgia Prison Farm in Milledgeville in the heart of the state. In the North, Slaton was cheered. In the South, he was jeered, accused of selling out to "Jew money." More damaging, he was attacked for an undeniable conflict of interests—Slaton was a law partner of Frank's lead counsel, Luther Rosser. Opinion was so hostile that Slaton ordered out the National Guard to protect the governor's mansion; he was hanged in effigy in half a dozen cities across the state.

In his first post-commutation writings, Tom Watson called for Frank's lynching. The call was heard by the leading citizens of Mary Phagan's ancestral home, Marietta, Georgia, twenty miles northwest of Atlanta. These men, using all their political influence, arranged for the bloodless abduction of Frank from the prison farm. He was then driven 150 miles via a circuitous route to Marietta. There, on the morning of August 17, 1915, Frank was lynched. Three months later, on Thanksgiving eve, a revived Ku Klux Klan was born at a cross burning atop Stone Mountain twenty miles east of Atlanta. At the same time, the newly formed Anti-Defamation League began to fight American anti-Semitism in earnest.

WRITING THE STORY

Down through the years, the story of Mary Phagan and Leo Frank has not surprisingly generated many books, movies, and plays. In the 1937 Warner Bros. film *They Won't Forget*, Lana Turner—in her first major role—played a part based on Mary Phagan. In 1968 a young Columbia graduate named Leonard Dinnerstein published a fine, albeit narrowly focused, study called simply *The Leo Frank Case*. Then there was the 1998 Alfred Uhry musical *Parade*. However, for all of this, I felt there had never been a comprehensive but compelling nonfiction book that did justice to the facts, yet brought to life the cast of extraordinary characters and illuminated the issues that animated them. This is what in 1986 I set out to accomplish.

I devoted nearly two decades to the research and writing of *And the Dead Shall Rise*. While this protracted birthing process owes something to procrastination, from the start my ambitions for the book were of the very highest order.

Because I wanted *And the Dead Shall Rise* to be different from the treatments of the Frank case that had preceded it, I began by discarding all preconceptions about the subject. I would approach it as if I'd awakened in Atlanta on the day of Mary Phagan's murder. To the extent possible, I would work only from original sources. Unlike most of those who'd previously written about the case, I was as willing to believe Frank guilty as I was to believe him innocent. Only the facts would determine what I wrote. My goal was simple and daunting—to find out what happened and then tell the story.

My first subject of inquiry was the Phagan murder, and I started by reading the daily newspapers published in Atlanta in 1913—the Hearst-owned *Georgian* and the then separate and locally owned *Journal* and *Constitution*. From the day of the crime to the day of Frank's conviction and on through the appeals, these papers carried thousands of stories, and I read and cross-referenced them all. I spent years sitting at microfilm machines. Such labor allowed me not only to ferret out lost pieces of evidence but to learn about the backgrounds of the key players. Moreover, it enabled me to reconstruct a missing document—the trial transcript, which disappeared from the Fulton County Courthouse in the 1960s. Because newspapers in the teens printed running accounts of major trials, the Q&A from the Frank proceedings was unofficially preserved. All that was required to retrieve it was diligence. At the same time I was conducting this research, I immersed myself in another heretofore ignored source—the files of the Pinkerton Detective Agency, which had been hired by Frank's employers to probe the murder. Because Pinkerton agents worked hand-in-hand with members of the Atlanta Police Department, these dossiers provided a fresh look at the daily activities of the detectives who compiled the evidence against Frank.

I also went as deeply as I could into the personal backgrounds of the case's principals. And it wasn't just the lawyers in whom I was interested.

The truth about Jim Conley—the state's black star witness—became an obsession for me. I sat in fellowship halls of churches in Vine City, Conley's raffish Atlanta neighborhood, interviewing aging men and women who might have known him. Eventually, I located a retired school teacher who as a college student had been close to Conley. I also found in a long overlooked piece of trial testimony the relevant fact that Conley's education was far better than that of most blacks of his era. He had been a student of two of Atlanta's most influential black educators—one a Spelman grad, the other an Atlanta University alumna. Conley was not only cunning—he was literate. He could well have authored the notes discovered near Mary Phagan's body as part of a plot to pin the Phagan murder on his white boss.

Not surprisingly, I was equally determined to discover who Leo Frank was. At Brandeis University I pored over Frank's early love letters to Lucille. These missives are stiff, courtly but oddly touching; I quote from them extensively in *And the Dead Shall Rise*. At the Atlanta History Center, I pondered the notebook that Frank, shortly after arriving in the South, used to inscribe chess gambits in order to learn the game. Also at the

History Center, I was transfixed by a simple, handmade Valentine card Lucille had given to Leo shortly after he proposed marriage to her.

As I was studying the Phagan murder, I also painstakingly pursued the story's other mystery. Leo Frank's lynching was long one of the great unsolved crimes in American history. There was never another lynching like Frank's. To begin with, the magnitude of the undertaking was enormous. At the time it occurred, Frank was America's most famous convict. He was held not in a county jail protected by an indifferent deputy with a shotgun across his lap but in a well-guarded state prison surrounded by gun towers that provided clear shots at anyone coming or going. The men who abducted Frank not only failed to draw fire, they were given the run of the place. Once the abduction was completed, these men faced no interference as they raced north through multiple jurisdictions back to Marietta. This was, for its day, remarkable—a three-hundred-mile round trip in the dead of night in Model-Ts on dirt roads. Whatever moral revulsion you feel, you have to acknowledge the audacity of the act and the efficiency with which it was conducted. Afterward, no one involved was even inconvenienced, much less arrested.

To learn how all this worked, the first thing I did was go to the Georgia Department of Archives and requisition the automobile tag records for all cars registered in Marietta between the years 1913 and 1915. Out of this group of just over one hundred vehicles were most of those that had been used in the raid on Milledgeville. I then took another basic step—I went to school on Marietta society. On Sundays during the teens, the Atlanta newspapers ran items on the previous week's dinner parties and social engagements in Marietta and other outlying towns. Not only are these stories a great source of fashion news and menu suggestions, but the guest lists reveal the connections among Marietta's leading citizens. It was a tight-knit world; day-by-day, night-by-night, these people were together. Finally, I matched the names of Marietta's car owners and power holders with the names of those who had made hostile remarks about Frank during the governor's clemency hearing or at other forums. Not surprisingly, the same names kept cropping up.

All of this fascinated me—and much of it ended up in *And the Dead Shall Rise*. Still, at this point, early in my research, I felt like someone with his face pressed to the window. I needed a point of entrée into the long-ago world of the two crimes. That entrée came through men and women who constituted what I term "the linking generation."

When I walked into the Sarasota, Florida, law office of seventy-five-year-old Gene Clay, he knew why I'd come. We'd been corresponding for months regarding his father, Herbert Clay, the scion of a famous Marietta family. Herbert's father, Alexander Stephens Clay, was a U.S. senator. Herbert's brother Lucius was military governor of Germany following World War II. At the time of the Frank case, Herbert was the chief prosecutor for much of north Georgia. No sooner had Gene Clay shown me to a chair than he broke into tears. "Yes," he said. "My father was one of the men who planned the lynching of Leo Frank." Out of this painful moment grew an unlikely friendship. Due to the fact that Gene's mother, after an early divorce, had raised Gene in the North, he had never really known the man whose name he bore. He wanted to find out what sort of person Herbert Clay was. I wanted to learn more about the role Herbert Clay had played in the lynching. Several months after our first meeting, Gene and I spent a long weekend together in Marietta, looking up people—many in their eighties—who could help us in our separate but related quests.

It's remarkable what a man who began practicing law in a small southern community sixty years ago, or a woman who opened a beauty parlor in the community at the same time, can tell you about the people who were then the town elders.

From a bond salesman who in the 1920s had been Herbert Clay's law clerk, I learned the particular ways in which Clay had used his personal charm to overcome obstacles to the lynch party's plans. From a former Superior Court judge who as a young lawyer had been a partner with two of Herbert Clay's partners—both of whom were also involved in the Frank lynching—I learned how Clay had staged a farcical grand jury investigation that absolved everyone in Marietta of responsibility for the crime.

Sometimes, lucky breaks come in clusters. On the same day I met Gene Clay in Sarasota, I spent several hours just up the road in St. Petersburg with Alan and Fanny Marcus, two Atlantans who'd retired to Florida. Alan was Lucille Frank's nephew. He'd grown up at her knee and borne witness to the devastation that the lynching had wrought in her life and in the life of Atlanta's Jewish community.

I'll never forget sitting with Alan and Fanny in a restaurant overlooking the water and asking them to talk about the impact of the lynching on Lucille. In response, Alan, in a matter-of-fact voice, told me an astonishing story. Following Lucille's death in 1957, her body was cremated. She wanted her ashes scattered in a public park, but an Atlanta ordinance forbade it. So for the next six years the ashes sat in a box at a local funeral home. One day, Alan received what for him was an upsetting call. The funeral home was conducting an inventory; the ashes needed to be disposed of. Alan didn't know what to do. In the years since Lucille passed away, the Temple—by this point moved to a neoclassical building on Peachtree Street—had been bombed. The event had set Atlanta's Jews on edge. It was no wonder that Alan didn't want to attract scrutiny by conducting a public burial. Thus, for months, he raced Lucille's remains around Atlanta in the trunk of his red Corvair. Early one morning in 1964, he and his brother Harold collected some garden tools and drove to the downtown Oakland Cemetery. There, under the cover of the gray dawn light, the two men buried this martyred figure in an unmarked plot between the headstones of her parents.

Alan's story moved me deeply, but more than that, it spoke to a larger truth about the impact of the Frank lynching on Atlanta's Jewish community, revealing a pain that had lasted a generation, a wound that had long been repressed.

During the same period I was getting to know Gene Clay and the Marcuses, and through them sensing the undercurrents of the Frank case that endure unto this day, I was grappling with both a philosophical and a creative problem. Most previous treatments of this story can be broken down into the phrase "Good Jews versus bad Yahoos." To me, this seemed a simplistic and polarizing formulation. But how could I get around it? As I struggled with that question, I made what I consider to be the most important breakthrough in my research. I learned about an extraordinary but little-known Atlanta lawyer who represented Jim Conley in the Frank case.

William Manning Smith was a man far ahead of his time. As early as the turn of the century, he was championing equal rights for blacks. That's why he took Conley on as a client. Not only did he believe Conley was telling the truth, he wanted to make sure that Frank's high-powered lawyers didn't run over the black man in court. All of this, however, I would learn later. What I learned first about William Smith involved something that occurred nearly forty years after Frank was lynched, and I learned it from Smith's son, Walter, who was there when it happened.

Walter Smith was for most of his life also an Atlanta lawyer. On a winter day in 1949, as his father lay dying in an Atlanta hospital, Walter witnessed a remarkable scene. William Smith was suffering from Lou Gehrig's disease, and like many so afflicted, he'd lost his power of speech.

But until the end, he remained mentally sharp, passing hand-written notes to Walter through a crease in a clear plastic oxygen tent. Most of the notes involved family matters—insurance policies and the like. But in the midst of conducting his final business, William Smith took the time to address a more significant subject. The note, which appears in my book, could not have been more profound: "In articles of death, I believe in the innocence and good character of Leo M. Frank. W. M. Smith."

As Walter described this emotionally fraught scene to me, I felt two things. On a human level, I wanted to cry. But as a writer, I couldn't wait to get the details down on paper. Almost instantaneously, I knew that *And the Dead Shall Rise* would revolve around William Smith. By telling the story of his transformation from a man who helped prepare Jim Conley to give the testimony that convicted Frank to someone who in his dying words declared Frank's innocence, I could bring a new perspective to the subject, one that avoided the tired clichés.

With Walter Smith's help, I learned everything I could about how William Smith had come to change his mind regarding the Frank case. Walter gave me scores of his father's personal documents and letters that threw light on the topic. Meantime, I spent weeks at the Georgia Department of Archives poring over William Smith's hundred-page study of the murder notes found by Mary Phagan's body. In this study, Smith proves beyond a doubt that Conley, not Frank, authored the notes. They were Conley's original compositions. They featured the same verb forms and sentence structures Conley used in other oral and written utterances. In 1914, a year after Frank's conviction, Smith went public with this contention. Though Smith believed that he was ethically free to come forward, other Atlanta lawyers disagreed. Smith's Atlanta law practice was destroyed.

In the end, the information that Gene Clay, Alan Marcus, and Walter Smith gave me about their relatives amounted to a large and exceedingly valuable bequest. So much so that I began to feel less like a reporter and more like the administrator of a sacred trust. I felt a fiduciary responsibility to do justice to these stories. This, I told myself, is the material of a lifetime. What a great book it will make. That was ten years ago.

To say that the research and writing of *And the Dead Shall Rise* was a battle in its own right is an understatement. When I started this book, I was a cocksure thirty-two-year-old with two dozen recently published pieces in *Esquire*, *Premiere*, and other magazines. I'd spent a year at Harvard as a Nieman Fellow. Journalistically speaking, I was in possession of a live fastball. By the time my book was finally published in October of 2003, I was a sobered and shockingly gray forty-nine-year-old—the epitome of the sage veteran who relies on off-speed stuff. Many were the times over the long, hard course that I wondered whether the writing of *And the Dead Shall Rise* was worth the cost. I was filled with doubts, most of them stemming from my fear that I was not equal to the task. A provocative and germane series of questions from T. S. Eliot's great poem "The Lovesong of J. Alfred Prufrock" ran often through my brain:

> "Do I dare disturb the universe?
> "Should I force the moment to its crisis?
> "Do I dare to eat a peach?"

What Eliot was talking about was the strength of will and volition needed to take action in the world. Did I dare? In the end, all I can say is that I did not quit. Luckily, because my wife believed in me and the book, she supported me through a long time of uncertainty.

In ways I could not have initially predicted, the lengthy process of writing *And the Dead Shall Rise* ended up working to the book's advantage. For instance, it was only in the summer of 2001 that Leo Frank's letters to a muckraking journalist who covered the case for *Collier's Weekly* were donated to the American Jewish Archives in Cincinnati. Thus, in my book, you will hear for the first time what Frank was thinking and feeling as he went through his ordeal. Similarly, I benefited from the bequest of the transcript of Governor Slaton's clemency hearings to the Emory University Library. This document, thick as a New York phone book, contains unexpurgated material regarding charges of sexual perversity leveled against Frank by Jim Conley. During the trial, Conley—who claimed to have served as a look-out during his boss's alleged sexual assignations at the factory—accused Frank of being a devotee of oral sex. He said that Frank preferred the act because he was "not built like other men." At the time, the description of Frank's purportedly impaired genitalia did great damage, but it wasn't until Slaton's hearings that Frank's lawyers were able to decipher exactly what Conley meant. To wit: Due to his own ignorance or at the instigation of the police, the state's star witness had voiced an anti-Semitic misrepresentation of the circumcision ritual, stating in words what eighteenth-century European anti-Semites had articulated with woodcuts.

Similarly, the nearly two decades I spent on the book gave me the time to explore at great depth the enigma of Frank's lynching. I interviewed at length the children of six of the principal participants. The daughter of one confirmed the names of everyone involved to me. (She kept her list in the family Bible.) I also actually got to know three people who were at the lynch site and saw Frank's body hanging there. One of these people—Narvel Lassiter—is pictured in my book, peering out from behind the famous oak tree. He was only nine years old. Most interesting of all, I ferreted out how the masterminds of the lynching in effect took over the state prison system. The lynching was conceived in Marietta, but it was run through the Georgia legislature. One of the crime's architects was chairman of the body's prison subcommittee. In that position, he was able to wield both the stick and the carrot over the board that administered the Milledgeville Prison Farm. The stick was blame for a typhus outbreak that had hit the facility early in 1915. The carrot was $30,000 in appropriations if Frank's abduction went off without a hitch. Shortly before the lynching, the threat of the typhus investigation went away. A month later, money from the state's coffers flowed and work on a new addition to the prison began. Simply put: the state of Georgia was briefly in the lynching business.

Now, at last, all of this is out in the open—the dead have, in a sense, arisen. That being so, what are we to make of it?

Ultimately, I believe Leo Frank was innocent.

For all of this, however, I leave the door regarding Frank's innocence or guilt slightly ajar in *And the Dead Shall Rise*. The physical evidence in the case from which contemporary forensic experts could make a conclusive determination long ago disappeared. So there will always be, at least in my mind, an iota of doubt. Why was Frank so nervous the morning Mary Phagan's body was discovered? Moreover, at the trial many female factory workers testified to Frank's penchant for making lewd comments to them and barging into the women's dressing room when they were unclothed. Were they all lying?

As for the saga's other great mystery, I believe there is now no doubt as to the identities of the Marietta citizens who planned Frank's lynching. I think there is also no doubt as to the culpability of the state of Georgia in the crime. But I did not write *And the Dead Shall Rise* in the spirit of a frustrated prosecutor going back into a cold case to arraign the guilty. I wrote in the spirit of understanding. The people involved in the lynching acted for a variety of reasons. Some of them never regretted their actions.

Others suffered and repented. Most accepted what they had done as a terrible but necessary act. Speaking of her father, the daughter of one of the men told me, "He was not proud, but he was not ashamed."

History can teach us nothing if we attempt to impose the standards and values of our own time on it. History's importance, in the words of Barbara Tuchman, is as a distant mirror. The participants in the Frank case—whether Atlanta's Jews, Marietta's vigilantes, or New York's newspaper reporters and activists—are the grandparents and great-grandparents of our present generation. For a long time, they have been trying to speak to us. In the pages of *And the Dead Shall Rise*, I believe they finally do.

Read More About It

David Carlton, *Mill and Town in South Carolina, 1880–1920* (Louisiana State University Press, 1982).

Leonard Dinnerstein, *The Leo Frank Case* (University of Georgia Press, 1987).

John Dittmer, *Black Georgia in the Progressive Era, 1900–1920* (University of Illinois Press, 1980).

Nancy MacLean, "The Leo Frank Case Reconsidered: Gender and Sexual Politics in the Making of Reactionary Populism," *Journal of American History* 78 (December 1991): 917–48.

Gene Wiggins, *Fiddlin' Georgia Crazy: Fiddlin John Carson, his Real World, and the World of his Songs* (University of Illinois Press, 1987).

C. Vann Woodward, *Tom Watson, Agrarian Rebel* (Macmillan, 1938).

Regional Stereotypes

Kudzu, hogs, rednecks, feuding, and rasslin' have real stories behind them.

Kudzu
A Tale of Two Vines

Derek H. Alderman and Donna G'Segner Alderman

Perhaps no other part of the natural environment is more closely identified with the South than this invasive and fast-growing vine. Courtesy of Dixie Pix.

ity leaders in Tallahassee, Florida, recently started a program that uses sheep to graze on large, troublesome patches of kudzu within the city. Several summers ago, Greenville, South Carolina, hosted the filming and the-atrical debut of "Kudzula," the story of a ten-year-old boy who saves a town from over-development with the help of a forty-foot kudzu creature.[1] As these incidents suggest, the story of kudzu is a "tale of two vines." Existing simultaneously in the realms of nature and culture, kudzu—like southern culture in general—is open to multiple interpretations and representations. In Tallahassee, kudzu is a pest. Like visiting relatives, the plant has overstayed its welcome. In Greenville, on the other hand, people not only pay $19 to watch a play about kudzu, but in that play, kudzu saves the day.

Perhaps no other part of the natural environment is more closely identified with the South than this invasive and fast growing vine. Yet relatively few academics have examined kudzu and its place within southern culture and the larger American experience. And southerners both endure and embrace this pervasive part of life. Some wage an ecological battle against kudzu, while others use and market the vine in creative ways. Both southerners and nonsoutherners identify with kudzu as a symbol and incorporate the plant into daily cultural expression, including the language used to characterize and understand social and environmental change. As a national news wire reports, "So aggressive is kudzu that the word has entered American English as shorthand for out-of-control growth."[2] In this respect, the plant illustrates the tremendous impact the American South has made, and continues to make, on national culture.

While kudzu may seem native to the South, it is an exotic species alien to the region and the country. The plant was introduced to America from Japan in 1876 at the Philadelphia Centennial Exposition and to the South in 1883 at the New Orleans Exposition. For the next few decades, kudzu served primarily as ornamental shade for homes, particularly porches. Later, despite early warnings about the vine's aggressive nature, the Department of Agriculture, the Soil Conservation Service, and other government agencies promoted kudzu as a public resource. Kudzu is comparable nutritionally to alfalfa and was first touted as a form of pasturage for feeding livestock—although cutting, handling, and baling the vine proved to be problematic. Kudzu reached the height of its popularity in the late 1930s as a tool in soil conservation, a means of replenishing nitrogen-poor soils and controlling erosion along fields and road banks. Historian Kurt Kinbacher has characterized the story of kudzu as "tangled" in the sense that the vine does not have just one historical role or identity in the region. Its value to humans has shifted with public opinion, advancements in science, and the changing demands of American agriculture.[3]

KUDZU AS PANACEA, PEST, AND PRODUCT

Kudzu rose in status through the careful cultivation of its image by several important individuals and groups. Kudzu's first promoters, Charles and Lillie Pleas of Florida, experimented with using kudzu as forage for animals in the early 1900s and later sold kudzu plants and rootstock through a mail order business. A roadside historical marker on Highway 90 in Chipley, Florida, recognizes their efforts in developing kudzu for agricultural use.[4]

Perhaps the most vocal and interesting of kudzu's supporters was Channing Cope of Covington, Georgia. Cope promoted the conversion of "wasteland" into kudzu pastures through his daily radio programs and articles in the *Atlanta Journal-Constitution*. He is credited with starting the Kudzu Club of America in the early 1940s, which had a membership of twenty thousand by 1943. The club embraced the goal of planting 1 million acres of kudzu in Georgia and 8 million acres in the South overall. In his 1949 book titled *Front Porch Farmer*, Cope equated the planting of kudzu on heavily eroded land to a physician's using strong medicine to fight a disease. Kudzu was the front porch farmer's life and perhaps even the reason for his death, according to Cope's friend Philip S. Cohen. Even after the government labeled the vine an ecological threat, Cope refused to let the county cut back the large kudzu patches on his property. The kudzu was so overgrown that it enclosed the road leading to his home, Yellow River Plantation. This dense kudzu canopy gave area teenagers the privacy to park and party without adult interruptions. Legend has it that when Channing Cope came off his porch one evening to run off these trespassers, he walked only three feet before dying of a massive heart attack.[5]

Arguably, the most influential kudzu promoter was the United States government, particularly the Soil Erosion Service, later renamed the Soil Conservation Service (scs). Naïvely optimistic regarding the plant's benefits, the scs established programs to plant kudzu throughout the South.

The agency raised 100 million kudzu seedlings in its nurseries between 1935 and 1942. Workers with the Civilian Conservation Corps (CCC) planted the vine on public lands. To overcome lingering public suspicion, the Department of Agriculture paid farmers and landowners as much as eight dollars an acre to cultivate kudzu. By the late 1930s, the "miracle vine" had been introduced to every state in the Southeast, and by 1946 the United States could boast of having 3 million acres of planted kudzu. Although the government stopped promoting kudzu years ago, this has not stopped the plant from spreading unintentionally inside and outside the South. Kudzu was discovered for the first time in Oregon in 2000. If sources are correct, it marks the first reported case of kudzu infestation west of Texas. In total, the vine has been sighted in at least twenty-eight of the fifty states.[6]

In the 1950s, the status of kudzu shifted from that of highly valued resource to lowly pest. In fact, by the 1970s, the Department of Agriculture had declared kudzu officially a "weed." In 1998 the federal government went a step further in demonizing a plant it once promoted when Congress placed kudzu on the "noxious weed" list, a designation that now makes the transportation of kudzu across state lines illegal if not approved by the Secretary of Agriculture. A year earlier, the county commission of Santa Rosa County, Florida, passed what is perhaps the nation's first ordinance aimed solely at controlling the spread of kudzu. It fines property owners fifty dollars for letting the plant invade a neighbor's property. Adding insult to injury, an end-of-the-millennium issue of *Time* magazine listed the introduction of kudzu to the United States as one of the one hundred worst ideas of the century.[7]

Although kudzu is an excellent soil stabilizer and drought-resistant forage, the vine's early proponents underestimated the plant's aggressive growth and extreme resistance to control. The Native Plant Conservation Initiative, a consortium of 10 federal government agencies and over 110 nonfederal cooperators, provides a graphic picture of the ecological threat posed by kudzu:

> Kudzu kills or degrades other plants by smothering them under a solid blanket of leaves, by girdling woody stems and tree trunks, and by breaking branches or uprooting entire trees and shrubs through the sheer force of its weight. Once established, kudzu plants grow rapidly, extending as much as 60 feet per season at a rate of about one foot per day. This vigorous vine may extend 32–100 feet in length, with stems

½–4 inches in diameter. Kudzu roots are fleshy, with massive tap roots 7 inches or more in diameter, 6 feet or more in length, and weighing as much as 400 pounds. As many as thirty vines grow from a single root crown.

While our attention is often drawn to the vine's fast growing foliage, the kudzu root system is unbelievably tenacious and represents the real nerve center of the organism. Although the plant produces seeds, most growth occurs through vegetative expansion from the roots, which can lie dormant for several years—lulling a landowner into a false sense of victory—and then suddenly generate new vines. Diane Craft, an avid gardener from Indiana, contributed this incredible account of her experiences with kudzu roots:

> I lived in Florida for twenty years. Before I knew how invasive it [kudzu] was, I collected a bag of roots and put them in a brown grocery bag and tucked them under the bottom shelf of a little closet thinking I would see if I could plant them the next spring. In the spring, while doing some cleaning, I decided to clean that closet, and after pulling a few things out, I noticed a white rope that I didn't remember having. I started pulling the rope, and pulling the rope, and pulling the rope, until finally I realized that it was not a rope at all. The kudzu root had grown to about fifty feet over the winter, in a bag and in the dark.[8]

Recognizing the problems associated with kudzu overgrowth, scientists and lay people continue the search for an effective means of control. Jeremy Farris, a whiz kid from Warner Robins, Georgia, discovered a fungal pathogen capable of destroying the weed. Farris's experiments parallel work by scientists at the U.S. Agricultural Research Service, who claim to have identified another common fungus that kills kudzu within hours. Scientists such as Kerry Britton, a plant pathologist with the U.S. Department of Agriculture Forest Service, are investigating the potential for controlling kudzu through biological means. She and several other colleagues, for example, have been working with Chinese scientists to find insects that eat kudzu in China. These insects will later undergo intensive testing in the United States. In another attempt to find a biological solution, David Orr, an entomologist at North Carolina State University, has done research on the development of a kudzu-eating caterpillar.[9] Despite these creative control measures—and conventional ones such as mowing, grazing, burning, and herbicides—there is no easy way of stopping the march of what poet James Dickey called those "green, mindless, unkillable ghosts."

Even in the harshest of environments, kudzu grows over houses, trees, utility poles, and junkyards. Perhaps most impressive is the ability of kudzu to climb. There are seemingly no limits to what the vine covers or hides, including death. In December of 1998, a maintenance worker for an Atlanta golf course discovered a murder victim face down in a kudzu patch. In 1995 at another Atlanta golf course, two early-morning golfers found a dead man in a car partially submerged in a creek. The car had plunged off the road into a kudzu bank before rolling into the creek. Perhaps the most infamous connection between kudzu and death is the early 1980s case of the Atlanta missing and murdered children, whose bodies were discovered in kudzu-covered vacant lots.[10]

On a less macabre note, kudzu can sometimes hide opportunities for development. When a couple bought an old apartment complex in De-Kalb County, Georgia, they began the task of clearing kudzu overgrowth. They eventually found a two-acre garden park with stone walls, walk-ways, waterfalls, and ponds. After this discovery, the couple decided to restore the gardens and upgrade the property. Rather than offer low-income housing as originally planned, they converted the buildings to condominiums.

The clearing of kudzu can, however, reveal uncomfortable truths about society. For instance, during the planning phase of Atlanta's Jimmy Carter Presidential Parkway in the early 1990s, controversy arose over the proposed displacement of a homeless colony hidden in a field of kudzu. A news report published at the time described their plight: "In huts amid honeysuckle and kudzu, where knives and forks hang from vines in the open-air kitchen and a sawed-off stump suffices for a dining table, a small colony of homeless people stands at a crossroad. Theirs is one in-town neighborhood whose residents are paying the price of progress. . . . Most of the colony's residents feel safer hidden in the kudzu, where they are out of sight of the police."[11] This case shows the centrality of kudzu to contemporary southern life and, in this instance, the politics of urban development. It also exposes the dual, contradictory place of kudzu in society: kudzu can be a barrier to development and "progress" for one group of people, a refuge and sense of community for another.

Clearly, kudzu is open to alternative interpretations. Recognizing this fact, sociologists Kathleen Lowney and Joel Best have documented historical shifts in scientific claims and opinions about kudzu. Currently, the hope of finding a productive use for the vine is challenging belief in total eradication. Biochemists at Harvard Medical School, for instance, have investigated its herbal and medicinal properties, noting that kudzu extracts curb the craving for alcohol in Syrian Golden hamsters. Herbal stores are presently marketing a Kudzu/St. John's Wort combination to help treat alcoholism. For the hamster or human who over-indulges, starch from the kudzu root is supposedly a popular hangover remedy in Asia. Experiments have also suggested that kudzu derivatives might be useful in treating high blood pressure. Kudzu leaves and stems are being made into paper, baskets, jewelry, and other crafts, and kudzu flowers into jams, syrups, jellies, and even soap. The production and marketing of these kudzu products represent a growing cottage industry for some southerners. *The Amazing Story of Kudzu*, a video documentary produced by Alabama Public Television, showcases the work of kudzu entrepreneurs such as Nancy Basket of South Carolina, Diane Hoots of Georgia, Edith Edwards of North Carolina, and Ruth Duncan of Alabama.[12]

Kudzu also lends itself to visual and artistic interpretation. Capturing some classic shots of kudzu overtaking barns, houses, and equipment, Georgia photographer Jack Anthony finds the vine strangely beautiful. Of special note are his pictures of kudzu flowers, which offer an alternative perspective—kudzu as a sweet smelling blossom. David Day, a Georgian transplanted to Connecticut, has experimented with infrared photographs of kudzu.[13] Because of the unique way foliage reacts to infrared light, infrared photography presents a very different world from the one we are accustomed to seeing. Day's photographs show kudzu with white leaves and vines, giving the appearance of clouds or snowfall rather than Dickey's "invading green ghosts." Long, thick expanses of kudzu may appear to take on the shape of animals or people. A kudzu formation—and local landmark—near Wall Doxey State Park in northern Mississippi resembles a crucifix.

KUDZU AND IDENTITY

It is easy to characterize kudzu as simply an ecological menace, a roadside photo opportunity, a novelty product, or, at best, a futuristic medicine. While the plant is all these things, we should not lose sight of the larger importance of kudzu within southern and even American culture. As historian Mart Allen Stewart declared, "Kudzu has become the stuff of folklore, joke, symbol, and metaphor." For National Public Radio celebrity and cowboy poet Baxter Black, kudzu is fodder for AG MAN, his comic strip about the adventures of the only agriculturally correct superhero of the planet. In Black's "Kudzu Katastrophe Series," an evil urban developer is pressuring a farmer to sell the family land. The developer, appropriately named "Slick," sabotages the farmer's soybean fields by planting an extremely destructive strain of kudzu, "pueraria tyranus." AG MAN and his sidekicks, Farm Boy and Cornsilk, discover that possum sweat kills this variety of kudzu. They herd 622 head of sweating possums into the kudzu-covered fields to save the day.[14] The grateful farmer says, "Thanks, AG MAN. The Kudzu is controlled, my soybean crop will pay the loan, and my farm won't become another subdivision." In addition to playing with kudzu as a point of comic fantasy, Black involves the vine in a biting satire about the loss of agricultural land to development and the very real disappearance of the family farm in America.

Although AG MAN and others in the agricultural community scorn kudzu, some embrace the vine as an important point of identification. Kudzu has become almost synonymous with the South, as illustrated by a postcard that pictures the Confederate battle flag and the vine, despite the fact that kudzu's heyday in the South came long after the end of the Civil War. The card reads, "Southern Revenge: Plant Kudzu Seeds Up Nawth," in effect making the plant a weapon in the continuing sectional animosity between North and South.

Some people identify with kudzu on a more personal level. Maxine Simmons of Georgia reserves a special place in her heart for the fast growing vine. One of her son's first words was "kudzu." In another family-related identification, Atlanta's Jim Downing named his racecar "Kudzu." According to a 1992 *Road & Track* article, "Downing's reasons for calling his car Kudzu are sentimental and emotional. Sentimental, because Jim's dad, a member of the Department of Agriculture in the Forties, was instrumental in reintroducing the kudzu vine to Georgia. Emotional because Jim and his wife, Connie, disliked 'he-man, macho man names' usually ascribed to racing cars and wanted a name they could be comfortable with. Kudzu, ubiquitous and practically a member of the family, was a natural." In perhaps the most personal and permanent identification with kudzu, geographer Ron Ward had an image of the plant tattooed on his lower leg. Ward, who drew the line-art for his own tattoo, is, ironically enough, not a southerner but wanted the tattoo as a reminder of his time spent in the South studying invasive plants and animals: "Of course, I knew about kudzu before coming down from Minnesota. I remember on the drive down looking out the window and anticipating the first sight of kudzu. Sounds strange, I know, but it was a thrill the first time I saw it."[15]

Patterns in naming further underscore the symbolic and cultural importance of kudzu. As sociologists such as John Shelton Reed and geographers such as Wilbur Zelinsky have observed, the names people attach to places, objects, organizations, and businesses provide insight into patterns of social identity and geographic location.[16] While it is common to name streets after trees and other natural features, southerners have extended the practice to include kudzu. Nineteen streets in the country have kudzu in their names, all found in seven southern states. The streets appear to be almost entirely residential and, indeed, nine (or 47 percent) of these nineteen streets are named "Kudzu Lane." This is not to suggest, however, that business owners do not identify or align themselves with kudzu. Perhaps seeing a commercial benefit in being associated with a widely recognized part of southern culture, thirty-three businesses in the United States have the word "kudzu" in their names. As with Kudzu streets, these businesses are located entirely within the South, albeit the one in Maryland may provoke debate. Southerners may be reluctant to eat kudzu like collard greens, but they show little inhibition about naming food establishments after the land-hungry vine. Such eateries include The Kudzu Cafe (Vicksburg, Mississippi, and Atlanta, Georgia), The Kudzu Bakery (Georgetown, South Carolina), The Kudzu Grill (Sandersville, Georgia), Kudzu on South Broad (Mooresville, North Carolina), and simply Kudzu's (Memphis, Tennessee). While kudzu covers much of the landscape, its business namesake—a hat shop—in Phenix City, Alabama, specializes in covering heads. Only two of these Kudzu establishments specialize in horticulture, Kudzu Landscaping (Lawrenceville, Georgia) and Kudzu Lawn Services (Madison, Mississippi). However, the name kudzu is connected with two other enterprises interested in the cutting and clipping of growth—beauty shops Kudzu & Cotton (Pine Hill, Alabama) and Kudzu Hair Salon (Jonesboro, Georgia). Despite the negative environmental reputation of kudzu, a public relations firm in Atlanta (Kudzu Communications) identifies itself with the vine. According to combined data on Kudzu streets and businesses, the practice of naming appears strongest in Georgia, Alabama, and North Carolina.

Kudzu has been identified, in name, with a host of things—including a gorilla at Zoo Atlanta (Kudzoo), numerous festivals across the region, a

Southern Streets and Businesses Named after Kudzu, by State

State	Streets	Businesses	Total
Alabama	3	5	8
Arkansas	1	0	1
Florida	0	1	1
Georgia	4	15	19
Louisiana	0	0	0
Maryland	0	1	1
Mississippi	2	3	5
North Carolina	4	5	9
South Carolina	3	1	4
Tennessee	2	2	4
Texas	0	0	0
Virginia	0	0	0
Total	19	33	52

Source: Compiled from Internet phone directories (www.teldir.com).

Georgia lottery scratch-off game (Kudzu Cash), a regular program on the Turner South cable channel (Kudzu Theater), a management style (The Art of Killing Kudzu), an alternative country-music band (Kudzu Kings), a 5K race in Birmingham (The Kudzu Run), a system of linked online library catalogs, and a southern comic strip by Doug Marlette, recently recast as a musical featuring the Red Clay Ramblers. A now defunct punk rock band named itself "Kudzu Ganja." As historian Kurt Kinbacher observed, "The band's image is a mixture of two noxious weeds. One chokes out competition while the other numbs the mind." Amazingly, kudzu's cultural importance is not limited to the terrestrial. The "miracle vine" also grows in cyberspace, as evidenced by the mass of Kudzu web pages that have sprouted up in the last few years. Southerners are increasingly going online, using the World Wide Web to construct what Stephen Smith called an "electronic folklore" about the region. Kudzu has a special place in these attempts to represent the South and southerners as culturally distinctive and unique. "The Kudzu Chronicles" web page clearly states, "For those who do not live in the South, the name 'Kudzu' means little. For southern landowners it means: Fear, holy terror, cancer in vegetation form." The "Y'all.com" Internet site also strongly suggested that kudzu was a "southern thing," going as far as instructing the nonsoutherner in pronunciation: "If you have to ask what it is, you aren't Southern. . . . In case you're not from around here and were wondering, kudzu is pronounced CUD-ZOO, like what cows chew and where gorillas live."[17]

TRANSCENDING TO METAPHOR

The importance of kudzu is not at all limited to the South, however. Aside from the botanical incursions of kudzu into other states (and the likelihood of these may increase with global warming), the vine has invaded the language and phraseology of the entire country. People use kudzu as a metaphor or point of comparison for talking about other issues and events. Metaphors convey meaning by linking together previously unrelated ideas or objects, which encourages a range of thoughts and associations while discouraging others. For example, when saying, "business is war," people think about fighting for market share. At the same time, however, one rarely thinks of working cooperatively. According to sociologists Gary Fine and Lazaros Christoforides, metaphors take two forms. First, metaphors can connect similar phenomena. Second, metaphors can connect seemingly different phenomena.[18] People employ kudzu in both these ways linguistically.

The word "kudzu" has become an important part of our vocabulary when characterizing the environmental threat posed by other invasive plants and animals. For example, in its report on the destruction of the Maryland Eastern Shore by nutria, aquatic rodents brought to the United States from South America, the *Philadelphia Inquirer* called this new ecological invader the "kudzu of the marsh." Although kudzu and nutria are indigenous to different continents and occupy different places in the natural order, people have proposed the same solution for controlling them—eat them. In some comparisons, people create a familial connection between kudzu and other nonnative species, a fitting use of language given the strong southern preoccupation with family relations and genealogy. "The Son of Kudzu" was the phrase used in a *New York Times* piece describing the problems surrounding the imported weed tearthumb. Called tearthumb because of the spines on its leaves and stems, *Polygonum perfoliatum L.* was brought to Pennsylvania accidentally in the 1930s and, in recent years, has crept south into Maryland and northern Virginia. Authors have extended the kudzu family metaphor even to invasive water species. For instance, when representing the damage caused by hydrilla—a plant introduced to Florida in the 1950s—a *Los Angeles Times* article stated, "First there was kudzu, which cloaked much of the land in the South with its tenacious tentacles. Now, a rampant weed described as kudzu's aquatic cousin is clogging Southern lakes." Lynne Langley of Charleston's *Post and Courier* described tropical soda apple (*Solanum viarum Dunal*), a pernicious shrub native to Brazil and Argentina, as "kudzu with thorns." Cattle and wildlife have presumably aided in the invasion of tropical soda apple by consuming the plant's fruit and spreading seeds through manure deposits. When asked to offer predictions on the impact of this new aggressive weed in the United States, a South Carolina extension service agent replied, "It will make kudzu look like a benevolent uncle."[19] As evident in these cases, the role of kudzu in environmental thought and dialogue stretches far beyond its natural characteristics. As a concept common to southern and even American culture, kudzu serves as a lens through which to view and understand other alien plants and animals. Like the proverbial older sibling, kudzu provides a yardstick by which to compare and evaluate the younger brothers and sisters—even when there is little resemblance.

It seems reasonable that kudzu would be used to frame the meaning of other, less well-known invaders. However, kudzu has made its way into conversations having little at all to do with the plant and animal kingdom. In a 1999 Capitol Hill hearing on urban sprawl, Vermont Senator Patrick Leahy testified, "Sprawl often steals unbidden in our midst, and it quickly wears out its welcome, much the same way our friends in the South have come to regard kudzu." In another committee hearing a few years before, James Young of Bell Atlantic invoked the kudzu metaphor in pressing for changes in telecommunications legislation: "Although Senate Bill 652 can be improved in several ways, the bill is an enormous step toward eliminating the regulatory kudzu that has been strangling our industry for the past decade." Newspaper databases yield numerous instances in which kudzu is used as a metaphor for characterizing the aggressive spread of business, housing, gambling, and even the Internet. Even lawyers and judges, famous more for legalese than flowery language, find kudzu to be a useful metaphor. In 1999 Judge James S. Sledge of the U.S. Bankruptcy Court wrote an opinion attacking the increased use of arbitration clauses in consumer contracts, comparing the practice to the creeping of kudzu vegetation across the South. Voicing concern over another area of unchecked growth in America's legal system, lawyer David Apatoff used the invasive vine as a rhetorical tool in representing what he saw as unnecessary prosecutorial invasions by the Justice Department: "For the past 12 years, the False Claims Act has grown like kudzu. It has spread from the field of government contracts into environmental health care and many neighboring areas of the law. Its tendrils have been spotted in the most unlikely enforcement proceedings. Today, it flourishes, in the words of Deputy Attorney General Eric Holder Jr., as 'one of the Justice Department's most powerful tools.' "[20]

If kudzu were a person, it would have a split personality. While landowners and other interests seek to outlaw the plant, curious observers from outside the region seek advice on how to plant and cultivate it. Expectations that kudzu would heal the southern landscape have waned, replaced with the hope of developing it into an actual medicine. The U.S. government reveled in kudzu cultivation in an earlier time and then later repudiated the rapid growth that it had set in motion. While continuing to overtake the physical landscape, the vine is firmly rooted in the fertile ground of our minds, words, and cultural images. Because the plant exists as a symbol and metaphor, it assumes a cultural presence in places and regions that may lie beyond physical or botanical thresholds. In this respect, kudzu is as much an "American" vine, as it is a "southern" one.

NOTES

This paper is a refinement and expansion of arguments found in Derek H. Alderman, "A Vine for Postmodern Times: An Update on Kudzu at the Close of the 20th Century," *Southeastern Geographer* 38 (November 1998): 167–79.

1. Catherine McNaught, "Counting on Sheep to Defeat Kudzu," *Tallahassee Democrat*, 5 April 1999, 1A; John Sevigny, "Low-tech Solution Chows Down," *Tallahassee Democrat*, 12 July 2000, 1B; a description of the Kudzula theatrical production is available online at www.spontaneous.net/1kudzula.shtml.

2. Michael Connor, "Kudzu 'Guru' Champions Plant Despised as Pest in South," *Reuters*, 7 May 1996, SIRS Researcher Record # 00849*19960507*848, www.sirs.com.

3. John J. Winberry and David M. Jones, "Rise and Decline of the 'Miracle Vine': Kudzu in the Southern Landscape," *Southeastern Geographer* 13 (November 1973): 63–67; Kurt E. Kinbacher, "The Tangled Story of Kudzu," *The Vulcan Historical Review* 4 (Spring 2000): 45–69.

4. C. Ritchie Bell and Charles Reagan Wilson, "Kudzu," *The Encyclopedia of Southern Culture* (University of North Carolina Press, 1989), 383–84.

5. Channing Cope, *Front Porch Farmer* (Turner E. Smith & Company, 1949), 26; Philip S. Cohen, interview with authors, 21 June 2000.

6. Mart Allen Stewart, "Cultivating Kudzu: The Soil Conservation Service and the Kudzu Distribution Program," *Georgia Historical Quarterly* 81 (Spring 1997): 156; Diane Hoots and Juanita Baldwin, *Kudzu: The Vine to Love or Hate* (Suntop Press, 1996), 19–21; Winberry and Jones, "Rise and Decline of the 'Miracle Vine,'" 64; John W. Everest, James H. Miller, Donald M. Ball, and Michael G. Patterson, "Kudzu in Alabama: History, Uses, and Control" (Alabama Cooperative Extension System Publications, ANR-65, 1991), available online at www.aces.edu/department/ipm/kudzu.htm; information on kudzu infestation in Oregon is available online at www.oda.state.or.us/Information/news/Kudzu.html; information on the geographic distribution of kudzu sightings is available online at www.invasives pe cies.gov/profiles/kudzu.shtml.

7. Winberry and Jones, "Rise and Decline of the 'Miracle Vine,'" 67; a copy of the U.S. Noxious Weed Act is available online at resource.lawlinks.com/Content/Legal_Research/US_code/Title_07/title_07_61.htm; "Kudzu Ordinance Ok'd," *Palm Beach Post*, 14 December 1996, 4B; "The 100 Worst Ideas of the Century," *Time: 100 Special Issue* 153 (4 June 1999): 37.

8. *Alien Plant Invaders of Natural Areas: Weeds Gone Wild*, an Internet-based project of the Plant Conservation Alliance, available online at www.nps.gov/plants/alien/fact/pulo1.htm; Doug Stewart, "Kudzu: Love It—or Run," *Smithsonian* 31 (October 2000): 68; Diana Craft, email correspondence with authors, 25 August 2000.

9. Joyce Bailey, "Kudzu & Daylillies," *Macon Telegraph*, 27 May 1999, 1B; Jeff Nesmith, "Kudzu Killer? South may rise again from pesky vine's clutches," *Atlanta Journal-Constitution*, 3 February 2000, A1; Kerry Britton, email correspondence with authors, 30 October 2000; Kirk Kicklighter, "The Taming of Kudzu," *Raleigh News and Observer*, 20 June 1998, A1.

10. "Police ID Body Near Golf Course," *Atlanta Journal-Constitution*, 9 December 1998, 6B; "Car, Dead Motorist Are Found in Creek," *Atlanta Journal-Constitution*, 29 October 1995, 2G; Jim Auchmutey, "True South Crazy Kudzu: Super-aggressive imported vine gives a whole region the creeps," *Atlanta Journal-Constitution*, 12 December 1993, M2.

11. Jill Elizabeth Westfall, "Condominium of the Week: Emerald Lake; Gardens Distinguish DeKalb Complex," *Atlanta Journal-Constitution*, 11 April 1999, 12HF; Cynthia Durcanin, "Homeless Threatened by Parkway," *Atlanta Journal-Constitution*, 3 September 1991, A1.

12. Kathleen S. Lowney and Joel Best, "Floral Entrepreneurs: Kudzu as Agricultural Solution and Ecological Problem," *Sociological Spectrum* 18 (1998): 89–110; Stewart, "Kudzu: Love It—or Run," 68; Max Shores, *The Amazing Story of Kudzu*, documentary (University of Alabama Center for Public Television & Radio, 1996); information on the documentary available online at www.cptr

.ua.edu/kudzu/; Jim Duke, "Eat Your Weedies," *Organic Gardening* 40 (July/August 1993): 31–36; Carol Bishop Hipps, "Kudzu," *Horticulture* 72 (June/July 1994): 36–40; Steve Nadis, "Kudzu: From Pest to Pulp," *Omni* 17 (December 1994): 40; Wing-Ming Keung and Bert L. Vallee, "Kudzu Root: An Ancient Chinese Source of Modern Antidipsotropic Agents," *Phytochemistry* 47 (1997): 499–506; an excellent example of the growing commercialization of kudzu is Juanita Baldwin's Kudzu Kingdom Web page, www.kudzukingdom.com.

13. A sample of Jack Anthony's kudzu pictures is available online at www.jjanthony.com/kudzu; a sample of David Day's infrared photography can be found online at www.tekelgallery.com.

14. Stewart, "Cultivating Kudzu," 154; in September of 1999, the AG MAN comic strip was available online at www.baxterblack.com/agman.html.

15. Maxine Simmons, interview with authors, 15 July 2000; Joe Rusz, "Tripping the (Camel) Lights Fantastic," *Road & Track* 43 (August 1992): 120; Ron Ward, interview with authors, 2 July 1999.

16. John Shelton Reed, "The Heart of Dixie: An Essay in Folk Geography," *Social Forces* 54 (June 1976): 925–39; Wilbur Zelinsky, "North America's Vernacular Regions," *Annals of the Association of American Geographers* 70 (1980): 1–16.

17. Kinbacher, "The Tangled Story of Kudzu," 60; a recent keyword search of Internet guide AltaVista Connections (www.altavista.com) produced 29,186 sites that referred to "kudzu"; Stephen A. Smith, *Myth, Media, and the Southern Mind* (University of Arkansas Press, 1985), 99–100; Derek H. Alderman and Daniel B. Good, "Exploring the Virtual South: The Idea of a Distinctive Region on the Web," *Southeastern Geographer* 37 (November 1997): 25; www.esdjournal.com/lightrd/kudzu/kudzu.htm; www.accessatlanta.com/global/local/yall/culture/kudzu.

18. On the importance of metaphor, see Trevor J. Barnes and James S. Duncan, *Writing Worlds: Discourse, Text, and Metaphor in the Representation of Landscape* (Routledge, 1992), 1–17; Gary A. Fine and Lazaros Christoforides, "Dirty Birds, Filthy Immigrants, and the English Sparrow War: Metaphorical Linkage in Constructing Social Problems," *Symbolic Interaction* 14 (1991): 375–93.

19. Conrad Grove, "Big rodents threaten marshes of Maryland's Eastern Shore," *Philadelphia Inquirer*, 1 January 1997, A1; William K. Stevens, "Invading Weed Makes a Bid to Become the New Kudzu," *New York Times*, 16 August 1994, C4; Cindy Roberts, "African Weed is Choking Lakes in the South," *Los Angeles Times*, 18 August 1991, A23; Lynne Langley, "Hungry deer may be aiding invasion of the soda apple," *Post and Courier*, 29 August 1997, B1; Lynne Langley, "Bad Apple: Tropical soda apple gains ground to become state's new kudzu pest," *Post and Courier*, 29 September 1997, B5.

20. Patrick Leahy, Capitol Hill Hearing Testimony on Urban Sprawl, Federal Document Clearing House Congressional Testimony, found online at Lexis-Nexis Congressional Universe (web.lexis-nexis.com/congcomp), 18 March

1999; James R. Young, Testimony to United States Senate Committee on the Judiciary Subcommittee on Antitrust, Business Rights, and Competition, Federal Document Clearing House Congressional Testimony, found online at Lexis-Nexis Congressional Universe (web.lexis-nexis.com/congcomp), 3 May 1995; "Arbitration Clauses 'Smell Bad,'" *Consumer Bankruptcy News* 8 (11 March 1999); David Apatoff, "Fraud Fought With Too Much Vigor," *New Jersey Law Journal*, 13 July 1998, 21.

A Short History of *Redneck*

The Fashioning of a Southern White Masculine Identity

Patrick Huber

The redefinition of redneck *speaks powerfully to the racial and class consciousness of self-styled rednecks. Courtesy of Jan Banning.*

*In the cotton counties along the river in Mississippi, where there are
three black skins for every white one, the gentlemen are afraid. But not
of the Negroes. Indeed, the gentlemen and the Negroes are afraid
together. They are fearful of the rednecks . . . who in politics and in
person are pressing down upon the rich, flat Delta from the hard,
eroded hills. They may lynch a Negro; they may destroy the last of a
civilization which has great vices and great virtues, beauty and strength,
responsibility beside arrogance, and a preserving honesty beside a
destructive self-indulgence.*

—*Jonathan Daniels,* A Southerner Discovers the South *(1938)*

*Arkie, clay-eater, corn-cracker, cornpone, cracker, dirt-eater, hillbilly,
hoosier, lowdowner, mean white, peckerwood, pinelander, poor buckra, poor white,
poor white trash, redneck, ridge-runner, sandhiller, tacky, wool hat.* . . . And this, of
course, does not exhaust the list. Rural poor and working-class white
southerners have endured a broad range of slurs throughout U.S. history,
many derived from geographic regions, dietary habits, physical appearance, or types of clothing. Epithets aimed at urban poor white southerners are fewer and tend to focus on cotton-mill workers: *cottonhead,
cotton mill trash, cottontail, factory hill trash, factory rat,* and *linthead,* for example. A few of the rural class slurs, especially *redneck* and *hillbilly,* are also
applied indiscriminately to southern white migrants working in factories
in Chicago, Detroit, Cincinnati, and other midwestern cities.[1]

For approximately the last one hundred years, the pejorative term
redneck has chiefly slurred a rural, poor white man of the American South
and particularly one who holds conservative, racist, or reactionary views.
In 1965, for example, John Silber backhandedly praised President Lyndon
Baines Johnson of Texas: "His manner and accent suggest a person
who might hold the racist views of a red-neck Southern bigot[,] yet he
has shown a moral vision as clear as Lincoln's on the race question."
Working-class white southerners are today, along with feminists and gays
and lesbians, among the few groups that one can publicly insult or lam-
poon with impunity. As southern historian C. Vann Woodward puts it,
redneck is "the only opprobrious epithet for an ethnic minority still permitted in polite company."[2]

But southern white working people—often poor, powerless, and non-
literate—have not accepted their place in the popular imagination without a fight. Rather they have time and again rehabilitated the derogatory
stereotypes ascribed to them by using language to fashion an identity as

honest, hard-working common folks. A good example of this identity-making process can be found in the changing definitions and connotations of *redneck* in the American language. The term *redneck* originated as a class slur in the late-nineteenth-century South, but white blue-collar workers—especially, but not exclusively, those from the South—gave it a complimentary meaning in the late twentieth century. The redefinition and use of the term by these self-styled rednecks speak powerfully to their racial and class consciousness as an economically exploited and yet racially privileged group.

THE ETYMOLOGY OF *REDNECK*

The term *redneck* emerged as a class slur in the lower Mississippi Valley region sometime in the latter half of the nineteenth century. The word did not appear in print, however, until late in the century.[3] According to the *Oxford English Dictionary*, one of its earliest examples came in 1893 when Hubert A. Shands reported that *red-neck* was used in Mississippi speech "as a name applied by the better class of people to the poorer [white] inhabitants of the rural districts." Eleven years later Joseph W. Carr heard the epithet in Fayetteville, Arkansas, where professional and middle-class whites used the term to refer to "an uncouth countryman" from the swamps, as opposed to a *hill billy*, "an uncouth countryman, particularly from the hills." Carr also recorded the expression *rednecked hill billy*. We do not know how much earlier the slur was in oral circulation among white Mississippians and Arkansans before Shands and Carr noted its use, but it was clearly in widespread currency in white southern speech by the 1930s. Black southerners of all classes, too, used *redneck*—along with *poor white trash*, *cracker*, *peckerwood*, and a host of other slurs—to poke fun at poor white country folks, whom they regarded as morally and socially inferior to themselves. Black sharecroppers, for instance, challenged the southern racial hierarchy in the twenties and thirties when they hollered while working in the fields: "I'd druther be a Nigger, an' plow ole Beck / Dan a white Hill Billy wid his long red neck."[4]

The compound word *redneck*, most scholars of the American language agree, originally derived from an allusion to sunburn. The prevailing view is that southern plantation owners and the urban white professional and middle classes coined the epithet to describe those white dirt farmers, sharecroppers, and agricultural laborers who had sunburned red necks from working fields, unprotected, under a scorching sun. Another explanation, however, traces the origin of *redneck* to black English and claims that it evolved from *peckerwood*, another, much older slur for a poor rural white southerner. According to this theory, African American slaves used *peckerwood*, a folk inversion of *woodpecker*, to refer to their poverty-stricken white neighbors who had sunburned necks while adopting the blackbird as a symbol for themselves. The red head of the woodpecker may in some way be related to the term *redneck*.[5] Whatever its derivation, the origin and early usage of the slur suggests that it ridiculed not only the sweaty, drudging labor of white farmers and sharecroppers but also their perceived deviation, at least a limited one, from a pale white complexion. From its earliest usage, then, the pejorative term *redneck* reflected clear connotations of both class and color difference.

A few students of the American language also speculate that southern white farmers and sharecroppers first became "rednecks" after some refused to wear their traditional wool hats any longer to protect them against sunburn. The reason for their refusal, scholars suggest, was a conscious effort to distinguish themselves in dress from the former black slaves who reportedly began adopting headgear in large numbers only after emancipation. A South Carolina writer lent support to this argument when, in 1877, he observed: "The negro men, as a general thing, did not wear hats before emancipation. But they have since displayed quite a zeal to procure head wear. . . ." More recently, southern journalists Billy Bowles and Remer Tyson have advanced another explanation. They propose that, after the Civil War, the white yeoman farmers of Georgia "stubbornly refused to wear the cool, wide-brim straw field hats favored by their former slaves" and instead opted for "sweaty, narrow-brim wool hats" that exposed their necks to sunburn as they stooped to work in the fields.[6] Both of the above explanations underscore the decision of rednecked farmers and sharecroppers to set themselves apart from their black counterparts. White farmers, whether landowners or tenants, sought to preserve their higher social and economic status and to undercut any opportunity for comparisons of themselves to black southerners, even at the cost of a painful sunburn. Obviously, a white racial identity held great significance in their minds and in southern culture generally.

The virulent racism of some poor and working-class white southerners also came to be closely associated with the word *redneck*, and as the twentieth century wore on, it was increasingly used to describe a racist, bigot, or reactionary. In 1938, for example, Harris Dickson, a white Mississippi plantation owner, simply explained to newspaperman Jonathan

Daniels, "Rednecks . . . are raised on hate." Some years later, "Gooseneck Bill" McDonald, a leading black Republican in early-twentieth-century Texas politics, suggested as much, implying that the words *redneck* and *racist* were synonymous. "Many of the whites I came in contact with in the country and elsewhere were extremely kind," McDonald recalled of his many years stumping for the Grand Old Party in the Lone Star State, "and I, for one, don't believe every Southerner is a 'redneck.' "[7]

By the midsixties the connection between redneck and racism was firmly cemented, especially for African Americans. At Oxford, Ohio, site of the training sessions for the 1964 Mississippi Freedom Summer, experienced instructors prepared northern college-age civil rights volunteers for the hatred and violence they expected to encounter, using a role-playing game called "Redneck-and-Nigger." In the scenario, journalist William Bradford Huie explained, "They would choose up [sides] and one group would be Rednecks, the others would be Niggers. Then the Niggers would try to see how long they could remain 'good-natured and smiling' while the Rednecks jostled them and called them 'black-assed coons.' " In 1973 during his bid to break Babe Ruth's all-time home run record, Atlanta Braves slugger Hank Aaron called a racist heckler a "redneck." In this sense the epithet has lost many of its class and regional connotations because African Americans apply it indiscriminately to any white racist, regardless of his or her class position or birthplace. "They were rich people, but that girl—oh—but I lived to see her get everything that she put out," Althea Vaughn, a southern cook and maid, bitterly recalled her white employer's daughter-in-law. ". . . I couldn't stand her for nothing in the world. She [was an] old redneck hoo'ger, those kinds that weren't used to nothing."[8]

THE STEREOTYPING OF THE REDNECK

Today the redneck is generally depicted in novels, films, and television shows as a greasy-haired, tobacco-chewing, poor southern white man with a sixth-grade education and a beer gut. He lives in a double-wide trailer with his homely, obese wife—who is probably also a first cousin—and their brood of grubby, sallow-faced children and a couple of scrawny coon dogs. He is, according to the stereotype, a rent farmer, a gas station attendant, or a factory worker, if he works at all. He enjoys guzzling six-packs, listening to country music, and hanging out with his buddies in pool halls and honky-tonks, that is, when he's not fishing, poaching deer, cruising in his pickup truck, going to stock car races, beating his wife, or attending Klan rallies. And, of course, the redneck supposedly hates blacks, Jews, hippies, union organizers, aristocratic southern whites, Yankees, and, for good measure, "foreigners" in general.[9]

In *A Turn in the South* (1989), a travel account of the southern United States, West Indian writer V. S. Naipaul recounts a conversation with a real estate salesman in Jackson, Mississippi, who provided a colorful description of what he took *redneck* to mean:

> A redneck is a lower blue-collar construction worker who definitely doesn't like blacks. . . . He is going to live in a trailer someplace out in Rankin County, and he's going to smoke about two and a half packs of cigarettes a day and drink about ten cans of beer at night, and he's going to be mad as hell if he doesn't have some cornbread and peas and fried okra and some fried pork chops to eat. . . . And the son of a bitch loves country music. They love to hunt and fish. They go out all night on the Pearl River. . . . They're Scotch-Irish in origin. A lot of them intermarried, interbred. I'm talking about the good old rednecks now. He's going to have an eight-to-five job. But there's an upscale redneck, and he's going to want it cleaned up. Yard mowed, a little garden in the back. Old Mama, she's gonna wear designer jeans and they're gonna go to Shoney's to eat once every three weeks. . . . If he or she moves to North Jackson, he'd be upscale [*sic*]. He wouldn't have that twang so much. But the good old fellow, he's just going to work six or eight months a year. . . . [The wife's] got some little piddling job. She's probably the basis of the income. She's going to try to work every day. . . . You see, he doesn't want to work all day long. He's satisfied by getting by. They don't like to be told what to do. . . . They have the same old attitude as the black people. Daddy is home a little more often. But they're tickled pink that they ain't got nothing. You wouldn't believe.[10]

While the real estate agent obviously knew his subjects intimately enough to notice the intricate nuances of consumption patterns and class differences, his description reflects stereotypes that are prevalent in popular culture.

The image of the redneck as a vicious, cross-burning racist is also widespread. In his song "Rednecks" from the 1974 concept album *Good Old Boys*, singer and songwriter Randy Newman comically depicts southern working-class whites as ignorant and belligerent hatemongers who "don't know [their] ass from a hole in the ground" and who are trying to keep "the niggers down." While he doesn't challenge the redneck stereotype, he does point out the hypocrisy of singling out southern white working people as the only racists in America. Not surprisingly, Newman's benighted redneck persona composes the song to defend Lester Maddox, the ax handle–wielding governor of Georgia, and his fellow southern rednecks against the mockings of "some smart-ass New York Jew." Yet he ironically and insightfully declares that "the North has set the nigger free"—but only "free to be put in a cage" in northern ghettos. Even a few country-and-western songs embrace the stereotype. For example, the Charlie Daniels Band's "Uneasy Rider" (1973) and Kinky Friedman's "They Ain't Makin' Jews Like Jesus Anymore" (1974) depict rednecks as intolerant, small-minded bigots who hate blacks, Jews, and hippies with equal passion.[11]

A host of popular jokes reinforces the negative stereotypes of rural southern white folks. Most of these jokes seem to be made up and told by middle-class whites—southerners as well as northerners—and are occasionally heard on cable-television comedy shows. Comic Jeff Foxworthy of Georgia has turned redneck humor into a cottage industry, publishing three best-selling books containing a total of more than four hundred jokes. Redneck and hillbilly jokes primarily poke fun at the stereotypical lower-class lifestyles, values, and manners of rural white southerners, especially their image as lascivious yokels given to drunkenness and sexual excess—often including bestiality, incest, and other aberrant sexual practices. "You might be a redneck," one Foxworthy jokes goes, "if you've ever heard a sheep bleat and had romantic thoughts." And another: "You might be a redneck if you view the upcoming family reunion as a chance to meet women."[12]

Redneck and hillbilly jokes not only ridicule and denigrate but also marginalize their subjects and mark group distinctions in much the same way as other ethnic and racial humor. They, in effect, convey exaggerated characterizations of rural white southerners that outsiders actually believe to be accurate. This is strikingly evident in the comments of Tony Isaac, a gay man from Michigan who cruised Chicago's "hillbilly bars" for sexual partners during the 1950s. "You found out that hillbillies first wanted a woman," Isaac concluded of his honky-tonk encounters with recently arrived southern white migrants, "and if they couldn't get a woman they'd take anything. I think they'd rather have a cow than a man but they'd take a man."[13]

To explain why poor and working-class white southerners have borne a disproportionate share of insults and stereotypes, we must begin by looking at the development of racial and class identity in the nineteenth-century South. Throughout that century and beyond, planters, overseers, and factory owners took advantage of such stereotypes of poor southern whites as a justification for exploiting them and paying them pitifully low wages. An Augusta, Georgia, cotton mill owner remarked, for instance, to traveler William Cullen Bryant of his female workers in 1849:

> These poor girls . . . think themselves extremely fortunate to be employed here, and accept work gladly. They come from the most barren parts of Carolina and Georgia, where their families live wretchedly, often upon unwholesome food, and as idly as wretchedly. . . . They come barefooted, dirty, and in rags; they are scoured, put into shoes and stockings, set at work and sent regularly to Sunday-schools, where they are taught what none of them have been taught before—to read and write. In a short time they become expert at their work; they lose their sullen shyness, and their physiognomy becomes comparatively open and cheerful. Their families are relieved from the temptations to theft and other shameful courses which accompany the condition of poverty without occupation.[14]

Other antebellum employers used stereotypes of southern white workers to rationalize the hiring of black slave or Irish immigrant laborers instead. Frederick Law Olmsted, a New Yorker who toured the southern coastal states extensively in the 1850s, frequently commented on the absence of native-born, white workingmen in southern agricultural work, canal-building, and other unskilled jobs. The planters and other employers whom he questioned repeatedly told him that they did not hire "poor whites" because such men "are not used to steady labour; they work reluctantly, and will not bear driving; they cannot be worked to advantage with slaves, and it is inconvenient to look after them, if you work them separately."[15]

Southern white workers, nevertheless, clung to their racial identity. From the nation's beginning, notions of whiteness and blackness developed in relation to one another in the South within the context of racial slavery, and eventually, whiteness became, by the turn of the nineteenth century, closely associated with the republican virtues of freedom, inde-

pendence, and manliness. At the same time, blackness came to symbolize its opposite qualities of slavishness, dependence, and emasculation.
"Euro-American culture in general valued a pale complexion," historian
Elizabeth Fox-Genovese writes, "but to [white] southerners paleness
assumed special importance by implicitly distancing [them] from the dark
skins of Africans." In effect, the nonslaveholding masses of southern
white men—small farmers, herders, squatters, day laborers, hunters, overseers, and riverboat hands—prized their racial identity because it distinguished them as free men and entitled them to political and civil rights. As
Emily P. Burke, a New Hampshire native who taught school in Georgia
during the 1840s, observed, the masses of "crackers, clay-eaters, and
sandhillers" in the state, "though degraded and ignorant as the slaves, are,
by their little fairer complexions entitled to all privileges of legal suffrage."
Race alone accorded poor whites a sense of superiority over blacks, slave
and free, "a sort of public and psychological wage," historian W. E. B. Du
Bois wrote in 1935. Of the lower classes of southern whites, Du Bois
asserted:

> They were given public deference and titles of courtesy because they
> were white. They were admitted freely with all classes of white people
> to public functions, public parks, and the best schools. The police were
> drawn from their ranks, and the courts, dependent upon their votes,
> treated them with such leniency as to encourage lawlessness. Their
> vote selected public officials, and while this had small effect upon the
> economic situation, it had great effect upon their personal treatment
> and the deference shown them.[16]

A pale white complexion also symbolized respectability, gentility, and
social status in the antebellum South, since planters and ladies, like the
nobility and gentry of Europe, did not perform manual work but rather
reaped the fruits of others' labor. In contrast, a sun-browned skin served
as a badge of agrarian toil, and few northern and European travelers
missed a chance in their journals to comment on the dark, weathered
complexions of southern white farmers and laborers. In 1817, for example, British traveler Elias P. Fordham described the differences of skin
color that he noted among the white classes of Virginia. "The gentlemen
[here] are fairer than Englishmen," he observed, "their faces being always
shaded by hats with extraordinary broad brims," while "the poorer people and the overseers are very swarthy." A fair-skinned complexion, then,
was not only an index of race but also an index of class.[17]

Although most were not slaveholders themselves, the masses of rural white southerners were often staunch champions of slavery because it established them in a superior social position to at least some people in southern society. According to southern historian Steven Hahn, white yeoman farmers and other small landholders "saw blacks as symbols of a condition they most feared—abject and perpetual dependency—and as a group whose strict subordination provided essential safeguards for their way of life." Fanny Kemble, an English actress who lived on a Georgia Sea Islands plantation during the late 1830s, claimed: "To the crime of slavery, though they [poor white southerners] have no profitable part or lot in it, they are fiercely accessory, because it is the barrier that divides the black and white races, at the foot of which they lie wallowing in unspeakable degradation, but immensely proud of the base freedom which still separates them from the lash-driven tillers of the soil."[18]

One example of rural southern white workers' efforts to maintain clearly defined economic and social distinctions between themselves and African Americans was these workers' occasional refusal to work under the supervision of a gang boss, or to perform certain types of agricultural wage labor such as tending cattle and hauling wood. They saw these tasks, traditionally performed by slaves, as "nigger work" that was beneath white folks, even the lowliest and most destitute, because it reduced them to a certain degree of equality with black southerners. As Frederick Law Olmsted explained, "To work industriously and steadily . . . is, in the Southern tongue, to 'work like a nigger; and from childhood, the one thing in their condition which has made life valuable to the mass of whites has been that the niggers are yet their inferiors."[19]

Ironically, this tactic to control their own labor won the masses of poor white southerners a reputation for being lazy and shiftless. Antebellum travelers and social observers condemned what they perceived as the laziness of poor white folks and their disdain for manual labor, and abolitionists in particular argued that manual work in the southern states was, as Fanny Kemble asserted, "the especial portion of slaves, [and] it is thenceforth degraded, and considered unworthy of all but slaves. No white man, therefore, of any class puts hand to work of any kind soever." Touring the war-torn southeastern seaboard states in late 1865, northern newspaper correspondent Sidney Andrews reported that "there can be no lower class of people than the North Carolina 'clay-eaters.' " Andrews believed that "the average negroes are superior in force and intellect to the great majority of these clay-eaters," who, he wrote, "are lazy and thriftless, mostly choose to live by begging or pilfering, and are more unreliable as farm hands than the worst of the negroes."[20]

After emancipation in 1865, slavery no longer provided a sharp distinction between white and black southerners. Despite the dire poverty, homelessness, and hunger that many poor white families suffered after the Civil War, white workers to a large degree remained steadfast in their refusal to do so-called "nigger work." True, some poor southern white men deliberately conformed to their imposed stereotypes and manipulated them by feigning ignorance or incompetence to avoid trouble or punishment from those more powerful than themselves. Slaves had sometimes done the same thing before them with the image of the shuffling, grinning Sambo. But this form of resistance was all too often self-defeating since it usually served only to reinforce dehumanized images of the group.[21]

The strategy certainly reinforced the views of industrious-minded factory owners and Victorian reformers who condemned poor southern white men for supposedly shirking their patriarchal responsibilities as family providers and instead placing the burden of their families' subsistence on their wives and daughters. Thus, these men forfeited any claim to manhood, honor, and respect, according to critics. In 1891, Clare De Graffenried, a U.S. Bureau of Labor investigator studying cotton mill workers in Georgia, put into words a stereotype that remains current today:

> The genius for evading labor is most marked in the men. Like Indians in their disdain of household work, they refuse to chop wood or bring water, and often subsist entirely upon the earnings of meek wives or fond daughters, whose excuses for this shameless vagabondism are both pathetic and exasperating. . . . The favorite occupation of the men is to spit, stare, and whittle sticks.[22]

As the New South began a spurt of industrialization in the 1880s, the promise of steady work and wages drew masses of rural white southern men and women to mills and factories. Again industry boosters used the popular stereotype of poor rural white folks to promote the social benefits of industrialization and to rationalize "the creation of a dependent, wage-earning white working class." Factory work and a capitalist work discipline, the owners argued, would civilize and transform shiftless "poor white trash" into productive, respectable citizens of southern society.[23]

For southern white workers factory jobs conferred not only a livelihood but also social and economic status since many owned no property and had nothing to sell but their labor. Consequently, they collaborated with factory owners to maintain rigidly segregated workplaces in the increasingly industrialized New South. In textile mills that sprang up in the Carolina and Georgia piedmont, for example, white workers demanded that all production line jobs be reserved for whites only and that blacks be restricted to such menial, undesirable jobs as sweepers, scrubbers, yard hands, and firemen. Such employment practices contained a trade-off for white mill workers. On the one hand, they protected their social and economic status as wage workers and gained a certain amount of job security by restricting the pool of unskilled laborers from which management could draw its employees. On the other hand, they accepted lower wages in return. For their part, textile mill owners benefitted from a less militant white workforce that identified not so much with the class interests it shared with black workers as it did with the racial interests of its employers. A racially divided workforce, moreover, dealt textile mill owners a trump card—the threat of replacing white strikers with black strikebreakers.[24]

These racist employment practices, as historian I. A. Newby has shown, were widely adhered to by textile mill owners throughout the South during the late nineteenth and early twentieth centuries. A 1907 survey of 152 southern textile mills, for example, found that none employed black men on the production line and that only a handful employed them to work outdoors. Any breach of segregated employment in mills and factories could result in outbreaks of lynchings and in other forms of racial violence against black workers or in labor strikes. Between 1882 and 1900, southern white workers in textile, railroad, and other industries staged at least fifty strikes to protest the employment of black workers in any but the dirtiest, lowest-paying, and most physically difficult jobs.[25]

One of the most famous of these strikes occurred at the Fulton Bag and Cotton Mills in Atlanta, Georgia, in August 1897, when more than 1,400 white mill workers walked off their jobs to protest the hiring of twenty-five black women as folders on the production line. The striking mill workers were outraged over management's suspension of racist hiring practices, despite the fact that the black folders worked in a segregated department of the mill. One millhand, for instance, expressed his anger at how "our wives [would] be forced to work along side nasty, black, stinkin' nigger wimmin [sic]." The strikers' demands were simple but carried significant meaning for their social and economic status as wage workers. "All we want you to do," a spokesman for the strikers told the president of Fulton Mills, "is to take out the niggers from this place, all except the scrubbers and the firemen." The strike lasted five days and resulted in an "overwhelmingly favorable" settlement for the strikers. No disciplinary action was taken against them, and the black folders were fired. Thus, the united white mill workers had successfully forced the company to make a major concession to their job security and to working-class respectability, and particularly to working-class white womanhood.[26]

THE PAIN OF PREJUDICE

It would be a mistake, however, to see the creation of rural southern white stereotypes as overtly conscious acts or to think that only a small segment of American society actually believed, maintained, and reproduced these stereotypes. Rather, they have long held wide currency among all classes of Americans, white and black alike, as realistic depictions of the poor white southerner. Many outsiders unfamiliar with southern white working people fear and intentionally avoid them on the basis of the negative, antisocial images. The *Chicago Tribune*, for example, reported in the late fifties that the city had been invaded by "clans of fightin', feudin', Southern hillbillies and their shootin' cousins," a reference to the approximately seventy thousand white migrants who left Kentucky, Tennessee, Arkansas, and Missouri during and after World War II in search of jobs in Chicago's factories, meatpacking houses, and stockyards. "The Southern hillbilly migrants, who have descended like a plague of locusts in the last few years," the paper continued, "have the lowest standard of living and moral code (if any), the biggest capacity for liquor, and the most savage tactics when drunk, which is most of the time." Midwesterners' fear of and hostility toward the migrants are also reflected in a 1951 Wayne State University study of Detroit residents, in which 21 percent of those surveyed identified "poor southern whites/hillbillies" as the most "undesirable people" who were "not good to have in the city" while only 13 percent of the respondents named "Negroes" and another 6 percent "foreigners." Only "criminals/gangsters," selected by 26 percent, ranked higher.[27]

Rural southern white stereotypes are often as powerful as other racial, religious, or ethnic prejudices. Listen, for instance, to Charles Strong, a black Vietnam War veteran from Pompano Beach, Florida, describing a white soldier in his company with whom he became close friends: "Joe was an all right guy from Georgia. . . . He talked with that 'ol' dude' accent. If you were to see him the first time, you would just say that's a redneck, ridge-runnin' cracker. But he was the nicest guy in the world." Strong was challenged and shocked by his previously almost unimaginable friendship with a "redneck, ridge-runnin' cracker" and was forced to rethink his prejudices—a painful but often enlightening experience.[28]

The epithets hurled at poor and working southern white folks can also be as damaging psychologically as slurs aimed at other minority groups. Victims often internalize the hateful messages of epithets, making them difficult to forget or escape. The point is made in a 1939 Federal Writers' Project interview of Jessie Jeffcoat, the wife of a third-generation share-cropper living in Durham County, North Carolina. "You ain't nothing but pore whites [*sic*]," a rich man's son cruelly teased Jessie's husband, Jim Jeffcoat, when he was a young boy growing up in northeastern Georgia. Later in his life, unable to rise above his poverty and to purchase his own land and mules, Jim Jeffcoat drank heavily and drifted from one farmstead to another. Jessie Jeffcoat confided that she believed that the "poor white" stigma was the cause of her husband's alcoholism. "Nobody ever called him 'pore white' anymore," she said. "But Jim still believes that people are thinkin' it. When they cuss him or 'pore Jim' him, he gets sore and keeps rememberin' and rememberin' that his folks were down near the bottom before the [Civil] War. Mister, I believe that's one reason Jim drinks so much. The only time he forgets that he came from pore folks is when he gits drunk [*sic*]."[29]

THE REDEFINITION OF *REDNECK*

Not all southern white working people remained victims of these damaging stereotypes and hateful slurs, however. Positive definitions of *redneck* also emerged. As early as 1910, for example, political supporters of Mississippi demagogue James K. Vardaman described themselves as "rednecks." Vardaman's constituency, comprised largely of poor and working-class white Mississippians, embraced the epithet and wore red neckties and kerchiefs to his political rallies to show their support for the candidate during a special Democratic senatorial primary race against opponent Leroy Percy. Historian Albert D. Kirwan, in *Revolt of the Rednecks: Mississippi Politics, 1876–1925* (1951), explains their adoption of the nickname:

In a speech at Godbold Wells on July 4, 1910, Percy, heckled by an audience with shouts of "Hurrah for Vardaman!" "Hurrah for [Theodore] Bilbo!" "Hurrah for Mary Stamps!" became angered and called them "cattle" and "rednecks." These names were adopted by the Vardaman following, and wherever Vardaman went to speak he was greeted by crowds of men wearing red neckties and was carried in wagons drawn by oxen. This accentuated the class division in the struggle.[30]

Yet it was not until the late 1960s and early 1970s that large numbers of poor and working-class white southerners began referring to themselves as "rednecks." Perhaps they chose this name partly because it conveyed their own emergent sense of racial and class solidarity in the midst of the civil rights movement, the counterculture revolution, and the women's liberation movement. In this sense the selection of the term may have been part of a larger southern white backlash to the social upheavals of the sixties. Regardless of the reasons for its widespread emergence, southern white workers redefined *redneck* to emphasize their industriousness and their white racial identity. As one blue-collar workingman told sociologists Julian B. Roebuck and Mark Hickson III: "Us rednecks are jes God-fearing Christians who don't cheat like niggers and the rich white man." As this quote suggests, rednecks first define themselves in relation to African Americans by accentuating their whiteness, from which they derived economic and psychological benefits. "Let the niggers suck in the welfare," another workingman baldly remarked. "Won't do them no good cause they're still gonna be niggers. We're gonna put food on the table and git by som'a how."[31]

Their identity involved more than race, however. Like the populist farmers of Georgia and South Carolina who termed themselves "wool hats" in the 1890s, modern-day self-styled rednecks define themselves in relation to southern white society by using the term *redneck* to mean an honest, hard-working workingman who identifies with traditional southern social and religious values. The chief characteristic that rednecks felt distinguished them from the other classes of white southerners is their masculine ethic of a hard, honest day's work. They see themselves as different from the "poor white trash," who are cast as lazy, good-for-nothing folks who never work but instead sponge off welfare as "niggers" supposedly do. Nor are they like the "big shots"—moneygrubbing upper- and middle-class southerners who exploit and get fat off workers' labor rather than doing honest work themselves. "We're jes po honest working folks who work for an honest day's pay," one self-avowed redneck explained. Another rankled redneck ranted, "Folks like us work for a livin'. The big guys are a bunch of phonies, know what I'ma talkin' bout?—phonies and bullshitters."[32]

In the midseventies a combination of political events and popular culture catapulted the word *redneck* to national attention. In 1978, for example, an obscure band named The Beaver Brothers released a song titled "Redneck in the White House" in the wake of a spate of country songs that celebrated the southern redneck as a working-class hero. That redneck in the White House was, of course, Jimmy Carter of Georgia, a wealthy peanut farmer and professional politician whose neck struck others as actually more pink than red. Nonetheless, Carter sometimes described himself—and during the 1976 presidential campaign was even sometimes described by Washington political reporters who didn't know any better—as "basically a redneck." He successfully ran as a self-styled "political outsider," a slick man-of-the-people packaging obviously designed for political purposes.[33]

It was the president's beer-drinking, straight-talking brother, Billy Carter, however, who came to epitomize the "genuine" redneck better than any other American public figure. The press hailed him as "America's newest folk hero," and Brother Billy, a self-avowed redneck, played the part admirably. On occasion he hammed for photographers in his "Redneck Power" T-shirt, with a cold Pabst Blue Ribbon in hand, or regaled reporters with his down-home anecdotes at his Plains, Georgia, filling station. In effect, Billy Carter embodied those characteristics that rednecks promoted in their campaign of self-definition. When his brother Jimmy ran for office in 1976, touting his own honesty, Billy told the press, "*I'm* the only Carter who'll never lie to you." On another occasion he identified his mainstream American lifestyle and values, remarking, "My mother joined the Peace Corps when she was seventy, my sister Gloria is a motorcycle racer, my other sister Ruth is a Holy Roller preacher, and my brother thinks he's going to be President of the United States. I'm really the only normal one in the family." For Americans disillusioned and embittered by Watergate and a lengthy Asian war, Billy Carter marked a refreshing return to those supposedly good old all-American values of honesty, hard work, pride, self-reliance, and commonness.[34]

To identify oneself as a redneck became fashionable during the Carter years, a national craze that writer and journalist Paul Hemphill termed "redneck chic." Suddenly, trendy white Americans across the country affected phony southern drawls, dressed up in Levi's and cowboy boots, sipped Lone Star and Pabst longnecks, tuned in to Waylon and Willie, and hankered for meals of fried pork chops, grits, greens, and biscuits and gravy. "Redneck chic"—which anticipated by half a decade the western-wear and bull-riding fad created by the blockbuster hit film *Urban Cowboy* (1981)—spawned its own distinct body of literature, to use the term loosely. Dozens of books and articles were published to teach redneck wannabes how to stomach greasy home cooking, speak with a proper accent, chug six-packs, fashionably dress down, chew tobacco and spit without opening their mouths, and convincingly act the part. One example was Nina Savin's 1981 article, "The Official Redneck Handbook," which appeared, oddly enough, in *Fashion For Men*. "Rednecks are cool. Not in an affected way, but fundamentally," Savin explained.[35]

Meanwhile, the term *redneck* cropped up in more and more country songs, with many of the singers referring to themselves as one: David Allan Coe's "Longhaired Redneck" (1975), Vern Oxford's "Redneck! (The Redneck National Anthem)" (1976), Jerry Reed's "(I'm Just a) Redneck in a Rock and Roll Bar" (1977), and Ronnie Milsap's "I'm Just a Redneck at Heart" (1983), to name only a handful. More often than not, country songs presented romanticized images of southern rednecks and frequently used the term as an affirmation of identity. Johnny Russell's well-known recording of "Rednecks, White Socks and Blue Ribbon Beer" (1973), for instance, celebrates the lifestyle of southern blue-collar workers who "don't fit in with that white-collar crowd" and who are "a little too rowdy and little too loud." More recently, The Charlie Daniels Band's solution to America's domestic problems, titled "(What This World Needs Is) A Few More Rednecks" (1989), underscores the term's emphasis on commonness, true grit, and hard work. A redneck, Daniels sings, is a working man who "earns his living by the sweat of his brow" and by "the calluses on his hands."[36]

Some rock 'n' roll songs also traded on the positive redefinition. In "Texan Love Song" (1972), British singer and songwriter Elton John's working-class hero threatens long-haired, drug-smoking hippie interlopers with violence, asserting, "We're tough and we're Texan with necks good and red." And Jan Reid coined the phrase *redneck rock* for his book, *The Improbable Rise of Redneck Rock* (1974), to describe the fusion of traditional country-and-western and rock 'n' roll pioneered in the early seventies by Michael Murphey, Willie Nelson, Jerry Jeff Walker, Kinky Friedman, and others involved in the *avant-garde* music scene in Austin, Texas. The terms *country rock*, *progressive country*, and *southern rock* were among the other catchy names created to refer to this hybrid of musical styles, and eventually its definition was extended to include such southern supergroups as the Allman Brothers Band, Lynyrd Skynyrd, and the Marshall Tucker Band.[37]

Used to mean a poor southern white man or worse, the term *redneck* is still considered an insult when used disrespectfully. But today, self-styled rednecks define themselves, and are even defined by some outside their group, as honest, hard-working, blue-collar white Americans with mainstream attitudes and values. University of Georgia historian F. Nash Boney, for example, argues, "In many ways rednecks are typical Americans with typical American attitudes. They as much as any group in our culture are representative Americans." The titles of both Randy Howard's "All-American Redneck" (1983) and John Schneider's "A Redneck Is the Backbone of America" (1987) emphasize this point. According to these two little-known country songs, rednecks are not only America's brawny workingmen and its chief producers but also the country's steadfast patriots and its moral pillars. In the latter song Schneider lionizes the redneck whose "heart [is] full of love for his family, his neighbors, his country" and who is "the reason this nation stands." Female derivatives of *redneck*, a traditionally masculine term, have also emerged, including *redneck girl*, *redneck mother*, and *redneck woman*.[38]

Even some white Americans who are neither of southern descent nor of working-class origins have adopted the term *redneck*. In 1977, for example, Sheriff Duane Lowe of Sacramento, California, a controversial political hard-liner and antihomosexual crusader, told an interviewer: "My detractors characterize me as a reactionary and as a redneck. And I'll tell you, I don't mind being called a redneck." Among blue-collar white workingmen, use of the word has spread beyond the South. Perhaps a Pittsburgh steel-mill worker, a Washington State logger, or a Detroit auto worker is as likely to describe himself as a redneck as is a Mississippi cotton farmer, a Birmingham construction worker, or an Atlanta mechanic. Moreover, no small number of professional and middle-class white southerners now refer to themselves as rednecks. "Some big shots is necks, too. . . . Fact is, it's hard to tell who be and who ain't a redneck," one blue-collar worker remarked. And another said: "Shit, anybody can be a redneck; it ain't who you be—but how you think." The real estate salesman interviewed by V. S. Naipaul marked distinctions between the rougher, lower-class "good old rednecks" and the more respectable, upwardly mobile "upscale rednecks." "I'm probably a redneck myself," the realtor added. Undoubtedly, an "upscale" one.[39]

The widespread success of *redneck* as a symbol of southern pride stems primarily from its synthesis of whiteness and industriousness, two attributes that historically have been central to the identity of the southern white working classes. First, *redneck* emphasizes a white racial identity. Although it denotes redness, the word ironically connotes whiteness because, as an allusion to sunburn, it naturally follows that only fair-complexioned persons sunburn or, rather, burn red. As one hack writer of humorous southern travel guides for "Yankees" curiously phrases it: "The South is [where], no matter how long he works in the sun, a black man never becomes a Red Neck."[40]

Second, *redneck* emphasizes the masculine values of hard, honest labor, a connotation that likewise stems from its origin. Since it evolved from an allusion to sunburn, *redneck* initially referred to a farmer who toiled for long hours exposed to the beating sun. In 1938 Jonathan Daniels cautioned readers of *A Southerner Discovers the South* that "rednecks" should not be confused with "po' whites," pointing out that "[Abraham] Lincoln and [Andrew] Jackson, to name but two, came from a Southern folk the back of whose necks were ridged and red from labor in the sun." In other words, self-described rednecks did not see themselves as the shiftless "poor white trash" of the popular imagination who lolled about on hot afternoons in the cool shade, intermittently suckin' on a jug of whiskey and dozing, while his long-suffering wife and daughters chopped wood and worked the land. Instead, they viewed their primary male role as family protector and provider, responsible for holding down a steady job, caring for their dependents, putting food on the table, and earning enough to make ends meet. As one southern blue-collar workingman remarked: "Hell with that ejacation [education] shit. . . . Me, I'd druther work. And alla my kids I'ma hoping will go to work early. Don't tell me about no future bullshit. My family's gotta eat today." Rejecting some of the bourgeois notions of manhood, rednecks fashioned their own code of working-class masculinity and respectability which placed a high premium on honesty, independence, and hard work.[41] Originally applied as a class slur, *redneck* emerged as an affirmation of identity for working-class white men throughout the United States—and even for some middle-class men—in less than a century.

CONCLUSION

The history of *redneck* in the American language strikingly demonstrates that words are a powerful force in fashioning class, racial, and ethnic identities. Confronted with an opprobrious epithet and stereotypical images projected onto them by those higher on the social scale, southern white working people reacted pragmatically by seeking not to replace the existing slur *redneck* but to redefine it to mean an honest, hard-working blue-collar man. In the process they robbed the pejorative stereotypes of much of their damaging psychological impact. Southern white working people's appreciation for the power of the spoken word was particularly significant since their rural southern folk society was based chiefly on an oral culture in which people transmitted stories, songs, superstitions, home remedies, and humor from one generation to the next. The spoken word was one of only a handful of means available to them with which to socialize their children, inculcate morality and social values, and defend their distinctive lifestyle and culture.[42] And their redefinition of *redneck* has been a process of resistance and empowerment, transforming a slur into a badge of racial, class, and gender identity.

But the story of poor and working-class white southerners is also a tragic one, and much more complex and fraught with contradictions than most historians have generally appreciated. On the one hand, southern white working people were constantly pulled toward a white racial identification and self-defeating racism as in the case of those who joined professional and middle-class white Americans in the Ku Klux Klan during the 1920s. On the other hand, they were also constantly pulled toward class solidarity and biracial labor alliances, as in the example of those who joined black sharecroppers to organize the integrated Southern Tenant Farmers Union during the 1930s.[43]

It would be a mistake, however, to see southern white workers as inevitably choosing to identify with either racial or class solidarity, although clearly the history of southern labor organization has been one of racism, white privilege, and black exclusion. Throughout the nineteenth and twentieth centuries, the masses of white southerners were—and continue to be—subject to racism and exploitation, albeit in a different sense and to a different degree from African Americans. White workers are at once both perpetrators and products, agents and victims, of that racism because they have so often and so tragically opted for the limited material benefits accorded by their whiteness and, in doing so, have accepted not only their own exploitation and oppression at the hands of employers but have also accepted, as historian David R. Roediger reminds us, "stunted lives for themselves and for those more oppressed than themselves."[44]

NOTES

This article was made possible in large part by the rich resource notes on *redneck* collected by the late Peter Tamony of San Francisco and now housed in the University of Missouri–Columbia's Western Historical Manuscripts Collection. The author wishes to thank, for critical reading, encouragement, and suggestions, Susan Porter Benson, Elaine J. Lawless, John Shelton Reed, Jacquelyn Dowd Hall, Alecia Holland, Karen D. Hayes, Peter Filene, Christine M. Stewart, LeeAnn Whites, Bob Pinson, Ronnie Pugh, Abra Quinn, Meghan Holleran, Tim Tyson, Lisa J. Yarger, and especially David R. Roediger, Archie Green, and Paul and Midge Huber. An earlier version of this article was presented at the Mid-America Conference on History in Springfield, Missouri, 19–21 September 1991. The epigraph is from Jonathan Daniels, *A Southerner Discovers the South* (Macmillan Co., 1938), 172–73.

1. J. Wayne Flynt, *Dixie's Forgotten People: The South's Poor Whites* (University of Indiana Press, 1979), 9; Raven I. McDavid Jr., and Virginia McDavid, "Cracker and Hoosier," *Names* 21 (September 1973): 163; and Lewis M. Killian, "Whites in Northern Cities," in Charles Reagan Wilson and William Ferris, eds., *Encyclopedia of Southern Culture* (University of North Carolina Press, 1989), 574–75.

2. John R. Silber, "Lyndon Johnson As Teacher," *The Listener* 73 (20 May 1965): 730; C. Vann Woodward, "Rednecks, Millionaires and Catfish Farms," *New York Times Book Review*, 5 February 1989, 7.

3. According to the *Oxford English Dictionary*, the first known appearance of the term in American print actually dates to 1830, when Anne Newport Royall, a Maryland traveler, reported that *Red Necks* was "a name bestowed upon the Presbyterians in Fayetteville[,]" North Carolina. Students of the American language have been unable to connect this antebellum Tar Heel usage of the word as a religious slur to its later widespread emergence in the Deep South as a class slur for poor whites. Anne N. Royall, *Mrs. Royall's Southern Tour, or Second Series of the Black Book* (1830) quoted in J. A. Simpson and E. S. C. Weiner, eds., *Oxford English Dictionary*, 2nd ed., 20 vols. (Oxford, 1989), 13:422.

4. H. A. Shands, *Some Peculiarities of Speech in Mississippi* (1893) quoted in ibid., 13:422; J. W. Carr, "A List of Words from Northwest Arkansas," *Dialect Notes* 2 (1904): 418, 420; the couplet is from a black worksong collected circa 1920 by Fisk University chemistry professor and amateur folksong scholar Thomas W. Talley and published in *Negro Folk Rhymes* (Macmillan Co., 1922), 43.

5. Hugh Rawson, *Wicked Words: A Treasury of Curses, Insults, Put-Downs, and Other Formerly Unprintable Terms from Anglo-Saxon Times to the Present* (Crown Publishers, 1989), 326; Robert L. Chapman, ed., *New Dictionary of American Slang* (Harper & Row, 1986), 318; Ken Johnson, "The Vocabulary of Race," in Thomas Kochman, ed., *Rappin' and Stylin' Out: Communication in Urban Black America* (University of Illinois Press, 1972), 143.

6. "A South Carolinian," "South Carolina Society," *Atlantic Monthly* 39 (June 1877): 680; Billy Bowles and Remer Tyson, *They Love a Man in the Country: Saints and Sinners in the South* (Peachtree Publishers, 1989), 47.

7. Harris quoted in Daniels, *A Southerner Discovers the South*, 175; and McDonald quoted in Arthur H. Lewis, *The Day They Shook the Plum Tree* (Harcourt, Brace, & World, 1963), 107.

8. William Bradford Huie, *Three Lives for Mississippi*, with an introduction by Martin Luther King Jr. (Signet Books, 1968), 62, "Not Everybody Cheers Aaron," *San Francisco Chronicle*, 13 April 1973, clipping in the Peter Tamony Collection, Western Historical Manuscripts Collection, University of Missouri–Columbia; and Vaughn quoted in Susan Tucker, *Telling Memories Among Southern Women: Domestic Workers and Their Employers in the Segregated South* (Schocken Books, 1988), 209. Tucker's footnote explains that *hoo'ger*, which is probably related to the southern slur *hoosier*, is "a slang term that blacks use to refer to a common white, usually a common white woman."

9. On the stereotypical portrayal of rednecks, and poor white southerners generally, in American popular culture, see, for example, Shields McIlwaine, *The Southern Poor-White: From Lubberland to Tobacco Road* (Cooper Square Press, 1970 [1939]); Sylvia Jenkins Cook, *From Tobacco Road to Route 66: The Southern Poor White in Fiction* (University of North Carolina Press, 1976); Jack Temple Kirby, *Media-Made Dixie: The South in the American Imagination* (Louisiana State University Press, 1978); John Shelton Reed, *Southern Folks, Plain & Fancy: Native White Social Types*, Mercer University, Lamar Memorial Lectures no. 29 (University of Georgia Press, 1986), 34–47; and F. N. Boney, *Southerners All*, rev. ed. (Mercer University Press, 1990), 33–38.

10. Real estate salesman quoted in V. S. Naipaul, *A Turn in the South* (Knopf, 1989), 206–8.

11. Randy Newman, "Rednecks," *Good Old Boys*, Warner Brothers Records; Charlie Daniels Band, "Uneasy Rider," *A Decade of Hits*, Epic Records; and Kinky Friedman, "They Ain't Makin' Jews Like Jesus Anymore," *Kinky Friedman*, ABC Records.

12. Jeff Foxworthy, *You Might Be a Redneck If...*, with a foreword by Rodney Dangerfield (Longstreet Press, 1989), 48, 50. See also Jeff Foxworthy, *Red Ain't Dead: 150 More Ways to Tell If You're a Redneck* (Longstreet Press, 1991) and *Check Your Neck: More of You Might Be a Redneck If...* (Longstreet Press, 1992).

13. Isaac quoted in Keith Vacha, *Quiet Fire: Memoirs of Older Gay Men*, ed. Cassie Damewood (Crossing Press, 1985), 202.

14. William Cullen Bryant, *Letters of a Traveller; or Notes of Things Seen in Europe and America*, 2nd ed. (Putnam, 1850), 358–59.

15. Frederick Law Olmsted, *The Cotton Kingdom: A Traveller's Observations on Cotton and Slavery in the American Slave States*, ed. Arthur M. Schlesinger (Knopf, 1953), 87.

16. For a discussion of the American cultural significance of whiteness and of blackness, see Winthrop D. Jordan, *White Over Black: American Attitudes Toward the Negro, 1550–1812* (University of North Carolina Press, 1968) and David R. Roediger, *The Wages of Whiteness: Race and the Making of the American Working Class* (Verso Press, 1991); Elizabeth Fox-Genovese, *Within the Plantation Household: Black and White Women of the Old South* (University of North Carolina Press, 1988), 197; Emily P. Burke, *Reminiscences of Georgia* (James M. Fitch, 1850), 205; W. E. B. DuBois, *Black Reconstruction in America: An Essay Toward a History of the Part Which Black Folk Played in the Attempt to Reconstruct Democracy in America, 1860–1880* (Russell & Russell, 1962 [1935]), 700–701.

17. Elias Pym Fordham, *Personal Narrative of Travels in Virginia, Maryland, Pennsylvania, Ohio, Indiana, Kentucky; and of a Residence in the Illinois Territory: 1817–1818*, ed. Frederic Austin Ogg (Arthur H. Clarke Co., 1906), 56.

18. Steven Hahn, *The Roots of Southern Populism: Yeoman Farmers and the Transformation of the Georgia Upcountry, 1850–1890* (Oxford University Press, 1983), 89–90; Frances Anne Kemble, *Journal of a Residence on a Georgian Plantation in 1838–1839*, ed. with an introduction by John A. Scott (Knopf, 1961), 182.

19. Olmsted, *The Cotton Kingdom*, 19.

20. Kemble, *Journal of a Residence on a Georgian Plantation*, 110–11; Sidney Andrews, *The South Since the War As Shown by Fourteen Weeks of Travel and Observation in Georgia and the Carolinas* (Ticknor & Fields, 1866), 177.

21. See for example John William De Forest, *A Union Officer in the Reconstruction*, ed. James H. Croushore and David Morris Potter (Anchor Books, 1968), 157.

22. Clare De Graffenried, "The Georgia Cracker in the Cotton Mills," *Century Magazine* 41 (February 1891): 488, 490.

23. Jacquelyn Dowd Hall, James Leloudis, Robert Korstad, Mary Murphy, Lu Ann Jones, and Christopher B. Daly, *Like a Family: The Making of a Southern Cotton Mill World* (University of North Carolina Press, 1987), xvi.

24. Hall et al., *Like a Family*, 66–67; I. A. Newby, *Plain Folk in the New South: Social Change and Cultural Persistence, 1880–1915* (Louisiana State University Press, 1989), 462–67.

25. Newby, *Plain Folk in the New South*, 465; C. Vann Woodward, *Origins of the New South, 1877–1913*, A History of the South, ed. Wendell Holmes Stephenson and E. Merton Coulter, vol. 9 (Louisiana State University Press, 1951), 222.

26. My discussion of the 1897 strike at the Fulton Bag and Cotton Mills is based on Newby, *Plain Folk in the New South*, 474–81. Mill workers quoted on pp. 476, 479.

27. *Chicago Tribune* quoted in Albert N. Votaw, "The Hillbillies Invade Chicago," *Harper's Magazine* 216 (February 1958); 64, 66; and 1951 Wayne State University study findings published in Lewis M. Killian, *White Southerners* (Random House, 1970), 98.

28. Strong quoted in Wallace Terry, *Bloods: An Oral History of the Vietnam War by Black Veterans* (Ballantine Books, 1984), 57.

29. Jessie Jeffcoat quoted in Tom E. Terrill and Jerrold Hirsch, eds., *Such As Us: Southern Voices of the Thirties* (University of North Carolina Press, 1978), 61–62.

30. Albert D. Kirwan, *Revolt of the Rednecks: Mississippi Politics, 1876–1925* (University of Kentucky Press, 1951), 212.

31. My discussion in this paragraph and the next is chiefly based on Julian B. Roebuck and Mark Hickson, III, *The Southern Redneck: A Phenomenological Class Study* (Praeger Press, 1982), v, 3, 65, 80. Rednecks quoted on pp. 64, 106.

32. On the Georgia Populists, see Barton C. Shaw, *The Wool-Hat Boys: Georgia's Populist Party* (Louisiana State University Press, 1984), 1, 10–11; Roebuck and Hickson, *The Southern Redneck*, 80 [quotation], 106; and David W. Maurer, "The Lingo of Good-People," *American Speech* 10 (February 1935): 19. According to linguist David W. Maurer, the term *redneck* used to mean "any honest working-man" dates to the turn of the century.

33. The Beaver Brothers, "Redneck in the White House," Scorpion Records, cited in Raymond S. Rodgers, "Images of Rednecks in Country Music: The Lyrical Persona of a Southern Superman," *Journal of Regional Cultures* 1 (Fall/Winter 1982): 71; and for examples of President Carter dubbed a "redneck," see assorted newspaper and magazine clippings in the Tamony Collection.

34. One of these photographs of Billy Carter appeared in the *San Francisco Examiner*, 25 April 1977, clipping in the Tamony Collection; Jeremy Rifkin and Ted Howard, comps., *Redneck Power: The Wit and Wisdom of Billy Carter* (Bantam Books, 1977); and Billy Carter quoted in Stanley W. Cloud, "A Wry Clown: Billy Carter, 1937–1988," *Time* 132 (10 October 1988): 44 [original emphasis].

35. Paul Hemphill, "Redneck Chic," *San Francisco Examiner*, 7 October 1976, clipping in the Tamony Collection; Richard West, "So You Want To Be A Redneck," *Texas Monthly* 2 (August 1974): 57–59; Kathryn Jenson, *Redneckin': A Hell-Raisin', Foot-Stompin' Guide to Dancin', Dippin' and Doin' Around in a Gen-U-Wine Country Way* (Perigee Books, 1983); Bo Whaley, *The Official Redneck Handbook* (Rutledge Hill Press, 1987); and Nina Savin, "The Official Redneck Handbook," *Fashion For Men* (Fall–Winter 1981): 75–78.

36. David Allan Coe, "Longhaired Redneck," *David Allan Coe: Greatest Hits*, CBS Records; Vernon Oxford, "Redneck! (The Redneck National Anthem),"

Redneck Mothers (various artists), RCA Records; Jerry Reed, "(I'm Just a) Redneck in a Rock and Roll Bar," *Redneck Mothers*; Ronnie Milsap, "I'm Just a Redneck at Heart," *Keyed Up*, RCA Records; Johnny Russell, "Rednecks, White Socks and Blue Ribbon Beer," *Redneck Mothers*; and The Charlie Daniels Band, "(What This World Needs Is) A Few More Rednecks," *Simple Man*, Epic Records.

37. Elton John, "Texan Love Song," *Don't Shoot Me I'm Only The Piano Player*, MCA Records; Jan Reid, *The Improbable Rise of Redneck Rock* (Heidelberg Press, 1974); Archie Green, "Austin's Cosmic Cowboys: Words in Collision," in Richard Bauman and Roger D. Abrahams, eds., *"And Other Neighborly Names": Social Process and Cultural Images in Texas Folklore* (University of Texas Press, 1981), 162–63; and Joe Nick Patoski, "Southern Rock," in Jim Miller, ed., *The Rolling Stone Illustrated History of Rock & Roll* (Random House, 1980), 357–59.

38. F. N. Boney, "The Redneck," *Georgia Review* 25 (Fall 1971): 336; Randy Howard, "All-American Redneck," Warner Brothers Records; John Schneider, "A Redneck Is the Backbone of America," MCA Records; Roebuck and Hickson, *The Southern Redneck*, v, 80; for female derivatives of the term, see Sharon McKern, *Redneck Mothers, Good Ol' Girls and Other Southern Belles: A Celebration of the Women of Dixie* (Viking Press, 1979), and The Bellamy Brothers, "Redneck Girl," *The Bellamy Brothers Greatest Hits*, vol. 1, MCA/Curb Records.

39. Lowe quoted in John Balzar, "A Loquacious Redneck," *San Francisco Chronicle*, 22 October 1977, clipping in the Tamony Collection; rednecks quoted in Roebuck and Hickson, *The Southern Redneck*, 65; and real estate salesman quoted in Naipaul, *A Turn in the South*, 209.

40. Bil Dwyer, *How Tuh Live In The Kooky South: A Fun Guide Book Fer Yankees* (Merry Mountaineers Publication, 1978), 22.

41. Daniels, *Southerner Discovers the South*, 183; and Roebuck and Hickson, *The Southern Redneck*, 80, 93–98. Redneck quoted on p. 64.

42. See Elliott J. Gorn, "Gouge and Bite, Pull Hair and Scratch: The Social Significance of Fighting in the Southern Backcountry," *American Historical Review* 90 (February 1985): 27–28.

43. David R. Roediger, "Gaining a Hearing for Black-White Unity: Covington Hall and the Complexities of Race, Gender and Class," in *Towards the Abolition of Whiteness: Essays on Race, Politics, and Working Class History* (Verso Press, 1994), 134–39.

44. Roediger, *The Wages of Whiteness*, 13.

"Where the Sun Set Crimson and the Moon Rose Red"

Writing Appalachia and the Kentucky Mountain Feuds

Dwight B. Billings and Kathleen M. Blee

Descriptions of moonshining and feuding did much to persuade middle-class readers of Appalachia's strange and peculiar nature. Mountaineer, ca. 1928, courtesy of the Collections of the Library of Congress.

In his 1901 essay "The Kentucky Mountaineer," novelist John Fox Jr. inscribed the mythic image of the southern mountaineers: "proud, sensitive, kindly, obliging in an unreckoning way that is almost pathetic, honest, loyal, in spite of their common ignorance, poverty, and isolation." But Fox also pointed out a *darker* side of the mountaineer that must have both fascinated and repulsed his middle-class readers. Noting the extensive violent conflicts then taking place in the mountain counties of Kentucky, he wrote, "It is only fair to add, however, that nothing that has ever been said of the mountaineer's ignorance, shiftlessness, and awful disregard for human life, especially in the Kentucky mountains, . . . has not its basis, perhaps, in actual fact."[1]

Accounts like Fox's profoundly shaped public perception of the southern mountains at the turn of the century. Along with descriptions of moonshining, popular and academic representations of mountain conflicts—sometimes described as "vendettas" but more often as "feuds"—did much to persuade middle-class readers throughout the United States of the region's strange and peculiar nature and apparently benighted population. Imagined to be "one of the most primitive regions of the United States," Appalachian Kentucky in particular was depicted as a place where "bloodshed is a pastime," where "cruel and cowardly murder goes unpunished," and where "assassination is . . . its passion."[2]

Literary, journalistic, and scholarly depictions of the Cumberland Mountains as a violent subculture shaped a discourse—a tradition of understanding—about Appalachia and its feuds. As literary theorist Edward Said observed, discourses are shaped by power and thus can "*create* not only knowledge but also the very reality they appear to describe." Thus, by characterizing Appalachians as quaint yet fearsome, popular understandings about feuding in the southern mountains paved the way for subsequent efforts to explain and justify the region's chronic poverty and suitability for resource exploitation.[3]

At the turn of the century, when feuds captured the popular imagination, violent community conflict was widespread throughout not only the post-Reconstruction South but also the developing West, the industrial North, and increasingly inter-racial urban America. Throughout the nation, such conflicts expressed new tensions but resulted in traditional and often violent forms of direct action: riots, mob action, labor struggles, vigilantism, racial and ethnic harassment, regulation, rebellion, and, most rarely, outright civil war. Such responses to conflict have existed in American society from colonial times to the present, from the Boston Tea Party and Shay's Rebellion to the most recent riots in Los Angeles. Despite the regularity and abundance of violent conflict in American history, the "Cumberland Gap region of Kentucky" came to be singled out as "one of the few dark spots on the map of the United States" and the Kentucky mountaineer as "a man of blood, governed more by hate than by justice."[4]

Historian Altina Waller's recent analysis of late-nineteenth-century press coverage of Appalachian feuds in the *Louisville Courier Journal* and the *New York Times* shows that both newspapers reported numerous examples of violent community conflicts throughout Kentucky and the wider South. It was not until about 1885, however, that they began to denote some of these as "Appalachian" conflicts and even later as "feuds." Before then, violence was deplored in newspaper reports and editorials, but such conflicts were interpreted as the expression of underlying political troubles. Once an episode was distinguished as "Appalachian," however, the origin of violence came to be seen as "personal, cultural, or even genetic" rather than political. "For the first time," Waller writes, "the mountain region of Eastern Kentucky was singled out as being uniquely guilty of producing individuals who possessed defective character traits . . . more savage, degraded and lawless than other Americans or even other southerners."[5]

It is not coincidental that also in the mid-1880s, popular writers began to draw a rigid distinction between the Kentucky Bluegrass and the Cumberland Plateau, even though both regions had been settled by the same population and were economically and politically interdependent throughout the antebellum period. In a travelogue published in *Harper's Magazine* in 1886, Bluegrass novelist James Lane Allen took the lead in creating a sense of regional difference. The "blue-grass country" of Kentucky, wrote Allen, which he referred to as "civilization," and the "primitive society" of the "eastern mountains" were "two worlds," separate and apart. He argued against speaking singularly of "the Kentuckians," and he introduced the literary device of the "two Kentuckies" to distinguish the highland and lowland sections of the state. Upon entering the Cumberland Gap country in the late nineteenth century, according to Allen, one encountered an "abjectly poor" population, "living today as their forefathers lived a hundred years ago; hearing little of the world, caring nothing for it; responding feebly to the influence of civilization . . . [and] lacking the spirit of development within."[6]

In 1890 the editors of the *New York Times* picked up the theme of the "two Kentuckies," quoting Allen as saying that the "highlander" and "lowlander" of Kentucky were "distinct in blood, physique, history, and ideas of life." In reference to the highlander, they cited Allen's remark that "the buying up of the mountain lands has, of course, unsettled a large part of these strange people" who, in the face of economic development, were found "to retire at the approach of civilization to remoter regions, where they may live without criticism or observation their hereditary, squalid, unambitious, stationary life."[7]

With few exceptions, Allen's distinctions between the Cumberlands and the Bluegrass became canonical among feud chroniclers. Thus, in a 1907 article in *Outing Magazine*, C. T. Revere assured readers that "in the central and western portions of Kentucky there is as high an order of civilization and advancement as can be found anywhere on the earth. But in the mountain counties of her eastern border, where the rugged and untaught minds are dominated by a crude and savage ideal of the meaning of honor, the deadly vendetta still races, and no one can say when it will cease." In this context it also became common to suggest that a criminal element of the trans-Appalachian settler population had peopled the mountainous portion of the state.[8]

In *Appalachia on Our Mind*, Henry Shapiro discusses how naming functioned as explaining in the process of identifying and understanding social problems in the southern mountains. Newspaper reportage of mountain violence represents a good example of this phenomenon. Community conflicts were used by nonlocal writers to define "Appalachia," and once established, the idea of "Appalachia" was used to explain the forms of violence that erupted there. Thus, according to the *New York Times*, the Kentucky State Guard was sent to Manchester, Kentucky, to bring order to Clay County in 1899 in response to the traditional and irrational violence of that section's "armed feudists." Less than a decade later, the guard was ordered to western Kentucky counties to suppress the even more violent and extensive campaign of arson, terror, and murder by planter-led tobacco farmers against the tobacco trusts, their buyers and warehouses, and the independent black-and-white farmers who sold their crops to them; notably, economics and power, however, not psychology, were understood to be at the root of the matter.[9]

The Garrard-White feud was one of the longest and most extensive of the feuds that contributed to Appalachian Kentucky's turn-of-the-century reputation as the "Corsica of America." It began in Clay County,

Kentucky, in the early 1840s and culminated in a violent struggle to control that county around 1900. This essay uses civil-court case records, data from state tax rolls, federal manuscript censuses, deeds, mortgages, wills, and corporate records to examine how newspaper, scholarly, and popular magazine accounts of Clay County's feud contributed to a popular understanding of Appalachia as a peculiarly isolated and violent subculture.

Clay County's feud was rooted in the economics of salt-making. As the first white farmers pushed into the Kentucky mountains at the beginning of the nineteenth century, so, too, did representatives of wealthy slave-owning families who began purchasing land and manufacturing salt. By 1817 Clay County salt was one of Kentucky's leading exports, and a few families had established local economic and political dynasties based on salt manufacturing, slave labor, and extensive landownership. Relations among these early entrepreneurial families were both interdependent and contentious. The absence of local banks bound entrepreneurs together in networks of financial obligation, but Kentucky's notorious system of overlapping land claims resulted in fierce conflict over land. The first eruption of Clay County's feud came in the mid-1840s—a time of increasing competition and decline in the local salt industry—when the two wealthiest and most powerful salt manufacturing families, the Whites and the Garrards, took opposing sides in the local murder prosecution of Dr. Abner Baker. This conflict created such a volatile situation that the governor deployed the Kentucky state militia to prevent an armed assault on the jail where the accused murderer was detained and to safeguard the circuit court.

From the late 1840s into the twentieth century, the Whites and Garrards engaged in internecine struggles—known outside Appalachia as "family feuds" and locally as "wars"—to control Clay County's political and economic life. Economic and political power in the county was contested frequently by the two families and their allies and those dependent upon them for protection or economic survival, but for nearly fifty years no faction was able to exert enduring control over county affairs. In the late 1890s, however, an outbreak of extensive violent conflict between the Whites and Garrards again spread throughout the county. Arsons and murders were commonplace, a sheriff was assassinated, and suspects refused to surrender, citing the danger of armed bands in court. Twice, the governor dispatched the state militia, but violence—including the courtyard murder of Tom Baker, a Garrard-allied prisoner, and assassinations of prisoners through the window of the county jail—continued unabated. In the words of one observer, "a perfect reign of terror exist[ed] all over Clay County," and the state debated whether to declare martial law or to dissolve the county altogether. At the turn of the century, a cataclysmic gun battle between Garrard and White forces at the county courthouse prompted a newly arrived county judge to negotiate the "great truce" of Clay County, and the feud officially came to an end.[10]

Contrasts between three principal findings from this study and examples of how nonlocal writers reported events in this and other "feuds" illuminate the discourse that informed the American imagination in regard to Appalachian violence. First, far from being the stereotypic poor, ignorant, and passive feudists of popular account, the principals in the Clay County conflict were wealthy, powerful, and politically active county leaders. From their ranks came numerous county magistrates, judges, sheriffs, legislators, state officials (including a secretary of state), and members of Congress (including a speaker of the United States House of Representatives). As could be expected, these prominent leaders did not always react passively to how they were portrayed in the mass media. Several partisans in the Garrard-White feud, for example, brought civil suits against Kentucky newspapers for how they reported local events. Louisa Combs sued the *Louisville Dispatch* Publishing Company in 1897; A. W. Baker sued the Louisville Press Company in 1898; Robert Lucas sued the *Louisville Courier Journal* and the *Louisville Times* in 1899; and B. P. White sued the *Louisville Evening Post* in 1900—each for what they considered slanderous or libelous reporting of their respective roles in feud-related violence. A Clay County dentist may have spoken for many non-aligned citizens in 1899 when a *New York Times* reporter opened up a rare discursive space that permitted him to say: "Manchester has been very unfortunate in having been misrepresented by writers more enterprising and sensational than they were truthful. . . . Nobody has been 'run out' of Clay, but one persistent falsifier has learned that he is no longer welcome, and the resentment against other falsifiers, some of them Kentucky newspaper writers, I regret to say has found expression in prosecution of the offenders for slander and libel."[11]

Second, although the popular press often portrayed feuds as irrational responses to petty conflicts, they can better be interpreted as struggles to control county power during periods of rapid social change. In both periods of active violence, economic interests of the Garrard family were pitted against those of the Whites. In the 1840s the families clashed over pricing in a declining salt industry. Fifty years later a county fiscal crisis propelled the families on a collision course when the Garrards' bank held a financial stranglehold over county government offices monopolized by Whites. In the 1890s, too, conflict between the families intensified as a frenzy of exploration and speculative investment in the county's timber, coal, gas, and mineral resources fueled dramatic increases in land values and the potential for massive profit-taking.

Finally, contrary to the assumption that Appalachians turned to violent means to resolve disputes because they were unfamiliar and inexperienced with the use of civil and criminal courts, so-called "feudists" were consistent and intense litigators throughout the nineteenth century. Civil cases involving feuding groups constituted between one-fifth and one-third of all such cases filed in the Clay County circuit court during the periods of peak feuding activity (1845–49 and 1896–1900) and represented a high proportion of the docket during periods of quiescence as well. Thus, besides being lawyers and lawmakers, Clay County's feudists routinely and consistently turned to local courts to redress grievances and resolve disputes. The local court and legal system did break down briefly during both periods of conflict, yet in both instances, those breakdowns were *consequences*, not *causes*, of political violence aimed at capturing local government.

When one looks at the huge body of popular and scholarly commentary in the national media that the Clay County feud and others like it stimulated, however, very different impressions of the character and causes of feuding are conveyed. Seen to result from poverty, ignorance, and isolation, feuds were portrayed as having been triggered by the most trivial of incidents, prolonged by primitive clan loyalties, and tolerated because of the ineffectiveness of or hostility toward legal institutions in mountain society. Each of these themes was articulated in a profoundly influential essay written by Ellen Churchill Semple, then a soon-to-be president of the American Association of Geography, that is still worth reading today as a compendium of turn-of-the-century error and exaggeration and as an important specimen of colonialist discourse in *fin-de-siècle* American social-science writing.

In "The Anglo-Saxons of the Kentucky Mountains," Semple argued that "isolation and poverty" had "fostered the survival of the blood-feud among the Kentucky mountaineers," an institution that she believed could "be traced back to the idea of clan responsibility among their Anglo-Saxon forbearers." Today we know that Appalachian Kentucky was more demographically diversified than commonly represented and that a mix of European and African populations settled the Cumberland Mountains two centuries after feuds had vanished from Scotland. Semple maintained, however, that "the same conditions that have kept the ethnic type pure have kept the social phenomena primitive," and she postulated various sociological and geographical factors such as "remoteness," "necessary self-reliance," and "extensive intermarriage" to explain "the clan instinct" and "the strength of the feuds which rage here from time to time."[12]

Like other writers of the era, Semple's claim to authority derived not only from the so-called "scientific" premises of her discipline, but also from her claim to first-hand observation based on "a trip of 350 miles [on horseback] through the mountains." Nonetheless, her description of specific events in Clay County—the particular case upon which her interpretation of feuds in general is based—appears, at least in part, to have been lifted without citation from a magazine article by J. Stoddard Johnson published two years earlier in the *Cosmopolitan*. For example, Johnson described an important episode in the Clay County trouble as follows:

> Now, Tom Baker did not relish the idea of giving himself up to the sheriff, Beverly T. White, brother of the man he had killed and kinsman to the clerk, jailer and judge. So he took to the hills until troops were sent to the county, when he surrendered himself to them.

Semple's account reads:

> In this same Howard and Baker feud, Tom Baker shot to death William White, an ally of the Howards and brother of the sheriff, as likewise kinsman of the county clerk, jailer, and judge. Naturally reluctant to give himself up to officials who were his personal enemies, Baker took to the hills until State troops were sent to the county, when he gave himself up to them.

Horace Kephart published a close variation of the Semple-Johnson description in 1913, adding an embellishment of his own that misnamed an additional Clay County combatant. This version of the original, along with Kephart's misnaming, was published in 1942 by Alvin Harlow.[13]

The point of comparing such passages is not to determine who copied from whom but rather to point out that much of what appears to be commentary on Kentucky mountain feuds was really commentary on *writings* about feuds as popular and scholarly authors alike read and borrowed from one another freely. Their close and generally unacknowl-edged mutual reliance suggests that the locus of what has been taken to be the reality of feuding was as much on the printed page as in the hills of Kentucky. Since we find a scholar, Semple, relying on a popularizer, Johnson, who, it turns out, had originally cited an often quoted passage from John Fox Jr.'s fiction as an authoritative description of the nature of feuds, it is reasonable to conclude that science, journalism, and fiction writing closely influenced one another in the creation of the popular image of feuding.

Examples of such borrowing without citation abound. Semple claimed that "together with the remoteness of the law," the "free, wild life" of the Kentucky mountaineers had made them "personally brave," while Hartley Davis and Clifford Smyth told readers of *Munsey's Magazine* that Kentucky mountaineers "have lived a wild, free life, governed only by such laws as it pleased them to observe." J. Stoddard Johnson described Appalachian Kentucky as a "vast Sargasso, a dead sea surrounded by an ocean of life," while a few years later Horace Kephart compared the peopling of "the stagnant eddy of highland society" to the process whereby "derelicts drift into the Sargasso Sea." The most liberal case of borrowing, however, was a Salvation Army publication reporting an effort by fifteen officers of the Salvation Army who traveled two hundred miles on horseback through the hills of eastern Kentucky to put a stop to feuds by spreading the "Christian gospel," a brave adventure described elsewhere as "one of the most dangerous missions ever to be undertaken." The Army's anonymous author of "Where Bloodshed is a Pastime" lifted ten paragraphs from Davis and Smyth's *Muncey's Magazine* article, including the claim that "the lust for human blood ha[d] become a malignant disease" among Kentucky mountaineers and its description of the Cumberland region as "a savage, primeval country, where have developed those fierce and terrible family wars, the American feuds, beside which the Italian vendetta is a childish thing, almost humane in comparison."[14]

More important, however, than the generous borrowing of meta-phors, phrases, and even paragraphs by one writer from another was the development among writers of a set of explanations for why Appalachian feuds occurred in the first place. Semple's claim that "isolation and pov-erty . . . [were] the explanation for the feud" resonated with the earlier fiction of John Fox Jr. and shaped most narrative accounts even when reported events and conditions contradicted this assumption as they so often did. The assumption of geographical isolation, hinged on the notion of the separateness of the "two Kentuckies," is one such example.

In her classic studies of early economic development and transportation improvements in Appalachian Kentucky, Mary Verhoeff shows that until about 1850, the mountainous region of Kentucky was closely interconnected with the more highly commercialized Bluegrass region and that its roads were not greatly inferior to those throughout the rest of the state. After that date, however, and for the next thirty to fifty years before railroads began to penetrate the mountains and as transportation elsewhere improved dramatically, the Cumberland Plateau did become somewhat disassociated from the rest of the state. Popular accounts of feuds, however, greatly exaggerated the region's isolation. Semple reported that "there are many men in these mountains who have never seen a town, or even the poor village that constitutes their county seat"; C. T. Revere bettered her, claiming to have "seen old men who have never been half a mile away from their homes." Women were portrayed as even more isolated. Claiming that some had never even seen a country store located within two miles of their cabins, Semple described women as being "almost as rooted as trees."[15]

Forget for the moment the question of how such an unperipatetic population could ever have traversed and settled the vast expanse of the Appalachian mountains; as the case of Clay County shows, the economic history of Appalachian Kentucky belies the myth of total isolation. The manufacture and sale of salt, produced by slave labor and shipped on flatboats down the Kentucky and Cumberland rivers or by wagon on through the Cumberland Gap, linked that locality to central Kentucky and more distant markets in Virginia and Tennessee from the earliest decades of the nineteenth century until the Civil War. Far from being an island of self-sufficiency, Clay County boasted one of antebellum Kentucky's most important industries more than one hundred years before railroads reached Manchester. Ironically, in fact, the tensions that led to permanent hostilities among the county's manufacturing elite first emerged when the local effects of the national depression of 1839–42 were most sharply felt in the commercial sector, which suggests that the notion of integration rather than isolation better captures that locality's even most distant economic past.[16]

Because of the importance of Clay County's local industry, the state of Kentucky made some of its earliest public investments in the county to facilitate the salt trade, including improvements on the Kentucky River and the establishment of three turnpikes during the antebellum period to help pay for local road building. As a result, no other county in Kentucky in 1908 had as many roads per square mile as Clay. Nonetheless, magazine writer E. Carl Litsey exaggerated Clay County's isolation in describing the road he took from London, Kentucky, to Manchester to investigate feuding: "The twisting, twinning road over which we went at varying degrees of speed was a sorry specimen. There had been no attempt to make a pike, nor macadamize. The 'right of way' had simply been established by custom and along this 'way' all things had to go that proceeded on wheels."[17] Here, the casual attribution of road building to blind custom and mere happenstance occluded the necessity of exploring what forms of historical agency and design had gone into building the local infrastructure as well as of questioning what forces might have been contributing to its apparent neglect at the time. Questions of rational agency and design did not necessarily arise, however, when one spoke about the "wild, free life" of the hills.

A corollary to the assumption of the geographical isolation of the feud country was the assumption of the primitiveness of its population. Thus, Litsey described entering Clay County as follows: "We swept deeper and deeper into the mountains, and traces of civilization became scarcer. Now and again we would pass a small hut. . . . Wild and poorly clad forms would appear in low doorways; faces almost expressionless would stare at us in a kind of apathetic wonder. . . . We were getting into the feudists' country, where the sun set crimson and the moon rose red." Once there, Litsey interrogated a young girl he had come upon about the whereabouts of her father:

> I asked a tousle-headed, brown faced little maid where her father was, having my own reasons for the question. A change came over the child's face, and she backed away in distrust; the guile of the serpent crept up and flamed in her fox-like eyes, and she answered quickly, and with a furtive glance around, "I don't know!" Then she ran as fast as her bare feet could carry her, and hiding behind a tree, peeped out at me like some wily animal I was seeking to entrap. Duplicity and cunning were bred in her bone, and had been fostered year by year as she grew.[18]

We like to imagine that this young girl, described in the primal and animalistic terms common to colonialist genres, was one of the feud leader General T. T. Garrard's well-educated granddaughters or perhaps young Laura White, daughter of the wealthy salt manufacturer and part-time feudist Daugherty White. But it is fanciful for us to think that the little girl thus described could have been Laura White, for by 1902, when Litsey was writing, she had much earlier completed her master's degree in architecture from the Sorbonne in Paris, after having been among the first class of women to graduate from the University of Michigan (her degree in mathematics) and after attending the Massachusetts Institute of Technology.

Such complications occasionally forced writers to acknowledge that the socioeconomic status of feud participants often reflected positions of power and privilege that their generalizations about poverty, ignorance, and isolation otherwise contradicted. Semple, for example, recognized that "the principals" of the Clay County feud "were men of prominence, influence, and means," and Davis and Smyth noted that the "chief families engaged in [that feud] have a distinguished lineage." Far from challenging their interpretation of feuds as the expression of "primeval, savage forces," however, the latter claimed that the participation of social elites in the feuds of Clay, Rowan, and Breathitt counties was an "exemplification of the fact that the refinements of education and civilization do not always check these murderous wars, and sometimes only make them more deadly."[19]

"Murderous wars" were taken almost universally by commentators as an indication of the essentially lawless quality of social life in the Cumberland mountains. Regardless of how implausible it was to imagine a people successfully reproducing their way of life outside of law and norms, the social scientist Semple nonetheless claimed that "when the law invaded this remote region, it found the feud [already] established and the individual loath to subordinate himself to the body politic." S. S. MacClintock, a sociologist writing in the *American Journal of Sociology*, concurred that in the Kentucky hills, "each man had been a law unto himself too long to be able to forget it immediately and look to civil law for protection." According to magazine writers of the time, the combatants of this county "set law at utter defiance, and curl their lips in scorn at a court of justice," although, as noted above, Clay County feudists relied routinely on civil courts to resolve their disputes. One *New York Times* correspondent was surprised to report that Manchester was actually "as serene as a sleeping child" when he visited there during the peak of troubles in 1899, but according to sensationalistic reports, Clay County was "tinged with the blood of the innocent and blackened by reasonless deeds of hate." It was said to be a place where "death stalks abroad at noonday like a roaring lion seeking whom he may devour." By another account, "there [was] scarcely an acre within the county boundaries that d[id] not hold a spot where some member of the populace has been shot from ambush."[20]

"In a region where the local agencies of the law are weak or indisposed to act," reasoned J. Stoddard Johnson, "resort to violence requires little provocation." Writers took their cues from John Fox Jr. who in his fictionalized account of "A Cumberland Vendetta" reported that "[w]hen the feud began, no one knew[;] [e]ven the original cause was forgotten"; they assumed not only the inherent lawlessness of the mountains but also the fact that the immediate causes of conflict there were "often of a trifling nature," as Ellen Semple put it. Feuds, she thought, could result from "a misunderstanding in a horse trade, a gate left open and trespassing cattle, the shooting of a dog, political rivalry, or a difficulty over a boundary fence." Although many accounts implicitly acknowledged the fact that mountain conflicts typically involved public officials, contested elections, and struggles over trials and courts, they nonetheless insisted, like Carl Litsey, that "the causes which lead to those long-lived vendettas are more often trivial than great. The bitterest and most hard-fought of them all arose from practically nothing. A fancied rebuff, a careless word, a stolen pig." According to Davis and Smyth, the feuds of Harlan, Rowan, and Perry counties were caused, respectively, by a "game of cards," a "ward-politics row," and "business jealousy." Finally, according to Johnson, "altercations between friends suddenly angered or drinking, disputes over business settlements, or family discords . . . may all lead to an outbreak the end of which may not be foretold."[21]

A variation of the claim that the causes of feuds were trivial was the equally strange notion that each of them could be traced back to a single, primordial feud which—like Fox's fictional case in "A Cumberland Vendetta"—was caused by some undetermined or forgotten event. Thus Emerson Hough told readers of the *American Magazine* that the seemingly separate feuds of the various mountain counties were "[a]ctually . . . all one feud and all . . . products of the old Highland clan spirit." "Today," he added, "no one knows the cause of the original feud. . . . It might have been property, it might have been women. But all the feuds date back to that ancestral warfare." Even more fanciful was the *New York Times*'s claim that each of the feuds in Appalachian Kentucky, and "3,000 graves," could be traced back to the falling out of the Whites and Garrards in Clay County that occurred in the 1840s:

> At first involving only two families and one town in it, it spread through the mountains until now it has many names and fills with implacable enmity the members of scores of families. In Perry and Leslie Counties it is known as the French-Eversole feud, in Harlan County as the Howard-Turner feud, in Letcher County as the Lee-Taylor feud, and in Clay County as the Howard-Baker feud. They are all branches of the same evil tree, and every one of them is green and vigorous. . . . Practically everybody in the whole region is ranged on one side or the other.[22]

If indeed the Clay County feud had been in and of itself important enough to have generated all the other county conflicts in Appalachian Kentucky, as the *New York Times* asserted, it seems likely that journalists and scholars would have made great efforts to investigate and report it carefully, but they did not. In 1909 the editors of the *Wide World Magazine* promised their readers an account of the Baker-Howard (Garrard-White) feud and others that would be not only "thrilling in the extreme" but would "spare no effort to make the narratives as accurate and fair to all parties as possible." Not surprisingly, however, their coverage provided no more reliable or consistent information than any of the magazine's competitors.

Most writers who reported scrupulously on the Clay County feud linked the conflict at the end of the nineteenth century to the earlier antagonism that began in the 1840s, but others questioned or overlooked this important connection. Johnson more or less accurately summarized the roots of the early Garrard-White conflict yet concluded that "the present feud has no relation to that difficulty." Litsey recognized connections between the early "political and business rivalry" of the Garrards and the Whites and later events, but mistakenly linked the Bakers to the Garrards through the unrelated antebellum murder trial of William Baker rather than that of Abner Baker, whom the Garrards supported. Coates attributed the fatal conflict between Abner Baker and his victim to Baker's teasing that the victim was as "yellow" as his hound dog, and he even illustrated his book, *Stories of Kentucky Feuds*, with a line drawing of the supposed event. Readily available surviving documents from the Abner Baker trial, however, offer nothing to suggest that such an argument ever occurred and are, in fact, quite clear about the actual source of that conflict. Nevertheless, journalist John Ed Pierce recently repeated Coates's "as yellow as that cur of yours" explanation of the original Clay County troubles in a 1981 article, and like several other writers collapsed the events of the 1840s and 1890s into a single episode that he described as "lasting 15 years" at the turn of the century.[23]

Just as they played fast and loose with the facts, writers were equally careless with the identities of participants in the Clay County feud. To give but a few examples, the salt manufacturer Daniel Garrard was confused with his father James Garrard, the second governor of Kentucky who never lived in Clay County. General T. T. Garrard, one of Appalachian Kentucky's most distinguished federal officers during the Civil War, was misidentified in one article as a hero of the Mexican War and in another as a southern sympathizer. U.S. Speaker of the House of Representatives John White was confused with his father, salt-manufacturer Hugh White, and misidentified as Abner Baker's father-in-law. Abner Baker, as we have seen, was apparently confused with William Baker by one writer and misidentified by another as Thomas Baker, a distant descendant centrally involved in the 1890s feud. Coates portrayed the Howards—key participants in the 1890s conflict—as aligned against the Garrards and Bakers during the 1840s, and Harlow described them as married into the White family during the same years. Both claims, however, were unlikely, since they occurred long before any of the Howards had migrated to Clay County.[24]

Popular and academic writers were able to play freely in their accounts with both identities and events because the accuracy of naming participants or investigating the actual causes of Appalachian conflicts did not really matter in this genre of regional representation and reporting. Instead, events and people were fluid and interchangeable in discourse about the southern mountain region. What mattered most—along with the thrilling stories and exotic descriptions that sold magazines and justified scholarly attention—was the discourse itself, not the specifics of Appalachian agency and action. Two versions of this discourse, each with its own motivations and effects, can be distinguished: a "discourse of uplift" and a "discourse of displacement."

For educators and reformers in the Kentucky mountains at the turn of the century, the occurrence of feuds and the vast amount of publicity they generated nationally provided both an embarrassment and an opportunity. In order to secure charitable donations for projects aimed at uplifting mountain people, these workers had a profound interest in portraying the moral (and racial) worthiness of the local population they were attempting to serve. The violence of feuds, however, threatened to call into question this very fact of worthiness. As Shapiro has said, "images of the mountaineer as pathetic and romantic gave way before a set of images of mountaineers as feudists and desperadoes, criminals and social deviants." At the same time, however, by placing mountain problems squarely at the center of public attention, feuds created opportunities to publicize the need for reform efforts. By interpreting feuds sympathetically as a regrettable but understandable consequence of ignorance and isolation, reformers could still justify their mission of uplift and make its urgency all the more apparent.

On the other hand, if feuds were represented unsympathetically as "the spawn of ignorance, prejudice, and a free giving-way to man's worst passions," their eradication could easily be linked to the advance of capitalist economic development rather than social reform—this at the very moment that corporate railroad, timber, and mineral interests were scrambling to acquire Appalachian rights and properties. Thus, the writer of the 1899 *New York Times* article "Cause of Kentucky Feuds: Isolation, Ignorance, and Whiskey Said to be Responsible; Railroads Much Needed" concluded that "what Manchester [Clay County] needs most next to schools . . . is the civilizing railroad. It has been too much by itself." This particular writer did not say but others (below) contended that if mountaineers resisted the so-called "civilizing" effects of corporate capitalist development, their recalcitrance—evidenced by the persistence of violence—might justify their displacement from the rich treasure house of natural wealth they inconveniently called "home."[25]

Authors of the discourse of displacement portrayed feudists in the worst possible light, claiming that "[n]ot a single deed of chivalry, not one act of generosity, not one ray of nobility or unselfishness, not even a suggestion of fair play, illuminates the blackness of the [feud] tales." Contributors to the discourse of uplift, however, were at pains to discern traces of misplaced courage and honor in Kentucky bloodletting in order to justify the moral worthiness of their client populations. Thus W. G. Frost, president of Berea College, proclaimed that "it gives us hope for their future that the frequent homicides [in Appalachian Kentucky] are not committed wantonly nor for purposes of robbery, but in the spirit of an Homeric chieftain on some 'point of honor.'"[26] General O. O. Howard, former head of the Freedmen's Bureau and founder of Lincoln

Memorial College, likewise attempted to put a favorable spin on feuding by claiming that "[m]uch of [the feud] spirit comes from the present and past necessity of a head of a family protecting his family" and by pointing out that "fortunately there is a reverence for women and children and they are spared" in feud confrontations.[27]

Subsequent contributors to the discourse of uplift followed the lead of Frost and Howard by describing feuds as the expression of the "great primal qualities" of "vigor and courage" in Appalachia's "Fighting Stock." Thus, an anonymous author in the *Berea Quarterly* concluded that mountain fighters' "impulses to avenge their own wrongs [were] not a degenerate tendency but the honest survival of the Old Saxon and Celtic temper" and further informed readers that "mountain homicides never occur as an accompaniment of robbery. They are performed invariably upon some 'point of honor,' and the ethical standard of the feudsman always protects women and children." Though decrying the conditions of isolation and ignorance and making a plea for the support of educational improvements in the mountains, Emerson Hough went even further in singing the praise of Cumberland feudists, calling them "a keen, bold breed of men . . . carrying on feuds as a religion . . . sweetly and graciously practicing the ancient laws of hospitality, sternly adhering to their ideas of personal honor, curiously unconventional, curiously unchanged."[28]

Once represented sympathetically, feuds could be used to justify rather than discourage charitable contributions in the region. In fact, agents of social reform and educational improvement in Appalachian Kentucky did much to keep a chastened image of feuds well before the public eye. At a meeting in Boston in 1900 to raise money for Berea College, President Frost opened his address to potential benefactors with a description of the Baker-Howard feud then raging in Clay County. He then told his audience that "[t]he mountain people are not so much a degraded population as a population not yet graded up" and asked them to contribute to Berea's educational efforts in the region. Three years later, while making a "great plea for the educational uplift of Appalachian America" before a Chautauqua Assembly in New York on the topic of "Mob Spirit in America," Frost again recounted the Clay County feud and the number of lives it had taken. This time he argued that "[t]he cure of the feud must lie in that moral progress which is called education," and he claimed that at Berea College, "[w]e are proposing not merely to prevent the mountain people from being a menace, but to bring the people of Appalachian

America over from the ranks of the doubtful classes and range them with those who are to be the patriotic leaders and helpers of the new age."

Elsewhere, Frost publicized Berea's extension work in the Kentucky mountains, including the value of a course offered on "How to Settle Family Feuds without Bloodshed." An anonymous article in the *Berea Quarterly* titled "The College and the Feud" later claimed that "Berea eradicates the feud spirit" and described "the work of Berea College as a prime force in the destruction of the feud." The cover of this particular issue of the *Quarterly* featured a provocative photograph of two supposedly armed feudists titled "Men Proud of Being 'Dangerous,'" and other issues of the *Quarterly* ran photographs of Berea students described gratuitously in captions such as "A Daughter of the Feud-Country."[29] Significantly, these articles and photographs were published roughly a decade after the termination of most mountain feuds.

Berea College was not the only educational institution in Appalachia to publicize and benefit from stereotypes about Kentucky feuds. Cora Wilson Stewart, who witnessed feud violence firsthand as a young child in Rowan County, used feuds as a justification for her campaign against illiteracy; O. O. Howard linked Lincoln Memorial University's educational mission to feud eradication, claiming that "good roads and good education, will surely cure the feud spirit!"; and James Anderson Burns, founder of the Oneida Baptist Institute in Clay County, claimed that his private academy grew "out of an indomitable purpose to stop the feuds and, in doing so, to conserve the manhood and the womanhood of the mountaineers." Following the well-trod path of W. G. Frost to New York City, Burns spent three months there in 1908 lecturing on "Feud Conditions in the Cumberlands" in order to elicit financial support for his school, and in 1912 the popular writer Emerson Hough publicized Burns's success nationally in the *American Magazine*, claiming, "They say that feudism and moonshining is done in Clay County; and they date that back to 1899 and the [founding of the Oneida Baptist Institute]."[30]

Not all commentators, however—especially those who portrayed the Appalachian population as benighted and degenerate—were confident about the ameliorative effects of education and social uplift. "Neither education, nor wealth, nor the refinements of civilization are as strong as the murder-lust in the Land of the Feuds," warned Davis and Smyth. "Its regeneration will come only through the introduction of outside influences, or people who will dominate not only intellectually but numerically." Thus, according to authors of what we call this "discourse of displacement," only with the domination of Appalachia and the displacement of its population by outsiders "will the Frankenstein of the Kentucky mountains receive its death thrust, and the Land of Feuds ... cease to be a blot on the map of these United States." Litsey agreed: "So long as their mountain defiles remain uninvaded by the emigrant; so long as their mountain sides intimidate the prospective railroad line; and above all, so long as their wild, barbaric blood remains uncrossed by a gentler strain—just so long will their internecine wars prevail."[31]

In his excellent study of the Appalachian settlement school movement, David Whisnant has shown how social reform work in the Kentucky mountains indirectly "facilitated the exploitation it sought to forestall" by falsely accepting mythical versions of mountain culture and failing to confront the devastating forces of corporate capitalist exploitation that were at work in the hills.[32] Despite important differences between them, the discourses of uplift and of displacement similarly reinforced one another. Each sensationalized feuds, each focused on perceived deficiencies in regional culture and mentality rather than investigating the sociological causes of local violence, and, ultimately, each diverted attention from the profound economic and political costs that were accompanying the industrialization of Appalachia and the rush to cash in on its natural riches.

Interpretations of the mountaineers' feuds as neither heroic nor evil incarnate but simply "the result of their environment" provided a middle ground between the highly polarized remedial visions of uplift and of displacement. This middle ground enabled commentators like J. Stoddard Johnson, who believed that the mountaineers' "unhappy fate [was] not from want of capacity, but of opportunity," to welcome the ameliorative effects of *both* educational improvements and industrialization, which he believed together would "break [the Kentuckians'] isolation and unlock the stores of wealth which lie latent among them." According to Johnson, "[h]elp has come to these marooned people" in the form of the Chesapeake and Ohio and the Louisville and Nashville railroads. Yet even a moderate like Johnson grew so troubled by the extent of violence in Kentucky, real or imagined, that he, too, demanded a forceful intervention in mountain affairs. Describing the events in Clay County that were unfolding as his article went to press in 1899, Johnson wrote hysterically:

Yet here at home a war is raging as savage as that in Luzon and no hand or voice is lifted to stay its bloody work. There is a provision in the Constitution providing for the intervention of the Federal government in certain cases when the state is impotent to quell disturbances. Yet there seems no indication of sending troops here. On the contrary, at London [Kentucky], almost within the sound of a Gatling gun in Clay County, there is a recruiting station for raising troops for the new regiments intended for service in the Philippines. Send a company, a regiment, a brigade, a division corps, or an army if necessary, but send something or somebody, if only to make terms, for the defenseless and innocent people, with those who have the law of Kentucky by the throat.[33]

The connection Johnson drew between the use of force in America's military adventure in the Philippines and its appropriateness at the same time in Appalachia helps bring to the surface the dimension of cultural imperialism that drove much of the writings about mountain feuding. In describing the relationship between culture and imperialism in western writing, Said points to "a structure of attitude and reference" that views "the outlying regions of the world [as] hav[ing] no life, history, or culture to speak of, no independence or integrity worth representing without the West." Alternatively, "when there is something to be described" in those regions, it is "unutterably corrupt, degenerate, irredeemable."[34] Both attitudes influenced how metropolitan writers in America viewed the Appalachian periphery before its industrialization.

On the one hand, according to the doctrine and discourse of uplift, Appalachia was a place where time stood still until its discovery and representation by social reformers who brought the region into the orbit of modern awareness, institutions, and progress. Thus, in a *Collier's Weekly* article titled "Children of the Feudists," Bruce Barton described the exploratory tour that William G. Frost made through the hills of West Virginia and Kentucky before assuming the presidency of Berea College as one of the "great voyages of discovery which have opened up unchartered continents and brought to light forgotten people." Much as if he had ventured to "darkest" Africa, Barton described Frost as having "uncovered the lost tribes of America: three million pure-blooded Americans who since the days when their ancestors first lost themselves in the mountains, have been as completely covered and forgotten as though the earth had opened to swallow them."[35]

If Appalachia at its best was viewed as latency and potentiality in the discourse of uplift, a space where American middle-class culture could effect its alchemy, it was portrayed as a place and a people far less subject to redemption in the discourse of displacement that called for the region's numerical domination by outsiders and for its "wild, barbaric blood" to be diluted by emigration. Here, the most strident version of the discourse on Appalachia echoed some of America's most blatantly imperialistic ideology.

By portraying the Kentucky mountaineer as a person who "by birth, tradition, and environment" was "taught to regard the taking of human life with as little concern as he would feel in removing a stone from his path," writers spun an imperial tale about savagery in Appalachia that was the narrative equivalent of numerous other colonialist discourses throughout the West. For example, Patrick Brantlinger's analysis of the British myth of the "dark continent" of Africa as a center of barbarism and evil shows that "Africa grew 'dark' as Victorian explorers, missionaries, and scientists flooded it with light, because the light was refracted through an imperialist ideology that urged the abolition of 'savage customs' in the name of civilization." Paralleling America's fascination with Appalachian feuds, the extreme western fascination with cannibalism, according to Brantlinger, marked Africa as a degenerate place earmarked for the kind of correction that only western forms of cultural and economic penetration could provide. Finally, not unlike the relationship we describe in Appalachian writings between uplift and displacement, imperialist sentiments in the British writings on Africa originated in anti-slavery reform discourses but culminated in demands, as one colonist put it, that "the natives must go; or they must work laboriously to develop the land as we are prepared to do."[36]

One need not, of course, turn to European colonialism for models of imperialist discourse since homegrown examples abound. Besides dehumanizing African slaves and indigenous peoples to justify their servitude or dispossession, American ideologues in part justified possession of Puerto Rico in 1898 because of the "tendency to lawlessness" among that island's "evil-disposed classes." Earlier, in the early 1840s, an advocate of American annexation of the Southwest had described Mexicans as "an imbecile, pusillanimous race of men . . . unfit to control the destinies of that beautiful [California] country. [They] must fade away before the mingling of different branches of the Caucasian family of the States."[37]

Few people outside the Kentucky hills were watching, or cared, in the

1840s when the Garrards and the Whites began their long-term struggles to dominate Clay County, Kentucky, but a half-century later, when the control of such timber and mineral-rich counties became a matter of great importance, voices predictably arose proclaiming that the time had come for obstinate hillbillies to fade away as well. "The power to narrate," according to Said, "or to block other narratives from forming and emerging, is very important to culture and imperialism, and constitutes one of the main connections between them."[38] By creating an impression of Appalachians as a people in need either of uplift or displacement, and the southern mountain region as a dark zone of chaos and violence in desperate need of what the *New York Times* called "the civilizing railroad," feud narratives gave American readers a framework through which to view the profound changes that were taking place at the turn of the century in Appalachian Kentucky and the spasm of violence that was accompanying its industrialization.

NOTES

The authors gratefully acknowledge support for this research by a grant from the Fund for Research on Dispute Resolution. We thank Pam Goldman, Sharon Hardesty, Lee Hardesty, and Lisa Wood for assistance and three anonymous reviewers for suggestions on an earlier version of this paper.

1. John Fox Jr., *Blue-Grass and Rhododendron: Out-Doors in Old Kentucky* (Charles Scribner's Sons, 1901), 52.

2. Hartley Davis and Clifford Smyth, "The Land of Feuds," *Munsey's Magazine* (November 1903): 161, 162.

3. Edward Said, *Orientalism* (Vintage, 1979), 94. In contrast, James C. Klotter, "Feuds in Appalachia: An Overview," *Filson Club Historical Quarterly* 56 (1982): 290–337, and Altina Waller, *Feud: Hatfields, McCoys, and Social Change in Appalachia, 1860–1900* (University of North Carolina Press, 1988), call attention to the economic and political context of feuds.

4. C. T. Revere, "Beyond the Gap: The Breeding Ground of Feud," *Outing Magazine*, 7 February 1907, 610. E. Carl Litsey, "Kentucky Feuds and Their Causes," *Frank Leslie's Popular Monthly* 53 (January 1902): 292.

5. Altina Waller, "Feuding in Appalachia: Evolution of a Cultural Stereotype," in Mary Beth Pudup, Dwight Billings, and Altina Waller, eds., *Appalachia in the Making: The Mountain South in the Nineteenth Century* (University of North Carolina Press, 1995).

6. Reprinted in James Lane Allen, *The Blue-Grass Region and Kentucky and Other Kentucky Articles* (Harper and Brothers, 1899), 232, 235, 231.

7. "The March of Progress in a Formerly Isolated Region," *New York Times*, 2 September 1890, 5.

8. Revere, "Beyond the Gap," 287; Davis and Smyth, "Land of Feuds," 172.

9. Henry D. Shapiro, *Appalachia on Our Mind: The Southern Mountains and Mountaineers in the American Consciousness, 1870–1920* (University of North Carolina Press, 1978); "Indict Kentucky Murderers," *New York Times*, 26 October 1899; Christopher Waldrep, *Night Riders: Defending Community in the Black Patch, 1890–1915* (Duke University Press, 1993).

10. Letter to President William Frost (Berea College, 1899); Kathleen Blee and Dwight Billings, "Violence and Local State Formation: A Longitudinal Case Study of Appalachian Feuding," *Law and Society Review* (forthcoming).

11. "Where Feuds Flourish," *New York Times*, 26 November 1899, 13. Records of the Clay County Circuit Court, Kentucky State Archives.

12. Ellen Churchill Semple, "The Anglo-Saxons of the Kentucky Mountains," *Bulletin of the American Geographical Society* 42 (August 1910), 586, 580, 566; Robert D. Mitchell, ed., *Appalachian Frontiers: Settlement, Society, and Development in the Preindustrial Era* (University Press of Kentucky, 1991), esp. 69–104.

13. Semple, "Anglo-Saxons," 564, 588; J. Stoddard Johnson, "Romance and Tragedy of Kentucky Feuds," *The Cosmopolitan* 27 (September 1899): 557; compare Horace Kephart, *Our Southern Highlanders* (University of Tennessee Press, 1984), 405, with Alvin F. Harlow, *Weep No More My Lady* (McGraw-Hill, 1942), 235.

14. Semple, "Anglo-Saxons," 589, 593; Davis and Smyth, "Land of Feuds," 172; Johnson, "Romance and Tragedy," 553; Kephart, *Our Southern Highlanders*, 446; Major Paul M. Kelly, "Foot Soldiers: An Anecdotal History of the Salvation Army in the Ohio Kentucky Area" (Salvation Army National Archives, n.d.), 54; "Where Bloodshed is a Pastime," *All the World* (January 1904), 44.

15. Mary Verhoeff, *The Kentucky River Navigation* (John P. Morton and Company, 1917); Semple, "Anglo-Saxons," 565; Revere, "Beyond the Gap," 612.

16. Tyrel G. Moore, "Economic Development in Appalachian Kentucky, 1800–1860," in Mitchell, *Appalachian Frontiers*, 222–34; Dwight B. Billings and Kathleen M. Blee, "Family Strategies in a Subsistence Economy: Beech Creek, Kentucky, 1850–1942," *Sociological Perspectives* 33 (1990): 63–88; Thomas Clark, "Salt, a Factor in the Settlement of Kentucky," *Filson Club History Quarterly* 12 (January 1938): 42–52; Roy R. White, "The Salt Industry of Clay County, Kentucky," *The Register of the Kentucky Historical Society* 50 (July 1952): 238–41.

17. Mary Verhoeff, *The Kentucky Mountains, Transportation and Commerce 1750 to 1911* (John P. Morton and Company, 1911), 176; Litsey, "Kentucky Feuds," 283.

18. Litsey, "Kentucky Feuds," 284.

19. Semple, "Anglo-Saxons," 588; Davis and Smyth, "Land of Feuds," 167, 170.

20. Semple, "Anglo-Saxons," 587; S. S. MacClintock, "The Kentucky Moun-

tains and Their Feuds II," *American Journal of Sociology* 7 (September 1901): 171; Litsey, "Kentucky Feuds," 287; "Where Feuds Flourish," *New York Times*; James M. Ross, "The Great Feuds of Kentucky II: The Baker-Howard Feud," *The Wide World Magazine* 140 (December 1909): 191.

21. Johnson, "Romance and Tragedy," 553; John Fox Jr., *A Mountain Europa, A Cumberland Vendetta, The Last Stetson* (Charles Scribner's Sons, 1911), 124; Semple, "Anglo-Saxons," 588; Litsey, "Kentucky Feuds," 290; Davis and Smyth, "Land of Feuds," 162, 164, 165; Johnson, "Romance and Tragedy," 553.

22. Emerson Hough, "Burns of the Mountains: The Story of a Southern Mountaineer Who is Remaking His Own People," *The American Magazine* (1912), 2; *New York Times*, 19 June 1899, 6.

23. Ross, "The Great Feuds," 191; Johnson, "Romance and Tragedy," 557; Litsey, "Kentucky Feuds," 288; Harold Coates, *Stories of Kentucky Feuds* (Holmes-Darst Coal Corporation, 1942); C. W. Crozier, *Life and Trial of Dr. Abner Baker, Jr.* (Prentice and Weissinger, 1846); John Ed Pearce, "The Kentucky Feuds," *High Hope 1981*, 24.

24. Davis and Smyth, "Land of Feuds," 167; Ross, "The Great Feuds," 192; Coates, *Stories*, 141, 142; Litsey, "Kentucky Feuds," 288; Harlow, *Weep No More*, 225, 227.

25. Shapiro, *Appalachia*, 102; Ronald Eller, *Miners, Millhands, and Mountaineers: Industrialization of the Appalachian South, 1880–1930* (University of Tennessee Press, 1982); "Cause of Kentucky Feuds . . . Railroads Much Needed," *New York Times*, 3 December 1899, 17.

26. Shannon H. Wilson, "Window on the Mountains: Berea's Appalachia, 1870–1930," *The Filson Club History Quarterly* 64 (July 1990): 384–400.

27. Davis and Smyth, "Land of Feuds," 162; Frost is quoted in Shapiro, *Appalachia*, 111; General O. O. Howard, "The Feuds in the Cumberland Mountains," *The Independent*, 7 April 1904, 787, 788.

28. "How to Make Something out of this Fighting Stock," *The Berea Quarterly* 16 (January 1913): 9; Hough, "Burns of the Mountains," 2.

29. William G. Frost, "The American Mountaineers," *The Berea Quarterly* 4 (February 1900): 12; "The Mountain Feud," *The Chautauqua Assembly* 27 (11 August 1903): 5; "University Extension in Kentucky," *The Outlook*, September 1898, 79; and "The College and the Feud," *The Berea Quarterly* 16 (January 1913): 7.

30. James McConkey, *Rowan's Progress* (Pantheon, 1992), 75; O. O. Howard, "Feuds," 786; James Anderson Burns, *The Crucible: A Tale of Kentucky Feuds* (Oneida Baptist Institute, 1938), 105; Hough, "Burns of the Mountains," 16.

31. Davis and Smyth, "Land of Feuds," 172; Litsey, "Kentucky Feuds," 287.

32. David E. Whisnant, *All That Is Native and Fine: The Politics of Culture in an American Region* (University of North Carolina Press, 1983), 20.

33. Johnson, "Romance and Tragedy," 553, 552.

34. Edward W. Said, *Culture and Imperialism* (Vintage, 1994), xxiii, xxii.

35. Bruce Barton, "Children of the Feudists," *Collier's Weekly* 51 (23 August 1913): 7–8, 29.

36. Litsey, "Kentucky Feuds," 287; Patrick Brantlinger, "Victorians and Africans: The Genealogy of the Myth of the Dark Continent," *Critical Inquiry* 12 (Autumn 1985): 166, 186.

37. Kelvin A. Santiago-Valles, *"Subject People" and Colonial Discourses: Economic Transformation and Social Disorder in Puerto Rico, 1898–1947* (SUNY Press, 1994): 77–78; quote from Harry L. Watson, *Liberty and Power* (Hill and Wang, 1990), 54.

38. Said, *Culture*, xiii.

The "Tennessee Test of Manhood"
Professional Wrestling and
Southern Cultural Stereotypes

Louis M. Kyriakoudes and Peter A. Coclanis

While professional wrestling has been popular in the South since at least the end of World War II, its American roots stretch back to a frontier tradition. By the 1920s, the modern variety of wrestling had risen with such stars as Irish Dan Mahoney, Ali Baba, and Stan Zbyszko (here). Courtesy of the Collections of the Library of Congress.

*I*n his *Georgia Scenes*, Augustus Baldwin Longstreet describes a fight between two early-nineteenth-century backcountry brawlers, Billy Stallions and Bob Durham. Each fighter was reputed to be the toughest in his locality, although their friendship had heretofore kept the issue of county champion unresolved. One day, however, after an exchange of insults between their wives, honor now aggrieved, Billy and Bob agreed to settle the matter in " 'a fair fight; catch as catch can, rough and tumble.' " It being market day in the county seat, word of the coming battle spread quickly through town, and a large crowd gathered, forming a ring in anticipation of the contest. Each combatant's supporters boasted of their man's impending victory.

"What's Bob Durham going to do when Billy lets that arm loose upon him?"

"God bless your soul, he'll think thunder and lightning a mint julep to it."

"Oh, look here, men, go take Bill Stallions out o' that ring, and bring in Phil Johnson's stud horse, so that Durham may have some chance!"

The spectators appealed to Squire Tommy Loggin—"a man . . . who had never failed to predict the issue of a fight in all his life"—for insight into the outcome, and his inscrutable gaze encouraged both parties that victory would be theirs.[1]

The fight began when Bob "dashed at his antagonist at full speed," grasping Billy in an " 'all under-hold' " that put Billy's " 'feet where his head ought to be.' " The struggle continued. Bob "entirely lost his left ear, and a large piece from his left cheek," while Billy lost "about a third of his nose," which was "bit off," and his "face [was] so swelled and bruised that it was difficult to discover in it anything of the human visage." Less one finger and upon having "dirt and sand" ground into his eyes, Billy ended the battle with a cry of " 'ENOUGH!' " The audience erupted in "shouts, oaths, frantic gestures, taunts, replies, and little fights."[2]

Present-day professional wrestling owes much to the type of fighting described by Longstreet. When examining the role of sport in southern culture, one inevitably must come to terms with these local contests. Nineteenth-century visitors to the southern backcountry noted the frequency of bloody brawls and the large crowds they attracted. So prevalent was such fighting, one might consider it, along with horse racing, the South's first spectator sport, albeit on an amateur level.[3] Today, professional wrestling's core American audience is southern, with some estimates placing 60 percent of the attendance at live matches in the South. Southern athletes also make up a disproportionate share of professional wrestlers.[4]

The catch-as-catch-can style of backcountry fighting, a free-for-all constrained by few meaningful rules, persists in creative combat in modern professional wrestling. Consider this description of a match between Crusher Blackwell, a "huge wrestler from the Georgia hills," and Bruiser Brody, a Texan. Upon their meeting in the ring, "kicks, punches, and gouging [became] the general order of the day." The two wrestlers carried their fight over the ropes to the floor below. "Blackwell rammed Brody's head into the iron post [and] Brody responded in kind . . . ripping a huge gash in the Crusher's forehead." The combatants turned to whatever was at hand to pummel each other, and the match "soon became an epic feat of arms, legs, cowboy boots, and even folding chairs." The match ended with the combatants "all saturated with somebody's blood, [and] the entire ring area looked like a Red Cross donors' bank."[5]

More than just unbridled violence connects the fight in the Georgia backcountry with present-day professional wrestling. Backcountry fighting and modern wrestling both are embedded in cultural contexts that draw audience and combatants—spectators and spectacle—together to create a larger competitive narrative. The Stallions-Durham contest was held before an audience that was keenly attuned to the drama of the fight and needed to consult an expert evaluation of the action in the opinions of Squire Logan. Like Longstreet's backcountry grapplers, present-day wrestlers arrive with their attendants, promoters, and "managers" who, like Stallions's and Durham's seconds, boast of their man's prowess and certain victory, and who don't always stay out of the fray. The spectators at the Stallions-Durham brawl invested the fight with meaning that went beyond the immediate contest. Because each combatant represented his section of the county, the affair was riven with overtones of local pride, honor, and bragging rights.

Contemporary professional wrestling similarly involves its fans in the spectacle by recreating loyalties and antagonisms not unlike those in the Stallions-Durham brawl. Wrestling does so by drawing upon racial, ethnic, and regional stereotypes, shamelessly scavenged from popular culture, to create stylized personas that will attract and hold fans' interest.

Wrestlers' personas drive the theatrical narrative, which pits hero against villain and creates the dramatic tension that intensifies the conflict in the ring. In a famous essay written over forty years ago, French critic Roland Barthes suggested that wrestling depicts a "purely moral concept: that of justice." Wrestling promoter Dick Steinborn has expressed the same idea more forthrightly by pointing out that wrestling is about "good overcoming evil." While wrestling's dramatic conflicts occur within this morality-play framework, every wrestling match does not end in the defeat of evil. Villainous characters pack the venues, and a skillful wrestling promoter will stage a rivalry between two wrestlers that can last a season or more and is only ended in a well-attended "grudge match." Wrestlers' personas can move between good and evil, and it is not uncommon to wrestle as a villain in one regional territory and as a hero in another.[6]

The sport's popularity in the South has meant that many individual wrestlers have drawn upon southern social types in formulating their personas, and southern cultural stereotypes have become an important element in professional wrestling.[7] The sport has been replete with hillbillies, rednecks, and good ol' boys, and the appeal of these characters has risen and fallen in relation to broader national views about the South and its place in the nation. Thus, the role of southern cultural stereotypes in wrestling tells us not only a great deal about sport in the South, but also about how southern identity has been constructed in American popular culture.

To be sure, some may object to calling professional wrestling a sport. Certainly, if a truly competitive outcome is the sine qua non of sport, wrestling does not qualify. In professional wrestling contests, "the outcome is generally known." Today's professional wrestling organizations carefully point out that they provide "sport entertainment" rather than truly competitive contests. Matches are scripted, moves are choreographed, and punches are pulled. As one World Wrestling Federation (WWF) official pointed out, their contests are "entertainment no different than when the circus comes to town."[8] An unnamed wrestling fan expressed a similar view: "I say the wrestling is like a good fiction book; it may be fake but it's very exciting."[9]

Nonetheless, professional wrestling is not without its dangers; injuries are common, and sometimes the blood is real. A recent example resembles Longstreet's backcountry fighters all too well. Michael Foley, who at the time wrestled under the name "Cactus Jack," had his right ear torn off after a botched attempt at performing the "Hangman" maneuver, in which his head and neck were to appear to be entwined in the middle and top ropes of the ring. Foley had successfully performed the maneuver some seventy-five times, but on this attempt the ropes were too taut, and his ear was ripped off as he tried to free himself during the match. Surgeons were unsuccessful in completely reattaching Foley's severed ear, and he now wrestles with a leather mask under the new name "Mankind."[10] Despite these occasional injuries, however, truly competitive professional wrestling is as much fiction as Longstreet's description of the fight.

The lack of a competitive outcome should not exclude wrestling from the world of sport. To most who ponder the role of sport in American life, the competitive element of the contest holds the least interest; such concerns are the province of collectors of statistics and play-by-play antiquarians. It is the social and cultural elements in modern spectator sports that draw scholars to study the phenomenon. Modern sport is an entertainment that draws spectators into an emotional involvement with individual sports figures and teams. Spectator sports have become narratives in which conflict is ritualistically reenacted. All modern sport is spectacle, a struggle between good and evil, between one's "team" and its despised rival.

Taken in this light, professional wrestling's scripted matches and predetermined outcomes make it no less a sport than any other bona fide sporting endeavor. Professional wrestling's formal theatrical conventions, or as Barthes put it, the "iconography" of wrestling, make "reading" its symbols a straightforward affair.[11] Like true theater, professional wrestling broadcasts its cultural and symbolic meanings with greater clarity than sports constrained by binding rules and truly competitive outcomes. Moreover, the mutability and elusiveness of wrestlers' identities, their self-conscious irony, and their willingness to flout, or "transgress," cultural and moral conventions make the sport especially well-suited to these postmodern times.

ORIGINS OF PROFESSIONAL WRESTLING IN THE SOUTH

While professional wrestling has been popular in the South at least since the end of World War II, its American roots reach back to the frontier tradition of itinerant wrestlers who would travel alone or accompany touring minstrel shows and fairs, challenging all comers. Mark Twain drew the prototype in *Life on the Mississippi* in the fighter named

"Sudden Death and General Desolation," whose boasting was nearly as effective as his strength in defeating his opponents. After the turn of the century, wrestling moved to northern cities and became a popular spectator sport. Early notable wrestling matches pitted Frank Gotch, an Iowa-born grappler, against George Hackenschmidt, the Russian Lion. The appeal of legitimate contests with paying spectators, however, was unpredictable. These truly contested matches could be long affairs, dominated by slow, defensive maneuvering that failed to hold fan interest, or they could end quickly in defeat. After a number of notable matches, including a 1909 Gotch-Hackenschmidt rematch in Chicago that attracted some forty thousand spectators, legitimate wrestling went into decline as a professional sport.[12]

In its place rose the modern variety of wrestling characterized by exaggerated violence, theatrical conflicts, and outrageous characters. Early professional wrestlers sought to appeal to the urban immigrant working class of northern cities that comprised the sport's base. Leading wrestlers of the 1920s included Irish Dan Mahoney, Turkish-born Ali Baba, and Stan Zbyszko. Jim Londos (Christos Theophilou), the Golden Greek, reigned as the leading wrestler of the 1930s. After World War II, Killer Kowalski, Bruno Sammartino, and Antonio "Argentine" Rocca, who billed himself as both Hispanic and Italian by virtue of his Italian-Argentine heritage, continued the tradition of ethnic wrestlers.[13]

The spread of television did much to broaden professional wrestling's appeal. Wrestling was a staple of early television broadcasts, especially for smaller stations seeking cheap programming that could appeal to family audiences. In the early 1950s, Chicago stood as the center of professional wrestling, hosting nationally broadcast wrestling cards on Wednesday and Saturday nights over the ABC and the now defunct DuMont television networks.[14]

Wrestling's burlesque antics, invisible on radio, were well-suited to the new visual medium, and television promoted the stylized violence and outrageous characters that have come to dominate the sport. The 1950s saw masked wrestlers such as Zuma, Man from Mars, and the Hooded Phantom; super patriots such as Mr. America and the thinly disguised homoerotic antics of "Gorgeous George" Wagner, who bleached his hair and disinfected the ring with perfume; and "Nature Boy" Buddy Rogers, who inspired the current wrestler Ric Flair. Midget and women wrestlers were also very popular. German and Japanese wrestlers enraged a public still seething with resentments from World War II, while Soviet wrestlers provided the new Cold War villains.[15]

As professional wrestling's popularity grew with the television boom in the early 1950s, it also moved South. The sport initially migrated below the Mason-Dixon line in the 1930s when wrestlers like the German-born Milo Steinborn toured the region's leading cities, becoming especially popular in the Southeast.[16] In the 1950s regional promotions such as Jim Crockett's Charlotte-based National Wrestling Alliance (NWA) attracted ever larger audiences and gave the "Mid-Atlantic" Carolinas-Virginia circuit the reputation as "the hotbed of professional wrestling."[17] Gulf Coast Championship Wrestling, operated by Dick Steinborn, son of Milo Steinborn, promoted wrestling in Alabama and Florida.[18] Other leading promotions centered around western Tennessee, especially Memphis, and Texas. By the early 1960s professional wrestling's popularity had declined in the North as more respectable mainstream sports, notably professional football, gained larger followings.[19] Conversely, wrestling's popularity increased in the South, which still lacked a base of major-league professional franchises. Since that time, the sport has thrived on southern soil and has enjoyed a dedicated regional following.

Like other loosely organized itinerant entertainment industries such as circuses and carnivals, the wrestling business has been a close-knit, family-organized affair. A remarkable number of wrestlers and promoters are the second or third generation in the business. Take, for example, Edward Welch, a wrestler and promoter who died at the age of seventy-one in 1996. The son and nephew of pioneering southern wrestlers and promoters, Welch wrestled and later promoted in the South under the name Buddy Fuller. His sons, Robert and Ronald, continue the family business. Robert Welch is better known as Colonel Rob Parker, a manager who adopts the persona of a southern gentleman. Welch's nephew also wrestles under the name "Bunkhouse Buck." Father-son combinations abound: Jerry and Jeff Jarrett, and Dusty and Dustin Rhodes. Sibling combinations are common, too: Jake "The Snake" Roberts and Sam Houston are brothers; their sister wrestles under the name Rockin Robin. Similarly, Lanny Poffo and "Macho Man" Randy Savage are brothers and are the sons of wrestler Angelo Poffo.[20]

The 1980s saw wrestling enjoy increasing national exposure for the first time since the early 1950s. Bolstered by the popularity of superstars such as Terry Bollea, an ex-body builder and failed rock musician from

Florida who wrestles as Hulk Hogan, professional wrestling rose to unprecedented levels of popularity. Hogan appeared in films and on television, and he even graced the cover of *Sports Illustrated*. Celebrities like rock musician Cyndi Lauper and comedian Andy Kaufman embraced the sport for its naïve extravagance and stylized artifice, qualities critic Susan Sontag has described as part of the essence of "camp." In 1985 professional wrestling returned to network television for the first time since 1955 with the airing of *Saturday Night's Main Event* on NBC. The series of wrestling extravaganzas known as WrestleMania became national sporting events. WrestleMania III, for example, drew 78,000 spectators to Michigan's Pontiac Silverdome.[21]

This growth of new cable television outlets for the sport sparked a consolidation in the industry in the 1980s. Like the networks in the 1950s, cable TV programmers were attracted to wrestling as an inexpensive way to fill air time. Seeing opportunities for growth in the sport on the new cable medium, wrestling impresario Vince McMahon Jr., a second-generation wrestling promoter, expanded his World Wrestling Federation (WWF) out of its traditional base in the Northeast. The WWF's roster of stars, including Hulk Hogan, and its popular and profitable WrestleMania and TV pay-per-view programs allowed McMahon to buy or drive out of business most of the smaller regional wrestling organizations. In 1984 McMahon moved his WWF into the South, purchasing a time slot on Ted Turner's Atlanta-based cable "superstation" WTBS. Personality conflicts between Turner and McMahon, as well as programming disagreements, prompted McMahon to sell his slot to Jim Crockett's NWA. The smaller NWA, however, was poorly prepared to compete with the WWF and was near bankruptcy by 1988. Turner, who needed programming to fill the airtime of his growing cable empire, purchased the NWA, renaming it World Championship Wrestling (WCW).[22]

Turner's Atlanta-based WCW and McMahon's WWF have been the reigning powers in wrestling ever since. The stakes are high, and competition between the two is intense and bitter. In 1995 the WWF and WCW grossed $58.4 million and $48.1 million, respectively, on cable television pay-per-view programs alone. Live-event receipts and merchandise sales push gross revenues higher.[23]

Professional wrestling targets males, age eighteen to fifty-four, although just over one-fifth of the sport's audience is under eighteen. While wrestling promoters are fond of pointing out that the sport appeals to a wide range of education and income groups, three-quarters of the sport's television viewership has earned only a high school education or less, and nearly 70 percent have household incomes under forty thousand dollars. Males are wrestling's target group, but as any spectator at a wrestling match would know, women have long comprised a substantial portion of the sport's audience. The chief sponsors of early televised wrestling were household appliance dealers who sought to reach an adult female audience. Today, 36 percent of wrestling's television audience is female. Something of the sport's appeal to women, particularly southern women, might be gathered from the fact that Lillian Carter, in her capacity as First Mother, once invited the masked wrestler "Mr. Wrestling II" to her Plains, Georgia, home for a visit.[24]

SOUTHERN WRESTLERS

While wrestling has not been a strictly southern phenomenon, southern wrestlers have been central to the sport, dominating the ranks of wrestlers and supplying an important source of characters for the theatricality of wrestling. A listing of current leading professional wrestlers reveals that 70 percent are from the United States. Of those American-born wrestlers, nearly half—49 percent—hail from the South, and of the five leading states of origin for wrestlers, three—Texas, Tennessee, and Florida—are in the South. Texas and Tennessee are the two leading sources of wrestlers, contributing 14 and 10 percent, respectively, of the wrestlers in the listing. Like country music, wrestling draws its performers from the southern periphery; both count Texas and Tennessee as the two leading sources of their performers.[25]

Given this southern-dominated roster, it is not surprising that individual wrestlers have heavily mined the popular images of southerners for the raw materials from which they construct their stylized wrestling personas. Identifiably southern characters in wrestling began to appear in significant numbers in the 1960s, when the sport took on an increasingly southern cast. Early southern stereotypes tended toward either the *Tobacco Road* and *Deliverance* view of the white South as home to a class of degenerate subnormals capable of horrific violence, or the popular romantic primitivism of the hillbilly uncorrupted by modern civilization best depicted in 1960s television programs like *Hee Haw* and *The Beverly Hillbillies*. Haystacks Calhoun, a 601-pound "mammoth super heavyweight" from Morgan's Corner, Arkansas, who wrestled in knee-length overalls, was a crowd favorite in Virginia and the Carolinas in the 1960s.

Crusher Blackwell, who weighed in at a mere 400 pounds, and Bruiser Brody, a Texan, also illustrated this stereotype.[26]

Crusher Blackwell is a good example of how wrestling integrates southern themes into its drama. Blackwell had largely wrestled as a villain, but in the 1970s, wrestling in Knoxville, Tennessee, he became involved in a plot line that cast him in the role of innocent victim. Blackwell was managed by Boris Malenko, a wrestling promoter skilled at building villainous characters that could inflame wrestling audiences. In the mid-1960s Malenko, himself the patriarch of an illustrious wrestling family, built his career posing as a pro-Soviet wrestler in the Cuban-dominated areas of South Florida. Casting Blackwell as a "reserved and kind man" who only wrestled because Malenko held the mortgage to his family's farm, the manager made it clear to audiences that he would foreclose on the farm if Blackwell did not use his strength to "destroy his opponents" in the ring. The climax to this drama came when the local hero, Ronnie Garvin, jumped into the ring, paid off the "mortgage," and thus released Blackwell from Malenko's clutches. Blackwell then turned his fury on his former master, to the delight of the audience. Blackwell thus became a reluctant warrior entering the ring only to prevent a decline into dependency that must have been all too familiar to a wrestling audience only one or two generations off the farm.[27]

The 1970s saw more positive images of southerners appear in wrestling. Dusty Rhodes (né Virgil Runnels Jr.), perhaps the most popular wrestler before Hulk Hogan's reign began in the mid-1980s, embodied this trend. Obese, with eyes that seemed perpetually swollen shut, Rhodes seemed every inch the common man he billed himself to be. Rhodes boasted of his working-class roots—he claimed to be a Texas plumber's son—and he bragged that he began his own working career at the age of eight digging ditches. Taking "The American Dream" as his epigraph, Rhodes wrestled as an "all around good guy, fighting for the American way of life."[28]

Rhodes's rivals were those who threatened the way of life he sought to defend. Chief among them was Kevin Sullivan, "a deranged madman" from Boston who claimed connections to devil worship and the occult. At one point the two met in a "Loser Leaves Florida" cage match in which the wrestling ring was enclosed by a chain-link fence and victory was had by clambering out over the top. Sullivan won, but only by concealing an unidentified "lethal weapon," which he used to "pound the great Dusty into a bloody American mess." Disguised as the Midnight

Rider, Rhodes returned later that season, and dedicated himself to ridding "the Florida rings of scum and vermin like Sullivan." Later, the two grappled again, and Rhodes again lost when Sullivan called to his aid an LSD-inspired sidekick known as "Purple Haze."[29]

Rhodes represented a new type of southern wrestler persona: urban and blue collar, a southern "embodiment" of the silent majority yet clearly still within the "good ol' boy" mold of regional stereotypes. Rhodes, however, also represented a broader trend in the 1970s. Tied to Jimmy Carter's election to the presidency and to the popularity of films like *Smokey and the Bandit*, this trend identified white southerners with mainstream American values. Sullivan's godless persona, with its clear association with the 1960s drug culture and satanism, was a perfect foil to Rhodes's traditional values of love of God and country. That Sullivan was a Yankee only heightened the struggle between good and evil in the minds of southern audiences.

The association of southerners with patriotism can also be seen in the character Sergeant Slaughter. A Parris Island marine drill instructor, Slaughter initially wrestled as a villain in the post-Vietnam 1970s, who was billed as having been discharged from the marines for "excessive cruelty to his troops in boot camp."[30] The Iranian hostage crisis presented Slaughter with the opportunity to transform himself into a heroic figure, and he became a superpatriot, standing for "love of God and country." Slaughter's "intense hatred for America's enemies and detractors made him one of the most respected men in wrestling." Through most of the 1980s, Slaughter's chief rival was the Iron Sheik, the "Madman from Iran." The Sheik would incite the crowd by waving a large Iranian flag, and Slaughter would promise that upon his defeat, the villain would "kiss my combat boots."[31]

By the 1980s black southern wrestlers could also fit the mold of superpatriot. Tony Atlas, Mr. USA, an African American body builder from Roanoke, Virginia, showed skill equal to Slaughter's in creating dramatic opportunity out of international crisis. Atlas's target was Ivan Koloff, a "Russian" wrestler by way of Charlotte, North Carolina. Atlas took Koloff's "insults against the United States as a personal insult." When Soviet fighters shot down a Korean Airliner that strayed into Soviet airspace, Atlas "made Koloff his personal target for revenge." Koloff soon joined forces with the hated Iron Sheik, and the two vowed to "stamp out all American snakes." Atlas, however, teamed up with an unlikely ally, Captain Redneck, and the two were able to defeat the "two double-dealers in villainy." The black southerner and the redneck, too busy to hate, crossed the racial divide to join forces against a common foreign threat.[32]

The African American superpatriot theme continued into the late 1980s with Ranger Ross. A former Fort Bragg, North Carolina–based airborne ranger who fought in the Grenada mission, Ross would pose in his service beret and jacket, saluting and carrying a large American flag. The latest manifestation of the type is Sergeant Craig "Pitbull" Pittman, who wrestles in camouflage pants, marine boots, and a tee shirt emblazoned with "Semper Fidelis."[33]

Wrestling personas have sometimes reflected the harder edge of the modern South. Such was the case with the trio of wrestlers known as "The Fabulous Freebirds" in the early 1980s. Adopting the reactionary white southern populism of the ill-fated rock group Lynyrd Skynyrd, the Freebirds also gave expression to white working-class resentments during a time of high inflation and unemployment. Billing themselves as the "fearsome threesome," the Freebirds were famous for pulling off their cowboy boots and using them as weapons against their opponents. Mimicking their inspiration, the Freebirds even recorded a rock song in the style of their inspiration entitled "Badstreet USA."[34]

Nonetheless, by the mid-1980s there were fewer and fewer mainstream southern wrestling personas in the mold of Dusty Rhodes, Tony Atlas, or Sergeant Slaughter. By then, interest in the South as a reservoir of an authentic Americanism had waned. Working-class America identified less and less with hard-bitten blue-collar personas as a wave of Republican optimism and prosperity swept the country. Carter had exited the presidential stage in defeat while Reagan began his ascendancy with the resolution of the Iranian hostage crisis. Southern voters had bought into the Reagan vision. Carter's South was clearly out, the glamour and glitz of Reagan's California was in, and professional wrestling responded in kind. Wrestlers who did adopt explicitly southern personas wrestled as fools or villains, atavistically drawing upon those elements in southern culture that had crystallized into larger-than-life icons of American pop culture, creating, in essence, parodies of existing parodies of the region. Memphis-based Elvis impersonator Wayne Ferris wrestled as the "Honky Tonk Man" in the late 1980s and early 1990s. Nearly always cast as a villain, Honky Tonk Man entered the ring dressed in the large-collar, rhinestone-studded jump suits favored by the original "King" and would often perform tunes such as "Hunka Honky Love." Honky Tonk's signature wrestling move was the "shake, rattle, and roll," and he briefly headed up a tag-team called the "Rhythm and Blues." He would often beat his opponents about the head with a guitar, and then gyrate his hips, Elvis-style.[35]

Also patterning his persona upon a notable southern rock-and-roll musician was the wrestler Johnny B. Badd. The Macon, Georgia, native cast himself as a Little Richard look-alike, complete with pencil-thin mustache and bouffant. Like Honky Tonk Man, Johnny B. Badd generally wrestled as a villain. He also played on the sexual ambiguities of the real Little Richard, dressing in "matching pretty-in-pink outfits" and wearing "more makeup than senior citizens at a Florida Condominium."[36]

Wrestling manager Colonel Robert Parker combined the image of the southern gentleman with allusions to Colonel Harlan Sanders and Elvis Presley's manager, Colonel Tom Parker, to create a composite of stereotypes. Dressed in a white wide-brimmed hat and white jacket, Parker is known for his shady dealings and willingness to break wrestling rules. When he wrestles on his own, his opponents are women, and even then he is known for cheating, much to the delighted outrage of wrestling audiences. Parker often faces another manager, Jimmy "The Mouth of the South" Hart. A Memphis native, Hart combines the look of a slick Nashville country-music producer with that of a used-car salesman who is pushy and loud, yet identifiably southern.

Southern religiosity has been mocked in wrestling, too. Brother Love, a wrestler turned manager and announcer, bases his character explicitly upon disgraced evangelist Jimmy Swaggart. Dressed in a white suit, red shirt, and white satin tie, with gold rings on each finger, Brother Love covers his face and neck with red makeup "to look like a redneck." Brother Love preaches "I love you" to the crowds, who know that this is just a "smokescreen to hide his selfish greed."[37]

This said, it should be noted that the real thing also exists among professional wrestlers. George South, a wrestler and promoter from Concord, North Carolina, wrestles with "John 3:16" airbrushed on the back of his tights. Tully Blanchard, one of a long line of West Texas State football players to wrestle professionally, was born again when "he met God in the person of Jesus Christ in a personal way Nov. 13, 1989" at his home in Charlotte. Blanchard, who still "competes," has gone on to direct "Ring of Truth Ministries" and serves as the minister of evangelism at Central Church of God in Charlotte.[38]

In some ways, then, wrestling has come full circle to the hillbilly images that were so prevalent in the 1960s and early 1970s. The most popular wrestlers to adopt a southern persona today are the "cousins" Henry O. Godwinn (H.O.G.) and Phinneas I. Godwinn (P.I.G.), who are managed by 1980s wrestling standout Hillbilly Jim. The two members of this tag-team bill themselves as pig farmers from Bitters, Arkansas. Overall-clad, they often enter the ring with their pigs, Priscilla and Pot-belly. Their "finishing" wrestling move is the Slop Drop, where they pour slop from a feed bucket onto the head of their opponent.

A recent "pig pen" match between Henry Godwinn and Hunter Hearst-Helmsley, "scion of a patrician Greenwich, Connecticut, clan," revived sectional tensions while reinforcing the Godwinns' populist appeal. By tossing Hearst-Helmsley into a mud-filled pig sty, Godwinn recapitulated the victory of a more notable "good ol' boy" from Hope, Arkansas, who also defeated a Connecticut patrician. Like Bill Clinton, as well, the Godwinns' weakness for the fairer sex can be their undoing. They lost a championship match at WrestleMania XII when the opposing team's "manager," Sunny, a shapely blond version of *Li'l Abner*'s Stupe-fyin' Jones, distracted Phinneas by posing suggestively before him. "I never saw anything like that down on the farm," was his explanation.[39]

Southern personas have been less popular in professional wrestling of late. The career of Ray Trayler, who once wrestled as the Big Boss Man, is instructive. Touting his home as Cobb County, Georgia, Boss Man was variously a southern prison guard and a violent police officer, complete with nightstick, who would rough up his opponents in the ring. Failing to succeed with that persona, Trayler then wrestled as Big Bubba, tattooing a Confederate flag on his arm. Just as Cobb County, increasingly domi-nated by Atlanta suburbanites, has become less "southern," Trayler now has abandoned his regional character for his latest moniker, the Guardian Angel.[40]

Southern wrestling personas seem to be losing their appeal as sports-minded southerners increasingly transfer their fan loyalty to the rising number of professional football, basketball, and, yes, even hockey teams now burgeoning in major southern cities. Perhaps as the South becomes more like the rest of the country—or the rest of the country more like the South, as the argument sometimes goes—the fascination with regional distinctiveness is relegated from the realm of the popular imagination to the arena of museums and preservation societies.

Moreover, the decline in popularity of regionally specific wrestling personas may also be the result of the internationalization of the pro wrestling business. Wrestling revenues in the United States have been flat or declining since the end of the boom of the 1980s. NBC canceled wrestling programming in 1991, while attendance at live matches has declined from 13 million in 1981 to 2 million in 1994. As a consequence, both Turner's WCW and McMahon's WWF have been looking to overseas markets, expanding into Europe, Asia, and Latin America. Overseas business now accounts for 15 percent of WWF's earnings, and the organization sells programming to Rupert Murdoch's BSkyB and Star TV, which reach Asian markets. The WWF also appears on German, Italian, French, and Spanish television, and Turner beams WCW into Latin America on TNT International. At the same time, traditional professional wrestling faces competition at home. A highly acrobatic style of wrestling from Mexico known as Luche Libre has proven to be very popular with Hispanic immigrant audiences as well as American audiences.[41]

While it is unclear if American professional wrestlers will soon hear Ross Perot's "giant sucking sound," the internationalization of the sport has helped to bring about a shift away from regionally specific cultural stereotypes. Wrestling's chief inspiration today seems to come from the developing global media culture. An example is the wrestler Galaxy, based upon the international TV superheroes, the Power Rangers. The sport's reigning stars such as Sting, Diesel, and the Giant are comic-book heroes that can appeal to many nationalities and cultures, and require no specific cultural referent.

Wrestling, alas, has not been immune to broader postmodern cultural and intellectual trends. A case in point is Goldust, the former Dustin Rhodes, son of Dusty, "The American Dream." Having failed as a cleaner-cut, upscale version of his father, Goldust/Dustin Rhodes saw opportunity in America's postmodernist tendency to render casual the distinctions between genders. His character is a transgendered, sexually ambiguous and rapacious cross dresser. Goldust enters the ring in gold pancake makeup, wearing fish-net stockings, garter belt, and bustier beneath a silver and gold lamé uniform, making provocative sexual overtures to opponents, fans, and himself alike. Initially a villain, Goldust has become one of the more popular good "guys" in the WWF, suggesting that postmodern ideas about sexuality are not confined to the academy and are leaching into the popular culture.

But the southern elements of professional wrestling still live on in the region, even in the face of postmodernity and the alleged Americanization, or even internationalization of Dixie.[42] On a recent cold February night in a National Guard armory in Butner, North Carolina, the wrestlers of Southern Championship Wrestling, one of many small-town, minor-league promotions, do their stuff. The highlight of the evening comes when two wrestlers go at each other in the "Tennessee Test of Manhood," an obviously painful ordeal that involves "swift kicks and private parts." Longstreet's "Fight" lives on.[43]

NOTES

1. Augustus Baldwin Longstreet, "The Fight," in *Georgia Scenes, Characters, Incidents, etc., in the First Half Century of the Republic, By a Native Georgian*, reprinted in *The Literary South*, compiled and edited by Louis D. Rubin Jr. (Louisiana State University Press, 1979), 230, 228, 229.

2. Longstreet, "The Fight," 230–31.

3. Elliot J. Gorn, "'Gouge and Bite, Pull Hair and Scratch': The Social Significance of Fighting in the Southern Backcountry," *American Historical Review* 90 (February 1985): 18–43; Timothy H. Breen, "Horses and Gentlemen: The Cultural Significance of Gambling Among the Gentry of Virginia," *William and Mary Quarterly* 34, 3rd ser. (April 1977): 239–57.

4. Randall Williams, "Tonight: The Hulk vs. Ox Baker," *Southern Exposure* 7 (Fall 1979): 30; "WCW: Where the Big Boys Play" (media brochure, WCW Media Relations Office, n.d.).

5. Bert Randolph Sugar and George Napolitano, "Crusher Blackwell vs. Bruiser Brody," *Wrestling's Great Grudge Matches: "Battles and Feuds"* (Gallery Books, 1985), 44–47; Roberta Morgan, *Main Event: The World of Professional Wrestling* (Dial Press, 1979), 204.

6. Roland Barthes, "The World of Wrestling," *Mythologies* (1957. Reprinted, Hill & Wang, 1972), 21; *Richmond Times Dispatch*, 13 June 1996, D-4. See also Gerald W. Morton and George M. O'Brien, *Wrestling to Rasslin: Ancient Sport to American Spectacle* (Bowling Green University Popular Press, 1985), 103–25 which places professional wrestling in the morality play tradition.

7. John Shelton Reed, *Southern Folk, Plain & Fancy: Native White Social Types* (University of Georgia Press, 1986).

8. Jim Tillman, a lobbyist for the World Wrestling Federation, commenting on the WWF's successful effort to defeat proposed legislation regulating professional wrestling as a competitive sport in Florida, *Atlanta Journal and Constitution*, 8 February 1992, D-2.

9. Quoted in Thomas Hendricks, "Professional Wrestling as Moral Order," *Sociological Inquiry* 44, no. 3 (1974): 177.

10. *Atlanta Journal and Constitution*, 2 March 1996, D-3.

11. Barthes, "World of Wrestling," 20.

12. Mark Twain, *Life on the Mississippi* (James R. Osgood and Company, 1883), 44–47; "Pro-Wrestling Illustrated," *The 1996 Wrestling Almanac and Book of Facts* (London Publishing Co., 1996), 99; Michael R. Ball, *Professional Wrestling as Ritual Drama in American Popular Culture* (Edwin Mellen Press, 1990), 42–43.

13. Hendricks, "Professional Wrestling as Moral Order," 178, 181.

14. Ball, *Professional Wrestling*, 54–55.

15. "It Pays to Sponsor Television Corn," *Business Week* (7 October 1950): 25–26; Jane and Michael Stern, "Professional Wrestling," *The Encyclopedia of Bad Taste* (HarperCollins, 1990), 258–59.

16. Williams, "Tonight," 31.

17. *Charleston Post and Courier*, 4 June 1995, B-10; Larry Bonko, "Stomping at the Greensboro Coliseum," *Esquire* 70 (November 1968): 116–17.

18. Williams, "Tonight," 34.

19. Benjamin G. Rader, *American Sports: From the Age of Folk Games to the Age of Televised Sports*, 3rd ed. (Prentice Hall, 1996), 250–53.

20. *Charleston Post and Courier*, 31 March 1996, C-24; George Napolitano, *The New Pictorial History of Wrestling* (Gallery Books, 1990), 71, 76, 95.

21. "Mat Mania: Hulk Hogan, Pro Wrestling's Top Banana," *Sports Illustrated* (29 April 1985), cover; *Tampa Tribune*, 7 July 1996, Business & Finance, 1; Susan Sontag, "Notes on 'Camp,'" *A Susan Sontag Reader* (Farrar, Straus, & Giroux, 1982), 105–19, esp. 106, 108, 110, 112.

22. *Tampa Tribune*, 7 July 1996, Business & Finance, 1.

23. Ibid.

24. "WCW: Where the Big Boys Play"; Morgan, *Main Event*, 134.

25. Calculated from a listing of currently active wrestlers (n = 389) in "Pro-Wrestling Illustrated," *The 1996 Wrestling Almanac*, 74–83. George O. Carey, "T for Texas, T for Tennessee: The Origins of American Country Music Notables," *Journal of Geography* 78 (November 1979): 221. The South is defined here as the eleven states of the former Confederacy plus Kentucky and Oklahoma.

26. Morgan, *Main Event*, 204–5; Sugar and Napolitano, *Wrestling's Great Grudge Matches*, 44–47.

27. Morton and O'Brien, *Wrestling to Rasslin*, 136.

28. Napolitano, *New Pictorial History of Wrestling*, 22.

29. Sugar and Napolitano, *Wrestling's Great Grudge Matches*, 156–57.

30. George Napolitano, *Wrestling Heroes & Villains* (Beekman House, 1985), 44, as quoted in Ball, *Professional Wrestling as Ritual Drama*, 106.

31. Sugar and Napolitano, *Pictorial History of Wrestling*, 35, 75; Sugar and Napolitano, *Wrestling's Great Grudge Matches*, 140.

32. Sugar and Napolitano, *Pictorial History of Wrestling*, 14.

33. Napolitano, *New Pictorial History of Wrestling*, 101; *WCW Magazine* (November 1996): 40–41.

34. Sugar and Napolitano, *Pictorial History of Wrestling*, 104; Sugar and Napolitano, *Wrestling's Great Grudge Matches*, 69.

35. Ball, *Professional Wrestling as Ritual Drama*, 128; Napolitano, *New Pictorial History of Wrestling*, 75.

36. "Pro-Wrestling Illustrated," *The 1996 Wrestling Almanac and Book of Facts*, 25.

37. Napolitano, *New Pictorial History of Wrestling*, 64; *World Wrestling Federation Magazine* 14 (March 1996): 6.

38. *Charleston Post and Courier*, 15 December 1996, C-14; 23 June 1996, C-12; *Chattanooga Free Press*, 1 November 1996.

39. *World Wrestling Federation Magazine* (September 1996): 34; Vince Russo, ed., *Showdown! Settling the Score . . . The Hard Way* (World Wrestling Federation, 1996), 49.

40. Napolitano, *New Pictorial History of Wrestling*, 46; *Charleston Post and Courier*, 25 December 1994, C-12.

41. *Financial World*, 14 February 1995, 112.

42. John Egerton, *The Americanization of Dixie: The Southernization of America* (Harper's Magazine Press, 1974); Peter Applebome, *Dixie Rising: How the South is Shaping American Values, Politics, and Culture* (Times Books, 1996).

43. *Raleigh News & Observer*, 26 February 1997, 4-E.

"How 'bout a Hand for the Hog"

The Enduring Nature of the Swine as a
Cultural Symbol in the South

S. Jonathan Bass

For almost two centuries, the southerner's best friend (the hog) has endured as the ideal symbol of the region. Porcelain pig lawn ornaments for sale, near Fayetteville, North Carolina, 1941, courtesy of the Collections of the Library of Congress.

Well, I've always heard, but I ain't too sure, that a man's best friend is a mangy cur. I kinda favor the hog myself. How 'bout a hand for the hog!
—*Roger Miller*[1]

The "King of the Road," Roger Miller, had a genuine understanding of the southern fondness for hogs. "In the scheme of things, in the way things go," wrote Miller, "you might get bit by the old Fido, but not that gentle porker friend. . . ."[2] For almost two centuries, the southerner's best friend (the hog) has endured as the ideal symbol of the region. In the Old South the swine served as the backbone of the southern farm and played a central role in the region's economy and culture. As the South changed from a rural-agricultural to an urban-industrial society, southerners relied on the hog in new ways: grocery stores met the demand for hog meat, agricultural fairs replaced the ritual hog killings, and barbecue restaurants perpetuated the region's dietary tradition of consuming pork.

Both symbolically and in reality the hog has become ingrained in the culture of the South. Much like cotton the hog developed from a simple economic staple to a broad cultural symbol. Some have theorized that southerners developed this swine compulsion because of the common nature they shared with the porky critters. In the antebellum South William Byrd noted that southerners lived "so much upon swine's flesh" that it not only inclined "them to the yaws" but consequently to the loss of "their noses" and made them "likewise extremely hoggish in their temper, and many of them seem to grunt rather than speak in their ordinary conversation."[3] This suggests that southerners and hogs have similar temperaments: slow, leisurely, independent, and hardheaded. Professional pork smoker Sy Erskine, owner of "Let's Eat Smoked Meat" restaurant of Hueytown, Alabama, agrees: "Hey man, it's the best way to be." Southerners have always enjoyed taking their time and not arriving "first at a gold rush."[4]

Many historians, writers, and other critical observers have emphasized only the most negative aspects of the southerner's leisurely, hoglike nature. Most critics have equated the South's slow pace of life with laziness. A writer described the poor whites of the antebellum South as so lazy they had to depend on self-sufficient "omnipresent hogs" for food rather than their own "weed-choked fields." It was commonplace in the 1850s for a northerner to denounce the South as a land filled with "lazy vagabonds" and "pitiable wretches."[5] Even one southerner, of a more noble character and class, described the bulk of these southern crackers as living in "barren solitudes" and spending their lives sowing "idle habits." They were "about the laziest two-legged animals" that walked "erect on the face of the Earth," he wrote. Even their "motions" were slow; their speech had a "sickening drawl"; and their thoughts and ideas appeared to "creep along at a snail's pace."[6]

Numerous expressions used to describe humans also emphasize the most negative characteristics of the hog: looking or acting dirty, greedy, or fat as a hog; acting pigheaded; pigging out or eating like a pig; going hog-wild or whole hog; living in a pig sty or pig pen; and the simple "pig" (which in politically correct terms means a male chauvinist, or one of the old standards: a police officer, a fat person, or a glutton). As hog connoisseur William Hedgepeth has noted, the question remains as to whether these expressions function as an "insult directed toward humans for acting some certain way . . . or toward hogs for the fact that undesirable people are drawn to parody and besmirch their patterns of behavior." Of course this is probably a chicken-and-egg debate.[7]

Nevertheless, most folks certainly maintain some sort of "half-suppressed" kinship with hogs. "At the very least," writes Hedgepeth, there exists enough "ritualized uses for the pig and a sufficient body of beliefs, superstitions, and folk tales" to intimate that most people have an "awful lot of faith" that the hog affects the happiness, well-being, and prosperity of their lives.[8] Southerners traditionally consume hog jowls and black-eyed peas on New Year's Day for the hope of prosperity in the coming year. Certainly hogs inspired Roger Miller to compose his ode to the hog: "The way I see it; it looks like this: either you ain't or either you is a true blue lover of the swine. How 'bout a hand for the hog!" Roy Blount Jr., a keen observer of the things that define southern life, found such great respect for the swine he waxed poetic: "You can't put a hog in a zoo. There's no telling what he will do. He may get loud and charge at the crowd, or just lie there not looking at you."[9]

The hog has become embedded in the culture of the South and remains the widespread symbol of the region and southern culture. As a symbolic "stand-in," Hedgepeth writes, the swine has "manifested itself throughout the past on all sorts of levels and dimensions." Even hogs seem to recognize the reciprocal nature of the southern disposition and the swine temperament. One old saying notes that "dogs look up to you; cats look down on you; and pigs think you're their equal."[10]

Despite the far reaching symbolism of hogs in southern culture, in reality the swine played a tremendously important role in the region's economy throughout the Old South. Antebellum southern farmers and herdsmen "looked upon the hog as one symbol of his success." If cotton ruled the South as a symbolic king, certainly the hog must be the crown prince. In 1860 hogs and other southern livestock had a value of $500 million—more than twice the value of that year's cotton crop. Southerners raised two-thirds of the nation's hogs, and ten southern states boasted a population of more than a million in 1860. That same year, hogs and other livestock slaughtered in the region were worth some $106,555,500, and southerners traded hogs five to eight times more than all other large animals combined.[11]

Planters and farmers were not the only southerners reaping the economic benefits of hogs. Legendary herdsmen (hog "drovers") drove hundreds of thousands of hogs great distances over rugged terrain to market and provided the "red corpuscles of the economic blood stream" in the region. As early as 1828 hog drovers had an impact on the economy of the South. "I am not making any money at present," wrote one Virginia farmer, "and cannot until I sell my corn to Hog-drovers from which I never have failed to make every fall something like four or five hundred dollars."[12]

Historian Sam Hilliard has estimated that southerners traded as many as one hundred fifty thousand hogs annually, and most trade routes headed toward the large markets along the east coast. Most successful drovers searched for markets outside of the lower South, where the mild winters of the region caused meat to spoil quickly, and this discouraged planters from slaughtering hogs and preserving meat on a wide scale.[13] Knoxville, Tennessee, emerged as the central location for hog routes radiating from Georgia and Alabama into the Carolinas. In the early years, thousands of swine clogged the passage through the mountains along the French Broad gorge route into North Carolina, prompting legislation to widen and improve roads. Even with the new roads the "hog traffic" continued to grow to "immense proportions." For most of the nineteenth century in east Tennessee, there were so many hogs going to market, one observer noted that it seemed as if "all the world were hogs and all the hogs of the world had been gathered there. . . ."[14]

The hog driving season lasted from mid-October to mid-December. The short fall days must have seemed "awfully lonely with nobody to talk to but the hogs." The drives consisted of herds ranging from three hundred to two thousand hogs, with one "pigboy" for every hundred swine and a manager for every herd. The hog driver's call "ho-o-o-yuh! ho-o-o-yuh!" had an "appealing resonance" that "resounded across the valley, rousing a throbbing expectation as it drew nearer and nearer, and held fast to the imagination as it receded into the distant and at last died away with only a faint echo." Hired help earned from twelve to fifteen dollars a month, with board and lodging provided. Drovers prodded the hogs down the trails about eight to ten miles a day before stopping at one of the "hog hotels" along the route. James Mitchell Alexander owned the most famous of the hog hotels along the French Broad route and provided drovers with "superior accommodations" including a hotel ("famous" from Cincinnati to Charleston), store, tan yard, shoe shop, harness shop, farm, blacksmith shop, wagon factory, gristmill, saw mill, "ferry, and bridge."[15]

The hog drives provided occasions for broad social interaction among southerners. The herdsmen gave local folks contact with people outside of their own isolated surroundings and access to oral recollections, political stories, and other "news items."[16] Local residents, however, viewed the drovers with a great deal of suspicion, and parents protected their daughters from herdsmen, whom they considered as "nomadic and careless as sailors." Folklorists wrote songs and told tales about hogmen, pigboys, and their herds. A popular "play-song" and game in the nineteenth century acted out a symbolic courtship involving hog drovers, a tavern keeper, and his daughter. The drovers had to convince the keeper to provide lodging and the opportunity for courtship: "Hog drivers, hog drivers, hog drivers are we, A courting your daughter so fair and so free. Can we get lodging, here, oh here? Can we get lodging here?" In the end the proprietor consents to the drovers' wishes.[17]

Throughout the nineteenth century hog meat was the staple item in the southern diet. Southerners filled their bellies with hog parts from the "sweet" snout to the curly tail and about the only part they didn't use was the squeal. "That's the reason hogs became such folklore in the South," said Van Sykes of Bob Sykes Barbecue in Bessemer, Alabama. "Southerners were just being smart. They had an animal that had a million different uses."[18] Although the farmer found "no use for the squeal," they dried the bladders and passed them "among the young folks to be blown up as balloons." In addition to the obvious hog portions—hams (back of legs), shoulders (front of legs), and bacon—farmers also converted the lights (lungs) and liver, together called "haslet," into a fresh stew, and cooked the fat into crisp "cracklin'" an essential ingredient in cornbread.

Guts became casings for sausage, and brains mixed with eggs graced the breakfast table. After pulling out the eyes and cutting off the end of the snout, southerners boiled the head, pulled the teeth, and picked off any meat left clinging. They crushed the meat (cheeks, ears, etc.) with herbs and spices and packed it tightly into muslin cloth for souse meat, also called hog's headcheese. The liver, feet, and especially the "knuckles" (the ankles) were "special delicacies." Southerners digested the backbone, tenderloin, tongue, ears, and tail soon after the ritualized hog killing.[19]

Local communities slaughtered hogs as part of harvest festival celebrations. Whatever the "pains, and penalties, discomforts and dejections" had been in hog raising, the hog killing days provided a "time of genuine joy" for the farmer and an entire community. North Carolinian Alberta Ratcliffe Craig remembered hog killings as "community occasions" for men, women, and children.[20]

Southern men symbolically expressed their "power over nature" in this grisly ritual. More than a "hot, ugly responsibility," killing a hog was a "tough, manly act performed in public."[21] Weak-kneed little girls often winced at the bloody process: "Oh, the shrill frightened squeals they made," recalled Belinda Jelliffe. "A sound accusing, asking for help, full of consummate awareness of annihilation! The completely unbearable fact that every pig was a member of the family."[22] The hog killing usually occurred after the first dash of extended cold weather or after the October full moon. The slaughter provided the first taste of fresh meat for a community "famished for it" and presented the symbolic "promise of meat through the long winter."[23]

The consumption of pork in the South has been described by historians as legendary and the distinctiveness of the southern diet as one of the region's most "outstanding" traits. Antebellum visitors and physicians, however, lamented the use of pork as the undisputed "king of the table" in the South. Bacon, instead of bread, emerged as the "staff of life" in the region, noted Emily P. Burke. "The people of the South would not think they could subsist without their swine flesh," she believed.[24] Dr. John S. Wilson of Columbus, Georgia, considered the southern frontier the center of the "great Hog-eating Confederacy" and the "Republic of Porkdom" in the United States. Wilson deplored the consumption of "fat bacon and pork" continually "morning, noon, and night, for all classes, sexes, ages, and conditions." Southerners also used the hogs' lard to fry all their meat, vegetables, and bread. They "indeed fried everything that is fryable [*sic*]," noted Wilson, "or that [which] will stick together long enough to undergo the delightful process . . . hogs' lard is the very oil that moves the machinery of life, and they would as soon think of dispensing with tea, coffee, or tobacco . . . as with the essence of hog."[25]

Southern farmers often placed the hams, shoulders, and bacon in the smokehouse for later use. Roasting (barbecuing) a large quantity of meat was usually reserved for the country get-together, the "big entertainment of customers and friends," the congregation, and the political rally. After all, "a barbecued hog in the woods, and plenty of whiskey, will buy birthrights and secure elections in America."[26] The "plain folk" in the Old South loved "good oratory," and politicians provided political debates and speeches to secure widespread support. To guarantee a large attendance at the event, organizers barbecued "scores of hogs" and served plenty of whiskey and lemonade.[27] One southerner described the kind of man he would support for public office as possessing the ability to "holler right, vote straight, and eat as much barbecue as any other man in the country." One visitor to Georgia believed barbecues had become such a powerful "social and political force" that it was "no exaggeration to say that many gubernatorial elections in Georgia had been carried by means of votes gained at barbecues, and no campaign for Governor is complete without a series of such popular feasts."[28] Apparently northerners found these activities quite peculiar: the southern "mode of living" was "entirely different" from the North's. "They live more heartily," wrote one northerner, and they "esteem" their "famous" barbecue "above all."[29]

The reason southerners ate so much pork stemmed from the efficiency of owning such an animal. Hogs remained self-sufficient during the spring, summer, and fall by foraging in the woods for roots, nuts, and berries. They also consumed sweet potato vines, fruits, and vegetables that had fallen from the vine, and unharvested grain and peas. During the fall months fattening a hog for slaughter remained a relatively easy process: farmers penned the swine and fattened him on corn for a few weeks. Digestively, hogs could convert the feed to meat at an extremely efficient rate—at almost six times that of cows and sheep.[30]

The Civil War had a tremendous impact on the herdsmen, the farmer's self-sufficiency, and his efficient friend, the hog. Some historians have emphasized the capital losses of animals destroyed during the war were as "important to the drovers, relatively, as were the capital losses to the planters that resulted from emancipation." In South Carolina the hog population had been reduced from 965,000 in 1860 to less than 150,000 in 1865, and one observer emphasized that the "larger portion" of the state had been "utterly stripped of its stock." Eight states of the former Confederacy produced 2.6 million fewer hogs in 1880 than they had in 1860.[31]

The closing of the southern range during the late nineteenth and twentieth centuries completely devastated open-range herding and the hog droving business. The end of the open range in the South reshaped the "social, economic, and political life of the region." Stock laws prohibited southern farmers from allowing hogs to forage freely in woods and fields. In Alabama, once counties enacted stock laws, the number of hogs per capita dropped significantly.[32] Stock laws deprived the hog drover of his historic "transportation system": the trail drive. Thus hog drives and hog drovers soon drifted into historical obscurity.[33]

With these changes—coupled with increasing agricultural commercialization, rising industrialization, and growing urbanization—economic reliance on the hog and the rural culture surrounding it declined. Southerners replaced the fading economic necessities and cultural events with new ones: Piggly Wiggly and other markets and grocery chains arose to meet the needs of the non-self-sufficient farmer and the urban southerner; state and county agricultural fairs replaced the ritual hog killings and most harvest celebrations; and barbecue restaurants perpetuated the southern obsession with hog meat.

The self-sufficient southern farm declined dramatically in the postwar period. Increasing debt and reliance on a lone cash crop ended the safety first production of corn and hogs. The cash economy drastically altered the southern farmers' mode of operation, and they relied heavily on store-bought supplies from nearby towns that rapidly modernized the southern economy and culture. As the farmers came to town more often, they demanded new products that opened new markets and led to more railroads, stores, and better roads.[34]

One of the greatest contradictions in the southern economy during the early New South period was the southern farmers' prevailing love of pork and growing hatred of hogs. Most southerners in the antebellum South considered raising hogs a relatively easy task, as long as the swine remained mostly self-sufficient. A pig kept in a pen required much more care than the range hog and was considered just another burden for a farmer struggling to make a living. Edmund Cody Burnett, who participated in some of the last hog drives in the 1880s, also shared the growing southern dislike of raising hogs. "If Satan would enter into all of them and make them rush headlong into the creek and get drowned," Burnett later reflected, "I was on the side of Satan in that job. There were, indeed, many times and occasions when the voluntary—or instinctive—conduct of the hogs would induce in either man or boy moods in which no pious thought could thrive."[35]

Southerners, however, continued to have a tremendous appetite for pork. Blacks, who had fled to Texas with their masters as Union troops advanced, returned east, complaining that the Lone Star State had "too much beef and too little pork."[36] One ex-slave told a folktale of deceitful Yankees that lured other freedmen to Arkansas with promises of "hogs just laying around already baked with the knives and forks sticking in them" ready for an eating jubilee.[37] Other southerners, who couldn't afford to buy pork at the store or raise a few scrawny pigs, simply took what they needed. Stealing hogs became such a problem in Mississippi, the legislature passed the famous "pig law" charging livestock thieves with grand larceny and sentencing the guilty up to five years in prison. The year following the passage of the law saw a sharp increase in prisoners from 272 to 1,072.[38] To satisfy the demand for pork, hungry southerners bought millions of pounds of hog meat shipped from Iowa, Illinois, Ohio, and Indiana.

This reliance on imported hog meat and the poor conditions of the swine had a tremendous effect on the economy and culture in the South. For the first time southerners were consuming high-fat, pen-fed hog meat. A penned range hog had been condemned to "filth," "disease," and "veritable extinction." This "unclean" meat aided the spread of pellagra and other vitamin deficiencies among southerners. In addition, farmers no longer walked out to the smokehouse for a slab of their own meat; as self-sufficiency faded southern farmers hitched their wagons and drove to town to buy salt pork sliced into five- and ten-pound orders. Store clerks sliced and sold the imported meat while disgruntled farmers loafed around the stores complaining about the "general" cursedness of a "hungry brood sow."[39]

One southerner, Clarence Saunders, used the hog as a symbol for his new concept in grocery shopping. Saunders modernized the small general store and transformed it into the modern supermarket. On a train ride in early 1916, Saunders noticed hundreds of hogs rooting around a farmyard near the railroad tracks. He reflected on an interesting analogy: clerks had to select merchandise for customers at the general store; when the store grew crowded customers flocked to the overwhelmed clerks like "piglets to their mother sow." This image of the hog inspired his store's name, Piggly Wiggly, and his efficient system of arrangement, self-service, and cash-and-carry.[40] The hog, as Saunders knew, had been the efficient backbone of the southern farm. "Piggly Wiggly will be born," he emphasized, "not with a silver spoon in his mouth, but a workshirt on his back." Credited by many as one of the "creators of twentieth-century culture," Saunders opened the first Piggly Wiggly store in Memphis, Tennessee, in 1916. By 1923 Saunders had become the pig-wig of the grocery business: he owned more than twelve hundred stores, each bearing the funny name and a smiling hog's face painted on every building. The hog continued to endure as a symbol of the southern obsession with pork and an ode to the bygone days of farmers' self-sufficiency.[41]

The hog endured—and adapted—even as self-sufficient family farming declined before the onslaught of agricultural commercialization and modernization. Most southerners abandoned the harvest festival, and as historian Ted Ownby has recognized, the hog killing ritual "lost its significance as a cultural event simply because of the decline in ownership of hogs for consumption."[42]

Southerners, however, adjusted to the new conditions of the twentieth century and replaced harvest festivals with county and state fairs. The local fair emerged as the "clearest continuation of the harvest celebration" and reflected the "changing ways in which farmers celebrated the harvest and the end of the work year." Fairs should be seen as agents of "modernization and centralization," not as an antiquated rural institution. Southerners celebrated their harvests in a "self-consciously modern way," and the fairs "reflected the changing directions" of southern culture in the twentieth century.[43]

Boys' pig clubs sprouted around the South to encourage youngsters to raise prizewinning hogs for fair contests. Agricultural newspapers in the 1910s and 1920s ran scores of stories in which boys told their secrets of raising a champion pig. The pig clubs became immensely popular throughout the South and prepared the "young for modern life" on the farm. Extension agents had the ulterior motive of encouraging a boy's father to try more modern techniques in hog raising.[44] As one fair proponent noted, education sent the farmer down the "pathway of progress," and set his "face in the right direction." The fair had "started a man upward, that but for the education and stimulus thus received, would have fooled all his life away. . . ."[45]

Modernization also transformed the traditional rituals. With precut, processed, and packaged meats available to southern farmers, the hog killing ritual slowly gave way to livestock shows and contests. Extension agents developed complicated scoring systems and categories for judging livestock. Judges examined a swine's color, face, snout, eyes, ears, jowls, neck, hair, skin, shoulder, back, side, flank, loin, ham, tail, legs, symmetry, condition, and style. A hog received five points for an "attractive and spirited" style, which indicated "thoroughbreeding and constitutional vigor." Judges deducted five to ten points for a "cross, restless, and quarrelsome" disposition.[46] One of the most popular and enduring contests at the fair remains the hog calling contest. Through the South the near-symphonic variations on a theme of "sooooooooo-weeeeeeeeeeeeee-piiiiiiiiiiiiiiiiiiiiiiiiiiiiiiig" echo as a tribute to the region's best friend.

The hog as a symbol of southern culture persists most noticeably in the region's continued obsession with pork consumption. As John Egerton notes, the hog has endured as a "beloved symbol of gastronomic excellence" in the region.[47] Historian Sam Hilliard has emphasized that the development and perpetuation of the southern reliance on pork had to do with the South's isolation from the "cultural shock" experienced in the North: industrialization, urbanization, and immigration. With the absence of these outside forces for most of the nineteenth century, traditional southern foods "survived the settlement years, a civil war, and more than a century of time to become a frontier 'relic' in the midst of twentieth-century American life."[48]

During the twentieth century the South began to "catch up" with the North and experience industrial and urban changes. Nevertheless, southerners continued to favor hog meat. Barbecuing a pork shoulder and ribs became the preferred method of cooking throughout the region. No one seems to know the origins of the word barbecue and its variant spellings: barbecue, bar-b-q, bbq, bar-b-que, and bar-b-cue. *Tar Heel* magazine has suggested the word developed out of a nineteenth-century advertisement for a combination whiskey bar, beer parlor, pool hall, and cafe that specialized in roast pork. The owner could not paint a sign with such verbosity on his storefront, so he simply used an abbreviation: "Bar-Beer-Cue-Pig!"[49]

In the early 1900s small restaurants gained popularity in the South, and barbecue made the transition from a special event meal to a widespread cultural phenomenon. The advent of hamburger buns and sliced white bread further spread the popularity of barbecue, and soon restaurants served sliced, chopped, or pulled shoulder meat and ribs on street corners from North Carolina to the Delta.[50]

Barbecue restaurant owner Sy Erskine envisions preparing barbecue as a sacred experience. "It's the mystic communion among fire, smoke, and meat in the total absence of water," he says. Erskine demonstrates his reverence by describing the succulent nature of slowly cooked pork over select hickory at a low temperature: the process seals the flavor and natural juices of the lean pork shoulder or ribs, resulting in a "tender, delicious, moist meat that almost melts in your mouth."[51]

Historian John Egerton has emphasized that the South's great barbecue tradition remains a "cultural gift" from black men like Erskine and other noteworthy pit men. Historically, blacks manned the barbecue pits, tended the fire, cooked the meat, and made the sauce for political events and other special occasions. Over the years black cooks have mastered the "ancient art," altered it to "their time and place in southern history," and passed the "wisdom on to others, black and white."[52] Erskine has traveled all over the world but hasn't found barbecue cooked like it's cooked in the South. "Southerners have been known to be slow traditionally in doing certain things," says Erskine. "It transfers right on to the cooking of the food. They sit down and take their time and let that meat cook instead of rushing things on and off the fire. It is a tradition strictly of the South."[53]

Good barbecue in the south knows no racial, social, or economic boundaries. "Barbecue is the dish which binds together the taste of both the people of the big house and the poorest occupants of the back end of the broken-down barn," wrote journalist Jonathan Daniels in the 1940s. Even at the height of Jim Crow traditions in the region, whites often frequented black establishments for "stealthy excursions for take out orders." Big John Bishop has operated the Dreamland Drive-Inn on the "black side" of Tuscaloosa, Alabama, since 1958. Bishop just "loves to sell meat," and folks travel from all over central Alabama to sample his ribs. "On busy weekends I get calluses from forking up so many ribs off the pit," he boasts. Menu choices are limited at Dreamland: patrons can order lots of ribs with white bread or a few ribs with white bread. Bishop says he has no secret sauce or historical pit tradition to pass down to the next generation. "I just cook 'em," he groans with a tight-lipped bite on his pipe. "I cook 'em."[54]

Today, many southerners recognize a great barbecue restaurant by the diversity of cars (pickups and Cadillacs) parked out front. As journalist W. J. Cash recognized, there are "many Souths" and "enormous diversity" within the borders of the region.[55] This holds true to the variety of southern pork barbecue served and the types of establishments serving the smoked meat. From North Carolina to the Delta, southerners serve up pork barbecue in an assortment of different ways: vinegar-, tomato-, mustard-, or mayonnaise-based sauces or no sauce; with white bread or on hamburger buns; cole slaw on top or on the side; and numerous choices of side items: beans, stew, fries, onion rings, corn, etc. The variations remain "closely tied to place" and an "emblem of home" for the southern barbecue enthusiast.[56]

Three distinct types of barbecue restaurants serve the most southern food on earth and help maintain this regional tradition: the black-owned and operated establishment (like Sy Erskine's and John Bishop's), the upscale, urban white establishments, and the lower-class white "joints."[57]

Charlie Vergos's Rendezvous located in downtown Memphis is a prominent example of the urban white establishment. Vergos, a Greek immigrant, spares the sauce while smoking the meat and serves customers ribs "rubbed" with a special blend of dry herbs and spices. In contrast, Van Sykes of Bessemer, Alabama, is a southern boy who has carried on the Sykes family tradition of smoking meat dripping with a twangy sauce. The noted "prince of pork," Sykes has dubbed his restaurant the "pork palace" and built a shrine to the swine on the roof of the building. The huge pig serves as a beacon for pork lovers in the area. A few years ago Sykes held a "name the pig" contest, and the winner received a color television. Most barbecue patrons at Bob Sykes think the pig's name is Maxine. "That's really my mother's name," says Sykes. "The pig is named Bubba. That's a good southern name."[58]

Of course, most folks named Bubba would probably visit one of the small white barbecue "joints." Simply honky-tonks with a menu, joints have a standard code of decoration: low ceilings, booths of unpadded plywood, neon signs, screen doors, hardwood floors, and a juke box. Oakland Barbecue, adjacent to Oakland Cemetery in Birmingham, Alabama, endures as a prime example. The owners have placed the notice: "We reserve the right to serve refuse to anyone" prominently over the barbecue pit to keep visitors humble. The place gets downright mean and ugly on Friday and Saturday nights. Crusty, yellow-stained one dollar bills litter the black enamel ceiling, as do the remains of several others, yanked down by some beer-guzzling patron as he stood on top of one of the tables and demonstrated to Hank Williams Jr. that all of his rowdy friends had not quite settled down. Patrons can certainly indulge in their cultural heritage at Oakland Barbecue while chasing a "neon rainbow" and living Alan Jackson's "Honky-Tonk Dream."[59]

Whether southerners patronize one of these unique places or any of the other hundreds of restaurants scattered throughout the South, barbecue remains a symbol of the region's obsession with hogs. Southerners, however, continue to consume just about all parts of the pig but the squeal. A well stocked Piggly Wiggly still carries Primrose Pickled Pigs' Feet, Golden Flake Pork Rinds, chitterlings, hocks, tongues, and tails (usually resting on the aisle with spam or spiced ham, potted meat, and vienna sausages). Pigs-in-a-blanket (sausage wrapped in a biscuit) remains a special treat for many folks in the region.

Chitterlings, or chitlins, also have a consumption cult of their own in many areas of the South. In the early twentieth century "The Royal Order of Chitlin Eaters" in Nashville had a popular following among a group of Methodist preachers and one intestine-loving Baptist minister "thrown in for good measure." Southerners threw chitlin parties throughout the region, and one participant described the affair as a "chawin' symphony." "If you find a tough one or another that is slick," he wrote, "swallow it whole. If you encounter anything else, swallow that, too. The real great pleasure is in getting these things down. . . ." In Salley, South Carolina, the Chitlin' Strut Festival is held each November in the cool autumn air to celebrate the often despised hog intestines. "Lord," said one chitlin cooker, "we'd never cook them things here in the summertime. That smell would kill every green thing growing." As many as twenty thousand people have gathered to eat five tons of chitlins, crown Miss Chitlin' Strut, and dance a twisting jig in tribute to the "way chitlins make you feel."[60]

Most southerners continue to have a variety of zealous feelings about hogs. Civil rights activist Fannie Lou Hamer used the swine in the war on poverty and the quest for racial equality in the region. Hamer raised a congregation of "Freedom Hogs" at the Freedom Farms Cooperative in Sunflower County, Mississippi, and opened a "pig bank" for needy families. The needy family received one female pig. Once the pig had a litter, the impoverished family gave two pigs back to the bank. Her "idea" had been to feed poor people and "make life better for ourselves and for the whites too." The pigs helped "us toward real freedom," she once said, whether they "knew it or not."[61]

Many of the dwindling number of rural, staunchly individual hog farmers in the South have rediscovered feelings of "joy, tranquility, and peace" in raising hogs. "You have to love to do it," says pig rancher Paul Williams of Tuscaloosa County, Alabama. "There's a lot of pride in it." Having your own pig farm enables true pork lovers to "strive for the best" in raising their meat. Williams speaks highly of the hog: "He's a rather smart animal," he said. "He requires a bit of attention, but there is joy in giving him the attention. What I like the most about them is their temperament. They seem to appreciate what you do for them, and they show it in their kind ways. They become rather gentle and real pets."

Williams and other hog raisers enjoy providing special names for their up-and-grunting friends. For the males most farmers prefer names that describe the boar's "enormous testicles": Golden Stretch, Tarzan, Bonded Intruder, Score Again, Go-Boy, Sir Prize, Sir Snort, Hams-A-Poppin', Kem-O-Sabe, and Mr. Standout. Williams named one of his favorite hogs, a big red Duroc, Bubba in honor of the burly men who drive mud-stained pickup trucks accompanied by friends named Earl and Junior. Bubba's "just something to see," Williams says. "He grew to be a pretty big pig— 750 pounds." Of course Williams usually has no regrets taking one of his porker friends down to the slaughter house. "It's not a problem unless he is one of your special pets," he says. "You become attached to some of them because of the gentleness, the closeness, and the time you spend with them."[62]

Most of the hogs raised in the South these days are mere oinks in an industrial process. A certain agricultural-industrial contrast exists between the rural yeoman farmer's delight in nurturing hogs and the agribusiness pig worker's disgust at raising the "slimy, stinking, squealing sons of bitches." Former pig worker Sheldon C. Giles says, "You just get tired of that shrill squeal, night and day. Constantly. Never ending. Sometimes it's real low and occasional. Sometimes it's nonstop with every one on the place squealing. That I hated."[63]

Giles, somewhat begrudgingly, served as a $3.35 an hour cog in a well-oiled, assembly-line system of breeding, raising, and selling hogs. A pregnant sow "drops out" a few piglets in the farrowing house, and after a few weeks the youngsters are moved to the "scientific" nursery where all they do is "eat and grow." When they grow even bigger, the pig workers take them to the finishing buildings for more gastronomic enlargement before they are shipped off to the slaughter house. A few "lucky" hogs might be taken to the breeding barn to "make more pigs" and start the process all over again.[64]

The endurance and evolution of the swine in the South demonstrate the interaction between the region's economic and cultural heritage. The development of the whole idea of the South as a separate and peculiar economic and cultural region has seemingly gone hand-and-hoof with the hog. Evolving from an antebellum economic necessity, dietary mainstay, and component in agrarian cultural rituals to a modern symbol, the hog has demonstrated remarkable adaptability. Throughout much of the nineteenth century, observers considered the hog a mark of southern backwardness. Nowadays most southerners look to the hog as a symbol of regional pride. The "noble" pig has been the "sustainer of the South" through "grief and glory" and will endure as a symbol of the region as long as there remains a distinctive South filled with hungry and loyal southerners.

NOTES

The author would like to thank two Pickens County, Alabama, pork lovers for their inspiration in this project: Virginia Gertrude Vaughn Driver (102 years old) and Lillian Etta Driver Bass (85 years old). Sincere appreciation must go to Dr. James C. Cobb for his guidance in this project and to the editorial comments of Jennifer Bass, J. Clint Clifft, Andrew Moore, and Dan Pierce.

1. Roger Miller, "Hand for the Hog," from *Big River* (Tree Publishing Company Inc., 1988).

2. Ibid.

3. Joe Gray Taylor, *Eating, Drinking, and Visiting in the South: An Informal History* (Louisiana State University Press, 1982), 22.

4. *Western Star*, 26 February 1992. Interview with Sy Erskine, Hueytown, Alabama, 20 February 1992.

5. Forrest McDonald and Grady McWhiney, "The Antebellum Southern Herdsman: A Reinterpretation" in *Journal of Southern History* XLI (May 1975) 2:153.

6. Daniel Hundley, *Social Relations in Our Southern States* (Louisiana State University Press, 1979), 254, 262.

7. William Hedgepeth, *The Hog Book* (Doubleday, 1978), 22–23.

8. Ibid.

9. Miller, "Hand for the Hog"; Hedgepeth, *Hog Book*, 42.

10. Ibid., 43, 22.

11. Sam Hilliard, *Hog Meat and Hoe Cake* (Southern Illinois University Press, 1972), 92; McDonald and McWhiney, "Antebellum Southern Herdsman," 147.

12. Edmund Cody Burnett, "Hog Raising and Hog Driving in the Region of the French Broad River," in *Agricultural History* 20 (April 1946): 88; McDonald and McWhiney, "Antebellum Southern Herdsman," 147.

13. Hilliard, *Hog Meat*, 196; Frank Lawrence Owsley, *Plain Folk of the Old South* (Louisiana State University Press, 1949), 37.

14. Burnett, "Hog Raising and Hog Driving," 86–89.

15. Ibid., 88, 100; McDonald and McWhiney, "Antebellum Southern Herdsman," 162.

16. William Lynwood Montell, *Don't Go Up Kettle Creek: Verbal Legacy of the Upper Cumberland* (University of Tennessee Press, 1983), 42–43.

17. Edmund Cody Burnett, "The Hog Drivers' Play-Song and Some of Its Relatives," in *Agriculture History* 23 (July 1949): 163.

18. *Western Star*, 26 February 1992; interview with Van Sykes, Bessemer, Alabama, 19 February 1992.

19. Harry Crews, *A Childhood: The Biography of a Place* (Harper & Row, 1978), 109–10; Burnett, "Hog Raising and Hog Driving," 96.

20. Ted Ownby, *Subduing Satan: Religion, Recreation, and Manhood in the Rural South, 1865–1920* (University of North Carolina Press, 1990), 90–91.

21. Ibid., 93.

22. Ibid.

23. Taylor, *Eating, Drinking, and Visiting*, 23.

24. Hilliard, *Hog Meat*, 41.

25. Ibid., 42.

26. Jonathan Daniels, *Tar Heels: A Portrait of North Carolina* (Dodd, Mead & Company, 1941), 257–58; Hedgepeth, *Hog Book*, 42.

27. Owsley, *Plain Folk*, 41.

28. John Egerton, *Southern Food: At Home, on the Road, in History* (Knopf, 1987), 155.

29. Hilliard, *Hog Meat*, 44.

30. Taylor, *Eating, Drinking, and Visiting*, 22.

31. McDonald and McWhiney, "Antebellum Southern Herdsman," 163.

32. J. Crawford King Jr., "The Closing of the Southern Range," in *Journal of Southern History* XLVIII (February 1982): 54, 68.

33. Forrest McDonald and Grady McWhiney, "The South from Self Sufficiency to Peonage: An Interpretation," in *American Historical Review* 85 (December 1980): 1116.

34. Ownby, *Subduing Satan*, 167–69.

35. Egerton, *Southern Food*, 216–17; Burnett, "Hog Raising and Hog Driving," 95.

36. Taylor, *Eating, Drinking, and Visiting*, 84.

37. Henry Green quoted in B. A. Botkin, ed., *A Treasury of Southern Folklore* (Crown Publishers, 1949), 551.

38. King, "Closing of the Range," 56–57.

39. McWhiney and McDonald, "The South from Self-Sufficiency to Peonage," 1116; Egerton, *Southern Food*, 216.

40. Mike Freeman, "Clarence Saunders: The Piggly Wiggly Man," in *Tennessee Historical Quarterly* (Spring 1992): 163.

41. Ibid.

42. Ownby, *Subduing Satan*, 182.

43. Ibid., 183.

44. Ibid., 186–88.

45. S. M. Shepard, *The Hog in America: Past and Present* (Indianapolis, Indiana: Swine Breeders Journal, 1886), 120.

46. Ibid., 123–31.

47. Egerton, *Southern Food*, 251.

48. Hilliard, *Hog Meat*, 68–69.

49. *Tar Heel* magazine quoted in Phillip Stephen Schulz, *Cooking With Fire and Smoke* (Simon and Schuster, 1986), 20.

50. Egerton, *Southern Food*, 150.

51. *Western Star*, 26 February 1992; Erskine interview.

52. Egerton, *Southern Food*, 253.

53. *Western Star*, 26 February 1992; Erskine interview.

54. Daniels, *Tar Heels*, 257–58; Egerton, *Southern Food*, 26, 152; *Western Star*, 4 March 1992; interview with Big John Bishop, Tuscaloosa, Alabama, 1 March 1992.

55. W. J. Cash, *The Mind of the South* (Vintage Books, 1941), viii.

56. Charles Reagan Wilson and William Ferris, *Encyclopedia of Southern Culture II* (Anchor Books, 1989), 474.

57. Some southern swine enthusiasts have even exported hickory smoked pork barbecue to such strange and foreign territories as Cambridge, Massachusetts. Southerner Chris Schlesinger opened Jake & Earl's Dixie B-B-Q with plenty of Yankee touches, including a wine cellar. And as one journalist commented, if the news of a barbecue restaurant with a wine cellar ever receives notice below the old Mason-Dixon, the South will certainly "have cause to rise again."

58. *Western Star*, 26 February 1992; Van Sykes, interview.

59. *Western Star*, 29 January 1992.

60. Wendell Stephens, "Hog-Killing Time In Middle Tennessee," in *Tennessee Folklore Society Bulletin* XXXVI (September 1970): 91; Alvin F. Harlow quoted in Botkin, *A Treasury of Southern Folklore*, 550; William Price Fox, *Chitlin Strut and Other Madrigals* quoted in Egerton, *Southern Food*, 166; Wilson and Ferris, *Encyclopedia of Southern Culture*, volume II, 479–80.

61. Hedgepeth, *Hog Book*, 54.

62. Ibid.; *Western Star*, 26 February 1992; interview with Paul Williams, 11 February 1992.

63. Interview with Sheldon C. Giles, 11 March 1994.

64. Ibid.

Southern Traditions

What interests, guides, and defines southerners is a diverse collection we can only begin to sample here.

Equine Relics of the Civil War

Drew Gilpin Faust

Abused and destroyed: a post-Vietnam sensibility projected onto a Civil War mount. The War Horse, designed by Tessa Pullan and donated to the Virginia Historical Society by Paul Mellon, courtesy of Lee Brauer Photography.

In the first battle of the Civil War, the only casualty was a horse. When the smoke lifted after the bombardment of Fort Sumter in April 1861, southerners hailed the "bloodless victory" that had yielded the federal fort into Confederate hands without the loss of a single human life. The death of an army horse in the shelling all but escaped notice. In the years of conflict that followed, horses played a critical military role, as mounts for officers and cavalry, as transport for artillery, and as all-purpose conveyance for the wide variety of army movements. Present in every Civil War camp and on every battlefield, horses suffered and died in numbers that rivaled even the Civil War's high rate of human devastation. An estimated 1,500,000 horses and mules were wounded or killed, or died of disease in the war, as compared with 970,000 military casualties.[1]

Civil War soldiers both noticed and ignored this slaughter, just as we ourselves have at once remembered and forgotten the Civil War horse. In the aftermath of the war's great battles, care of the human wounded and dead took obvious priority. As Confederate general Richard Ewell once explained to a distraught civilian horrified by a horse rotting near her house, he "had more important business on hand just then than burying dead horses." Yet soldiers' commentary on battlefield scenes almost inevitably included remarks about the dead animals strewn across the ground. After Shiloh, as one soldier observed, it was possible to walk from one side of the field to the other stepping only on horse carcasses.[2]

Disposal of horses' remains was of course a real problem. After the battle of Gettysburg, for example, as many as five million pounds of horse flesh had to be removed from the field. But dead horses represented more than simply a logistical challenge. Soldiers sentimentalized horses, often projecting onto them feelings they suppressed about the human cost of war. One Union soldier remarked after the 2 July 1863 fighting at Peach Orchard, "The poor horses had fared badly and as we passed, scores of these ungazetted heroes stood upon their maimed limbs regarding us with a silent look of reproach that was almost human in expression." A Georgia officer regarded the death of his beloved mount Barnaby at Chickamauga as a symbol of the injustice and irrationality of war: "He had done no one any harm, but his faithful work for man was now to be rewarded with a grape shot from a cannon's cruel mouth. His fate breathes a reproach and cries out against this inhuman war." As a Union chaplain observed about a horse brutally killed at Chancellorsville, "I hardly remember a sight that touched my heart so keenly during the entire battle. The innocent animal had no part in the fight, but he was a silent victim."[3]

The horse's innocence has remained an important part of twentieth-century memory. But the Civil War horse lives on as more than a victim. The best known of the animals have been glorified as soldiers and campaigners, themselves honored as veterans of the war. Americans of the second half of the twentieth century have in a quite literal sense been able to come closer to the Civil War horse than to any of the conflict's other veterans. Dead soldiers, Union or Confederate, privates or generals, heroes or bounty jumpers, were interred or entombed, hidden from sight, memorialized in statues or in photographs that for all their realism are clearly just representations on paper or in stone. But real Civil War horses —or at least parts of them—have actually been preserved. Stonewall Jackson's Little Sorrel and Philip Sheridan's mount—variously known as Rienzi or Winchester, after his most famous battle—had their carcasses stuffed. Old Baldy, the horse of General Meade, victorious Union commander at Gettysburg, was buried for several days before two of Meade's former soldiers were inspired to preserve him, so only his head and shoulders were successfully disinterred and sent to the taxidermist. Robert E. Lee's fabled Traveller died in 1871, the year after his master, and his articulated skeleton ended up on display at the renamed Washington and Lee University—only a few hundred yards from the Virginia Military Institute (VMI) home of the more corpulent Little Sorrel. Legend has it that disrespectful student pranks led to the decision in the 1970s to consign Traveller to the safety of the ground, where he now rests beneath a memorial slab regularly adorned with the honorific apple or carrot.

To many late-nineteenth-century Americans, Traveller, Little Sorrel, Winchester, and Old Baldy were relics, objects venerated by the faithful because of their association with a sacred person. As vestigial remnants of the great men they had carried, they were less horses in their own right than extensions of their masters. All four not only survived battle, but lived well into the postwar era. Traveller was the first to go in 1871, but by the time Winchester died in 1878, Old Baldy in 1882, and Little Sorrel in 1886, Reconstruction's bitter conflicts had been suppressed, and many Americans North and South had begun to sentimentalize the war and its remembrance. For more than a century, the horses have served as both repository for and representation of memory of the war that defined us as a nation.

Old Baldy—or his mounted head and neck—is today the most popular exhibit at the Civil War Museum and Library in Philadelphia. The horse occupies a glass case, the place of honor, in a room named for his master General George Meade. A discussion group that meets at the museum on the second Thursday of each month marks its esteem by calling itself the Old Baldy Civil War Roundtable. Curator Steve Wright describes the affection museum volunteers feel for the horse. Many converse with Baldy, greeting him when they arrive and bidding farewell when they walk out the door. Wright explains that Old Baldy is the "closest thing" to a real veteran these Civil War enthusiasts will ever see, and he muses about the stories the horse would tell "if he could talk."[4]

Old Baldy could tell a lot. The horse was shot in the nose at First Bull Run, the leg at Second Bull Run, the neck at Antietam, the chest in his master's triumph at Gettysburg, the ribs a year later at Petersburg. Wounded fourteen times in all, Old Baldy was lucky to have a carcass left to be stuffed. A bright bay with a notoriously uncomfortable gait slightly slower than a trot, Old Baldy was nine years old when Meade purchased him in September 1861. Baldy carried the general through the most important battles of the Virginia campaign, but earned his retirement after being seriously wounded by a spent shell in the summer of 1864. Meade rejoined his mount in Philadelphia after the war and used him as a saddle horse for a number of years before turning him out to pasture in a rural area near the city. When Meade died in 1872, the twenty-year-old horse followed his master's body in the funeral procession to Mount Laurel Cemetery. But Old Baldy marched once again, joining the parade of the Grand Army of the Republic (GAR) that honored General Grant on a visit to Philadelphia in 1879. Hailed by the crowds lining the city's streets, Baldy had taken his place in the pantheon of war heroes.

By December 1882 Old Baldy had grown so feeble that his caretaker decided to have him put to sleep. General George Gordon Meade Post #1 of the Grand Army of the Republic, part of an emerging network of veterans' organizations devoted to the war's memory, learned of Old Baldy's death two days later, and they quickly agreed that some relic of the valiant horse had to be preserved. Two members of the post secured permission from Old Baldy's last owner to exhume the horse and sever his head. "Armed and equipped" for this last campaign, as they described it, "with a knife, hatchet and overalls," they performed the task on Christmas Day itself. No doubt they were thankful Old Baldy had not died in the summertime.[5]

By February 1883 the taxidermist had finished his work, and a formal presentation and celebration took place at Post Headquarters, where Old Baldy was hung behind the Post Commander's Chair. Oral tradition holds that Philadelphia's GAR Post #2, composed of less socially prominent veterans, quickly procured a stuffed mule head to keep pace. Whatever its origins, the mule proved no rival to the veteran war horse and now hangs largely ignored, relegated to the Civil War Museum's attic. On the main floor, Baldy is enshrined as the premier attraction, almost as good as new after his 1975 restoration by a local taxidermist—Baldy's "hair stylist," as Steve Wright describes him. Phil Ewaka of West Chester, Pennsylvania, says he was honored to be chosen to refurbish Old Baldy, a job quite unlike his usual practice preserving game birds and fish for proud outdoorsmen. The work on Baldy involved mending a split in the neck and a number of skin cracks around the nose, as well as applying a considerable amount of wax and glue to restore the ears. Ewaka saw clear evidence of Baldy's many wounds, places on his nose and neck marked with scars of darkened hair. Ewaka judges that in the carefully controlled climate in which Baldy now lives, his "tune-up" might last as long as thirty years.[6]

WINCHESTER'S LONG RIDE

Union General Philip Sheridan's horse Winchester has had his own share of refurbishments that make him still a popular sight in the Armed Forces Hall at the National Museum of American History of the Smithsonian Institution. Sheridan was himself responsible for the horse's preservation when Winchester died in 1878. After sending the carcass for treatment to Ward's Taxidermy in Rochester, New York, Sheridan donated the animal to the Military Service Institution, an officers' organization founded just about the time of Winchester's death to promote military professionalism, "patriotism . . . and historical research." Winchester represented an early and valuable accession to the institution's new museum on Governor's Island in New York. The horse served as one of a collection of "relics," along with a variety of military portraits (including one of Sheridan), Revolutionary War bullets and buttons, Indian weapons, Civil War battle flags, a piece of the ironclad *Merrimack*, and a section of fence post from the notorious prison camp at Andersonville.[7]

Sheridan attached a letter to his donation, detailing the horse's biography. Born in 1859, the black gelding was presented to Sheridan by his troops at Rienzi, Mississippi, in 1862 and was called by the name of that place until the general's momentous victory at Cedar Creek, near Winchester, Virginia, in the fall of 1864. A popular poem, "Sheridan's Ride," celebrated the horse's crucial role in delivering the general to the battle in the nick of time, and Rienzi was subsequently renamed in honor of the triumph. The tiny general, who was five-feet five-inches tall, and the enormous horse, five-feet eight-inches at the shoulder, made a striking duo, and "Sheridan's Ride" turned the "steed that saved the day" into a factor in Lincoln's reelection. Sheridan reported that he rode Winchester in "nearly every engagement in which I took part" and enumerated forty-seven such events, culminating with Lee's surrender at Appomattox.[8]

By the turn of the century, the Military Services Institution and its museum had fallen on hard times. With the outbreak of World War I, Winchester and the other exhibits were removed to storage in a clock tower on Governor's Island to make way for pressing military needs. At the close of the war, the institution began negotiations with the Smithsonian about transferring the animal to its care. Nearly sixty years after the Civil War's end, Winchester became embroiled in another conflict. Fading memories had created an identity crisis for the Union relic. The horse described in the popular poem as black now seemed to be only a dull bay. Had he faded, or had the poet of the 1860s engaged in a little fantasy to make him appear more dashing? And exactly how many engagements had he really participated in? Forty-four? Forty-seven as Sheridan had said? Or as many as fifty? And what was his name anyway?

Invoking standards of scientific accuracy, officials at the Smithsonian proposed exhibiting the horse under the name Rienzi, arguing that their research indicated that Winchester was a "name which seems to have been borne by the stuffed animal but not by the living animal." The secretary of the Military Service Institution was outraged, replying, "That is just the point. He is stuffed and not living. . . . He was called Rienzi for about 5 years and he has been called Winchester for 58 years, during 14 of which years he was alive." A compromise offered by the Smithsonian to label him simply as "Sheridan's horse" elicited an even more scornful response from the prospective donors. In a society so recently engaged in a struggle to identify and name all the Civil War's human dead, the proposed removal of a name from an equine veteran seemed especially unfeeling. The debate continued with efforts to tap Mrs. Sheridan's memories of the past as well as those of individual soldiers in Sheridan's command. Although these investigations suggested that Rienzi was indeed the name used throughout the war, the fact that Sheridan called the horse Winchester at the time of his original donation—and that the donors were so insistent upon that name—ultimately proved decisive. The horse would be labeled Winchester.[9]

Ten years after this original controversy had subsided and the horse had been installed in the museum's galleries for a decade, a Smithsonian curator was called upon to assure a troubled visitor that Winchester was indeed accurately identified. The official conceded, however, that perhaps the name Rienzi should be added to his label. The debate over the name of Sheridan's horse had elicited an important inquiry into the reliability of memory, as well as the potential for conflict between the power of myth and the lure of science in historical interpretation. In a 1922 letter, a member of the museum staff reflected on the lessons of the Winchester controversy about the changing nature of historical understanding. "History is a subject," he wrote, "which is constantly receiving new treatment in the light of information recently acquired. It is almost impossible to regard any historical label as a final and completed product, because the discovery of new information regarding historical objects necessitates changes in the original form of such labels." Winchester/Rienzi might have been dead for decades, but his name, his label, and his historical meaning remained subject to change. Today he is marked with both names; " 'Winchester' or 'Rienzi' " looks out across three cannons and a figure (not stuffed) of a soldier in Yankee uniform toward a display of the "Drive to Victory" in which he so long ago participated.[10]

The controversy over the horse's identity only intensified the attention directed at his departure from New York for Washington. All but forgotten in the clock tower during the first World War, Winchester became a hero once again. Members of the GAR organized a ceremony of farewell at Governor's Island in June of 1922 and printed formal invitations outlining a program that included music, a recitation of "Sheridan's Ride," and, as culmination, a "Cheering of Winchester" by the assembled crowd. A number of veterans of the Civil War Battle of Cedar Creek attended the New York festivities, and others greeted the horse upon his arrival in the capital after what the *Washington Star* described as his "last journey." A newspaper photograph shows Winchester upon his arrival flanked by, on one side, two elderly Civil War veterans and, on the other, a youthful World War I soldier in full uniform standing at attention. In the background stands a caisson bearing artillery of this modern twentieth-century war.[11]

In his new home, Winchester confronted new dangers, described by the Smithsonian curator as "the ravages of souvenir hunters" eager for a bit of his mane or tail. A glass case seemed the best solution, though at first the tilt that had appeared in Winchester's stance worried the curators lest the horse tip over and shatter it. Today, Winchester stands behind glass, his posture adjusted and erect, protected from his enthusiastic visitors.[12]

TRAVELLER'S REST

The only way to protect Robert E. Lee's Traveller proved to be finally to bury him. But his route to his final resting place just outside the chapel at Washington and Lee University turned out to be anything but direct. From the time of Lee's purchase of Traveller in 1862 the two were nearly inseparable, and the iron-gray—Lee called him Confederate gray—horse became with his master an enduring symbol of the southern cause. Traveller was born in 1857 in what is now West Virginia and attracted Lee's attention early in the war. Lee persisted in efforts to acquire the horse, at last persuading his owner to sell the mount named "Jeff Davis" for $200 in 1862. What Lee described as a "perfect understanding" evolved between Traveller and his new master, and the general confessed to missing the horse "dreadfully" whenever they were parted. Lee believed Traveller's sterling qualities worthy inspiration for artist or poet. Only a person of elevated sensibilities could fully render "his fine proportions and muscular figure," as well as his moral qualities: "his endurance of toil, hunger, thirst, heat & cold . . . his sagacity and affection & his invariable response to every wish of his rider." He sounded not unlike the ideal slave.[13]

Traveller carried Lee through the rest of the war and retired to Washington College in Lexington when Lee became its president in 1865. The two rode together across the Virginia countryside nearly every afternoon until Lee's death. Draped in crepe, Traveller followed the general's body when it was transported to lie in state in the college chapel.

The horse passed the remaining eight months of his life as a "privileged character" with freedom of the Lexington campus. But in June 1871 a small nail in his hoof led to tetanus and an agonizing death. Eight people attended Traveller's burial in a ravine behind the university. By

1875 the horse had been disinterred, though tradition varies in explaining how this happened. One story maintains that vandals tried to seize the bones for exhibition at the Philadelphia Centennial of 1876. In all probability, however, Henry Ward of Rochester—the same Ward who later stuffed Winchester—was involved in procuring the horse's remains in anticipation of exhibiting them in a museum of natural history to be established at the university.

But not until 1907 did Traveller's bones finally return from Rochester and take their place on display as an articulated skeleton in Washington and Lee's Brooks Museum. From the outset, students showed little reverence for this scientific exhibit, transforming the horse into a kind of totem on which they inscribed their initials in order to ensure good luck on their examinations. Pranks and hoaxes bedeviled the skeleton, even after a glass case was installed to protect its physical integrity. A rumor that the bones were not really Traveller's led a student publication to produce an extended satire reporting that the skeleton actually belonged to one of Ulysses Grant's mounts—a profane rather than a sacred relic. And when the bones of a miniature horse were placed on display near Traveller's skeleton, students insisted to visitors that this was Traveller as a foal.

By the late 1920s, any scientific interest Traveller might hold had clearly been eclipsed by his historical significance, and his skeleton was moved from the natural history museum to the chapel. By the early 1960s, the deterioration of this mausoleum required that it be closed for renovation and Traveller moved to storage. But the deterioration of the horse, unlike the chapel, could not be reversed, and Traveller's weary graffitied bones were at last reinterred. Watch fobs and brooches decorated with wisps of Traveller's tail suggest the indignities to which his celebrity had subjected him in life; the inscriptions on his skeleton extended this treatment after death. In a grave recently relandscaped by the United Daughters of the Confederacy, Traveller's remains today receive only reverent affection—and a steady ration of carrots and apples.

FROM "SORRY SIGHT" TO HERO

Stonewall Jackson's Little Sorrel endured the same costs of celebrity during his lifetime. After the battle of Cedar Mountain in 1862, a Union prisoner waiting to be interrogated stood beside Sorrel and stealthily plucked hair from the animal's tail. When Jackson asked what he was doing, the soldier replied, "Ah, General, each one of these hairs is worth a dollar in New York."[14]

Little Sorrel was himself Yankee in origin, for Jackson purchased him after he was seized from a federal supply train at Harpers Ferry in 1861. The eleven-year-old gelding—smaller than fifteen hands high—became Jackson's preferred mount and was carrying the general when he was fatally wounded at Chancellorsville in 1863. Originally named Fancy, the horse was in fact anything but, and Jackson's troops, who found him "scrubby," began to call him Little Sorrel to distinguish him from a larger horse captured at the same time. Jackson's wife Anna described him as "round and fat," but, however unprepossessing in general appearance, the horse had "intelligent and expressive" eyes and a wonderfully calm and comfortable gait that suited his master's awkwardness as an equestrian. It may have in fact been more the responsibility of Little Sorrel than of Jackson himself that the two stood so staunchly at First Bull Run— "like a stone wall." Little Sorrel apparently maintained his stamina and demonstrated his equanimity throughout the war by lying down like a dog whenever the army stopped to rest.[15]

Little Sorrel continued to attract attention because he did not, as one soldier put it, "look much like a charger," and because he and his master made such an "ordinary," even "sorry" sight. Neither Jackson nor his horse fit the conventional model of military prowess. The rider was a Presbyterian elder, not a scion of the southern chivalry; his mount an "ugly" gelding of uncertain origins, rather than a blooded stallion. Perhaps this made it possible for his devoted soldiers to love him all the more, but it also generated considerable commentary. One member of Jackson's staff even compared the general's horse to his slave: "The servant and 'Old Sorrel' being about the same color—each having the hue of gingerbread without any of its spiciness their respective characters were in a concatenation accordingly. For they were equally obedient, patient, easy-going and reliable; not given to devious courses nor designing tricks; more serviceable than showy and, altogether, as sober-sided a pair of subordinates as any Presbyterian elder with plain tastes and a practical turn, need desire to have about him."[16]

The only account of Little Sorrel losing his calm describes the moment of his master's mortal wound at Chancellorsville. In the terror and confusion after Jackson was shot, Little Sorrel ran off toward enemy lines and remained missing for several days. After Jackson's death, Sorrel accompanied the widowed Anna to her father's farm in North Carolina, where he served as a saddle and harness horse for the remainder of the war. In 1883, when Sorrel was over thirty, Anna Jackson decided she could no longer care for him and returned him to be reunited with his master at VMI where Stonewall Jackson was buried on the parade ground. But Little Sorrel was not yet ready to die. After a triumphant journey by train to Virginia, with crowds of veterans greeting him along the way, Little Sorrel took up his new life in Lexington, wandering about VMI's parade ground much as Traveller had roamed the adjacent campus of Washington and Lee.

Despite his advanced age, Little Sorrel was not to be permitted a life of leisure. In the emerging climate of Confederate nostalgia and commemoration, the horse provided a valuable connection to the Lost Cause. Sorrel began to make public appearances, riding by train up and down the Shenandoah Valley in order to embellish country fairs. Responding with animation to the strains of "Dixie" or the firing of guns, the horse demonstrated himself to be, according to one observer, "a glorious warrior, game to the end." His performances were "heart appealing in the extreme."[17]

The VMI Board of Visitors began to contemplate sending him to the 1885 New Orleans World's Fair in hopes of raising money for a Jackson memorial. Anna Jackson had ideas of her own, however, about how he might fit into the national mood of Confederate celebration. Insisting that she retained ownership of the horse, she began to make plans to exhibit him in New Orleans for different commemorative purposes. An undignified quarrel over who should pay Sorrel's transportation costs resulted in VMI's refusal to accept any further responsibility for care of the horse. After several months in New Orleans, Sorrel returned to Richmond, where he was stabled by the Robert E. Lee Camp for Confederate Veterans at their home for aged soldiers. He certainly qualified. Before long, the horse was too feeble to stand unaided, but the inventive veterans devised a hoist that could raise him to his feet to greet visitors. One day early in 1886 the contraption slipped and Little Sorrel seriously injured his back. When he died several weeks later, he had lived only three years less than Stonewall Jackson himself.

Well before his death, Little Sorrel had been examined and measured by a taxidermist. The systematic organization of Confederate memory had gained a momentum and a force it had lacked at the time of Traveller's death more than a decade earlier. Little Sorrel had become a southern symbol and a kind of media star even in his own lifetime, and appropriate preparations were made for him to continue in this role after his death. The taxidermist prepared a plaster-of-Paris model of the living horse over which his hide could eventually be stretched. The mounted animal was placed on display at the Richmond Soldiers' Home, while the taxidermist, as part of his fee, removed the bones to the Carnegie Museum in Pittsburgh.

By the 1940s Sorrel's hide and bones had returned to VMI, where the horse went on display in the institute's natural history museum, and the bones served instructional purposes in the biology department. By mid-century Little Sorrel had moved to the institute library, where even a diligent custodian's efforts to keep enough water nearby failed to provide adequate humidity. Fabled as the only man in history to water a dead horse, the caretaker could not prevent the appearance of an alarming tear in Little Sorrel's chest and the loss of considerable hair from the desiccated hide. When VMI began to design a new museum in the 1960s—not a fusty temple of natural history but a tribute to its own illustrious past— Little Sorrel seemed an obvious feature for the Stonewall Jackson display. But something had to be done about what one newspaper called the horse's "sorry state." A visit from the Smithsonian's large-mammal expert and three of his assistants restored the horse at a cost of nine hundred dollars. Since that time, Little Sorrel has served as the premier attraction in the institute's museum, a touchstone of verisimilitude and a central part of the story of VMI's role in America's military glory.[18]

Perhaps it was the ever-increasing popularity of the horse—and of his postcards, plush likenesses, and refrigerator magnets—that led VMI officials to decide in 1997 to make better and more respectful use of Little Sorrel's bones. Unlike the horse's hide, they no longer served any purpose —either scientific or commemorative—and had long since been sent by the biology department to the institute's museum for storage. After all, "how many things can you do with bones?" asks Keith Gibson, the museum's current director.[19]

Gibson, in fact, has managed to do quite a lot. On 20 July 1997, the Virginia Division of the United Daughters of the Confederacy (UDC) sponsored a public Ceremony of Interment for the cremated bones of Little Sorrel. On the parade ground at VMI on a stiflingly hot summer day, Confederate military reenactors, women in period dress, and a crowd of curious onlookers gathered for a solemn ceremony, though not all approached it with equal earnestness. A *Washington Post* reporter remarked that with Little Sorrel's interment only a few hundred yards from Traveller's last resting place, "in matters grave, Lexington no longer can be called a one horse town." Tony Horwitz, reporter for the *Wall Street Journal* and author of *Confederates in the Attic*, was perhaps more direct: "The world will little note nor long remember what was said here, but many will never forget the weirdness of what they did here this week." For many of the participants, however, this was a very serious business. Juanita Allen, head of the Virginia UDC, was the moving force behind the occasion. She had found it strange and "sad" that Little Sorrel had never been buried, and she had been galvanized to act by a visit to the horse's bones in their storage box in the museum. "I picked up his teeth and rubbed his nose bone. I was petting it and talking to him, telling him how sorry I was and how we'd take care of him."[20]

A procession of cavalry, a fife and drum corps, a color guard, an escort of honorary pall bearers, and a bevy of UDC ladies in hats and flowered dresses accompanied a VMI cadet carrying a walnut box with Little Sorrel's ashes to a spot just in front of Stonewall Jackson's imposing statue. A local Presbyterian minister invoked God's blessing on the occasion; distinguished Jackson biographer James I. Robertson Jr. offered an address on Little Sorrel's life and wished him well in the "boundless pastures of heaven," and a member of the U.S. Cavalry Association intoned a Prayer for Horses. Or at least a prayer for Confederate horses. This was no equal opportunity commemoration; Union steeds were pointedly excluded from the whole occasion. Horses were not to be remembered as innocent victims of man's violence and warlike propensities. Like the UDC members who planned it, the event was a decidedly partisan occasion. As one UDC speaker explained, the burial was intended to embody "our love and honor for our Confederacy and our great General Jackson."[21]

One observer, dressed in full nineteenth-century mourning garb, complete with hooped petticoats, gloves, fan, and veil, shielded herself from the sun with a twentieth-century black umbrella as she explained the meaning of the ceremony. It was rare, she noted, that a Confederate memorial service had an actual, authentic body to physically connect the past and the present. This sense of living tradition, she insisted, must be kept alive, for the Confederacy represented values—"family values, Christian values"—that are disappearing in modern society. Honoring Little Sorrel, she continued, was a way of affirming that past. A way, too, another female reenactor added, of making a statement against the transformation of values that would be represented in just a few short weeks by the admission of women to VMI to comply with the Supreme Court's decision. Little Sorrel's cremated bones were bearing a considerable burden of meaning. It might have been easier when all he had to carry was General Jackson.[22]

After a rousing rendition of "Dixie," a presentation of wreaths of laurel, apples, and carrots (including one from the Little Sorrel chapter of the Children of the Confederacy), and a volley of rifles that the re-enactors' experienced mounts hardly noticed, the formal ceremony came to an end with an invitation to the assembled crowd. In his remarks, Keith Gibson had reminded the gathering that the interment offered an opportunity not just to witness, but to participate in a moment of Civil War history. After the last words of the closing benediction, that opportunity for participation became real. United Daughters of the Confederacy from across the state had gathered soil from Jackson's birthplace and from the fourteen battlefields where he and Little Sorrel had ridden together. Members of the audience pushed forward to scatter handfuls of this hallowed dirt on the horse's walnut coffin, now lowered several feet beneath the surface of the parade ground in a still uncovered grave. A reception followed in the VMI Museum, enabling admirers to pay their respects to the stuffed version of the animal they had just interred. The wonders of taxidermy had made it possible to have your horse and bury him too.

THE LAST RIDE

Less than two months later and fewer than a hundred miles away, Virginia again honored the Civil War horse. But if the interment of Little Sorrel was intended to represent the horse as triumphant—and partisan—warrior, the ceremony in Richmond on 17 September 1997 embraced an alternative image of innocent victim. Politicians, Virginia horse breeders and trainers, historians, and interested citizens gathered in front of the imposing structure of the Virginia Historical Society to dedicate its first memorial statue: a commemoration of the Civil War horse. Paul Mellon, wealthy Virginia philanthropist and horseman, had donated a life-sized bronze statue in memory of "the one and one-half million horses and mules who were killed, wounded, or died from disease in the Civil War." Neither Union nor Confederate, the statue was commissioned in honor of all the animals slaughtered in military service. After an uproar the preceding spring over Governor George Allen's proclamation of April as Confederate Heritage and History Month, and after the many other battles Richmond had fought over its racial and especially its Confederate past, the publicly supported Virginia Historical Society was not about to risk accusations of Lost Cause partisanship. Only recently had controversy subsided over another statue, that of Richmond native Arthur Ashe, finally installed just blocks away among the Confederate heroes along Monument Avenue. Historical society and state officials—and perhaps even Paul Mellon himself—had no desire for the gift to open another round of conflict over the meaning of Virginia's past.

But the character of the statue itself—not just its nonpartisan identity —mitigated against such an outcome. Although Little Sorrel's interment was meant to be a kind of funeral, it smacked of celebration. In contrast, the dedication of the horse statue in Richmond underscored not the glory, but the tragedy of war. This horse is on his last legs. He cannot hold up his head or tail; his reins have fallen over his neck; his ribs protrude; "poverty lines" are visible in his quarters. A legendary Virginia equestrian, Ellie Wood Baxter of Charlottesville, her eye ever ready to evaluate horse-flesh, commented as she examined the statue after the ceremony that he was "way down in the pasterns," that even the shape of this bone between his foot and his ankle showed him on the edge of collapse. Sculptor Tessa Pullan of Rutland, England, explained that as she designed the statue, she shared her ideas and preliminary drawings with Paul Mellon. He kept urging her to make the horse look worse, more oppressed, more damaged. At last, lacking any model for such misery, she turned to the Royal Society for the Prevention of Cruelty to Animals for photographs of misused horses that she could use as a basis for her design.[23]

War has abused and destroyed, not glorified this horse. This is a dramatic departure from traditional commemorations of the Civil War. This is not a general's mount, but a nameless common soldier, who has done his duty and paid his price. Such sacrifices, not more conventional notions of heroism, are what many late-twentieth-century Americans are most comfortable remembering and honoring in war. This statue represents a post-Vietnam sensibility, projected onto a Civil War horse.

At night, lights cast an enormous shadow of the horse against the wall of the Historical Society, creating an image that is even more dramatic than that of the statue itself, an image that has captured the imagination of much of the city of Richmond. One community newspaper suggested that the horse was so striking that it should become the design for a new city seal (though dissident voices argued that the chalked outline of a homicide victim would be more appropriate given Richmond's high murder rate). The Richmond *Guide*, a publication distributed to tourists at hotels and motels, featured a photograph of the horse at night for the cover of its Fall 1998 edition.

On a morning soon after the dedication ceremony, a Virginia Historical Society guard was shocked to discover another use to which the new statue had been put. Reviewing routine security videotapes made the previous night of the exterior walls of the Society building, he was treated to a performance by a young woman in Godiva attire who had come to give the horse a late-night ride. Society officials quickly designed a new landscaping plan for the statue—a collection of fast-growing, prickly shrubs.

Horses—stuffed, cremated, cast in bronze—have provided twentieth-century Americans with a means of touching what they see as an authentic past. Horses seem timeless, familiar in a way many other historical artifacts do not. Compared with humans, or clothing, or buildings, or weapons, their appearance has changed very little in the past century and a half. Moreover, as animals lacking independent will or responsibility, they can serve as repositories for the changing ideas about the past we wish them to represent. At once victims and heroes, they enable us simultaneously to celebrate and to deplore war, thus capturing an ambivalence at the heart of American culture. We can use them—both the terrible suffering represented by the Richmond statue and the courage and nobility embodied in Traveller or Old Baldy—to remind ourselves of what Robert E. Lee so eloquently observed more than a century ago: "It is well that war is so terrible, else we should grow too fond of it." But perhaps most important, horses are tangible and in some cases even real. Old Baldy, Traveller, Little Sorrel, and Winchester were there, and by being with them, we feel in some sense we are there as well. The Civil War's equine relics are participatory monuments, carrying us beyond imagination into a history populated by the conflict's only remaining accessible veterans.

NOTES

I would like to thank the following individuals for help with this essay: Albert Beveridge III, Thomas Camden, Michael Cavanaugh, Tyson Gilpin, Ann Greene, Tony Horwitz, Jim Hutchins, Frances Pollard, Charles Rosenberg, Margaret Vining, and Steve Wright.

1. Thomas Smyth, *The Battle of Fort Sumter* (Columbia, SC: Southern Guardian Steam Power Press, 1861); Charles W. Ramsdell, "General Robert E. Lee's Horse Supply, 1862–1865," *American Historical Review* 35 (1930): 758–77.

2. Richard Ewell, quoted in Blake A. Magner, *Traveller & Company: The Horses of Gettysburg* (Farnsworth House, 1995), 37.

3. Francis Moran, quoted in Magner, *Traveller & Company*, 26; Benjamin Abbott to Green Haygood, 26 September 1863, Georgia Department of Archives and History, Atlanta; William Corby, *Memoirs of Chaplain Life* (Notre Dame, Indiana: Scholastic Press, 1894), 160.

4. Steve Wright, conversation with the author, November 1997, Civil War Library and Museum, Philadelphia.

5. W. B. Hervey and A. C. Johnston, manuscript, 1883, Old Baldy Papers, Civil War Library and Museum, Philadelphia. See also Michael Cavanaugh, "'Old Baldy': General George Gordon Meade's Veteran War Horse," *North-South Trader* (March–April 1982): 12–34.

6. Phil Ewaka, telephone conversation with the author, September 1998.

7. *Journal of the Military Service Institution of the United States* 1 (1880): 21, 22; 6 (1885): 98–99.

8. "Isolated Relics," ibid., 1 (1880): 77, 126; John Fleischman, "The Object at Hand," *Smithsonian* 27 (November 1996): 28–30.

9. William deC. Ravenel to Edmund Banks Smith, 23 August 1922, Edmund Banks Smith to William Ravenel, 25 August 1922, Winchester File, National Museum of American History (NMAH), Smithsonian Institution.

10. William Ravenel to Edmund Banks Smith, 16 October 1922, ibid.

11. "Winchester: Lieutenant General Sheridan's Battle Horse," printed program, 3 June 1922, Winchester File, NMAH; undated clipping [June 1922], *Washington Star*, ibid.; see also *New York Times*, 5 June 1922.

12. Theodore Belote to William Ravenel, 25 April 1930, Winchester File, NMAH.

13. W. Donald Rhinesmith, "'Traveller': Just the Horse for General Lee," *Virginia Cavalcade* (Summer 1983): 42; Robert E. Lee, dictated to Eleanor Agnes Lee [1866], George Bolling Lee papers, Virginia Historical Society.

14. Daniel Sutherland, *Seasons of War: The Ordeal of a Confederate Community, 1861–1865* (Free Press, 1995), 156.

15. Louise K. Dooley, "Little Sorrel: A War-Horse for Stonewall," *Army* (April 1975): 34, 35; Mary Anna Jackson, *Memoirs of Stonewall Jackson* (Louisville: Prentice Press, 1895), 171–73.

16. W. H. Andrews quoted in James I. Robertson Jr., *Stonewall Jackson: The Man, the Soldier, the Legend* (Macmillan, 1997), 499; John Hinsdale, quoted in ibid., 486; William W. Blackford, quoted in ibid., 471; Alexander Boteler, quoted in ibid., 291.

17. Dooley, "Little Sorrel," 37.

18. Jerrie Atkin, "Stonewall Jackson Horse Restored for Museum," newspaper clipping [1969], Little Sorrel Press Package, Virginia Military Institute, 1997.

19. Peter Finn, "Lexington, Va., Bids Fond Farewell to a War Horse," *Washington Post*, 21 July 1997, B1.

20. Finn, *Washington Post*, B5; Tony Horwitz, "How a Rebel Mount Endured to Become the Stuff of Legends," *Wall Street Journal*, 25 July 1997, Al, A6.

21. Horwitz, *Wall Street Journal*, A6; "Little Sorrel: Ceremony of Interment," printed program, Virginia Military Institute, 20 July 1997.

22. Unnamed female reenactors, personal conversations with the author, 20 July 1997, Lexington, Virginia.

23. Ellie Wood Baxter and Tessa Pullan, personal conversations with the author, 17 September 1997, Richmond, Virginia.

The Most Southern Sport on Earth
NASCAR and the Unions

Dan Pierce

Red Byron, who won the inaugural NASCAR Strictly Stock championship in 1949, relaxes after a dirt track race. The following year, Bill France would strip Byron of all his championship points for participating in non-NASCAR events. Courtesy of the International Motor Sports Hall of Fame.

entlemen, I won't be dictated to by the union." Six-foot-five, 240-pound Big Bill France loosened his tie, removed his glasses, and proceeded to put the "fear of God" into his workers. Before he had "this union stuffed down [his] throat," he swore, he would shut down his entire operation, plow it up, and plant corn. France also pledged that no known union member could work in his organization. "And if that isn't tough enough," he vowed, "I'll use a pistol to enforce it. I have a pistol, and I know how to use it. I've used it before."[1]

For most observers of the piedmont South in 1961, this was an all-too-typical scene in the region's textile mills, furniture factories, and tobacco processing plants. As late as 1976, only 7 percent of the nonagricultural labor force in both Carolinas belonged to a union. As the majority of Bill France's workers knew, the threat to shut down his operations was not an idle one. Other business owners in the region—such as textile magnate Roger Milliken in Darlington, South Carolina—had shut down rather than submit to unionization. The setting for Bill France's tirade was not a mill, however, but Bowman Gray Stadium in Winston-Salem, North Carolina. France's workers were not mill hands, but the drivers of the National Association for Stock Car Auto Racing's (NASCAR) elite Grand National Division, now known as Winston Cup.[2]

Perhaps no better metaphor exists for both the changes and lack of change in the piedmont South in the past fifty years than NASCAR stock car racing. A product of post–World War II economic and social transformations, NASCAR Winston Cup racing has become the second most popular spectator sport in the United States. Despite its national growth and ever-widening appeal, NASCAR's top division remains firmly rooted in the red-clay soil of the region. Although NASCAR's headquarters is located in Daytona Beach, Florida, the vast majority of Winston Cup team garages, crews, and drivers are located within a hundred-mile radius of Charlotte, North Carolina. The relationship to the piedmont South extends to the language, the customs, even the religion practiced in the typical NASCAR garage. Perhaps the most glaring example of NASCAR's deep regional roots is its unique form of management and the lack of union representation for its drivers and mechanics: NASCAR's style of management is more typical of a cotton mill than a modern, billion-dollar, professional sporting enterprise.

Stock car racing in the South originated just before World War II in a mill-village environment with few choices and little excitement besides moonshining. "Trust me, there was nothing to do in the mountains of North Carolina back in the 30s, 40s, and 50s," North Wilkesboro native and former Winston Cup driver Benny Parsons recently asserted. "You either worked at a hosiery mill, a furniture factory, or you made whiskey." It was also a question of lifestyle for these young men, many of whom "would rather die violently in [a] car than of boredom in a production line somewhere, punching a time clock to begin the day."[3]

As many observers have recorded, southern stock car racing evolved out of informal competitions between moonshiners who tested their skills as mechanics and their courage as drivers. As the popularity of these events grew, local entrepreneurs bulldozed tracks out of the red clay and the sport became more formalized, offering an escape from working-class realities. "[Bobby] Isaac didn't have any education whatsoever," former Grand National driver Paul "Little Bud" Moore recently observed. "He came out of the mills, just like David Pearson and a lot of other people. Stock car racing was a way to get away from that." The same type of escape applied to race fans as well, who, according to historian Pete Daniel, "took to racing in part because drivers personified both wildness and success, transgression and acceptance, and were people much like themselves who had become stars."[4]

Although stock car racing's popularity grew rapidly in the mid-to-late 1940s, the sport lacked organization. Promoters often reneged on paying promised purses. Track owners neglected even basic maintenance of the racing surface and demonstrated little concern for the safety and comfort of spectators and drivers. And with an alphabet soup of sanctioning agencies, fans and drivers had no way of comparing performances at various tracks. Into this chaotic situation strode William Henry Getty France, a Daytona Beach garage owner and racing promoter. On December 12, 1947, France gathered thirty-five men—promoters, drivers, and manufacturers' representatives—in the Ebony Bar above the Streamline Hotel in Daytona Beach. The group featured Erwin "Cannonball" Baker, an honored racing champion from Indianapolis; Bill Tuthill, a racing promoter from New York; Atlanta moonshine baron Raymond Parks; and Red Vogt, an ace mechanic from Atlanta, who built race cars for Parks and prepared cars for both moonshiners and revenue agents.[5]

After three days of meetings, the group adopted a set of rules to standardize the cars, making them safer and more equal; create a points system to declare a national champion; arrange insurance for drivers; and guarantee drivers that promoters would pay announced purses. They established three divisions of competition: "modified stock," "roadster," and, in a stroke of genius, "strictly stock"—the division that would later become Grand National, and then in 1971, Winston Cup. France defended the novel concept of racing automobiles right off the showroom floor: "If you race a junky-looking automobile—even if you take a new Cadillac, take the bumpers off, and let it get real dirty—then in people's minds it would still be a jalopy. We need to have races for the most modern automobiles available. Plain, ordinary working people have to be able to associate with the cars. Standard street stock cars are what we should be running."[6]

After establishing the rules, the group elected France as president and "Cannonball" Baker as commissioner of racing. Red Vogt came up with the somewhat redundant name of National Association for Stock Car Automobile Racing when participants discovered that a small group in Georgia had already claimed the preferred acronym, nascra—National Stock Car Racing Association. In February 1948, NASCAR was incorporated and issued one hundred shares of stock—fifty owned by Bill France, forty by Tuthill, and ten by Daytona lawyer Louis Ossinsky.[7]

Although the organizers created NASCAR ostensibly for the benefit of the drivers and as a drivers' association, it soon became apparent that the competitors themselves would have little input into its management. Almost from the beginning the organization became the personal fiefdom—perhaps milltown would be a more appropriate metaphor—of Bill France and his family. France soon bought out his partners and gained complete control of the organization.

From the first running of a strictly stock race on June 19, 1949, at the Charlotte Fairgrounds, France demonstrated that his word would be law in NASCAR. He disqualified race winner Glen Dunnaway when inspectors discovered an illegal modification in Dunnaway's 1947 Ford—a wedge placed in the springs to keep the car stable in the turns, an old bootlegger's trick. (In fact, the winning car had been used to haul moonshine earlier in the week.) After the race Hubert Westmoreland, the car owner, sued NASCAR for $10,000. NASCAR and France won a huge victory when Judge John J. Hayes recognized NASCAR's authority to enforce its rules and threw the case out of court.[8]

With his authority legally verified, France proceeded to exercise his power. In the second season of strictly stock racing, France stripped defending champion Red Byron of all of his championship points for competing in non-NASCAR events. Later in the year, France took away all of Lee Petty's points when he competed in an "outlaw" event during a three-week lull in NASCAR-sanctioned events. Petty would have won the 1950 championship if he had retained those points. In 1951 France did the same thing to eight drivers, including Red Byron and stars Curtis Turner, Marshall Teague, and Bob Flock.

The seeming capriciousness of many of France's decisions angered drivers. In 1954 Grand National star Tim Flock temporarily quit racing when France disqualified him after his victory in the Daytona Beach/Road Race for a minor carburetor infraction. It was "one of the toughest decisions I have ever had to make," asserted France, but one made "for the advancement of the sport." Later in the 1954 season, Flock's brother Fonty walked away from NASCAR over an incident at Lakewood Speedway in Atlanta. Four racers treated the crowd of over twenty thousand to door-to-door competition for the entire hundred-mile race. A flat tire late in the race cost Fonty Flock the victory and Herb Thomas took the checkered flag. NASCAR penalized Thomas a lap, however, for "improperly rejoining the race after a pit stop." Officials proceeded to declare Buck Baker the winner, but then observers pointed out that Baker had committed the same infraction as Thomas. If France had upheld the rules, then Gober Sosebee would have finished first with Fonty Flock second. For inexplicable reasons NASCAR reversed itself, waived all penalties, and declared the results official as the drivers had crossed the finish line. Similar incidents throughout NASCAR's early days convinced many drivers that France played favorites and enforced the rules only at his convenience.[9]

This type of incident earned France a reputation. "Now there are two dictators in Daytona Beach," wrote reporter Max Muhlman in his 1959 *Charlotte News* article featuring Cuban dictator Fulgencio Batista's move into exile in France's hometown. France seemed intent on demonstrating the accuracy of Muhlman's assessment when he flew his airplane to Charlotte and unsuccessfully attempted to get the editor of the *News* to fire the reporter. "Bill France had total control. It was a dictatorship," noted Smokey Yunick, legendary NASCAR mechanic.[10]

As drivers increasingly complained about France's iron hand, they also realized that many of his decisions benefited them. When auto manufacturers pulled their financial support of selected race teams in 1957, France convinced promoters to increase the prize money and make sure that those who finished from fifteenth to thirtieth received at least $300 in "travel money." In addition, he helped engineer a number of under-the-table deals with the automakers for favored drivers. In the early 1960s, driver Ned Jarrett picked up new cars from a Chevrolet dealership in Melbourne, Florida, with France's friend B. G. Holloway acting as paper owner and intermediary with General Motors. France also ensured that promoters paid the posted prizes. When a Grand National event first came to Riverside, California, in 1958, France became concerned that ticket money collected from the crowd would not cover payment of the announced $20,000 purse. He delayed the start of the race for over an hour while track employees counted all of the money from the ticket booths. When the amount came to only $16,570, France insisted that track owner Al Sloanaker write him a check for the remaining $3,430 before the race could begin. Pete Daniel recently commented on France's mastery of the personal style of management favored by southern planters and mill owners: "Cajoling, threatening, and punitive, Bill France brilliantly mixed the smile, the handshake, and the clenched fist."[11]

France and NASCAR also worked to improve the safety of racing. In 1953 NASCAR issued safety regulations requiring roll bars and locking seats that would not slide on impact. The next year the organization worked with the Pure Oil Company to produce the first special tires for stock car racing. That same year NASCAR encouraged its drivers to use the newly developed GenTex 70 racing helmet and flameproof coveralls.

A WORKING MAN'S PLIGHT

Despite France's paternalism, however, by the late 1950s drivers had become increasingly frustrated. The lack of correlation between gate receipts and race purses topped the list of complaints for most drivers. As early as 1949, NASCAR driver Marshall Teague noted that gate receipts often substantially exceeded purses at NASCAR modified races. He argued that the organization needed to follow the policy of the American Automobile Association, which ran Indy-car racing at the time, in allocating 40 percent of gate receipts for the purse. In response to this criticism, Bill France suspended Teague for "actions detrimental to auto racing," preventing the driver from competing in the first strictly stock race in Charlotte.[12]

Money worries increased as NASCAR Grand National racing grew in popularity through the 1950s and early 1960s and racing became more competitive and more expensive for drivers and owners. "Ten years ago NASCAR was paying $4,000 purses for 100-mile races," complained driver Curtis Turner in 1961. "Then it cost $3,000 to build an automobile. Today, NASCAR is still paying $4,000 purses for 100-mile races. But it costs $6,000 or $7,000 to build a first-class automobile." *Charlotte Observer* reporter George Cunningham estimated that a 1961 race at Bristol, Tennessee, attracted twenty-five thousand fans who paid on average $8 a ticket to produce gross revenues of $200,000. "Forty-two drivers divided a purse of $15,000 which included about $4,000 put up by manufacturers," wrote Cunningham. "We weren't making no money," observed Tim Flock. "We were only getting a thousand dollars for first place in most races. They were probably paying about 7 percent of the gross."[13]

Drivers also became increasingly concerned about inadequate insurance coverage, especially given the sport's inherent danger. In an all-too-common case, Bobby Myers died when he crashed head-on into Fonty Flock's stalled car in the Southern 500 at Darlington in 1957. "When my dad died, he didn't have any insurance, didn't have anything," recalled Myers's son, Danny "Chocolate" Myers, a member of the late Dale Earnhardt's race crew. "I can remember someone bringing a bucket of change into the house. NASCAR gave us whatever they could collect in a five-gallon bucket." Although his injuries did not threaten his life, the same crash ended Flock's nine-year Grand National career. He had little to show for it, despite finishing among the top five in points three times.[14]

Poor track conditions provoked the ire of many drivers. Ned Jarrett noted that "the promoters made very little effort towards the care of the tracks." Dirt tracks often had huge holes, mud, and blinding dust. "When a race started, there was always mud, because they had just watered the track down," Richard Petty recalled. "You'd have to reach outside the car and try to wipe it off the windshield. Then by the time you'd run fifty laps, it got so dusty you couldn't see a thing. There was as much dust on the inside of the windshield as there was the outside, so you had to wipe off on both sides. You finally just had to take your goggles off, because the dust would get on the inside, and you'd sweat and that turned it to mud. My eyes were as red as the clay for two days after a race."[15] Drivers fared little better on many of the paved tracks. At the first World 600 at Charlotte—now Lowe's—Motor Speedway in 1960, holes began to appear in the newly paved track during qualifying runs. "You could have half-ridden a big Chevrolet Impala in some of those holes," Buck Baker groused. In order to compete, drivers fabricated wire-mesh screens to prevent flying rock and asphalt from puncturing radiators and smashing windshields. "Most of the cars looked like army tanks," observed Lee Petty. Jack Smith led much of the race but had to retire on lap 352 of 400 when a chunk of asphalt punctured his fuel tank.

Grievances went both ways. France and NASCAR officials had their hands full trying to regulate and organize the independent, free-spirited individuals attracted to racing. In the early years of Grand National racing, NASCAR and track owners had difficulty promoting races because the drivers refused to fill out entry forms far enough in advance so that the names of the drivers in the race could be advertised. "If they showed up, they would race. If not the promoter would know by their absence," noted NASCAR historian Greg Fielden.[16]

Much of the time race drivers were too busy fighting among themselves to unite and appeal to NASCAR for improved conditions. Many drivers had reputations for violence and roughhousing and most felt obligated to maintain a tough-guy persona just to survive. One race at Bowman Gray Stadium in the mid-1950s turned into a two-man demolition derby between Bobby Myers and Curtis Turner. After the race, an angry Myers went looking for Turner with tire iron in hand. He found him sitting on the back of his truck, but stopped short when Turner produced a pistol. "Bobby, where are you going with that tire tool?" Turner asked. "I was just looking for a place to lay it down," Myers responded.[17]

In addition to the general rowdiness of many of the drivers, it became apparent from NASCAR's earliest days that circumventing NASCAR regulations would be an important part of the game. "Cheating had always been a way of life with racers," Richard Petty once argued. "Some of the mechanics did things they knew they might get caught at, but they figured those guys couldn't find everything." Suspecting that mechanic Smokey Yunnick had done something illegal to increase the capacity of a car's fuel tank, inspectors removed the tank and carefully measured the contents. While the fuel tank passed inspection, NASCAR officials gave Yunnick a list of nine infractions that had to be corrected before the car would qualify. Yunnick proceeded to the car, started it up with the fuel tank still on the ground, and drove away, calling out to inspectors, "Better make it ten." To this day, the popular adage around the NASCAR garage is "It's only cheating if you get caught."[18]

By 1961, however, drivers had finally realized the need to form a union to represent their interests. Ironically, the rowdiest and most free-spirited driver of them all, Curtis Turner, a former moonshine runner from Virginia, became the catalyst for the movement. Turner lived his life like he drove a car—at full throttle. His drinking, marathon parties, womanizing, and practical jokes were as legendary as his win-or-blow-up style of driving. He made and lost millions in business ventures ranging from timber sales to movie theaters. Such a business venture gone wrong, the construction of Charlotte Motor Speedway, brought Turner together with another legendary figure, Jimmy Hoffa.[19]

Turner and his partner, racing promoter Bruton Smith, began building the 1.5 mile speedway in 1960, selling stock in the enterprise out of the backs of their cars. Cost overruns began to mount soon into the project. Construction expenses, plus the high costs of staging the first race—despite attracting over thirty-five thousand fans—put the project into a deep financial hole. In June 1961, frustrated stockholders ousted Turner as the speedway's president. In order to regain control, Turner approached Hoffa and the Teamsters with a deal. If the union would lend him $850,000, Turner would organize Grand National drivers as part of a Teamsters' program to organize all professional athletes into a branch of the union known as the Federation of Professional Athletes (FPA).[20]

With the aid of Nick Torzeski, the Teamsters' point-man for the FPA, Turner began soliciting drivers for the union. He told them that union membership would bring them higher purses, "a pension plan, death benefits, health and welfare benefits, a scholarship fund for children of deceased members, strong and meaningful complaint procedures, and assurance of adequate safety conditions." Within weeks the top drivers in NASCAR—including Fireball Roberts, Tim Flock, Ned Jarrett, Junior Johnson, Glen Wood, and Rex White—signed union cards. "The way Turner explained it to me, it sounds like a good deal for drivers, car owners and racing in general," Glen Wood told a reporter as he signed a union card. "It will only cost me $10 to find out. I have been at races before when drivers would want to strike because of a low purse and a large crowd." Three-time Grand National champion Lee Petty and his son, rising NASCAR star Richard, became the most notable hold-outs, primarily because of their personal antipathy for Turner, Lee Petty's bitterest racetrack rival. Despite the Pettys' unwillingness to join, the union movement in NASCAR appeared unstoppable.[21]

Turner and the Teamsters, however, had greatly underestimated the determination and force of personality that Bill France would bring to opposing the union movement. Drivers soon found out that union membership would cost them much more than $10. Although France had grown up in the Washington, D.C., suburbs and lived in Daytona Beach, Florida, he had traveled the South for years promoting stock car racing and had obviously learned a great deal about controlling labor from piedmont millowners. The NASCAR boss employed practically every tried and tested method of keeping unions out, from threats and intimidation, to "yellow dog" contracts, to accusations of communism, to propaganda, to blacklisting.

As soon as Turner went public with the union, France immediately flew to Winston-Salem to confront the Grand National drivers before the August 9 race at Bowman Gray Stadium. In an hour-long meeting with drivers, he threatened to "plow up my two-and-a-half-mile track at Daytona Beach and plant corn in the infield." France also immediately banned all union members from competing in the next scheduled Grand National race at Asheville-Weaverville Speedway. He then proceeded to point out the problems unionization would produce: "If you unionize, any support from the factories will be withdrawn. And all of you car owners, if you hire a mechanic, as you will, then you'll have to pay him time and a half on Saturday and double time on Sunday." He also argued that drivers were not employees of NASCAR. They were "independent contractors" and therefore responsible for their own insurance and pension. France defended his actions by arguing that banning the union was a "safety measure." He pointed out that union drivers might threaten non-union drivers during a race, coercing them to join. "A Fireball Roberts or a Curtis Turner will drive alongside you on the track and say, 'Hey you signed up yet?' I'm not going to allow that to happen. I'm protecting NASCAR drivers by not letting union members compete." Finally, France dropped a bombshell on the group when he revealed that Turner and the Teamsters planned to bring pari-mutuel betting to NASCAR racing. "As far as pari-mutuel betting is concerned, we know it won't work with auto racing. Auto racing is a clean sport. We've never had a scandal. And I will fight any pari-mutuel attempt to the last tilt."

France offered drivers a chance to sign cards nullifying their union membership and proceeded to set up a special grievance board of drivers, promoters, and car owners to deal with driver complaints. Almost all of the drivers who had signed union cards immediately pledged their allegiance to NASCAR and dropped out of the FPA. "I joined this union. And I've been thinking about it ever since," said Rex White at the time. "Drivers have legitimate beefs. And the drivers want a fair deal and more money. But let's let this board France has appointed decide what's good for racing, not some union. . . . I'll admit the union offer of a retirement plan sold me. But from now on, I'll think for a while before I sign anything else." When asked if his offer of amnesty applied to union officers Curtis Turner, Fireball Roberts, and Tim Flock, France replied, "Maybe. Just maybe. If they make an affidavit and swear on the Bible."[22]

France also launched a public offensive by issuing a prepared statement characterizing his fight against the union as a defense of the nation and the Constitution: "A recent newspaper story suggests that I might be some rootin', hootin', shootin' cuss, waving a pistol and itching to shoot up anyone who might disagree with me. Honest, I'm nothing like that. But I am an American who believes our constitution and our laws—and that bearing arms to repel invasion is a part of our great American Heritage." In a statement to reporters, France clarified what he meant by his reference to repelling invasion: "I don't think people realize the seriousness of this Teamsters move. There is only one promise I'll make. And that is that I will always do everything I can to keep them from taking over the country. The ultimate aim of that man that's heading the Teamsters [Jimmy Hoffa] is to control the country."[23]

Roberts fired back: "Curtis and I fully realize just how far we have our necks stuck out. We know our careers in auto racing are at stake, but we're not backing down. We've made no demands, made no moves other than to try and sign up drivers for the union. We must have grabbed Mr. France where it hurts, though, from all the things he's said in the papers." If drivers looked at how France tried to strong-arm the union leaders, Roberts continued, they would realize that their best interests lay in supporting the union. He further argued that affiliation with the Teamsters Union would give the FPA the leverage and backing needed to gain the concessions from NASCAR that all of the drivers agreed were needed.

France, however, marshaled his forces to overwhelm the already weakened opposition. He lined up most of the track owners and promoters to speak out publicly against the union. "I think it would be the devil for that union outfit [the Teamsters] to get in. I believe all the promoters are going to stick with Bill," argued Gene Sluder, owner of the Asheville-

Weaverville Speedway. France also traveled to Washington, D.C., with Darlington track owner Bob Colvin and allegedly received assurances from an assistant attorney general that NASCAR was on solid legal footing. "Drivers are individual contractors according to the entry blanks they sign," Colvin told reporters. "There is no form of union for individual contractors. We will have the FBI at Darlington for the Labor Day Southern 500. The law states that pickets, etc., for independent contractors are illegal and anyone participating in such or trying to stop the race will be liable for prosecution." Colvin noted no irony in their plan to prevent union organizing at a Labor Day race.[24]

The death knell for the union movement sounded when Fireball Roberts succumbed to pressure, resigned as FPA president, and severed his ties with the union. The day after publicly defying Bill France, Roberts made a decision on a slow drive from Charlotte to Asheville, the site of the next race: "My motives in the FPA were quite clear. I simply wanted to better the positions of race drivers, car owners, myself and racing in general. I can see now that by affiliating the FPA with the Teamsters that we could possibly accomplish more harm than good for racing. I feel if I do anything to hurt the least man in racing, I will be doing a disservice to my fellow drivers who have been my friends for fifteen years. And I'll have no part of it." France quickly welcomed his most popular star back into the fold: "I think in future years Fireball will regard this move as the best thing he ever did for sports in America."[25]

With Roberts's defection, Curtis Turner and Tim Flock stood alone against France. The NASCAR president banned both drivers from NASCAR racing "for life." The two sought injunctions to prevent NASCAR from blackballing them for their attempt at unionization. The courts dismissed all of their petitions and the ban on both drivers stood. Bill France had won. Any piedmont factory owner could look with pride at the manner in which France defeated the union effort.[26]

Ironically, the race held at the Asheville-Weaverville Speedway in the midst of the union controversy aptly demonstrated many of the problems faced by NASCAR drivers. Word of a possible confrontation between France and Turner had attracted an unusually large crowd of over ten thousand. While Turner didn't show, the race generated a major confrontation of its own. About 60 laps into the scheduled 500-lap race, holes began to appear in turn four of the race track. "The holes soon became gaping monsters," observed *Asheville Citizen* reporter Bob Terrell. When driver Bunk Moore hit one of the holes on lap 208, bounced off the outside wall, careened into a temporary pit area, smashed through the pit wall, hit a pickup truck, and injured a spectator, officials threw the red flag, temporarily stopping the event. While track workers tried to sweep up debris and make track repairs, Pat Purcell, executive manager of NASCAR, called all of the drivers together. He informed them that because of track conditions the drivers would run only 50 more laps and left the drivers with the reassuring thought: "I hope you can make it." Race officials failed to tell the spectators that the race would be shortened.[27]

When the flagman threw the checkered flag at lap 258, abbreviating the race by 242 laps, pandemonium broke out. Bill France and other NASCAR officials had conveniently changed out of their black and white NASCAR uniforms and left the track before the end of the race. Four thousand enraged fans blocked the exits to the track to prevent the drivers from leaving. "I paid five bucks to see a 500 lap race. Somebody owes me some laps or some money," one member of the mob demanded. "Fist fights broke out in the crowd," Terrell observed. "Someone was thrown in the lake at the western end of the infield and two persons who attempted to quiet the crowd were heaved bodily from the track over the pit wall." Part of the mob hoisted a pickup truck and placed it across the exit road, trapping the drivers and crews inside the track for three and one-half hours. Sheriff's deputies called to the scene failed to disperse the crowd. Finally, six-foot-six, 285-pound Pop Eargle, a crew member for car owner Bud Moore, approached the mob's ringleaders to convince them to let the drivers go. When one of the leaders jabbed Eargle in the stomach with a two-by-four, "Eargle grabbed the big piece of wood and whacked the mobster in the head." Shortly after, the crowd allowed the drivers to leave. Local hospitals treated four individuals for injuries incurred in fights, and sheriff's deputies arrested three members of the mob. As they finally headed for their homes, the drivers had to wonder if they had not made a big mistake in failing to back the FPA.[28]

France did make some concessions, most notably the formation of a special advisory committee to oversee Grand National racing. He appointed driver Ned Jarrett, driver/car owner Lee Petty, car owner Rex Lovette, promoters Clay Earles and Enoch Staley, and NASCAR officials Ed Otto and Pat Purcell. NASCAR instituted some minor changes as a result of committee activity—primarily increases in prize money and insurance benefits, and improved track conditions. As Ned Jarrett recalled, however, the committee met "off and on for a couple of years and then it just sort of died out."[29]

In the years immediately following the organization and crushing of the FPA, NASCAR began a period of transition as more and more of its events moved from the dirt tracks to new and longer paved speedways. Ford and Chrysler sponsorship of cars also returned, bringing needed money and material to many of NASCAR's top Grand National drivers. Attendance at events increased and NASCAR's popularity swelled.

Driver frustration, however, did not go away, and in many ways complaints became even more serious. Rapidly escalating speeds brought on by a combination of faster tracks and the intense competition between Ford and Chrysler topped the list of driver complaints. In 1964 alone, three drivers—Joe Weatherly, Fireball Roberts, and Jimmy Pardue—died in accidents. Countless other drivers suffered serious injury. "It's reached the point at the superspeedways where it's a big relief when a race ends and you're okay, no matter where you finished. It's become a pretty jumpy game," noted driver Buck Baker. After he cut an artery and almost bled to death in a July accident at Daytona, Fred Lorenzen asserted that the cars "are just too fast. I'll never run another race unless they slow the speeds down."

One of the chief problems drivers faced was that tire technology had not kept pace with the demands of the faster cars and the new superspeedways. At the April 1964 race in Atlanta, only ten of the original thirty-nine cars finished the race. Wrecks caused by blowouts eliminated most of the competitors. "We haven't learned enough to keep the cars handling safely at the speeds we can travel," complained a frustrated Junior Johnson. "And the tire companies are having trouble developing compounds that will give adequate tire wear."[30]

Drivers also became disconcerted over the seemingly constant wrangling between Bill France and the automakers. In 1965 France banned Chrysler's Hemi engine. Chrysler retaliated by ordering its drivers to boycott much of the season. In 1966 France banned Ford's overhead cam engine, resulting in a Ford boycott for much of that season. Drivers became increasingly irritated with France's handling of these problems because he often bent the rules and reversed earlier decisions to try to keep fans in the seats. France even lifted his "life-time" ban on Curtis Turner when a rival organization, the Grand American Racing Association, began talking to Turner about headlining its events.

France's capriciousness reached new heights in August 1966 when he bent beyond recognition the rules on "stock" characteristics of Grand National cars to prevent Chrysler products from totally dominating the series. Junior Johnson fielded an alleged Ford in the Dixie 500 at Atlanta International Raceway for his driver Fred Lorenzen. "It was supposed to carry some resemblance bestowed by the original car maker—Ford Motor Co. But somewhere along the line, it missed the boat," NASCAR historian Greg Fielden observed. The car, nicknamed the "yellow banana," had an extra-low roof line, a severely sloped front windshield, and a front end that rode low with a jacked-up rear end. "It looked weird enough to be put together by committee," one observer quipped. In the same race, Smokey Yunick entered a Chevrolet Chevelle with off-centered wheels and a hand-crafted spoiler on the roof. NASCAR inspectors allowed the cars in the race, despite the fact that they both featured numerous nonproduction features, a previous NASCAR no-no. France defended his decision to allow modifications in some "gray areas": "I admit the rules were bent at Atlanta. After Fred Lorenzen drove Johnson's car in Atlanta, it sort of opened the door for any of the other Ford drivers to return to racing if they wanted to. The entire deal happened at the last minute and there was no time to prepare another body for the car. We are going to stick to the rule book and everybody knows it. Junior knows it. He is rebuilding the Ford and putting a new body in it."[31]

Despite the addition of new tracks—most notably the expansion of NASCAR Michigan International Speedway—and an infusion of new stars —David Pearson, Bobby Isaac, Bobby Allison, Cale Yarborough, and LeeRoy Yarbrough—driver frustration increased as they remained underpaid pawns in a game dominated by Bill France, Chrysler, and Ford. As a result, NASCAR lost three of its best drivers in the prime of their careers: Junior Johnson, who stayed on as a car owner, Fred Lorenzen, and Ned Jarrett. "I got to looking at the security, or the lack of security really, that this sport offered," two-time champion Jarrett said recently. "I wanted to spend more time with the family, the kids were growing up, and so I made my decision to retire then at the end of the 1966 season."[32]

Driver rebellion once again surfaced in 1969. This time around the organizers proved more effective in maintaining secrecy and retaining the loyalty of top drivers. On August 14, 1969, eleven drivers organized the Professional Drivers Association (PDA) in Ann Arbor, Michigan. The group elected the sport's reigning superstar Richard Petty as president of the organization, Cale Yarborough and Elmo Langely vice presidents, and a board of directors composed of Bobby Allison, Buddy Baker, LeeRoy Yarbrough, David Pearson, Pete Hamilton, Charlie Glotzbach, Donnie Allison, and James Hylton. The success of players' organization efforts in the National Basketball Association (NBA), Major League Baseball, and the National Football League encouraged the drivers. The PDA hired Lawrence Fleisher, who had spearheaded the organization of NBA players, as general counsel. The organization's goals differed little from those of the FPA: retirement and insurance plans, improved facilities for driver convenience, improved driver safety, and higher purses. "All of a sudden the cars started running 190, 195 mile-an-hour," recalled Richard Petty. "We was running on some of these race tracks that it wasn't safe to really be in the pace car. Also, . . . there's more people coming but the purses ain't going up." Bobby Allison also defended the organization of the PDA: "We formed an organization because we felt foolish in not forming one. Every other major sport has its players' organization. . . . A guy devotes his life to racing, and he gets only $7,500 if he gets an arm torn off. If he gets killed, his wife gets $15,000. We've never had a voice in planning or scheduling. They might have a 500-mile race and two days later, a 100-miler a thousand miles away."[33]

Once again France responded in a tried-and-true manner with a combination of amazement that Grand National drivers could be disgruntled, threats, and a like-it-or-leave-it attitude: "NASCAR has been pretty great to this bunch of people. Some of these fellows have gotten to be big heroes and they have apparently forgotten how they got there. . . . We're not planning to change NASCAR. We'll post our prize money and they're welcome to run if they want to. If not, that's their business. There are no contracts with NASCAR. But these fellows had better realize that they can't go very far without factory cars. And I'm sure the factories would put someone in their cars if they should think about a strike or something." France also used the classic "outside agitator" tactic when he expressed concern about the involvement of "New York interests" in an obvious reference to PDA lawyer Lawrence Fleisher. Once again, he called on track owners and promoters for support. Larry LoPatin, owner of four tracks that ran Grand National races, came to France's defense: "I think this sport has a long way to go before pressure groups start making demands from it. A driver's organization may be fine, but Bill France and Bill France Jr. are no patsies. I believe their interest in the drivers is sincere."[34]

France's ownership of tracks and dominance of NASCAR gave him control over the drivers not unlike the millowner's control over his employees when he owned their housing, the company store, the school, and even the church. France was unique in American professional sport not only because he owned and ran NASCAR, but also because he owned its most important venue, Daytona International Speedway. With the building of the even faster Talladega speedway in 1969, the union issue came to a head when France severely overplayed his hand.

France discovered the perfect site for his new track at an abandoned World War II airstrip near the milltown of Talladega, Alabama. Fifteen million people lived within a three hundred-mile radius of the tiny town, fifty miles east of Birmingham and one hundred miles west of Atlanta. The property became even more attractive when France's good friend, Alabama governor George C. Wallace, agreed to speed up construction of the Alabama portion of I-20, which ran by the site, and build new roads to the track.[35]

In May 1968 France broke ground for the massive 2.66 mile superspeedway, with thirty-three degree banking. Anxious to recoup his investment, he scheduled the first race at the track for September 14, 1969. Bad weather, however, caused contractors to rush the paving job, with less than satisfactory results for drivers who tested the new track. After making a lap at over 193 miles-per-hour, Bobby Allison sounded an alarm: "This place is rough as a cob. It would be a beautiful speedway if it was smooth. The roughness bounces the car around so much it feels like it's tearing the wheels off in the corners. . . . The only way they're going to fix it is to repave it." Other drivers expressed their concerns that tires would last for only a few laps at these unprecedented speeds of nearly 200 miles-per-hour combined with rough track conditions.

With the formation of the PDA and concerns over the Talladega track brewing, France tried to quell any potential uprising among his Grand National drivers. France himself got behind the wheel of a Ford Grand National car and turned a lap at 175 miles-per-hour on the high-banked track. "It's a world record for a 59-year-old man," he proudly announced to the press. He then applied for membership in the PDA when he filed an entry for the Talladega 500 eight days before the race. When asked about France's request, Allison replied, "I'd say he would be a foolish old man. He wants to get into the PDA any way he can."[36]

When the drivers arrived for race practice and qualification, safety concerns mounted. In many cases, tires blistered and cracked after only 2 laps at 190 plus miles-per-hour. "They ought to call this race. Nobody has tires any good for more than 15 laps," driver Charlie Glotzbach argued. Even tire company representatives admitted that they did not have any tires that could withstand such pressure. On Friday evening before the

Sunday race, Firestone officials, fearing a disaster, withdrew their company's tires. "The drivers' concern for their safety is legitimate," said one unnamed tire manufacturer's representative. "As much as I hate to admit it, the tires just won't withstand the pressure of running 200 miles-per-hour. This is a whole new realm for us and it shows. The right side tires are virtually falling apart after only five or six laps." Buddy Baker spoke for the drivers: "Every man down there wants to race, this track is so exciting. But we don't want to race under these conditions. I'll be tickled to come back here and race when the various things are all straightened out. Not now, though. I like me. I've grown accustomed to living."

Bill France fired back that a "foreign substance" on the track cut the tires. He pledged that his crews would sweep the track to remove the problem. A Goodyear spokesman countered France's assertions: "The reason the tires are lasting only four or six laps is because of high speed, the poor condition of the track surface, and tires. There's no such thing as a foreign substance. We didn't have enough time to test here. This was a rush-rush race." France, however, refused to budge. He had too much tied up in the race to cancel or postpone it: "We will have a race here. Right now I don't think we have a major problem."

On the Friday night before the Sunday race, Petty met with PDA members individually, polling them about boycotting the race. The next morning Petty informed France that the PDA drivers would not run the race. "There will be a race tomorrow," France shot back. "If you don't want to be in it, pack up and leave." Petty proceeded to load his car on his trailer, and several other drivers followed suit. A few hours later, France confronted Petty and a group of PDA drivers. "What you hot-dogs do is your business," France shouted. "But quit threatening the boys that want to race. If you want to go home, then go." The NASCAR boss then tried to convince the drivers to stay around and observe what happened in that day's Grand Touring race: "I tell you the wear isn't going to be as bad as you say." Bobby Allison argued that comparing tire wear on the smaller and lighter Camaros, Mustangs, Javelins, and Cougars run in Grand Touring races would be comparing apples to oranges. "Don't try to fool us," he sneered.

France then advised the drivers that if they were so concerned about tire wear and safety, they could just run at slower speeds. LeeRoy Yarbrough jumped in: "Bill, we can't put on a decent show the way things are now. Sure we can go out and run 175 and not wear any tires, but is this fair to the guy that's paying $25 for his seat?" Petty countered, "We don't want to run. We want to race." Bobby Allison then launched into sarcasm: "Can we start on foot and get paid by position? Wait, I take that back, the track is so rough we'd probably trip and fall before we got to the first turn." Violence almost erupted when Petty called a meeting and France tried to follow. Cale Yarborough angrily blocked his way: "Where do you think you're going?" This is a "drivers' meeting and only drivers are coming in." France backed down, but it was soon obvious that he was not to be deterred in running the race.

Even as the top Grand National drivers pulled out and headed for home, France employed another common union-busting tactic to fill the field for the Sunday race—hiring scabs. His power as both head of NASCAR and speedway owner/promoter gave him a tremendous advantage in combating the union as he once again threw out the rulebook in order to hold a semblance of an official race. Bobby Isaac, shunned by the PDA because of his independent streak, and nine journeyman, independent drivers (drivers without factory backing) were the only Grand National drivers in the field. France filled the rest of the field by allowing twenty-five Grand Touring drivers with their smaller cars—in clear violation of NASCAR rules—to enter the headline event. The NASCAR boss also provided Grand Touring driver Tiny Lund with the Holman-Moody Ford that he had previously driven around the track. The Ford never went through track inspection, another blatant violation of NASCAR rules.[37]

As the race approached, France demonstrated not only his toughness and determination, but also his mastery of public relations. France knew his core customers, the piedmont working class, and like many southern union busters before him, he played their distrust and suspicion of unions masterfully. As spectators arrived, track ushers handed them a statement from France that placed all of the blame for the boycott on the drivers:

I am very much surprised that some of our drivers and car owners would wait until the last day prior to a major race and withdraw their automobiles from a race. Track officials and NASCAR officials worked until the last moment to get the drivers to fulfill their obligations to the fans who traveled some distance to see the event. Everyone expected they would race.

It would be unfair to the spectators who traveled to Talladega to see a race to postpone it. It would also be unfair to drivers and car owners who wish to compete.

France went on to offer a free ticket for a future race to anyone who had purchased a ticket to the opening Talladega race. To his great relief, over sixty-two thousand fans showed up for the race, many attracted by the controversy of the previous weeks. After the race, France told reporters, "With what we planned—the ticket arrangement—I felt sure that fans wouldn't be mad at the speedway or NASCAR, and they weren't."[38]

In order to avoid a race marred by tragedy, as the PDA drivers feared, France directed the flagman to bring out the yellow caution flag every 25 laps so that drivers could pit and change tires. The drivers themselves kept their speeds down until late in the race to prevent blowouts.[39]

Independent driver Richard Brickhouse won the race driving a factory-backed Dodge Daytona originally intended for Charlie Glotzbach, one of only three cars running on the lead lap. A PDA member, Brickhouse had resigned from the organization over the public address system prior to the race. In presenting the winner's check and trophy, an overjoyed Bill France announced to the cheering crowd: "Winners never quit, and quitters never win." In the next day's *Charlotte Observer*, Tom Higgins captured the essence of the previous day's proceedings: "Bill France, who has survived some harrowing crises in 20 years as head of the NASCAR organization he created, pulled a rabbit out of the hat again Sunday."

Now NASCAR's top drivers knew they had little leverage left to gain any sort of concessions from France. Although France had said that drivers wouldn't be penalized for pulling out of the race, technical inspector Bill Gazaway allegedly told one driver that if he boycotted the race, he "might as well turn [his] car into a farm tractor, 'cause it won't ever get through inspection again." France himself gave the PDA drivers cause for worry when he told the press, "As far as I'm concerned, the boys that raced today saved this track, and they saved NASCAR racing. . . . The boys who pulled out owe their future to the drivers who ran today—if they have a future."[40]

The PDA publicly defended their boycott, but France was now in the driver's seat. He added a new clause to future Grand National entry forms prohibiting employees from joining a union: "Therefore, we agree to compete in the event if humanly possible unless the event is postponed, canceled or if the car fails to qualify for the starting field." This "yellow-dog" contract ensured that there would be no repeat of the Talladega boycott. France also "sweetened the pot" by offering appearance money to top drivers. By the early 1970s, drivers like Richard Petty could make more than $100,000 in appearance money alone. "Whatever political notions, if any, these wild men had in the early days of racing, prosperity made them Republicans," noted Pete Daniel.[41]

After a meeting at Charlotte on September 24, 1969, the drivers agreed to sign the new forms and backed down from almost all of their demands. "We wanted to assure the motor companies, the promoters, the fans and everybody concerned that we are going to race the rest of the races this year and next," Petty explained. Drivers had just wanted "someone to talk to" about their problems. France had won again, probably ending the organization of drivers in racing forever.[42]

Ironically, four years later the independent drivers/scabs who broke the union's back at Talladega attempted to convince NASCAR that they needed more money if they were going to continue to fill fields and finish at the back of the race. Independent driver Bill Dennis rented a track at Rougemont, North Carolina, and organized the "Independent 250," a race that allowed only owner/drivers to compete. Dennis and other independents hoped that a crowd of five to six thousand would convince France that they could attract an audience in their own right, an implicit threat to organize a competing series. Although France recognized the threat, he kept a low profile and hoped the race would prove a failure. The race attracted a solid field of the likes of Dave Marcis, Coo Coo Marlin, Cecil Gordon, James Hylton, Elmo Langely, Wendell Scott, and Richard Childress (now owner of Dale Earnhardt's car), but the location, date, and weather worked against success. On a day threatening rain, at a track on the back roads of Orange County, North Carolina, the November 25 race attracted only two thousand paying customers, effectively crushing the hopes of the independents. Bill France had won again, this time without really lifting a finger. "We work on such a low budget, not one of us could afford to get out of line now," conceded James Hylton. "I would say that if one of us started talking to France about how things were, he'd break that driver's back before he could even step out of line. If you had a meeting, only seven drivers would show up, and they'd be too scared to do anything anyway." Richard Childress echoed Hylton's sentiments with a lament often heard by labor organizers in the Piedmont: "You'll never get all the drivers together. It's just not the nature of the guys."[43]

Today, little evidence remains of NASCAR's red-clay roots. State-of-the-art superspeedways surrounded by condos and luxury suites, not dirt tracks with rickety wooden bleachers, dominate the NASCAR landscape. Competitors no longer come to racing to escape the tedium of the mills.

Instead, they are drawn by multi-million-dollar contracts. Spectators now pay sixty to a hundred dollars for tickets and number not in the hundreds but in the hundreds of thousands. Some things, however, have not changed. NASCAR remains the one major sporting organization without significant representation from the competitors themselves, and drivers still complain about the lack of correlation between gate receipts and prize money and their overall powerlessness. "They [NASCAR] still don't let you be involved in anything. They still run the show," Richard Petty recently commented. Dave Marcis noted the low prize money—especially for those drivers who, unlike Dale Earnhardt and Jeff Gordon, are not raking in millions on endorsement: "Charlotte [Lowe's] Motor Speedway is a perfect example. It's basically been trying to be the premier racetrack and build these fancy grandstands and these suites and these restaurants and all this kind of stuff. They pay the worst purse on the circuit and have for quite a few years. . . . All the drivers talk about it when they're together, and they'll be talking about it again this week."[44]

Because the France family has a virtual stranglehold on the sport, drivers in NASCAR Winston Cup racing today have even fewer opportunities to redress grievances. NASCAR is still a privately held corporation controlled by the France family, and since 1972, when Big Bill France turned the day-to-day operation of his NASCAR/International Speedway Corporation (ISC) empire over to his son William Clifton France (known as Bill Jr.), the Frances have taken an even larger piece of the NASCAR pie. Although it is now a publicly traded company, ISC is also controlled by the Frances. Bill France Jr. is chairman of the board, while his brother Jim France is president and daughter Lesa France Kennedy is executive vice president. In recent years, ISC has come to own or control twelve tracks hosting Winston Cup events. In 2001 these tracks will host eighteen of the thirty-six Winston Cup points races, giving NASCAR/ISC unprecedented power and control over a professional sport. Herb Greenberg, a columnist for *TheStreet.com* market analysis website, recently compared the relationship between NASCAR and ISC to a hypothetical scenario in which the "NBA owned over half of the stadiums, promoted the games and then paid the teams whatever they felt like paying."[45]

Ironically, when asked about their view of Bill France and the France family, those involved with NASCAR generally come up with only accolades. "It [the growth and success of NASCAR] wouldn't have happened without them. . . . They've done one heck of a job to make it work," said Richard Petty. Dave Marcis expressed his respect for Bill France Sr.: "If he told you something, you could bank on it." Max Muhlman, the sports writer whom Bill France had once tried to get fired, mused, "Over the years France became more and more of a benevolent dictator. Now I see what he did and what he had to put up with and how difficult it must have been. Some of the things he did by themselves maybe he shouldn't have done, but on balance, on which hopefully most of us are judged, clearly the man was a genius."[46]

To be sure, today's Winston Cup drivers, much like their predecessors, seem content with their place and encouraged by the growth of their sport. Perhaps this attitude points again to the ongoing connection between the piedmont South and NASCAR Winston Cup racing. Much like the millhand whose nonunion job with J. P. Stevens is now a much better paying nonunion job with BMW, they are thankful for the work.

NOTES

1. Almost any book that covers the history of NASCAR includes an account of this incident. I have relied primarily on Greg Fielden, *Forty Years of Stock Car Racing*, vol. 2, *The Superspeedway Boom, 1959–1964* (Galfield Press, 1988), 93–100; and Ned Jarrett, interview with author, 14 September 1998.

2. For the purposes of this essay, I define the piedmont South as that region running roughly between the coastal plain and the Appalachian Mountains and from Richmond, Virginia, to Birmingham, Alabama. Information on unionization of southern industries is from James C. Cobb, *Industrialization and Southern Society*, 1877–1984 (Dorsey Press, 1988), 68–98; and Jacquelyn Dowd Hall, et al., *Like a Family: The Making of a Southern Cotton Mill World* (University of North Carolina Press, 1987); and Allen Tullos, *Habits of Industry: White Culture and the Transformation of the Carolina Piedmont* (University of North Carolina Press, 1989).

3. "The Fifty: Sincerely, Bill France," video (Indianapolis: Lingner Group Productions for ESPN Video); Peter Golenbock, *American Zoom: Stock Car Racing —From the Dirt Tracks to Daytona* (Macmillan, 1993), 21; and Paul Hemphill, *Wheels: A Season on NASCAR's Winston Cup Circuit* (Simon & Schuster, 1997), 78.

4. Golenbock, *The Last Lap: The Life and Times of NASCAR's Legendary Heroes* (Macmillan, 1998), 91–92; and Pete Daniel, *Lost Revolutions: The South in the 1950s* (University of North Carolina Press, 2000), 117.

5. Fielden, *Forty Years of Stock Car Racing*, vol. 1, *The Beginning, 1949–1958* (Galfield Press, 1988), 5–9; and Hemphill, *Wheels*, 118–19.

6. Golenbock, *American Zoom*, 71.

7. Fielden, *The Beginning*, 5–6.

8. Fielden, *The Beginning*, 7–9; and Hemphill, *Wheels*, 119–20.

9. Fielden, *The Beginning*, 20–21, 43–44, 139–40.

10. Golenbock, *The Last Lap*, 139; Golenbock, *American Zoom*, 59.

11. Fielden, *The Beginning*, 299; Jarrett interview; and Daniel, *Lost Revolutions*, 99.

12. Fielden, *The Beginning*, 109, 140, 7.

13. *Charlotte Observer*, 10 August 1961, A-1; and Golenbock, *Last Lap*, 220.

14. Golenbock, *Last Lap*, 69; and Fielden, *The Superspeedway Boom*, 285–86.

15. Jarrett interview; and Richard Petty with William Neely, *King Richard I: The Autobiography of America's Greatest Auto Racer* (Paper Jacks, Ltd., 1987), 149.

16. Fielden, *The Superspeedway Boom*, 52–53; and Fielden, *The Beginning*, 108.

17. Golenbock, *Last Lap*, 66.

18. Petty, *King Richard*, 192; and Golenbock, *American Zoom*, 49–50.

19. Practically every book on NASCAR has a section on the life and antics of Curtis Turner. A few of the more notable include Golenbock, *American Zoom*, 23–34; and Golenbock, *Last Lap*, 27–51.

20. Golenbock, *Last Lap*, 217–20; and Fielden, *The Superspeedway Boom*, 94–96.

21. *Asheville Citizen*, 10 August 1961, 26; *Charlotte Observer*, 10 August 1961, A-1; and Fielden, *The Superspeedway Boom*, 94.

22. *Charlotte Observer*, 10 August 1961, E-1.

23. Fielden, *The Superspeedway Boom*, 97; and *Charlotte Observer*, 13 August 1961, E-1.

24. *Asheville Citizen*, 11 August 1961, 22, 23.

25. *Charlotte Observer*, 12 August 1961, 6-A.

26. Fielden, *The Superspeedway Boom*, 99–100; and *Charlotte Observer*, 22 August 1961, 5-B.

27. *Asheville Citizen*, 14 August 1961, 1.

28. Ibid.; and Fielden, *The Superspeedway Boom*, 127–28.

29. *Charlotte Observer*, 23 August 1961, 4-B; and Ned Jarrett interview.

30. Fielden, *The Superspeedway Boom*, 239.

31. Ibid., 7–15 and 61–66.

32. Ned Jarrett interview.

33. Richard Petty, interview with author, 23 September 1998; and Fielden, *Forty Years of Stock Car Racing*, vol. 3, *Big Bucks and Boycotts, 1965–1971* (Galfield Press, 1989), 211.

34. Fielden, *Big Bucks and Boycotts*, 210.

35. Hemphill, *Wheels*, 204.

36. Fielden, *Big Bucks and Boycotts*, 210–12.

37. The information on the Talladega speedway episode came from the *Charlotte Observer*, 13 September 1969, 9-A; 14 September 1969, 1-D, 3-D; and 15 September 1969.

38. Fielden, *Big Bucks and Boycotts*, 214.

39. Ibid., 214, 255; and interview with Richard Petty.

40. *Charlotte Observer*, 15 September 1969, 13-A.

41. Fielden, *Big Bucks and Boycotts*, 216–17; and Daniel, *Lost Revolutions*, 99.

42. *Charlotte Observer*, 25 September 1969, C-1.

43. Jonathan Ingram, "The Battle of the Independents," *Southern Exposure* 7.2 (1979): 92–99.

44. Richard Petty interview; and Dave Marcis, interview with author, 29 September 1998.

45. International Speedway Corporation website, www.iscmotorsports.com/ischistory.html; Herb Greenberg, "Herb's Hotline: The Value of Bond Analysts," www.thestreet.com/funds/herbgreenberg/975164.html, 23 June 2000.

46. Richard Petty interview; Dave Marcis interview; and Golenbock, *Last Lap*, 140–41.

African American Humor and the South

Trudier Harris

Famed author Zora Neale Hurston (here) reportedly once used classic southern humor in a courtroom encounter to play on segregation-era double standards. Courtesy of the Collections of the Library of Congress.

lack folks *in* the South. Black folks *and* the South. Black folks *from* the South. Black folks *against* the South. Black folks *with* the South. Black folks *above* the South (as in *up*south, New York or Chicago). Black folks *under* the South (as in the "foot on the neck" image of oppression). These reflect some of the tensions and paradoxes involved in thinking about a people whose American roots are primarily in the South but who have such a strange relationship to it.

One strand of African American history is the saga of migration out of the South and into the urban areas of the North, where formerly enslaved persons or those who were drawn by the hopes of the Great Migration found a healthy antithesis to the environment from which they had presumably escaped. Or they perpetuated a healthy mythology about the North even when it did not exist. And they made their annual pilgrimages home—frequently in rented Cadillacs—designed to impress their "backward, country" relatives. The South was anathema, epitomized in the story of the pregnant black woman who visits relatives in that region, where her pregnancy extends into the tenth and eleventh months. When a baffled doctor finally puts a stethoscope to the mother's stomach, the baby is heard proclaiming, "I won't be born down here. I won't be born down here." So black folks who had migrated north generally stayed out of the South—until 1974 or thereabouts, when inflation hit and the price of sugar rose to two dollars and forty-nine cents for a five pound bag, and when heating oil bills in colder climates skyrocketed. Then, all of a sudden, those southern peas and greens, open spaces, and sunshine became attractive. It became chic for black folks to migrate back to the South.

Yet for all the migration in and out, and the ambivalence in attitudes, the South, with all its connotations of repression and violence, remained and remains an active force in the African American creative imagination. In belles lettres, popular culture, and folk culture, the South as a place of mixed memory and the site of the creation of a particular brand of determination led black Americans to replay its meanings again and again. While James Baldwin asserted in his 1979 novel *Just Above My Head* that black Americans could look at a map of the territory below the Mason-Dixon line and scare themselves to death, Toni Cade Bambara, Toni Morrison, and Alice Walker reversed the trend of leaving the South and transformed the soil into a healthy, regenerative force for their characters. Bambara crated a mythical southern town in *The Salt Eaters* (1980) that rivals in tolerance and cuisine any place on earth. Morrison sent Milkman

Dead to Virginia in *Song of Solomon* (1977) in order for him to find an ancestry that transcended not only Michigan but American soil; her revisionist approach to the experiences of enslaved Africans in *Beloved* (1987) left us with several memorable and mythical southern characters. Walker's claiming of Georgia soil for several of her works, including *The Third Life of Grange Copeland* (1970) and *The Color Purple* (1982), illustrates yet again how contemporary black writers allow characters to grow, prosper, and reach their full potential in a territory that previously only meant death and repression to them.

On the lighter side, the black folk imagination—from tales of encounters with sheriffs to dealing with generic forms of confinement—has demonstrated that the South has always been fertile soil on which to work out the blues motif (laughing to keep from crying) inherent in being descended from a people so strongly identified with that territory. The humor reflects a mixture of love and revulsion, immersion and transcendence. Comedians such as Jackie "Moms" Mabley have done their share in "inventing" (as Morrison would say) the South, for as long as the exorcising force of humor was operative, African Americans could never be defeated by racial ugliness. In a sense we could argue that African American humor—as folk narrators and popular comedians presented it—did more for black people's attitudes toward the South than any legislation. Put simply, for African Americans, humor made the South not only endurable but transcendable, for humor reduced the South to a laughably manageable level of insanity.

The love-hate relationship blacks have with the South is manifested in everyday life as well as in the humor. Expressions such as "down home" used in reference to the South locate the point of origin for most black Americans. It has been documented that, when asked the question, "Where are you from?," black people invariably identify their southern homes even if they have lived out of the South for two or three decades. In fact, William Wells Brown used the title *My Southern Home: Or, The South and Its People* for a collection of essays he published in 1880; Richard Wright would similarly draw upon connotations between slavery and the South in *Uncle Tom's Children* (1938). The South is home just as America is home, and black people have exhibited their claims to the territory by asserting the right to criticize it. Criticism, Baldwin argues of his relationship to America, is ultimately what one earns by *loving* one's country. I cannot speculate on how many black people would say they *love* the South, but demographics would certainly suggest that they are more comfortable in it than history might warrant—or perhaps it is precisely history that occasions that comfort.

I should point out that, in the humor on southern territory, black people frequently draw upon racial stereotypes and derogatory self references as a part of the laughter. It seems to me that the nature of humor is such that abbreviated references, especially to stereotypical habits, are frequently preferred to those that are spelled out and that commonplace or slang references take precedence over more formal ones. It is common, therefore, in the humor to see black people paint themselves as driving Cadillacs, wielding razors, stealing, or referring to themselves as "niggers."[1] Black men may stereotypically be in pursuit of "the white woman"—less, it seems, for the woman herself, than for what she represents. She is objectified into a prize to be won or a metaphor for overstepping the bounds or limitations imposed upon black men. If the subject matter of the humor is at times brutal, it reflects the brutal circumstances from which it is derived.

The subject areas upon which the humor focuses are wide-ranging. Many deal with how whites try to maintain the status quo and how black people are caught in the web of negotiations involving the pushing of legal, physical, and psychological limits of confinements. Attempts to change laws, for example, from obtaining voting rights to eating in diners, are fair game for the humor. The broad areas of integration (of bus stations, restaurants, and schools) in an effort to broaden access to democracy perhaps serves as the prime subject area for sources of humorous interactions between blacks and whites. The territory on which custom and law clash, that is, practices governing private interactions between blacks and whites in the South, also find their way into the humor. For example, law may determine that blacks and whites can intermarry, but custom forbids the practice. Those who violate such customs—usually black men in liaisons with white women—are punished swiftly. Crossing geographical, legal, and interpersonal boundaries —those were the taboo actions that led to much civil rights legislation and that define much African American humor about the South. All of these areas of negotiated access were clearly serious and often involved lifethreatening issues, yet these are the areas in which we see humor serving its primary function: that of release. Humor is the balm against pain, the laughter in the face of insane actions and customs directed against black individuals and black people generally.

Instead of reflecting upon the severe slap to dignity that refusal of service in a diner would mean, a black person unceremoniously informed that, "We don't serve niggers here," could reply with, "I don't eat 'em."[2] A similar saving of face in the possible loss of dignity is the following anecdote. A black man goes into a restaurant, orders, and is served a whole chicken. Just before he begins eating, a group of white men gathers around his table and asserts, as punishment for his violation of taboo, that they will do to him whatever he does to the chicken. He sits awhile, desperately thinking how he can get out of the situation, then he turns the chicken up, kisses its rear end, and gets up, and walks out. The joke turns upon the stereotype of the chicken-loving black person that dates back to enslaved persons being caught in the slaveowners' henhouses. It also is a tribute to the black man of wits who is able in a pinch to outwit his hostile opponents. Turning the tables, changing the joke, and slipping the yoke (as Ralph Ellison would say), or simply having the lucky foresight to say, "You've got the old coon at last," as the salvation to identifying a raccoon in a box are but a few instances of black people using their wits to get out of near fatal situations. The seeming ease with which black people negotiate these racial waters reflects the depth of their familiarity with the territory on which they are forced to play as well as their knowledge of their opponents in that territory.

While many black people may consider the South home, it is clear that they have repeatedly been treated almost as strangers, or worse than strangers, as if they were in a foreign country. I borrow the phrase "foreign country" in reference to the South from Moms Mabley, and it is Moms who has provided us with many humorous accounts of adventures in as well as responses to the South. She has joked about the voting registration situation, about segregation in general, and about specific racist encounters. She has the uncanny ability, like poet Sterling Brown, to make the absurd manageable by making it laughable. On the impossibility of blacks voting in the South, she says:

> Now hear this. Mom just got back from down there. Behind the scorching curtain in Selma. While I was down I even hear 'em give a boy a literacy test where them cats have to go thru before they can vote. And this boy happened to be a college graduate, you see. So he went up to the desk; the fellow behind it say, "Let me hear you say the Constitution backwards." He's giving a literacy test and he's talking about the Constitution backwards. Said, "Let me hear you say the Old and New Testament frontwards and backwards." He said it forwards

and backwards. He give him a Chinese newspaper. He said, "Let me hear you read that paper." Fellow looked at it. He say, "What does it say? What does it say?" "Says don't make no difference what I do you ain't gonna let me vote nohow."[3]

If prejudice in the South extended to maintaining the status quo in voting, it certainly extended to more personal, private relationships. Law might allow one thing, but custom governed more often than not. Says Moms:

> Colored fellow down home died. Pulled up to the [heavenly] gate. St. Peter looked at him, say, "What do you want?" "Hey man [the guy says], you know me. Hey Jack, you know me. I'm old Sam Jones. Old Sam Jones, man, you know me. Used to be with the NAACP, you know CORE and all that stuff, man, marches, remember me? Oh man, you know me." He just broke down there. "You know me." He [St. Peter] looked in his book. "Sam Jones," he say, "No, no you ain't here, no Sam Jones." He said, "Oh man, yes, I am. Look there. You know me. I'm the cat that married that white girl on the Capitol steps of Jackson, Mississippi." He [St. Peter] said, "How long ago has that been?" He said, "About five minutes ago."[4]

If Mississippi justice was so swift that Sam Jones did not get his reward (the prized white woman) on earth, then surely he cannot be denied entry into heaven. His desperation enhances the urgency of that desire. And the joke obviously allows laughter at the absurdity of taboos, injunctions against marriage across racial lines.

As a political commentator and observer of social norms who appointed herself adviser to President Lyndon B. Johnson, Moms Mabley seldom passed up an opportunity to comment on the southern racial climate. Of the many caricatures she created of herself, she placed herself in the South in several of these joking situations. One involves the play on language that is a key ingredient for African American humor.

> I just come back from down there, you now. I didn't want to go but, you know, my children now are young children in school, in college, and they buy my records, and they wanted to see Mom. I wanted to go and I didn't want to go cause I just bought me a brand new white car, you know. And I didn't want to paint it all up! Cause you know you have to be the same color your car is down there. And I thought a brown car with black wall tires would look terrible, you know. But I

went on, you know, and I got down there and I tried to pass, you know. Well, I'll try to let me pass for anything except what I am, you know, I'd make it, you know. And some of my friends from Montana, some of my children out there sent me a cowgirl outfit. So I got, I wore that down there and wore it the whole time I was there I wouldn't wear nothing but this cowgirl outfit, but I was trying to pass. They were nice to me, you'd be surprised. They didn't treat me bad at all. In fact, they called me after Will [Roy] Rogers' horse, you know, Trigger. Yeah, everywhere I go they'd be saying, "Hello Trigger, hi Trigger!" At least I *think* that's what they said.[5]

How do human beings salvage dignity in impossible situations? By pretending that the offense is something else, because in that "foreign country," anything is liable to happen.[6]

In traditional African American literature and folktales, travel through the South has been particularly perilous, for it may frequently involve violations of spatial taboos that whites hold sacred. Many are the tales of signs posted on various off-limits southern territories that assert: "Nigger, read and run. If you can't read, run anyhow." Or "No niggers or dogs allowed." However, some black folks are better able to traverse those forbidden boundaries than others. One notable negotiator is Slim Greer, a character Sterling Brown created and incorporated into many of his poems. Slim, who is "no lighter / Than a dark midnight" nonetheless manages to pass for white and court a white woman in Arkansas until his blues-playing ability makes a suspicious white man conclude: "No white man / Could play like that. . . ." In another poem Slim goes to hell only to discover that it is Dixie. But one of his real stops in Dixie is especially noteworthy; it highlights a peculiar practice in Atlanta.

Down in Atlanta he encounters two hundred black folks lined up to get into a "telefoam booth," because "De whitefolks got laws / For to keep all de niggers / From laughin' outdoors." Slim jumps the line and enters the booth to laugh at the sight. Soon there are "*Three* hundred niggers there / In misery.— / Some holdin' deir sides, / Some holdin' deir jaws, / To keep from breakin' / De Georgia laws." The sight provokes Slim to still more laughter. Finally an ambulance is called and "De state paid de railroad / To take him away; / Den, things was as usual / In Atlanta, Gee A."[7] Slim escapes punishment because his unusual actions can be cast into the "crazy nigger" syndrome, that realm of permissibility into which black males in the South managed to violate law or custom and live in spite of the violation. They are the kind of men about whom Richard Wright writes in an essay entitled "How Bigger Was Born"[8] in reference to his creation of the character Bigger Thomas in *Native Son* (1940).

It is also worth noting that the joke hinges upon a concept that black people cultivated historically, that is, a specific space for the containment of sound, such as a pot placed in the middle of a forbidden, impromptu religious gathering in the woods near a plantation. Of this phenomenon, folklorist and cultural analyst Alan Dundes writes: "If a Negro wished to laugh out loud at his master, he might do so only at considerable risk. So he suppressed the desire to laugh and went instead to the 'laughing barrel,' where he could laugh to his heart's content without fear of being heard. This traditional outlet is strikingly similar to the custom of placing an inverted wash kettle in the center of the floor during a prayer meeting so that the sounds of the singing might go into the pot and thereby not disturb the white folks at the plantation house."[9] It is interesting, therefore, that Brown appropriates this tradition from African American culture as the site for illustrating the absurdity of southern Jim Crow laws and, in this case, the humorous consequence for a traveler who violates them.

Black travelers on southern territory are frequently held accountable for violating economic taboos, that is, for the cars they drive and the clothes they wear. Many are the tales of black men in the Jim Crow South who owned "white" cars, in that white people considered the cars too "good" for black folks. In order to keep their dignity, their persons, and their cars undamaged, these men would wear chauffeurs' caps when they went driving and pretend that they were working for wealthy whites.[10] Various versions of a joke portraying a black man in a Cadillac depict the following encounter. "This fellow, you know, came down South. . . . He rolled in, had one of these big, long Cadillacs, one of these $400 suits thrown on, diamond rings." He saw a white man chewing tobacco in front of a gasoline station and asked him, "Fill the tank up, will you chief?" The white man asked him if he knew just where he was, and said, "Well, down here, you say 'mister' and you say it snappy, you hear." The colored man replied, "Now, I don't say 'mister' to nobody." So the white man pulled his gun and blew a fly clear off the top of a nearby bush, without ever touching the bush. He said, "That's what happens when you don't say 'mister,' boy." The colored man asked if he were trying to show off and asked for a saucer. "Throw it in the air," he asked of the white man. The colored man got an apple from his car and threw it in the air. While the apple was still in the air, he "took a straight razor, whipped it out, 'fore the apple hit the ground, peeled, cut the core out, sliced it up so thin that it land in the saucer, hit the ground, it was apple sauce." And the white man saw this and jumped up and said, "What you want, sonny?" "Just regular."[11]

This joke, obviously of more recent political times in its twist ending, allows the black man to become an active force in his own fate—in contrast to Slim Greer. Ellison's notion of changing the joke and slipping the yoke is even more striking. By using a weapon stereotypically associated with black males, the black man turns the tables on his presumed enemy by a superior show of skill. The added dimension is that the white man is portrayed as willing enough to admit a level playing field, to recognize and give way before the superior skill—a fact that would not have happened in earlier such tales. The black man here violates speaking taboos, patterns of interracial social interactions, and the presumed psychological space that is traditionally assigned only to the white man. For a competition to be concocted, played fairly, and culminated by the success of the black victor is a milestone in the humor. The tale is so popular that Moms Mabley has a version of it, and there are at least three others I have discovered in addition to the one just quoted.

In another Cadillac tale, a black man uses the vehicle as the particular expression of his desire to violate taboo:

"This Black guy say, [excitedly] I'm gon' get me a *white* woman, a *white* Cadillac, and a *white* suit, and ride down the roads o' Georgia in dat car!"

The (other black guy) say, "Well, you go right ahead—you know what I'm gon' do. I'm gon' get a *black* woman, a *black* Cadillac, a *black* suit, and ride down them same roads o' Georgia—and see your black ass hanging."[12]

Custom renders the local version of justice swiftly, but the joke also posits acceptable laughter at a black person who is so gleefully insensitive to the tragic consequences of trespassing established racial taboos. The second speaker knows that history—knows that whites will respond in a certain way, knows that racial taboos may as well be immutable, for violation is tragic and fatal. Any black man remotely accused of improper conduct with a white woman was subject to death by lynching. Sensible black males, therefore, would not place themselves in situations that allowed for such a possibility.

The arena of legal justice in the form of courtroom encounters, however, also find their way into the humor. Southern blacks find themselves jailed or fined for not saying *Mister* Mule when the mule happens to be white or for not putting sufficient emphasis upon *Miss* in requesting Miss Muriel cigars. And there is the standard joke of a black person being arrested for walking against a red light and, when taken to court, offering this explanation: since the white folks walked with the green light, he or she just assumed that the red light was for black folks to walk (even Zora Neale Hurston reputedly once used this as an explanation).

African American humor focusing on the South and race relations in general may well be called "dark laughter," the title of Oliver W. Harrington's collection of political, social, and racial cartoons. For situations that are frequently life threatening, it is at times hard to imagine guffaws associated with them. Yet black people managed to create the essence of the blues—to laugh to keep from crying—in and about a land that was as much hell as it was home. And for all the migration North, for all the justified complaint about treatment in the South, I have never heard a black person say of the South: "It's a nice place to visit, but I wouldn't want to live there." As more and more black people are living "there," it is clear that a healthy sense of humor is a prerequisite for that experience.

NOTES

1. It is difficult, even in the most altruistically intended context, to argue positive connotations for this word. Yet, African Americans invariably use it among themselves, most often affectionately but sometimes derisively. Whites generally still only intend it derogatorily. For example, at the conference at which I presented an earlier version of this paper, a white man who has lived in the South all his life and wanted to illustrate "the changing same" asked privately if he could tell me a joke he had heard recently. He wanted to ensure that I would not be offended by it. The joke took the form of a question: "What do you call a nigger?" Answer: "An African American who has just left the room."

2. For two other versions of this tale, see Daryl C. Dance, *Shuckin' and Jivin': Folklore from Contemporary Black Americans* (Indiana University Press, 1978), 201.

3. Jackie "Moms" Mabley, *The Best of Moms Mabley* (Mercury Records).

4. Jackie "Moms" Mabley, *The Best of Moms Mabley* (Chess Records).

5. Ibid.

6. In her autobiography, *Zami: A New Spelling of My Name* (Freedom, California: The Crossing Press, 1982), Audre Lorde recounts how, when she was growing up in New York, her mother would attempt to ignore white people spitting

on her daughters by asserting that they were spitting into the wind and the spittle just accidentally sprayed her daughters' clothing. Lorde comments: "But it was so typical of my mother when I was young that if she couldn't stop white people from spitting on her children because they were Black, she would insist it was something else. It was so often her approach to the world; to change reality. If you can't change reality, change your perceptions of it" (18).

7. *The Collected Poems of Sterling A. Brown*, selected by Michael S. Harper (New York: Harper Colophon, 1983), 81–82.

8. Richard Wright, "How Bigger Was Born," printed in the introduction to *Native Son* (Harper and Row, 1966), vii–xxxiv.

9. Alan Dundes provides this explanation in entitling his early collection of essays on African American folklore *Mother Wit from the Laughing Barrel* (Prentice-Hall, 1973), xii–xiv.

10. Mildred D. Taylor, who has written several books about the Jim Crow South in Mississippi, deals with that taboo in *Roll of Thunder, Hear My Cry* (Dial, 1976), in which the young female narrator's uncle, visiting from the North, drives a "silver Packard" "a few months newer" than the one belonging to the most prestigious white man in town.

11. Roger Abrahams, *Deep Down in the Jungle: Negro Narrative Folklore from the Streets of Philadelphia* (Chicago: Aldine, 1970), 237–38; for a tale that uses the apple cutting motif without the car and gasoline components, see Dance, *Shuckin' and Jivin'*, 217.

12. Dance, *Shuckin' and Jivin'*, 107–8.

Sister Act
Sorority Rush as Feminine Performance

Elizabeth Boyd

Alumni chapters, in-house "poop groups," and a vast network of family and friends are called upon to verify sorority applicants' reputations and class status. Dancing at a Chi Phi party, 1966, courtesy of the North Carolina Collection at the University of North Carolina Library at Chapel Hill.

he scene inside Fulton Chapel is almost enough to make you forget that it is two o'clock on a late August afternoon in Mississippi. Despite the sweltering heat, the melting humidity, and the lack of air conditioning, the atmosphere inside is not one of languidness, but of high anxiety. Here some 665 incoming female students are seated in groups of seventy. They are chattering, they are excited, they are nervous. It's the opening scene of sorority rush, and at the University of Mississippi—known by one and all as "Ole Miss"—rush is serious business.[1]

In the next few days these young women (or girls, as they refer to themselves and each other) will submit to a process of evaluation that will determine the course of their social life for the next four years. For some, the stakes will be for life. But right now they're all equal—at least equally nervous—and they're checking out the competition.

If the air is filled with tension, the scene reveals nothing but composure and preparation. Here the rule is flawless skin; tasteful manicures; healthy, glossy hair that's just been trimmed, highlighted, deep-conditioned. All vision has been corrected. All hair is at least shoulder length. The clothing is "studied casual"—shorts, sundresses, new sandals. A few false eyelashes. Full makeup, professionally done.

Roaming the crowd are the rush counselors, those twenty-five knowledgeable rising seniors who have given up their sorority affiliations for the week to help guide and advise the new rushees. They hold meetings, say "yea" or "nay" to dresses, shepherd the rushees around from house to house. For them, this Convocation—the official opening of rush—is old hat. Dressed in Panhellenic T-shirts, khaki shorts, and cross-training shoes, they roam the auditorium with an air of purpose and self-assurance. Not for them the rushee's complete makeup incongruously paired with casual shorts and sandals. The counselors are wearing day makeup, tastefully blended. And they're hauling around enormous backpacks, which they'll soon use to carry the rushees' essentials from house to house.

A couple of hours later, we meet in the back of Brown dorm. The casual clothes of the afternoon have been replaced by demure, long, swingy sundresses (the small-town Tennessee girls); contemporary, short-sleeved suits (the Dallas girls); matching, slightly out-of-date pants suits (the Delta girls); and bright floral, sixties pop-art sundresses (the Jackson girls). And everywhere, as if it had washed up in an Irish tide, a virtual sea of linen. Not linen-blend or "linen-like," but sure-enough, my-family-can-afford-it linen. Suit-weight and handkerchief. The genuine article. The shoe of the hour is chunky, brown or black, and generously strapped. The girls have stuffed their essentials—keys, lipstick, all manner of Clinique—in labeled, plastic bags, which will be schlepped up and down Sorority Row for them by the rush counselors.

Outside the Theta house, the rushees learn the pattern of the evening. Waiting in the stifling heat, they suddenly hear what sounds like war whoops and pounding coming from inside the front door. At the strike of five, the Thetas, two hundred strong, throw back the door and appear in formation, crowding the door from floor to sill with Theta faces, radiating Theta love, and singing a Theta song. Then they burst from the door, each calling a particular rushee's name: "Heather! Ashley! Brooke!" The Thetas are dressed in different shades of the same scoop-necked shift; together, they create a linen rainbow. Taking the rushees by the hand and scooting them indoors, the Thetas proceed to "rush" them—to woo them with party chatter and giant, unrelenting smiles—for exactly twenty minutes.

Inside the Theta house, it's cool and tasteful: apricot walls, country French antiques, floral arrangements in front of every gilt mirror, oriental rugs. After a frenetic few minutes of socializing, the girls are herded into the meeting room for a slide show highlighting Theta life and its many advantages: formals with fraternity men, parties and more parties, "sisterhood." Then, more high-volume meeting and greeting in the front rooms, and on to the next house. But not before the Thetas once again crowd the doorway, this time to sing goodbye.

ACTING FEMININE, ACTING SOUTHERN

Sorority rush is a feminine stratification ritual performed each year at scores of college campuses across the country. Consisting of a series of increasingly selective "get acquainted" parties, rush is a proving ground of competitive femininity cloaked in the guise of gracious hospitality and collegiate spirit. If at first glance rush appears all fresh-scrubbed good looks, lilting laughter, and nonstop smiles, a closer look reveals something else entirely: a scrutiny session in which women are assigned a social value based on looks, status, and feminine competency.

Rush is a daunting social obstacle course wherever it's enacted, but nowhere are the expectations higher, the standards more stringent, or the consequences so crucial as in the South, where many a feminine future still depends on a few days in August. If schools in other parts of the country have gradually adopted more relaxed rush procedures—featuring casual get-togethers, shortened rush schedules, and bidding practices geared towards inclusion rather than exclusivity—the large southern schools have been slower to change, hanging on to old forms and arcane formalities that, at century's end, make a southern rush increasingly distinctive.

As a laboratory of southern womanhood, sorority rush is perhaps unsurpassed. And at Ole Miss, the annual performance represents a pinnacle of sorts, an apex of feminine enactment with its own regional meanings, yardsticks, and habits. Here, in a mere five days of careful choreography, time-honored gender standards are upheld and celebrated, as intertwined ideas about family and femininity, race and place, are mapped on the bodies of young women. Demanding the performance of a fairly specific rendition of womanhood, rush momentarily resurrects the Southern Lady—strong yet demure, chaste but fertile, ethereal yet grounded, knowing but silent—in all her contradictory mythological splendor. In the process, regional feminine ideals are maintained, class and race structures are reaffirmed, and the Old South exists ephemerally in the New.

In truth, rush demands a particular feminine performance that combines attributes of the Lady with those of her iconographic counterpart, the Belle.[2] That the Belle's polished surfaces—her high-wattage allure, her conversational dexterity—should prove useful during rush is not surprising. But her true advantage is found beneath the gloss, in her strategic mind, selfish nature, and determined heart. On first witnessing rush, it might be easy to assume that somewhere along the way the Lady and Belle figures have become fused in the popular imagination, with a single, hyperfeminine persona the result. But to give the participants credit, the rushee is a situational construction, a pragmatic feminine character with the deft ability to display the appropriate Lady or Belle characteristics in turn, as circumstances demand. As if instinctively understanding rush for what it is, a crucial rite of passage between the carefree ways of youth and the more serious demands of southern womanhood, the able rushee navigates expectations on cue, alternately exhibiting the bright sparkle of the Belle and the sincere empathy of the Lady. Meanwhile, behind the scenes, both actives and rushees operate from decidedly Belle-like positions: cold calculation and opportunism. The successful rushee is the one who performs the pertness of the Belle while evidencing the promise of the Lady. In the final analysis, rush comes down on the side of the Lady, for a Lady would never embarrass her sisters.

It should come as no surprise that such stylized performance should reach its zenith at Ole Miss, where in recent years an extended public debate has raged over the university's symbols. The use and meaning of such contentious signs as the Confederate flag, the song "Dixie," and the university's planter-gentleman mascot, "Colonel Reb," continue to endure scrutiny, with opposing camps largely stalemated between claims of "tradition" and "heritage" on the one hand and "racism" and "backwardness" on the other. On a campus still haunted by the James Meredith integration "crisis" of 1962, social progress has been real, but it is also understood to be hard-won, and campus symbols, potentially explosive.[3] When a chancellor-led campaign to improve perceptions of the university caused Confederate flags to all but disappear from the football stadium, that potent symbol migrated to the bodies of young women, who continued to sport it in the form of whole-flag wraparound skirts and Greek T-shirts incorporating the insignia. Officially "gone," but not forgotten, the flag never so much went away as it went underground, where in some circles it now enjoys the status of renegade booty: its visibility curtailed, its circulation improved, with femininity and the flag now explicitly, corporally linked.

The flag controversy is just a single example of what one critic calls "hidden in plain sight," the phenomenon of southerners' inability—or refusal—to acknowledge the cultural mechanisms they see working clearly before them.[4] Many mechanisms that serve to maintain race and gender hierarchies, for example, do their work so seamlessly they rarely draw recognition, despite their public nature. So persuasive yet so pervasive, they are so much a part of the warp and weft of southern life (so "natural," so "traditional"), they largely go unnoticed by participants and observers alike. Perhaps least recognized of all are those rituals that shore up conservative notions about race in the process of reiterating prescriptive gender ideals. For all the ink spilled and the breath spent on the South's twentieth-century racial symbols, little has been noted about its contemporary gender signs, much less the link between the two.

Sorority rush hides much in plain sight. Not far from the athletic fields thrives a symbol sport of another sort. Across the Grove on Sorority Row, the Southern Lady returns each season for a cameo appearance that in its precision and predictability offers comforting reassurance. Gone for the week are the slummy baseball caps and Birkenstocks that typify the sorority girl's class-day wardrobe. In their place appear demure, churchy frocks that in their dated modesty speak volumes about our longing for an earlier, bygone innocence. Out of character with day-to-day college life, the scene is in sync with only rush itself—and perhaps a pervasive regional anxiety about a changing South. The dramatic contrast between the performative style of the everyday and that of rush, if not purposely exaggerated, nevertheless takes on heightened significance, visible evidence that for many rush remains a sacred space, a ritual link between nineteenth-century ideals and twentieth-century imaginations. With acting feminine and acting southern twin criteria, rush is a two-act performance, and accepted standards of breeding, grooming, lineage, appearance, and class are the markers the successful rushee must not only possess but tastefully display. What with rushees and actives attempting to assess each other's social value while demonstrating their own, and rushees trying to land themselves in a "good house" so to do their families proud, there's a lot of cultural work going on behind the lipstick and laughter.

But don't for a second think this romantic ritual is some self-conscious Confederate commemoration. That's not magnolia blossoms you smell, it's dry cleaning. And out in the street, there's not a horse-drawn carriage in sight, just late-model BMWs, Acuras, and sport utility vehicles as far as the eye can see. These days, nostalgic longings are best pursued with contemporary equipment and postmodern techniques. Hopeful rushees are burning up their cell phones and e-mail checking in with Mom and the hometown crowd, while harried actives put the finishing touches on multimedia presentations and gather computer Opscan sheets for voting. Yet here are the columned mansions, the wide verandahs, the plantation shutters, the shady oaks. For just as antebellum society placed a gender icon—the Southern Lady—at the center of its racial and economic rationale, then measured status and place through so many movements and approximations of etiquette, so too does sorority rush demand proof of a particular feminine competence, then sorts out the campus pecking order on the basis of execution. It's a command performance, and the ability to "do" southern womanhood—Lady *and* Belle—is once again, suddenly, strangely, in high demand. Tara may have been bought out by agribusiness, but for a few days in summer, sorority rush is surely a living symbol, a romantic ritual that conserves much more than it changes. Once again, being received in the right houses depends on lineage, on pure blood, on being able to claim—and visually represent—a direct line of honorable descent. Perhaps most of all, it's what makes rush at Ole Miss so "hard core," "cut throat," even "brutal," as participants describe it. According to a junior Tri Delt from Houston, Texas, friends back home going through rush at the University of Texas were warned ahead of time that theirs was a "hard rush" and that only one other in the country was known to be tougher—that at Ole Miss.[5] As a close-up look reveals, a southern rush, although in many respects similar to rituals taking place on far-flung campuses, is distinguishable in both obvious and subtle ways.

The texts, settings, and performance of rush emphasize feminine competency and its necessity to social success. The rush party's multiple texts—including the lyrics of sorority songs, skit scripts, the one-on-one party talk between active and rushee, and the sorority president's persuasive monologue—all articulate a singular rite of homosocial wooing that is ultimately in the service of heterosexual romance.

The physical setting of rush—especially the antebellum-mansion-like architecture of the Ole Miss sorority house and its ultra-feminine décor—holds out the promise of inhabiting a real, grownup woman's home. By joining a sorority, the fledgling woman's feminine, domestic destiny is assured; cachet is granted.

In this realm of feminine intimacies, the older, seemingly glamorous and sophisticated actives seek out new members who already appear to possess a high level of feminine competence, performed via clothing, cosmetic know-how, manners, and sociability. Girls who are likely to prove "an asset to the house" contribute positively to the overall public profile of the group by being any or all of the following: cute, popular, a campus leader, a beauty, an athlete, a student with good grades, a member of an old, established, and recognized family.[6] Rushees, in turn, seek out a group in which they feel "comfortable" but in which they can also imagine improving themselves—a group the rushee considers "like me, only better."

Throughout it all, the performance of authenticity is central, as each sorority endeavors to posit itself as the one group that "really does" value diversity and where a new member "really can" find a home. In turn, the rushee strives to appear as sincerely interested in one sorority as the next, in effect not showing her hand. Both active and rushee play roles in a ritual that, through its annual performance, reinscribes a conservative, prescriptive rendition of gender.

The things at issue during rush—looks, family, status, feminine power, social value—make their appearance along a performative axis balancing innocence and knowledge. Both actives and would-be members attempt to perform innocence while acquiring knowledge. Both parties attempt to find out more about the other, while keeping the revelations selective. Both try to see the other's hand, without showing their own. In this parlor game, knowledge is power. But so is innocence. This dichotomy is evident in even the simplest mechanics of rush.

"I felt really intimidated [the first day] because all the sorority girls knew exactly what was going to happen," recalls one Phi Mu. "You kind of knew even then which sororities knew which girls. I kind of caught on that day. They don't know who the heck I am and they *know* that girl in my rush group."[7]

A freshman met up with this imbalance in knowledge even earlier—at the Oxford Wal-Mart the week before rush. Stocking up on dorm-life essentials, she encountered group after group of letter-wearing sorority girls, who met her friendly glances with only silent, knowing stares. The sudden realization that "they know exactly who I am and where I'm from and everything about me and I have no idea who any of them are" was enough to warn her away from appearing in public that week without first getting "dolled up."

At the parties, says one freshman, "You're sitting there talking and you know that they're critiquing you and they know that you're critiquing them. It's their objective to make you think that *you* are the one that they want, out of everyone in the room."[8]

Once a rushee gets used to all the attention, ignorance is a poor substitute for knowledge. "They all knew my name," recalls a Tri Delt of her first visits to the house. "It was overwhelming. Then . . . when you go to a house and they [have to] look at your nametag, you're kinda [unimpressed]. At one house, they mispronounced my name, and I was like, Oh, well, they obviously don't *know* me."[9]

The rotation groups employed during the rush parties represent a classic split between knowledgeable active and naive rushee. In an effort to make party circulation appear natural—and rushees feel cherished—actives perform a tightly choreographed version of musical chairs, moving from seated rushee to rushee. Designed to create an illusion of popularity and adoration, the goal is to make each rushee feel as if *she* were the center of attention. Like most illusions, this one requires elaborate timing and considerable practice. All the rushee sees is a nonstop stream of actives coming to surround her, like bees to a flower. What she mustn't see is that her treatment is not so special after all. As with so many aspects of rush, notes one Phi Mu, "the rushee's really not supposed to know what's happening."[10]

At the Alpha Omicron Pi house, the presence of Santa and Mrs. Claus, numerous lighted Christmas trees, boughs of holly and ivy, and plenty of elves attest to members' claims that their house is "the only thing close to the feeling you get at Christmas."[11] (It also attests that Jewish rushees are not anticipated.) Like all the other sororities, the AOPis make claims of authenticity that by definition posit their competition as fake. In this battle for authenticity, two rush scripts are consistently employed: the "home away from home" script (or the narrative of the "lost rushee"), and the "diversity" script.

In the first, the lost rushee is away from home for the first time. Stripped of her identity and bewildered by university life, she enters rush in search of a home. Only through sorority membership will the fledgling girl-woman acquire the knowledge necessary to social success. The lost rushee knows she's come home when she gets that Christmasy feeling at AOPi.

Closely related to this script is the narrative of diversity. In this disingenuous script, each sorority—an exclusive organization by nature—attempts to "out-diverse" the others with claims of inclusiveness, sincerity, and acceptance. It's only at *their* house that you can really be yourself. At the AOPi house the diversity skit features four drum majors, one dancing to her own beat.

"You're trying to sell authenticity," says one Phi Mu active. "I try to keep it all authentic. Because I have girls in my sorority who don't. They lie about everything. They . . . tell the rushees, 'Oh, I had the hardest decision to make, and my mother was here, and da-da-da.' You know, trying to get the legacies to come over. And they lie, lie, lie."[12]

At the Kappa Delta house, 250 young women with some of the largest smiles in Mississippi emerge from the columned mansion, dressed in little girls' pinafores, Peter Pan collars, white tights and ballet slippers, and tossing pigtails over their shoulders. It's the Munchkins, and they're positively squealing with little-girl delight. In probably the most professionally performed skit on the sorority circuit, the KDs posit Dorothy as the "Lost Rushee."

But the naivete stops there; this definitely isn't Kansas. The KDS have some crucial messages to get across as Dorothy skips down the yellow brick road toward KD sisterhood. Informants' perceptions of campus status place the KDS a solid but constant third, behind Chi O and Tri Delt. Strong in activities, grades, and pledge numbers, they nevertheless suffer from a party-girl reputation that keeps the highest prestige just out of reach. They're known as being a little bit *wild*.[13]

But is that so bad? Not to see the KDS do it. Like the Chi Os, the KDS are hip. But, their skit demonstrates, they're a lot more fun. After a sweet, fairy tale introduction, the Wicked Witch of the West rips into a raucous R & B rendition of "R-e-d-s-h-o-e" to the tune of Aretha Franklin's "Respect." When Dorothy is timid about setting off for Ole Miss, and wonders how she'll ever find her place in campus life, Auntie Em reassures her that she'll find a home at KD, where she'll also find entrée to the important parts of college: "There'll be the boys, the new friends, the boys, the professors, and most of all, the boys!"[14]

The KDS aren't lacking in the class department, either. When Dorothy meets the "Dollypop girls," they are Dolly Parton send-ups with huge balloons for breasts and a countrified appearance. Smacking gum, they suggest that Dorothy will find her place "at the shoppin' mall." In this class-based put-down of some other, unnamed sororities, Dorothy confides, *sotto voce*, "I don't think they're the group of girls for me." This, the script points out, is no house full of hayseeds.[15]

At the Pi Beta Phi house, actives dressed in sporty gym shorts and dainty tennis shoes sink at the feet of rushees perched on chintz sofas and wing chairs. The actives gaze up into their guests' eyes with visible love and adoration. All around the room, this is the picture: a rushee attempting to talk and sit in a ladylike manner; a beaming, adoring active wooing her from below. They positively drink each other in.

And it's not just happening at Pi Phi, either. For what is rush if not a whirlwind romance amongst women? Until 1994, in fact, a fourth party was a part of the rush schedule. Held the first night of rush, "Ice Water" was a frenetic, ten-minute party at which rushees were literally "swept off their feet" by actives attempting to introduce them to as many sorority sisters as possible.[16] Largely homosocial in nature, the sparking that goes on during rush represents a courtship of sorts, but one with a dual dimension. While the primary act of persuasion is a performance conducted between women, the secondary audience is surely the heterosexual romance waiting in the wings. Through successful romance with the right women, the right man will also be delivered.

Men are ever-present during rush but rarely mentioned. When they are, it's in the most programmatic fashion. Guys appear in the multimedia presentations sororities present as evidence that theirs is an active and popular group on campus. And men are the unspoken presence behind the tabletop display of photographs on view at many houses during rush: the tableaux of homecoming queens, Pike calendar girls, fraternity little sisters, and the like. Ostensibly evidence of members' campus accomplishments, these feminine shrines point the lost rushee along a path to success only reached through heterosexual romance.

"It kind of isn't!" exclaimed one Tri Delt when asked if trying to impress women during rush is different than trying to impress a man. "It kind of isn't! There are no men around, and we're not trying to impress men, we're trying to impress other women."[17]

But if "talkin' about guys" is considered tacky during rush, masculinity is hardly absent. In fact, it is necessary to the performance. During the Chi Omega skit party—based on a *Jungle Book* theme—a battalion of jockish actives decked out in camouflage T-shirts and military-like khaki shorts rush back and forth from kitchen to chapter room, serving as the rushees' personal waiters. There's nothing like a woman in uniform. At the end of the party, the room is suddenly hushed, as the Chi Os gather to whisper a song: "Tie a little ring around your finger; Chi O, Chi O; Any little thing to make you linger; Chi O, Chi O." During the singing of the song, some heavy-duty wooing is going on; actives kneel before the rushees, pleading with them to let them tie a ring of ribbon around their fingers while they tell about what Chi O has meant to them. The obvious referent for this scene is the prototypical, heterosexual marriage proposal, with kneeling supplicant and coy, noncommittal feminine object.[18]

At the Tri Delta house, short-haired actives play the male roles in a fifties-style rock 'n' roll skit from the musical *Grease*. Here, the gender play is more obvious, with drawn-on mustaches and chest hair, low-slung jeans and lots of swagger. Laughs one mannish active to another, "Remember when I came through? They had put you on me and I swear, I thought you were a guy!" At the AOPi house, a "Brady Bunch" skit features actives who impersonate the TV show's teenage male characters. They saunter through the aisles, point out favored rushees, and mock-whisper, "I'm checkin' you out!"[19]

Masculine appearance, then, has its place in rush, as long as it remains cloaked in play. In a similar way, racial spoofing is okay as long as it is clearly an act. Just as the wailing, Aretha Franklin-ish witch at KD gets the biggest laughs and applause, the Tri Delts' Motown skit, complete with Supremes, gets the biggest hoots. With plenty of laughing at themselves and each other as they let loose, gyrate, and shout, there is an insider-joke quality to it all, as if to say, "Isn't this funny? This is what the blacks do!" In the Kappas' circus-themed skit, clowns with brightly colored, Afro-like wigs and large, painted lips take the stage. What begins as an improvisational, standup-comedy routine quickly deteriorates into shucking and jiving in a surreal, if unintentional, approximation of the black vernacular. Within the safe seclusion of the sorority house, the already chosen feel free to play around with cultures decidedly Other. In contrast, the members' elite, chosen status stands out in sharp relief. As recently as 1979, the Chi Os performed a skit in blackface at their annual party. (The "Chi Omega choo-choo" skit featured a blackface mammy emcee.)[20]

In fact, it is the sororities with the highest campus status and the best track record of delivering the marriageable male goods that venture the farthest in race and gender play. Veering too near realism, however, is dangerous. In a realm where one sorority is cautioned before every party to "Remember, we're all Phi Mu ladies," actually looking like a boy can spell trouble. One Phi Mu recalls the "problem" her chapter had the year the friend of an active came through rush looking too masculine for their tastes.

"She'd come in looking kind of real boyish, and she didn't wear any makeup and she was a real tall, tall, big, big girl," she said. "And it was really hard because she had a friend in the sorority and I think we ended up cutting her. Someone stood up and said, 'Well, she kinda looks like, you know, she's not very attractive, and she kinda looks like a boy or whatever.'"[21]

At the Chi Omega house, the decor is that of an English hunt club, complete with plate racks on the walls, polished mahogany furniture, plush carpets, and glossy maroon walls. In the meeting room, oversized plantation shutters shield the windows and crystal chandeliers twinkle overhead. These are the moneyed Delta girls, and their privilege is quietly evident. If the KDs pointedly verbalize their claims to sophistication and status, the Chi Os don't have to; each year, they take their membership largely from legacies and from Mississippi girls they already know quite a bit about. Place—in all its permutations—plays a significant role in rush.

As in most rushes, of utmost importance are where you're from and who you know. But make no mistake: this is a southern rush, and place doesn't stop with hometowns and heritage. In everything from architecture to adornment, place is performed during rush, allowing actives to place rushees and rushees to learn their place.

"She didn't realize that they were *so* into southern girls," a Phi Mu from California said of her mom, herself an Ole Miss alumna. "She didn't realize how hard it was going to be on me, coming in and people not knowing you. Because a lot of these girls in the sororities *know* these girls from when they start ninth grade or from when they're *born*."[22]

"Just the fact that I wasn't from Mississippi was a minus," claims a freshman from Louisiana, who says she didn't stand a chance against the Jackson girls who knew all the Chi Os and Tri Delts. As she remembers it, "half of them are like *quadruple* legacies. They come up, they'd gone to high school with all these girls, so they *know* them."[23]

But the high school connection can be a curse as well as a blessing. A Theta from Georgia recalls her dismay at learning the Jackson girls had spent their high school years in vigilant protection of their reputations, lest the Ole Miss sorority girls catch wind of any drinking bouts (or worse). "These girls were prepping and training for rush as of their sophomore year [of high school]," said the Theta. "And if the girls at the university found out about [any questionable behavior], they would be screwed."[24]

To remedy her situation, the California Phi Mu "kind of made it known that I had southern roots, some sort of connection to the South." She also sent her mother on a reconnaissance mission to Mississippi boutiques. "I *expected* to get into a sorority, which is *stupid* here," she recalls. "I expected to be treated good because I was from someplace they're not. . . . As opposed to being treated like I was, which was, 'Hmmm, well, we don't really know who she is.'"[25]

How do they know who they are? In a nutshell, by using a system of rushing that emphasizes hometowns, insider knowledge, and maintenance of lineage. Active members hoping to promote rushees from their hometown advertise them within the sorority house via posters featuring photographs of the favored rushee and lists of her interests and attributes. But having a friend in the house isn't enough. Alumni chapters, in-house "poop groups," and a vast network of family and friends are called upon to verify applicants' reputations and class status. "Trust your sister" is an adage sororities turn to when in doubt.[26] Furthermore, all hometowns are not created equal. In an effort to consolidate alumni support, individual towns in Mississippi receive separate consideration, while the entire state of Tennessee, for example, is in some sororities treated as one hometown.

Back in those hometowns, certain groups are favored over others. "In Meridian, it's Tri Delt, Chi O, KD," reports an extremely popular Tri Delt. "And there's kind of pressure to do one of those top three. I mean, I had a *good* rush . . . but there were girls from Meridian who didn't. And I mean, the talk of the town is what happened to so and so during rush."[27]

Pity the poor Yankee. "I think it's hard on them, because they're from a completely different culture, and they don't come down here to change the way they are," notes an out-of-state active. "They just want to be involved in a group. So when they get down here and realize, pretty much, if you're not southern, no matter how you talk . . . you have so much less of a chance of getting into anything here."[28]

A junior Tri Delt from Texas recalls arriving on campus accustomed to wearing flashy silver earrings and concho belts, only to discover her Mississippi counterparts given to dainty heirloom trinkets, especially rings and necklaces handed down for several generations. "They also had these big necklaces with their initials carved out in them," she said. "And I remember I thought that was funny. Because they would just really deck themselves out in those."[29]

MAKING THE CUT

On Pref Night, fraternity men in expensive convertibles circle sorority row, checking out the new women on campus and waiting to find out how Pref went at their girlfriends' houses. But they must wait. In candle-light seclusion, the actives are still turning up the heat, romancing their prey. The Kappas present handwritten letters to the rushees. The Delta Gammas press their own membership pins into the palms of favored prospects. A rondo ripples across the heavy August air: "It's just me and Tri Delta from now on." "Search your heart," echo the Chi Os. "In your heart, you'll know."

"Oh! It comes down to how much you cry!" laughs a new active about Pref. "They *all* cry. They're kind of telling you more about them, what it feels like to be a Whatever . . . and they sing really . . . cheesy, sentimental songs, and *everybody* cries!"[30]

Laugh she may, but at the conclusion of another Pref Night at Ole Miss, the rushee tears are flowing. Lining their verandahs and sidewalks, the actives, dressed in full-length damask gowns and cupping burning tapers, gather to sing farewell and bid a dreamy adieu.

Sorority members past and present report conflicted feelings about sorority life. Even the most enthusiastic members lament the exclusivity of their social clubs. Others credit sororities with offering opportunities for leadership. My informants articulate similarly mixed feelings. But one thing seems clear: being able to "do" Southern Lady, to trot her out and put her on at will, remains important to many southern women. And sorority rush provides a ritualistic stage for reiterating through performance a fairly specific, regional understanding of gender. Through speech, gesture, and adornment, through codes of conduct and choreography, a regional, racialized definition of gender gets performed, again and again. Only by first performing this particular rendition of gender—by demonstrating that this anachronistic version of womanhood features in her repertoire and is readily accessible—is a woman admitted to a dubious sisterhood.

Over the years, Ole Miss has earned its share of headlines. In recent years, attention has focused on the campus as a conservative political training ground—the stomping grounds where U.S. Senators Trent Lott and Thad Cochran, for example, made important alliances and learned their craft. But the culture of Ole Miss, in addition to serving as a proving ground for masculine political power, nurtures one of feminine social power as well, with sorority rush at its heart. At a time when the university is going through a cathartic debate about its symbols, a time when Ole Miss will likely set a precedent for how Old South fantasies will exist in the New, sorority rush remains largely untouched. Hidden in plain sight, it performs a prescriptive idea of gender, year after year. For the Southern Lady, tomorrow is truly another day.[31]

But outside Fulton Chapel, their final bid sheets signed, such deep concerns are absent among the spent rushees. A brunette from Arkansas greets an old friend from Meridian, and they tease each other about their atypical, dolled-up appearance. "I don't think I've ever seen you in a dress!" shrieks one, and they huddle to compare notes about the week. Bucking better advice, they've cashed in the game; one is "suicidin' for Kappa," the other, for Phi Mu. Turning to me, they are pragmatic about the performance of rush and their part in the act. "They're fake, we're fake, the whole thing is fake," says the would-be Kappa. "Tomorrow we get our bids, and we'll all divide up, and by next week, things will start getting back to normal."[32]

NOTES

1. This article stems from my ongoing field research of sorority rush in Mississippi and is based on taped interviews and ethnographic observation of participants in the white rush system at the University of Mississippi during August 1996 and October 1997. (Panhellenic Rush was moved to the mid-Fall semester beginning in 1997.) Interviews were conducted between February 1997 and April 1998. Informants who requested anonymity are identified here as "Informant A," "Informant B," etc. All interview tapes, papers, and transcripts are in the possession of the author.

2. For recent interpretations of the Lady and the Belle, see Donna Tartt, "The Belle and the Lady," *The Oxford American* 26 (March–May, 1999): 94–105; and essays by Drew Gilpin Faust, Jacquelyn Dowd Hall, Anne Goodwyn Jones, and Patricia Yaeger in the forum "Coming to Terms with Scarlett," *Southern Cultures* 5:1 (Spring 1999): 5–48.

3. On symbolism at Ole Miss and on recent progress in race relations at the University, see Kevin Pierce Thornton, "Symbolism at Ole Miss and the Crisis of Southern Identity," *The South Atlantic Quarterly* 86:3 (Summer 1987): 254–68; Curtis Wilkie, "A Region Apart," *The Boston Globe Magazine*, 14 September 1997, 14–22; and, Kevin Sack, "The Final Refrains of Dixie," *The New York Times*, 1 November 1998, sec. 4A, 20–35.

4. See Patricia Yaeger, "Race and the Cloud of Unknowing in *Gone with the Wind*," *Southern Cultures* 5:1 (Spring 1999): 21–8.

5. Interview with Informant F, 28 February 1997.

6. On "feminine intimacies," see Jackie Stacey, *Star Gazing: Hollywood Cinema and Female Spectatorship* (Routledge, 1994).

7. Interview with Tana Triplett, 19 March 1997.

8. Interview with Informant B, 27 February 1997.

9. Interview with Informant E, 4 March 1997.

10. Interview with Tana Triplett.

11. Alpha Omicron Pi Skit Night Party, August 1996.

12. Interview with Tana Triplett.

13. This characterization is drawn from my pool of informants' reports.

14. Kappa Delta Skit Night party, August 1996.

15. Ibid.

16. Pi Beta Phi Skit Night party, August 1996; "Ice Water" incident from an interview with Informant F.

17. Interview with Informant F.

18. Chi Omega Skit Night Party, August 1996.

19. Overheard at Tri Delta Skit Night party, August 1996. On such gender proxy phenomena, see the H-Women archives for a discussion thread about Takarazuka, the all-female Japanese dance troupe in which the women who play the male roles are wildly popular with female audiences. See also Jennifer Robertson, *Takarazuka: Sexual Politics and Popular Culture in Modern Japan* (University of California Press, 1998); Alpha Omicron Pi Skit Night party, October 1997.

20. Tri Delta Skit Night party, August 1996, and Kappa Kappa Gamma Skit Night party, October 1997; *Rush* (P. Bottom Pictures, 1980).

21. Interview with Tana Triplett.

22. Ibid.

23. Interview with Informant B.

24. Interview with Informant D, 26 March 1998.

25. Interview with Tana Triplett.

26. Interview with Honea Henderson, 26 February 1997.

27. Interview with Informant E.

28. Interview with Tana Triplett.

29. Interview with Informant F.

30. Interview with Informant B.

31. Jerry Gray, "At Ole Miss, They Learned to Play Hardball," *The New York Times* (national edition), 2 June 1996, front page. Anne Goodwyn Jones's ruminations about the continued ideological power of the Southern Lady provided early impetus for this project. See "Dixie's Diadem," in Anne Goodwyn Jones, *Tomorrow Is Another Day: The Woman Writer in the South, 1859–1936* (Louisiana State University Press, 1981).

32. Conversation with Allie Grisham, Pref Night, August 1996.

The Death of Southern Heroes
Historic Funerals of the South

Charles Reagan Wilson

*Funerals for public leaders and cultural heroes are among the most significant
ways the South and southerners have sustained their identity. Jefferson Davis's
funeral procession, 1889, courtesy of the Historic New Orleans Collection.*

*D*espite pronounced divisions and decades of change, the South and southerners have sustained their identity through institutions, customs, and rituals. Funerals for public leaders and cultural heroes are among the most significant. They affirm the community's values and continuity: the society will survive its loss. Over history, prominent funerals show how the South's sense of itself has changed.[1]

The funerals of early southern leaders differed little from those of other American heroes. When a George Washington or a Thomas Jefferson died, eulogists hailed him as a great nationalist or as a citizen of his state. John C. Calhoun's death, shortly after the passionate debates that led to the Compromise of 1850, did evoke sectional emotions in the South, but the funerals of southern heroes did not take on well-defined regional dimensions until the Civil War.

By the late nineteenth century, public funerals included overtly "southern" rhetoric and symbolism, and death served to remind southerners of their cultural differences from the rest of the nation. Symbols of Dixie were prominently displayed and eulogies explained the hero's contributions not just to the local community or the nation but to the South as a whole. The most prominent funerals, such as those for Robert E. Lee and Jefferson Davis, were aristocratic ceremonies for military and political figures. They honored the Lost Cause and reinforced white racial identity.

In the twentieth century, large-scale public rituals have been more democratic, celebrating the heroes of common people. There have still been massive funerals for populist politicians like Huey Long, but even greater public outpourings have appeared for heroes of popular culture such as Hank Williams and Elvis Presley. Martin Luther King Jr. was controversial, but the formal public rituals honoring him showed how much the South had changed from the time when public funerals were occasions for affirming white racial identity.

The evolution of southern funerals suggests that southerners now think of the South mainly as a cultural region. After the Civil War the political and military significance of the South waned; for southerners, the South became a place held together by its music, food, humor, values, myths, and customs. Public ritual, including funerals for prominent regional figures, nurtured the growing popular belief in a southern cultural identity.

After the Civil War, the funerals for military heroes were the clearest regional displays, reflecting the region's psychic involvement with its warriors. The most memorable funerals were for military figures, combining martial symbolism with religious ritual and imagery. They were elitist affairs, aristocratic in tone and style. Through elaborate ceremonies advocates of the Lost Cause defined a tradition that reinforced regional orthodoxies about race, religion, and the meaning of southern history.

Robert E. Lee should have received the grandest funeral in the region's history. He was a beloved father figure and a symbol of unity for southern whites. He also represented both military values and the aristocratic South—the cultured, educated, romantic cavalier. When he died in the isolated village of Lexington, Virginia, on 12 October 1870, at the age of sixty-three, the South was in the midst of Reconstruction, and he remained a controversial symbol of national division, even though as president of Washington College he had avoided politics. Still, he was the central embodiment of Confederate symbolism, and his death brought a genuine outpouring of southern sentiment. Schools across the region closed, businesses shut down, legal proceedings were interrupted, flags flew at half-staff, memorial meetings were pervasive, and cities displayed the black and purple bunting of mourning.

Nevertheless, Lee had requested a simple funeral, and the ceremonies were noteworthy for their stately simplicity. For a day and a half Lee lay in state in the college chapel. A flood impeded travel into the village, and the waters even washed away the available caskets, but thousands of people managed to view the general, who was dressed in a simple suit of black rather than in his wartime uniform. Evergreens and flowers covered the casket, but the Virginia flag was the only flag displayed. On the day of the funeral a mile-long procession marched by nearby Virginia Military Institute to the sound of booming artillery and the slow cadences of a funeral dirge. A military escort of ex-Confederates led the way, followed by faculty and students, politicians, family, and friends. Crepe, the prime Victorian emblem of mourning, was everywhere. Lee had requested that there be no funeral oration, and his wish was honored. The traditional rites of the Episcopal church were performed at a simple burial service as mourners placed the casket in a vault in the chapel basement. Services ended outside in the brisk autumn air with the singing of Lee's favorite hymn, "How Firm a Foundation."

Lee's death was a reminder of the end of the Confederacy only five years earlier. The Civil War had brought death and devastation to the South and Lee's demise was a reminder of human limitation, mortality, and other lessons southerners had graphically learned in the war. Lee himself was as death-obsessed as any southerner has ever been. Despite his image as a cavalier, he embodied the pronounced streak of puritanism in southern Protestantism. He was melancholy, a Calvinist at heart and a stoic by nature, tendencies only reinforced by war and defeat.

Lee's funeral ranks as one of the South's most admirable public funerals—tasteful, one might say, in a way that many later ones were not. It was what a southern gentleman would have wanted.[2]

THE SOUTH MOURNS JEFFERSON DAVIS

When Jefferson Davis died nineteen years later, on 6 December 1889, Reconstruction had ended, but sectional differences remained intense. In the North, Davis's death was not front-page news. Editorials mostly urged sectional harmony, but the news awakened old hard feelings. The Department of War, where Davis had once been secretary, refused to lower the American flag to half-staff or to drape Davis's portrait in crepe. In the South, by contrast, Davis's death caused the most intense mourning in Dixie since Lee's funeral and the greatest outpouring of sectional unity since the Civil War. His funeral showed the amazing degree to which he had recovered from his negative image at the end of the war. His performance as president, criticized by many southerners during the war, had become insignificant by 1889; he had become a symbol of the South.

The southern press urged southerners to make Davis's funeral, as the *Charleston News and Courier* put it, "the most memorable event in the history of the South since the war" because "he died for the South while yet he was alive—and though dead he should live forever in the heart of his countrymen, the great martyr of the Confederate cause." Every bell that tolled, every patriotic speech from southern lips, every flower on the bier of the South's preeminent leader would "testify to the world that though we have passed through the storms of war and revolution, we have preserved our identity and our honor." The *New Orleans Times-Picayune* agreed, saying that Davis represented for the South, "more than any other, the cause for which a million of her most chivalrous sons drew their swords."

Many southern cities competed to serve as Davis's final resting place. Atlanta, New Orleans, Richmond, Montgomery, Vicksburg, and Macon all put forward their cases. An *Atlanta Constitution* editorial argued, for example, that no other city had "paid the penalty of devotion to principle to the extent that did Atlanta." Its ringing conclusion was "Let Atlanta have his body—let Georgia, the state of Stephens and Toombs, keep it!" New Orleans was chosen, although Davis was later reinterred in Richmond's Hollywood Cemetery. Rumors soon began circulating that Yankee grave robbers from Chicago were headed South.

New Orleans went all out, as somber colors draped private and public buildings. A leading New Orleans undertaker, Frank R. Johnson, embalmed the hero, and Davis's body, in a gray suit, was placed in a dark metal coffin. He lay in state in the council chamber of the New Orleans City Hall, the Victorian symbols of death around him. Heavy black drapery was everywhere, and flowers, evergreens, and ferns blanketed the chamber. Flower arrangements were in the form of hearts, anchors, pillows, hands, swords, and guns. Above the casket and in one of the largest floral arrangements, the crossed flags of the United States and the Confederacy were intertwined. Confederate battle flags hung across the casket. Sentries kept watch. Small firearms and two brass howitzers behind the catafalque strengthened the military emphasis. The cannons had been named Redemption and Resurrection, adding a religious motif. The whole scene gave the impression that the deceased was dug in, ready to fight again. On the first day an estimated thirty thousand people had seen Davis lying in state, and by the time of the funeral seventy thousand had passed by his bier.

Unfortunately, Johnson had botched the job. The body was only partially embalmed, and the heat and humidity made the problem worse. When Davis's body was first displayed on Sunday, 8 December, it had "a familiar appearance," in the words of one reporter. On Tuesday, when the body was next on display, careful observers noticed a wasted look on the chin and cheeks and a dark, dingy hue on the cheeks and nose. It looked more like the body of a dead man than it had two days earlier. By the day of the funeral, when a plate was finally placed over the glassed upper part of the casket, one hand had begun to perish. In retrospect, the image of the Confederate president deteriorating before the eyes of his people evokes a scene from Flannery O'Connor or William Faulkner. As a final irony, both the casket and the embalming fluid had come from the North.

Jefferson Davis's funeral on 11 December was a great Victorian death ceremony, a political and military ritual, and a grand southern pageant. The crush of humanity on New Orleans streets was the equal of Mardi Gras. Guns were fired throughout the day at the head of Canal Street and at the intersection of Claiborne and Canal. The services were held on the portico of city hall, overlooking Lafayette Square. The Confederate flag lay on the casket, along with Davis's saber from the Mexican War, and armed sentries surrounded the catafalque. All of the officiating ministers had been Confederate chaplains. The Episcopal priests read the funeral ritual of their church, to the accompaniment of cannonfire, clanging bells, and organ music.

A dozen militia companies from Georgia, Texas, Mississippi, Alabama, and Louisiana marched in the funeral procession, which stretched four miles and took an hour and a half to pass on its way to Metairie Cemetery, two and a half miles from City Hall. More mourners came from the city in streetcars, special trains, carriages, and on foot. Police estimated the crowd at ten thousand. At the graveside, mourners heard rifle volleys and bugle calls. Episcopal bishops John Nicholas Galleher and Hugh Miller Thompson read the church burial ritual as a soldier played "Taps." The choir sang an anthem, and everyone recited the Lord's Prayer and sang "Rock of Ages." Davis was then laid to rest in the underground vault of the Army of Northern Virginia and the Confederate flag removed from his casket. Because of the rumors of grave robbers, the tomb was sealed with a granite boulder. Two police officers were stationed as guards; a private detective agency also joined the protective effort.[3]

The South had paid homage to Davis and to the Lost Cause. Grand in its scope and achievement, his funeral set a high standard for later ones. The growing Lost Cause movement reflected more than simple nostalgia. The year of Davis's death, 1889, was a turbulent one for southerners, the beginning of a decade of dramatic events. Industrialization and the growing New South ideology were eroding older self-conceptions of southerners. Social tensions had reached a new intensity, with lynchings, agrarian discontent leading to the Populist revolt, and southern whites poised to force racial disfranchisement and statutory Jim Crow segregation. Despite these growing tensions, the ritualization of the Lost Cause memory through Davis's funeral represented stability amid turmoil and emphasized the unifying effect of the wartime past. That identity was, of course, for whites only—fitting the mood of this New South in the decade to come.

Politicians continued to receive the largest funerals in the South until well into the twentieth century, but the new hero was of a radically different character. As Louisiana governor and then United States senator, Huey Long was a demagogue who built one of the most ruthless and corrupt political machines the country has ever seen. By the time he was assassinated in September 1935, the Lost Cause had faded and the South was deep in the Depression. Long's appeal was not to the aristocratic past, but to the aspirations of poor whites.

Long used a folksy manner and autocratic methods to promote the political and social interests of the masses. As governor, he pushed through tax favors and a free-textbook law, improved roads and schools, expanded the state university, built a state hospital intended to provide free treatment, and generally improved services. In the Senate, his keynote was his Share-the-Wealth program, which he proposed in 1932 and continued to refine until his death. His plan called for liquidation of personal fortunes, a guaranteed family allowance of $5,000, a minimum worker's income of $2,500, old-age pensions (the Social Security Act did not pass until 1935), bonuses for veterans, and a guarantee of a college education for all qualified students. By the time he died, Long claimed more than twenty-seven thousand Share-the-Wealth Clubs and had a file of more than seven million names.

Long's funeral was ironically elegant for a hero of the oppressed and disfranchised. He lay in state for two days at the Louisiana Capitol, dressed in a tuxedo, starched white shirt, and black bow tie. He lay beneath a bas-relief portrait presented by the United Confederate Veterans, which was how he would have wanted it. More than a thousand floral arrangements surrounded the casket; they covered an entire acre and cost more than $25,000. Eight Louisiana guardsmen stood on duty, along with two Louisiana State University students and four members of the LSU band wearing the purple and gold uniforms Long had designed. Most of those who passed by were Long's people. "They showed up in dusty overalls, ill-fitting Sunday clothes, rubbing shoulders with city folk in tailored suits," a reporter noted. More than twenty-two thousand people viewed the body.

The funeral was on Thursday, 12 September. Schools throughout the state were closed, and cars clogged the roads into Baton Rouge. It was a scorching day, with temperatures in the nineties. Soda pop, hot dog, and ice cream vendors arrived early and contributed to the chaotic scene. One hundred thousand people came to see the Kingfish buried. At 4:25 the funeral procession appeared on the Capitol steps and the huge crowd outside quieted. The Reverend Gerald L. K. Smith, a minister with political ambitions, delivered the eulogy before leading the walk to the grave. The procession was accompanied by the muffled beat of a drum and a dirge composed from Long's song "Every Man a King."

Smith's eulogy stressed Long's compassion for the poor. "His spirit shall never rest as long as hungry bodies cry for food, as long as human frames stand naked, as long as homeless wretches haunt this land of plenty," Smith said. He argued that Long was a man of destiny, whom God had taken to the quiet of eternity, and that "his torch was left to light the way." Smith made it clear that he intended to seize the torch, to the distress of Russell Long, Huey's son. "[It] was a political speech to himself," Russell said. "He appointed himself as Long's successor."

Long was an insurgent politician who represented the democratic masses. He was surely identified with the South, although not in the same way as Davis and Lee. He was a hero of the poor and working classes. By their massive turnout and display of emotion at his funeral, the southern plain folk forcefully asserted the centrality of their hero and his ideology for their region.[4]

HANK WILLIAMS AND THE RISE OF POPULAR CULTURE

Since Long's time, most of the South's historic, large-scale public funerals have been for those who, like him, were heroes of the plain folk. But the nature of such heroes has changed dramatically. The most notable death ceremonies have been not for politicians but for cultural celebrities closely identified with the South.

These celebrities have not been the heroes of high culture. Despite the South's achievements in literature, the deaths of great southern writers have not been met with outpourings of public affection. Even the funeral . of William Faulkner, certainly the South's most celebrated writer, was a modest affair.

No, the most historic funerals in the contemporary South have not been for writers. But some have been for musicians, who have come to be numbered among the popular-culture heroes of modern America, not just the South. The public response to the death of country singer Hank Williams—and later Elvis Presley—stands in marked contrast to the reaction to Faulkner's death.

Faulkner had a simple funeral after his death on 6 July 1962, near Oxford, Mississippi. The most memorable aspect of it seems to have been the Mississippi heat. Faulkner's publisher, Bennett Cerf, arrived in an air-conditioned car and recalled later that "the heat was overpowering, like walking into a steam bath." William Styron, who covered the death for *Life* magazine, noted that the heat was "like a small mean death itself, as if one were being smothered to extinction in a damp woolen overcoat." Electric fans whirred as mourners ate a buffet lunch of southern food—turkey and homemade bread, stuffed tomatoes, and gallons of iced tea. Meanwhile, Faulkner lay in a closed plain wooden casket in the parlor.

After the Episcopal rites, a procession wound up South Lamar Street, through the crowded center of town. It took much persuasion by the newspaper editor and a few others, but most of the merchants on the square did close for the hour of the funeral. Faulkner's funeral was a curiosity to the people of his hometown. As one of them noted, if a deacon in the local Baptist church had died, reporters would have seen a real turnout.[5]

Hank Williams, on the other hand, was an authentic hero of the southern masses. He embodied a southern propensity for paradox. He was drunk and rowdy and packed a pistol, but he also wrote and sang sacred songs. He was brutally realistic in writing of love, but he also was a sentimental man who doted on his mother. He was a national figure, but his popularity in the South was phenomenal. As his son has written, "When you said 'Hank' south of the Mason-Dixon line, there was never any doubt that you were talking about Hank Williams." He was popular with many kinds of southerners, but he was especially notable for giving cultural voice to the traditionally powerless southern poor white.

Williams's funeral—dramatic, emotional, and traditionally southern—illustrated the growth of mass popular culture. This trend was not confined to the South. The hysterical reaction to the death of actor Rudolph Valentino in the 1920s, for example, revealed the peculiar passion the modern cultural celebrity could evoke. Just as Valentino's funeral revealed much about ethnic and urban culture, Williams's was part and parcel of southern life.

Most country-music funerals have been evocative of the South. Maybelle Carter's was restrained—genuine sadness and grief, but little show. It was the best of simple country ceremonies, even though she was a celebrity. On the other hand, the deaths of Patsy Cline and two other country music entertainers in an airplane crash in 1963 evoked extravagant displays of emotion. The same was true with Hank Williams. His funeral, like these others, was a celebrity event, almost as if the star were performing.

Hank died on 1 January 1953 in the back seat of his powder-blue Cadillac, on the way to a performance in West Virginia. He was twenty-nine. The autopsy concluded that he died of heart failure, but the actual reason was undoubtedly a combination of alcohol and painkillers, along with years of general dissipation. Williams was a death-obsessed southerner, a man who had seemed to court death. His music was particularly melancholy. His hit song on the charts at the time of his death was "I'll Never Get Out of This World Alive."

The funeral was held in Montgomery, Alabama, where Williams had launched his career. Reporter Eli Waldron described the events as "the greatest emotional orgy in the city's history since the inauguration of Jefferson Davis." Williams's mother took charge of affairs and put him on display in a silver casket in the living room of her frame boarding house. Thousands of people came to pay respects, to bring food, and to drink coffee and iced tea. Hank looked bloated in his coffin—not his old emaciated, lean and hungry self. Family and friends stayed up all night with the body, in the regional tradition of the "sitting up" ceremony. There was a bitter argument between Hank's mother and his new bride Billie Jean, who made the mistake of wearing slacks. The funeral director eventually restored the peace by limiting each woman to a thirty-minute period with the hero.

The funeral itself was held on Sunday, 4 January, a sunny, cold winter day. Hank's promoter arranged the funeral, which took on the trappings of a Williams concert. The Montgomery city government provided the city auditorium free of charge and put large numbers of police and firefighters on duty to prevent chaos. Cars jammed the streets, and about twenty thousand people milled about near the auditorium, many consuming homemade sandwiches and thermoses of hot coffee. The city set up loudspeakers outside the auditorium for those who could not see the ceremony. Two Montgomery radio stations broadcast the funeral.

Inside the auditorium, the scene was hardly serene. It was a flashbulb funeral. Photographers were everywhere, strutting about the stage and around the bier, snapping photographs of the hero at rest. Flowers covered the stage, with arrangements in the form of guitars, pillows, and wreaths. Many had been brought south in a two-ton truck by a Nashville florist. The biggest arrangement was in the shape of a Bible, with the first notes of Hank's religious song "I Saw the Light" across the cover.

Mourners lived up to the southern tradition of emotional expression of grief at funerals. Most of those who passed by the open casket before the funeral were women. Four women fainted as they gazed at the corpse and a fifth had to be carried away screaming. Blacks were surprisingly numerous among the mourners; they filled the segregated balcony. In the front row Hank's mother, his sister Irene, his first wife Audrey, and his new wife Billie Jean sat side by side, each in intense grief, each nursing suspicion and hatred of one or more of the others. It was a good southern family gathering.

The service included both gospel and country music. The Statesmen Quartet, a white gospel group, sang "Precious Memories," and a black gospel group, the Southwind Singers, performed "My Record Will Be There." The Nashville music presence was notable. Ernest Tubb sang "Beyond the Sunset," Roy Acuff did Hank's "I Saw the Light," and Red Foley delivered "Peace in the Valley" with tears streaming down his face.

The Reverend Henry Lyon of Montgomery's Highland Avenue Baptist Church delivered a great southern funeral sermon about sin and depravity, guilt, and the possibility of redemption. He portrayed Hank as a rags-to-riches American hero who had achieved the "heights of immortal glory" and then "answered the call of the last roundup." He preached that Hank would want everyone to repent. If you liked Hank, in other words, then follow him to the arms of Jesus. More weeping occurred as pallbearers carried out the casket. The streets were so crowded and events so disorganized that no stately procession was possible. Mourners simply jumped in their cars and headed for Oakwood Cemetery, where thousands viewed the brief graveside services.

Williams's body was soon reinterred in a larger plot in the cemetery, beneath a Vermont granite monument enlivened with etchings of heavenly sunlight and his song titles, a bronze plaque of him playing his guitar, and a marble cowboy hat at the base. Plans were made but never carried out to move Williams to a grave at the toe of an eighty-foot-high cowboy-boot monument estimated to cost $750,000.

Hank Williams's funeral evoked more sentiment among rural southerners than most large public funerals. In its emotionalism, religious attitudes, family behavior, and essential customs, it was authentically regional in style and tone. It also recognized the rise of country music as an art form associated with the southern plain folk. By the early 1950s, country music had chronicled the struggles of rural folk like Williams who flooded to the cities after World War II. Williams expressed their aspirations, frustrations, sufferings, tragedies, and achievements. His music expressed a new southern identity—the country boy gone to the city, but still recognizable to fellow southerners like those who turned out for his funeral.[6]

MARTIN LUTHER KING JR.: A SOUTH DIVIDED

As black mourners sat in the balcony at Hank Williams's funeral in 1953, *Brown v. Board of Education* was still being argued. It was not until the next year that the United States Supreme Court ruled de jure school segregation unconstitutional. It would be another decade before the Civil Rights Act of 1964 provided a statutory guarantee of equal employment opportunity and equal access to public facilities and the Voting Rights Act of 1965 guaranteed blacks the right to vote.

The public reaction to the assassination of Martin Luther King Jr. on 4 April 1968 in Memphis, Tennessee, revealed a South in transition, but still deeply divided on the issue of race. King was surely no hero to most southern whites, but he was the cherished champion of black southerners. To the nation and the world he represented a South different from Jefferson Davis's or even Huey Long's, a black southerner struggling against an evil South. In his own way, like Hank Williams, King was an outsider whose funeral reflected the rise of his people. His death had overtones not just of martyrdom but of redemption for the South, and yet his funeral was the most overtly political in southern history, an occasion to express political opposition.

King's funeral was historically important because a significant number of whites were among the 150,000 to 200,000 people who took part in the formal tribute to the black leader. His funeral was rich in ceremony and meaning, showing a southern black receiving honor in his homeland. King was a national and international figure and drew on sophisticated intellectual foundations. Yet, he also drew from southern black traditions in attacking regional ways. The funeral ceremony made conscious reference to those for southern rural blacks, including the pilgrimage to the cemetery in a mule-drawn farm wagon. A half-century earlier, Booker T. Washington's funeral in Tuskegee, Alabama, had been both grand and simple, but it was an almost entirely segregated affair.[7]

The response of the white establishment was deeply ambivalent. Atlanta, which had carefully nurtured its reputation as "The City Too Busy to Hate," responded with full support for King's family. When Mayor Ivan Allen Jr. heard of the death, he rushed to King's home and drove Coretta King to the airport. Described by a reporter as "grim faced and near tears," Allen said that King's "unnecessary death is a great tragedy." When the body arrived, he was there to meet it and he went to the funeral home. Vice-Mayor Sam Massell called King's assassination "a tragic loss to the free world," adding that "every man of good will, white and black, must search his heart asking forgiveness for this disgrace." Atlanta's police chief went to comfort the widow and family. The *Atlanta Constitution* responded with editorials and columns of shocked lamentation. The city's schools and many businesses closed to honor King.

The state of Georgia's response, however, reawakened old images. The governor was Lester Maddox, one of the prime symbols of extreme and even violent defense of segregation. He expressed regret over the killing, but urged respect for law and order and refused to close state offices. Needless to say, he did not attend the funeral. Maddox opposed lowering flags to half-staff, but left the decision to the secretary of state, who approved the gesture because President Lyndon B. Johnson had authorized it. Outside Atlanta, schools did not close. The response of other southern politicians was even more revealing. Although a few southern congressmen and senators issued polite statements regretting King's death, none attended the funeral.

On Monday, 8 April, more than twenty-five thousand mourners viewed the body at Atlanta's Spelman College as an organist played hymns and a muted rendition of "We Shall Overcome." Many cried softly, and some stopped in line to take pictures of the body. The next day, King lay in an open African mahogany coffin topped with a cross of white carnations at Ebenezer Baptist Church. Almost eight hundred people attended the private funeral service, which included moving tape recordings of King speaking. In the months before his assassination, King had become death conscious, seemingly aware of his destiny and accepting it. "If any of you are around when I have to meet my day, I don't want a long funeral," he had said, as though speaking from beyond the grave. "And if you get someone to deliver the eulogy, tell them not to talk too long. . . . I'd like someone to mention that day that Martin Luther King, Jr., tried to love somebody." The choir sang "Softly and Tenderly," and mourners began to cry and wipe their eyes. Two Baptist ministers from Atlanta read from the Psalms and the New Testament, and one of King's professors at Boston University spoke briefly.

After the service, two Georgia mules pulled an old farm wagon carrying the casket more than four miles from the church to the campus of Morehouse College. A remarkable procession (or "pilgrimage," as Ralph David Abernathy called it) followed. The pilgrims wore African-style clothes, dark suits, miniskirts, jeans, and work clothes. Prominent politicians, popular entertainers, international statesmen, and average citizens were all there. The march had a somber quality and great dignity.

In keeping with King's achievements, the symbolism of the procession was ethnic, regional, national, and international. The heat was surely southern—it was a hot and humid spring day and the dogwood was in bloom. Hundreds fainted from the heat. The mourners sang southern black hymns and anthems like "Swing Low, Sweet Chariot," "We Shall Overcome," "We are Climbing Jacob's Ladder," and "Precious Lord, Take My Hand." The marchers participated in an old southern tradition by partaking of funeral food. Churches and restaurants fed more than twenty-six thousand people, with tons of fried chicken, ham, sandwiches, eggs, doughnuts, and Coca-Cola from the hometown company.

But King transcended the South, and his funeral procession reflected this. The crowd sang not just southern black religious and protest songs, but other American songs as well. The flags of the United States and the United Nations were displayed, as well as a Christian emblem. Rabbi Abraham Joshua Heschel read from the prophet Isaiah, a West Coast minister offered prayers, and representatives of the World Council of Churches participated in the ceremonies. The symbolism was complex because the man and the time were complex.

After ceremonies at Morehouse College, the body was taken to the South View Cemetery for temporary burial near the graves of King's grandparents. Abernathy, his assistant, delivered a graveside eulogy, and the body was placed in a crypt, sealed behind walls of Georgia marble. Mrs. King was composed, but wept quietly. "Daddy" King, in the words of a reporter, "placed his head on the crypt and wept openly as the casket was placed inside." The epitaph on the tombstone quoted an old spiritual King had used in a famous speech, "Free at last; free at last; thank God almighty I'm free at last."

If Jefferson Davis's funeral in 1889 expressed a regional identity growing out of the white southern Civil War experience, King's was subversive of that identity. The scale of his funeral and the commitment of Atlanta's government were early signs of a changing southern regional public identity that would become clearer in the 1970s and after. King was a hero of the central southern event of the twentieth century, the civil rights movement. While race relations remained troubled, the end of de jure racial segregation and the political enfranchisement of African Americans helped to create a new biracial public identity that was embraced by southern governors and other public officials by the early 1970s. At the time, King's funeral was interpreted in national terms and in terms of the black community, but it was also an early indicator that the South was redefining its public culture at the insistence of its black citizens.[8]

THE SOUTH BIDS FAREWELL TO THE KING

The death of another post–World War II southerner also embodied aspects of the changing South. Elvis Presley died on 15 August 1977. His was one of the biggest funerals in American history, and the tremendous outpouring of public grief was in good southern tradition. Less than twenty-four hours after the announcement of Presley's death, eighty thousand people had gathered in front of Graceland. Fans came to Memphis from far away, many of them simply abandoning normal responsibilities. More than 250 journalists came to cover the event. The activities were chaotic. The funeral was an attempt to combine the funeral customs and ceremonies of southern common people with the grand funerals of the past. It did not come off, but that is hardly surprising. It was as if the Bundren clan in Faulkner's *As I Lay Dying* had tried to plan a large-scale funeral.

Presley died at Graceland of massive drug abuse that led to heart failure while he sat on the toilet reading a book on the Shroud of Turin. He was discovered face down on the plush red carpet. He led an isolated, tormented life, but he had a well-developed sense of his God-ordained destiny. Raised a Pentecostal, he came naturally to a kind of mysticism, which took undisciplined directions in his later life. He became fascinated with unorthodox spiritual phenomena, reincarnation, life after death, and millennialism. He also had an obsession with death, probably triggered by his mother's death in 1958, a loss so traumatic that he compensated by believing in her survival in mystical realms. Presley's interest in death was not simply philosophical. He was fascinated with corpses and frequently visited cemeteries and funeral homes, especially the one in Memphis where his mother had been laid out. He would go there in the middle of the night and wander among the embalmed bodies. He liked to talk about the embalming process and had seen his own friends embalmed.

The official reaction to Presley's death suggested that his significance transcended his celebrity. Tennessee governor Ray Blanton said that Presley's "career was an American dream come true"; Mississippi governor Cliff Finch declared an official day of mourning, calling Presley, in his rise from poverty, the "personification of the American dream." Praise for the King came from around the world. President Jimmy Carter issued a statement saying that Presley's death "deprives our country of a part of itself." He did not say which part, but the statement characterized the entertainer as a prime symbol "of the vitality, rebelliousness and good humor of this country."

Presley lay in view in Graceland, a setting every bit as ornate as the one that had surrounded Jefferson Davis's body a century before, but with quite different elements. He lay under a crystal chandelier, near a glass statue of a nude woman, surrounded by plastic palms, black velveteen paintings, and scarlet drapes with gold tassels. Flanking the bier were burly bodyguards and six members of the Tennessee National Guard. The flags of the United States and Tennessee were on view. Elvis lay in a nine-hundred-pound, satin-lined, seamless copper casket flown in from a manufacturer in Oklahoma City. The plump body appeared swollen even more than in his last days of life. Nonetheless, he presented a dazzling image. He was dressed in a cream colored suit, a light blue shirt, and a silver tie. On his hand was his gold and diamond "TCB" ring (initials for "Taking Care of Business") with its two lightning bolts. He wore diamond cuff links and a diamond stickpin. Presley's funeral had more flowers than any other in American history. The president of the American Floral Trade Association came to Memphis to coordinate activities. Flower supplies in Memphis had been quickly exhausted, so massive airlifts of flowers took place, with five tons coming from California and Colorado. Flowers filled every room at Graceland and lined the front of the house and the circular drive. The arrangements recalled Presley's hit songs (guitars, hound dogs, teddy bears, blue suede shoes) and symbols of the King (broken hearts, bibles, and especially crowns). Most flower shop requests were simply for red, yellow, or pink roses.

The mood of the mourners outside the gates of Graceland was at first marked by despair and depression. The landscape itself seemed to brood. Flags were at half-staff, signs on the Memphis streets carried messages of love for the King, and radio stations played only Presley songs. The throng included "hikers, businessmen, children, Shriners in clown shirts, and phalanxes of middle-aged women, many of them sobbing," according to journalist Chet Flippo. It was predominantly a white, working-class crowd, with women clearly in the majority. Most were from the South or Midwest. Some of the women had abandoned jobs and families to come. As one mourner said, "They're here because it's the only way the common people can pay their respects." The city was awash with emotion— genuine love, sentimentality, and mawkishness. People suffered much discomfort to show their feelings. Hundreds fainted in the stifling heat, scuffles occurred as everyone maneuvered for position, and the Red Cross erected first-aid tents on the lawn at Graceland.

Atlanta reporter Jerry Schwartz described the crowd the first night as "emotional, a bit gaudy and distinctly southern." By the second day the mood had shifted to near hysteria. Police were afraid that pent-up feelings and wild rumors might lead to violence. A National Guard Unit was called out, and sentries were posted in front of the house. At three in the afternoon the gates of Graceland opened to allow fans to pass by the casket. Between seventy thousand and one hundred thousand people waited in line, but only twenty thousand to thirty thousand saw the hero before the gates were closed at 6:30. Frustration ended in tragedy at 4:00 the morning before the funeral when a drunk driver careened into the crowd outside Graceland, killing two teenage girls from Louisiana and critically injuring a third.

On the day of the funeral the crowd was smaller than the previous day, when everyone had hoped to see the body, and Graceland took on a carnival atmosphere. Vendors hawked "Elvis in Memoriam" T-shirts and bumper stickers reading "Elvis Lives" and "Long Live the King." Soft drinks, snow cones, and ice cream kept the crowd cool.

Fifty family members were among the two hundred mourners who attended a private service in the mansion's Music Room. It was an improvised ceremony, lacking unity or grandeur. There were Bible readings, prayers, and a eulogy by Las Vegas comedian Jackie Kahane. Religion was represented by a local Church of Christ minister and by television evangelist Rex Humbard. Their remarks represented a generalized sense of religion rather than traditional southern evangelical themes. The saving grace of the service was gospel singing by the Blackwood Brothers and Presley's buddy J. D. Sumner.

After the funeral, an impressive motor cortege carried the hero down Elvis Presley Boulevard to his burial. Eighteen white Cadillacs, plus additional cars, carried official guests and the press. Tens of thousands of mourners lined the three-mile route. Elvis was entombed next to his mother in a white marble mausoleum. The tomb was sealed with a double slab of concrete and an outer slab of marble because of the real danger of grave robbery. After the burial the family and close friends returned to Graceland for what Caroline Kennedy, who covered the funeral for *Rolling Stone*, described as a "southern supper."

The self-consciously southern imagery was less overt in the Presley funeral than in the death ceremonies of Lee and Davis a century before. That in itself was testimony to the region's changes. But the funeral was still southern in rhetoric and in the behavior of the mourners, both those inside Graceland and those outside. In trying to explain their unreasoning attachment to the King, mourners mentioned that he was religious, was good to his family and loved his mother, that he was a gentleman and a generous spirit who had nurtured his roots by living in the South. All those qualities might be admired by nonsoutherners, of course, but they are traits especially identified with the South. The overriding point is that southerners claimed him as one of their own; even if he was a national and international celebrity, he was a southerner first.[9]

THE BURDEN OF SOUTHERN HISTORY

The funerals of public figures provide ritual support for southern identity. In an episodic way, these commemorative events reveal aspects of southern society, its self-understanding, and its internal structures. Although the rhetoric and the patterns of behavior at these funerals have been shaped by common southern customs and have revealed the emotional, sentimental southern response to human mortality, these events have also reflected the diversity of the South.

Southern death ceremonies have sometimes been admirable in their simplicity, dignity, and grandeur; others have been embarrassing and even bizarre. They show, nonetheless, that the region's culture has evolved from a political-military identity in the days of Lee and Davis to a cultural identity today. In the late nineteenth century, these ritual outpourings reflected and promoted the social cohesion of southern whites around an ideology of white power and a hierarchical, tradition-bound society. The funerals of such twentieth-century figures as Long, Williams, King, and Presley represent the triumph of a democratic South: all were, in varying ways, not only heroes of the common people but common people themselves. The elite, gentleman's funeral with military overtones no longer has popular appeal. A popular culture figure like Elvis may be today's quintessential southerner, as the southern identity has become commercialized.

These dramatic southern funerals have been for men who reflected the region's sobering historical experience. Lee and Davis were defeated southerners, the frustrated embodiment of a lost cause; Long and King were leaders of the South's dispossessed in the struggle against economic and racial injustice; Williams and Presley died young, poor boys burned out by the temptations of material success. Southern heroes and their melancholy deaths have not just illustrated but embodied southern historian C. Vann Woodward's idea of the "burden of southern history."

NOTES

1. See Richard Huntington and Peter Metcalf, *Celebrations of Death: The Anthropology of Mortuary Ritual* (Cambridge University Press, 1976).

2. John Esten Cooke, *The Life of Gen. Robert E. Lee* (D. Appleton & Co., 1873), 499–507, 513–38; "Historic Funerals: Gen. Robert E. Lee," *American Funeral Director* 62 (August 1949): 41, 507, 513–16, 531; Thomas L. Connelly, *The Marble Man: Robert E. Lee and His Image in American Society* (Alfred A. Knopf, 1977), 191–93, 12; Douglas Southall Freeman, *Robert E. Lee: A Biography*, vol. 4 (Scribner's, 1934–35), 326–28; Marshall W. Fishwick, *Lee after the War* (Dodd, Mead & Co., 1963), 216–21; Robert B. Dickerson Jr., *Final Placement: A Guide to the Deaths, Funerals, and Burials of Notable Americans* (Reference Publications, Inc., 1982), 144–45.

3. Seabury Quinn, "The Burial of Jefferson Davis," *American Funeral Director* 62 (October 1939): 68–70; *Atlanta Constitution*, 7–12 December 1889, reproduced in A. C. Bancroft, ed., *The Life and Death of Jefferson Davis* (J. S. Ogilvie, n.d.), 163–76, 195–221, 222, 225, 230.

4. George Brown Tindall, *America: A Narrative History* (W. W. Norton & Co., 1984), 1077–78; *New Orleans Times-Picayune*, 11–13 September 1935; David H. Zinman, *The Day Huey Long Was Shot* (I. Oblensky, 1963), 183–91; Howard Dorgan, "Gerald L. K. Smith and the Huey P. Long Funeral Oration," *Southern Speech Journal* 36 (Summer 1971): 378–89.

5. Joseph Blotner, *Faulkner: A Biography*, vol. 2 (Random House, 1974), 1838–46; Bennett Cerf, *At Random: The Reminiscences of Bennett Cerf* (Random House, 1977), 135; William Styron, "As He Lay Dead, a Bitter Grief," *Life*, 20 July 1962, 39; Hughes Rudd, "The Death of William Faulkner," *Saturday Evening Post*, 20 July 1963, 32–34.

6. Hank Williams Jr., with Michael Bane, *Living Proof: An Autobiography* (G. P. Putnam's Sons, 1979), 9–10; Dickerson, *Final Placement*, 225–28; Ellis Nassour, *Patsy Cline: An Intimate Biography* (Tower Books, 1981), 364–76; Eli Waldron, "The Death of Hank Williams," *Reporter*, 19 May 1955, 35–37; Chet Flippo, *Your Cheatin' Heart: A Biography of Hank Williams* (Simon and Schuster, 1981), 207–9, 240; recorded tape of the funeral at the Country Music Foundation, Nashville, Tennessee; Roger M. Williams, *Sing a Sad Song: The Life of Hank Williams* (University of Illinois Press, 1970), 223–28; Jay Cares, *Hank Williams: Country Music's Tragic King* (Stern and Day, 1979), 213–17.

7. *Atlanta Constitution*, 15 November 1915; Dickerson, *Final Placement*, 229–30; Louis R. Harlan, *Booker T. Washington: The Wizard of Tuskegee, 1901–1915* (Oxford University Press, 1983), 454–57.

8. *Atlanta Constitution*, 5–10 April 1968; Stephen B. Oates, *Let the Trumpet Sound: The Life of Martin Luther King Jr.* (New American Library, 1982), 455–58, 473, 486.

9. Neal and Janice Gregory, *When Elvis Died* (Washington Square Press, 1980), 68, 78, 93–109, 179; Albert Goldman, *Elvis* (McGraw-Hill, 1981), 282–89, 573–76; Brian C. Kates, "The Elvis Presley Funeral," *American Funeral Director* 100 (October 1977): 44–47; *Memphis Commercial Appeal*, 17 and 21 August 1977; Red West, Sonny West, and Dave Hebbs, *Elvis: What Happened?* (Ballantine Books, 1977), 158–72; *Atlanta Constitution*, 17, 18, and 20 August 1977; *Memphis Press Scimitar*, 17–18 August 1977; Brian C. Kates, "The Elvis Presley Funeral," *American Cemetery* 50 (October 1977): 30; Chet Flippo, "Funeral in Memphis," *Rolling Stone*, 22 September 1977: 40; *New York Times*, 18 August 1977.

About the Contributors

Derek H. Alderman is associate professor in the Department of Geography at East Carolina University. He is a former editor of *Southeastern Geographer*, and his research focuses on the cultural geography of the American South, with special attention to the interplay between landscape, regional identity, and representation.

Donna G'Segner Alderman is a teacher of special education in the Pitt County Schools in Greenville, North Carolina. She is an avid traveler and observer of the South. For the past several years, she has been collecting stories and other information about people's experiences with the kudzu vine.

S. Jonathan Bass is associate professor of history at Samford University in Birmingham, Alabama. He is the author of *Blessed Are the Peacemakers: Martin Luther King Jr., Eight White Religious Leaders and the "Letter from Birmingham Jail,"* which was nominated for the Pulitzer Prize.

Dwight B. Billings is professor of sociology at the University of Kentucky. His most recent book, coauthored with Kathleen M. Blee, is *The Road to Poverty: The Making of Wealth and Hardship in Appalachia.* He is a past president of the Appalachian Studies Association and recent editor of the *Journal of Appalachian Studies.*

Catherine W. Bishir is author or coauthor of numerous articles and books on North Carolina architecture, including *North Carolina Architecture* and a three-volume guide to the historic architecture of the state's regions, as well as, most recently, *Southern Built: American Architecture, Regional Practice.*

Kathleen M. Blee is Distinguished Professor of Sociology at the University of Pittsburgh. She is the coauthor, with Dwight B. Billings, of *The Road to Poverty: The Making of Wealth and Hardship in Appalachia* and author of several books on organized racism in the United States.

Elizabeth Boyd writes and teaches about the American South in Emory, Virginia. Her *Southern Beauty: Region, Remembrance, and the Feminine Ideal* is forthcoming from the University Press of Kansas.

James C. Cobb is Spalding Distinguished Professor of History at the University of Georgia. A former president of the Southern Historical Association, he has written widely on the history and culture of the American South. His most recent book is *Away Down South: A History of Southern Identity.*

Peter A. Coclanis is associate provost for international affairs and Albert R. Newsome Professor of History at the University of North Carolina at Chapel

Hill. He works primarily in the fields of economic and business history and is the author of many works in these areas. His most recent book is *Time's Arrow, Time's Cycle: Globalization in Southeast Asia over la Longue Durée*.

Joseph Crespino is assistant professor of history at Emory University. He received his Ph.D. in American History from Stanford University and is the author of *In Search of Another Country: Mississippi and the Conservative Counterrevolution*.

Drew Gilpin Faust is the 28th president of Harvard University. A historian of the Civil War and the American South, she is also the Lincoln Professor of History in Harvard's Faculty of Arts and Sciences. She previously served as founding dean of the Radcliffe Institute for Advanced Study.

franklin forts is a Ph.D. candidate at the University of Georgia and is currently working on his dissertation, "Cool Like Dat: Compulsive Masculinity in the African-American Community, 1965–2000." He presently serves as Diversity Scholar in the Social Sciences and assistant professor of history at Allegheny College in Pennsylvania.

David Goldfield has been Robert Lee Bailey Professor of History at UNC-Charlotte since 1982. His most recent books include *Still Fighting the Civil War: The American South and Southern History* and *Southern Histories*.

Larry J. Griffin is coeditor of *Southern Cultures* and teaches sociology, history, and American Studies at the University of North Carolina at Chapel Hill.

Adam Gussow is assistant professor of English and southern studies at the University of Mississippi and the author of *Seems Like Murder Here: Southern Violence and the Blues Tradition* and *Journeyman's Road: Contemporary Blues Lives from Faulkner's Mississippi to Post-9/11 New York*.

Trudier Harris is J. Carlyle Sitterson Professor of English and Comparative Literature at the University of North Carolina at Chapel Hill. Her most recent works are her memoir, *Summer Snow: Reflections from a Black Daughter of the South*, and *Reading Contemporary African American Drama: Fragments of History, Fragments of Self*.

Patrick Huber is associate professor of history at the University of Missouri-Rolla and the coauthor of *The 1920s: American Popular Culture Through History*. His *Linthead Stomp: Southern Millhands and the Creation of Hillbilly Music, 1922–1942* will be published this year.

Louis M. Kyriakoudes is associate professor of history at the University of Southern Mississippi. He is the author of *The Social Origins of the Urban South: Race, Gender, and Migration in Nashville and Middle Tennessee, 1890–1930* and is currently writing a history of cigarette smoking.

Melton McLaurin taught at the University of South Alabama before chairing the UNC-Wilmington Department of History until retiring in 2004. He is the author or coauthor of nine books and numerous articles on the history of the American South and race relations, including *Separate Pasts: Growing Up White in the Segregated South* and *Celia, A Slave*.

Michael Montgomery is Distinguished Professor Emeritus of English and Linguistics at the University of South Carolina. He has written extensively on the English of the American South, and he is coeditor of Volume 5, *Language*, of *The New Encyclopedia of Southern Culture*.

Steve Oney is the author of *And the Dead Shall Rise*, the winner of the American Bar Association's Silver Gavel Award, the Jewish Book Council's National Jewish Book Award, and the Southern Book Critics Circle prize. He is a senior writer for *Los Angeles* magazine.

Theda Perdue is professor of history at the University of North Carolina at Chapel Hill. She is the author of *Slavery and the Evolution of Cherokee Society*, *Cherokee Women*, *"Mixed Blood" Indians*, and other books on southern Indians.

Dan Pierce is associate professor of history and chair of the department at UNC-Asheville. He is the author of *The Great Smokies: From Natural Habitat to National Park* and numerous articles on the Great Smoky Mountains and the history of stock car racing in the southern piedmont.

John Shelton Reed is William Rand Kenan, Jr. Professor Emeritus of Sociology at the University of North Carolina at Chapel Hill and has written or edited over a dozen books on the South. His articles and essays have appeared in professional and popular periodicals ranging from *Science* to *Southern Living*. He is founding coeditor of *Southern Cultures*.

Mart Stewart is professor of history at Western Washington University. He was a Fulbright Scholar in 2000–2001 and a Fulbright Senior Specialist in 2003 in Vietnam. He also is the author of *"What Nature Suffers To Groe": Life, Labor and Landscape on the Georgia Coast, 1680–1920*.

Thomas A. Tweed is professor of religious studies and adjunct professor of American Studies at the University of North Carolina at Chapel Hill. He is the author or editor of six books, including *Asian Religions in America: A Documentary History* and *Our Lady of the Exile: Diasporic Religion at a Cuban Catholic Shrine in Miami*.

Timothy B. Tyson is senior research scholar at the Center for Documentary Studies at Duke University. He is author of *Blood Done Sign My Name*, *Radio Free Dixie: Robert F. Williams and the Roots of Black Power*, and, with David S. Cecelski, coeditor of *Democracy Betrayed: The Wilmington Race Riot of 1898 and Its Legacy*.

Anthony Walton studied at Notre Dame and Brown University, and is the author of *Mississippi: An American Journey* and *Go and Tell Pharaoh: The Autobiography of the Reverend Al Sharpton*. He also has written for a wide variety of publications, including the *New York Times*, *7 Days*, and the *New York Times Magazine*. He currently lives in Brunswick, Maine.

Harry L. Watson teaches southern history at the University of North Carolina at Chapel Hill and directs its Center for the Study of the American South. He joined with John Shelton Reed to found *Southern Cultures* in 1993.

Charles Reagan Wilson is Kelly Gene Cook Sr. Chair of History and Professor of Southern Studies at the University of Mississippi. He is former director of the Center for the Study of Southern Culture and general editor of *The New Encyclopedia of Southern Culture*.

C. Vann Woodward was a Pulitzer Prize–winning storyteller, historian, and expert on race relations, who chronicled the South and its culture in numerous works including *The Strange Career of Jim Crow*, *Tom Watson: Agrarian Rebel*, and *Origins of the New South*.

Index

Aaron, Hank, 307
Abernathy, Ralph David, 475
Accent in South. *See* Southern accent
Acuff, Roy, 151, 472
Adair, James, 218, 220
Adolescence in southern autobiography, 195–207
Adventures of Huckleberry Finn (Twain), 35, 39, 177
Affirmative action, 188
African Americans: autobiographies of, 195–207; and barbecue, 381–84; and black English, 104; and blues music, 156–72, 436; as characters in *Gone with the Wind*, 39; as characters in *To Kill a Mockingbird*, 182–83, 187; in Chicago, 22–31; and Confederate symbols, 119, 127–28, 133–42; disenfranchisement of, 66, 67, 87 (nn. 21–22), 126, 438–39; double-consciousness of, 40; education of, 201–2, 240; as elected officials, 126; and fatalism, 29–30; humor of, 435–43; Jews' relationship with, 235–41; lynching of, 169, 170, 314, 442; and magical thinking, 30; in Mississippi, 11–12, 24–25, 28, 119, 127–28, 156–57, 164, 169–72; and Mississippi flag, 119, 127–28; in movies, 39; in North Carolina, 260; northern migration of, 22–31, 178, 435; police killing of, 11, 17; prison time for, 253; and *redneck* as term, 305–7; reparations to, 18; and Republican Party, 87 (n. 22); and symbolism of whiteness vs. blackness, 310–12; violence against, 5–11, 15, 17, 28, 30, 65, 156–57, 169, 170, 199–200; voting rights for, 126; as wrestlers, 363–64. *See also* Civil rights movement; Racism; Segregation
Agriculture, 378, 380. *See also* Swine
Agriculture Department, U.S., 290, 291, 294
Alabama: Baptists in, 257; civil rights movement in Montgomery, 249–51; flag of, 124; religious diversity and immigrants in, 259; stock laws in, 378; violence against African Americans in, 199–200
Alexander, James Mitchell, 375
Ali Baba (wrestler), 353, 358
All About Love (hooks), 162–63
Allen, George, 404
Allen, Ivan, Jr., 474
Allen, James Lane, 330–31
Allen, Juanita, 403
Allen, Mel, 110
Allison, Bobby, 423–27
Allison, Donnie, 423
Al Qaeda, 252
Amazing Grace (Kozol), 15
American Revolution. *See* Revolutionary War
Ames, Jessie Daniel, 180, 240
Anderson, Benedict, 137–38
Andrews, Sidney, 312–13
And the Dead Shall Rise (Oney), 276–84
Angelou, Maya, 197, 202
Anthony, Jack, 293
Anti-Defamation League, 276
Anti-Semitism, 231–35, 237–38, 274–76, 280, 282. *See also* Jews
Apatoff, David, 298–99
Appalachian feuds, 329–49
Appalachian settlement school movement, 346

Naipaul, V. S., 308, 321

Nairne, Thomas, 217

Namath, Joe, 110

NASCAR: and appearance money for drivers, 428; and cheating by drivers, 416; and competition between Ford and Chrysler, 422–23; and fighting among race drivers, 416; finances of, and prize money, 413–15, 421, 428, 430; Big Bill France's dominance of, 409–14, 416–31; injuries and fatalities during races, 415, 422; and insurance for drivers, 415, 421, 424; and labor unions, 410, 417–31; and mob reaction to shortening race, 420–21; in 1950s, 412–16; in 1960s, 420–28; organizers of, 412–13; and parimutuel betting, 418; and Professional Drivers Association, 423–28; and promoting races, 416; rules of, 411–12, 416, 422–23, 427; and safety concerns, 414, 422, 424–27; and speed of cars, 422, 424, 425–26; and Talladega speedway boycott, 425–28; tire technology and speed of cars, 422, 425–26, 428; and track conditions, 415–16, 420–21

Nash, Dianne, 253–54

National Association for the Advancement of Colored People. *See* NAACP

National Council of Jewish Women (NCJW), 239, 240

Nationalism, 137–38

National Organization for European American Rights, 261

National Wrestling Alliance (NWA), 359, 360

Native Americans: land ownership of, 221; marriage of, 216–19; Poca-

hontas and John Smith, 211–13; and tattooing, 214; women's sexuality among, 212–22

Native Plant Conservation Initiative, 290–91

Native Son (Wright), 441

NCJW. *See* National Council of Jewish Women (NCJW)

Neilson, Melany, 200–201, 206

Nelson, Willie, 320

Newby, E. A., 314

Newman, Randy, 308–9

New Orleans, La.: Jefferson Davis's funeral in, 462, 465–67, 476

New York, N.Y.: blues music in, 159; poverty and violence in, 15; September 11 terrorist attacks, 253; speech-change course in, 98; violence against blacks in, 11

Nixon, E. D., 249

"No Deed but Memory: Historical Memory and Southern Identity" (Brundage), 36

Noland, William G., 79

North Carolina: Asians and Latinos in, 260–68, 269 (n. 9); Democratic Party in, during late nineteenth century, 57, 62–69, 77, 83; Fusionists in, 62, 63; historical and patriotic groups in, 67–68, 89 (n. 36); and Jamestown Tercentennial Exposition (1907), 81–83; population of, 84 (n. 2), 260; Populists in, 62; religious diversity in, 261–68, 270 (n. 15); Republican Party in, during late nineteenth century, 62, 63, 65; secession of, 61; segregation in, 66; State Capitol of, 53, 54, 59, 72–73, 74; white supremacy crusade in, 62–67, 70–71, 86–87 (n. 17). *See also* Raleigh, N.C.; Wilmington, N.C.

Robertson, Ben, 207 (n. 4), 229–30
Robertson, James I., Jr., 403
Rocca, Antonio "Argentine," 358
Rodgers, Jimmie, 150–51, 247
Roebuck, Julian B., 317
Rogers, Stewart, 77
Romans, Bernard, 216
Roosevelt, Franklin R., 12
Rose, William P., 79–80
"A Rose for Emily" (Faulkner), 35
Ross, Ranger, 364
Rosser, Luther, 274, 275
Rountree, George, 87 (n. 21)
Royall, Anne Newport, 323 (n. 3)
Royko, Mike, 110
Rubin, Louis D., Jr., 234–35
Rush, Benjamin, 214
Russell, Daniel, 62
Russell, Johnny, 319
Russia. *See* Soviet Union/Russia
Ruth, Babe, 307
Ryan, Abram Joseph, 265

The Salt Eaters (Bambara), 435
Salvation Army, 336
Sambimb, Phramana Somsak, 264
Sammartino, Bruno, 358
Sarup, Madan, 135–36
Saunders, Clarence, 379–80
Savage, Kirk, 87–88 (n. 26)
Savin, Nina, 319
Scarlett: The Sequel to Margaret Mitchell's "Gone with the Wind," 34
Scherman, Tony, 151, 153
Schneider, John, 320
Schwartz, Jerry, 478
Scottsboro trial, 178
Scruggs, Earl, 151
Sculpture. *See* Confederate monuments
SCV. *See* Sons of Confederate Veterans

"The Search for Southern Identity" (Woodward), 12–14
Secession, 61
Segregation: and African American humor, 439–41; in Chicago, 29; impact of, on children, 180, 206; and Jim Crow laws, 66; in Mississippi, 6, 157; in North Carolina, 66; of schools, 201–2; and "separate but equal" doctrine, 16, 87 (n. 22); in southern autobiography, 195–207; at University of Mississippi, 157, 449; Woodward on, 16. *See also* Racism
Semple, Ellen Churchill, 334–35, 336, 340
Separate Pasts (McLaurin), 199
September 11 terrorist attacks, 253
Sessions, William, 252
Shands, Hubert A., 305
Shapiro, Henry, 331
Shepherd, Kenny Wayne, 159
Sheridan, Philip, horse of, 393, 395–98
Silber, John, 304
Simmons, Furnifold M., 63, 86 (n. 14)
Simmons, Hazel, 24
Simmons, Maxine, 294
Simone, Nina, 15
Simpson, Lewis, 229
Skaggs, Ricky, 152
Slaton, John, 233, 234, 275–76, 282
Slaton, Mattie, 234
Slaughter, Sergeant, 363
Slavery: as cause of Civil War, 125, 136; in *Gone with the Wind*, 39, 40; and religion of slaves, 238; and rural white southerners, 312–13; and slave revolts, 236
Sledge, James S., 298
Sloanaker, Al, 414
Sluder, Gene, 419–20

Smiley, Glenn, 250
Smith, Benjamin, 16
Smith, Bruton, 417
Smith, Frank E., 207 (n. 5)
Smith, Gerald L. K., 469
Smith, Jack, 416
Smith, John, 211–14, 222
Smith, Lillian, 180–81, 192, 195
Smith, Samuel Stanhope, 215
Smith, Walter, 280–81
Smith, William Manning, 280–81
Smokey and the Bandit (film), 363
Smyth, Clifford, 336, 340, 345–46
SNCC, 203
Social class. *See* Class
Social Venture Network, 161
Society of the Cincinnati, 67, 70, 72
Soil Conservation Service (SCS),
    289–90
Song of Solomon (Morrison), 435–36
Sons of Confederate Veterans (SCV),
    8, 117, 122–23, 127–30, 133, 141
Sons of the Revolution, 67, 72
Sons of Union Veterans, 129
Sontag, Susan, 360
Sorority rush, 446–61
Sosebee, Gober, 413
South, George, 365
South Carolina: flag of, 8, 115, 117,
    118; hog population in, 377–78. *See
    also* Charleston, S.C.
Southern accent: and black English,
    104; and British speech patterns,
    102–4; changes in southern speech,
    105–9; characteristics of southern
    drawl, 100–101, 109, 111; and cli-
    mate and pace of life, 101; histor-
    ical derivation of, 101–5; and
    "Homogenization Factor," 96, 108;
    and Linguistic Atlas projects, 99–
    100; of Lower South, 99–100, 107;
    persistence vs. disappearance of,

95–96, 106–9; and "Snowbird Fac-
    tor," 96, 107–8; and social status,
    109–12; and southern attachment
    to southern speech, 97–99, 108;
    and "Special Education Factor," 96,
    108; and television programs and
    sportscasters, 109, 110; and tem-
    perament of southerners, 101; of
    Upper South, 100, 107; and urban-
    ization, 107; and "Walter Cronkite
    Factor," 96, 106–7
Southern Belle image, 448–51
Southern Changes, 204
Southern Christian Leadership Con-
    ference, 117, 191
Southern Colonial architecture, 75,
    76–82
A Southerner Discovers the South
    (Daniels), 304, 321
Southern Exposure magazine, 15, 199–
    200, 202
Southern Historical Society, 136
Southern Lady image, 448–51
Southern Living magazine, 15
Southern Regional Council, 204
Southern Tenant Farmers Union,
    322
Southern White Knights, 121
Soviet Union/Russia, 33, 179, 250,
    363
Spanish-American War, 69
Sports and sportscasters, 109, 110,
    366–67. *See also* Baseball;
    NASCAR; Wrestling
Sprunt, James, 61–66, 70, 71, 78, 80–
    81, 89 (n. 34), 90 (n. 45), 93 (n. 54)
Sprunt, Luola Murchison, 70, 78, 80–
    81, 90–91 (n. 45), 93 (n. 54)
Staley, Enoch, 421
Steel, Danielle, 34
Steinbeck, John, 35
Steinborn, Dick, 356, 359

Stepto, Robert, 24

Stereotypes: hog symbolism of southerners, 372–73; in humor of African Americans, 437; in movies and
on television, 190, 307–8; redneck
as, 304, 307–9, 315–16, 322; and
wrestling, 356, 361–68

Stern, Caroline, 229

Stevens, Gavin, 192

Stewart, Cora Wilson, 345

Stewart, Mart Allen, 293–94

Stock car racing. *See* NASCAR

Stoneman, Ernest V. "Pop," 149

Stowe, Harriet Beecher, 35, 39

Strachey, William, 214

The Strange Career of Jim Crow (Woodward), 16

Strikes. *See* Labor unions

Strong, Charles, 315–16

Styron, William, 470

Sullivan, Kevin, 362–63

Sumner, J. D., 479

Sundquist, Eric, 177, 184

Supreme Court, U.S. See *Bakke* case;
Brown v. Board of Education; *Plessy v.
Ferguson*

Swaggart, Jimmy, 365

Swine: and boys' pig clubs, 380; as cultural symbol of South, 371–86; and
current conditions of hog raisers,
384–85; economic importance of,
374; and hog drives, 374–75; and
livestock shows, 380–81; loss of,
during Civil War, 377–78; and
"pig pen" wrestling match, 366;
pork in diet of southerners, 375–
77, 379, 381–84; slaughter of, 376,
380

Sykes, Van, 375, 383

Taj Mahal, 159

Tan, Amy, 34–35

Taylor, Helen, 48 (n. 13)

Taylor, Mildred D., 444 (n. 10)

Teague, Marshall, 413, 414

Teamsters, 417–20

Television and radio: cable television,
360; Confederate symbols on, 130;
music on radio, 149–50, 158; redneck stereotype on, 307–8; South
and southern accent on, 109, 110,
361; speech patterns of newscasters, 96, 106–7; wrestling on
television, 358–61, 367

Tennessee, 259, 476–79

Terrell, Bob, 420, 421

Texas, 257, 259–60

They Won't Forget (film), 276

The Third Life of Grange Copeland
(Walker), 436

Thomas, Herb, 413

Thompson, Bennie, 129

Thompson, Hugh Miller, 467

Till, Emmett, 6, 28, 178

A Time to Kill (film), 189

Tindall, George B., 138, 232

To Kill a Mockingbird (Lee), 175–92

Torzeski, Nick, 417

Travis, Randy, 152

Trayler, Ray, 366

Tubb, Ernest, 472

Turner, Curtis, 413, 415–20, 422

Turner, Lana, 276

Turner, Ted, 360, 367

Turner, Victor Witter, 24

A Turn in the South (Naipaul), 308

Tuthill, Bill, 411, 412

Twain, Mark (Samuel Langhorne
Clemens), 35, 39, 46 (n. 4), 177,
275, 357–58

Twain, Shania, 152

Tyson, Alonza, 245

Tyson, Jack, 245

Tyson, Remer, 306

Watson, Tom, 275, 276
WCW. *See* World Championship
  Wrestling
Weatherly, Joe, 422
Webster, Noah, 105
Welch, Edward, 359
Welch, Robert, 359
Welch, Ronald, 359
Welty, Eudora, 247
Welwood, John, 162
West, Cornell, 191
Westmoreland, Hubert, 412
Whisnant, David, 346
White, B. P., 333
White, Beverly T., 335
White, Daughterty, 339
White, Hugh, 342
White, John, 81, 342
White, Laura, 339
White, Rex, 417, 419
White, William, 335
White Citizens' Councils, 122, 158,
  231–32
Whiteness and white supremacy: and
  Lost Cause ideology, 125, 128; in
  North Carolina, 62–67, 70–71, 86–
  87 (n. 17); and redneck images, 321;
  and symbolism of whiteness vs.
  blackness, 310–12. *See also* Ku Klux
  Klan; Racism; Segregation
Wildmon, Donald, 116, 131
Wiley, Bell, 236
Williams, Hank: funeral of, 463, 469–
  73; music of, 147, 151–52
Williams, Hank, Jr., 153, 383
Williams, Paul, 384–85
Williams, Tennessee, 97
Williamson, Sonny Boy, 156
Wills, Bob, 151
Wilmington, N.C.: architecture and
  monuments in, 69–71, 77–78, 80,
  92 (n. 53); elites in, as shapers of

public memory, 56–57; homes in,
  77–78, 80, 92 (n. 53); and white
  supremacy crusade and race riot in,
  63–66, 70–71
Wilson, August, 165–66, 169
Wilson, John S., 376–77
Wilson, William Julius, 30
The Wind Done Gone (Randall), 34, 36,
  39, 40, 41
Winston, Francis, 63, 72, 86 (n. 14), 87
  (n. 21), 88 (n. 27)
Winter, William, 157
Witherspoon, John, 105
Wolfe, Charles, 149
Wolfe, Thomas, 229, 230, 247
Women: Appalachian women and
  girls, 337–39; autobiographies of,
  197–206; memorial to Confederate
  women in Raleigh, N.C., 72; sexuality of Native women, 212–18;
  sorority rush as feminine perfor-
  mance, 446–61; Southern Lady/
  Belle image of, 448–51; and wres-
  tling, 361
Wood, Frank, 72
Wood, Glen, 417
Woodward, C. Vann: on burden of
  southern history, 480; on collective
  experience of southern people, xiii,
  xiv; on landmarks in South, xii; on
  redneck as term, 304; "The Search
  for Southern Identity," 12–14; on
  segregation, 16; *The Strange Career of
  Jim Crow*, 16
World Championship Wrestling
  (WCW), 360, 367
World's Columbian Exposition (1893,
  Chicago), 55–56, 76
World War I, 125
World Wrestling Federation (WWF),
  356, 360, 367
Wrestling: audience for, 360–61; con-

temporary nature of, 355–57, 366–68; dangers of, 356–57; internationalization of, 367; nineteenth-century style of backcountry fighting, 354–55; origins of professional wrestling in South, 357–61; southern wrestlers, 361–65, 368; as spectator sport, 356, 357; stereotypes in, 356, 361–68; television coverage of, 358–61, 367

Wright, Richard: on anti-Semitism, 238; *Black Boy*, 196–97, 201–2, 205, 207 (n. 2); compared with other writers, 206; *Native Son*, 441; and southern identity, 247; *Uncle Tom's Children*, 436

Wright, Steve, 394, 395

WWF. *See* World Wrestling Federation

Wyatt, Henry Lawson, 71–72

Wynette, Tammy, 27, 247

Yarborough, Cale, 423, 427

Yarbrough, LeeRoy, 423, 426

Yoakam, Dwight, 152

Young, James, 298

Your Blues Ain't Like Mine (Campbell), 167–68

Yunnick, Smokey, 413, 416, 423

Zbyszko, Stan, 353, 358

Zelinsky, Wilbur, 295